# The New Yorker
# Book of War Pieces

# The New Yorker

# Book of

# War Pieces

*Essay Index Reprint Series*

BOOKS FOR LIBRARIES PRESS
FREEPORT, NEW YORK

Library of Congress Cataloging in Publication Data
Main entry under title:

The New Yorker book of war pieces. ③ Freeport, N.Y., Books for Library
(es Pr. [1971, c1947])
(Essay index reprint series)   , xiii, 512 p. ② 24 cm. ③
    Articles originally published in the New Yorker, Sept. 1939-Aug. 1946.
    1. World War, 1939-1945--Addresses, sermons, etc.
2. World War, 1939-1945--Personal narratives.
I. The New Yorker (New York, 1925- 4 )
D743.9.N4 1971        940.53        75-167394
ISBN 0-8369-2470-3

PRINTED IN THE UNITED STATES OF AMERICA
BY
NEW WORLD BOOK MANUFACTURING CO., INC.
HALLANDALE, FLORIDA 33009

# Publishers' Note

The articles that make up this book first appeared in *The New Yorker*. They have been selected and arranged with the assistance of *The New Yorker*'s editors. The dates printed in brackets above the titles are the magazine's dates of issue.

# Contents

LETTER FROM LONDON, *September 3, 1939*
MOLLIE PANTER-DOWNES     3

LETTER FROM PARIS, *September 10, 1939*
JANET FLANNER     6

LETTER FROM PARIS, *October 22, 1939*
A. J. LIEBLING     9

DEPARTURE FROM POLAND
PRINCESS PAUL SAPIEHA     11

LETTER FROM LONDON, *May 12, 1940*
MOLLIE PANTER-DOWNES     21

LETTER FROM PARIS, *May 12, 1940*
A. J. LIEBLING     24

LETTER FROM PARIS, *May 18, 1940*
A. J. LIEBLING     27

LETTER FROM LONDON, *May 24, 1940*
MOLLIE PANTER-DOWNES     30

LETTER FROM LONDON, *June 15, 1940*
MOLLIE PANTER-DOWNES     33

LETTER FROM LONDON, *June 22, 1940*
MOLLIE PANTER-DOWNES     36

PARIS POSTSCRIPT
A. J. LIEBLING     39

LETTER FROM ENGLAND, *August 18, 1940*
MOLLIE PANTER-DOWNES     54

LETTER FROM LONDON, *August 25, 1940*
MOLLIE PANTER-DOWNES     56

LETTER FROM LONDON, *August 30, 1940*
MOLLIE PANTER-DOWNES                               *59*

LETTER FROM LONDON, *September 8, 1940*
MOLLIE PANTER-DOWNES                               *62*

LETTER FROM LONDON, *September 14, 1940*
MOLLIE PANTER-DOWNES                               *65*

LETTER FROM LONDON, *September 29, 1940*
MOLLIE PANTER-DOWNES                               *68*

LETTER FROM LONDON, *January 4, 1941*
MOLLIE PANTER-DOWNES                               *71*

PARIS, GERMANY
JANET FLANNER                                      *74*

A DAY IN TOWN
REBECCA WEST                                       *84*

PADDY OF THE R.A.F.
A. J. LIEBLING                                     *89*

DUE CREDIT TO HULL
A. J. LIEBLING                                     *99*

THE ARMY LIFE—MY DAY
E. J. KAHN, JR.                                    *107*

FOURTEEN FOR THE NAVY
ST. CLAIR MCKELWAY                                 *111*

THE SPINNER OF BOMB BAY
ST. CLAIR MCKELWAY                                 *119*

THE ARMY LIFE—SOMEWHERE IN NEW GUINEA
E. J. KAHN, JR.                                    *127*

THE ARMY LIFE—BUSY IN PAPUA
E. J. KAHN, JR.                                    *130*

GUERRILLA FROM ERIE, PA.
A. J. LIEBLING                                     *136*

THE FOAMY FIELDS
A. J. LIEBLING                                     *145*

MOLLIE
A. J. LIEBLING                                        *154*

THE ESCAPE OF MRS. JEFFRIES
JANET FLANNER                                        175

EIGHTY-THREE DAYS
MARK MURPHY                                          *202*

SEALED SHIP
GEORGE SESSIONS PERRY                                *231*

THE TAKING OF FICARRA
WALTER BERNSTEIN                                     *235*

BUSY MORNING
WALTER BERNSTEIN                                     *245*

ANZIO, FEBRUARY 10TH
JOHN LARDNER                                         *256*

THE MAYOR OF FUTANI
JOHN LARDNER                                         *264*

DUMPLINGS IN OUR SOUP
BRENDAN GILL                                         *273*

YOUNG MAN BEHIND PLEXIGLAS
BRENDAN GILL                                         *280*

SURVIVAL
JOHN HERSEY                                          *292*

LETTER FROM LONDON, *May 7, 1944*
MOLLIE PANTER-DOWNES                                 *303*

LETTER FROM LONDON, *May 21, 1944*
MOLLIE PANTER-DOWNES                                 *305*

LETTER FROM LONDON, *June 4, 1944*
MOLLIE PANTER-DOWNES                                 *308*

LETTER FROM LONDON, *June 11, 1944*
MOLLIE PANTER-DOWNES                                 *310*

CROSS-CHANNEL TRIP
A. J. LIEBLING                                                                                    312

SECOND MAN OUT
GUY REMINGTON                                                                                     339

LETTER FROM ROME, *July 7, 1944*
DANIEL LANG                                                                                       341

LETTER FROM FRANCE, *July 14, 1944*
A. J. LIEBLING                                                                                    348

LETTER FROM FRANCE, *July 20, 1944*
A. J. LIEBLING                                                                                    353

LETTER FROM FRANCE, *August 4, 1944*
A. J. LIEBLING                                                                                    358

MY DEAR LITTLE LOUISE
A. J. LIEBLING                                                                                    362

LETTER FROM PARIS, *September 1, 1944*
A. J. LIEBLING                                                                                    368

THE YELLOW FLOUR
DANIEL LANG                                                                                       373

LETTER FROM FLORENCE, *August 25, 1944*
DANIEL LANG                                                                                       384

SEARCH FOR A BATTLE
WALTER BERNSTEIN                                                                                  389

LETTER FROM LUXEMBOURG, *October 10, 1944*
DAVID LARDNER                                                                                     399

THE FIRES ON SAIPAN
EUGENE KINKEAD                                                                                    403

LOVELY AMERICANS
ROBERT SHAPLEN                                                                                    409

THE NICEST FELLOWS YOU EVER MET
ROBERT LEWIS TAYLOR                                                                               415

THE SUSPENDED DRAWING ROOM
S. N. BEHRMAN                                                                                     421

THE DUGGANS OF WAPPING

MOLLIE PANTER-DOWNES                                       *433*

PERSIAN GULF COMMAND—THE HEAT

JOEL SAYRE                                                            *452*

PERSIAN GULF COMMAND— YOU DON'T FOOL
AROUND WITH A RAILROAD

JOEL SAYRE                                                            *458*

D DAY, IWO JIMA

JOHN LARDNER                                                      *462*

LETTER FROM LONDON, *May 12, 1945*

MOLLIE PANTER-DOWNES                                       *472*

LETTER FROM ROME, *May 8, 1945*

PHILIP HAMBURGER                                              *477*

OKINAWA

JOHN LARDNER                                                      *481*

LETTER FROM BERCHTESGADEN, *June 1, 1945*

PHILIP HAMBURGER                                              *497*

LETTER FROM BERLIN, *July 14, 1945*

JOEL SAYRE                                                            *502*

HIROSHIMA

JOHN HERSEY                                                         *507*

# The New Yorker
# Book of War Pieces

# LETTER FROM LONDON

MOLLIE PANTER-DOWNES

*September 3, 1939*

FOR a week everybody in London had been saying every day that if there wasn't a war tomorrow there wouldn't be a war. Yesterday people were saying that if there wasn't a war today it would be a bloody shame. Now that there is a war, the English, slow to start, have already in spirit started and are comfortably two laps ahead of the official war machine, which had to await the drop of somebody's handkerchief. In the general opinion, Hitler has got it coming to him—or, in the local patois, " 'E's fair copped it."

The London crowds are cool—cooler than they were in 1914—in spite of thundery weather that does its best to scare everybody by staging unofficial rehearsals for air raids at the end of breathlessly humid days. On the stretch of green turf by Knightsbridge Barracks, which used to be the scampering ground for the smartest terriers in London, has appeared a row of steam shovels that bite out mouthfuls of earth, hoist it aloft, and dump it into lorries; it is then carted away to fill sandbags. The eye has now become accustomed to sandbags everywhere, and to the balloon barrage, the trap for enemy planes, which one morning spread over the sky like some form of silvery dermatitis. Posting a letter has acquired a new interest, too, since His Majesty's tubby, scarlet pillar boxes have been done up in squares of yellow detector paint, which changes color if there is poison gas in the air and is said to be as sensitive as a chameleon.

Gas masks have suddenly become part of everyday civilian equipment and everybody is carrying the square cardboard cartons that look as though they might contain a pound of grapes for a sick friend. Bowlegged admirals stump jauntily up Whitehall with their gas masks slung neatly in knapsacks over their shoulders. Last night London was completely blacked out. A few cars crawled through the streets with one headlight out and the other hooded while Londoners, suddenly become homebodies, sat under their shaded lights listening to a Beethoven Promenade concert interspersed with the calm and cultured tones of the B.B.C. telling motorists what to do during air raids and giving instructions to what the B.B.C. referred to coyly as expectant mothers with pink cards, meaning mothers who are a good deal more than expectant.

*3*

The evacuation of London, which is to be spaced over three days, began yesterday and was apparently a triumph for all concerned. At seven o'clock in the morning all inward traffic was stopped and A.A. scouts raced through the suburbs whisking shrouds of sacking off imposing bulletin boards, which informed motorists that all the principal routes out of town were one-way streets for three days. Cars poured out pretty steadily all day yesterday and today, packed with people, luggage, children's perambulators, and domestic pets, but the congestion at busy points was no worse than it is at any other time in the holiday season. The railways, whose workers had been on the verge of going out on strike when the crisis came, played their part nobly and the London stations, accustomed to receiving trainloads of child refugees from the Third Reich, got down to the job of dispatching trainload after trainload of children the other way—this time, cheerful little cockneys who ordinarily get to the country perhaps once a year on the local church outing and could hardly believe the luck that was sending them now. Left behind, the mothers stood around rather listlessly at street corners waiting for the telegrams that were to be posted up at the various schools to tell them where their children were.

All over the country the declaration of war has brought a new lease of life to retired army officers, who suddenly find themselves the commanders of battalions of willing ladies who have emerged from the herbaceous borders to answer the call of duty. Morris 10s, their windshields plastered with notices that they are engaged on business of the A.R.P. or W.V.S. (both volunteer services), rock down quiet country lanes propelled by firm-lipped spinsters who yesterday could hardly have said "Boo!" to an aster.

Although the summer holiday is still on, village schools have reopened as centers where the evacuated hordes from London can be rested, sorted out, medically examined, refreshed with tea and biscuits, and distributed to their new homes. The war has brought the great unwashed right into the bosoms of the great washed; while determined ladies in white V.A.D. overalls search the mothers' heads with a knitting needle for unwelcome signs of life, the babies are dandled and patted on their often grimy diapers by other ladies, who have been told to act as hostesses and keep the guests from pining for Shoreditch. Guest rooms have been cleared of Crown Derby knickknacks and the best guest towels, and the big houses and cottages alike are trying to overcome the traditional British dislike of strangers, who may, for all anybody knows, be parked in them for a matter of years, not weeks.

Everybody is so busy that no one has time to look up at the airplanes that pass overhead all day. Today was a day of unprecedented activity in the air. Squadrons of bombers bustled in all directions and at midday an enormous number of vast planes, to which the knowing pointed as troop-carriers, droned overhead toward an unknown destination that was said by two sections of opinion to be (a) France and (b) Poland. On the ground, motor buses full of troops in bursting good humor tore through the villages, the men waving at the girls and howling "Tipperary" and other ominously dated ditties that everybody has suddenly remembered and found to be as good for a war in 1939 as they were in 1914.

London and the country are buzzing with rumors, a favorite one being that Hitler carries a gun in his pocket and means to shoot himself if things don't go too well; another school of thought favors the version that he is now insane and Göring has taken over. It is felt that Mussolini was up to no good with his scheme for holding a peace conference and spoiling what has become everybody's war. The English were a peace-loving nation up to two days ago, but now it is pretty widely felt that the sooner we really get down to the job, the better.

# LETTER FROM PARIS

JANET FLANNER

*September 10, 1939*

THIS is a queer war so far—thank God! Since it started a week ago today, Paris has been thrice visited by enemy planes, but not bombed. Most shops except food stores are closed, with their shutters pulled down, and behind these shutters families are still living. Paris is not empty. Were it not for the existence of war, the knowledge, for example, that it is against the law to go onto the street without your gas mask slung ready over your shoulder in its little khaki case, this Sunday would just be a beautiful Indian-summer day.

News does not arrive, or maybe it does not exist. What is going on along the eastern front you learn from the communiqués. As for what is going on along the western or Franco-German front, one can only say that the information all us journalists try to get and the comments we try to make are very soundly and strictly censored here. *Le Jour* has just appeared with nothing left of the last half of its leading editorial except the capital letters "P.S." of a postscript that was not printed. *Gringoire* has come out with a picture of a pair of scissors occupying a blank column on its front page.

All that can be truthfully and properly reported from France today is that what is going on in no man's land is strategically strange. It would seem, indeed, as if efforts are still being made to hold the war up, prevent its starting in earnest—efforts made, perhaps self-consciously, by government leaders reluctant to go down in history as having ordered the first inflaming shots, or efforts made as a general reflection of the various populations' courageous but confused states of mind. Certainly this must be the first war that millions of people on both sides continued to think could be avoided even after it had officially been declared. For months there has been a rumor here that at the last minute—a later last minute than history has even seen—something would be arranged, and that the arrangement would not be appeasement but a plan. The outline of the supposed plan was that war would be threatened or, as a desperate gamble, even entered upon as an aid to the anti-Nazis in Germany in their efforts to free their country from the present regime. After that, according to this theory, there would be a cessation of hostilities and the beginning of talks. In certain high circles it is still believed that there is such a general plan.

In the last war, newspapers played an important part. In this war, they are too slow. Only the radio can act quickly enough. Before the French papers had been distributed the morning of September 1st, the seven-o'clock German news hour had broadcast Herr Hitler's announcement of his attack on Poland. From September 1st through September 3rd, anybody in France with a short-wave radio powerful enough to get New York was receiving amazingly complete and nearly instantaneous European news. And anybody whose wireless could get only the French and British stations was receiving in comparison very little news at all. The C.B.S. and N.B.C. broadcasts in French rendered an unforgettable—although sometimes, static being bad, inaudible—service to listeners all through this land on those anxious days. It is our impression that at first, anyhow, the news from the French and British stations was infinitely less voluminous not because of censorship, as now, but because their organizations, being neither so expansive nor expensive, lacked the enormous and ubiquitous personnel of the American companies. To French people, bewildered by events, stunned by their own pathetic previous determination to believe the events could not occur, and dazed by the necessary sparsity of official French news, it was staggering to listen to European news that had gone out to America and returned before it had been announced in Europe itself. The New York broadcasts only added to the sense of unreality that the French felt, and that the French sti.. feel.

As the most pleasant phase of the unreality in which everybody seems to be living, the French seized on the incredible flight of the British fliers over Germany and their gallant and dangerous distribution of pamphlets. This paper raid created a tremendous impression among the French, who immediately talked of it as though it were a gentle and legendary act such as might have been performed in the so-called darker ages by knights on horseback. The unfortunately more modern sinking of the Athenia caused anxious comment, invariably summed up in two questions: "Will the Athenia be like the Lusitania? Will the Americans come in?" The third much-discussed event was President Roosevelt's declaration of neutrality. The French felt as if they had just lost a battle. Nor does Italy's neutrality in any way reassure or disarm them. While Hitler's unexpected announcement that he would not ask his friend to help him make war was at first hailed as meaning that Mussolini was boldly wavering away from the Axis, it is now suspected that Italy's neutrality is actually a complicated piece of Hitlerian strategy and a further sign of Mussolini's helpless loyalty.

Since, because of unprecedentedly strict censorship, the French people are told little so that the Nazi Secret Service won't know everything, the average Frenchman is largely left to his own speculations. He believes he will fight bravely, because he is shrewd enough to see that if he doesn't it's his turn to be gobbled up next. On the whole, however, there is a feeling of dry theory about this entire war, at least until it turns wet with blood, that confuses not only the French but apparently myriad Germans as well.

Women of *sangfroid,* as the appeals describe them, have been requested to register with the various French passive defense organizations. American women who own automobiles have been aiding the evacuation from Paris of the lame, halt, and blind. The American Committee for Devastated France, which functioned so splendidly in the last war, is being reorganized in Paris by Miss Anne Morgan as the Comité Américain pour le Secours Civil. It is already doing evacuation work in the north, with five American lady car-drivers and four nurses to attend the sick, and is also making its first appeal for funds.

Never have nights been more beautiful than these nights of anxiety. In the sky have been shining in trinity the moon, Venus, and Mars. Nature has been more splendid than man.

[October 28, 1939]

# LETTER FROM PARIS

A. J. LIEBLING

*October 22, 1939*

PARIS at this writing is a city in which people are tentatively picking up the threads of ordinary existence—tentatively, and a little sheepishly, as if ashamed of their initial agitation. Theoretically, there is as much danger from the air this week as on the first day of War '39, as Frenchmen call this one to distinguish it from the other, but habit is stronger than reason. Wives who were rushed to the country at the outbreak now want to come back to rejoin their husbands in Paris, and in most cases the women are having their way. People buy newspapers as mechanically as they light cigarettes and, after looking at the headlines, leave them on café tables virtually unread because there is no news. The public at first blamed censorship but has now begun to sense that simply nothing has happened, and in the French fashion it has begun to make fun of the baffled journalists. One of the favorite butts is Mlle. Geneviève Tabouis, of *L'Œuvre,* who writes circumstantially every day of events in Germany, where, of course, she isn't. She has many less eminent imitators.

Paris newspapers have never carried so much German news as now, when the sources of this news are inaccessible. One reported Monday that Hitler had confided his testament of thirty pages to Göring, who presumably was decent enough to count them for the Allied press. Havas announced later that the Führer was practicing revolver shooting at moving targets, a sign he feared assassination. Another journalistic genre, already hackneyed, is the conducted visit of illustrious correspondents to the front. The correspondents, often members of the Académie Française or Goncourt, are invariably taken to Strasbourg, which was cleared of inhabitants when the war began. Each Academician compares Strasbourg to a dead city or a sleeping beauty, according to his taste, and professes to have been startled by the sound of his own footsteps in the empty streets. One columnist wrote, after reading a series of these *rapportages,* "Monsieur X was not frightened by his own footsteps, but by the fourteen correspondents behind him." Serious editorialists, like Gallus, of *Paris-Soir,* have felt impelled to reprove such public levity and to warn their readers that the situation remains potentially grave.

9

The French have an enormous confidence in their army, especially now that the Germans have let slip the opportunity for a surprise attack. They suspect that the German High Command will not attempt a great offensive unless its hand is forced by *ce fou d'Hitler,* and discussions of strategy in the cafés invariably hinge on just how *fou* Hitler is. As for air raids on great cities, the public senses now that the Germans are loath to begin; while waiting, people say, it is no use torturing oneself.

A few theatres have reopened. The Comédie-Française gives several performances a week, the evening ones beginning at six-fifteen, and the companies of the Opéra and Opéra-Comique share the latter's home on the Rue Favart, each on a one-show-a-week basis. Several music halls have begun their season, and night clubs are struggling against the handicap of an eleven-o'clock closing. Les Halles, where restaurateurs used to go to market long before dawn, now operate in daylight from noon to three in the afternoon, but there is all the old profusion of *primeurs* and game, rock lobsters and oysters. Nothing reassures Parisians more than this gastronomic normality. As they eat, lovingly and with discrimination, they like to talk about the short rations *chez l'ennemi;* it is that, they are convinced, which will provoke a German revolution.

To the visitor returning to Paris for the first time since the beginning of War '39, no major change is apparent in the city by day. There are the air-raid-shelter signs, the strips of paper pasted over shop windows to stop glass from flying in case of an air raid, and sandbags around some public buildings; one soon becomes accustomed to these. The streets are well filled and those favorite subjects for water-colorists, the fishermen and book merchants of the Seine, pursue the placid, meagre tenor of their lives. There are a great many uniforms everywhere, but uniforms never were rare in Paris, and a French soldier seems a normal enough feature of civilian life.

At night, of course, all this changes; windows and street lights cast only the dimmest of rays. Behind the café fronts, however, shrouded by blue paper, one finds groups of people made sociable by the war, consuming their beer and coffee and demonstrating with matches on the tables the strategies that could quickly win War '39. This willingness to talk to almost anybody resembles the fraternization of speakeasy days in New York.

Parisians, always grumblers, are beginning to complain about the air-raid restrictions now that they realize the first alarms were only for practice. "Let's have the lights again," one owner of a *bistro* said to a group of customers a day or so ago. "Light is like the butterflies and the verdure that lifts the spirits." "And if the light attracts the bombers of Monsieur Hitler?" a customer asked. "Then turn off the lights," the *bistro* man said. "All you have to do is press a button."

# DEPARTURE FROM POLAND

PRINCESS PAUL SAPIEHA

SINCE March, everyone in Poland had been uneasy. Few days passed without a threat or two from Germany. It was as if, wherever you went, some stranger followed. I persistently refused to believe, however, that anything would actually happen. All the people around me had known the bleak insecurity of war in their own lifetime, and it was only natural, I thought, that they exaggerated the present danger. I was unable to bring myself to take a possible shortage of food or a possible attack from the air seriously. Having been born in New York and having lived in America until six years ago—when I married a Pole and moved to his family estate near Lemberg—I had no memory of hardships to guide me. My childhood recollections of the war were limited to parades on Fifth Avenue, a plethora of flags, much advertising of Liberty Bonds, and the fact that after the war was over I was told that the atrocity stories had been merely propaganda and that the German and French and other armies had been composed of simple men who hated to kill one another and suffered mostly from cold hands and wet feet.

I was visiting friends in Poznań when the news of the pact between Germany and Russia was announced. We were only thirty kilometres from the German frontier. The first thing my hostess did was to pack up her silver and linen and send them to Warsaw. There were frequent telephone calls from neighbors, asking advice. "Should we buy gas masks?" they asked. "What about sending the children eastward?" "What about digging a trench in the garden?" People came for tea and said, "We Poles are not the Czechs. We won't give in." "It's not just a question of Danzig," they said, "it's the principle of the thing." They talked about the English and French Commissions in Poland, about tactics, about what various ambassadors had said. Plans for the evacuation of danger zones were discussed. The guests agreed that the Germans would open their attack, through Slovakia, in Silesia, and, of course, along the northwestern frontier. They envied me, they said, because it would surely be safe around Lemberg.

Before dinner my host proposed a toast that went, "Ladies, gentlemen, and Germans." We all laughed. In the back of my mind I kept apologizing for what I felt was my friends' hysteria. The flowers in their garden still

*11*

bloomed abundantly under a spotless sky. For once, the Polish autumn was mild. I had brought along on the visit a young daughter, who went wading at noon in a lake on the grounds and stuffed herself with the first plums and grapes. Nature was putting on her best face. It seemed unreasonable to listen to the warnings about me. I was so strongly convinced that the war would not materialize that I planned to leave my child in these pleasant surroundings until the middle of September. It was only when my hostess murmured something about the problems of being responsible for someone else's child in a time of crisis that I decided to take her home.

Our journey from Poznań took us along the German border, through Silesia, to Cracow, and then Lemberg. In the stations and on the trains there were crowds of people with children. Everyone was very quiet. There was nothing unusual in the air except this extreme quiet.

It was the twenty-fourth of August when my little girl and I reached our home, a sprawling estate situated in the middle of a forest outside the town of Rawa Ruska, near Lemberg. My husband was not there to greet us but arrived a few hours later, rather breathless, and told me that he had been mobilized and would have to leave for Lemberg at once. He seemed more annoyed than worried. We fished out a uniform he had worn twenty years ago, moved the buttons of the coat, which he had outgrown, and pinned on a few medals. He wrote out a check and a page of instructions for me. I was to be responsible for our family, which consisted of the little girl, a baby son, and my husband's mother and sister, and for the entire estate, which included our house, a large staff of servants, a farm, some mills, some timberland, the foremen of these various projects, and thirty families of farm hands. I was to take charge of all business matters, about which I knew almost nothing, and was to sit in the estate office, open the mail, give instructions, and order supplies. Chiefly, I was to represent moral authority. My husband left hurriedly, telling me that war was a nuisance but he would be back in a few days.

The question of supplies soon came up. I had no idea myself what was needed, but I was not long left in ignorance. The estate foremen and various members of the household, well acquainted with my inadequacy, came to me with advice. Soap, matches, candles, naphtha, oil, gasoline, medicines, sugar, tea, and coffee were among the absolute necessities. In what quantities? No one seemed to know. When would the shortage begin? Immediately.

The foreman of the farm telephoned to say that no peasants were coming to work. There was not enough money on hand to pay them. They felt that they would be mobilized at any moment. They preferred to stay at home and talk things over and perhaps, in the night, dig up a few of our potatoes for their wives and children. Some of the servants had set to work digging pits and opening up ancient cellars in which to stow away guns, silver, and wines. I was glad that they were busy, so I did not interfere, but I still felt that we were all children playing Indians and that when the excitement petered out we would feel somewhat sheepish.

The telephone rang constantly, either to bring bad news or to ask for help. There was no more sugar to buy. It was already too late to get more than one barrel of gasoline and one barrel of naphtha. The army had stopped the sale of oil. We could not expect to keep our power plant, which provided our electricity, going for more than a month. Someone proudly brought home two boxes of candles; there were no more to be had. A neighbor was dying of dysentery, and his daughter, caught in Lemberg, could not come to him as the trains and autobuses were no longer open to civilian passengers. We had cars and chauffeurs, but I could not offer them because we had too little gasoline.

Peasant women whose husbands had already been mobilized drifted in quietly with children in their arms. "We have army receipts," they said, "but no one knows when we can be paid. Last night the children had no supper. There's nothing in the house. What shall we do?" I took them to the kitchen, but the cook met me with a discouraging look. We had no flour ourselves because the grain that I had ordered ground was still at one of our own mills and the army had taken over the mill. I had to stave off the hungry women and children with promises.

My mother-in-law and sister-in-law, who had been away on a vacation in Austria, returned. We hovered anxiously over the radio, learning what ambassador had flown where, listening eagerly to the grandiloquent reassurances from England, quailing at the bombastic shouts from our German neighbors. There was an evening when the Polish news broadcast announced that there were strikes in the German steel industry, and we went to sleep with a small, sneaking hope that these strikes had not come too late. Everyone told everyone else what Hitler was planning. The kitchen girls, unable to read or write, could nevertheless assure us that the Germans were weak and starving, that Mussolini would maintain the peace. We knew what Chamberlain thought, and with whom Göring had a conference, but we did not know what would become of us tomorrow.

Late on the night of the twenty-ninth, my husband drove up to the house in a car. He was wearing a field uniform and carrying a gas mask over his shoulder. He came into the house and asked to be served supper quickly. Then he left for his post. Suddenly I knew what I had not before admitted to myself. This war was not just a nuisance and he would not be coming back in a few days.

After that we got no mail or newspapers. It was about noon of September 1st that I learned the war was on. "Moscicki has declared a state of war," the radio said. It did not mention that already, at dawn, the Germans had bombed Cracow.

Many of the men on the estate now left, most of them without saying goodbye. There was no handkerchief-waving; no one sped them cheerfully on their way. Under the monotonously brilliant sky the place lay still, in a sort of paralysis. There was no sound of work in the forest, of peasant wagons ambling past, of bustle around the house. Only the telephone continued to ring and the voice of the radio echoed under the trees. The Polish broadcast said that six hundred English bombers had arrived in Warsaw, that they were bombing Berlin, that Bremen, Cuxhaven, and Hamburg had been badly damaged. From the French, Swiss, and English we learned only that the Germans were advancing in Poland and that the English were dropping millions of seditious leaflets behind the German lines.

Our farm foreman, an Austrian who had lived in Poland for thirty-five years, received notice to leave the country at once. He did not know where to go and could take no money with him. After two days of telephoning officials and unsuccessfully pleading his cause, I had to send him off, tears running down his cheeks. It was essential to put someone in his place, so I asked one of our office employees, a forestry engineer, to take charge. That left only a cashier and a woman bookkeeper to work with me at the office. The cashier had to carry on without cash, because the bank in Rawa Ruska had already run out of funds. Meanwhile, German planes were rumored to have flown over Lemberg. In Rawa Ruska the alarm sounded often.

I received a telephone call to the effect that forty wives and children of army officers were on their way to the estate with a hundred kilograms of baggage apiece. They had been evacuated from Poznań and might arrive for billeting any day. I would be responsible for their shelter, light, heat, and cooking facilities. We prepared as many rooms as we could in the various houses on the estate. We distributed wood for the stoves, hay to sleep on, and what ramshackle furniture we could muster. I ordered an extra supply of milk and sent to town for bread in order to be able to prepare a first meal for my guests.

Since all our horses had been taken by the army, the only person who could still get to town to attend to our business was the cashier, who had managed to hold on to a bicycle. It sometimes took him a whole day to accomplish one errand, however, because at each alarm the townspeople vanished into cellars or doorways for an indefinite stay. Still, I did not altogether believe that we were in any actual physical danger. I wrote to my mother, living in America, that our place was a little island of safety. The children continued to play happily in the woods, I wrote, and I had my books and pictures, my new tiled bathroom, and my dear bed, in which to take refuge at the end of each confused day.

On September 5th two small silver planes flew quite low over the house. Shortly afterward another small plane, with red and white marks under its wings, darted past, apparently pursuing them. Some of the servants and I stood on the lawn to watch them out of sight. About a half hour later we heard the thin wail of the Rawa Ruska alarm mounting over the trees. We then heard a deep throb of motors, growing rapidly louder. I stood on the lawn again and searched the sky against the strong sun. At first I saw nothing. Finally I saw three planes, so high that they looked like giant mosquitoes, circling above us. There was no guessing how far off they were at that height. They turned in formation and flew toward Rawa Ruska. From under one of them, something—infinitesimal, it seemed—fell out. There was a dull detonation, then a second. The planes sank lower and lower, and then I heard a succession of rattles and saw, simultaneously, little dark streaks headed toward the earth. The planes rose again swiftly. The powerful throb faded. They were gone.

Until then I had been motionless. I had not known whether I was alone or not. Now I felt buttery in the knees. My mouth felt hot. I looked about me. A dozen people were standing there. "What are you doing?" I shouted suddenly, in a voice that did not sound as natural as I intended. "Get back to your work. Nothing's happened." I remembered the children. Where were they? In the woods, of course. I began to run. I only stopped when I saw them sitting with their nurse on a sand pile in the sun.

When I got back to the house, nothing seemed to have changed. Everyone was busy. Luncheon would soon be ready. "We'll get used to it," one of the servants told me. Later I called the telephone operator and asked what had been bombed in Rawa Ruska. She told me that one bomb had fallen in a field, and that the second had knocked off the corner of the railroad station but no one had been hurt. There had also been some harmless machine-gun fire from the planes. I hastened to tell the household. "You see," I said, "these bombs aren't so bad. Their bark is worse than their bite." I felt quite cheerful.

I later received a telephone call from the military headquarters in Lemberg. After a long wait, during which I had time for some unpleasant speculation, someone said, "A message has come for you as follows: 'First, I am well. Second, please keep the house absolutely dark at night. Third, see that no one stands out in the open during an air raid. Fourth, I am sending you my proxy by mail.' That is all."

At breakfast time the next day some bombers flew over the house but dropped no bombs. At noon they reappeared; this time there were bombs, and the house shook a bit from the detonations. "Where are they now?" my little girl asked. "What do they want to do?" I told her that bombs were too precious to drop on such unimportant people as ourselves, but she did not eat her lunch.

In the afternoon the officers' wives and children, whom we had been expecting for a week, arrived. They said that their train had been bombed every day. They had sometimes spent hours lying face down in potato fields. There had been days when they had no food. They looked numb but strangely tidy. They spoke in patient voices.

On the same day some unexpected people also arrived. There was an aviation major with his wife and a child and two carloads of possessions. "The next town from here is burning," he said. "When they saw our cars at a standstill, they bombed us. They even bomb cows." There was another couple, who had walked by night from beyond Warsaw, three hundred kilometres away. Could they please have a night's sleep here? There was a woman in ski trousers and cap with a six-month-old baby in her arms. She showed me her identification papers. She was a general's wife. Could we take her in? It was growing dark outside, but not too dark to see that wagons and automobiles were still coming out of our forest road and hesitantly slowing down near the house. "Where do you come from?" I called to these people. Some said from Warsaw, others from Przemyśl.

In the evening we discussed all these migrating people. Where could they go? Who would feed them? The still, bright night came and the shadows of the forest closed around us. In the woods there were hares and foxes and deer and wild boar, cuddled down among warm leaves in the underbrush. Even when winter came, they would know what to eat and where to sleep. But these new inhabitants of the forest, these restive human families moving among the trees, were helpless.

The next day I telephoned the mayor of Rawa Ruska for some advice, and it took me an hour to reach his office. Then I was told that he was not there. I tried to get a call through to a doctor. His telephone did not answer. I tried the town bank. It was closed. Someone sent word that if we needed anything, we must go to town after seven at night. The population of Rawa Ruska was taking to the woods for the day and creeping home at night to carry on the business of living.

After the next air raid, when the bombers were already out of sight, I noticed little white specks fluttering down in the sunlight. As they came nearer, I saw that they were leaflets. I caught a few. They were printed in Polish and in Ruthenian. "Poles," they began, "you are lost. We have taken Silesia, Cracow, Czestochowa, Poznań, Danzig, Gdynia, etc. Your government has failed you. Your army is broken. It is up to you to make the peace." They described the terrible conditions under which Poland had been living for the past twenty years and said that the Germans came as redeemers.

On Sunday morning, September 10th, most of the household went to our chapel for Mass, but I could not make myself go. Once in there, I knew, it would be impossible to leave until the service was over, without causing a stir, and I had determined to let no bombers fly over us unseen by me. I had the feeling that if I kept my eyes on them they would not bomb us. I sent my children to the woods and waited restlessly for the approaching hum.

There were nine planes this time, flying three by three. I stood under a tree. The sound clogged my ears and my whole body was shaken by the vibrations. An officer and his wife and grown son who had slept in our house the night before came out and lay face down under another tree nearby. The planes moved off, then turned and thundered back again. There were no anti-aircraft guns within miles. One crash, then another drowned out the roar of the motors. The bombs had fallen not far off this time. Suddenly the lawn was full of people. They rushed down the path from church. Servants and peasant girls in Sunday kerchiefs, a nun with her black skirts billowing behind her, small girls dressed in white for their Communion huddled together, ran this way and that, then stopped to stare at the bright sky. I did not know what to do. My maid, who had been standing with me, charged into them, shouting, "To the woods with you! Get out of sight!" I followed her, shouting too. We threatened and pushed and drove them on till they reached the forest.

When the planes had gone, my mother-in-law, who had stayed in church throughout the Mass, came quietly down the path, prayer book in hand. "We prayed for you," she told me.

I went into the house and sat down in the drawing room, hoping to cool my head. It was the first time I had been in there for the ten days since the war had begun. There was a film of dust over everything. There were crumbs from last week's tea, a comb from someone's hair, a pile of disordered magazines, cigarette stubs in the ashtrays, some knitting sprawled on a chair. I hurried out to look for the servants. They were standing in the courtyard behind the house. "This house is dirty," I said. "I'm ashamed." No one answered and no one moved. Finally one of the older servants said, "What's the use? The Germans will soon be here. Why should we clean and dust when they're coming?" There was nothing I could say.

The radio brought no comfort that afternoon. From Katowice came German dance music; from Cracow, German news. Warsaw gave no signal at all. There was too much static to catch foreign stations. I went to play with the children and all I could do was to marvel that they were still there, running about among their toys, laughing their normal laughter.

That night, at about eight o'clock, I suddenly heard my husband's whistle in the hall outside my room. He rushed through the door. His eyes looked hard in his pinched face. His uniform hung loosely about him. He told me I must leave right away with the children. I protested, saying that the children were in bed, that nothing was packed, and that I did not know where to go. He told me it was now or never and that everything had been prepared for the journey, that our passports had been fixed, and that I would go first to Rumania and then to Hungary. I asked him about himself—where he had been, where he was going, what had happened to him—but he refused to talk about anything except arrangements for my getting away with the children. He convinced me that I had no choice, that I would have to go.

By ten o'clock the children were prepared to leave, dressed in winter things, their faces drowsy but not alarmed. The nurse and my maid sat packed and ready in the nursery. The servants carried down the luggage through the darkened house. I looked for a last time at my room, at the candlewick curtains, at the beds which I had painted myself, at the golden Polish Virgin hanging above them. Everything was still in its place. I had worked so carefully to make this room my own.

Downstairs my husband was leaving instructions with the staff. "The Germans may be here by tomorrow," he said. "If there's any shooting, take to the woods, all of you, and don't come back till it's over." He told the men who were not yet mobilized to leave in the morning. "Go east," he said. "It doesn't matter where, but don't let them get you. Keep going."

This departure was not real. Though our things were packed and we stood ready to go, I did not believe it. I pleaded with my mother-in-law to go with the children in my place, arguing that I was an American, after all, and that nothing could happen to me. "My children are in Poland," she answered. "I'm an old woman now. I will not go."

My sister-in-law went upstairs to bring down the children. I went out to see if the two cars that we were to use were ready. The night was lit only by a dim moon. The baggage was placed in one car, which would lead the way. We piled the nurse, the maid, and the children into the back of the other car. I got into the front seat with my husband. We drove off through the woods. My mother-in-law and sister-in-law stood in front of the house to see us go.

At first the night concealed everything. We had to drive without lights, so the familiar road and the fields were a black blur against which I could distinguish nothing. Then I began to see that the night was alive. People shuffled along on foot, carrying bundles. Trucks stood still at the sides of the road, piled high with the gray shapes of sleeping figures. Small cars crept along with branches strewn over their roofs as camouflage. Everywhere, something moved in the dark.

"We're going, we're going," the baby murmured behind me. "Papa is there, Mama is there. We're going." "When are we going to bed?" my little girl asked. "You must sleep," I told them. "We'll have a long ride. We must all sleep."

A torchlight flared at us suddenly. Someone ordered us to stop. My husband got out and showed his papers. We drove on again, slowly weaving in and out among the cars, the wagons, and the plodding figures. Everyone was going our way, toward Lemberg. There was nothing coming to meet us.

Beyond Rawa Ruska the line of cars was jammed to a standstill. Two men were filling a deep hole in the road where a bomb had fallen. We crept over a narrow ridge of fresh earth. The chauffeur switched on the lights for a second. "Lights out, damn you!" someone said.

I tried to talk to my husband. What was he going to do? Where would he go? He said he didn't know, that he would go wherever his general went. Could I write him? He said I could try. How long could it last? Not much longer, he thought, but no one knew.

After some time we saw a dull red haze ahead of us on the horizon. My husband told me that it was the station in Lemberg and that it had been burning for three days. As we approached Lemberg, we saw several smoldering red patches of light where before there had been factories and warehouses.

We drew up in front of the hotel in the center of the city. It was even darker here than in the woods at home. It was two o'clock in the morning, but the streets were full of people. My husband went to rouse the Rumanian consul for our passport visas. I stood by the cars. Now and then some passerby said a few words in a low voice, but for the most part the stream of people moved in silence. Peasants passed us, pushing wheelbarrows laden with sacks. Wagons full of children sitting up stiffly, sound asleep, rattled over the cobblestones.

I stood there a long time. Still my husband didn't return. He had told me we must reach the frontier before the morning raids began. I looked at the sky. It seemed a little paler. Why didn't he come? I took out a cigarette. When I struck a match to light it, a hand reached out and stopped me. "No smoking," someone mumbled in my ear.

At last my husband came back. He had the passports in his hand. "Get those children to safety," he told me. "That's what you have to do. God bless you." He kissed the children and me.

"Drive on," he said to the chauffeurs sharply. "And don't stop, whatever you do." As we drove off, he waved his cap.

For the rest of the night I kept my eye on the tiny red tail-light of the car in front. We passed groups of soldiers, autobuses, camouflaged cars. The dust on which no rain had fallen for weeks filtered in upon us, stinging our eyes. The children cried. Wherever we stopped to show our papers, there were people about us, lying under bushes and in the ditches at the sides of the roads. I listened all night to the sound of the motor, waiting to hear it weaken or splutter, clenching my hands when it balked on the hills. All night, in my mind, I was driving those two cars of ours as fast as I could.

The sky grew gray, white, pink, and finally blue. It was after nine o'clock when I looked behind and saw that my little girl had been sick. I decided to stop. We got out. I unpacked some milk and crackers. Unconsciously, I listened for a distant hum, and then it came. Louder and louder, high over our heads, flew the planes I had been expecting. I flung open the door of the car, pushed in the nurse, the maid, the children, the milk, and the crackers, and got in beside the chauffeur again. "Hurry, hurry," I told him. We sped on, trailing yellow dust.

The next afternoon, in a toylike train consisting of an engine, a passenger car, and a baggage car, we travelled the three kilometres that lay between the last Polish station and the first Rumanian station and crossed the frontier into safety. "Will there be bombs in Rumania?" my little girl asked. "No more bombs now," I told her. "There's no war here. We're going where it will be sunny and where children can play wherever they please."

"But when are we going home to Papa?" she asked.

I could not answer.

# LETTER FROM LONDON

## MOLLIE PANTER-DOWNES

*May 12, 1940*

IT IS difficult to remember that this is Whitsun, the long weekend on which Londoners usually acquire the tan that must last them until their August vacation, and nothing has impressed them more as an indication that the government is really getting a move on than the decision to cut out the sacred holiday. People say that it feels like September all over again—same sort of weather, same sort of posters, same sort of empty sensation as the news came through of the bombing of Brussels, Calais, and Louvain—and the bus changing gear at the corner sounds ridiculously like a siren for a second, as it used to do in the first edgy days of the war.

On the Friday that began with the invasion of Holland, Belgium, and Luxembourg and ended with the resignation of Mr. Chamberlain, London itself seemed much the same as usual except that everyone carried a paper and most people for the first time in months carried a gas mask (ladies who felt like taking in a Whit Saturday matinée were warned by the radio that they would probably be refused admittance to the theatres without one). Air Raid Precautions workers, who have spent the last seven months playing darts and making themselves endless cups of tea, stood ready. Householders checked up on their blackout facilities and ran through the instructions for dealing with an incendiary bomb: you shovel sand over it and rush it out of the house in a bucket, after which, as the Ministry of Home Security cheerfully adds, "you will then have to deal with the fire which the bomb has started."

This being notoriously an inarticulate nation that likes to express its feelings at home and not in public at a café table, there were no excited crowds in the streets, and the only place where voices were raised above the average British monotone was Soho, where unemployed Italian waiters stood at the street corners or crowded into their favorite bar on Frith Street, vigorously arguing as to whether Mussolini is coming off the fence now, in which case they will be on the wrong side of an internment camp's barbed wire, or will wait for his friend to give him fresh proof of military prowess in the Low Countries.

21

Events are moving so fast that England acquired a new Premier almost absent-mindedly, without any excessive jubilation from Winston Churchill's supporters, who had been fearful that even at the last moment Mr. Chamberlain would hang on to the office, since he was said to feel, in his mystical Berchtesgaden manner, that it was his sacred duty to lead the nation to ultimate victory. Those who still believed him capable of doing so were mostly to be found in the middle class, for the aristocrats and the working people, who frequently plump on the same side in matters of policy, had long been resentful of his habit of surrounding himself with loyal but fumbling yes-men, and of the inflexible provincial caution that caused M. Osusky, the late Czech Minister to Paris, to observe, *"Monsieur Chamberlain n'est pas un homme d'état; il est un businessman de Birmingham."*

In Winston Churchill, people feel that they have a leader who understands exactly what risks should be taken and what kind of adversary they are up against; the iron of appeasement had burned too deeply into British souls for them ever to be quite sure again of Chamberlain on that second point. Diehard Tories, who once looked on Mr. Churchill as "a dangerous fellow," now passionately proclaim that he is just what the country needs. It's paradoxical but true that the British, for all their suspicious dislike of brilliance, are beginning to think that they'd be safer with a bit of dynamite around.

Many people want to see Lloyd George in office, arguing that his age would be discounted by the youthful fire and vigor that he can still bring to the attack. It is certain that his appointment as minister without portfolio would be popular with the sentimental British, who have a weak spot for veteran public servants and are delighted that Admiral Sir Roger Keyes, the hero of Zeebrugge, has been plucked from the retired list and sent bustling off as special naval attaché to Brussels. His fighting speech was certainly one of the sensations of Tuesday's tumultuous debate, another being the effective .use of Cromwell's famous speech dismissing Parliament by Mr. Amery, who vehemently addressed the startled Treasury bench as "old, decayed serving men and tapsters and such kind of fellows."

In the country, bus services have been suddenly cut to a skeleton schedule because buses have been commandeered to serve as emergency ambulances. The hard-working ladies of the Women's Voluntary Services are standing by for a new evacuation of London, which may start at any moment; this time, only children of school age are to be sent, but it is thought that if the ports are bombed first, which many think probable, there may be a frantic unofficial evacuation of people of all ages from them, with which it will be extremely difficult to deal.

Since the public has been asked to look out for parachute troops at dawn and dusk, there has been a great deal of argument as to what a person should do who suddenly sees a German soldier tumbling from the clouds. One publication urged its golfing readers to carry a rifle in their golf bags, but this was not recommended by the *Times,* which observed, "It would not be correct for country gentlemen to carry their guns with them on their walks, and take flying or running shots as opportunity is offered. Such action would put them into the position of francs-tireurs and should therefore be avoided." The proper procedure, in case you're worrying, said the *Times,* is to telephone the police as calmly as possible.

Britons are certainly calm in the present crisis. They are neither excessively pessimistic nor optimistic over the news as it comes in, because they remember the initial optimism over what turned out to be the Norwegian reverse. It is probable that good will come out of this reverse in the long run, if only because it has stopped people from chirping, "Ah well, we always start badly" or "We English always lose every battle but the last." There's a feeling now that in this war the last battle may not be recognized until it is over, and anyway, after Chamberlain's unfortunate colloquial remark about Hitler's having missed the bus, snappy slogans aren't so popular as they were.

It takes a good, stiff dose of adversity to release the formidable strength in what Harold Nicolson has called "the slow-grinding will power of the British people." To that has been added for the first time the quickening realization that they are fighting for their lives.

# LETTER FROM PARIS

A. J. LIEBLING

*May 12, 1940*

THE new phase of the second World War was announced to Parisians at daybreak Friday. People had gone to bed Thursday night in their habitual state of uncertainty; the governmental crisis in London was still the chief subject of preoccupation. With the dawn came the air-raid sirens, startling a city that had heard no *alerte* during the daytime since the first weeks of the war. At once, each of the innumerable residential squares in Paris took on the aspect of an Elizabethan theatre, with tiers of spectators framed in the opened windows of every building. Instead of looking down at a stage, however, they all looked up. All wore nightshirts, which, since the prosperity of tenants in a walkup is in inverse ratio to their altitude, appeared considerably dingier on the sixth and seventh floors than on the second and third.

The anti-aircraft guns, which nobody heeds now unless an *alerte* has sounded, were intoning such an impressive overture that startled birds flew out of the trees in at least one of the squares and circled nervously in squadrons over the roofs. As they did so, a large, formless woman in a gray nightshirt, making her entrée at a top-floor window, waved her right arm toward them and shouted *"Confiance!,"* putting all her neighbors in hilarious good humor.

The guns kept up their racket, and a number of tracer shells were fired to light up the early-morning sky. The noise of airplane motors was distinctly audible, but there was no way of telling whether they belonged to bombers or to French pursuit planes looking for Germans. At last, one airplane appeared, flying so high that it looked like a charm-bracelet toy, and as it passed overhead, there seemed to be a deliberate lull in the firing. (The disadvantages of knocking down a bomber directly over Paris are obvious.) People stared uneasily at the plane, as they would at a stinging insect near the ceiling, but it went away harmlessly enough, and then the guns opened up again.

The morning air was chilly, so most of the spectators soon closed their windows and went back to bed. In the Square Louvois, the neighborhood milkman, with his wagon drawn by two enormous old gray stallions, came along a few minutes after the plane, and the crash of his cans on the cobbles brought a few nervous folk back to their windows under the impression that bombing had begun.

The episode differed so from previous alarms, in which no planes were seen, that nobody seemed astonished to learn from newspapers consisting mostly of headlines that the real war—the war on the Western Front—had begun. *"Finie la drôle de guerre,"* people said to each other with a kind of relief. Even the war in Norway had seemed *"drôle,"* because it was so remote. The rush to news kiosks was such that policemen had to shepherd would-be purchasers into queues, which in some cases were half a block long. As the men and women of Paris read of the bombings in other French cities, they became united in a furious, personal anger that had as little in common with copybook patriotism as it had with the spirit of Locarno.

The public reaction to the first of what surely will become a series of air raids was so fearless that the authorities immediately became worried; all the newspapers at the moment are harping on the necessity of keeping off the streets and staying away from windows when an *alerte* sounds. The *Intransigeant* declared gravely that "block captains reported that all good Parisians went down to the air-raid shelters carrying their gas masks within five minutes of the first signal." Actually, almost nobody did, but caution is bound to increase as air raids become more frequent. Street illumination has been reduced to what it was at the beginning of October.

The drawing together of the French in time of danger is not a fiction invented by correspondents in 1914, and it did not seem in the least strange to learn within twenty-four hours after Germany invaded the Low Countries that such last-ditch Rightist Deputies as Louis Marin and Jean Ybarnegaray had joined a Reynaud ministry that already included Socialists. Hitler has within a year imposed ferociously anti-German governments on the two great democratic powers in this hemisphere. A few months after Munich, he declared that terrible things would happen if men like Churchill and Eden ever attained power in Great Britain, and that, of course, made their rise inevitable; in March, his radio speakers gloated over what looked like Reynaud's defeat, and that kept the little Frenchman in—until the end of the war, from the way it looks now. The Führer has also managed to get himself into trouble with most of the neutrals whose ports once supplied him with raw materials, to scuttle his own ships, and to drive the Allies into providing themselves with the greatest merchant marine in the history of the world.

News of military operations is, as one might expect, much scantier in Paris than in New York, or even London; it is confined to the military communiqués of the five Allies—France, Britain, Belgium, Holland, and Norway—and to what the experts can embroider on what the armies give out. Parisians have been enormously encouraged by the report, which seems indisputable, that the Dutch are fighting hard. France has not been immune to pessimistic talk, and it had been whispered that the Dutch were Nazis at heart, that they wouldn't fight, and that, even if they did fight, the Germans would go through Holland "as through butter"—all rumors which, it now seems, were unfounded.

Since the beginning of the war, the French have had confidence in the Belgians, but the most reassuring element in the situation for people here is the feeling that their own army—the one article of faith uniting all Frenchmen—is now engaged on a terrain that French soldiers have known for a thousand years, against an enemy France has usually succeeded in beating.

[May 25, 1940]

# LETTER FROM PARIS

### A. J. LIEBLING

*May 18, 1940*

THE Académie Française, working away on its great dictionary of the French language, this week completed its studies of the verb *"aimer."* At an auction gallery on the Rue Drouot, a fine 1734 edition of Molière sold for 12,500 francs. Sirens sounded at four o'clock yesterday afternoon, and hundreds of mothers led their children out of the Tuileries Gardens, where the young ones had been playing in the sun, to the shelters under the arcades of the Rue de Rivoli; the children carried sand pails and sailboats, few of them cried, and the mothers did not hurry them unduly, for it is an axiom here that you must not frighten a child. No firing was audible, but the government reported this morning that sixteen bombers had been sighted, headed for Paris, and that four had been brought down.

The increased frequency of *alertes* and the near-blackouts in the evenings are the most obvious outward signs of the new seriousness of the war; truck-drivers and shopgirls and cobblers go about their business with the same calm as the Academicians. People, naturally, worry about friends or relatives in the thick of a battle which the newspapers describe as the greatest in history, but this is such a universal and troubling preoccupation among Parisians that it is regarded as unnecessary and inconsiderate to talk about it.

Another phenomenon of the present turn of the war is the comparatively large number of automobile drivers who head in the wrong direction on one-way streets and receive only courteous admonitions from the usually caustic police. The drivers are Belgian refugees, unfamiliar with Paris's complicated traffic regulations. Some of the Belgians' cars are small and old, with mattresses and household goods strapped on their roofs; others are sleek Chryslers and Minervas. The wealthiest refugees, having the most powerful cars, got here first, and Paris hotels were soon filled with characteristically large Belgian families. The children in such families seem to think of the exodus as a junket, while their parents worry about what they are going to do for a living when their cash runs out.

The poor, and therefore most numerous, refugees are those who come by train. Among these are waxen-faced mothers dragging drowsy babies, and

27

very old couples who remind you of New Englanders—respectable, reserved, and exasperated—lugging cowhide suitcases and parrot cages, and repeating, after an interval of twenty-six years, the great trek they made in the previous war, when they were already middle-aged. There are blond doxies from the boulevards of Brussels who, when the fright and fatigue of the journey are over, stare hopefully around at the great city that they have read about in serials, and there are, of course, a great many nuns.

Committees for the welcome of Belgians meet them at the Gare du Nord and distribute billets for lodging and coupons for food. No men of military age get off the incoming trains, but there is a steady stream of soldiers northbound out of Paris—men who have been on sick leave and *permissionnaires* held here until the authorities could locate their corps in the great, suddenly imposed mêlée. The soldiers, like the refugees, are weighed down under duffels and cooking utensils and wine bottles, and many of them, also like refugees, carry little dogs. They go back, these components of various corps, without the lift that comes from mass enthusiasm, but as sure of themselves as riveters going to work.

The real war cry of France in these difficult moments is *"Les salauds!"*—which means the Germans and is, as you probably know, emphatic and impolite. The impact of the Germans, especially the rapidity of the advance across the Meuse and the great striking power of the armored divisions, undoubtedly impressed the French, who had become so used to thinking themselves safe behind the Maginot Line they had forgotten that the northern frontier was protected only by the much more fragile barrier of two neutral countries and the bodies of men. The French, however, have never been frightened; the 1914 veterans in Paris say, with confidence, that though the Germans always strike hard to begin with, they sooner or later slow up, while the French hang on and on.

Last Thursday, though it was marked by a comparative lull on the front, was a day of black rumors among foreigners and café strategists in Paris: the Germans, people whispered, were practically in the suburbs. The rumors failed to affect the ordinary Frenchman, nor did they upset the experts, who say they are "rather optimistic" that the drive is losing momentum.

"The events" is the current phrase for the horrors north of here—in France and in the Low Countries. Nobody speaks of a crisis or a defeat, or even of an offensive. "Because of the events," the French say, "the autobuses are not running today" or "Because of the events, police are carrying rifles." The rifles are for use against parachutists or Fifth Columnists, and the police, who are more likely to be provincials than Parisians, are deadly serious about such precautions, which is a good thing. A young Japanese Embassy attaché told a friend that it was nice to be a Japanese, since no policeman could possibly suspect him of being a parachutist.

As pathetic in some respects as the refugees are the bewildered statesmen of recently neutral countries, who visit Paris on their way to or from London and give press conferences in which they try to explain that the disasters encountered by their governments are the result of an attitude of excessive good will—an attitude which, they don't bother to point out, used to save a lot of money on their armament budgets. Mynheer van Kleffens, the Netherlands' Minister of Foreign Affairs, recounting with real emotion the story of the war that lasted four days, virtually asked the rest of the world to protect the great wealth the Netherlands had accumulated in the Indies and had been too high-minded to spend in order to create an effective fighting force. When Parisians hear things like that, they are inclined to remark that had each democratic power contributed to collective security in just proportion to its potentialities, the dictators could have been reduced to impotence before this war ever started.

# LETTER FROM LONDON

## MOLLIE PANTER-DOWNES

*May 24, 1940*

WHILE the greatest battle in history is being fought on the other side of the Channel, which has suddenly shrunk in most people's minds to something no bigger than the Thames, an equally great revolution has been taking place here. In a single day so much constitutional ballast was heaved overboard in order to lighten the unwieldy ship for this swift and deadly new warfare that a number of revered statesmen must have positively writhed in their graves. If the British people had their way, several more—who were once revered but are now revealed in all their heavy guilt of responsibility for placing the country in its present critical peril—would shortly be joining them.

Even the slowest minds in a race not famed for lightning perceptions have grasped at last, with anger and bitterness, the exact extent of that peril to which the years of complacent leadership have brought them, and they are ready emotionally for the most drastic measures Mr. Churchill may choose to take. On the day the act was passed empowering the Government to require all persons "to place themselves, their services, and their property at the disposal of His Majesty," a coster on a donkey cart possibly summed up the universal comment on the announcement of Britain's total mobilization when he shouted to a crony, "That's right! All in it together to knock 'is bleedin' block off!"

All in it they certainly are, donkey cart and Rolls-Royce alike. "There must be no laggards," warned Mr. Attlee. "Victory is our goal. We must and shall attain it." Nobody doubts that to do so the Government will use its new powers, more complete than any government has held since Cromwell's time, to the utmost. The Englishman's home is no longer his castle but a place that can be commandeered at a moment's notice if the state needs it. Landowners must be prepared to give up their land; employers to close down their businesses or to carry on under government control, and perhaps at a loss; employees to change their jobs as they may be directed by the Ministry of Labour. It's the stiffest dose of totalitarian principles that a democracy has ever had to swallow in order to save the democratic ideal from total extinction, but there's a feeling of relief that the country is now united under a fighting leader who is not afraid to tell hard truths and to call for hard deeds when circumstances require them. Britons suspect that the present situation must be just as critical as it can be, because the King is to broadcast to them tonight and they have come to associate royal broadcasts with solemn national moments, such as abdications, the beginning of a reign, or the beginning of a war.

London has been a tense place in these last days of waiting, though the morale has been excellent. The first thing that strikes one is the unusual absence of khaki on the streets; the soldiers seem to have melted away, and with them has gone the booming prosperity of the theatres and restaurants, both of which are suffering badly. It's a fine time to shop in the big stores, for they're practically empty; the salesgirls huddle together, chatting in the middle of the departments and eying a potential customer as a group of mermaids might eye a deep-sea diver.

Barbed-wire entanglements have been erected around government buildings in Whitehall, and other barricades are halting road traffic into London for inspection at various key points. One beautiful spring evening recently, troops in their shirtsleeves were to be seen setting up sandbagged machine-gun and observation posts near the Houses of Parliament, watched by the usual expressionless group of loiterers, who might have been watching them erect gala flag standards for some bit of royal pageantry.

It's ironical that this summer looks as though it were going to be the best, as far as weather and growing things go, that England has had in years. The displays of tulips in the parks have been so magnificent that it's too bad the garden-loving Britons haven't had more heart to go and see them; the tulips in the big beds outside Buckingham Palace are exactly the color of blood. People have no heart for reading, either, unless it's the papers, which as yet have contained only one list of casualties—possibly incurred in the Norwegian campaign. Since they can't settle down to read a book or sit through a movie, they have to talk.

Atrocity stories that everyone over thirty remembers from the last war have turned up again, as good as new but with different details. They produce, together with the photographs of refugees pushing heaped perambulators along Belgian roads, a horrifying sense of living the same old nightmare all over again.

In the country, farm laborers and gentlemen with estates are flocking to enlist in the local defense corps formed to deal with what a B.B.C. announcer referred to in an absent-minded moment as American, instead of enemy, parachutists. A quarter of a million such recruits have been given rifles as well as uniforms or armlets, without which they're liable to be shot out of hand as francs-tireurs, and the job of patrolling lonely spots looking for an air armada.

Rifles must be left with the authorities and not carried home, lest they fall into the hands of local Quislings.

The Fifth Column menace is taken very seriously here, as well it might be. Motorists have been warned to remove not only the ignition key but also the distributor from their cars if they intend to leave them for any length of time unattended, and it is particularly requested that garage doors be carefully locked at night.

Since many people believe that Eire is on the Nazi map as a jumping-off place for the attack on England, those who evacuated their families to the west in September are wondering if they picked such a safe spot after all. Many more believe that with even the sleepiest hamlet not a stone's throw, as the bomber flies, from some camp, airdrome, ammunition dump, or aircraft factory, the beautiful word "safety" has temporarily gone out of circulation. In the south of England, the guns can be plainly heard pounding away all through the day, and at night the nightingales are drowned out by the drone of planes on patrol or coming back from a bombing raid.

# LETTER FROM LONDON

MOLLIE PANTER-DOWNES

*June 15, 1940*

THE fall of Paris was the culmination of a tragic week for the British people. Stunned by the brilliant speed and organization of the German drive, and bewildered by the press, which alternately warned them against undue pessimism and easy optimism, they took refuge in the classic national formula for disaster: calmness, and an increasingly dogged determination to hold back for bitter months—or years, if necessary—a juggernaut that everyone now knows is out to annihilate the nation in weeks. "Our turn will come," said a man grimly one morning this week, as he watched the newspaper-seller on a pitch on St. James Street chalking up "Germans Enter Paris" on the boards that have taken the place of posters.

One hears nothing but admiration for the heroic French resistance, and no kind of criticism of Weygand's command; the feeling seems to be that a magnificent fighting weapon has been crushed by a steam roller. All the criticism is reserved for the criminal complacency of former leaders on both sides of the Channel who refused to see that this war would be one of steam rollers, not of gentlemen's weapons, and prepared only to fight the last war over again in spite of the helpful hints of things to come given out by German armored divisions in Poland and by Italian dive-bombers in Spain. There's a growing tendency here to ask the un-British and healthily pugnacious question "Why?" Why, for instance, the munitions and aircraft factories waited until three weeks ago to double and treble their output, and why the maximum effort was not called for in the early days of September.

There are so many more urgent and frightening problems to think of at the moment (such as how to induce stubborn East End mothers to evacuate their children so that the defense of England will not be delayed by tragic fleeing hordes like those that blocked the roads out of Brussels and Paris) that these and similar questions must wait to be answered. However, the slow but formidable British anger, roused by the thought of young Englishmen firing rifles at oncoming tanks, makes it certain that there will have to be a pretty comprehensive answer someday. It's also certain that the end of the war will

*33*

find a changed—perhaps a better, possibly a less pleasant—England, in which Englishmen will no longer be able to give their loving and undivided attention to the cultivation of their gardens.

On the night that the Germans entered Paris, Queen Elizabeth broadcast to the women of France, and at the close of her touching little speech, which was made in careful, schoolgirlish French and was followed by the "Marseillaise" and the sober swell of "God Save the King," many people were unashamedly weeping. It has been a week of historic broadcasts, starting with Mr. Duff Cooper's on Monday evening after Italy's entry into the war. Next day, there were protests from some members of Parliament who deprecated Mr. Duff Cooper's bellicose tone and his impolite references to Caporetto, and who deplored the fact that such blusterings would only unify whatever split factions there may be in Italy when an appeal to religious conscience might have divided them further. To this, Mr. Duff Cooper replied briskly, indicating that Englishmen had heard a great deal too much in the same strain directed toward the German people at the beginning of the war, and that if the honorable gentlemen wanted someone to be kind and sympathetic to the Italians, they could go elsewhere—sentiments with which the majority of the public heartily agreed.

No serious-minded citizen would deny that Italy's entrance into the war at such a juncture was likely to have highly dangerous and unpleasant results for the Allies, but the average simple Briton believes that all the possibilities of the genteel approach were tried out only too patiently in September, 1939. The reminiscent ring of the announcement that pamphlets had been dropped on Rome caused a good deal less satisfaction than the news that oil tanks had been destroyed near Venice, which was hailed with delight by many people who, a short time back, would have blanched at the very thought of a bomb anywhere near a Giorgione.

On the evening of Mussolini's declaration, windows of macaroni joints in Soho were broken by excitable crowds. Italian restaurant owners elsewhere pasted notices in their windows to the effect that they were one-hundred-percent British. In spite of this loyal enthusiasm, many arrests were made and the ranks of Mayfair's restaurateurs were noticeably thinned, the Quaglino Brothers and Ferraro, the popular maître d'hôtel at the Berkeley, being among those removed.

People who had listened to Mr. Duff Cooper sat up until quarter past twelve to hear President Roosevelt's great speech, which came through perfectly and for millions of Britons provided the one gleam of light in a dark and menacing week. The answer that anxious Britons make to the new universal question, "Will the Americans come in?," is by no means as hopelessly negative as it would have been a short while ago. There is an increasingly trusting belief in American assistance—first with guns and planes, and eventually with men. People simply cannot believe that the great power whose chief representative spoke to them so nobly on Monday night can continue to contemplate these horrors unmoved. Time, however, is the principal factor, as André Maurois said in his recent heartbreaking appeal for France, in which he observed that one division then, even if badly equipped, would be worth more than several divisions, magnificently equipped, in two months. Time, which was once said to be on the side of the Allies, has turned out to be, after all, Hitler's man.

# LETTER FROM LONDON

MOLLIE PANTER-DOWNES

*June 22, 1940*

ON MONDAY, June 17th—the tragic day on which Britain lost the ally with whom she had expected to fight to the bitter end—London was as quiet as a village. You could have heard a pin drop in the curious, watchful hush. At places where normally there is a noisy bustle of comings and goings, such as the big railway stations, there was the same extraordinary preoccupied silence. People stood about reading the papers; when a man finished one, he would hand it over to anybody who hadn't been lucky enough to get a copy, and walk soberly away.

For once the cheerful cockney comeback of the average Londoner simply wasn't there. The boy who sold you the fateful paper did it in silence; the bus conductor punched your ticket in silence. The public seemed to react to the staggering news like people in a dream, who go through the most fantastic actions without a sound. There was little discussion of events because they were too bad for that. With the house next door well ablaze and the flames coming closer, it was no time to discuss who or what was the cause and whether more valuables couldn't have been saved from the conflagration.

Similarly, people were more reassured by the half-dozen sentences which the Prime Minister barked into the microphone that Monday evening than they would have been by any lengthy, prepared oration. Mr. Churchill's statement the next day was less stirring than sensible—a carefully reasoned balance sheet of the chances for a British victory, well suited to the grimly sane public mood.

Tuesday afternoon the newspaper-sellers were chalking "French Army Still Fighting" on their signs, to which one or two had added "Vive la France!" In the almost deserted residential streets, cars full of luggage and people moved away from newly shuttered houses and turned into the traffic going toward the big roads out of London. Oxford Street crowds were buying strawberries from hawkers who handed out their usual hoarse philosophy to the customers.

Few people remembered that Tuesday was the anniversary of the Battle of Waterloo, another occasion when disaster trod very close on the heels of this country, and when it seemed impossible that the British squares could stand up to the assault of the greatest military machine in the world, led by the greatest commander. "Hard pounding, this, gentlemen," said Wellington to his staff at one stage of that battle. "Let's see who will pound the longest." "Don't worry, lidy," one of the strawberry-barrow proprietors said on Tuesday to a stout and apprehensive matron, " 'e'll find us an 'ard nut to crack and no mistike."

It's possible that the anniversary of Waterloo was celebrated unconsciously this year, after all. The determination to keep pounding the longest is the only thing that people have been able to see clearly in the past dark and bewildering week. News from France has been scarce. Rumors about the French Navy and Air Force continue to get around, and every other person claims to have seen a strange-looking squadron flying with Gallic lack of formation in the direction of some British airfield.

It would be difficult for an impartial observer to decide today whether the British are the bravest or merely the most stupid people in the world. The way they are acting in the present situation could be used to support either claim. The individual Englishman seems to be singularly unimpressed by the fact that there is now nothing between him and the undivided attention of a war machine such as the world has never seen before. Possibly it's lack of imagination; possibly again it's the same species of dogged resolution which occasionally produces an epic like Dunkirk. Millions of British families, sitting at their well-stocked breakfast tables eating excellent British eggs and bacon, can still talk calmly of the horrors across the Channel, perhaps without fully comprehending even now that anything like that could ever happen in England's green and pleasant land.

The authorities are certainly doing their best to drive the idea that it could deeply into the public consciousness. From now on, ringing of church bells for any reason except to warn of approaching invaders will be forbidden—a nice throwback to Napoleonic England which fits in well with squires watching the skies from the hilltops and peasants cleaning old shotguns in the villages. A movement to provide parashots with hand grenades is afoot, sponsored by Beaverbrook's *Express,* which manufactured the slogan, "A hand-grenade dump by each village pump," and opened a whole new vista of horrible possibilities by insisting that every schoolboy who could throw a cricket ball was perfectly capable of throwing a grenade.

One morning this week, postmen slipped official pamphlets in with the mail, telling householders just what to do if Britain is invaded. Official advice is to stay at home unless told by the proper authorities to leave, "because, if you run away, you will be machine-gunned from the air, as were civilians in Holland and Belgium." People were also warned not to believe rumors, not to supply any German with food, petrol, or maps, and to overcome their natural inclination to mind their own business sufficiently to go to the police if they see anything at all suspicious.

Apart from the Prime Minister's statement that the bulk of the new B.E.F. contingents had been withdrawn safely from France, the best news of the week for most people was the appointment of Mr. Stimson and Colonel Knox to President Roosevelt's Cabinet. Although the irrepressible British love of a joke, even in the most desperate situation, led the irreverent to christen the refugee ship Washington the S.S. Gone With the Wind Up, the majority of Britons hope and believe that before long there will be many more ships making the crossing—this time from west to east.

# PARIS POSTSCRIPT

A. J. LIEBLING

ON SATURDAY, May 11th, the day after the Germans invaded Holland and Belgium, I had a letter from Jean-Pierre, a corporal in one of the two French armored divisions, which were created after the Polish campaign. They were good divisions, and Jean-Pierre had no way of knowing that the Germans had six times as many. "The real rough-house is about to begin," he wrote. "So much the better! It will be like bursting an abscess." Jean-Pierre, whose parents were my oldest friends in France, was a strong, quiet boy who in civil life had been a draftsman in an automobile factory. He liked to play ice hockey and collect marine algae. He had not wanted a soft job in a factory during the war because he did not want to be considered a coward.

On the same morning, I had a telephone conversation with another friend of mine, Captain de Sombreuil, who had just arrived from Alsace on furlough. Upon reaching the Gare de l'Est, he had learned that all furloughs were cancelled, so he was going back by the next train. He called me up to say that he wouldn't be able to go to the races at Auteuil with me as he had planned. "It's good that it's starting at last," he said. "We can beat the Boches and have it over with by autumn."

In the afternoon I went to Auteuil alone. I watched a horse belonging to Senator Hennessy, the cognac man, win the Prix Wild Monarch for three-year-old hurdlers. The track was crowded with people whose main preoccupations seemed to be the new three-year-olds and the new fashions being worn by the women. That day the Germans were taking Arnhem and Maastricht in Holland and attacking Rotterdam with parachutists. Nobody worried much. Everyone was eager principally to know whether French troops had yet made contact with the enemy. "The Boches have business with somebody their own size now!" they said pugnaciously. "They will see we are not Poles or Norwegians!" It was conceivable, of course, that the Germans would win a few victories, but it would be a long war, like the last one. All France, hypnotized by 1918, still thought in terms of concentrated artillery preparations, followed by short advances and then, probably, by counterattacks. Even if the Allied troops should fail to save Holland, they would join the Belgians in holding the supposedly magnificent fortified line of the Albert Canal. At worst, the

*39*

armies could fall back to the Franco-Belgian frontier, where, the newspapers had been proclaiming since September, there was a defensive system practically as strong as the Maginot Line. Confidence was a duty. The advertising department of the Magasins du Louvre discovered another duty for France. The store's slogan was "Madame, it is your duty to be elegant!" "They shall not pass" was considered *vieux jeu* and hysterical. The optimistic do-nothingism of the Chamberlain and Daladier regimes was, for millions of people, the new patriotism. Ten days before the war began in May, Alfred Duff Cooper told the Paris American Club, "We have found a new way to make war—without sacrificing human lives."

The news of the break-through at Sedan, which reached Paris on the fifth day of the offensive, was, for a few Parisians who were both pessimistic and analytical, the beginning of fear. But it happened so quickly, so casually, as presented in the communiqués, that the unreflective didn't take it seriously. The Belgian refugees began to arrive in Paris a few days after the fighting started. The great, sleek cars of the de-luxe refugees came first. The bicycle refugees arrived soon after. Slick-haired, sullen young men wearing pullover sweaters shot out of the darkness with terrifying, silent speed. They had the air of conquerors rather than of fugitives. Many of them undoubtedly were German spies. Ordinary destitute refugees arrived later by train and as extra riders on trucks. Nothing else happened at first to change the daily life of the town.

Tuesday evening, May 14th, I climbed the hill of Montmartre to the Rue Gabrielle to visit Jean-Pierre's parents. Henri, Jean-Pierre's father, had long limbs and sad eyes; he combined the frame of a high jumper and the mustaches of a Napoleonic grenadier. He was a good Catholic, and by birth and training he belonged to the wealthier bourgeoisie. By temperament, which he had never been allowed to indulge, he was a bohemian. A long struggle to succeed in business, which he secretly detested, had ended in a defeat just short of total. When war was declared, he was working for a firm of textile stylists whose customers were chiefly foreign mills. Since September, business had fallen off drastically and Henri had had nothing to do except drop in once in a while to keep up the firm's desultory correspondence. Henri spoke English, German, and Dutch in addition to French, and sometimes sang in a deep voice that sounded like a good but slightly flawed cello. He often said that he was happy to be living, at last, high on Montmartre, just under Sacré-Cœur. His wife, Eglée, would never have permitted him to live there for any reason less compelling than poverty. Eglée, before her marriage to Henri, had been a buyer in a department store. Recently she had devised a muslin money belt for soldiers to wear under their shirts. She worked an average of sixteen hours a day, making the belts with a frantic dexterity, but about once a fortnight she got so exhausted that she had to stay in bed for two or three days. She had placed the belts in several of the department stores, but her profit was small. Eglée and Henri were both about sixty years old. For thirty-five years, Henri had pretended to like trade in order to hold his wife's respect, and Eglée had pretended to loathe trade in order to hold Henri's affection. Neither had succeeded in deceiving the other. He brooded, she scolded, he drank a little, they quarrelled incessantly, and they loved each other more than any two people I have ever known.

As I came into their apartment Tuesday night, Eglée was saying she felt sure Jean-Pierre was dead. Henri said that was nonsense. She said he was an unfeeling parent. Henri became angry and silent. Then he said that often, when he was at Verdun, Eglée had not heard from him for a week at a time. She said that Henri was always talking about Verdun and belittling "Jean-Pierre's war." "To think that after these years of preparing to avoid the old mistakes," Henri said, "the Germans are now eighty miles from us. If they get to Paris, it's all over." Eglée said he was a defeatist to mention such an eventuality. He said, "I am not a defeatist. I am an old soldier and also an old travelling man, and I know how near they are to Paris." I tried to console him by saying that the Dutch, at any rate, were fighting better than anyone had expected. Henri had cousins in Holland. Eglée said the Dutch were Boches and would before long prove it.

The next morning there was a radio announcement that the Dutch had surrendered in Europe but were going to continue the war in the East Indies. In the afternoon, some of the American correspondents, including myself, went to the Netherlands Legation to meet Mynheer Van Kleffens, the Netherlands Minister for Foreign Affairs, who had arrived from London to explain the Dutch decision. Van Kleffens, accompanied by the Netherlands Minister to France and the Netherlands Minister for National Defense, received us and the journalists of other neutral countries in the Legation garden. While we were talking, sadly and quietly, among the trees, the French were losing the war. On that Wednesday, May 15th, the Germans made the deep incision which a few days later was to split the Allied armies. The Foreign Minister, a blond, long-faced man, had a pet phrase that he repeated many times, as a man does when he is too tired to think of new forms for his thought. "The Germans tried this," he would say, recounting some particular method of the German attack, and then he would add, "It failed." "It failed," he would say, and again, "It failed"—until you thought he was talking of a long, victorious Dutch resistance—and then finally, "But to fight longer was hopeless." "We will fight on" was another recurrent phrase. When we asked him whether the Dutch had any planes left to fight with, he said, "No. We had fifty bombers. The last one flew off and dropped its last bomb and never returned."

Holland, with one-tenth the population of Germany but with several times the wealth per capita, had presented fifty bombers against five thousand. It had been comfortable to believe in neutrality, and cheap. Norway, with the fourth largest merchant marine in the world, had not built the few good light cruisers and destroyers that might have barred the weak German navy from its ports. France herself had economized on the Maginot Line, had decided it was too expensive to extend the fortifications from Luxembourg to the sea. The democracies had all been comfortable and fond of money. Thinking of the United States, I was uneasy.

The first panic of the war hit Paris Thursday, May 16th. It affected, however, only the most highly sensitized layers of the population: the correspondents, the American and British war-charity workers, and the French politicians. In Paris, because of censorship, news of disaster always arrived unofficially and twenty-four hours late. On the evening of the catastrophic May 15th, even the neurotic clientele of the Ritz and Crillon bars had been calm. But on Thursday people began telling you about Germans at Meaux and south of Soissons, points the Germans didn't actually reach until over three weeks later. There was a run on the Paris branch of the Guaranty Trust Company by American depositors. I lunched in a little restaurant I frequently went to on the Rue Ste.-Anne, and after the meal, M. Bisque, the proprietor, suggested that we go to the Gare du Nord to see the refugees. M. Bisque cried easily. Like most fine cooks, he was emotional and a heavy drinker. He had a long nose like a woodcock and a mustache which had been steamed over cookpots until it hung lifeless from his lip. Since my arrival in France in October, he had taken me periodically on his buying trips to the markets so that I could see the Germans weren't starving Paris. On these trips we would carry a number of baskets and, as we filled one after another with oysters, artichokes, or pheasants, we would leave them at a series of bars where we stopped for a drink of apple brandy. The theory was that when we had completed our round of the markets we would circle back on our course, picking up the baskets, and thus avoid a lot of useless carrying. It worked all right when we could remember the bars where we had left the various things, but sometimes we couldn't, and on such occasions M. Bisque would cry that *restauration* was a cursed *métier,* and that if the government would permit he would take up his old rifle and leave for the front. But they would have to let him wear horizon blue; he could not stand the sight of khaki because it reminded him of the English. "They say the English are very brave at sea," he would say, winking slowly, "but who knows? We don't see them, eh?"

The trip to the Gare du Nord was solemn. M. Bisque dragged me to see various mothers sitting on rolls of bedding and surrounded by miauling children; his eyes would water, and he would offer a child a two-franc piece, and then haul me to the buffet, where he would fortify himself with a glass of Beaujolais. At the buffet I remember meeting a red-bearded gnome of a colonial soldier who kept referring to himself as "a real porpoise." "Porpoise" was the traditional Army term for a colonial infantryman. "A real porpoise," the soldier repeated dreamily, "an old porpoise, and believe me, Monsieur, the Germans need *somebody* to bust their snouts for them." He had two complete sets of decorations, one from the old war and one from the new. He was going north to rejoin his regiment and he was full of fight and red wine.

Saturday morning I had another note from Jean-Pierre. He enclosed a bit of steel from a Dornier shot down near him. "How I am still alive I have not time to write to you," he said, "but chance sometimes manages things well." The letter produced the same effect on me as news of a great victory. I called up Henri. He and Eglée had had a letter too.

On Saturday, May 18th, I went to a press conference held by the Ministry of Information, which had just organized an Anglo-American press section, with quarters in a vast, rococo ballroom at the Hôtel Continental called the Salle des Fêtes. Pierre Comert, chief of the section, held conferences for the correspondents at six every evening, when he would discuss the day's developments from the government's point of view. This evening he announced that Paul Reynaud had taken over the Ministry of National Defense. He also announced that Reynaud had recalled Marshal Pétain from Spain to advise him. General Weygand had already arrived from Syria and it was understood that he would take over the high command in a few days. The two great names, in conjunction, were expected to raise national morale. The two old men, however, were military opposites. Pétain, cautious at sixty, when he had defended Verdun, was at eighty-four incapable of conceiving any operation bolder than an orderly retreat. Weygand believed in unremitting attack. One staff officer later told me, "Weygand's ideas are so old-fashioned that they have become modern again. He is just what we need." Strategically, the two men cancelled each other, but politically they were a perfect team. Both were clericals, royalists, and anti-parliamentarians. There is something about very old soldiers like Hindenburg and Pétain that makes democrats trust them. But Pétain was to serve Laval's purpose as Hindenburg had served Hitler's. However, we were cheerful on the evening we heard about the appointments. The German advance was apparently slowing down, and all of us thought that Weygand might arrange a counterattack soon. A week earlier we had been expecting victories. Now we were cheered by a slightly slower tempo of disaster.

There was a hot, heavy pause the next few days. I took long walks on the boulevards, and up and down dull, deserted business streets. The wartime population of Paris had slowly increased from late November until April, as evacuated families returned from the provinces, but since the beginning of the offensive the population had again decreased. All the people who remained in town seemed to concentrate on the boulevards. It gave them comfort to look at one another. They were not yet consciously afraid, however. There were long queues in front of the movie houses, especially those that showed double features. You could get a table at a sidewalk café only with difficulty, and the ones that had girl orchestras did particularly well. One girl orchestra, at the Grande Maxeville, was called the Joyous Wings and its bandstand and instruments had been decorated with blue airplanes. There were no young soldiers in the streets, because no furloughs were being issued.

It is simple now to say, "The war on the Continent was lost on May 15th." But as the days in May passed, people in Paris only gradually came to suspect how disastrous that day had been. There was a time lag between every blow and the effect on public morale. I can't remember exactly when I first became frightened, or when I first began to notice that the shapes of people's faces were changing. There was plenty of food in Paris. People got thin worrying. I think I noticed first the thinning faces of the sporting girls in the cafés. Since the same girls came to the same cafés every night, it was easy to keep track. Then I became aware that the cheekbones, the noses, and the jaws of all Paris were becoming more prominent.

There was no immediate danger in Paris unless the Germans bombed it, and when the news was in any degree encouraging, I did not think of bombing at all. When the news was bad, I thought of bombing with apprehension. It helped me understand why troops in a winning army are frequently brave and on the losing side aren't. We heard anti-aircraft fire every night now, but there were no air-raid alarms, because the planes the guns were firing at were reconnaissance planes. The heaviest shooting would begin in the gray period just before dawn. You wouldn't really settle down to sleep until the morning shooting was over, and you wouldn't wake up until noon.

On the night of May 21st, after Paul Reynaud announced to the Senate that the Germans were at Arras and that France was in danger, I had a *frousse* —a scare—of such extreme character that it amounted to *le trac,* which means a complete funk. It was an oppressively hot night, with thunder as well as anti-aircraft fire, interspersed with noises that sounded like the detonations of bombs in the suburbs. When I lay on my bed face down, I couldn't help thinking of a slave turning his back to the lash, and when I lay on my back I was afraid of seeing the ceiling fall on me. Afterward I talked to dozens of other people about that night and they all said they'd suffered from the same funk. The next morning's papers carried Weygand's opinion that the situation was not hopeless. This cheered everybody. It has since been revealed that May 21st, the day of the great *frousse,* was the day set for the counterattack that might have cracked the Germans. It never came, and by May 22nd, when we were all beginning to feel encouraged, the opportunity had been missed.

Later that day, word got around among the correspondents that negotiations were already on for a separate peace and that if the French didn't sign it the Germans might arrive in Paris in a few days. This counteracted the effect of the Weygand message. Still later, I felt encouraged again as I watched a city gardener weed a bed of petunias in the Square Louvois, the tiny park under my hotel window. Surely, I thought, if the old man believed the Germans were coming in, he would not be bothering with the petunias.

The greatest encouragement I got during those sad weeks came from Jean-Pierre. Shortly after the Reynaud speech, I went up the hill to Montmartre to take some flowers to Jean-Pierre's mother. For once, Henri and Eglée were smiling at the same time. "You should have been here early this morning for a good surprise!" Henri shouted. "At five there was a knock at our door." "And who do you suppose it was?" his wife cried, taking over the narrative. "Suzette?" I demanded, naming their married daughter, who lived in Grenoble. I was sure that it had been Jean-Pierre, but I wanted to prolong Eglée's pleasure. "No," Eglée announced happily. "It was Jean-Pierre. He was magnificent. He looked like a cowboy." "He came with his *adjudant,*" Henri broke in, "to get engine parts they needed for tanks. The boy has no rest, you know," he said proudly. "When the division goes into action, he fights. When they are in reserve and the other fellows rest, he is head of a repair section. He is a magician with engines. And his morale is good! He says that the first days were hard, but that now they know they can beat the Boche." "On the first day of the battle, Jean-Pierre's general was arrested," Eglée said, with a sort of pride. "What *canaille!* Jean said it was fantastic what a traitor the general turned out to be. And there were German spies in French officers' uniforms!" "They met a regiment of artillery without officers," Henri said, "but completely! 'So much the better,' the artillerists said. 'They were traitors anyway. But where in the name of God are we supposed to go?' Fifteen German bombers appeared over Jean-Pierre's unit. 'We're in for it,' he said to himself. But the boy was lucky. The Germans had dropped their bombs elsewhere. Then Jean-Pierre's unit met German tanks. He says our fellows rode right over them. 'There may be a great many of them,' he said, 'but we are better than they are. Our guns penetrate them, but they do not penetrate us. As for the spy problem, we have solved that. We simply shoot all officers we do not know.' Jean-Pierre and the *adjudant* stayed for breakfast. Then they had to go away."

Although I knew that an individual soldier had no chance to understand a military situation as a whole, Jean-Pierre's optimism raised my spirits considerably. I believed fully the details of the encounter with the German tanks. Jean-Pierre was of that peculiar race of engine-lovers who cannot lie about the performance of a mechanical thing.

When I returned to my hotel, I passed along Jean-Pierre's confident report to Toutou, the hotel's cashier, with whom I often discussed the war. She was a patriot but a congenital pessimist. All the employees slept on the top floor of the hotel, and as soon as Toutou had read of the German parachutists in Holland she had bought a revolver and cartridges. "If one lands on the roof, I'll pop him!" she had said. "Or perhaps as he descends past my window!"

In each week of disaster there was an Indian summer of optimism. On the third Sunday after the offensive started, I had dinner with Henri and Eglée. We teased one another about our forebodings of a fortnight earlier. "Do you remember how sure you were that the Germans would be here momentarily?" Eglée said to me. "And how you were certain that Jean-Pierre was no longer alive?" Henri asked Eglée. "It seems a year ago," I said sincerely. "I must admit that the French have their heart well hooked on. Any other people would have caved in after such a blow. I wonder where Weygand will make the counterattack." "In Luxembourg, in my opinion," Henri said. "If he made the counterattack too far to the west he would not catch enough Boches. A good wide turning movement, and you will see—the whole band of them will have to scramble off. They will be on the other side of the Albert Canal again in a week."

We talked and listened to the radio, and, as usual, I stayed for tea, then for supper, and then for the final news bulletin broadcast at eleven-thirty. The bulletins earlier in the day had been dull. But something in the speaker's voice this time warned us, as soon as he commenced, that the news was bad. We began to get sad before he had said anything important. Then he said, "Whatever the result of the battle in Flanders, the high command has made provision that the enemy will not profit strategically by its result." "What can he mean?" Eglée asked. "He means that they are preparing to embark that army for England," Henri said. "Unless the enemy captures the army, his victory is tactical but not strategical." "But why must they embark?" Eglée asked. "I do not know," Henri said almost savagely. That was the day—though none of us knew it—that King Leopold told his Ministers he was going to give up. Eglée began to cry. "Now they are coming to Paris," she said, "now they are coming to Paris."

As late as Monday, May 27th, people in Paris still believed that the Allies stood a chance of closing the gap between their southern and northern armies. That evening, Pierre Comert announced at a press conference I went to that operations in the north were "proceeding normally" and that the high command expected the Battle of Flanders to last at least another two weeks. I slept well that night, awakened only a few times by moderate anti-aircraft fire. In the morning, Toutou stopped me as I was going out of the hotel and said, "Did you hear Reynaud on the radio? The King of the Belgians has surrendered his army." She had been crying.

I walked about the streets stupidly the rest of the morning. I had the map well in mind. The Belgians, by their surrender, had laid bare the left flank of the Franco-British armies in Flanders, and I thought the armies would soon be surrounded. Perhaps the French and British in the north would become demoralized and surrender. If they had been seeking an excuse to quit, they had a good one now. People on the streets were saying to each other, "And that isn't the worst of it. All the refugees probably are spies." They did not seem depressed. A man wheeling a pushcart loaded with wood stopped and shouted to a colleague on the other side of the street, "Say, old fellow, did you hear the news? Ain't we just taking it on the potato!" In his voice was a note of pride.

I walked around the Place Vendôme a couple of times; the luxury-shop windows had for me a reassuring association of tourists and normal times. Charvet was showing summer ties. I bought a couple from an elegant and hollow-chested salesman. I didn't want to talk to him about the war because he looked sad enough already, but he began to talk about it himself. "We are an indolent people, Monsieur," he said pleasantly. "We need occurrences like this to wake us up." Paris reminded me of that conversational commonplace you hear when someone has died: "Why, I saw him a couple of days ago and he looked perfectly well." Paris looked perfectly well, but I wondered if it might not be better for a city in such danger to show some agitation. Perhaps Paris was dying.

That night, when the shock of the Belgian surrender had begun to wear off, I had a late dinner with two American friends in a little Marseillais restaurant on the Rue Montmartre. We were the only customers. We had Mediterranean rouget burned in brandy over twigs of fennel. Although all three of us knew that the war was lost, we could not believe it. The rouget tasted too much as good rouget always had; the black-browed proprietor was too normally solicitous; even in the full bosom and strong legs of the waitress there was the assurance that this life in Paris would never end. Faith in France was now purely a *mystique;* a good dinner was our profane form of communion.

Incredibly, beginning the day after the Belgian surrender, there was a great wave of exhilaration, based on the heroic action of the British and French armies fighting their way out of Flanders. People with relatives in the northern armies had, when they heard of the capitulation, resigned themselves to the capture or death of the trapped men. The German government, in radio broadcasts, had threatened that even if the Allies were able to make a stand at Dunkirk the Germans would sink every boat that tried to embark troops. It was one German threat that didn't come off. People in Paris began to receive telegrams from relatives who had safely arrived in England. Several of my acquaintances received such messages, so we assumed that the number of troops saved was very large.

Henri and Eglée had not worried about Jean-Pierre, because, having seen him on leave since the Germans drove the wedge between the Allied armies, they knew he was south of the Somme. But Henri's brother Paul, who at fifty had been called back into service as a lieutenant of artillery, was with the army in Flanders. One evening shortly after the Belgian surrender, I climbed up to the Rue Gabrielle to visit Henri and Eglée, and found them in a happy mood, because Paul had reached England. I tried to talk to Eglée about what she and her husband would do if the Germans turned toward Paris after they finished the Dunkirk job. Her answer was simply that she had an order from the Galeries Lafayette for five dozen money belts and that after she completed the order she would have to wait eight days for payment, so how could she think of leaving Paris? As for Henri, he said he now constituted the whole office force of the textile-design company and couldn't leave without giving a month's notice. Peacetime thought patterns were mercifully persistent.

Everyone now was doing his best to forget that the Allied forces had had too few tanks and guns to begin with, and that now the evacuated armies had lost what little they had. We consoled ourselves with stories of individual heroism and with the thought that the Allies, after all, controlled the sea. Only when the evacuation was completed did the enthusiastic French suddenly take cognizance of the fact that there were no more British troops on their side of the Channel. As if spontaneously, the German gibe "England will fight to the last Frenchman" swam into the popular consciousness and began to seem like a portent.

Two kinds of person are consoling in a dangerous time: those who are completely courageous, and those who are more frightened than you are. Fernand, the night porter at my hotel, was completely courageous. "Well, what do you know?" he would ask me when I came home at night. Before I answered, he would say, "We will have them yet, the camels. It takes a few defeats to get our blood up. They poison our lives by provoking the anti-aircraft into making a noise at night. A surprise is preparing itself for those cocos!" It was a pleasure to see him during the frequent early-morning *alertes*. Hearing the sirens, he would go out into the small park in front of the hotel and, shielding his eyes with his hands, search the sky for airplanes. Seeing none, he would shake his head disgustedly and shout up to the female guests at the windows of the hotel, "Do not derange yourselves, Mesdames, it is for nothing again!"

The most frightened man I saw in France was a certain well-known French journalist who wrote under various names in a dozen Parisian newspapers of varying political color. He had a broad, paraffin-textured face which, when he was alarmed, appeared to be on the point of melting. Long before the offensive began in May, he had tried to explain to me why Laval, the appeaser, and Paul Faure, the left-of-Blum Socialist, together with Georges Bonnet, representative of the great banking house of Lazard Frères, were all planning a move to get rid of Paul Reynaud in order to liquidate the war as quickly as possible. They wanted to put Daladier back in Reynaud's place because they knew that as long as Daladier headed the government there would be no effectual war—that eventually the war would die of dry rot, which was what ninety per cent of the French politicians and all the French Communists, along with the Germans, wanted. I had asked naïvely why Laval didn't try to become Premier himself. "Because, of course," my journalist friend had said impatiently, "then everybody would *know* he was going to make peace. Then there would be mutiny in the Army." Personally, he used to say, he was a decided partisan of both Reynaud, who wanted to fight, and of Laval, who wanted to make peace. You were always running up against things like that in French politics.

When I met my journalist at lunch one day the first week of June, he was in as spectacular a funk as I have ever observed. "What a terrible mistake to have provoked those people, my dear!" he shrieked. "What madness to concern ourselves with Poland! Laval was so right to have wished to conciliate Mussolini. I am going to give my dog a lethal injection. He could never stand the nervous shock of those bombs that whistle. Working people are so insouciant. They know they have us in their power. I cannot get a man to dig a trench in my garden for me until tomorrow afternoon, and the bombers may be here any minute!" As he stuffed asparagus into his mouth, large tears welled out of his eyes. "Peace, quickly, quickly!" he shouted, after swallowing the asparagus.

Sunday, June 2nd, I visited the country home of a French newspaper publisher who lived with his large, intelligent family near the town of Melun, thirty miles south of Paris. The countryside, hot and rich and somnolent, and the family, sitting on the lawn after a chicken dinner, made me think of Sundays on Long Island. It was as if no war had ever been. We sat around in lawn chairs, fighting against drowsiness, talking unintently, resisting the efforts of one woman to get up a game like charades. We spoke with no originality whatever of all the mistakes all the appeasers in the world had made, beginning with Ethiopia. We repeated to one another how Italy could have been squelched in 1935, how a friendly Spanish government could have been maintained in power in 1936, how the Germans could have been prevented from fortifying the Rhineland in the same year. We talked of the Skoda tanks, built according to French designs in Czechoslovakia, that were now ripping the French army apart. The Germans had never known how to build good tanks until Chamberlain and Daladier presented them with the Skoda plant. These matters had become for every European capable of thought a sort of litany, to be recited almost automatically over and over again.

Women in the train that took me back to town that evening were talking about the leaflets German planes had dropped, promising to bombard Paris the next day. The word "bombardment" had a terrible sound, evoking pictures of Warsaw and Rotterdam. The train arrived at the Gare de Lyon after eleven. There were no taxis. In the last month they had become increasingly scarce even in the daytime; the drivers simply refused to risk their necks in the pitch-black streets at night. I could not distinguish one street from another. There was a cluster of dim, moving lights at a distance, like a luminous jellyfish seen by another fish at the bottom of the sea. I started toward the lights and tripped over a plank, skinning my knee. When I reached them, I found they came from the electric lanterns of a group of policemen who were stopping pedestrians and examining their papers. They were polite and quiet. One of them told me how to get to my hotel, which took me almost an hour.

The promised bombardment came at about one o'clock the next afternoon, an anticlimax to its advance notices. It was preceded by a tremendous noise of motors in airplanes too high to be seen, and by the angry hammering of anti-aircraft guns. Technically, I was later given to understand, it was, from the German standpoint, a very good bombardment. Two hundred and fifty planes participated, the largest number that had been assembled for a single operation in this war. The bombing, considering the height at which the planes flew—twenty thousand feet—was commendably accurate. However, the results looked nothing like the photographs of Warsaw and Rotterdam, because Paris was reasonably well defended. "The anti-aircraft fire was well nourished," the French said, "so the bombers stayed high." The pursuit squadrons, although they failed to intercept the bombers on their way to Paris, were on their tails so closely that the Germans dropped their bombs quickly and left. If there had been no defending batteries or planes, as at Rotterdam, the bombers would have loafed along a few hundred feet above the main thoroughfares and dropped their high explosives like roach powder. The bombs hit the huge Citroën factory on the Quai de Javel and knocked down a few scattered apartment houses, but the total effect on public morale was tonic. Forty-eight hours after the bombardment, M. Dautry, the Minister of War Industry, took a group of correspondents through the Citroën plant, which had been the chief German objective. There we found a smell of burnt paint, and a great deal of broken glass on the floor, but no serious damage to the great automobile-assembly lines or the part of the plant where shells were made. The women making shells worked on as calmly as girls in an American candy factory.

The day we visited the factory, June 5th, was also the day the Germans began their second attack, the push southward across the Somme that was to carry them to the Spanish frontier. "It is the beginning of the second round," Pierre Comert announced at the press conference that evening. None of us could admit to ourselves that the war might be a two-round knockout. The French would surely be dislodged from the Somme-Aisne line, we conceded, but it would take weeks to do it. Then they would defend Paris and the line of the Seine, then the line of the Loire. By that time, perhaps, the British would be able to do something. Even the United States might begin to understand what was at stake. But this fight was not to have even a decent second round. The rest after the first round had not been long enough; the French were still out on their feet. Unarmed and outnumbered, they were led by two old men who were at loggerheads. As for Reynaud, he had called into his government Ybarnegaray and Marin, two reactionaries whose only surface virtue was a blustering show of war spirit. Raised to power by Socialist votes, Reynaud had turned toward men whom he trusted because they were of his own Rightist background—Pétain, Mandel, Ybarnegaray, Marin. All his Rightist friends except Mandel joined in smothering him. They felt that by making war against Hitler he was betraying his own class.

When I got back to my hotel that night, tired and discouraged, Fernand the porter, looking radiant, said to me, "What they must be digesting now, the Boches!" He showed me a copy of Le Temps, which said the German losses were stupefying. All the attacks had been "contained," but the French Army had executed a slight retreat in good order.

By now there were perceptible changes in the daily life of Paris. There was no telephone service in the hotels, so you had to make a special trip afoot every time you wanted to tell somebody something. Taxis were harder than ever to find. My hotel, which was typical, had six floors. At the beginning of the war in September the proprietor had closed the fourth, fifth, and sixth floors. Now I was the only guest on the second floor, and there were perhaps a half dozen on the first. The staff, naturally, dwindled like the clientele. Every day somebody said goodbye to me. One by one the waiters left, and then it was the headwaiter, who had been kept on after all of his subordinates had been dismissed. The next day it was Toutou, who left the bookkeeping to the housekeeper. A couple of days later, the housekeeper herself left. Finally, there were only a porter and one chambermaid in the daytime, and Fernand at night. "Perhaps, if the line holds, there will be an upturn in business," the proprietor said.

It was at about this time that my restaurateur friend M. Bisque decided to close his restaurant. It was not that the Germans worried him, he explained to me, but there were no more customers, and also his wine dealer was pressing him to pay his bill. M. Bisque, and his wife, who kept the books, and his daughter Yvette, who possessed the tour de main for making a soufflé stand up on a flat plate, and his son, who had been an apprentice in the kitchen of the Café de Paris, and Marie-Louise, the waitress, were all leaving the city to run the canteen in a munitions factory south of Fontainebleau. I wished them Godspeed.

For a few days I had lacked the heart to visit Henri and Eglée. Then Henri had come to my hotel to tell me joyfully they had had another letter from Jean-Pierre, who said he had been working twenty-one hours a day repairing tanks for his division. On Sunday, June 9th, which was a warm and drowsy day, I returned Henri's call. On the way I stopped at a florist shop and bought some fine pink roses. The woman in the shop said that shipments from the provinces were irregular but that fortunately the crisis came at a season when the Paris suburbs were producing plenty of flowers. "We have more goods than purchasers," she said, laughing. When I arrived at the apartment, I found Eglée busy making her muslin money belts. Henri was amusing himself by reading a 1906 edition of the Encyclopaedia Britannica, one of his favorite possessions, and drinking a *vin ordinaire* in which he professed to find a slight resemblance to Ermitage. "This time I think the line will hold," Henri said. "I served under Pétain at Verdun. He will know how to stop them. Only I don't like that talk of infiltration near Forges-les-Eaux."

"Infiltration" was a grim word in this war. The communiqué never admitted that the Germans had pierced the French line, but invariably announced, "Motorized elements have made an infiltration. They have been surrounded and will be destroyed." Two days later the "infiltration" became a salient, from which new infiltrations radiated. When I left the apartment, Henri walked down as far as the Place des Abbesses with me. He wanted to buy a newspaper. As we stood saying goodbye, we heard a series of reports, too loud and too widely spaced for anti-aircraft. "Those sound like naval guns mounted on railroad cars," Henri said. "The Boches can't be so far away, then." That was the last time I saw Henri.

At six o'clock that evening, I went to another Anglo-American press conference at the Hôtel Continental. We were told that the Ministry of Information was planning to provide us with safe-conduct passes to use in case we left Paris. That made us suspect that the government would move very soon. Then M. Comert told us that Jean Provoust, who had just been appointed Minister of Information, wanted to talk to all the American correspondents. M. Provoust, the dynamic publisher of *Paris-Soir,* received us in his office with the factitious cordiality of a newspaper owner about to ask his staff to take a pay cut. He said that he didn't want the United States to think the situation was hopeless. "From a military standpoint," he said, "it is improving steadily. Disregard reports of the government quitting Paris. We will have many more chats in this room." John Lloyd, of the Associated Press, who was president of the Anglo-American Press Association, waited to see Provoust after the talk and invited him to be guest of honor at a luncheon the correspondents were having the next Wednesday. The Minister said he would be charmed, and then hurried away.

On my way home I saw a number of garbage trucks parked in the middle of the streets to balk airplane landings. Evidently Paris would be defended. I didn't think, after Provoust's talk, that I would have to leave Paris immediately, but the situation looked so bad that I decided to begin getting my passport in order.

Early the next morning, Monday, June 10th, I set out in a taxi—which the porter had taken two hours to find for me—to go to the Spanish Consulate General to obtain a transit visa. This was easy to get if you already had the Portuguese visa, and luckily I already had one that was good for a year. My taxi-driver came from Lorraine, where, he said, people knew what patriotism meant. He had fought the other war, four years of it. The country needed men like Poincaré, a Lorrainer, now. "The politicians have sold us out," he said. "And that Leopold," he shouted, "there is a fellow they should have got on to long ago!" Now, he expected, the Germans would come to Paris. But it would be defended, like Madrid. "They will come here, the animals," he said, "but they will leave plenty of feathers! Imagine a tank trying to upset the building of the Crédit Lyonnais! Big buildings are the best defense against those machines." He did not know that the real-estate men would never encourage such an unprofitable use of their property. "Even ten centimes on the franc is something," the rich men were already telling one another, "when one has a great many francs."

From the Spanish Consulate, I went to the Prefecture of Police, where I asked for a visa that would permit me to leave France. A woman police official, a sort of chief clerk, said, "Leave your passport and come back for it in not less than four days." "But by that time, Madame," I said, "the Germans may be here and the Prefecture may not exist." Naturally, I didn't leave the passport, but I was foolish to question the permanency of the Prefecture. The French civil servants are the one class unaffected by revolution or conquest. The Germans were to come, as it turned out, but the Prefecture was to stay open, its personnel and routine unchanged. Its great accumulation of information about individual Frenchmen, so useful for the apprehension of patriots and the blackmailing of politicians, was to be at the disposal of the Germans as it had been at Philippe-Egalité's and Napoleon the Little's and Stavisky's. The well-fed young *agents* were to continue on the same beats, unaffected by the end of the war they had never had to fight in. Yesterday the Prefecture had obeyed the orders of M. Mandel, who hated Germans. Now it would obey Herr Abetz, who hated Jews. Change of administration. *Tant pis.*

Afterward I stopped at the Crillon bar, where I met a Canadian general I knew. "The French still have a fine chance," he said. "I am leaving for Tours as soon as I finish this sandwich." I walked over to the Continental to see if M. Comert had any fresh news. As I arrived at the foot of the staircase leading to Comert's office, I met another correspondent on his way out. "If you're going up to the Ministry," he said, "don't bother. The government left Paris this morning." Then he began to chuckle. "You remember when John Lloyd stopped Provoust last night and invited him to the Wednesday luncheon?" he asked. Yes, I remembered. "Well," he said, "Provoust was in a hurry because he was leaving for Tours in a few minutes." I said maybe we had better leave too, and we did.

# LETTER FROM ENGLAND

MOLLIE PANTER-DOWNES

*August 18, 1940*

A COUPLE of mornings ago, the little village in which this is written became a ringside seat for total war. One of the mass air raids that were launched against Britain from dawn to dusk that day was directed at an objective about a dozen miles away from here. This particular raid was close enough to dawn to catch all but the most hard-working members of the community in their beds, from which they were quickly drawn by a racket suggesting that most of the Luftwaffe was practicing stunts overhead. The sky, which was cloudy, seemed to have become one vast, roaring airplane engine. Villagers said to each other, "Maybe this is it," meaning, of course, the invasion, and one or two still sleepy souls imagined the din was the clatter of tanks and lorries going along the highroad a couple of miles off.

The raiders were flying high and couldn't be seen, but suddenly there were several loud explosions and a burst of machine-gun fire coming from a distance which the country-trained ears of the listeners estimated with, it turned out later, remarkable accuracy. The village folk hung out of their windows or stood among their bean rows and dahlias looking on with a bland disregard for safety which worried the air-raid wardens, who went around on bicycles begging people to take cover. One lady made a gracious concession to authority by hopping briskly into a pigsty with a corrugated-iron roof, from which she and a startled but amiable white sow observed events companionably together.

Someone armed with binoculars called a warning as the first raider came swooping out of the clouds, a harmless, pretty-looking thing gleaming in its white camouflage. Another plane came and then another, until the sky seemed full of them—Junkers, the knowledgeable said. Still flying high, the raiders went round and round like horses in a circus, only this was a deadly sort of circus—the detonations of more bombs and the rattle of machine-gun fire, even though it sounded as innocuous as a child's popgun at that height, told us that. It was difficult at the start to be sure which were bombers and which, if any, were British fighters, but suddenly one of the Junkers detached itself from the rest and made off, fast and fairly low, toward the north, with black smoke pouring ominously from its tail. Soon another Junker came turning

54

and twisting out of the clouds in what the watchers at first took to be complicated aerial acrobatics but quickly recognized as a crash. After it vanished among the trees, there was a cloud of smoke, a pause, and then a tremendous explosion that shook the panes in cottage windows. Finally, two British fighters circled low, went into a few exultant loops, and made off to look for more trouble. After a bit, the noise grew less, moving away like a storm into the distance.

It was difficult to believe that the battle wasn't a dream and that this wasn't just another summer morning, in which about the only mechanical sound would be the rattle of reaping machines in the cornfields. A farmhand, turning up at a cottage with the milk, admitted cautiously that he'd "heard something close," but seemed more interested in finding out how much cream the household wanted. Later, a delivery boy bringing news of the outside world reported that the raid hadn't done much damage, most of the bombs having fallen in open country. Several Germans had been brought down in the neighborhood, however. The rector of a nearby village, after seeing nine Germans bailing out over the Common, hurried off to his church and started hauling away at the bells, mindful of the official warning that more than five men bailing out at once might mean parachute troops. The disappointment of the home guard was intense when the rector's fears proved unwarranted.

This community has adapted itself placidly to the necessary adjustments of the blitzkrieg. People going to the station to pick up weekend guests are resigned to finding that the train is anything up to an hour late, a mildly annoying everyday hazard of travel which is now accepted as philosophically as a cow on the tracks would be in Ireland. Cottagers are no longer surprised to discover tanks nestling on the village green or a couple of soldiers flat on their stomachs by the pond, apparently training a Lewis gun on the vicarage gate. The sound of men marching no longer brings children running.

What has impressed everybody in this neighborhood more than any such signs of war is the incident of the lady owner of a Tudor house, which is one of the show places here, who arrived home from a short visit the other day to find a party of soldiers engaged in cutting down a group of historic cedars on her front lawn. The officer in charge explained regretfully that it was necessary because the trees were right in his line of fire. The house itself, the slightly dazed owner was told, might have to be pulled down later. To country people, who lose trees as grudgingly as they would a tooth, this drastic step can only mean that the authorities expect their homes to be in the front line of the battle that has already started. To descendants of the tough peasants who centuries ago welcomed successive waves of invaders with boulders, scalding water, and hot pitch, this seems just as it should be.

# LETTER FROM LONDON

MOLLIE PANTER-DOWNES

*August 25, 1940*

LONDON has accepted its sirens with the usual exciting British display of complete impassiveness. Inasmuch as everybody feels deep down in his bones, and in the uncomfortable area of the stomach, where most people keep their courage, that the first of the big raids are upon us at last, the universal calm has seemed almost ostentatious. People have queued up for the public shelters as quietly as if waiting to see a motion picture. When the first of the sirens went off early one evening, the lights went off too in the bar where a group of us happened to be, but the barman continued to arrange sprigs of mint in some drinks as though absorbed in this artistic effort. Running footsteps and blowing whistles sounded from the street. It was instructive to watch the behavior of persons who turned up, panting slightly, to meet their friends for a drink. "I ran all the way from Bond Street," said a pretty, hatless girl to a young naval officer, who seemed to take it for granted that pretty girls should choose this form of exercise on a warm August evening. We all went on chatting pleasantly while pretending that we were not listening for the first crash of the bombardment or calculating how long it would take to duck down to the basement. When the all-clear sounded after a period of eventless waiting, there was a little stir of gaiety and most of the customers ordered another drink.

Since then, there have been plenty more sirens, but the raiders have not got farther than the outer suburbs, where the gunfire was especially heavy in the night raid a week ago. Every other person one meets can give exact details of damage and casualties, details that unfortunately never tally. It was announced that a hundred and fifty girls had been killed in the bombardment of the Coty factory, but the story was denied next day by the Coty people themselves, who said that the girls were not working at the time of the raid. This is the kind of thing which starts rumors and makes the public suspect that it is not being told all it should be, and it was a relief to learn that from now on official lists of the killed and injured will be posted as soon as possible outside borough town halls. Monthly totals of casualties are to be announced in the press.

Failure to sound the sirens in one of last week's raids was the subject of a question in the House of Commons which drew from the Minister of Home Security the uncomfortably insecure statement that citizens must be prepared not only to be warned without being bombed but also occasionally to be bombed without being warned. The problem is a difficult one, since to sound sirens in all towns within likely range of the raiders' course would be to throw a spanner into industrial output by day and into workers' precious sleep by night. However sensible this argument seems, it is unfortunately only human nature to feel aggrieved when the first intimation one receives of hostile aircraft overhead is a bomb splinter landing at one's feet. Considering the terrible opportunities for practice that this country is likely to get in the near future, some more universally satisfactory system will probably be worked out before long.

Now that raids are obviously going to become part of the day-to-day routine for millions of people, there is a good deal of fervent discussion as to the best place to make for if one is unlucky enough to be caught out of doors when the sirens start. Shoppers prefer Harrods, where chairs are provided and first-aid workers unobtrusively but comfortingly hover about. In the public shelters, it is usually a case of standing room only, which becomes hard on the feet after an hour or so but is less of a hardship to most than the ban on smoking.

On the whole, the general feeling seems to be one of relief that "it" has come at last, although there is no doubt in anyone's mind that the raids on the London area so far have been little more than reconnaissances. Still, the first round of the mass offensive in the air is over and the result has certainly been overwhelmingly in Britain's favor. The second round may bring some harder hitting, but the public is confident and cheerful. The ordinary individual is magnificent in a moment like this. Recently the Ministry of Information launched a series of advertisements which, in the form of the soul-searchings of an unattractively smug and breezy citizen, gave the public the Ministry's notions of correct British behavior under every possible stress and strain: "What do I do in an air raid? I do not panic. I say to myself, our chaps are dealing with them, etc." The campaign would seem to be another of the Ministry's unfortunate bloomers, since under stress every charwoman reacts with the courage, restraint, and humor traditionally expected of aristocrats.

In spite of the alarms of the past week, London still looks a good deal safer than many a country district that has unexpectedly found itself right in the center of the blitzkrieg. A person living near a well-guarded military objective frequently discovers he has passed a less harassing night than his friend in some village on the other side of the county, where raiders, chased by the R.A.F., were jettisoning bombs all around.

In the beautiful fruit-growing country, over which in happier days the Paris airliners peacefully droned, fag ends of last week's raids upset the harvesting of the plum crop until exasperated farmers hit on the notion of digging trenches in their orchards so that the pickers could remain in the fields during dogfights overhead, snatching another bushel or so at every lull. Country people continue to be sturdily unimpressed by visitations from the enemy. "I just turned over and went to sleep again," said one old man, relating how a bomb had fallen a hundred yards from his cottage gate.

The Prime Minister's most recent speech and the successful action against Italian ships raised everybody's spirits. Anthony Eden is curiously uninspiring. Alfred Duff Cooper, after one first-class broadcast, turned in a series of outbursts which set the teeth of even the not particularly sensitive on edge. Mr. Churchill is the only man in England today who consistently interprets the quiet but completely resolute national mood. The sinking of the Italian ships was a tonic chaser to the nasty taste that the evacuation of Somaliland had left in the public's mouth. For most Britons, one of the bitterest of the many bitter consequences of France's capitulation was that it has made operations against Italy vastly more difficult. The feeling of this country about Italy has an angry, personal quality, as though it were directed against someone who has been guilty not of crime on a heroic scale but of mean behavior, such as bilking at a race meeting or pinching the poor box of a church.

# LETTER FROM LONDON

### MOLLIE PANTER-DOWNES

*August 30, 1940*

THE nightly nuisance raids of the past week continue. Since the damage they have done has been slight, their objects would seem to be reconnaissance and interference with the civilian population's sleep. Their immediate result has been a sudden display by Londoners of a talent for taking cat naps in all sorts of places. On Tuesday, the morning after the longest air-raid warning to date, which stranded hundreds of suburbanites in town without a toothbrush among them, matrons snoozed in buses and clerks devoted their lunch hour to dozing under trees in public squares and gardens. By the middle of the week, people were accepting the daily performances of what they now call the "Wailing Willie" as a dull routine instead of an alarming novelty. During a raid last Monday night, when some cinema managers interrupted their programs to give audiences the choice of leaving or of moving into greater safety at the back of the auditorium (a suggestion that brought to many of their hearers qualmish visions of being the meat in the sandwich between the balcony and the floor), most people stayed put, even if their enjoyment of the entertainment was understandably diminished. Pubs remained open and companionable parties gathered. At Queen's Hall, a Wagner concert ran to greater length than "Götterdämmerung," while the immortal Richard's compatriots droned somewhere in the vicinity; when Sir Henry Wood's official program ended, members of the symphony orchestra obliged with solos and the indefatigable audience filled in with community singing and amateur talent until the all-clear came, around three. "Was it [the air-raid siren] Siegfried's horn or Fafner's growl or both together?" asked the *Times* music critic in a facetious mood next day. Since experts agree that night raids are likely to become more numerous, Londoners are adapting themselves sensibly and courageously to this new phase of the war. On Wednesday, the manager of the Empire had only to walk out on the stage and say "I suppose you know why I'm here" to get the biggest laugh of the evening.

The damage of the most severe night raid was confined to the part of Pepys' London where the crooked, mazy lanes are dotted with blue plaques

59

announcing the site of such-and-such a building that was destroyed in the Great Fire of 1666. After a good deal of coy hesitation, the censors revealed the fact that the affected area was Cripplegate, where a potential Great Fire of 1940 was put under control by the prompt action of the fire services. Strangely enough, the fire station, just a street's width away from where one of the bombs fell, was the only building in the block in which no windows were broken. The rest of the houses were a mass of staring desolation. For a couple of blocks, what had been office buildings were blackened shells inside which one could get glimpses of charred wreckage. If the bombs had fallen in the daytime, the casualties in this closely packed area would have been tragic.

By midweek, the work of reconstruction was already going ahead. Men were running up scaffolding around the damaged buildings, hurrying to and fro, like ants in a heap that someone had just kicked apart. What had been an ill wind for many people had blown good to the glaziers, from whose vans, backed against the pavement, hundreds of square feet of glass were being lifted out of straw packing. The danger from falling glass and odd bits of masonry was still considerable, and police barricaded the surrounding streets to anyone who couldn't show a pass or prove legitimate business there. Opposite St. Giles, the church where Milton is buried, the front had been blown out of a dark and Dickensian little eating house, and two men in bartenders' aprons sat together discussing events among the broken mahogany hatracks and scattered spittoons. A notice tacked up outside announced business as usual. Around the corner, in Aldersgate, a sign in front of a delicatessen shop that had suffered the same fate proclaimed cheerfully, "We are wide open." It was doing a good trade among customers who did not seem to be moved by the fact that they could leave by the conventional door or through the space where the window had been.

At St. Giles, a bomb had fallen slap on the sandbags protecting a stained-glass window, blowing a hole in the wall and toppling Milton off his plinth outside. A George Belcher charlady in rusty black was leaning mournfully against the broken railings, regarding the fallen poet among the debris of sand, glass, and masonry. "And 'im one of our finest poets, too," she said. "Ow, it's shocking!" On the vacant plinth were still inscribed Milton's own curiously appropriate lines: "O Spirit . . . what in me is dark illumine, what is low raise and support."

Naturally, there has been a good deal of hopeful talk this week about retaliatory raids on Berlin, but it is realized that such reprisals, though satisfactory, would do less good than the present devastating R.A.F. raids on Germany's centers of war production. A campaign of destruction of factories, power plants, and airdromes is more useful than the German policy of hitting and running where no possible military objective can exist. Incidentally, the announcements of the first air-raid deaths are beginning to appear in the obituary columns of the morning papers. No mention is made of the cause of death, but the conventional phrase "very suddenly" is always used. Thousands of men, women, and children are scheduled to die very suddenly, without any particular notice being taken of them in the obituary columns. To observers here, it sometimes seems that more than Milton has been toppled off his plinth. All that is best in the good life of civilized effort appears to be slowly and painfully keeling over in the chaos of man's inhumanity to man.

# LETTER FROM LONDON

## MOLLIE PANTER-DOWNES

*September 8, 1940*

THE air blitzkrieg started in earnest yesterday—Saturday—with the first big raids on London. It is as yet too early to report on the full extent of the damage, which has certainly been considerable, especially in the dwelling-house sections of the East End. Observers of the Spanish War methods of terrorizing civilian populations have frequently remarked that in Spain the heaviest bombardments were directed on working-class districts—structurally more vulnerable and emotionally more prone to panic than less crowded areas of a city. The job of providing homeless and frightened people with shelter and food is one that workers have apparently tackled heroically. They are probably going to have increasingly and tragically frequent opportunities for practice. The figure of four hundred killed, which has just been announced, may well mount higher in future bulletins, in the same way that the figure of raiders brought down was given as five in last evening's reports but by this morning, with fuller information coming in all the time, had totalled eighty-eight.

Those who were weekending in the country guessed the magnitude of the attack from the constant roar of aircraft passing invisibly high up in a cloudless blue sky. At dusk, a red glow could be seen in the direction of London, but it died down as the stars and the searchlights came out, and again waves of bombers passed overhead at intervals of about ten minutes. In between waves, one could hear the distant racket of the anti-aircraft guns picking up the raiders that had just gone by, and at the same time one half heard, half sensed the unmistakable throbbing of the next waves of engines coming nearer over the quiet woods and villages. This morning it was difficult to get a call through to London, probably because so many anxious people in the country were ringing up to find out what had happened and to try to get in touch with members of their families who were in town. Further big attacks were expected today, but the attitude of those who were returning to the city was sensible and courageous. "Let them send plenty. There will be more for the boys to bring down" was a typical comment.

Up to yesterday, the raids on London had not been developed beyond a point that indicated that they were merely reconnaissance or training flights to accustom enemy pilots to night work over the capital. Sirens had become tiresome interruptions, which Londoners learned to expect at fairly regular intervals during the day, roughly coinciding with the morning and evening traffic rush and with the lunch hour. Unless shooting accompanied the alarms, they were ignored, as far as possible, except by especially nervous individuals. The dislocation of office and factory work schedules was more or less remedied by the posting of spotters on rooftops to give the warning when things really become dangerous locally. Until the warning comes, workers have been getting on with the job, sirens or no sirens. No part of the Premier's speech last week was better received, by the way, than his statement that the whole of the air-raid-warning system is to be drastically revised and a new ruling concerning it announced in the near future; what he described as "these prolonged banshee howlings" are apparently more alarming to a great many people than an actual bombardment.

Life in a bombed city means adapting oneself in all kinds of ways all the time. Londoners are now learning the lessons, long ago familiar to those living on the much-visited southeast coast, of getting to bed early and shifting their sleeping quarters down to the ground floor. (After recent raids on the suburbs, it was noticeable that in all the little houses damaged by anything short of a direct hit people on the upper floors had suffered most, and that in surprisingly many cases those on the ground floor had escaped injury entirely.) Theatres are meeting the threat to their business by starting evening performances earlier, thus giving audiences a chance to get home before the big nighttime show warms up. The actual getting home is likely to be difficult, because the transportation services have not yet worked out a satisfactory formula for carrying on during raids. The busmen's union tells drivers to use their own discretion, and the London transportation board's orders are that buses are to go on running unless a raid develops "in the immediate vicinity." The drivers grumble that it would take a five-hundred-pounder in the immediate vicinity to be heard above the din of their own engines.

The calm behavior of the average individual continues to be amazing. Commuting suburbanites, who up to yesterday had experienced worse bombardments than people living in central London, placidly brag to fellow-passengers on the morning trains about the size of bomb craters in their neighborhoods, as in a more peaceful summer they would have bragged about their roses and squash.

Earlier in the week, the first anniversary of the declaration of war passed peacefully and found Britons in a state of encouragement which less than three months ago would have seemed downright fantastic. The Anglo-American agreement was a birthday present that was received with tremendous satisfaction. Officially, it was greeted as "the most conspicuous demonstration that has yet been given of the general American desire to afford the utmost help, compatible with neutrality, to a cause now recognized as vital to the future of the United States." Ordinary comment was less solemn, but no less grateful. The successful conclusion of the agreement, combined with the superb work of the R.A.F. and the significant new spirit in the French colonies, has been responsible for a big increase in public confidence which reacted favorably on that sensitive plant, the stock market. In spite of the dark times ahead, it is believed that better things are coming into sight beyond them.

# LETTER FROM LONDON

## MOLLIE PANTER-DOWNES

*September 14, 1940*

FOR Londoners, there are no longer such things as good nights; there are only bad nights, worse nights, and better nights. Hardly anyone has slept at all in the past week. The sirens go off at approximately the same time every evening, and in the poorer districts, queues of people carrying blankets, thermos flasks, and babies begin to form quite early outside the air-raid shelters. The blitzkrieg continues to be directed against such military objectives as the tired shopgirl, the red-eyed clerk, and the thousands of dazed and weary families patiently trundling their few belongings in perambulators away from the wreckage of their homes. After a few of these nights, sleep of a kind comes from complete exhaustion. The amazing part of it is the cheerfulness and fortitude with which ordinary individuals are doing their jobs under nerve-racking conditions. Girls who have taken twice the usual time to get to work look worn when they arrive, but their faces are nicely made up and they bring you a cup of tea or sell you a hat as chirpily as ever. Little shopkeepers whose windows have been blown out paste up "Business as usual" stickers and exchange cracks with their customers.

On all sides, one hears the grim phrase "We shall get used to it." Everyone takes for granted that the program of wanton destruction, far from letting up, will be intensified when bad weather sets in and makes anything like accuracy in bombing impossible. Although people imagined early in the war that vicious bombardments would be followed by the panic-stricken departure of everybody who could leave the city, outward-going traffic on one of the major roads from London was only normal on the day after the worst of the raids. The Government, however, has announced new plans for the evacuation of children who were not sent away under former schemes or whose mothers last week had the unhappy inspiration to bring them back to town for a holiday at home.

The East End suffered most in the night raids this week. Social workers who may have piously wished that slum areas could be razed had their wish horribly fulfilled when rows of mean dwellings were turned into shambles overnight. The Nazi attack bore down heaviest on badly nourished, poorly clothed people—the worst equipped of any to stand the appalling physical strain, if it were not for the stoutness of their cockney hearts. Relief workers sorted them out in schools and other centers to be fed, rested, and provided with billets. Subsequent raids killed many of the homeless as they waited.

The bombers, however, made no discrimination between the lowest and the highest homes in the city. The Queen was photographed against much the same sort of tangle of splintered wreckage that faced hundreds of humbler, anonymous housewives in this week's bitter dawns. The crowd that gathered outside Buckingham Palace the morning after the picture was published had come, it appeared on close inspection, less to gape at boarded windows than to listen to the cheering notes of the band, which tootled away imperturbably at the cherished ceremony of the Changing of the Guard. This was before the deliberate second try for the Palace, which has made people furious but has also cheered them with the thought that the King and Queen are facing risks that are now common to all.

Broken windows are no longer a novelty in the West End, though the damage there so far has been slight. In getting about, one first learns that a bomb has fallen near at hand by coming upon barriers across roads and encountering policemen who point to yellow tin signs that read simply "Diversion," as though the blockage had been caused by workmen peacefully taking up drains ahead. The "diversion" in Regent Street, where a bomb fell just outside the Café Royal and did not explode for hours, cut off the surrounding streets and made the neighborhood as quiet as a hamlet. Crowds collected behind the ropes to gaze respectfully at the experts, who stood looking down into the crater and chatting as nonchalantly as plumbers discussing the best way of fixing a leaking tap. Police went around getting occupants out of the buildings in the vicinity and warning them to leave their windows open, but even with this precaution, when the bomb finally went off that evening there were not many panes of glass left.

The scene next morning was quite extraordinarily eerie. The great sweep of Regent Street, deserted by everyone except police and salvage workers, stared gauntly like a thoroughfare in a dead city. It would have been no surprise to see grass growing up out of the pavements, which were covered instead with a fine, frosty glitter of powdered glass. The noise of glass being hammered out of upper windows, swept into piles at street corners, and shovelled into municipal dust vans made a curious grinding tinkle that went on most of the day. The happiest people there were two little boys who had discovered a sweetshop where most of the window display had been blown into the gutter, and who were doing a fine looting job among the debris. Around the corner, the florid façade of Burlington Arcade had been hit at one end, and an anxious jeweller was helping in the work of salvaging his precious stock from the heap of junk that a short while before had been a double row of luxury shops. Scenes like these are new enough to seem both shocking and unreal; to come across a wrecked filling station with a couple of riddled cars standing dejectedly by its smashed pumps makes one feel that one must have strayed onto a Hollywood set, and it's good to get back to normality among the still snug houses in the next street.

Wednesday night's terrific, new-style anti-aircraft barrage reassured people, after scaring them badly. A.R.P. workers, who have been heroic all the week, were told to warn as many as possible that something special and noisy was going to be tried out that evening, but all over town persons who hadn't been tipped off thought that the really terrifying din was a particularly fierce bombardment. Houses shuddered unceasingly until the all-clear sounded in the dawn, when everyone felt better because, although Londoners had had a bad night, the raiders must have had a worse one. The behavior of all classes is so magnificent that no observer here could ever imagine these people following the French into captivity. As for breaking civilian morale, the high explosives that rained death and destruction on the capital this week were futile.

# LETTER FROM LONDON

## MOLLIE PANTER-DOWNES

*September 29, 1940*

ADJUSTING daily life to the disruption of nightly raids is naturally what Londoners are thinking and talking most about. For people with jobs to hold down, loss of sleep continues to be as menacing as bombs. Those with enough money get away to the country on weekends and treat themselves to the luxury of a couple of nine-hour stretches. ("Fancy," said one of these weekenders dreamily, "going upstairs to bed instead of down.") It is for the alleviation of the distress of the millions who can't afford to do anything but stay patiently put that the Government has announced the distribution of free rubber earplugs to deaden the really appalling racket of the barrages. Plans to improve accommodations in air-raid shelters by the addition of bunks, heating, and better sanitary arrangements were announced at the same time, to the relief of physicians who had been figuring out that if winter comes, a really first-class epidemic can't be far behind. This announcement was also welcome news to Londoners who use the shelters nightly and are ready with fight and staying power so long as the authorities do the right thing by them. In some boroughs, relief organization isn't so intelligent as it might be and homeless people have to wait interminably and needlessly at rest centers while billets are found for them. Often the billets are bombed the first night and the homeless are back at the rest centers the next day, angrier than ever. Relief workers report that anger is the first reaction of people who have lost everything, and that old people feel the loss worst of all.

Excellent unsentimental work is being done in rest centers of the hard-hit districts by the Women's Voluntary Services. Besides billets, new wardrobes are provided there, and money for current expenses is advanced by the public-assistance funds; the pitiful bundles of belongings salvaged from the wrecked homes are carefully checked and stored. Mothers who wish to be evacuated with their children are sent to out-of-town billets, and the authorities hope that twenty thousand children a day will shortly be leaving the city to which too many of them, alas, were brought back by parents when things looked quiet. The rest centers also deal with inquiries from soldiers and sailors who return on leave and find their homes gone and their families missing. An appeal was recently broadcast to relatives of service men asking them not to forget the daily or weekly letter that can save endless anxiety for those in uniform. It was also announced that an organization to trace missing relatives in bombed areas will be set up at once.

The courage, humor, and kindliness of ordinary people continue to be astonishing under conditions that possess many of the merry features of a nightmare. Nobody imagines that England has seen the worst tricks the Germans have up their sleeves. There is a good deal of talk about gas. People seem calmly certain that it will be used before long, if civilian morale shows no signs of cracking, and that with it will come a characteristically elaborate story about British fliers having used it first over Berlin. There was a strong feeling of confidence last week, in spite of Dakar. Events there are still obscured by a lot of high-flown language and little real news. The papers quite obviously couldn't think what to think, but the public had no difficulty in reaching the disappointed decision that de Gaulle's withdrawal showed the usual unhappy lack of coördination between the Intelligence and the War Departments.

The Battle of London, however, was naturally more important to those in the thick of it than anything happening on the coast of Africa. The morale on the home front certainly inspires confidence. East Enders, who had suffered most, stuck up paper Union Jacks in the heaps of rubble that used to be their homes. Women pottered placidly in and out of a big Oxford Street store that had been badly damaged but had the usual uniformed doormen standing outside its boarded-up windows, over which stickers had been pasted declaring that all departments were open.

Things are settling down into a recognizable routine. Daylight sirens are disregarded by everyone, unless they are accompanied by gunfire or bomb explosions that sound uncomfortably near. A lady who arrived at one of the railway stations during a warning was asked politely by the porter who carried her bag, "Air-raid shelter or taxi, Madam?" As anyone else here would have done, she took a taxi. To those who live in apartments, a good night is now one in which the whole block doesn't start swaying; if it merely shudders gently, people remark that things are nice and quiet tonight. It's dusty work getting around London these days. Objects that feel like small rocks have a habit of lodging in one's eyes and turn out to be grit from the debris of wrecked buildings. Often the first intimation that a place of business has been hit is a small notice in the *Times'* personal column saying simply that Messrs. So-and-So are opening up in a day or two at a new address. Gieves, the famous military tailor on Bond Street, whose shop was completely gutted, ran a stately advertisement regretting that it was necessary to inconvenience clients for a few days, as though the fuss had been caused by a bit of spring redecorating.

Some of the damage has been curious. A section of one big block of flats was taken out as neatly as a slice carved from a cake. Homes on Dover Street were opened up like doll houses, so that passersby could see pictures still hanging on a wall or some trivial little ornaments still arranged neatly on a mantelpiece that was dangling in space; it seemed as though people's lives as well as their inanimate possessions were being dissected in public. The exact whereabouts of bomb damage is concealed with irritating coyness by the censorship bureau, which yesterday admitted playfully that "a church famed in a nursery rhyme" had been hit. Any child who has played oranges and lemons will be glad to step up and give you the answer, which is a sad one for those who have loved the last bits of Wren's London all their lives.

# LETTER FROM LONDON

### MOLLIE PANTER-DOWNES

*January 4, 1941*

LAST Sunday night's big fire raid may have produced some good results to balance tragic losses. The authorities and the public showed signs for the first time of realizing that arson was going to be used as a major weapon in the war. As usual, the British learned their lesson expensively, and it was poor consolation to be told that quite a bit of the damage could have been prevented if fire-watchers had been organized, as they now are, on a compulsory-service basis. Lord Beaverbrook's lively *Daily Express* has been saying for some time that fire-spotters ought to be thus organized and that every householder should be made responsible for preventing fire bombs from igniting his own premises. With the heart of the City still smoldering, Mr. Herbert Morrison, the Minister of Home Security, went on the air to ask that this be done. It was also announced that a census would shortly be taken of the entire able-bodied manpower in the shelters, which pleased many people who feel that too much has been said and written about the courage of the crowds that spend the nights down below and too little about the truly courageous men and women who remain above guarding other people's property.

Up to that Sunday night, incendiaries were looked upon as tiresome annoyances incidental to a raid. Now that the really serious gap in the air-raid precautions of the big cities has been seen, there is talk of possible hasty legislation providing for the imprisonment of owners of industrial plants that are destroyed by fires that spread because of neglect of proper precautions. Citizens also have been asked, and have shown a willingness, to form communal fire-fighting squads, which are to take turns patrolling the streets, armed with the keys of absent neighbors, so that fires in empty houses can be quickly reached and controlled. For the reserved and suspicious British, this represents a step forward not only in civic discipline but also in the un-English mateyness which is one of the few pleasant things to come out of the war so far.

Meanwhile, the debit side of the Sunday raid was heavy. Some years back, lovers of the antique raised a howl of protest when it was proposed that the scantily attended Wren churches in the business section be demolished. Now that so much of the demolition has been accomplished overnight, not only

71

the lovers of the antique are horrified but also citizens who for a lifetime had been cozily conscious that the churches were there without ever feeling compelled to go inside them. Thousands have gone to mourn over St. Lawrence Jewry and the quaintly named St. Andrew by the Wardrobe—now that they are in ashes—who would hardly have been able to recognize one steeple from the other when those steeples were still elegantly vertical.

In the general lamentation over the national treasures that have been lost, there is a tendency to overlook the fact that a good deal that wasn't precious but only unhygienic, inconvenient, and an offense to civic pride has also gone down in the flames. Wren churches can be rebuilt (it is rumored that one wealthy young man has offered to duplicate the Guildhall as soon as the war is over), but there are also many dark and noisome spots which Londoners hope won't be restored when the time for planning a new town arrives. Already there are brisk discussions over the advisability of setting up all the old monuments again in precisely the same historic spots they used to occupy. One school of thought, headed by Clough Williams-Ellis, the architect, is all for resurrecting Wren churches with the exactness that meticulous records make possible, but wants them resurrected on more convenient sites, where millions instead of a few conscientious tourists can admire and see them. The other school deprecates slavish imitation and hopes that rebuilding will strike out along bold contemporary lines, emphasizing the point that Sir Christopher himself did not dig up the old blueprints when he was commissioned to rebuild St. Paul's. The St. Paul's assignment may yet again fall to someone or other, for in the last raid the great dome was spared only by a margin which a chance breeze, blowing sparks from nearby blazing warehouses, might easily have narrowed to disaster.

Taking a walk through the damaged section at the beginning of the week, one had to pick one's way over the hoses that lay coiled across the dark little alleys. Some of the fires were still smoking and the firemen were hard at work in their tin hats, thigh boots, and dirty uniforms, which they probably hadn't scrambled out of since Sunday. Some of the streets had been roped off so that the Royal Engineers could blow up dangerous buildings, and the ropes were used as a kind of necklace along which were strung flapping bits of paper giving the temporary addresses of firms that had been burned out. An enormous Union Jack flew from the Guildhall's one undamaged roof, but the main body of the building was a sad sight, with blackened statues looking down on the mass of debris where the famous Gog and Magog have disappeared in the ruins of the proudest link with the City's history.

It was thought by many that the raid might be the first of a devastating series leading up to an invasion, which is again forecast for a variety of dates in the near future. Both the informed and the uninformed seem to feel that an attempt will be made as soon as the screws have been tightened sufficiently by the Nazi air and submarine forces. Faced with such a menacing new year, most Londoners celebrated their parting with the tragic old one in a quiet fashion. In spite of the good news from the Libyan front and the heartening effect of President Roosevelt's fireside talk, no one was inclined to underrate the dangers ahead in what may well be a critical year not only for the British Empire but also for men of good will everywhere.

# PARIS, GERMANY

JANET FLANNER

PARIS is now the capital of limbo. It is a beautiful French city on the banks of the Seine which only Berlin, the capital of Germany, knows all about.

This was to have been remembered as the century of perfected human communications—of swift air-mail letters flying over oceans and lands, of radio stations comfortably crackling sparks of news into the night, of wireless-telephoned headlines presumably announcing that mankind was all well, and of streamlined trains hustling across continents with unimportant postcards. From Poland, from Denmark and Norway, from Holland and Luxembourg and Belgium, there have been few communications in recent months. Johannesburg, South Africa, however, recently reported capturing storks that had just migrated from Holland. Around the birds' legs had been wrapped messages that read, "The German occupation of Holland is hell" and "The Dutch people are dying under injustice." As there are not many storks at any season in France, as French carrier pigeons have been forbidden to fly by the Nazis, and as French postmen may not, under penalty, cross the boundary from the Occupied Zone into the Unoccupied, written communications, even smuggled, have been rarer from Paris and the rest of Occupied France than from any other German-conquered territory. In the autumn of 1940, the French of Nazi France communicate even with each other principally by word of mouth. With the rest of the world, they don't communicate at all.

Information about Paris brought back to America by French refugees, American expatriates, members of volunteer ambulance units, and the like, is also only oral. With their tongues they tell you what they saw and heard with their own eyes and ears, but they have no papers to prove it. The only documentation on Paris today is in Berlin. Still, on three or four particulars, all these informants agree.

First: Anybody who loved Paris and grieves at its plight is fortunate not to see it now, because Paris would seem hateful.

Second: Parisians permit themselves exactly two words to describe their conquerors; Parisians say that the Germans are *corrects* and that they are *emmerdeurs*. This superficial adjective and this scatological substantive, taken together, are probably important historically. By *corrects,* the French mean that physically, militarily, one might almost say socially, the Germans have up to now conducted themselves with disciplined decorum. By the second word (now used as practically political terminology by polite Parisians who never before used such a word for anything), Parisians mean that they find the German mentality, its shape, its principles, its whole Teutonic mentation, boring to a malodorous degree. These two curious words so far represent merely the intellectual periphery of a vocabulary not yet filled in with words for the despair and anguish that some of the conquered French are beginning to feel not with their brains but with their stomachs and hearts.

Third: Owing to the Germans' mania for systematic looting—for collecting and carting away French bed linen, machinery, Gobelin tapestries, surgical instruments, milk, mutton, sweet champagne—the French will have to become a race of liars and cheats in order to survive physically. For example, milk is now sold only for babies, pregnant women, and people over seventy. Parisian housewives stand outside dairy shops for hours with rented babies in their arms, or with pillows stuffed under their apron fronts, or with borrowed grandparents hanging on their shoulders. In the old days, soldiers, Christian or pagan, looted with disorderly enthusiasm—raping, robbing, staggering down roads with booty and with blood on their hands. In the new Aryan looting manner, Nazis ring the French front-door bell while an Army truck waits in the street, and soldiers do the job of fanatical moving men.

Fourth: The German passion for bureaucracy—for written and signed forms, for files, statistics, and lists, and for printed permissions to do this or that, to go here or there, to move about, to work, to exist—is like a steel pen pinning each French individual to a sheet of paper, the way an entomologist pins each specimen insect, past struggling, to his laboratory board. For years, Parisian liberals had suspected that their Republic's increasing tendency toward petty bureaucracy was weakening France. As totalitarians, the Germans seem sure that their bureaucracy, organized on the grand scale, is their strength. Even the suburban fisherman now must have written permission to fish in the Seine, though they haven't caught anything in generations worth writing a line about. As one old fisherman cried, "Soon even French minnows will have to learn to read and write German!"

At least three conscious psychological attitudes characterize the German treatment of Paris. The first attitude is that of moderation, almost of consideration, toward Parisians, provided such moderation gets a good name for the Germans. Their treatment of the French has the quality of a cruel but polite *opéra bouffe*. With political shrewdness, and out of racial egomania, they want the French to refer to them as *des braves types, tout de même* ("nice fellows, after all"). This cynical moderation is part of a carefully calculated publicity program. By chance, it often slightly benefits the French, but if it doesn't help German publicity more, it's cut short. Or, to quote the French, "The Nazis

offer us, let's say, twelve grains of rice and then take away from us eleven potatoes. But if they're not praised by the populace for donating twelve of something small and taking only eleven of something large, they take both the rice
and potatoes, which makes the score twenty-three to nothing." The rice and
potatoes are purely figurative. Rice is so scarce that it is not given out except
on a doctor's certificate, pure starch having already reached pharmacopoeial
ranking. As for potatoes, by August the Germans had their soldiers guarding
the fields while the potatoes were still in the French ground. The French
rarely see potato bugs, which they elegantly call *doryphores*. This summer
there was a pest of them, and of German soldiers, whom the French grimly
nicknamed after the bugs. *"Ja,"* admitted one German soldier, "we're the
*doryphores*. We will eat the potatoes and you will eat nothing."

The second psychological attitude of the Nazis is that Parisians must be
equalized. There is an effort to reduce the individualistic French to a common
level. For example, a French doctor who has been an expensive heart specialist
is forced to become a general practitioner at small fees; a lawyer who has been
used to pleading only before the highest courts is forced to handle petty litigation. This equalization policy is also applied materialistically. Because German *Hausfrauen* lack bedsheets, since German looms have been working only
for the Army, many Paris housewives have been forced to give the Nazis all
their sleeping equipment except two pairs of sheets, one blanket, and one
mattress for every occupied bed in their homes. If the sheet owner lives in a
château and possesses, as one old chatelaine did, sixty pairs of fine yellow linen
sheets left from her trousseau, the Germans do not even leave one pair but
take them all as punishment for her plutocracy. By this policy of equalization,
the Germans hope to unsettle the modest French into hating the clever or
rich and into admiring the Nazis for what Nazis call their special sense of
social justice.

The third psychological attitude of the conquerors applies only to themselves, but it enormously affects the French. Oddly enough, each local German
*Kommandant,* or *chef,* is free to interpret Nazi policy according to his own
judgment or temperament. Thus the German *Kommandant* in one Paris
*arrondissement* took bedsheets from every house on only one side of the street,
whereas another took them from every other house on both sides of the street.
Such uncertainties add to the demoralization of the unhappy French. A *Kommandant* in Neuilly expressed his individuality by charging his French mistress's
new wardrobe and his florist bill to the *mairie,* which, after a scandalized
protest, was forced to pay. On the other hand, the *Kommandant* of a town
near Saint-Malo has become noted for his strict honesty and justice toward the French. The *Kommandant* at Fontainebleau, however, has another
notion of justice. He punished the mayor for having fled his post of duty when
the Germans arrived, forcing him, on his return, to quit his mayoral mansion
and live in a furnished room. Because an insouciant little Fontainebleau boy

made a *croque à jambe*—stuck his foot out—and tripped a German soldier, all citizens of Fontainebleau are compelled to step into the gutter when a Nazi approaches them on the sidewalk.

In the application of only one of their better-known Nazi psychological devices have the Germans been remiss in Paris. Though addicted, when at home, to book-burning and the destruction of criticism in print, not until the last of July, five weeks after they marched into the capital of highly literate France, did the Germans get around to suppressing anti-Nazi books. In all, only one hundred and sixty-two books, including, as a belated addendum, "France and Its Army," by Charles de Gaulle, now of the Free France movement, have been put on the index, though for the five years before the collapse France was fuller of anti-Nazi literature than it was of any other means of self-defense. As for German *Lieder* and other German music, only Germans are permitted to perform them in Paris, since foreigners, the Nazis say, would demean both the racial melodies and the noble language. A stranded American baritone who offered to sing Schumann's "Dichterliebe" at a private concert was informed that he might sing only degenerate music, such as Debussy or Ravel.

Before the German Occupation, Paris was the world's greatest news-publishing and news-reading center, having eighteen major daily newspapers, one of them, the *Paris-Soir,* with the Continent's largest daily circulation—two and a half million. Only a handful of the papers remain, and all of them function entirely under the German eye and reflect its news squint, though the actual writing of the Paris newspapers is done by French journalists, since a job is still a job. The *Paris-Soir* had the distinction of being the only paper to have its printing plant (which was a new one and considered the best in Europe) actually handed over, with the door keys, to the Germans immediately after they made their entry into Paris. The rich gift was tendered by *Paris-Soir's* Fifth-Column Alsatian elevator man. Prepared for any emergency, however, the Germans had brought to Paris with them several fonts of French type— easily distinguishable from French-manufactured type—which they now use to print their official Paris daily, *Les Dernières Nouvelles.* Under the Germans' solemn efficiency there are, comically enough, two editions of *Le Matin*—a morning *Morning* and an evening *Morning.* The Nazis have also started a labor paper, sternly entitled *La France au Travail,* which is a substitute for the old sitdown-strike backer, the Communist *L'Humanité.* Except when a sort of crazed hunger for news, even false, seizes the Parisians (a new neurasthenic phenomenon that can visit a civilized population strait-jacketed for months, cut off from world communication), most of them refuse to buy the Nazi French papers, because they don't believe the news.

The most blatant of the new Nazi papers is the anti-Semitic, anti-Free Mason weekly *Au Pilori,* which already has acquired a reputation for the obscene cartoons it publishes. It is sold on the street by the young Gardes Françaises, the new French Hitler Jugend, to which all French girls and boys from twelve to fifteen must now belong. The July 26th *Au Pilori* contained an editorial entitled "Egalité," which opened, "The democracies only govern by lies. They've made us swallow that fantastic yarn that one man is as good as another." The policy is against "anonymous and international capitalism," favors the so-called "capital-labor" of National Socialism, demands that the French admit France erred and deserved her fate, and features a "Noblesse de Ghetto" society-chat column which accuses a Prince de Ligne and a Duc de Gramont of having married Rothschilds. In an article headed "No; No Trials!," it argues against letting lawyers fuss to defend the former French leaders at Riom and begs instead for "the good, rapid, direct, ineluctable justice of the street . . . the death of Blum, Daladier, Mandel, Reynaud and Paul-Boncour" by *"lynchage."*

Utterly different, infinitely more delicate as propaganda, is *Signal,* the *"édition spéciale de la Berliner Illustrirte Zeitung."* This is a pictorial weekly containing some excellent color photographs and astonishingly dignified text which refers to the French as "the enemy," and which furnishes remarkable documentation on the Battle of Flanders, the March into Paris, the French refugees, and other similar subjects. Photographs show the inefficiency with which "the enemy" blew up its bridges and the skill with which France's enemy reconstructed them within an hour. Photographs also show London jobless in their lying-down-in-the-streets strike of 1938 and London hovels in the East End over the caption, lifted from Lord Halifax, "If Hitler wins, it will be the end of all that makes life worth living." Various editions of *Signal,* printed in Paris in English, French, German, Portuguese, and Spanish, have been put on sale in Lisbon, so that people, many of them leaving Europe forever, can take it with them as a souvenir of what happened in France, according to the Germans, in the summer of 1940.

In general, a strained air of venality hovers over Paris. The Germans who are there have money in their pockets for the first time in twenty-two years and can buy French luxuries the like of which some of the younger Germans have never laid eyes on since they were born. For centuries, *les élégances de Paris* have been regarded all over Europe as a sort of civilized, fabricated soul of France. This particular soul of France is perforce for sale for German cash. Like termites that have been walled in for years and on a diet, the Germans, since the middle of June, have steadily advanced through the Paris shops, absorbing, munching, consuming lingerie, perfume, bonbons, leather goods, sweet silly novelties—all the chic, charm, and *gourmandise* of Parisian merchandise. In order to save for themselves what little they themselves have allowed to remain in the city's stores and warehouses, the Germans have just decreed that all the big Paris shops and department stores must close from noon till two o'clock, hours in which French employees normally go out for lunch and shopping, but also hours in which the Germans are housed in their garrisons or *Speiselokale,* eating their slowest, largest meal. Under the new ruling, the empty-handed French go back in to work just as the Germans, digesting, come out to buy again.

With their curious capacity for convenient metaphysics, certain of the more educated Germans see in their ability to purchase unlimited French silk stockings the operation of an almost occult law. When recently a Frenchwoman in the Trois Quartiers protested against her being forbidden, in the interest of conservation, to buy more than one pair of stockings when she wanted three, while at the same moment a German officer was buying a dozen pairs to send home to his wife, he explained to her in his puffy French that because French legs had worn silk while Germans had worn only cotton, it was now, as a matter of philosophical justice and moral evolution, the Germans' turn.

In a more vulgar manner, Paris has been frankly presented as the Promised Land to the common soldier lucky enough to be detailed there. Bliss takes queer, violent forms in young people who, through force or fanaticism, have for years been practicing self-denial. Eyewitnesses say that some of the earliest German soldiers in their first free hour in Paris stuffed their mouths with oranges and bananas without taking the skins off and spread butter on their chocolate bars. All one Austrian soldier wanted of Paris was to eat tinned pineapple and to moon over Napoleon's tomb. In the Paris cafés, the German soldiers still order what was their first favorite series of drinks—a beer, then a coffee, then what they generically call *"liqueur."* When the French *garçon* asks, *"Mais quelle liqueur?,"* they simply repeat, uncritically, *"Liqueur."* During an evening they will mix whatever the waiter brings—Chartreuse, Bénédictine, Cointreau—with gluttonous indifference.

The German officers go in wholeheartedly for champagne. It's like a liquid symbol of their conquest of Gay Paree. Having a naïve belief in the Nazi theory that French degeneracy was brought on by high living, they demand and expect champagne wherever they go. As one peasant said, *"Ces cochons,* they come into my cottage and ask me for champagne—I, who have never given myself anything better than a bottle of *mousseux,* even for my son's first Communion."

Whatever the German soldiers buy in Paris, it's really the French who pay for it by footing the staggering occupation bill, which includes the unusually high pay given to Nazi soldiers in Paris. The mark that the Germans print in Paris, expressly for use in France, on presses they brought with them, is used concurrently with the franc in Paris business transactions. In a restaurant, a French diner may hand the waiter a hundred-franc note to pay his bill and have to take two German marks and some French centimes in change. The French marks are cleared through the Banque de France. There are probably about twenty thousand Nazi men in uniform in Paris. No official figure is

known. All the French do know is that there are too many. The Nazi soldiers
are constantly shifted to prevent fraternization with the French. The ratio of
officers to men is unusually high; Germany discovered that even the model
Nazi soldiers failed to remain model, in France, if left without strict
supervision.

On June 10th, just before the Occupation, a *sous-directeur* of the Hôtel
Ritz phoned Minister of the Interior Mandel, saying that he was nervous for
Mme. Ritz's sake and hadn't they better close her hotel. Mandel replied that
the Germans would not be in Paris before the fourteenth and that if the Ritz
closed, the German officers would requisition it as being unused, whereas if it
remained open, it would probably get the German *Kommandantur* as paying
guests (paying guests at the expense of the French government, as it has since
turned out). The staff was warned that those who left would not be taken
back and that those who remained would sink or swim together. A number
of them left. In a dignified, traditional manner, to fill the vacancies, the elevator men became concierges and the pageboys became elevator men. Olivier,
most famous maître d'hôtel of Europe, is believed to be still at his post, because the restaurant service remains impeccable. One old French waiter said
that between overwork and anguish he lost ten pounds the first week the
Germans were there, but that it was no moment in the history of France to
let the Ritz service down, too.

At first the Rue Cambon side of the hotel was closed. Now the long passage between the Cambon and the Place Vendôme wings is shut, but the
Cambon side has been opened again, for the use of non-Germans only. The
Germans have the exclusive use of the Place Vendôme wing. Before its porte-
cochère stand two Nazi soldiers on guard, with a third to signal "Psst!" as a
warning to present arms when an officer approaches. The small writing room,
to the left on entering, is now a checkroom for rifles and pistols. The old
mixed bar is reserved for men only. In the big, formal dining room no one but
the *Kommandantur* and guests now dine; the regular officers' mess is in the
famous back room, which is shared by the few remaining French patrons, who
maintain a wide, empty space, which they consider *de rigueur,* between themselves and the Germans. It is thought bad form for loyal French to recognize
the Germans socially when in the Ritz, though the same Frenchmen may have
been struggling for better terms with them in their *bureaux* all day. For the
first time, the Ritz serves a sixty-franc table-d'hôte dinner; it begins and ends
with whipped cream. Caviar, which had been missing since the beginning of
the war, came back to the Ritz with the Germans; brioches appear on the
breakfast menu on Thursday, Friday, Saturday, and Sunday, but the delicious
little *croissants* are no longer there. The French and foreigners who, by habit,
continued to live at the Ritz were criticized by their friends for dwelling amid
the enemy—until the friends realized the Ritz guests were bringing them a

certain amount of unprinted political news. By tradition, the Ritz room keys always hang, when not in use, in the elevators. The sudden absence from their hooks of ten or twenty keys on a single floor meant that a mysterious delegation of somebodies had arrived from somewhere to see the Germans about something—delegations of Spaniards, say, who were there to sign on the dotted line, to try to wiggle off it, to palaver, to protest, to promise, to try and take part, with or without hope, in changing the trembling boundaries of the new map of Europe.

War and conquest are, in some small ways, humanizing disasters. The Ritz staff, formerly trained to show not even indifference, under conquest (and with the door closed) now sometimes show their beating hearts. That is to say, recently one old French room waiter, first asking permission of Madame, rolled up his trouser leg to show his battle wounds from Verdun and wondered aloud if his son had received the same or worse, or had indeed been killed, when the cathedral at Beauvais was bombed. One old chambermaid showed snapshots of her peasant sisters, who had fled from the Ardennes family farm as refugees and of whom there had been no news since; she also asked Madame's permission to consume the second brioche and the part of the café-au-lait which Madame always left.

For a soldiers' mess, the Germans have taken over the Champs-Elysées Taverne Alsacienne, which had doubtless been a Fifth Column station, since, significantly, it was opened only a few years ago, with German beer, waitresses in Alsatian costume, and not enough French patronage to warrant staying in business. The upstairs room of Bofinger, formerly the Bastille businessmen's *fin-bec* eating place, has also been taken over by the Germans. The French may still lunch downstairs, provided the Germans don't overflow. The de-luxe Rex and Marigny movie houses have been made exclusively German, both as to patrons and pictures; American films are forbidden and there aren't any new French films. This segregation of the Germans from the French is sought by the German command in as many ways as possible. One way has been to tell the German soldiers that all French women are diseased.

The German soldiers, because of the high pay they receive in Paris, come into closer public contact with their officers than they ever did before in the German Army. Whereas the Nazi soldier at home receives per diem one German mark (about forty cents), in Paris he gets two French marks, which is fifty times what the French soldier was paid for active service in the current war. This pay is probably the highest ever received by Continental troops in Europe's military history. In the first World War, our A.E.F. got a dollar a day and ranked as millionaires. As a result, the Nazi ranks turn up often enough in the same cinemas, cafés, and restaurants as their superiors. In theory, the Nazi soldier eats in his cheap *Speiselokal,* where he absorbs the heavy German victuals that are deemed to be Nordic and virile, as distinguished from the degenerate, tasty French diet. Nevertheless, they stray. Eyewitnesses tell about two bewildered German soldiers who found their way into the Crémaillère, formerly international society's hangout and now patronized by the *Kommandantur*. On leaving, the soldiers pulled down their tunics, stiffened, and got ready to goose-step and *heil* two German officers seated by the door. The officers made embarrassed signs, to signify *"Um Gottes Willen, nein."* The acrobatics of the German salutes, the presenting-of-arms outside the officers' hotels (with little French boys capering in imitation), the integral, muscular, Teutonic solemnity that meant so much morally to the Nazis at home have been found to mean nothing, beyond the snicker they arouse, to the French. This baffles the Germans.

When the Radio-Paris, which the Nazis have taken over to blare out their official news, is broadcasting, French children sing, to the tune of "La Cucaracha," *"Radio-Paris ment, Radio-Paris ment, Radio-Paris est allemand"* ("Radio-Paris lies, Radio-Paris lies, Radio-Paris is German"). To Parisians, the most trusted radio news is what they get from the American short-wave broadcasts; strangely, the French are still permitted to listen to all short-wave programs, though only in private. Some of the bitterer Parisians have begun to head their letters to each other "Paris, Germany." *"Veni, vidi, Vichy"* is the only bon mot Pétain has produced. Apparently, the best thing about Parisian morale is that Parisians remain, under the Germans, just what they were under the French. Parisians grumble, argue in cafés about the new politics as they did about the old, are logical, critical, disgusted, sardonic, witty, realistic, civilized as they always were, but they have an earnest, a desperate and humble, hope that is new. The blackout is severer under the Nazis, though Paris has not been bombed by the English, than it was under the French when they were still at war with Berlin. For carelessness during blackouts, the Germans warn a householder twice. The third time they fire a pistol shot through the offending lighted window. *Ils sont très corrects.*

Outside of Paris, the roads to Senlis, Laon, Beauvais, Les Andelys, and Vernon are deserted except for occasional bicycles. These towns are deserted in proportion to the destruction they suffered. Along the roads still lie the debris of the catastrophic refugee trek. Through the summer there also lay the remains of French soldiers, unnamed, unmarked, half earthed-over where they dropped. With that appalling efficiency which still leaves the French speechless, the German dead were neatly buried wherever they fell, whether in some villager's chrysanthemum bed or in some peasant's wheat field, always beneath wooden crosses which the Germans, who apparently thought of everything, brought to France with them. The graves are marked with name plates and German helmets are placed on them, like headstones. If several German dead lie together, there is often a German spread eagle decoratively patterned in pebbles on the well-tended, well-heaped earth.

The new French morale, the reaction that will permanently count, will surely consist not only of what the French see of the Germans at close range but also of what the French, when their bitterness dies down, remember about themselves. In the meantime, the rich French industrialists, whom the French Communists accused of being pro-Nazi, are, naturally, getting from the Nazis the treatment that the Nazis at one time would have dealt out only to the French Communists. That is, the rich French industrialists are being systematically ruined. Ninety million francs' worth of machinery in the Hispano-Suiza factories has been earmarked for shipment into Germany, and the French Ford plant (belonging to the Matford company, in which the American Ford company has a controlling interest) has already lost about fifty million in machinery. In Lyon, the fine-textile center of Europe since the fourteenth century, looms have been ripped out and shipped to Germany. What silk printing is still being done is restricted to two colors; formerly up to fifty colors were used. Designers trained through generations for delicate artistic invention are ordered to experiment with fabrics made only for durability and often of *ersatz* yarns. The great French dressmakers, around whom literally hundreds of thousands of French workers revolved in ramified industry, have been invited to work in Berlin. The 1940 autumn dress collections in Paris were made up in fabrics left from the autumn of 1939. This autumn, when the Paris stores and shops should have been displaying wool and furs in their windows, the display of beach frocks and sandals dragged on. Paris *couture* had been bought up, cleaned out, cut down before it was ready to sell, even to the Germans.

Biarritz is the secondary Promised Land for the Germans. As a reward for being German, troops by the hundred are sent down in trucks for a look at Biarritz. During the summer, German generals strolled the beach and other German officers on holiday leave renewed their domesticity with their dowdy wives, dazed at having a good time. The majority of Germans have never seen the ocean. Nazi youth has been taught to swim in the tideless German rivers. At first, in the chilly, treacherous Biarritz surf, many German soldiers were drowned. Then a system was worked out. In September, an American on the beach watched a platoon of German soldiers march out on the sand, led by an officer, who ordered them to stand in three rows, facing the sea. At a command, they all stripped to their shorts, folded their clothes in a neat pile in front of their boots, and, crossing their arms and ankles, sat down behind their boots. The officer, advancing from his own piled-up wardrobe, walked knee-deep into the ocean and tested the water's swish and temperature with his hand. He then commanded the first row of soldiers to march into the water to swim, while he kept paternal watch. After their plunge they filed out and sat down behind the two dry rows of soldiers, who, one row at a time, then took their turn. Finally, all the soldiers, on command, dressed, pulled on their boots, and marched away. These are the boots, this is the system, marching around half of France.

[January 25, 1941]

# A DAY IN TOWN

REBECCA WEST

BEFORE I could leave with Mrs. Raven, who was going to drive me to the High Dashwood station, I had to chase our ginger cat, Pounce, and lock him into the pantry. This war has revealed cats as the pitiful things they are—intellectuals who cannot understand the written or spoken word. They suffer in air raids and the consequent migrations exactly as clever and sensitive people would suffer if they knew no history, had no previous warning of the nature of modern warfare, and could not be sure that those in whose houses they lived, on whose generosity they were dependent, were not responsible for their miseries. Had Pounce found himself alone in the house and free, he would probably have run out into the woods and not returned to the dangerous company of humans.

"Well, you've lost the eight-forty-seven," said Mrs. Raven, looking at her watch and chuckling. All the world over, the most good-natured find enjoyment in those who miss trains or sit down on frozen pavements.

"Yes, we've lost the eight-forty-seven," I said, with the proper answering chuckle, and we loaded in the basket of vegetables I was taking up to my sister. We set off through the shining morning, with the sky an innocent blue over the thin gold plating of the stubble fields. But for the nests of sandbags and barbed wire at the turns in the lanes, it could have been pretended that England had not a trouble in the world. The Georgian red brick of High Dashwood was glowing rosily in the sunshine, the very color of contentment. And luck was with us, for a London train was waiting in the station.

"What train is this?" I asked a porter, looking at my watch. It was twenty to ten.

"The eight-forty-seven," he answered.

There were two men in the compartment I took, London office workers who had come down to stay the night with relatives in High Dashwood because their homes were in the heavily bombed areas of south London and they had felt the need of a night's unbroken sleep. "One night in five I must have my rest," said the one, "so my old auntie looks for me Monday, and then Saturday again, and so on." "I can't get that many," said the other, "what with being in the Home Guard and all." They compared notes on the easiest way

84

of getting from point to point in the City, avoiding the damaged tube stations and the roped-off areas. "Ah, but you hadn't thought of Porkpie Passage. Never even heard of it, I shouldn't wonder," the one said triumphantly, but broke off because, while the train was standing at a station, we heard the wail of an air-raid warning. "They're late this morning," he said, and shook his pipe at the window. "There's a pretty sight for you," he said. From an airdrome behind some houses, a squadron of fighters was rising in battle formation, as precisely aligned and synchronized as an ideal *corps de ballet*.

Nothing worried these two very much, I gathered, except the delay in the mails, which, they said, showed faulty organization, not to be excused by the present circumstances. "Ought to be able to do better than that," one of them said, "considering things haven't been so bad, really." They were still grumbling about it when we reached our terminus, which was looking more cheerful than I had ever known it. This was because all the smoke-dimmed glass had gone and the sunshine was pouring in through the iron ribs. There were no taxis in the station, as it had been impossible to sweep up all the finer splinters of glass, so I carried the vegetable basket till I got clear of the building, and then set it down at a street corner and looked round for a taxi. The streets about seemed oddly empty. I assumed that there had been a bad raid the night before and that people were not yet about again.

Across an otherwise trafficless patch of street, I saw a taxi, which had just deposited its fares at a house in a side street and was driving off. I ran to catch it, and while I was running the all-clear sounded. That is why I did not hear the shouts of a young policeman who was running after me and presently caught me by the arm. "You're running straight toward a time bomb," he said. "Can't you see that notice?" "No," I said, and then I mentioned a fact that had always before seemed to be not a disadvantage but, rather, a shield from unnecessary distractions. "I'm so short-sighted that I can't read notices," I said. "Get yourself some spectacles then," he said, and wiped his brow. "My God," he breathed, "you move fast for your age."

I carried the vegetables for another block, and found myself in a crowded street. Everyone wore the expression characteristic of people in a raided town. It is not unlike the look on the faces of pregnant women. It is as if they were drained of their strength by a condition against which there can be no rebellion and of which they are not ashamed. I found a taxi, which took me by roundabout ways to the square where my husband and I live. Down one of the streets I saw a house where I have often dined, its whole front laid open and its familiar wallpapers brightly lining its nothingness.

Before our apartment house the janitors stood pale and heavy-eyed. The one who took the basket out of the taxi said, "A bomb fell in the square gardens last night, but only on the soft earth. Nobody was hurt and the glass hasn't gone." The old man who took us up in the elevator said, "Did you know that John Lewis's has gone? It's gutted, gutted to the ground floor, and I nearly died of it. Just listen what happened to me. You know, me and my wife live at 8 Harley Street—we're caretakers there now all the doctors there have gone into the Army. Well, what would my wife do but every night put on her hat and go out to the shelter under John Lewis's. I often reasoned with her about it. 'What's the good of doing that?' I said. 'What's the good of going to a great store like that, which sticks its head up and asks to be bombed? Why not stay here, in a house that's just a house, among a thousand just the same as itself?' But she would have her way, and away she'd go every evening as soon as the sirens went. And last night she'd gone off as usual, and I was sitting in our basement snug as could be, and all of a sudden I heard one of those awful bombs, and I said, 'Sure as knife's knife, that's over by John Lewis's,' and I ran out into the street, and there I saw it blazing, and I hared along to the shelter, the way I haven't since I was a boy, and I said to the chap at the door of the shelter, 'Look here,' I said, 'look here, my wife's down there,' and he said, 'What if she is? They're all coming out now,' and, believe me or not, she was the very last to come out, and when she comes along, I said to her, 'Well, where's your new rug and your new cushion what I bought you for the shelter yesterday?,' and she said, 'Oh, I was so upset I couldn't think of anything like that,' and of course I couldn't be angry with her, being so glad she was all right, but of course we'll never see them again, though I've asked. But this morning, after breakfast, I said to her, 'Now you've got to go down to your sister at Chipping Norton as quick as we can put you on a train,' and I sent her off at half past eight, for there's some people that can't cope with emergencies, and though she's been as good a wife as I could wish, I don't feel she's been sensible, not over these air raids."

Inside my apartment, I looked at my shopping list with distaste. I had meant to buy some more blackout lampshades, some extra parts of a dinner service, and some electric-light fittings, all from John Lewis's, and I did not know where else I would get them. I would have to find somebody who could tell me which stores had been bombed and which hadn't. But first I had to hurry off to deliver the vegetables at my sister's apartment. She is a lawyer, and she lives in one of those old Inns, as they are still called, which are inhabited chiefly by lawyers. She lives on the top two floors of the tall Regency house where Charles Dickens once worked as an office boy. I carried the basket of vegetables up the four flights, and the door was opened by the Austrian Jewish refugee, a friend of my sister's, who does the housework, a colored handkerchief about her head, a broom in her hand. She was a doctor of philology and had been a happy and patient scholar in the field of medieval poetry. Now the opportunity to handle a broom represented an unhoped-for run of good luck. She murmured, *"Ach, die gute Gemüse!* We are so glad of them, for it is so hard to do shopping now. Whenever I take the basket and go out, the warning goes and all the shops shut, and when the all-clear goes I am sure to be making jam or seeing one of the refugees from your sister's committee."

At that moment, the warning went, and I fled. All over London, when sirens go, people spring apart. If the warning finds one too far from home, one may be forced to take refuge in a public shelter and waste precious hours, and when the all-clear sounds, one runs out to take advantage of the fact that the shops and post offices are open. My taxi whirled me homeward through poorer quarters than I had yet seen that day, where the damage had an unchivalrous air. At a corner, a rag-and-bone shop and three stories of frowsty lodgings over it were still recognizable for what they had been, but were twisted like barley sugar. It seemed unnecessarily presumptuous of the Germans to spoil what had, in its essence, never been unspoiled. During the latter part of the journey, I made myself dizzy by swivelling round to look out of the back window to see, against the blue sky, the trails of exhaust fumes which marked a fight between a German and an English plane.

At home, the butler gave me a lunch of coffee, tinned tongue, and bread and jam, which I ate off a tray in the lounge, with machine guns tapping at each other somewhere overhead. I wondered how, with so much going on, I was to get up to Hampstead, where I was to have a conference with a friend who owns a paper of which I am one of the editors. But the telephone rang, and it was my friend. She had left Hampstead and gone to her house in the country for the excellent reason that there was a time bomb in her Hampstead garden. We settled a matter about book-reviewing. Then the all-clear sounded and I ran out to find lampshades otherwhere than John Lewis's, to change my books at the Times Book Club, and to buy a chest of drawers I had seen in a shop window and needed for the country house.

Back in my apartment, I found my husband sitting in the lounge. He had three days' holiday before him and was to drive me back to the country. I thought he was looking rather pale, and I asked him if anything was the matter. He said, "Yes, it has all been very unfortunate. When I got to the Ministry this morning, I found that the whole front porch had been blown up and that you had to go in at the back entrance. And I was not unhappy about this till, in the middle of the day, I suddenly learned what everybody had supposed I knew: that Black, one of my colleagues whom I got on with best, an older man whom I liked and respected, with whom I had had a lot of pleasant talk, had been killed by the blast."

The butler brought us tea and said, "I was wondering if I might keep this as a souvenir, seeing that it fell in the kitchen." He held out to us a piece of shrapnel the size of a man's hand. "But did it not smash the windows to smithereens?" I asked "It made a hole exactly its own size," he replied, "but the splintered glass held. That varnish we painted the windows with seems very serviceable."

While we were drinking our tea, my husband said, "Are those two women ready?" For we were taking down not only the housemaid but the cook. "I can hear them packing up things in the kitchen," I said. "What things?" he asked. "Oh, china, cruets, boot-polishing kits—all sorts of oddments we had forgotten in the hurried move to the country," I said. "Well, we had better take down something of the things we really value," he said. "What would you like to take?"

We looked round the lounge without much interest. "Let us go through the whole flat and look at what we have," I said, and we pushed back the tea table and walked through our rooms. Everything we saw seemed a victim of a sudden, irreparable depreciation of value. It was no longer worth its price, because of the people who lay dead under the whorled laths and plaster of a hundred rag-and-bone shops. It was sometimes distressing, because of other, less corporeal deaths. We have a Rembrandt drawing, a minute, cunning, loving piece of magic, a few strokes of a pencil which show, receding into an immense distance, mile upon mile upon mile of Holland. We have a Dufy that shows Burgundy as it is after the vines have been sprayed with copper sulphate, a blue land, deep bright blue, delphinium blue. They had become portraits of enslaved countries, unvisitable, dangerous.

Nothing in the apartment was now as dear to me as the few fields we owned in the country, as our haystacks, as our Jersey cows, or the bullocks we are fattening for the market. Yet, when we opened the drawing-room door and saw the long, narrow Empire table which throughout my married life has stood in front of the window, I felt all my muscles go tense. "What has happened to it?" I asked. "What has happened to it?" Each of the three panels that made up its top bulged unevenly, as if forced apart by some inner strain. Its two wide legs were thrusting clumsily outward, and the bar that joined them was ready to drop out of its sockets. I went up and touched it, and saw that every joint was gaping. Nothing had hit it, but it stood there like something dead and unspeakably mangled. Under the gentlest blow, this honestly and beautifully made article of furniture would have fallen to pieces on the floor. I felt a sick yet distant anger that was extreme and not quite my own, an anger that might have been felt by the long-dead cabinetmaker who had made this table. Behind me, the butler said, "It was like that when I came in this morning. I understand several people have noticed that the furniture under their windows has been affected like this. It has something to do with the vibrations from the blasts." Beyond the table, through the obscuring varnish on the windowpanes, I could see London, veiled by the smoke that was still rising from the ruins of John Lewis's store.

[December 6, 1941]

# PADDY OF THE R.A.F.

A. J. LIEBLING

THE few British fighting men who have become popular legends during this war have done so without the connivance of His Majesty's Government. German and Russian communiqués are studded with the names of individual heroes, but even the R.A.F., although garrulous compared to the British Army and Navy, believes fliers should be almost anonymous. Whereas the Luftwaffe would announce that the late Werner Mölders had shot down his ninety-ninth plane—and, incidentally, British airmen would take no stock in his score—the Air Ministry says merely that a pilot attached to one of its squadrons scored his eleventh victory. Weeks later, perhaps when the pilot is due for a decoration, his name will appear in the London *Gazette,* a government newspaper few civilians read. For this reason, a high score is not enough in itself to make a fighter pilot a new personality. He has to have some particularity that the public can remember. Flight Lieutenant Brendan Finucane—Distinguished Service Order and Distinguished Flying Cross with two bars—has established himself in the public mind by being profoundly Irish, so Irish that strangers spontaneously address him as Paddy, which is also what his friends call him. He is neither Ulster Irish nor Anglo-Irish nor public-school-and-Oxford denatured Irish but middle-class Dublin Irish, and so proud of it that he has a big shamrock painted on his Spitfire. It is a shamrock designed by the adoring Yorkshire rigger and Canadian fitter who look after his plane. The shamrock has the initials "B.F." in the center and is surrounded by thorns. The rigger says he knows that thorns belong on a rose, but he feels they are appropriate, and Paddy agrees with him. The same rigger once, after the pilot had shot down his twenty-first plane, thought he would please him by painting twenty-one little swastikas around the periphery of the shamrock. Paddy got angry at this, saying they were an affectation of elegance, and made the rigger remove them. Paddy is twenty-one years and a couple of weeks old, and has a boyish eagerness to avoid any implication of swank. The way he got his most serious war injury fits in almost miraculously with his public personality; he broke his right foot jumping over a wall at a wake.

Being Irish is not itself a rare distinction in the R.A.F. At least five hundred citizens of Eire wear pilots' wings on their tunics and about fifty have been decorated. What made Paddy identifiable even before the public knew his name was his being both Irish and attached to an Australian squadron. When the Londoner at his breakfast table reads, for example, about a Polish pilot in the R.A.F. shooting down a plane, he has no way of knowing whether or not it is the same Pole he read about last Thursday, but the designation "an Irish pilot officer attached to an Australian squadron," which began to thread its way through the communiqués last June, gave Paddy his public identity. Subsequently the Londoner could follow Paddy's promotions as well as his triumphs, because the communiqués, which early last summer mentioned him as an Irish pilot officer (a pilot officer being the equivalent of an American second lieutenant), later spoke of him as a flying officer and then as a flight lieutenant. The last rank is like our captaincy. Finucane's decorations piled up even faster. He began the summer with a Distinguished Flying Cross left over from 1940, when, as a comparative novice, he had shot down five "certains," as the unquestionably disposed-of planes are called, in the Battle of Britain. As the summer progressed, he added two bars to the cross, and then, just before his birthday, he received the Distinguished Service Order. A couple of days later he broke his foot. By that time he had accumulated twenty-three "certains" and about a dozen "probables." He doesn't try to remember the planes he damages but does not bring down.

There are a good many men in the R.A.F. who think Flight Lieutenant Finucane is the most accomplished fighter pilot of the war, although he has not actually downed the most planes. In support of their argument, they point out that he made almost all his kills last summer and that 1941 was a poorer season for German planes than 1940 had been. Firth, Paddy's Yorkshire rigger, holds this point of view. In 1940, he says, there were "oondreds of jerries—all you'd to do was fly oop in air and poosh booton. But this year, when Paddy wants one, he has to go to France for it." Also, the technique of air fighting has been much refined since 1940. As there has been no general mêlée this year, German and British veterans alike have had time to teach the new pilots their tricks. None of the other pilots in Paddy's outfit, Squadron 452, had fought before last June, though they were the pick of the first lot to enter training in Australia. They had continued their training in Canada and Scotland. Paddy, who had been in the R.A.F. since 1938, joined them last spring at their first fighter station, which was in England, with the assignment of teaching them by example. They were the high-scoring squadron in England in August and September. They were nosed out by the American Eagle Squadron in October, while Paddy was nursing his foot, as he still is.

The wake at which Paddy broke this foot was expressly an Australian fliers' variant of the rite. All squadron members leave a couple of extra shillings in a kitty each time they settle their mess bills; then, when a pilot goes missing, the survivors drink up what he has left. The day before this particular observance, a sergeant pilot had been shot down over France. He had left two pounds ten, which was enough to finance only a modest wake. That, Paddy says, is why it was emotion and not drink which was responsible for his accident. The sergeant had been a close pal of his, and when, at the party, Paddy came upon a wall, he decided to jump over it, as a gesture of respect. There was a blackout, he says, and the wall looked like any other wall in the same circumstances. However, there happened to be a twenty-foot drop into an areaway on the other side, so he broke his foot. He was consoled a couple of days later by the news that the sergeant was safe in a prison camp. "In a way, the whole party was a waste," he says, "but I don't bear him any hard feeling." The hospital ward to which he was immediately afterward assigned was devoted entirely to R.A.F. leg injuries, and every pilot present, except himself, had been hurt either in a motorbike accident or a Rugby match. This excess of animal spirits may result in the loss of some flying hours, but it is also a sign that the men are in prime condition.

Paddy Finucane is an unusually serious young fighting man except when he is actually in the midst of the Australians, which is perhaps why he likes them so much. One Australian flight lieutenant, called Blue because he has such red hair, says, "We had to teach Paddy to play the fool when he came to us. The poor man had been with an English squadron so long he was trying to act dignified." The Australians, though few of them are older than Paddy —one pilot officer with a magnificent drooping mustache is nineteen—are relatively worldly types. One, upon returning recently from what the fliers call a sweep, remarked that he had shot a German into the Channel and that after the plane had struck, a bright-green stain had appeared on the surface of the water, something he had never seen before. "Heavy crème-de-menthe drinker, no doubt," he concluded. Most of them, before joining the Force, were university undergraduates or students in Australian public schools, whereas Paddy, right before he enlisted in the R.A.F., was an assistant bookkeeper in an office in London. Yet today, on all questions pertaining to air fighting, the Australians defer to Paddy's advice and obey his instructions. When he is flying with them, he sometimes, by radio-telephone, directs four dogfights simultaneously. "Has one of those beautifully efficient minds that work along just one line," a disciple of his says. "He can remember the positions of a dozen planes at once, although they change by the split second. And he has phenomenal eyes. Some fellows say Paddy smells Messerschmitts, but what really happens is that he sees them before anybody else can."

This exceptional vision may be the one quality all great pilots have in common. Once Paddy's mates saw him going after two Messerschmitt 109 Fs, of which he downed one. The second plane flew into a cloud and was lost to view. Finucane flew in after it, opened fire while in the cloud, and a moment later flew out of the other side as the German fell out of it, trailing flames.

Another time, when the Australians and a New Zealand squadron were taking part in a sweep, Paddy, three miles away, saw some Messerschmitts flying near the New Zealanders and warned them before they were aware of their own danger. He isn't a "suicide fighter," his comrades say. He will sometimes maneuver his section for five or ten minutes before he sends it in to the kill, but when he does, every Spitfire is apt to be on a German plane's tail. "The idea isn't just to get a plane for yourself," Finucane himself says. "You want to see the other fellows get some shooting, too." He derives more pleasure from helping a new pilot to his first certain than out of increasing his own bag. Paddy thinks his squadron is perfect. "All the Australians are mad," he says in a tone of heartiest approbation. "Waggle your wings, and they'll follow you through hell and high."

Paddy is of almost exactly medium weight and height; he is probably an inch too short for the New York police force. He boxed as a welterweight on the R.A.F. team in a match against the combined Scottish universities just before the war began, which means he weighed a hundred and forty-seven pounds, or ten stone seven in the national jargon. He is a few pounds heavier when he isn't in boxing trim, and he has the strong neck, the wide cheekbones, and the broad jaw of a good Irish ring type. He has wavy dark-brown hair, blue eyes, and a pink-and-white complexion that looks like a soap ad; he reddens to his ears when flustered. He was wild about boxing until he turned to air fighting, which he thinks a more exhilarating form of competition, and constantly draws analogies between the two. "Some pilots roll better to their right than to their left," he may say, "the way some boxers move better to one side." Or he says, "You have to take the play from the other fellow, just like boxing. I don't let them dither around." It isn't that Paddy is frivolous or brutal; in his direct way, he has made a mental adjustment that he couldn't have bought from a psychoanalyst for under a million dollars. "The personality never enters my mind," he says. "I always think to myself, 'I'm just shooting down a machine.' Some things get you rather angry, though," he adds. "For instance, if they shoot at our chaps after they've bailed out. That's like hitting a man when he's down." He has never seen this happen, he explains, but he has talked to fellows who say they have. He used to like Rugby almost as well as boxing. When the Army beat the R.A.F. at Rugby this fall, 30–3, Paddy took it as hard as missing three Germans. He watched the game on crutches.

He has never been shot down or wounded or forced to bail out, although during the 1940 hurly-burly he got a number of bullets through various Spitfires he was piloting. All last summer his planes were unscathed, a proof of his skill at maneuvering. Pilots like to find a couple of bullet holes in their planes after they get safely back to the airdromes, because it gives them something to talk about at mess. Once this year Paddy landed with holes in the tail fin of his plane, but they proved to have been made by the branches of a tree he had scraped. His rigger and fitter say he was much disappointed. He has never fought in anything but Spitfires, and has had them in all their editions. During the summer he ran through five planes—three early Spits and two of the latest Spit fives. He cracked up two machines on his own airdromes, stunting near the ground. Stunting is an officially discouraged but universal custom among fighting pilots. He is very careful about selecting a plane; he not only puts it through all the tricks he knows but he fires several trial bursts with its cannon and machine guns. If a cannon jams, he gets out instantly and walks away from the machine. Once he has picked a Spit, he leaves it in the care of his rigger and fitter, who work with an armorer, an electrician, and a radio man. Aircraftsmen in the last three categories take care of three planes apiece, so they are not identified with one pilot as a rigger and a fitter are. Finucane does not fancy himself an engineering shark. When he comes in from a sweep, he may say to his retainers, "She's flying left wing down," or "right wing down," but he leaves the remedy to the ground crew. This delights them. Firth, the rigger, who is dark, solid, and snaggle-toothed, says, "When Spit's been in dogfight, she's oopsey." His tone implies that the ordeal is rather like a childbirth for a delicate woman. Moore, the fitter, who is small and blond, says, "Some officers get a big head when they down one or two planes, but not Paddy." They both carry decks of snapshots of Finucane in their pockets.

After Paddy has chosen a plane, his shamrock and the letter "W" are painted on it. Each plane in a squadron is identified by a letter, as moviegoers who saw "Target for Tonight" know. Senior pilots usually get low letters, but Finucane insists on his "W," for sentimental reasons. It stands for Wheezy Anna, a nickname he gave his first Spit because its engine made such strange sounds. In those days the R.A.F. was short of planes and young pilots took what they could get. "Wheezy was a good old girl," Paddy says. "I cracked her up so hard I had the mark of the stick on my chest for a month."

When Paddy is on leave, as he is now on account of his foot, he lives with his parents, a small brother named Joseph, and two sisters, Monica and Claire, aged eleven and seven, in Richmond, the London suburb south of Kew. He has another brother, Raymond Patrick, who is nineteen and a sergeant air gunner in the Bomber Command. The house looks like several thousand others in suburban London and America. It is Tudor of a recent vintage, complete with the path of irregular concrete flagstones from gate to front door. Paddy's father is a night office manager at an airplane-parts factory that works the clock around. He is black-haired, energetic, witty, and a firm teetotaller. He looks a good deal younger than his forty-nine years and used to be an amateur soccer star in Ireland. Mr. Finucane pronounces his surname "Finewcan," but Paddy says "Finoocan." Paddy, who admires his father, has never developed a taste for beer or whiskey. Recently, in an effort to keep up with the Australians, he has learned to order a bottled drink called Pimm's No. 1, which is like a sweet Tom Collins. Mrs. Finucane is good-natured and hospitable. When Joe, the small brother, gets home from school, his favorite reading is a monthly publication called *Rockfist Rogan of the R.A.F.,* the adventures of a British Superman with a war slant. Rockfist, typically, will jump from his flying plane into that of a wounded brother pilot, drag him from the cockpit, and make a double parachute jump to safety, perhaps lassoing the propeller of a Heinkel on the way down and hauling the crew into captivity. This serial greatly increases Joe's respect for his older brothers. Paddy himself prefers more realistic books about flying. There is a recently published one called "Fighter Pilot," which he describes as wizard, his favorite adjective of praise. He uses it, too, to describe the two Australian flight lieutenants who roomed with him at the airdrome up to the time of his jumping over the wall. One, the red-haired fellow called Blue, is addicted to mystery stories and the other reads poetry, forms of composition that Paddy runs down at every opportunity, out of a spirit of contradiction. The poetical Australian says he knows Paddy has a poetic soul, a suggestion that drives Paddy into a picturesque fury. The mystery-story Australian, who has downed ten German planes, wears the jacks of spades, hearts, clubs, and diamonds inked on his "Mae West," as the fliers call their bulbous yellow inflatable life-saving jackets, because these cards are the sign of a fictional detective he admires.

The mantelpiece in the Finucanes' dining-sitting room is decorated with cutouts of Snow White and the Seven Dwarfs made by Monica, a large square clock with an inscription saying it was presented to Flight Lieutenant Brendan Finucane by the night staff at the factory where his father works, and a bronze cigarette lighter in the form of an aircraftsman spinning a propeller. This last is a gift to Paddy from his girl friend. He doesn't think it a good idea to get married during the war, he says, because "someday I might be going on a sweep and I would have it in the back of my head that I wanted to get back that night and that would distract me." Even now, he acknowledges, he sometimes has "a funny feeling in my tummy" just before he takes off, and he is afraid that marriage might make it funnier. He is a devout Catholic and attends Mass whenever he gets a chance. The Australians, he says regretfully, are "free and easy" about spiritual matters. He gives you a feeling that this worries him a little. He is always worrying about the fellows he flies with. Blue says that Paddy once woke him at four in the morning by shouting "Break, Blue! There's a Messerschmitt on your tail!" "I guess he dreams about air fighting all night," Blue says.

The Finucanes' move from Dublin to Richmond took place early in 1938. In Dublin, Paddy had attended a wonderful institution of learning called the O'Connell School, where the headmaster was a retired Army officer who had held a service boxing title. Like headmasters the world over, this one believed in his own favorite sport as a character builder. Every morning at eight-thirty, according to Paddy, the boys were turned out under a large shed in the school-yard and told to whack each other. Paddy developed such a taste for whacking that the future pattern of his life lay clear before him when he came to England; he was destined to be a fighter pilot. He was too young to enlist in the R.A.F. immediately, so he worked without pleasure at an office job until May, 1938. Then, on the precise day that he became seventeen years and six months old, the minimum age allowed, he enrolled for a course leading to a short-term commission. Richmond had seemed somewhat humdrum after the O'Connell School, and the Finucane brothers, during their first few months there, found the English rather "standoffish." After Paddy joined the R.A.F., things went much better. He is still, however, a vocally patriotic Dubliner. Being an R.A.F. officer, he does not go in for political arguments, he explains, but occasionally somebody says something about Eire which betrays a lack of understanding, and then Paddy puts him right.

Men accepted for the course Paddy took were supposed to put in four years of active service and then pass to the volunteer reserve for six more. That was considered the expedient way to raise a body of fliers for what some people thought might be an emergency. The British did not sufficiently hurry the training of their pilots even after the war began to give Paddy an opportunity to fly in France with the expeditionary squadrons. He did not get into action until June, 1940, a couple of weeks after Dunkirk. He was first posted to the East India Squadron at an airdrome in the south of England. The squadron got its name from the fact that people in India had contributed money for its Spitfires. Most of the pilots were British. That is a fine squadron, Paddy says; he had a good deal of fun there. "First the Germans started pushing over high-flying fighters, and then bombers with fighter escort," he reminisces happily. "There was something doing all the time." On his first flight with a formation in combat, he says, he was so preoccupied with keeping his place in the formation that he "could not see a sausage." The squadron broke up an incursion of eighty German fighters, but Paddy says he wasn't much help. Afterward formation flying became automatic, and then he began to enjoy himself.

In the East India Squadron days, the pilots slept with their flying suits on when the weather was clear, and their planes were kept warmed up constantly. One time, Paddy remembers, the squadron was just taking off when some Heinkels started bombing the field. A number of Spitfires bumped over fresh bomb craters as they got into the air. A bomb dropped directly in front of a pilot named Kenny Hart, and the blast stopped his propeller. He scrambled out and ran for a shelter trench, with bombs continuing to drop about him, while his mates, gaining height, took after the Heinkels. "We shot down a couple of them," Paddy says, "but seeing Kenny run was the cream of it." On another occasion the boys were gathered around a table in the middle of the field, having afternoon tea before taking off for a sweep. Unexpectedly, some Messerschmitts dived on the field and started plunking cannon shells into the tea service. The pilots, conspicuous targets in their yellow Mae Wests, dashed for shelter while the ground defenses had a go at the Germans, who got away intact. "Things like that amuse us when we think of them," Finucane says. He shot down five certains while he was with the East Indias and contributed to the destruction of other enemy planes, and the Fighter Command tabbed him a coming man.

There is nothing unorthodox about Finucane's methods. The secret seems to be that he does everything exactly right, and a fraction of a second before his opponent. A fighter pilot aims at his adversary by means of a small, electrically operated arrangement called a reflector. When the enemy shows in the reflector he is in line with the guns, although, of course, he may be at a quite impractical range. There are two ideal shooting positions: one close behind the other plane, the other head on. Paddy prefers the first. The inconvenience of the second is that you are at the same time in line with the other fellow's guns. Polish pilots like this position. Even if you are hit, they say, you can ram the German before it is possible for him to pull out. You are therefore certain of your German. Paddy has a high regard for Polish pilots, but his mind does not run in the same channel.

The most difficult style of attack is called deflection shooting. This means firing as an enemy plane flies across your path. The angles of approach, rates of climb or descent, and speeds of the two planes all enter into the instantaneous guess the pilot must make as he pushes the button which operates the cannon and machine guns. Inexperienced pilots usually fire behind the other plane. Old hands have a tendency to fire in front of it. Paddy is a wizard shot, but he does not consider that deflection shooting pays. "Sometimes you take a long squirt at something that way and see bits fly off it, but you don't see it crash," he says. "What you want to do is get on their tail, close in. I give them a squirt in the tank and if they break up, I'm quite happy." A squirt is the burst of cannon and machine-gun fire that results from pressing the button and holding it down a couple of seconds. Paddy gets on the other fellow's tail in various ways: by pouncing, if he has an initial advantage in height; by waiting for the German to dive and then getting him as he pulls out; or by facing him at a safe distance and then circling him, as a mongoose goes around a cobra, finishing up at the back of his neck. A Spitfire can out-turn a Messerschmitt, although it cannot out-climb one. By practicing rigid economy in shooting, which is usual with him, Paddy once was able to down three German fighters in a single trip and arrive back at his airdrome with a quarter of his ammunition. It was his best afternoon's work. The squadron, collectively, got eight. The Australians had been "squatting on top of the bombers" that afternoon; that is, flying just above some Blenheims that were going to France for a daylight raid. A big formation of German fighters had dived from a great altitude, ignoring the Spitfires and going straight for the bombers. They dived right past the bombers without getting any. Then, as the Messerschmitts pulled out of their dives, Paddy, who was commanding the whole squadron that day, led the Spits above and at them.

Paddy has no personal feeling against Germans. His contacts with them have been limited. He remembers once seeing a couple at the Dublin Horse Show, and last August, after the East Indias shot down a Dornier near their airdrome, he and some other pilots went over to a hospital to visit the wounded German pilot and observer. "They had never flown together before," he says. Crews in the British Bomber Command rehearse their teamwork many times before they go out on a serious job.

Paddy's assignment to the Australian squadron was a masterpiece of psychology, as well as a good technical selection, because the Australians might have taken less kindly to a more formalized version of the British officer. At almost any time five or six of them are likely to be found around a table in one of the squadron's huts playing poker and saying, on any provocation, "Ectualleh." One boy will say "Two cards," and the dealer will say "Ectualleh?" The next will say "I'll have three," and the dealer will say "Ectualleh?" again. Then another will say "I'll stand" and the dealer will shout "Ectualleh!" and they will all roll on the floor with laughter because they believe that a certain type of Englishman never says anything but "ectualleh." Their own favorite interjection is "bloody oath," which they consider more spirited and democratic. They also say "very crook" when they mean put-out, and "fair dinkum" to indicate good faith. By this time Paddy is so steeped in their patois that it is sometimes hard to tell whether he is talking Irish or Australian. All the Australians are given to puns, and Paddy, who affects to be above them, used to run around punching the punsters on their biceps. One night some Australians went out and painted kangaroos all over his Spit's shamrock, an outrage that excited him for days. The Australians love to tell Finucane stories, and they think he is wonderful.

When Paddy is to go on a sweep, he usually sleeps late in the morning and then takes an extremely hot bath. Most athletic trainers say hot baths are enervating, but Paddy says they just make him feel relaxed. He then has tea and goes to receive the day's orders from the commanding officer. Last year R.A.F. fighter squadrons generally had the mission of intercepting German bombers. This year they escort British bombers to France and protect them from enemy fighters. In a sweep, which may involve a dozen squadrons, each has a special role. Sometimes the Australians fly closely above the bombers, sometimes they fly beneath or among them ("on the deck"), and sometimes they go very high, looking for Messerschmitts in ambush in the sub-stratosphere. The last is the assignment that Paddy likes best. The conventional order that goes with it is "Seek out and destroy." The only mission he really dislikes is a Balbo, which is an R.A.F. term for a reconnaissance in formation without any particular object. It is named after the late Italian aviator, who always flew high and never hurt anybody.

There are days when no large general operation is planned and the planes go off in pairs, flying very high, looking for some object of innocent merriment, like a little train on a *chemin de fer départemental* that may be carrying German Army supplies, or a lorry loaded with middle-aged Landsturm men on a road. Coastal steamers are particularly agreeable sights to them. When they fix on a target, they come plummeting down as straight as a stalk and squirt twenty-millimetre cannon shells just to see what will happen. Paddy remembers that one time he hit a steamer and it flew to pieces with a report that was heard on both sides of the Channel. "It must have been full of ammo," he says. The best day's sport he ever had resulted from another patrol. He and a pal were flying high and got into a cloud bank. Suddenly the cloud dissolved and they saw that they were sitting in among twenty Messerschmitts. "Twenty was a wee bit too many," Paddy says, "because we had the height and the sun against us, so I said to my mate, 'Come on along and beat up some gun positions,' and we left. We got down to about ten thousand feet and ran into another forty Messerschmitts, so we gave them a squirt to help them on their way and continued. Then, way down below us, just over the Channel, we could see two Messerschmitts attacking a lone Spitfire. We went along down and each shot one of them into the water. That brought me pretty low, and I was just above the surface when I saw cannon shells splashing into the water in a steady stream, so I could figure that one of the big bunch of Jerries had followed me on down and was in back of me. It is a very good position to be in in a fight, because you can judge the angle of fire by the splashes, and then you know where your man is. As the angle gets smaller, you can figure he's getting in line with you. Just before that happens, you give a quick turn. If he tries to follow, he goes in the drink, because he won't be able to pull out quick enough. If he doesn't follow, you whip up behind him, and there you are. I got him and went home quite happy, with the other lad."

Paddy doesn't know what he will do after he goes back to active duty, or rather what the Fighter Command will tell him to do. He may get a new outfit to whip into shape next spring, by which time, other R.A.F. officers say, he is fairly sure to be a squadron leader. What he would like most is to travel to the Middle East, or anywhere else, even if it's only by bomber. "My brother Raymond Patrick has all the luck," he says. "He goes to Bremen and other fascinating places every week, but I hardly get out of the country." His pet scheme, which the Fighter Command probably won't endorse, is to get to the United States as the pilot of a Catafighter. A Catafighter is a land plane carried on a merchant ship and launched from a catapult whenever one of the big German flying boats appears. The pilot shoots down the flying boat and then tries to get to the nearest land on the petrol he has left. If he can't make it, he lands in the water and hopes for the best.

"That would be wizard," Paddy says. "Free passage and all. Besides, I have an aunt and uncle and three cousins in Detroit, all named O'Callahan."

[February 14, 1942]

# DUE CREDIT TO HULL

A. J. LIEBLING

KINGSTON UPON HULL, generally known just as Hull, is an east Yorkshire city about as big as Providence, Rhode Island. Like most cities of that size, Hull has great civic pride, which has been increased by the circumstance that it firmly believes it has had more bombing than any other place in England. Describing bomb damage is nowadays a great outlet for municipal enthusiasm in Britain. Towns want it to be known that they have suffered as much as their neighbors in the common cause, and their inhabitants enjoy reviewing past crises much as convalescents enjoy discussing their operations. It is incautious to arrive in a medium-sized city, the center of which seems unscarred by bombs, and say to your hosts cheerfully, "Why, this town is practically as good as new." They will look at you with icy eyes and say, "You haven't had time really to see what's what. There is a place a hundred yards square in back of the jam factory that we have been told is quite as bad as anything in Plymouth." When you get to Hull, you are not likely to be guilty of any such *gaffe;* one look out of the train window and not even the president of the Coventry Rotary Club would deny that Hull has had a bit of a do.

This state of affairs, however, does not nearly satisfy the loyal citizens of Hull. They want fair recognition from the outside world. All through the past summer and fall, while the rest of England was learning to take quiet nights as a matter of course again, Hull had intermittent air raids. After each of these, London papers would announce, under a small heading, "Enemy raiders were again reported over a northeastern port last night," generally adding, "Bombs were dropped. There were some casualties." It was a little convention of the censors which almost all newspaper readers understood. A contractor named Robert G. Tarran, who is sheriff and chief air-raid warden of Hull and the city's most articulate civic booster, used to fly into a rage whenever such a report was printed. "It is bad enough to be bombed," Mr. Tarran would write to the authorities in London, "and anybody who says he likes it is a liar. But we ought at least to get credit for it." I did not learn about this grievance of Mr. Tarran's until I went up to Hull, but I had heard about the repeated German raids over the city.

Hull is situated near the mouth of the Humber in what is called a protected area, which means that an alien cannot go there without a permit. As an American journalist, I got a permit through the good graces of the Ministry of Information, which notified its local representative of my coming. The Ministry of Information man in Hull, a Mr. Peddie, was waiting at the reception desk of the Royal Station Hotel when I registered there, and he had a municipal councillor and an A.R.P. deputy controller with him. "At least they haven't hit the hotel," I said, without intending any reproach, after we had introduced ourselves. "Aye, but did you note the great department store across from the station when you came from the train?" Peddie asked defensively. He sounded like a Californian who hears a complaint about the weather in his state. "A complete ruin, that is. And a stock that must have been worth a hundred and fifty thousand pounds. Perhaps you'd like to have a look at it before we take you for a drive about in a motorcar." I said, naturally, that I would like a look, and so I checked my bag and walked across the station plaza with Peddie and the others to the shell of what, for a provincial city, had evidently been a very large store. "It happened at night," Peddie said, "so there were no casualties—the fire watchers got out all right. But it was very inconvenient. You see, every large draper's shop in the city had been blitzed, and a great many families had lost their houses, too, and all the clothing in them. Well, when this store went, the ladies had no place to go to buy new clothes. To hear them, you would have thought it was worse than if they had been killed."

"Aye," said the Councillor, "it hurts everyone in a different spot. I remember meeting a chap I know named Harrison, and 'Oh,' he says, 'did you hear? The Grapes is gone, and the Mitre, and the Marquis, and the Farmer's Glory, and the Spread Eagle, and the Shakespeare's Head'—all pubs, you know. 'Oh, the good beer,' he says, 'the crying, wasteful shame of it.' "

"It didn't put the shops out for long, though," Peddie assured me. "The government paid them out for what they'd lost and allowed them to restock. This big firm here is in operation again around the corner. They've taken a whole street of small shops and set up in them." I said I would like to see that, and we walked to a side street that ran behind the wrecked building. Each department of the firm was housed in a separate shop; instead of a single store, there was now a whole shopping district. Only two of the old tenants in the long row of individual shops had stayed on. One ran a pub, which snuggled between children's overcoats and the knit-goods department, the other was a fishmonger, appropriately sandwiched between perfumery and delicatessen. Women shoppers were fighting their way in and out of the narrow doorways, which became relatively narrower as the customers accumulated packages. Bombing does not seem to dull a woman's appetite for bargains.

"I'll wager you haven't seen anything like that in London," the Councillor said, and when I admitted I hadn't, everybody smiled.

"I can't understand why the hotel hasn't been hit yet," Peddie said, musingly. "Maybe they'll hit it tonight."

The Controller interrupted Peddie's reverie. "Now," he said, "we'll just run you around in the motor and give you a general idea of the damage." We walked back to where they had left their automobile in front of the hotel. I got in the rear seat with Peddie, the Controller drove, and the Councillor, who wore a bowler hat and a chesterfield, just like a municipal statesman at home, sat in front of me and waved his arm at points of interest. "If you could publish the number of buildings we've had hit," he said solemnly, "it would put Coventry's eye out."

The number of buildings, which I knew he was right in assuming·the censor wouldn't pass, was impressive, but the number of people killed in Hull since the beginning of the raids is, as is true all over Britain, amazingly small compared to the property damage. Naturally, many of the bombed buildings that normally would have had people sleeping in them were empty at the time they were hit, because the occupants had moved to shelters. Others were business structures, mostly empty at night. The number of casualties was also limited by the circumstance that working-class houses in Hull are small affairs of one or two stories. Even when an occupied house is hit, my guides reminded me, the possible number of casualties is slight compared to what it is in the boxlike four-story tenements of Glasgow, or, as I reflected, to what it would be in a six-story old-law Manhattan walkup. Hull is a horizontal rather than vertical town.

It was about four o'clock in the afternoon, and I said I would like to see some of the boys on the local paper. Since the war started, I had often wondered what it would be like to work for years as a reporter in some quiet town, grousing time and again that "nothing ever happens in this burg," and then suddenly to have the biggest stories in the world start popping all around: local characters killed by bombs or making heroic rescues, enemy planes crashing in the back yards of prominent citizens, fire and slaughter in familiar buildings everywhere. The entrance to the editorial rooms of the *Daily Mail,* the Hull paper, reminded me so much of the setup of a newspaper on which I once worked in New England that I half expected to recognize the elevator man. "What is the circulation of this paper?" I asked Peddie, who accompanied me into the building, and when he said "Eighty-seven thousand," I answered absently, "Ours was eighty-eight thousand." Peddie looked startled.

Mr. Robinson, the *Mail's* editor, a lanky man with a mop of dry hair, had a pinched appearance, reminiscent of New England too. I said I was curious as to how a newspaper covers a continuous blitz on its own town, and Robinson replied that it was a difficult problem but he'd be glad to try to explain. The worst feature of blitzes, from the point of view of an editor in a bombed town, he said, is that nothing specific may be printed about them. Even though half a dozen of the city's best-known buildings may have been knocked down and all the citizens may be gaping at the wreckage, the newspapers are not permitted to identify the structures, since doing so might acquaint the enemy with the effectiveness of his bombing. Newspapers are not even allowed to publish the names and addresses of casualties. Lists of these are posted inside the doors of police stations as soon as compiled, and the townspeople go there to read them. Newspapers can prepare a vivid but indefinite account of a blitz, but this must be passed by the censorship office in London before it is published; it is generally read to a censor over the telephone. Sometimes the censor "embargoes" the news of a raid, and then for the time being nobody is allowed to publish anything about it at all. The *Mail* is part of a chain, I was told, and arrangements have been made to print it in some other plant of the same ownership, at Leeds or Manchester or Grimsby, if it is bombed out in Hull. So far, Robinson said, it hadn't had a serious hit. Peddie looked a trifle embarrassed at that.

We left Robinson, who I could see had a lot of work to do, and went down to the street to rejoin the others. The Councillor was just suggesting that I might like to visit some more ruins when we heard a long wail, less strident than that of a New York police-car siren and not so dramatic as the *alertes* I remembered in Paris. It was polite but insistent. All three of my hosts seemed pleased, as if the sound justified the reputation of Hull as the air-raid metropolis of England. "This would be a fine chance to go over to the control center," the Controller said. "We'll show you just how the Civil Defense machinery works during a raid. We have plenty of time, as that's only the first alarm. People in the factories go right on working until they get a second alarm, which we call the industrial. I'll drive around slowly for a few minutes so you can observe the reaction of the populace. You will please notice how Jerry has got our wind up." This last remark was Yorkshire irony, which has the same gossamer quality as Yorkshire pudding.

We drove to the control station through a number of streets with wonderful names; one, I recall, was Land of Green Ginger. Nobody seemed to have paid the slightest attention to the siren. The bicyclists, of whom there are more, proportionately, in Hull than in any other British city, because the terrain is so flat, continued to glide along at practically nothing an hour. People standing in queues at bus stations continued to read their newspapers while they waited for their conveyances. "Buses to the suburbs run right through the blitz," the Councillor said. "Those women bus conductors are wonderful." When we arrived at the control station, which had served as some sort of municipal building before the war, the Controller led us inside and down a long corridor to a room which is the brain center of the city during attacks. One of his assistants was in charge. It was an unexciting sort of place, with several large maps on the walls, among them one showing Hull, the Humber, the North Sea, and the rest of eastern England. The Controller glanced at it hopefully; if there were planes around, he said, markers on this map would show us their position. There were no markers to be seen. He looked let-down as, turning to the man in charge, he asked in a vexed tone, "Where did they go?" The assistant, who didn't know how disappointed his superior would be, said happily, "They skedaddled. There were only a couple of them, and they crossed the coast here." He put his finger on a point about twenty-five miles north of Hull. "They just turned around and went back without dropping any bombs. Probably just a training flight. There goes the all-clear now." We could hear the wobbling voice of a siren as the assistant went to write something in a ledger that lay open on a desk. "I always record the time of the first alert and of the all-clear, even when they don't drop anything," he told me.

"How many alerts does that make altogether, George?" Peddie asked, and the assistant mentioned a figure well up in the hundreds.

"Hull is the nearest English port to Germany," the Controller said. "We're straight across the North Sea from it, about three hundred miles apart. And the Humber, which is three miles across at its mouth, makes a good signpost, except on the darkest nights. So their young pilots learn navigation by bombing Hull. And after all, it's one of the great ports of England, and the Germans know that even if they just chuck out a few bombs at random from a great height, they may hit something interesting. I think that's why we get all these little raids. We got it even in the last war, being where we are, only then it was mostly Zeppelins. So we're used to raids." Motioning toward the map again, he said, "The sound of enemy planes is picked up by our observers and their positions are relayed to anti-aircraft headquarters here, which passes the information on to us. Of course, we don't send out an alert unless the planes seem to be definitely headed for Hull. By moving markers on this map, we keep track of the position of each plane, or each group of them, until they get here and pass over or turn back. The markers have different denominations, depending upon their color, like poker chips—one plane, five planes, ten planes, and so on."

Next the Controller led me over to a large-scale map of Hull that was almost covered by pins with heads of various colors. At the bottom was a neatly printed explanation of what the colors stood for—incendiary bombs, oil bombs, parachute bombs, high-explosive bombs, and a few others. "The idea at first was to mark every site of bomb damage," he said, "but along about last March we found that there were places where we had no room to stick in another pin and, besides, the supply of pins was getting to be a problem, so we gave it up. That was before the really heavy raids on Hull began. Some of the heaviest we had came in late July, while London was enjoying that lull we read so much about in their papers."

Another large-scale map showed every block in the city, with all its Civil

Defense arrangements. On it the city was divided into about thirty districts, each with a warden's post, and the districts grouped in four areas, each with a central office known as a report center. I was told that when a bomb drops, the warden in whose district it falls telephones the details to his report center. A standard form is used for taking down these details; it calls for information under such headings as "Position of occurrence," "Type of bombs," "Casualties (approx. number, whether any trapped under wreckage)," "Fire (if reported, write word 'Fire')," "Damage to mains (water, coal gas, overhead electric cables, sewers)," "Names of any roads blocked," "Position of any unexploded bombs," "Time of occurrence (approx.)," and "Services already on the spot or coming." On the basis of this information, the officer in charge of the report center notifies whatever services seem needed—rescue, stretcher, fire, and so on—picking the squads nearest where the bomb fell. "When there are so many incidents that the services inside a report center's area can't handle them," said the Controller, "the officer calls on the control center—that's here—and we shift services from quiet districts to the places where they're needed. It's like the G.H.Q. of an army during a battle. Sometimes, in very heavy raids, our telephone communications are damaged. Then we use small boys on bicycles as messengers. We've had kids of fourteen riding through the barrage all night."

It was dark by now, and Peddie suggested that I might like to visit some shelters. Shelters, it turned out, were the Councillor's specialty, just as air-raid precautions were the Controller's. "I'll take you out to a group of shelters where we are sleeping twelve hundred people every night," the Councillor said, when we were back in the car. "You mustn't think that bombing has no effect on morale. People react wonderfully during a blitz; they've plenty of pluck then. The trouble comes later, when they haven't got a roof over their heads and when for nights on end they can't get a decent night's sleep. A chap can't put in a real day's work at the docks if he's been trying to sleep in a half-blitzed house with shrapnel falling around him and maybe his old lady or his mother a bit on the windy side—there's usually one nervous one in a large family—and wondering whether it was a sin not to have sent the kids into a safe area. At least where we're going everyone has a clean bunk to sleep in and before long we'll have a heating appliance in each shelter and some shower baths in a school nearby that they can all use. We've got several places of this type going, and we'll soon have more." When a family starts coming to a shelter colony every night, the Councillor said, it is assigned to some particular shelter. Each shelter has a kind of house committee made up of women who see that it is kept clean; the men share the odd jobs. There is thus no need of a permanent staff.

We drove for a while in the darkness and then turned down a side road, bumped briefly along it, and stopped. A man carrying a flashlight, which he kept trained on the ground, came up to the car. The Councillor introduced him as the superintendent of the shelter colony. Behind the superintendent I could make out the silhouettes of some of those permanent surface shelters you find these days in any city in England—rectangular, narrow structures, about eight feet high, with flat roofs. They are always built of yellow brick and look rather like the New York comfort stations of the unimaginative pre-Mosaic era. My companions led me inside one. There were two tiers of bunks along each wall, with wooden frames painted bright red, which gave the place a touch of kindergarten gaiety, but otherwise it was as bare as you might anticipate from its exterior. There were a number of people already in the bunks and others preparing to go to bed. I have been in shelters on several occasions and I have always felt like an intruder. The English working people are incredibly patient about this; if I had been bombed out of my house and someone woke me up in a shelter to ask me how I was getting on, I am afraid I should try hard to punch him in the eye, but not these English. The Councillor, announcing me as a gentleman from America, asked a woman with a cold in the nose how she liked her new billet. "It's champion," she said, without conviction. "Better than sleeping on the floor, eh?" the Councillor insisted. The woman said, "Yes." That sounded reasonable.

Peddie said, "The mobile canteen should be here by now, shouldn't it, Councillor?" The Councillor said he thought it should, so we went out to look. Canteens, each of which carries enough hot soup and tea and bread to feed several hundred people, visit all the clusters of shelters every evening, in addition to feeding people in bombed areas immediately after a blitz, which is their primary function. The municipality furnishes the food at nominal cost— a penny for tea and twopence for soup with bread—and the Y.W.C.A. provides attendants. My companions were right; a canteen had arrived, as we discovered by the faint glow of its shielded lights. It was built on a Chevrolet chassis, which its driver, a city employee, called "a swell crate." "Having a left-hand drive makes me feel like a real he-man," he said in a matter-of-fact way, as if a left-hand drive were all it took to make a man feel up to churning around through the Hull blitzes for three quid a week. He said that his machine had been donated by a Chevrolet dealer in Oneonta, New York—a fact written in chalk under the hood. The surrounding darkness must have been full of children, for they swarmed around the faintly illuminated serving end of the canteen like May bugs pressing to a light. It was not cold; there was a clinging, steamy mist, the sort they call in Hull a sea roke. One boy, with a penny in his hand, wanted soup and was told by the Y.W.C.A. woman that soup cost twopence. "That's not right," the Councillor said. "They should sell a half-portion of soup for a penny. I'll take it up with the Council." The driver didn't say anything but slapped down another penny on the counter, and the boy got the soup.

We returned to the car and drove back toward the center of town. Before we had gone a quarter of a mile, the sirens began blowing again. The Controller drove with his usual unconcern. It was eight o'clock by now and I was quite hungry, but my hosts insisted we stop off at a pub on our way to the hotel. "The finest sight in Hull is the froth on a glass of beer," Peddie remarked. We stopped unerringly in front of a pub, even though it showed not even a glimmer of light, and went in and ordered four pale ales. The pub was a large, bare place with a few chairs and a cheap wooden counter and none of the pseudo-Tudor woodwork and pseudo-pewter ornamental mugs that English brewers give most retail establishments; it looked like a converted store, which Peddie said it was. The original premises had been fifty feet down the street and, owing to enemy action, they no longer existed. Two soldiers were playing a game of darts at a board over which was a sign reading "Game Postponed at Gunfire." The barmaid, a substantial middle-aged woman in a black woollen dress, knew my guides and asked them if they had read the latest snub to Hull by the London press.

At that moment all the anti-aircraft artillery in eastern Yorkshire opened up simultaneously, or so it sounded. The two soldiers went on with their darts game, heedless of the sign. The barmaid, who was mopping the counter, looked worried and glanced at a shelf on which a number of glasses were jigging up and down. "I know they won't fall off," she said. "The shelf is quite wide enough, but sometimes a glass cracks with the vibration. Down in the old place I lost two that way in one night last winter. And you know how hard they are to buy nowadays." The Councillor finished his ale and said, "Well, we may as well stay until it blows over. Have another. Funny, but every time I go out without my tin hat we get shrapnel." We had another round of drinks and the firing died away. Peddie winked. "Brief but sharp," he said. Ten minutes later the all-clear sounded.

The next evening, back in London, I was looking through a newspaper and happened to notice a short communiqué from the Ministry of Home Security. "There were a few raiders over a northeastern port last night," it read. "Bombs were dropped and there were some casualties."

[November 15, 1941]

# THE ARMY LIFE
## MY DAY

E.  J.  KAHN,  JR.

O NE of the questions frequently asked of a selectee by civilians he en-
counters on the rare excursions he makes into their sheltered world is
"Well, what do you *do* all day, anyway?" Well, we do lots of things. The
component parts of my routine at Camp Croft, South Carolina, where I am
receiving thirteen weeks of basic infantry training, are varied slightly from day
to day, but on the whole I find it hard to tell one day from another. On my
typical day I am aroused, along with thirty or so roommates, at five-thirty in
the morning by a fellow who has spent the night in charge of company headquarters and who bounds briskly into the barracks, snaps on the lights with a
flourish, shouts, "Let's go," and vanishes again into the darkness outside before I have had time to say thanks. A bugle is also blown, but we don't always
hear it. We have only ten minutes in which to prepare for reveille, so most
of the boys, having dislodged themselves from their beds, hurriedly start
putting their clothes on, at the same time encouraging reluctant risers near
them, by a stiff nudge or two, to follow their example. At five-forty a staff
sergeant's whistle blows and we line up in front of our barracks for roll call.
When we have been found all present and accounted for, we scramble back
indoors. We are then completely at leisure, until breakfast at six-fifteen, to
wash, make our beds, sweep under them, arrange our shoes neatly under the
beds, tie the laces on the shoes we have arranged, and dust the whole display.
We perform some of these chores to the musical accompaniment of Stan
Shaw's all-night phonograph-record program on one of the boys' radios, a
broadcast some of us used to listen to in New York as we went to bed.

At the sound of another whistle, we walk to our company mess hall, a long,
low building a hundred yards away, and as we file in we pause at the door to
receive our daily ration of milk, a half-pint bottle. About two hundred and fifty
men eat there, seated ten at a table. Our food has already been set out by soldiers who are on duty as waiters for the day, and we begin eating when a cook
blows a whistle. Before each of us is a thick china cup, a china plate, a knife, a
fork, a spoon, and, at some breakfasts, a cereal bowl. We are continually informed by our mess sergeant, a man evidently unimpressed by such conversation-

*107*

ally worth-while meals as those that once took place at the Mermaid Tavern, that it is pointless and in fact improper to mix talking with eating and that our table repartee should be limited to "Pass the butter, please" and "Reach for it yourself." After breakfast some of us line up in front of the barracks and then roam across the company area, stripping it of such undesirable matter as cigarette butts, matchsticks, and bits of paper. The rest of us return to our barracks to finish sweeping and to wipe off any ledges or shelves we suspect an inquisitive officer might finger.

By seven-fifteen, we are ready to go to work. Most of our days are divided into hourly periods. We work for fifty minutes and then have a theoretically ten-minute break, which is rarely longer than ten minutes and is frequently shorter, depending on how many things we are required to do during it. Each break begins and ends with a whistle blast, and in between we often run in and out of the barracks to gather up equipment as orders are shouted to us. We sometimes change our accessories as often as a débutante. One morning, for instance, we were told to fall out in khaki hats. After doing so, we were told to go back inside and get our denim hats. We neatly stowed our khaki hats away and fell out in denims, only to learn that at Camp Croft they are worn exclusively by prisoners. It developed that what we should have done was to wear our khakis and carry the denims, which were to be turned in at the supply room, where they would presumably await our admittance to the guardhouse.

On a typical day our work starts off with a brisk dose of calisthenics, which we perform not to musical rhythms but to our own raucous count. Each exercise we do, we're told, develops some especially useful muscle, and the officers who serve as physical-education instructors, while warning us not to bend those knees as we strive earnestly to touch our toes, are apt to urge us on by announcing that every uncomfortable position we get outselves into is for our own good. You don't have to be in the Army long to learn, from some superior or other, that everything you do, or that is done to you, is for your own good.

During the ten-minute break allotted to us after calisthenics we return to the barracks and pick up the resplendent accessories of our regular drill uniforms, which consist, all told, of blue denim fatigue blouses and trousers; canvas cartridge belts, with canteen, bayonet, and first-aid kit attached; rifles; leggings; and wide-brimmed khaki field hats that have recently been issued and will no doubt eventually inspire some little Daché creation that all the smart girls will be wearing. From eight-fifteen until nine o'clock we are occupied with close-order drill, without which we would never be able to give a decent account of ourselves in a Fifth Avenue victory parade. Close-order drill consists of marching in formation. We move at attention, maintaining, when underway, a steady speed of one hundred and twenty steps to the minute, holding our rifles on our shoulders at identical angles, and looking straight ahead at the neck of the fellow in front of us, a monotonous and singularly unappealing view.

Close-order drill is followed by fifty minutes of what is called extended-order drill, which we are learning for use in areas more combative than Fifth Avenue. During this period we move around a field in squads of a dozen or so men in long, loose lines, and at frequent intervals are compelled to fall flat on the ground, no matter how unreceptive the ground may appear to be. More often than not, we are running when we get the order to drop. The Army has an approved way of performing every movement, and we have been given explicit instructions about falling. You hit the ground first with your rifle butt, which is clasped firmly in the right hand. Your knees hit next, and, a fraction of a second later, your whole left side. Immediately you roll over into a prone position, bring your rifle butt up to your right shoulder, and there you are, ready to shoot. Very simple.

We are finished with extended-order drill at ten o'clock, by which time we are tired enough to call it a number of days. We are accordingly astonished when we learn that our schedule now demands a five-mile hike. On hikes we march at route step—keeping in step not required and talking permitted—with our rifles slung by their straps over our shoulders and our packs, like overweight jockeys, riding high on our backs. We get back to the barracks just in time to collect our mail before lunch, which is served at noon. We receive mail twice daily, and once on Sunday. Two letters and a medium-sized package of cookies are regarded as fair compensation for a hike. Probably the saddest fellow in the camp the day we returned from our first long march was the one who stopped lamenting a blister long enough to open a promising-looking envelope forwarded to him from his home, only to discover that it contained a letter from his draft board. It wanted to know where he was.

We are usually finished with lunch, known in the Army as dinner, by twelve-twenty, and we have the next forty minutes to ourselves, unless, of course, somebody with more authority wants them. At one o'clock our afternoon begins. We are likely to spend the first two hours of it at a movie theatre, where we divide our time impartially between cat naps and films about the training of an infantryman. The majority of our pictures are produced by the Signal Corps and, considering their purpose, would probably receive an extremely low rating from a Senate investigating committee. The actors are almost all Army men, who accomplish with dexterity and poise various movements our officers hope we will someday be able to duplicate. The only member of any of the casts known to us as a non-professional is a silver-haired Hollywood actor of whose identity we are uncertain. As a wise old medical officer, a sort of antiseptic Frank Craven, he plays the narrator's role in an animated treatise on sex hygiene we have so far witnessed twice. When he turned up a few nights ago in a regular Hollywood picture about a reformed jewel thief, his first appearance on the screen drew more cheers from the audience than a sweater girl would have.

After our siesta at the movies, we go back to our company drill ground for bayonet practice. We stand in two facing rows and, at appropriate intervals, we growl ferociously at our supposed opponents and make threatening gestures at them. Bayoneting is as precise a sport as fencing, with a set of conventions no less strict. We are taught a series of ten movements designed to wear down the resistance of, if not actually cut to small pieces, the most formidable enemy, and we are taught to execute them in a definite order. The only thing that worries us about bayonets is that our opponents may have a set of movements of their own that will interfere with the proper completion of ours, or that they may refuse to coöperate by simply not remaining erect long enough for us to go all the way through our lessons.

Our working day ends at four-thirty in the afternoon. However, there are still plenty of things to keep us from feeling idle. If, for instance, we have carried our beds and bedding outside in the morning, we naturally have to carry these inside and reassemble them. At five twenty-five we go to retreat, presenting arms in formation while the camp colors are lowered. While waiting for this ceremony to occur, we take showers and shave, if we have time; otherwise, we clean up after supper. The Army expects every soldier to shave once a day.

Supper comes immediately after retreat, and after supper we are free. Frequently, however, we have a few incidental extra-hour duties to perform, such as cleaning our rifles, turning in our laundry, receiving our laundry, signing the payroll, getting paid, receiving or turning in equipment, or writing letters home. Some men, of course, go to the movies or hang around at the canteen. At nine o'clock the lights in the barracks go out. By eleven every man is required to be in his bed. It may seem like a long day, but, as one sergeant explained to a new private who happened to remark that at home he had enjoyed the luxury of a fifty-hour week, "In the Army, fellow, your day begins at midnight." And when, the private hopefully inquired, did it end? "Midnight," the sergeant said.

# FOURTEEN FOR THE NAVY

ST. CLAIR MCKELWAY

THE S.S. Comet, of the Colonial Navigation Company, lay alongside Pier 11 in the Hudson one afternoon last week, ready to start at six o'clock on her regular overnight voyage up Long Island Sound to Providence, Rhode Island. There were about a dozen passengers on board, including myself. A man named Roundtree, who had a Kiwanis button on his coat lapel, had confidently asked the purser for his usual dollar-fifty stateroom, had got it, and had explained to the colored steward who took his bag that, by God, the sensible way for a Providence businessman like himself to get back home, if he had to go to New York on business, was to use one of these boats—have a good night's sleep and a fine breakfast and be on the job before eight-thirty. Two rather flashy women in flimsy black dresses and cloth coats had come aboard together and were sitting in the smoking room, along with the other passengers, reading a pair of film magazines. A young fellow in Broadway clothes, who carried a guitar case, had taken a three-bunk stateroom for himself, his young wife, and her younger sister, a slim and pretty girl who must have been about seventeen. They looked as if they might have been going to Providence for some kind of night-club engagement. There was a middle-aged couple, sulky and a little drunk. "I can certainly use that bar when it opens," the woman said, and the man shook himself and nodded. There was an elderly lady in a tweed suit who sat in a corner gazing at the Jersey shore through a porthole. That was all. Then, a few minutes before six o'clock, fourteen young men of New York who had just joined the Navy walked up the gangplank in column of twos and the S.S. Comet was transformed.

At first, as the young men swarmed into the smoking room to wait for the purser to get the keys to the seven staterooms the Navy had engaged for them, the rest of the passengers appeared to feel that the ship's social tone had been abruptly and offensively lowered. They stared sourly at the newcomers. The recruits were not in uniform and, except for three who wore topcoats, they looked as if they had just come from a scuffle on a vacant lot. Most of them were bareheaded and wore polo shirts open at the neck, and sweaters or windbreakers. One wore khaki pants and an old woollen shirt with a gaudy em-

*111*

blem on the sleeve that said "New York World's Fair Guide." They all stood around solemnly and seemed abashed.

These fourteen were named Barba, Brantwein, Brown, Cochario, Dowling, Foley, Jenks, Kennedy, Lieber, McHugh, O'Connor, Pavitt, Rafferty, and Sullivan. Of the several thousand young men who jammed the recruiting offices of the Army, the Navy, and the Marine Corps all last week, they were among the first to get through the formalities and into the armed forces. Before nine o'clock on the Monday morning after the bombing of Pearl Harbor, they had gone from their homes in Manhattan, in Brooklyn, in the Bronx, and on Long Island to the Navy recruiting office in the Federal Building downtown and volunteered. It was now Wednesday afternoon. Except for hurried trips home to get birth certificates (if they had neglected to take them along) and to obtain in writing their parents' permission to enlist (if they were under twenty-one), they had been in the recruiting office for three days and two nights, along with hundreds of others like themselves. They had slept on the floor of the office Monday and Tuesday nights so they wouldn't lose their places in line as they waited for the overworked Navy doctors to give them their physical examinations; they had hung around all day, too, until the Navy, eager to have them but unprepared for the unprecedented number of volunteers, had finally got around to taking them. They were now on their way to the Naval Station at Newport for a short period of training before being assigned to active duty at sea.

As the stewards began to lead them off to their staterooms two by two, Mr. Roundtree, the businessman, suddenly called out, "So you're in the Navy now!" All fourteen looked at him. "I thought so," said Mr. Roundtree, as if in disgust, and picked up his newspaper. The sailors went off to their staterooms, sheepishly.

"A lot of 'em will be wishing they were back in their mothers' arms by tomorrow night," Mr. Roundtree remarked to the smoking room at large.

The passengers glanced at him suspiciously.

"You suppose these are the boys that have been joining up in the Navy since Honolulu got bombed?" asked the woman who was waiting for the bar to open, looking around at the other passengers.

"Sure," said Mr. Roundtree, in apparent disdain.

"Well!" said the elderly lady aggressively, turning away from her porthole and sitting up straight. "I think they're just fine! I must say I couldn't imagine who they could be when they came in here all at once like that, but I think they're just fine!" She looked at Mr. Roundtree with hostility, and so did the other passengers.

"Sure," said Mr. Roundtree inscrutably, and went back to his paper.

Then, as the passengers ignored him and began to talk among themselves about the war, he looked up and said, "I notice they're putting two of these rookies to a stateroom. They used to pack us in four to a stateroom when they shipped us back and forth from Newport to New York on these boats in 1918."

"Oh, so you were one of them yourself then!" said the old lady, looking at him sharply.

"Sure," said Mr. Roundtree, with a thin smile. "The Navy'll teach them to take care of themselves. But I'm telling you all this is no joke for those kids."

Everybody seemed relieved about Mr. Roundtree. The S.S. Comet edged into the Hudson, rounded the Battery, and steamed up the East River on the way to the Sound. The sailors, having taken off their sweaters and windbreakers, began to drift back into the smoking room again, the passengers smiled at them and spoke to them, and, as soon as the bar opened, Mr. Roundtree invited two of them to have a beer on him. "Wait till you try to sleep in one of those damn hammocks," he was saying over his shoulder as they followed him into the bar.

The middle-aged couple stood up; the husband went over to one of the recruits and said, "Look, my wife, she don't do nothing but play the slot machine in a bar. You come and have a drink with me, huh?" The three of them walked off together, the woman laughing and saying, "I want the slot machine *and* a drink."

I had seen and talked briefly with some of the fourteen at the recruiting office the day before and had arranged to meet them on the ship and go along with them to Newport. One of the youngest, named Kennedy, came into the smoking room and looked around uncertainly, and I asked him if he would like to have a beer. "I'd appreciate it very much," he said, and we went in and stood at the bar. Kennedy is eighteen years old, slight, and wiry, with clever gray eyes and an unchanging look of wonderment on his face. "Had an ordeal at home today," he told me. "Mother crying and so forth—you know. It's inevitable, I guess. She signed the permission papers all right, but it was tough when I left this afternoon."

Kennedy's home is in Bay Ridge, Brooklyn, where he has been living with his mother and father and a younger sister and brother. His father is a machinist. Kennedy gave up a $32-a-week job as a ferryboat deckhand to join the Navy. "I think I'll try for gunner's mate or something like that," he said, sipping his beer. He pointed an imaginary anti-aircraft gun at the ceiling of the bar and grinned. "Want to get a crack at the Japs." Then he shoved his beer away from him, looking like a guilty child. "Don't want to get too much of this alcohol in the system with those tests coming tomorrow. I already had one beer with the guys on the way over. Say, we certainly have suffered severe losses in the Pacific, haven't we? What with the sinking of the Repulse and the Prince of Wales, I mean."

We were talking this over when Foley, another of the fourteen, came up to the bar, ordered a beer, and joined us. After a few minutes Kennedy yawned elaborately, said, "Guess I'll write up a couple of postcards before dinner," and left.

Foley and another recruit, named Cochario, had been designated by the Navy to be in command of the group on the trip to Newport. A bus was to meet them at Providence the next morning and take them to the Naval Training Station. Foley was feeling his responsibility and said he hoped the guys wouldn't stay up all night. "I figure my authority doesn't call for me to remonstrate with them or anything along that line," he said, "but I just hope they don't stay up raising hell and fighting." I told him I didn't think they would, and he said paternally, "They're a good bunch, aren't they?"

Foley is twenty-six. He was working as a counterman in a luncheonette in the Thirty-fourth Street station of the B.-M.T. subway up to Monday, but when he went to enlist he took along several letters of recommendation from former employers showing that he had worked as an electrician, and the Navy tentatively rated him as an electrician's mate, third class. He will have to pass some examinations, of course, to hold the rating. He has been living on Fortieth Street in Manhattan, far over on the West Side.

One of the women in the flimsy black dresses came in with one of the fourteen (whom we might call Buck), and the two of them sat down cozily at a chromium-trimmed banquette and ordered Scotches. "My God!" said Foley. The other woman came in with another of the recruits and the four sat together. "I wonder if they're professional," Foley said in a low tone, and finished his beer at a gulp. "I hope dinner is ready soon. I'm going to round them all up as soon as it's ready." Just then the dining steward came through announcing the first call for dinner, and Foley, looking pleased, went off to find Cochario to help him.

Mr. Roundtree had five of the recruits around him at the other end of the bar by now. One of them had taken out of his pocket a booklet the Navy had given him, and Roundtree was looking through it, pointing to the various insignia of the naval ratings and reading off the terms, holding the booklet so that all five could see the emblems. "That's pharmacist's mate, that's yeoman or clerk, that's gunner's mate, that's cook," he was saying. They seemed fascinated.

In the smoking room the old lady was talking away cheerfully to a very young recruit. He was a short, blond, red-cheeked boy in tennis shoes, brown slacks, and polo shirt, and he was listening intently and looking at her in amazement from time to time. "I also met General Pershing one time in Paris at the end of the war," she was saying as I went by. "He was a very fine man and still is." The guitar player from Broadway was sitting on a couch with his two young women and listening tolerantly while two of the recruits told about their experiences of the past three days. Foley and Cochario came through the smoking room, followed by six or seven of their men, and Cochario went into the bar to get the rest while Foley said self-consciously to the three in the smoking room, "I guess we'd better be going down to dinner now, you guys." Cochario came back from the bar with Buck and the others, and they all went off together in column of twos.

After dinner there were the customary ship's movies, and the smoking room and the bar were completely free of recruits until the movies had been run through. Then all but five or six of them went to bed. Cochario, the co-commander, told me he was going to go to bed himself and that Foley, who claimed he wasn't particularly sleepy, was going to stay up for a while and keep an eye on things. Cochario is twenty-eight, a husky, healthy-looking fellow who was drafted into the Army, although he had wanted to go into the Navy, and then released about two weeks ago under the age-exemption clause then in effect. He was trying to make up his mind what to do when the Japanese bombed Pearl Harbor. He then decided to go into the Navy, as he had always wanted to do. "I said goodbye to my old man this afternoon," he told me. "My old man's seventy-two and we've always been sort of pals. I said goodbye and started down the street, and I looked around, and there he came after me, just like a little dog. Ever see a little dog, I mean, follow you when you want him to stay home? He caught up to me and didn't say anything, and we walked on to the corner and then we shook hands all over again, and I made him go back home. He's a swell guy, my old man."

Back in the bar, the slot-machine woman was playing intently, muttering mild curses and telling her husband and two of the recruits that there were only three things she loved in this world and one of them was playing a slot machine. Buck and his friend and the two flashy girls were back at their banquette. Buck had one arm around his girl and was holding her hand, letting it go now and then to pick up his drink. They were telling stories and giggling. Kennedy came through one door of the bar and went right out the other, giving me a look that plainly said, "Do you see what I see?" Mr. Roundtree was at his place at the bar, telling clean and rather long anecdotes. Once he grew rankly sentimental. "I'll never forget one thing, boys," he said. "That Christmas, here I was at Newport, lonely and homesick, and what do you suppose happened? A dame in Kansas City—in *Kansas City,* see?—who I'd never heard of or seen or anything like that, sent me a sweater she had knitted, a carton of cigarettes, and a wristwatch. Imagine it! They used to pick names off the service lists and send them presents—to guys they never saw or knew or anything like that. I've never forgotten it, never." His listeners seemed enchanted.

One of the recruits, a man obviously older than the others, and wearing a business suit, was talking to the bartender at the other end of the bar. I joined him. "Boy, you don't know how I feel," he said happily. "Have a drink. No, I'm buying—I mean it. This afternoon I took a suitcase full of old deeds and insurance policies and Lord knows what and took them to my brother-in-law and dumped them on the floor and I said, 'Here!' Just 'Here!,' like that, I said." He drank and brushed a lock of hair out of his eyes. "That Pearl Harbor stuff was all I needed. I wasn't drafted, because I'm over that twenty-eight limit, but I didn't enlist because—well, you know how it is. You just couldn't be sure they were all really against us until this happened."

I asked him what sort of business he was in.

"Printing," he said, "or, rather, color reproduction. I was assistant superintendent of our plant, a fair-sized one. I was going to open my own business a year ago, but what the hell, you can't start a business with the priorities and everything. But you don't know how I feel *now!* That's what I'm talking about! Oil burners and plaster cracking in the basement and the roofs needing painting. I own three one-family houses on Long Island, see? Oh boy, am I rid of them! This is like starting a new life, honest to God. You know a funny thing I just thought of? In the business world you got to fight. Get it? That's one reason I'm joining the Navy. I'm not kidding myself. Because in the business world you got to fight all the time. What the hell!"

The recruit who had been sitting with Buck and the two women got up and came over to us. He was the one who had the World's Fair Guide emblem on his sleeve.

"Tired of that Frenchy-Frenchy, talkie-talk junk," he said, and we asked him what he meant by that. "They're French girls, or claim to be," he said. "My pal there is going at it all the wrong way around—soft and sloppy. Look at him." Buck still had his arm around his girl, was still holding her hand, and was now rubbing his cheek against her cheek. "He looks like a calf, and maybe he is a calf," said Buck's pal.

"There's a bunch of English and Irish stock in this crowd," said the ex-houseowner to the young man. "I'll bet you're Irish."

"Me?" said Buck's pal. "I'm Irish, Scotch, English, and Russian. My name's Pavitt, would you believe it? Owen K. Pavitt, P-a-v-i-t-t. My old man's a Russian and a screwball and a hell of a guy all round. So's my mother. I can drink a cocktail with her and tell her a funny story or anything. She's Irish, English, and Scotch. My old man is a hell of a guy, though. You won't believe me, but he installed all the rails and stuff on the Trans-Siberian Railway. Over here he was a big importer and exporter and ran through two fortunes, and now we live in a fourteen-room house in Brooklyn and it has a mortgage on it would knock your eye out. Yeah, boy!"

"This is something," said the ex-houseowner appreciatively.

"You know what I think, if you don't mind my talking my head off, because I always do it when I can?" said Pavitt. "There's going to be public ownership of natural resources after this is over."

"What the hell are you doing, pal, with a World's Fair Guide shirt on?" the ex-houseowner asked.

"Why take good clothes to the Navy? Mom, she tried to make me wear my best suit, but I said to her, 'What the hell, Mom! Gimme my old World's Fair Guide shirt that I had when I was a World's Fair Guide and I'll guide myself up to Newport.' You oughta seen her laugh. But you have interrupted me, my friend, and I don't want to be interrupted. The only way to interrupt anybody who is Irish, English, Scotch, and Russian is to hit them on the head. Now, I'm serious. I'm not saying I'm a Socialist or a Communist, but the natural resources of a free country—the mines and the rivers and the trees and the land—ought not to belong to any one man just because he finds some coal or something under the earth. I'll tell you. I was in Hollywood last year, in California, and the houses of the rich people there would make you sick to your stomach. I say houses and not homes. They're not homes. They're houses. They would make you sick to your stomach to see them, they would make you nauseous."

"Wow, is this something!" said the ex-houseowner.

"I will now go back to the Frenchy-Frenchies and their goddam talkie-talk for one drink, and then I am going to bed—alone—because I have sense," said Pavitt.

The young girl who was with the Broadway guitar player and his wife came into the bar with one of the recruits, and the ex-houseowner looked at them dully and said, "Well, I'll be damned. I thought sure that was a private party. Maybe it was, for that matter. Well, I'm going to bed myself. That recruiting office pretty much finished me off, and I don't mean maybe."

After a very short time the young girl left her sailor rather suddenly and walked out. He sat for a few minutes more, looking at the table, and then left the bar himself. Mr. Roundtree and his followers were saying good night to each other, Foley had given up, and I decided to go to bed. Down the corridor I saw the Broadway guitar player standing in the doorway of his stateroom, arguing patiently with the recruit who had just left the bar. "Look, sailor," he was saying. "One of them is my wife and the other one is a virgin." The sailor was weaving and grinning and saying over and over, "O.K., O.K., O.K."

The bus was to leave the pier in Providence at eight o'clock, and the recruits had breakfast at half past seven. The S.S. Comet had docked at six and most of the other passengers had eaten breakfast and gone. I found out later that the elderly lady had bought three large boxes of candy for the recruits at the ship's store and left them with the purser, and that the guitar player and Mr. Roundtree had each left five cartons of cigarettes. After breakfast the recruits sat around waiting for the bus and started to eat the candy. "I don't know how they do it," the ex-houseowner said to me.

There were no women now, only the recruits and the stewards, and a gay wave of obscenity swept over the smoking room, wholesome, friendly, and human. A recruit named Sullivan, who had been quiet the night before and had gone to bed immediately after dinner, suddenly assumed a dominating role. He had heard about Buck at breakfast.

"How old was she?" asked Sullivan, among other things. "Fifty? Sixty? I'd say fifty-eight, hey guys?"

Buck was silent, morose, and superior.

"I have sense, personally," said Buck's pal, the former World's Fair Guide, "because I'm no Don John."

Foley and Cochario came into the smoking room and Foley called out, "All right, guys! Let's get the bus!"

"Hop to it, you lugs," said Sullivan, and all the way off the ship and out to the street he contrived to keep alive the new, lewd spirit, fresh and cheerful.

It was a merry, wild ride through the sunny winter morning, across the Providence River, and down the bay shore to the sea. Everything we passed was sharply observed and appraised. The landscape was compared to that of the Brooklyn coast and to the marshes of the Bronx. Girls on street corners were hallooed and nobody cared. Kennedy seemed ecstatically happy, his eyes wide with unutterable wonder. The ex-houseowner appeared to have dropped ten years, and halfway to Newport was exchanging ribaldries with Sullivan and holding his own. Foley relaxed. Buck perked up and forgot his superiority and his shame.

"There it is!" yelled Sullivan as we got through the town of Newport and came out on the bay, with the open sea beyond. "There's the old training ship. I seen pictures of it. It can't move, and it wouldn't float if you unhooked it. It's the old U.S.S. Nevergo." This got a unanimous laugh, which was cut off suddenly as the bus drew up at the gate of the Training Station and an armed Marine, with bayonet fixed, came over and opened the door. I had to leave the sailors there. They got out, buttoning up their sweaters and windbreakers against the sea wind—Barba, Brantwein, Brown, Cochario, Dowling, Foley, Jenks, Kennedy, Lieber, McHugh, O'Connor, Pavitt, Rafferty, and Sullivan. Then they marched off up the road to the reception center.

[March 7, 1942]

# THE SPINNER OF BOMB BAY

### ST. CLAIR MC KELWAY

ALBERT HOLLINS is what is known as a worker. He has been an employed worker and an unemployed worker, an unskilled worker and a skilled worker. For a while he was a defense worker. Now he is a war worker. Approximately once a minute for eight hours, five days a week, he performs a dangerous operation on a piece of pipe. He operates on it with a machine called a spinner. When the piece of pipe comes to him, it looks like something you might find in a junk yard—a section of metal tubing of the sort used for gas mains. It is about three feet long, as big around as a gallon jug, and open at both ends. When Hollins is through with it, one end has been fashioned into a neat, tapering point and it has begun to take on a businesslike appearance. After a number of other things have been done to it by various other workers, it will be a bomb.

When Hollins has finished his operation on a piece of pipe, a helper removes it from Hollins' machine and starts it on its way down the assembly line of the bomb factory in which he works. At the other end of the assembly line a freight car is waiting. As the bomb-to-be moves away from Hollins and another helper puts a new one into his machine, Hollins lifts his left hand and wiggles the fingers, once. The gesture has become automatic and rhythmical. It represents in concentrated form a more elaborate blessing he gave the bombs the day after the Japanese attack on Pearl Harbor. On that Monday morning, Hollins waved to each bomb as it left him and said out loud, "Now go get the sonsabitches!" As the days went by, he cut this down to "Get the sonsabitches!," then to "Sonsabitches!," and finally he stopped talking to the bombs altogether. But he still waves to them. "I musta made enough of 'em to blow up the whole world," he has been saying lately. "When they going to start *dropping* 'em?"

Hollins is one of a dozen or so men at his plant who operate spinning machines. He sits behind a wire screen at a control board crowded with gauges and levers. In front of him, just to the right of the screen, is a gas furnace, which heats one end of the piece of steel tubing until it is white-hot. Also in front of him, at the left of the screen, is his machine, the spinner, which his levers control. One of Hollins' two helpers pulls a piece of tubing from the furnace and shoves it down a metal slide and into the spinner. As soon as it is in the spinner, the two helpers run back and stand beside him, behind the screen. Hollins pulls a lever and the spinner clamps down on the unheated end and begins to revolve the tube at high speed. He pulls another lever and two acetylene torches, held by mechanical arms, move close to the heated end, to keep it from cooling. Then Hollins pulls a third lever and a steel roller moves up to the spinning tube and begins to press and mold the white-hot metal into a point. Fragments of fiery steel break off now and then and fly through the air like shooting stars. The screen protects Hollins and his helpers from these. The real, though remote, danger in the operation is that the bomb, spinning at something like two thousand revolutions a minute, may work its way out of the spinner. The screen would not be of any use to Hollins and his helpers if that happened and the bomb came their way. A bomb got loose from one of the other spinners a few months ago and, though it didn't hit anybody, it went through the wall of the plant and onto the railroad tracks outside. Hollins has to watch closely and stop the machine if the bomb starts to work its way out of the spinner. He also has to know how much pressure to apply and how to make the point taper off to the proper specifications. On a good day he puts perfect points on several hundred bombs.

After the bomb leaves Hollins, a somewhat similar operation has to be performed on its tail; then both nose and tail have to have threads machined on them so that caps can be screwed on; steel lugs have to be welded onto its sides so that it can be fastened to a bomber's rack; it has to be painted to prevent rust; and, finally, after it leaves Hollins' plant in a freight car, it has to go to a government arsenal to be loaded with high explosives. Hollins is inclined to think that what he does to the bomb is the most essential of all these operations. "If its nose wasn't pointed, what the hell kind of a bomb would it be?" he has asked some of his co-workers. They have argued variously that spinning the tail, putting on the threads, welding the lugs, and painting are the most important parts of the job of bomb-making. The argument has never been settled, but the workers in Hollins' plant agree that the job of loading the bomb at the arsenal is extremely simple and easy. "All they got to do when we finish with her," said one of the painters recently, "is hold her up and pour the stuff in her."

The steel mill in which Hollins is employed is in a small town in Pennsylvania. The section he works in is known as Bomb Bay, a bay being a portion of any large plant devoted to the manufacture of a particular article. One reason Hollins stopped talking to the bombs was that nobody could hear what he was saying to them. Bomb Bay is a good deal like a boiler factory, except that the bombs are not quite as big as boilers. All day and all night the bombs clang and ring, the furnaces roar, the heavy cranes rumble as they move overhead. The gas furnaces make the air smoky and the white-hot steel gives off acrid fumes, hard on the throat.

Hollins, like most of his fellow-workers in Bomb Bay, is not particularly conscious of the noise or the smell. Working in a steel plant seems to him the natural thing for a man to do. During the depression, when he was looking for his first job, he couldn't get work in any of the steel plants in his home town or nearby, and although he found work as a counterman in restaurants and once had a good job in a gas station, he didn't like those ways of making a living. He felt uncomfortable working at jobs that had nothing to do with the steel industry. He felt out of things. When he looked for other kinds of work, he went away from home to find them because he didn't want people in his town to see him working in restaurants or gas stations. Then the steel mills began to hire men again and he quit his gas-station job and got into one of the plants, even though he had to take less money at first than he was making at the gas station. Now, when he gets to talking to somebody in a bar or at the roller-skating rink where he spends a lot of his spare time, and is asked what he is doing, he says with easy satisfaction, "Oh, I'm over at Bomb Bay making bombs. I'm a spinner."

Hollins is just under thirty, short and slim, strong and healthy, with mild manners and an attitude that is reasonable rather than aggressive. He is not a tough guy. He hasn't been in a fight since he was a schoolboy and he looks down on what he considers the lower element in his town, the first-generation families of immigrants from Central Europe. From the point of view of the steel companies, he is more civilized than the steelworkers of earlier times; from the point of view of the labor unions, he is more repressed. He is proud, jealous of his individuality, and would be the last man on earth to say that he is a slave. He considers the company he works for an adversary rather than a master. Sometimes he feels good-natured about the company, sometimes indignant about it. He will argue passionately with workers who have a more radical outlook than his, who claim that the steel companies have exploited labor for generations. He prefers to think of the capital-labor situation as a struggle in which he sometimes loses, sometimes wins.

Like most of his fellow-workers, Hollins belongs to the local C.I.O. affiliate and pays his dues of a dollar a month. Like more than half of the union members, he doesn't take an active interest in the union and doesn't go to union meetings regularly. When he has a complaint, he usually takes it up with his foreman. He prefers to settle his own difficulties with the company in his own way and won't take his case to the union unless he is sure he can't make the company see his point by himself. "A union ain't necessarily got a man's best interests at heart," he says. "I've seen too many labor leaders who are just getting themselves fixed up, taking care of themselves and nobody else. Maybe if you got a hundred-per-cent union membership, you got something. But if you ain't got a hundred-per-cent union membership, you ain't got nothing. You got to know what you're doing and how to do it, that's all. You got to know how much you ought to get paid and how to get it."

Hollins makes, on an average, about $44 a week just now. He thinks he should be making no less than $50 a week. "I know how hard I work and how quick I turn out the bombs, and I know it's worth a hundred bucks every two-week payday," he says. Along with several other spinners of Bomb Bay, he has been complaining regularly to the foreman, as well as to the plant superintendent when he gets a chance. His complaint is that the piecework bonus plan has, as he puts it, been figured out all wrong. "You can't spin them bombs no quicker than we're spinning 'em lately," he says, "and if the piecework bonus plan was figured out right we'd be drawing down a hundred bucks every two-week payday. I think the company'll change it pretty soon so's we get that much. The government says the company can't make no more than a ten-per-cent profit. All right. Let them make that, but give us some profit, too. If the piecework bonus plan was figured out right, we'd be getting those twelve, fourteen more dollars every two-week payday."

On most public questions, Hollins is as conservative as a New York taxi-driver. He voted for Willkie for President, as most of the steelworkers seem to have done, some of them influenced, perhaps, by the anti-Roosevelt stand of John L. Lewis. Hollins has his own theories about Roosevelt. "You get a man like Roosevelt, a friend of labor and all, and that's mighty fine and sweet," he says, "but when you got a job to be done, I say get a man who's been a company boss himself. I ain't saying Roosevelt ain't doing all right now, but, anyhow, that's why I voted for Willkie. I seen these friends of labor work out wrong many a time trying to run a plant. They trick it all up with recreation rooms and free parking and I don't know what-all sorts of goddam dewdads, and what happens? The plant goes busted and everybody gets thrown out. Or else the guys that plays the best basketball gets all the breaks and bonuses in the shop. You gimme a tough boss who knows his business and I can take care of myself without his being no friend of labor or a friend of mine—or my uncle's."

Hollins was born in the town he now works in and has lived there all his life except for a couple of years during the depression, when he travelled over the country, finding work wherever he could, not eating very regularly, and sleeping in freight cars a good deal of the time. He was six years old when the first World War ended, seventeen when the depression started. His father, who was killed by an automobile last August on his way home from work, had spent fifty-one years in the steel mills and had raised a family of five children, all either steelworkers themselves now or married to steelworkers. The Hollins home was a seven-room frame house in a residential district that might be compared to the cheaper sections of Flushing. The house was built on a plot of about half an acre. Both the elder Hollins and his wife were industrious people of English and Pennsylvania Dutch stock. They had chickens, and they had a vegetable patch that covered the front and back yards, except for a small square of grass just outside the front door. In the good years, from the beginning of the first World War until 1929, the family felt almost prosperous. There was always a car, usually a Chevrolet, and all the children had plenty of food and good enough clothes. During the depression, when the head of the family seldom had more than one day's work a week at the mill, the chickens and the vegetable garden helped the family to survive. "It was bad, bad as could be," said Hollins' mother recently, "and I don't know what we would have done without the chicken farm. When I saw that movin' picture, called 'Mutiny on the Bounty,' about that Captain Bligh a couple of years ago, I said to Mr. Hollins, 'That was us.' We were rationin' and rationin' down to almost nothin' for a while there, just like they did in the open boat in that picture. But we were a whole lot better off than most of the folks around here."

Albert was the oldest of the children. He went through grade school and started high school, but after a couple of years of that, he says, he wasn't learning anything more that he wanted to know and he quit. It was 1930 and he was seventeen. "There weren't no jobs and I couldn't stand it around the house, everybody was so down in the mouth," he says now. "I told 'em I was going to travel around for a while and I started out. Lots of kids were doing the same thing then, you know. I got out West, hitchhiking and on the freights, and I followed the harvests around, picking beets and potatoes and working in wheat fields and stuff like that. Some of the time I was hungry and some of the time I wasn't. I had a break in Wyoming—town named Rock Springs. I got in a walkathon contest and won a second prize—two hundred and fifty dollars. Oh boy! That gave me some influence. I met a lot of people, like the mayor and all, and then I got into the C.C.C. with their help. I was in that about a year. Then a buddy of mine in the C.C.C. and me, we took out for Georgia, where his home was, and his old man set us up in a little restaurant —well, a counter and four or five stools it was. We were doing all right, but I didn't like it down there. The dames in Georgia are silly as hell and everybody, guys and dames and everybody, talk silly and kind of hang around all the time, laughing and talking. I got sick to my stomach with them and came on home.

"Things weren't as bad back home, but they were bad enough. The mills still wasn't hiring much and I got this gas-station job over around Pittsburgh, where I didn't know nobody. I was pretty young, I guess, and kind of stuck up—well, anyway, I didn't want to be seen working in no gas station. I got up to twenty-seven fifty a week in a year, and then Dad, he told me he thought I could get on as a laborer up at the plant—same plant he had always worked in —with a chance to work into machining, and so I got on and quit the gas station. I started at twenty-five dollars a week and I been there ever since, and

when Bomb Bay got going a year and a half ago I'm promoted to this spinner's job, making bombs. I been lucky, I guess, all in all."

Seven years ago, Hollins married a girl who had grown up in the same
neighborhood. He was twenty-two then and she was seventeen. Working on
his days off from the gas station, he had built a three-room bungalow in the
back yard of his father's house in anticipation of their marriage, and they
settled down in it after a weekend honeymoon in a Pittsburgh hotel. A baby
girl was born to them a year later, and when Hollins got his job as a spinner
they rented a five-room house about a mile down the highway from his
father's. They live there now. Young Mrs. Hollins does all her own work, including the washing and ironing. She has to keep house with considerable ingenuity. For five days her husband works from seven in the morning until
three in the afternoon, for his five days the next week he works from three in
the afternoon until eleven at night, and for the next five days from eleven at
night until seven in the morning. When Hollins is on the shift from 11 P.M. to
7 A.M., he and his wife go out a good deal in the afternoon and evening—to the
roller-skating rink or to the movies or to a friend's house for dinner—but in
spite of that they both prefer the shift from 3 P.M. to 11 P.M. That way, Hollins comes home about half past eleven at night, gets a long sleep, and still has
all morning and half the afternoon to fool around the house, play with the
baby, and do a few chores. That seems normal to them. Both hate the 7 A.M.-
to-3 P.M. shift; Hollins can't seem to relax in the evening and doesn't want to
go out when he knows he has to get up so early the next morning.

Hollins feels secure on his present wages. "Hell, we have everything we
want," he said recently, "except a car." The rent for the house is $35 a month
and food costs them about $35 more. "Besides that," he says, "there's five bucks
a month for electricity. The rest is for luxuries." He seems to consider clothing, occasional doctors' bills, and such items luxuries. Both Hollins and his
wife have new coats and new shoes, Hollins has a new suit, and Mrs. Hollins
has three new dresses suitable for going to the movies or the skating rink. Both
are experienced roller-skaters and they like roller-skating more than any other
form of recreation they know. The rink has a juke box, a beer bar, and a
lunch counter where you can buy a sandwich if you get hungry. They gave
each other ice skates for Christmas and tried them out on a nearby lake one
afternoon, but came back home rather disappointed. "You skate on the ice,"
says Hollins. "All right, you skate on the ice. But where's the fun in that?"

Every week some of the Hollinses' surplus income goes to the furniture
store where they bought most of their furniture on the installment plan. Their
house still isn't fully furnished, but they think it is comfortable. There is a
living room, which has a three-piece suite (a davenport and two overstuffed
chairs, all of modern design), a cabinet radio, and a table with a lamp on it.
They use this room rarely. They usually sit in the kitchen, which has a dinette

in a corner, and when they want to listen to the radio they turn it up loud so that they can hear in the kitchen. Upstairs are three bedrooms, but Hollins and his wife and the baby all sleep in the same room. "We don't know what the hell to do with them other two rooms," Hollins says. "I guess, when the baby gets older, we'll put her in one of 'em."

Hollins likes to work with his hands, likes the satisfaction of doing something for himself instead of paying somebody to do it for him. His father-in-law has a coalpit in his back yard, a vein of coal so close to the surface of the ground that it can be dug out with a pick and shovel. On one of his days off, Hollins usually goes over to the pit and digs coal for a couple of hours, bringing back a few large scuttlefuls for the kitchen stove. He likes the idea of digging his own coal. When anything in the house needs to be fixed, he fixes it. In the summer he always goes over to his mother's house and helps her can the vegetables from the garden. Nobody in the Hollins family ever has to buy vegetables. Every summer his mother puts up enough to last all winter. "Why pay the old A. & P.?" Hollins would like to know.

The war doesn't concern Hollins in the way it concerns many of his fellow-citizens. "Before I started making bombs," he says, "I used to read all the papers and worry about this and worry about that and argue this way and that way about whether we should get in or stay out or what the hell. But when I started making bombs, I figure we'll be getting in it all right and I figure I don't have to worry any more as long as I make bombs and make 'em as fast as I can. It's a break that way for me to be making bombs. I don't worry. Now I got a friend, fellow works in a factory over the way, and you know what he makes? Hairpins! Yes, sir, he makes hairpins. Well, he worries all the time. I tell him what the hell, they gotta have hairpins, but it ain't no use. He feels bad and he tells me the other day his production's lousy and getting lousier.

"But the guys I feel sorry for in this war is the soldiers. I be damn if I can see what's fair about the way they're treated. You know how much they get? Twenty-one or maybe thirty-one a month, for the love of God, and they got to pay their own laundry bills. Of course, they get their housing and their food, but even so, they work hard and, on top of that, they've got to risk their lives. Well, why can't they be paid as well as I am, or nearly as well, anyway? If the company can afford to pay me, why can't the government afford to pay them? I don't think it's fair and I can't figure it out. It's a hell of a note."

Hollins goes to work with a friend who lives out his way and works at the plant. The friend charges twenty cents a day for the ride there and back. He picks up five or six workers besides Hollins and is using the money to pay for his 1941 Chrysler. Most of Hollins' friends are men he grew up with in his old neighborhood, and most of them work in Bomb Bay or in another steel plant. Like him, they are members of the town's old families, and they don't mingle with the first-generation workers. Hollins and his friends had a favorite bar last spring where they used to meet sometimes in the evening, but, according to Hollins, "a sort of a bad crowd—hunkies and so on" began patronizing the place, and Hollins and his friends had to find a new one.

Hollins doesn't get much chance to make friends at Bomb Bay. There is no time for casual conversation, and if the men did try to talk to each other, they would have to shout because of the noise. Hollins works through his eight hours with hardly a break, because he wants to turn out as many bombs as he can. His helpers are also paid on a piecework basis and are as eager as he is to speed up production. Although Hollins and all his fellow-workers thought they were working as fast as they could for the year and a half before the Japanese bombed Pearl Harbor, the daily production of bombs in Bomb Bay has increased about six per cent since then.

The workers bring their lunches with them and eat quickly, standing up, or sitting on a cool bomb. Hollins and his helpers usually have their lunch while their machine is being oiled and cleaned by the millwrights, who come around once during the eight hours. Sometimes Hollins takes four or five raw wienies with him and roasts them over a red-hot bomb he has just worked on. A good many workers have seen him doing this and have begun to bring hot dogs themselves. "It makes a good meal instead of the cold sandwiches," says Hollins, "and it don't take no time at all to roast a dog over one of them bombs."

# THE ARMY LIFE
## SOMEWHERE IN NEW GUINEA

### E. J. KAHN, JR.

WE AMERICAN soldiers who have arrived finally in New Guinea travelled many thousands of miles by rail, water, and air during the early stages of the war, but we moved into our first bivouac area here, prosaically, by truck. The fact that we did not have to walk was probably something to be grateful for, since this is not a land on which civilization has yet made many appreciable inroads, or, for that matter, outroads. The dirt trails we bounced along for weary hours were in much better shape, we were pleased to learn, than they had been before the Japs began to filter across the island. The road we mainly followed was, not so long ago, merely a trail wide enough to accommodate a couple of natives abreast carrying a load of bananas. Today a heavy six-wheel truck can lumber over it without difficulty, but the passengers are not likely to compose testimonials to the roadbed. We rolled up and down some of the countless hills of which New Guinea seems largely to consist, through patches of jungle with vines hanging down to lash at the heads of tourists who forget to duck, through coconut-palm groves and banana plantations, through tall, wavy fields of grass, and past clumps of rubber trees and other vegetation peculiar to this outdoor hothouse.

Although we were riding along what I suppose would locally be called a highway, we saw no towns, for the simple reason that New Guinea has almost no towns. The largest settlement we passed was a native village of a half-dozen thatched huts on stilts, clustered about a relatively substantial church with an English name over its door. The church, we gathered, had been put up by missionaries, whose influence is frequently observable in these parts. One group of natives chanted as they worked. Their song didn't have any clearly recognizable tune, but every now and then an English phrase or two would crop up in it—the remnants of an old hymn. Some of them know a little English, others know none except the words "smoke" and "cigarette," which they use whenever they meet a soldier who might conceivably give them one. As we rode past the settlements in our trucks, we tossed cigarettes down to the natives, and they occasionally offered us a coconut in return. Most of them were little boys, often wholly naked, who sometimes indicated that they were not altogether unaccustomed to soldiers by offering us their crude version of a military salute—just like the little boys who used to salute us back home long ago when we marched by them on maneuvers.

Though for some reason or other we saw no little girls, we passed plenty of older ones, many of them as becomingly undressed as if they had just finished posing for the *National Geographic*. They were, inevitably, subjected to admiring whistles. Some of them seemed unmoved by these tributes, but others, on the shy side, retreated modestly behind trees. A few of the women had tattooed faces, and almost all of the men had huge heads of hair, fairly close-cropped at the rim of the skull but flaring out wildly six or seven inches up. We felt self-conscious about this because, just before taking off for New Guinea, most of us had had our hair cut extremely short, in what we then thought would surely be the style in a notoriously hot climate. There are supposed to be head-hunters and cannibals all around this region, but the natives we've met so far have been very friendly and haven't even hinted that they would enjoy eating us. One of them, in fact, perhaps to assure us of his strictly vegetarian intentions, chased the truck I was in for several hundred yards in order to bestow upon us a handful of small, sweet tomatoes he had just picked. They were quite refreshing and helped to sustain us through a trip so dusty that by the time we arrived at our destination we were as black as the natives.

We have set up camp on a rubber plantation, a restful and appealing spot, even though the mail service is irregular. We are less concerned with the price-less substance inside the tall gray trees—to which we fasten our clotheslines—than with the ill-mannered red ants that frolic on their trunks. We are getting used to having insects of various sizes, species, and stings around us, however, and wouldn't think of going to bed without first tucking in the edges of our mosquito netting. Our bedsteads are made of bamboo poles. Vines, we have found, make an acceptable substitute for springs, and palm leaves can be turned into an adequate mattress, but a restless sleeper faces the danger of cutting himself on its fringes. We spend a good deal of time in bed, having nothing else to do after dark. In the absence of better-qualified entertainers, we some-times sing ourselves to sleep, using as lullabies ancient numbers on the Hit Parade. We have never heard the tunes now popular at home.

In an area like this the biggest problem, for soldiers or anyone else, is the transport of supplies. It is impossible to get fresh meat or vegetables or butter or milk to us, and therefore almost everything we eat comes out of cans. We'll probably soon forget how to wield a steak knife, since hash (sometimes re-placed by beans or spaghetti) is our main dish. Our potatoes come canned and dehydrated, our milk and eggs powdered, most of our fruit dried. We have no ice, of course, and the other night, when the mess sergeant, using some lemons a soldier had picked down the road, stirred up some delicious lukewarm lemonade, we considered it a real treat. Soldiers, as everyone knows, are inordinately fond of eating between meals. At the moment our off-hour nibbling is confined to coconuts. We have become reasonably adroit at puncturing them, drinking the milk, and then chewing the meat after cracking them open with the long, sharp knives we bought before leaving Australia— the most valuable pieces of personal equipment we possess.

Isolated as we are, we naturally hear little news. For a while, until someone found a radio station in the hills not far away, to which we now make daily trips for worldly enlightenment, we were entirely cut off from information about current events, even those taking place in other sectors of this island. Scarcely had the dusty wake of a passing truck died down when the magnificent rumors that soldiers are supremely capable of brewing began to flow. At one time or another we were more or less convinced that Russia had invaded Japan, that Turkey, Eire, and Spain had declared war on Germany, that the Japs had withdrawn from the Philippines, and that the Yankees had won the World Series. This last bit of misinformation was probably the most annoying, since it resulted in the erroneous settlement of several small bets.

As an urban selectee's military career progresses, he changes gradually from a preponderantly indoor being into a wholly outdoor one. In New Guinea the last characteristics of the former have finally vanished. We no longer regard it as curious or improper to walk entirely nude along a highway, or to bathe in full view of traffic, since the traffic is invariably military and thus presumably shockproof. Right now we do our bathing, as well as our laundry, in a tropical stream nearby. We have no diving platforms, but we can grab a vine on the bank and swing ourselves out over the water, just as' we once swung over water on ropes while going through obstacle courses in our training-camp days. The chief difference is that then we were supposed to come to rest on the opposite shore, whereas now we let go in mid-air and fall happily into the stream. There are said to be some crocodiles in it, but so far they have been as little in evidence as the Japs. Though we haven't yet seen any of the enemy, we are suspicious of all rustlings in the woods, many of which appear to be caused by small animals—with the bodies of opossums and the heads of anteaters—that walk and breathe just about the way we suspect Japanese patrols do. Although we would like to run into some Japs soon, we don't mind the comparatively peaceful nature of the life we're leading. It has its minor inconveniences, but after all it's far less risky than the lives a lot of people, who enjoyed a few more metropolitan luxuries, were leading in London two years ago.

# THE ARMY LIFE
## BUSY IN PAPUA

E. J. KAHN, JR.

A SOLDIER'S estimate of the number of things he can accomplish during a calendar day rises amazingly as his service continues. Selectees fresh from the dawdling civilian world are usually downright appalled by the Army's assumption that they can keep going at a prodigious number of physically taxing activities from before dawn to dusk; older hands are merely irked by schedules as crowded—and including tasks as unsavory—as the Black Hole of Calcutta; and even soldiers in combat, who don't have to bother about schedules because their day never ends anyway, are sometimes startled, in the few brief moments allowed them for reflection, by their own durability. As a selectee, an older hand, and lately a member of an American task force in New Guinea, I have been in turn appalled, irked, and startled.

At ten o'clock one recent evening, at our Army camp in a tiny native village on the coast north of the Owen Stanley Mountains in Papua, I was notified that I was about to participate in a little expedition which, as it turned out, kept me rather fully occupied for nearly twenty-four hours. I was just going to bed when the news came. I hadn't had much sleep the night before because a lot of planes had been flying around overhead, and I had put in what I judged to be a fairly creditable day's work since. When I was told that I was to be permitted to go up to the front on a tour of inspection along with an officer and one other soldier, I abandoned all notions of sleep and spent the next two hours getting ready, which consisted mainly in taking an inventory of what possessions I would leave behind. Anybody planning a trip in the New Guinea combat zone selects his impedimenta with great care and with a negative approach, knowing that whatever he decides to take along will undoubtedly have to be carried for the greater part, if not all, of the journey on his own back. After a good deal of deliberation, I gambled that we'd return by the next night and accordingly ruled out everything except a rifle, a bandoleer of ammunition, and a filled canteen.

The officer, the other soldier, and I were able to save considerable walking, which is ordinarily the only way of getting about in this area, by making

*130*

part of the trip forward on a small trawler that was moving up the coast under cover of darkness, carrying ammunition to the front-line troops. Shortly before midnight a dim shape appeared offshore and the three of us were rowed out to it. We swung up over the rail and onto a deck piled high with cases of ammunition, where we made ourselves as comfortable as one can be on top of boxes of grenades. The master of our trawler, a drab vessel some forty feet long, was a scrawny Australian wearing only a pair of shorts and a sleeveless sweater several sizes too big for him. His assistant was a fat fellow with what I took to be an Italian accent; he was dressed merely in pants. The rest of the crew consisted of a handful of Filipinos, every one of them a triumph of sartorial inelegance.

It was almost one o'clock when the captain gave the order to get under way, and we started chugging along at six or seven knots. We couldn't smoke because of the possibility that a glowing cigarette would be spotted by some enemy plane cruising hopefully above. We had watched plenty of Zeros in action and knew what one or two of them could do to a trawler that was able to defend itself only with a couple of machine guns on anti-aircraft mounts. Also, if we were attacked, we would probably be exposed, surrounded as we were by ammunition, to a display of fireworks much more dangerously impressive than the gaudiest nightmares of a National Safety Committee spokesman. A full tropical moon was shining down on us, and under it we felt somewhat conspicuous.

We cruised along uneventfully until about two-thirty, when we suddenly came to a quiet, firm halt. The captain announced that we had run aground on a sand bar, a common hazard in these parts, and added gloomily that in his professional opinion we were badly stuck. We were still quite a few miles from our destination. Knowing that a trawler, however stationary, would naturally arouse the curiosity and attract the fire of any roaming Zeros as soon as daylight broke, we asked him if there was any chance of getting the ship off before dawn. After a consultation with his fleshy assistant, who was equally depressed, he told us that it might be done if we shifted a few tons of ammunition from the stern toward the bow. We devoted the next half hour to hauling heavy cases forward. The boat still wouldn't budge. Then the captain sent a dinghy to drop anchor about thirty feet off to one side, ran a rope from it to the winch on the trawler, and tried to make the trawler pull itself off by its own power. We didn't move a nautical inch.

Hoping at least to get the cargo off by dawn, we Americans decided that we would proceed to our goal by whatever means was possible and send back an unloading party. None of us had ever been in the neighborhood before, so we had no idea of where to look for the trail through the jungle that fringed the coast. The captain said that our best bet would be to row to the mouth of a certain river that cut the trail in two, proceed up the river until we came to the trail, and then take it. He said the river mouth was about a mile ahead. We finally prevailed upon him to pilot us and he got into the dinghy with us. By this time clouds had obscured the moon and we couldn't see much except a desolate shoreline. Our confidence in the captain as a guide would probably have been less wholehearted than it was had we known, as we found out the next day, that the river mouth he had mentioned was actually within fifty yards of where we struck the bar. We rowed along steadily, taking turns at the oars and keeping a watchful eye on the shore for signs of life.

It had been rumored in the afternoon that the Japs might attempt a landing somewhere along the coast that night, and we knew that whatever of our troops were on guard at the water's edge would be highly suspicious of our craft and might easily mistake us for an enemy patrol. After we had rowed along for about an hour and a half without finding the river mouth, it became obvious that the captain was getting nervous. He pointed to floating logs and whispered hoarsely that they were boats and he took every dark object on the beach for a soldier with his finger on a trigger. He finally stated his conviction that we had passed not only the river mouth but also the town we were heading for and the American lines, and were about to bear down embarrassingly on a village serving at the moment, we all knew, as a Japanese base. Fairly certain that we hadn't gone by any of the distinctive clumps of coconut palms that indicate a village on this seacoast, the three of us military men outvoted the captain and decided to continue. A half hour later, a telltale group of trees loomed up.

As we drew in to shore, our officer told me to call for a guard, despite the captain's anguished protest that the response might be *"Banzai"* or some other unaffectionate cry. I yelled out. A few seconds later a figure emerged from the shadows on the beach and stood at the water's edge, pointing a rifle at us and demanding, in English, the password. We hadn't any idea what the current one was but gave him an old one in which the letter "l" appeared several times. The sentry was satisfied to the extent of agreeing to take us to the officer we had been told to report to. We left the Australian captain on the beach with his dinghy, after promising to send back a detail of men to unload his cargo, and finally reached the command post we were looking for shortly after five o'clock. At five-thirty, after arranging for the ammunition-unloading detail, we readily accepted the suggestion of an officer there that we take a nap. Somebody lent me a blanket and I spread it out on one of the few patches of ground in this dense jungle large enough to accommodate it. I took a head net out of my helmet, pulled it over my head, and dropped down on the blanket. There were a couple of knobby roots underneath it, but I scarcely felt them. I probably fell asleep in mid-air.

A little over an hour later the three of us were awakened. We had breakfast in a crude kitchen, where a cook prepared pancakes and coffee in old biscuit tins over an open fire. Shortly after seven we set out up the trail toward the front, about three miles away. We walked past several ammunition dumps, camouflaged artillery positions, first-aid stations making ready to handle the day's inevitable traffic, and numerous muddy foxholes and trenches containing soldiers who had slept in them the night before and were preparing for a morning attack. They were wearing the same clothes we were—twill jackets and pants dyed a mottled green and dirtied by weeks of living in the mud— and many of them had greenish paint smeared on their faces and hands. One rifleman, as we approached, proudly pulled up the bottoms of his trousers and showed us that he had paint daubed all over his legs, too, evidently so that he could remain obscure even if his pants were shot off. On the way up we also passed a couple of well-trodden spots in the jungle where, we were told, the Japs had had machine-gun emplacements before the American advance had begun. We asked if any enemy prisoners had been taken there. None had.

We eventually reached our destination, which was the most forward command post. It consisted simply of a field telephone in a foxhole and a couple of empty ration cases to sit on whenever it wasn't necessary to duck. In jungle fighting it isn't possible to see much, even a short distance away, but you can hear plenty. When the morning's attack began, there was first the sound of our own planes skimming the treetops on their way to strafe the enemy positions. Now and then we would catch a glimpse of them tearing by overhead. After the planes came an artillery barrage, launched by the guns we had passed. We could hear the shells bursting up ahead of us. At the same time, from dozens of foxholes scattered throughout the jungle—in front of us, behind us, and on both sides of us—light and heavy mortars opened up. Then came the command for the infantry to drive forward, and the ping of our rifle bullets and the stutter of our machine guns began to blend with the noise of the heavier weapons. The Jap machine guns answered them, and the Jap mortars, searching for our own mortar positions, started to drop shells in around us. We could hear the shells coming long enough in advance to take shelter in trenches or down among the roots of the huge mangrove trees. Mangroves, which, like most jungle flora, are afflicted with elephantiasis, grow horizontally as well as up. Sometimes six enormous branches, all pointing in different directions and each as large as a giant oak, will sprout from a single mammoth trunk. Whenever a heavy mortar shell landed nearby, even the mangroves seemed to quiver as the concussion rippled along the floor of the fantastically lush battlefield.

After a while the medical "collecting" troops, with Red Cross brassards on their arms, began to come slowly back along the trail, carrying and escorting wounded men toward the first-aid stations. There was a constant flow of men along the narrow track. In addition to the casualties, sweating officers covered with dirt and frequently bleeding from minor wounds would return to report

on the progress their troops were making. At the same time a stream of soldiers kept moving up, some of them to carry on the attack, others to deliver
ammunition. We stayed at the command post for a couple of hours, and then
our officer decided to begin the return trip. It was about eleven o'clock, and the
attack was still on. We had a fourteen-mile walk ahead of us back to the camp
we had left the night before, and much of it was over soft sand, over which
we knew we couldn't make very rapid progress. We walked back to where
we'd slept earlier in the morning, had lunch, and then started out on the last
eleven miles of trail, a stretch, incidentally, involving the crossing of eleven
streams.

A mile or so out, we picked up an itinerant sergeant from Brooklyn who
had been waiting on the trail for someone to come along and keep him company. We noticed with surprise that he wasn't armed, and he explained that
he was assigned to a non-combatant unit called Graves Registration, which has
the responsibility of burying men killed in action and making detailed records of the circumstances. He had run out of official forms, he told us, and
was heading toward the rear to replenish his supply before, he added with
deep concern, his work piled up on him. For the rest of the way he regaled
us with anecdotes about his wartime specialty, for which he had prepped, he
told us, at a place in which the opportunities for useful experience were un-
paralleled—the morgue at Bellevue. As we listened to him, we realized that
at last we had found the perfect example of a selectee placed by the Army's
classification experts in the most suitable martial niche.

For more than half the way the trail followed the beach. We plodded
along with the sun beating down on us and our feet sinking into the sand at
every step, soon reaching the river near which we had been forced to disem-
bark from the trawler the night before. That was when we learned how far
our geography had been wrong when we began our cruise in the dinghy. The
trawler, presumably unloaded, was still there, held firmly on the sand bar.
We crossed the stream by means of a bridge some of our engineers were just
finishing up. We had moved on a mile or so farther down the coast when we
heard planes overhead. They were Japs. They flew low past us, the red balls
on the under part of their silver wings disturbingly large and clear, and we
could hear the rattle of their machine guns and a few moments later the dull
explosions of bombs. We were protected from aerial detection at that point by
mangroves, so we climbed out on some of their horizontal limbs to try to get
a better view of the proceedings. A number of our fighter planes came down
out of the sky, and we saw the start of a couple of dogfights. Then all the
planes disappeared into the clouds. Later we heard that the trawler and the
bridge had both been damaged.

Although the destruction of a bridge is of course a decided inconvenience, it is not necessarily a calamity. The natives here, who wear nothing but loin-cloths and seem rather to enjoy getting wet, don't bother with bridges at all unless the water they want to cross is over their heads. Then they build a bridge by simply throwing a single log across the stream. Americans are more used to bridges, but they can learn to get along without them. Of the eleven rivers we had to cross, only four were bridged at all, three by logs so slim and slippery that after contriving to get across them we felt as smug as tight-rope walkers. The seven other rivers we forded. At first we carefully removed our shoes and stockings each time and, when it seemed advisable, stripped from the waist down. As we grew more and more tired in the late afternoon, we took to not bothering with this, a bit of neglect which we always regretted when we got to the other side and had to hike on with water sloshing around inside our shoes. Near the end of the trip we came to a stream which at its shallowest fording point had a maximum depth of about five and a half feet, near the far side of the crossing. On this occasion we stopped, removed all our clothing and equipment, and piled it on our heads. I rolled my stuff into a compact bundle, balanced it on my helmet, and put my rifle on top of every-thing else. I got along all right until I hit the deep spot. Then my helmet came down over my eyes, the water came up over my nose, a nasty current grabbed at my legs, and I felt that my rifle was slipping off, a feeling that turned out, a second later, to be regrettably accurate. When I finally retrieved the rifle from the river bed, after considerable underwater groping, it was a pathetic-look-ing weapon, full of sand and the promise of untold rust. As I carried it for-lornly toward camp, which we finally reached at seven-thirty in the evening, I realized that the necessity for cleaning it as soon as possible had dispelled whatever lingering uncertainty I had had about my activities upon arrival. I knew then that I wouldn't be frittering the whole night away sleeping.

[February 13, 1943]

# GUERRILLA FROM ERIE, PA.

A. J. LIEBLING

A MINOR accident knocked the artificial cap off one of Major Philip Cochran's upper front teeth last fall, putting a gap in his grin. This is perhaps the most striking feature of his appearance. Up to a month ago the thing about Cochran that you noticed second was his mop of hair, the color and apparent texture of steel wool, which he wore in a pompadour and long in back, like the late Buffalo Bill. The dust lodged in his hair made it look even grayer than it naturally is. Cochran, then, as now, living at an airfield in southern Tunisia, was flying two or three missions a day himself and was in charge of running a guerrilla air war above an area of twenty thousand square miles. "If we ever get a rainy day out here so I can't fly, I'll have time to get a haircut," Cochran used to say. On the evening of January 13th, while he sat astride a wooden bench in his hut at the field, eating a mess of scrambled eggs out of a canteen cup, he allowed Private First Class Ralph Otto of California to shear away part of his mane. "I never cut human hair back home on the farm, but I used to clip all our horses," Private Otto said. "Civilization is creeping up on us on this front, so why the hell struggle against it?" Cochran grumbled. He could see that the vast region which for a month had been his private battleground was turning into a major front of formalized warfare, and he felt depressed. On that very day he received an oblique reproach for his unsoldierly appearance from the first brigadier general he had seen in several weeks. Cochran, ever since he landed in Africa last November, has worn the same leather jacket, pants, and British flying boots. He sleeps in them, too. The general had said, "Major, if you are captured in those clothes, you will have to wear them until the end of the war, and they look about ready to fall off now." "Can you tie that?" Cochran said later to one of his pals. "There is nothing the matter with these clothes except they are full of dust." Cochran's ideas of military dress have never been regulation. He remembers that while he was in the R.O.T.C. at Ohio State University, a general making an inspection found him wearing black-and-white shoes with his uniform. "I told him they were the only ones I had to my name," Cochran says. "I imagine I was lying."

The dust in Cochran's part of Tunisia is so heavy that a group of Messerschmitts once came in on the tail of a dust storm and started strafing his field before anybody knew they were there. This left him speechless, a rare state for him, because he can usually anticipate what the Germans are going to do. His own Curtiss P-40 fighter was on the field and got shot full of holes. "It was already just a lot of holes tied together with piano wire," Cochran says. "They even shot away the connections between the holes. I had seen one of those Messerschmitts at about twenty thousand feet that morning and I knew he was casing the joint for a strafe job, but I didn't think they'd pull it that way."

A few days later, Cochran rolled out of bed and predicted that a combined force of German bombers and fighters would appear over the field at two-thirty in the afternoon. He was wrong. The bombers and fighters—seven Junkers 88s and eight Messerschmitts—appeared at two-twenty-eight. Cochran had seven fighters in the air waiting for them and they shot down a Messerschmitt and two Junkers. "I felt they would come then because they had been over a couple of times at dawn and a couple of times just before dark and they would want to do something different." He says it is like sensing when to hop on or off a guy who is shooting craps.

"On the day after the two-twenty-eight raid," Cochran recalls, "I have a hunch that if they do not come over at ten-thirty A.M. they will come over at a quarter to six, with bombers." It was due to get dark at six. The Germans did not come at ten-thirty. Consequently, Cochran put eight planes, including his own, in the air at a quarter to six, but nobody appeared. At five-fifty-five he decided to come down and ordered the other planes down by radio. He was low over the field and had his landing wheels half down when the man in the field's control room—a circular hole in the ground with a radio telephone in it—called, "Enemy planes reported." Cochran started to climb into the gathering dark, and by the time he got to seven thousand feet he saw some flak and, looking down to find out why, saw that three Junkers 88s were bombing his field. "I dived for the first one and hit him, but he gave it the blossom—gave it the gun, you know—and got away over a hill to the south," Cochran says when he tells the story. A lieutenant named Bent got on this plane after it had escaped Cochran and shot it down behind the hill. "Then I got on the second one and just flew formation with him," Cochran says. "I kept on shooting tracers into him, and the lights turned green and orange when they hit, like the Fourth of July. You never know how pretty tracers are until you see that effect. I went around him and saw the gunners die. The one on top stopped firing first, and then the side gunner. The one in the belly lived longest. The plane went down and down into the valley and me after him, and dark as hell, and I kept saying, 'Go down, you sucker. Go down.' Then I saw a big flare of light, and it wasn't gunfire, and it stayed in one place, and I left the plane burning in the valley and pulled up, not knowing where I was, but I found my friend the river—that *wadi,* which shows light tan in the dusk—and I started to follow it home. When I tell it, it sounds like a movie.

"Then I began to hear one of the kids over the radio saying he was lost, asking for directions." This was a lieutenant named Thomas, of Ada, Oklahoma, who had hopped the third Junkers and chased it out into the night fifty miles before bringing it down. It was when Thomas was pulling up from his kill that he found he was lost. He was not a veteran pilot like Cochran and lacked the older man's photographic memory of the region. "I tried to keep up his spirits by insulting him," Cochran says. "I thought he was somebody else, anyway—a fellow named Brown. I would say, 'I don't mind losing you, you stupid lug, but we can't afford to lose another P-40. Try and see the lights on my ship and steer a thirty course.' The kid would answer very politely, 'I don't see your lights, sir.' He never forgot to say 'sir.' But he was confused. Of course he couldn't see the lights we had out on the field, so I got an idea. I phoned down to the control room to tell the ack-ack to fire. I told him to tell the battery at the west edge of the field to fire, and then the one to the east, and so on, to outline the field. And then all together. I stayed up with my lights on. The kid saw the field all right and got his direction, and we both came down. When you tell about it, it sounds just like a movie." The German bombers didn't damage a single American plane.

Cochran is a barrel-chested one-hundred-and-fifty-pounder of medium height. He has high cheekbones, a jaw extremely broad at the base, and white teeth that are generally visible in a smile. He is a first lieutenant in the Regular Army, a captain in the Army of the United States, and a major in the Air Forces. Cochran was at first the ranking officer at his post but is now outranked. There are at least four lieutenant colonels above him. However, because of his knowledge of the country, he is still the one who selects and directs the post's missions, as he did during his guerrilla days. He is thirty-two and has been in the Air Forces ever since he left Ohio State nearly eight years ago with a degree in business administration and advertising. He had never been in combat before last November, but he had enjoyed a certain fame in the Air Forces as a tactical pilot and instructor of other pilots, as well as a certain vicarious celebrity with several million young Americans who follow the syndicated cartoon strip called "Terry and the Pirates," in which he appears under the name of Flip Corkin. Milton Caniff, the creator of the strip, went to college with Cochran and used him as a model for Flip, who is an aviator.

The attention that the Germans pay to Cochran's field is not unsolicited. He thinks that the way to fight anybody is to keep pushing him off balance and he is constantly devising new ways of pushing. For instance, there was his one-man expedition to Kairouan, a Tunisian city within the German lines. Cochran had heard that a German divisional commander had his headquarters in a certain building near the town and he had earmarked a bomb to drop on him, but for a couple of weeks he couldn't find time to do it. He didn't want to send anybody else, because the idea of dropping a bomb on a general amused him and also because dropping a bomb from a P-40 with any degree of accuracy calls for considerable experience. He kept putting the venture off, like his haircut, until he had a day coming up with nothing important on his early-morning schedule. The evening before, he told his armorer to put a bomb on his plane. "I woke up a couple of times during the night, laughing at what I was going to do in the morning," Cochran says. "In the morning I got up and climbed into my plane and went over the joint once very high, just at dawn, and nobody spotted me. I had a good look at the target and then I went around and came in from the north, which was just where they wouldn't expect me, and I made my run so low that I had to pull up to get over the building." When he tells the story, he totters forward with bent knees, like a little man carrying a big load, to show how he toted the bomb up to the target. "When I was right over the target, I let the bomb go and gave her the blossom," he says. "Then I looked over my shoulder, and there were pieces of building flying all around me. I looked over my shoulder again at the Kairouan airfield and made sure that nobody had taken off after me—or so I thought. Then I decided to have a look over the French advanced positions to see if I could spot any German tank concentrations before I went home. About forty miles from Kairouan, I noticed a lot of flak. I thought that this was a funny place for flak, so I looked around again, and a guy in a FW-190 was shooting at me with a cannon and by that time he had shot away my right aileron and most of my tail, so I headed for home. He came after me, and I decided I would have to make a crash landing, so I started down. It was just like a movie. He got so close to me that I figured I would have to turn or he would shoot hell out of me, but the only way she would turn was to the right, and that was into him. So I fired one burst, and he gave it the blossom and went back toward Kairouan. He must have figured I had been kidding him when I'd started down. Then I said to myself, 'If she can steer at all, maybe I can get her home after all,' so I did."

At his airfield, Cochran has a small entourage of admirers who give him the anxious care a singing teacher and manager expend upon an opera star. He lives in a *gourbi,* a Tunisian hut sunk into the ground and banked with sand on all sides. Unlike most *gourbis,* his has a wooden floor and walls and a tin roof, but the roof has been covered with sand and alfa grass has been planted on top for camouflage. His *gourbi* was built by a French corporal out of material foraged by a French Jewish lieutenant named Léon, who is the liaison officer between the French forces and Cochran's fliers. Only Léon, a talented forager, could even have suspected the survival of such a quantity of building material in North Africa. Léon, who lives with Cochran in the *gourbi,* likes to talk American slang; when he hears that something seems to be stirring in a certain direction, for instance, he may tell Cochran, "Up by

Fondouk there is something cooking in. It is really boiling. Hot intelligence."
Cochran, though he can't speak a word of Arabic, knows the terrain so well
that he needs only a casual reference to any *chott* (dried lake) or *oued* (river
bed) or *djebel* (mountain) to get into his plane and go there. He doesn't need
a map any more.

Another resident of Cochran's *gourbi* is Captain Robert Wylie, of 1060
Park Avenue, in peacetime an executive of the American Radiator & Standard Sanitary Corporation. Wylie, a leathery, middle-aged gentleman who
won a Croix de Guerre while serving with a Yale ambulance unit in the last
war, is always the first one up in the morning. He gets the stove going so that
Cochran, who rises an hour before dawn, will not catch cold. Léon is a
brilliant amateur cook. Whenever he thinks Cochran's appetite is failing, he
prepares special dishes, which he and Wylie try to induce Cochran to eat.
As a matter of fact, Cochran's appetite is good, but he neglects it because of
his chronic preoccupation with flying. When he remembers that he is hungry,
he wolfs quantities of scrambled eggs, accepting them gratefully from anybody
who happens to be around and equipped with a mess tin to cook in. Cochran's
list of chefs in Tunisia has included enlisted men, visiting Tank Corps officers,
war correspondents, French pilots, and even a British booby-trap expert, who,
out of consideration for Cochran, was careful not to put any high explosive
in the eggs. The booby-trap man, a captain in the Royal Engineers, is continually inventing devices for blowing people up when they step on them and
refers to these engines of destruction as rather amusing. He puzzles Cochran,
who once said, "I can *tell* when an American is crazy."

Cochran was born in Erie, Pennsylvania, and his parents still live there.
His father, Bernard Cochran, is a lawyer and a real-estate expert for the city
government and is known to most of the population as Barney. Cochran's
mother, a woman of strong character, never liked this public familiarity with
her husband, so she long ago decided that she would give all her sons solid
saints' names that would not lend themselves to conversion into chummy nick-
names. "We got names like Paul and Philip," Cochran says. He has four
brothers. "The only trouble was that my oldest brother, Paul, got the nickname
of Shanty, which has been a handicap to him in his profession as a lawyer.
Mother was very displeased." Shanty, who is thirty-six, is now an enlisted man
in the Navy. One of Phil's younger brothers is an ensign and the youngest
of the lot is an Army Air Forces cadet. "Paul used to have a beautiful contralto
voice when he was a kid," Cochran recalls, "but it is bass now. Anyway, he
was the means of getting me into singing as an altar boy and in a choir of
fifty-two boys we had at our church. You know, 'Little Town of Bethlehem'
and stuff like that. It came in handy later, when I sang with a band to work
my way through college. "Erie is not a bad joint," Cochran says loyally. "There
are a lot of beer clubs that you can join for fifty cents a year, so you can drink

on Sunday, and the clubs are always planning to do something ambitious, like run a clambake, but it always mucks up." Cochran went to Central High School and played football, even though he then weighed only a hundred and fourteen pounds. "I was substitute for the All-State Scholastic quarterback, and I used to sit on the bench and pray for him to break his leg so I could play," he says. "It would have been horrible if he had, because I stank. But he played every minute of every game. They only sent me in once, and as I ran out on the field the gun went off and ended the game. I was so nuts about football that I wouldn't go to college until I was big enough to play, so I stayed out for two years and carried ice, the way Red Grange used to. My muscles developed, but I only weighed one twenty-eight then and I figured it was no use waiting any longer or I would just be in the ice business for life."

At Ohio State, which Cochran calls "a good poor boy's school," he worked his way through, like at least half the student body. He waited on table at the Sigma Alpha Epsilon fraternity house for his meals and picked up some cash by singing with dance bands in dives around Columbus. "My longest engagement was at the Ritz," he says without pride. "That was an eatery across the street from the campus where dinner is fifty cents if you take pot roast and seventy-five cents for steak. My singing was like stealing money. Every now and then I catch myself singing 'Stormy Weather' or something else from that period of my life. I wonder I am not in prison. There was a roadhouse called Valleydale near Columbus where I used to get eight dollars a night three nights a week until the depression got terrible." Cochran's income fell off after he had finished three years of college, so he went back to Erie to regroup, as he says, and worked two years in the Hammermill paper factory. He returned to Columbus for his senior year and was graduated in 1935, when he was twenty-five. Shortly after that he decided to take an examination for the Air Forces cadets. He had never flown, but he thought he would like to. The examination was to be held in Detroit and to finance his trip from Erie he sold the gold case of a watch his maternal grandfather had left to him and played a game of semi-professional football, having by that time attained his full growth. "I never thought I'd pass the test, but I did," he says, "and so I got a blue uniform and seventy-five dollars a month for two years." He received a Reserve commission as second lieutenant in June, 1937, and remained on active service, drawing officer's pay. It wasn't until September, 1939, that Cochran got his Regular Army commission. "It took me three years and eight months to become a real second lieutenant," he remarks.

As the expansion of the Air Forces was speeded up, promotion became more rapid and he was soon a major and in command of a squadron. It was at about that time that Milton Caniff, the "Terry and the Pirates" artist, decided to document himself on aviation. "He remembered me from Ohio State," Cochran says, "so he looked me up. I had a squadron up at Groton, Connecticut, and he came up and lived with the boys and learned the lingo, and we put on dogfights for him, and he began drawing us into his strip. The Air Corps liked it because it was great stuff for recruiting. About half the people I know call me Flip now, after the comic-strip character. One thing that causes trouble, though, is that he has me—that is, Flip—all mixed up with a beautiful nurse named Taffy in this strip, and people get curious when they meet me and want to know who is Taffy. There is no Nurse Taffy, as far as I am concerned. I like hat-check chicks and showgirls."

One of the things Cochran sometimes says when he feels lonely is "The hat-check chicks are certainly going to catch hell when I get back to New York." He thinks the Copacabana is the finest spot in America and sometimes says he is going to spend all his time there after the war. "I had a squadron out at Mitchel Field a year ago," he says. "We were big operators. One of the fellows had a girl who was a hat-check chick at the Larue, and when we had a new kid that didn't know his way around New York we would send him to the Larue, where he would say, 'Hello, Sport, Major Cochran sent me,' and she would say, 'Roger Wilco,' which means, in radio procedure, 'Message received. Will coöperate,' and she would see that he got along all right."

During his stay in Connecticut, Cochran got his only American decoration so far, the Soldier's Medal, for rescuing a student pilot from a burning plane. He received a Croix de Guerre a couple of weeks ago for his work on the Tunisian front.

Cochran entered Africa by way of Casablanca. Before that, in the States, he had trained and lost a few squadrons, which were taken out from under him and shipped abroad while he was left behind to teach new batches of fliers. This made him rather irritable. Finally he was ordered to take thirty-four young fliers and thirty-five planes to Africa. The idea was that the kids were to be replacements for pilots who might be killed. Shortly after the kids arrived, they decided that since few pilots were being killed, their only chance to see action was to form their own squadron, which might get to the front by mistake even though it had no official existence. Cochran took them to Rabat, Morocco, for further training and christened them the Joker Squadron, because they had no number. They had no table of organization, no mechanics, no mess fund, and no medical attendance, and they sponged on other outfits. Sometimes they messed with an infantry regiment which, as Cochran puts it, they found in the brush, and sometimes with a unit of engineers. They slept in pup tents and went to a French military hospital with their afflictions. They practiced gunnery by towing canvas engine covers aloft and firing at them. By the time the higher echelons of the Twelfth Air Force staff, which had jurisdiction over them, discovered what they were up to and ordered their dispersal, a number of the boys had developed into pretty hot pilots. Cochran, who was now a major without a command or function, was directed to take his seven brightest pupils and fly to Tunisia, where they were to be posted to some squadron or other. When they got to an airport called Oudjda, in eastern Morocco, another order came through grounding the seven Joker pilots and assigning their planes to more experienced men. Cochran was ordered to stop at Oudjda, too, but he flew on alone anyway, since by that time he was getting fed up with not fighting. He reversed the procedure of the celebrated soldier who made an advance to the rear, by telling airport officials at every stop in his journey that he was going back to Casablanca and then taking off and flying east.

When Cochran finally arrived at an airfield in southern Tunisia, he found a squadron of P-40 fighters on a bare plain without much idea of what they were doing or should do there. Southern Tunisia was sketchily defended by a few French battalions with about twenty-five rounds of rifle ammunition to a man, a few old seventy-fives, and a few score American parachutists. Luckily, the German and Italian forces in the region were small, but it was evident that this was a critical area, into which Rommel might move from the southeast to form a junction with the Axis forces in Tunisia. Or Axis troops in Tunisia, if dislodged by the Allies before Rommel moved, might attempt to join him in Tripolitania. The situation called for officers who were good at guessing, bluffing, and guerrilla tactics, and Cochran found himself in the spot he had dreamed of all his military life. He was not officially in command of the airfield, but he ranked any officer there and was moreover the only one of the lot with much idea of what to do in such an irregular situation. "So I called the boys together one day after they had mucked up something terrible on a raid by following the wrong line of railroad track and getting lost and finding the wrong target and having their rump shot off, and I told them that I was going to run the field," Cochran says. "It was just like something you'd see in a movie. After that Léon came here, and the French began to call us up and tell us about tanks and trucks they saw on different roads, and we would go out and look for them, and quite often they were there. We were big operators. One day Captain Levi Chase, my operations officer, went out by himself and destroyed eighty-four trucks and a few guns. We must have destroyed about three hundred trucks altogether, and for the last three weeks, incidentally, the Germans and Italians haven't moved a truck over a road anywhere in Tunisia by daylight.

"After doing that for a while, we got to know the country pretty well ourselves and began to think of other things to do. We knew the enemy had only about a dozen locomotives on all the little lines down here, so we got to blasting them, and also went after oil dumps and munition dumps. Chase was the best man I ever saw at spotting those things from the air. One time he strafed a lot of haystacks and they all exploded, proving he was right. We used to hunt light tanks all over southern Tunisia. We would strafe them with our fifty-calibre machine guns and they would play dead, and then at night the crews would run them into Arab courtyards or dry gullies and camouflage them, and we would have to find them again and shoot some more holes in them before they could be repaired. We didn't have armament to blast them, but we kept them out of action. We would observe troop movements and report them to the French and then go back and strafe them, and the French would occupy one more town.

"Then the people back at headquarters saw we were doing so well that they sent us a squadron of bombers to fool around with, and we had fun thinking up bombing missions and then escorting the bombers. Escorting is nice, clean work for fighters. It is a thing they are supposed to do in textbooks. A lot of fighter pilots at home would think that wrecking transport and strafing tanks and giving ground cover was unconventional. A P-40 can't climb like a German fighter or dive like one, and they can pull away from us on the straight, but it has quite a wallop and it can take an awful beating and bring you home safe. If you know how to use a P-40, you can get a Messerschmitt or even a Focke-Wulf 190. You just have to wait for them to dive and then turn into them as they get down to your level. If you climb after them, they've got you. In our first month of operations we got thirteen planes for six and we only had one pilot killed."

Cochran has a high respect for German fliers. "They are big operators," he told two war correspondents not long ago. "They are very methodical Joes. When they are going to start an offensive, they lay off you, conserving their forces. Then, when they think you are going to attack, they attack you to draw you and get you off balance. They expect you to play it the same way. I am in favor of attacking hell out of them all the time, and then they never know what to expect. Another thing they do is let you get away with something a couple of times and pretend they don't notice it and then come in and catch you right. For instance, the way our transport planes come up here and land on the field and stay right where they land until they take off again. I used to send out and tell them I wouldn't have my men service them until they dispersed, but it's no use. Someday those guys are going to get it." Cochran delivered himself of this particular speech while saying goodbye to the two correspondents, who were walking down to the runway to board a transport. Ten minutes later one correspondent was hiding under a jeep and the other was lying flat on his belly on the runway while sixteen-millimetre explosive shells from some Messerschmitts were digging furrows all around them and miraculously missing them and the transports. "If I keep on calling the turn like that," Cochran said afterward, "I will find myself up on Park Avenue after the war with a thing around my head, charging twenty-five dollars a reading."

# THE FOAMY FIELDS

A.  J.  LIEBLING

IF THERE is any way you can get colder than you do when you sleep in a bedding roll on the ground in a tent in southern Tunisia two hours before dawn, I don't know about it. The particular tent I remember was at an airfield in a Tunisian valley. The surface of the terrain was mostly limestone. If you put all the blankets on top of you and just slept on the canvas cover of the roll, you ached all over, and if you divided the blankets and put some of them under you, you froze on top. The tent was a large, circular one with a French stencil on the outside saying it had been rented from a firm in Marseille and not to fold it wet, but it belonged to the United States Army now. It had been set up over a pit four feet deep, so men sleeping in it were safe from flying bomb fragments. The tall tent pole, even if severed, would probably straddle the pit and not hit anybody. It was too wide a hole to be good during a strafing, but then strafings come in the daytime and in the daytime nobody lived in it. I had thrown my roll into the tent because I thought it was vacant and it seemed as good a spot as any other when I arrived at the field as a war correspondent. I later discovered that I was sharing it with two enlisted men.

I never saw my tentmates clearly, because they were always in the tent by the time I turned in at night, when we were not allowed to have lights on, and they got up a few minutes before I did in the morning, when it was still dark. I used to hear them moving around, however, and sometimes talk to them. One was from Mississippi and the other from North Carolina, and both were airplane mechanics. The first night I stumbled through the darkness into the tent, they heard me and one of them said, "I hope you don't mind, but the tent we were sleeping in got all tore to pieces with shrapnel last night, so we just moved our stuff in here." I had been hearing about the events of the previous evening from everybody I met on the field. "You can thank God you wasn't here last night," the other man said earnestly. The field is so skillfully hidden in the mountains that it is hard to find by night, and usually the Germans just wander around overhead, dropping their stuff on the wrong hillsides, but for once they had found the right place and some of the light anti-aircraft on the field had started shooting tracers. "It was these guns that gave away where we was," the first soldier said.

"Only for that they would have gone away and never knowed the first bomb had hit the field. But after that they knew they was on the beam and they come back and the next bomb set some gasoline on fire and then they really did go to town. Ruined a P-38 that tore herself up in a belly landing a week ago and I had just got her about fixed up again, and now she's got shrapnel holes just about everywhere and she's hopeless. All that work wasted. Killed three fellows that was sleeping in a B-26 on the field and woke up and thought that was no safe place, so they started to run across the field to a slit trench and a bomb got them. Never got the B-26 at all. If they'd stayed there, they'd been alive today, but who the hell would have stayed there?"

"That shrapnel has a lot of force behind it," the other voice in the tent said. "There was a three-quarter-ton truck down on the field and a jaggedy piece of shrapnel went right through one of the tires and spang through the chassix. You could see the holes both sides where she went in and come out. We was in our tent when the shooting started, but not for long. We run up into the hills so far in fifteen minutes it took us four hours to walk back next morning. When we got back, we found we didn't have no tent." There was a pause, and then the first soldier said, "Good night, sir," and I fell asleep.

When the cold woke me up, I put my flashlight under the blankets so I could look at my watch. It was five o'clock. Some Arab dogs, or perhaps jackals, were barking in the hills, and I lay uncomfortably dozing until I heard one of the soldiers blowing his nose. He blew a few times and said, "It's funny that as cold as it gets up here nobody seems to get a real cold. My nose runs like a spring branch, but it don't never develop."

When the night turned gray in the entrance to the tent, I woke again, looked at my watch, and saw that it was seven. I got up and found that the soldiers had already gone. Like everyone else at the field, I had been sleeping in my clothes. The only water obtainable was so cold that I did not bother to wash my face. I got my mess kit and walked toward the place, next to the kitchen, where they were starting fires under two great caldrons to heat dish water. One contained soapy water and the other rinsing water. The fires shot up from a deep hole underneath them, and a group of soldiers had gathered around and were holding the palms of their hands toward the flames, trying to get warm. The men belonged to a maintenance detachment of mechanics picked from a number of service squadrons that had been sent to new advanced airdromes, where planes have to be repaired practically without equipment for the job. That morning most of the men seemed pretty cheerful because nothing had happened during the night, but one fellow with a lot of beard on his face was critical. "This location was all right as long as we had all the planes on one side of us, so we was sort of off the runway," he said, "but now that they moved in those planes on the other side of us, we're just like a piece of meat between two slices of bread. A fine ham sandwich for Jerry. If he misses either side, he hits us. I guess that is how you get to be an officer, thinking up a location for a camp like this. I never washed out of Yale so I could be an officer, but I got more sense than that."

"Cheer up, pal," another soldier said. "All you got to do is dig. I got my dugout down so deep already it reminds me of the Borough Hall station. Some night I'll give myself a shave and climb on board a Woodlawn express." Most of the men in camp, I had already noticed, were taking up excavation as a hobby and some of them had worked up elaborate private trench systems. "You couldn't get any guy in camp to dig three days ago," the Brooklyn soldier said, "and now you can't lay down a shovel for a minute without somebody sucks it up."

Another soldier, who wore a white silk scarf loosely knotted around his extremely dirty neck, a style generally affected by fliers, said, "What kills me is my girl's brother is in the horse cavalry, probably deep in the heart of Texas, and he used to razz me because I wasn't a combat soldier."

The Brooklyn man said to him, "Ah, here's Mac with a parachute tied around his neck just like a dashing pilot. Mac, you look like a page out of *Esquire*."

When my hands began to feel warm, I joined the line which had formed in front of the mess tent. As we passed through, we got bacon, rice, apple butter, margarine, and hard biscuits in our mess tins and tea in our canteen cups. The outfit was on partly British rations, but it was a fairly good breakfast anyway, except for the tea, which came to the cooks with sugar and powdered milk already mixed in it. "I guess that's why they're rationing coffee at home, so we can have tea all the time," the soldier ahead of me said. I recognized the bacon as the fat kind the English get from America. By some miracle of lend-lease they had now succeeded in delivering it back to us; the background of bookkeeping staggered the imagination. After we had got our food, we collected a pile of empty gasoline cans to use for chairs and tables. The five-gallon can, known as a flimsy, is one of the two most protean articles in the Army. You can build houses out of it, use it as furniture, or, with slight structural alterations, make a stove or a locker out of it. Its only rival for versatility is the metal shell of the Army helmet, which can be used as an entrenching tool, a shaving bowl, a wash basin, or a cooking utensil, at the discretion of the owner. The flimsy may also serve on occasion as a bathtub. The bather fills it with water, stands in it, removes one article of clothing at a time, rubs the water hastily over the surface thus exposed, and replaces the garment before taking off another one.

There was no officers' mess. I had noticed Major George Lehmann, the commanding officer of the base, and First Lieutenant McCreedy, the chaplain, in the line not far behind me. Major Lehmann is a tall, fair, stolid man who told me that he had lived in Pittsfield, Massachusetts, where he had a job with the General Electric Company. When I had reported, on my arrival at the field, at his dugout the evening before, he had hospitably suggested that I stow my blanket roll wherever I could find a hole in the ground, eat at the general mess shack, and stay as long as I pleased. "There are fighter squadrons and some bombers and some engineers and anti-aircraft here, and you can wander around and talk to anybody that interests you," he had said.

Father McCreedy is a short, chubby priest who came from Bethlehem, Pennsylvania, and had been assigned to a parish in Philadelphia. He always referred to the pastor of this parish, a Father McGinley, as "my boss," and asked me several times if I knew George Jean Nathan, who he said was a friend of Father McGinley. Father McCreedy had been officiating at the interment of the fellows killed in the raid the evening before, and that was all he would talk about during breakfast. He had induced a mechanic to engrave the men's names on metal plates with an electric needle. These plates would serve as enduring grave markers. It is part of a chaplain's duty to see that the dead are buried and to dispose of their effects. Father McCreedy was also special-services officer of the camp, in charge of recreation and the issue of athletic equipment. "So what with one thing and another, they keep me busy here," he said. He told me he did not like New York. "Outside of Madison Square Garden and the Yankee Stadium, you can have it." He wore an outsize tin hat all the time. "I know a chaplain is not supposed to be a combatant," he said, "but if parachute troops came to my tent by night, they'd shoot at me because they wouldn't know I was a chaplain, and I want something solid on my head." He had had a deep hole dug in front of his tent and sometimes, toward dusk, when German planes were expected, he would stand in it waiting and smoking a cigar, with the glowing end of it just clearing the hole.

When I had finished breakfast and scrubbed up my mess kit, I strolled around the post to see what it was like. As the sun rose higher, the air grew warm and the great, reddish mountains looked friendly. Some of them had table tops, and the landscape reminded me of Western movies in Technicolor. I got talking to a soldier named Bill Phelps, who came from the town of Twenty-nine Palms, California. He was working on a bomber that had something the matter with its insides. He confirmed my notion that the country looked like the American West. "This is exactly the way it is around home," he said, "only we got no Ayrabs." A French writer has described the valley bottoms in southern Tunisia as foamy seas of white sand and green alfa grass. They are good, natural airfields, wide and level and fast-drying, but there is always plenty of dust in the air. I walked to a part of the field where there were a lot of P-38s, those double-bodied planes that look so very futuristic, and started to talk to a couple of sergeants who were working on one. "This is Lieutenant Hoelle's plane," one of them said, "and we just finished putting a new wing on it. That counts as just a little repair job out here. Holy God, at home, if a plane was hurt like that, they would send it back to the factory or take it apart for salvage. All we do here is drive a two-and-a-half-ton truck up under the damaged wing and lift it off, and then we put the new wing on the truck and run it alongside the plane again and fix up that eighty-thousand-dollar airplane like we was sticking together a radio set. We think nothing of it. It's a great ship, the 38. Rugged. You know how this one got hurt? Lieutenant Hoelle was strafing some trucks and he come in to attack so low he hit his right wing against a telephone pole. Any other plane, that wing would have come off right there. Hitting the pole that way flipped him over on his back, and he was flying upside down ten feet off the ground. He gripped that stick so hard the inside of his hand was black and blue for a week afterward, and she come right side up and he flew her home. Any one-engine plane would have slipped and crashed into the ground, but those two counter-rotating props eliminate torque." I tried to look as though I understood. "Lieutenant Hoelle is a real man," the sergeant said.

I asked him where Hoelle and the other P-38 pilots were, and he directed me to the P-38 squadron's operations room, a rectangular structure mostly below ground, with walls made out of the sides of gasoline cans and a canvas roof camouflaged with earth. A length of stovepipe stuck out through the roof, making it definitely the most ambitious structure on the field.

Hoelle was the nearest man to the door when I stepped down into the operations shack. He was a big, square-shouldered youngster with heavy eyebrows and a slightly aquiline nose. I explained who I was and asked him who was in charge, and he said, "I am. I'm the squadron C.O. My name's Hoelle." He pronounced it "Holly." There was a fire in a stove, and the shack was warm. Two tiny black puppies lay on a pilot's red scarf in a helmet in the middle of the dirt floor, and they seemed to be the center of attention. Six or eight lieutenants, in flying togs that ranged from overalls to British Army battle dress, were sitting on gasoline cans or sprawled on a couple of cots. They were all looking at the puppies and talking either to them or their mother, a small Irish setter over in one corner, whom they addressed as Red. "One of the boys brought Red along with him from England," Hoelle said. "We think that the dog that got her in trouble is a big, long-legged black one at the airport we were quartered at there."

"These are going to be real beautiful dogs, just like Irish setters, only with black hair," one of the pilots said in a defensive tone. He was obviously Red's master.

"This is a correspondent," Hoelle said to the group, and one of the boys on a cot moved over and made room for me. I sat down, and the fellow who had moved over said his name was Larry Adler but he wasn't the harmonica player and when he was home he lived on Ocean Parkway in Brooklyn. "I wouldn't mind being there right now," he added.

There was not much in the shack except the cots, the tin cans, a packing case, the stove, a phonograph, a portable typewriter, a telephone, and a sort of bulletin board that showed which pilots were on mission, which were due to go on patrol, and which were on alert call, but it was a cheerful place. It reminded me of one of those secret-society shacks that small boys are always building out of pickup materials in vacant lots. Adler got up and said he would have to go on patrol. "It's pretty monotonous," he said, "like driving a fast car thirty miles an hour along a big, smooth road where there's no traffic. We just stooge around near the field and at this time of day nothing ever happens."

Another lieutenant came over and said he was the intelligence officer of the squadron. Intelligence and armament officers, who do not fly, take a more aggressive pride in their squadron's accomplishments than the pilots, who don't like to be suspected of bragging. "We've been out here for a month," the intelligence officer said, "and we have been doing everything—escorting bombers over places like Sfax and Sousse, shooting up vehicles and puncturing tanks, going on fighter sweeps to scare up a fight, and flying high looking for a target and then plunging straight down on it and shooting hell out of it. We've got twenty-nine German planes, including bombers and transports with troops in them and fighters, and the boys have flown an average of forty combat missions apiece. That's more than one a day. Maybe you'd like to see some of the boys' own reports on what they have been doing."

I said that this sounded fine, and he handed me a sheaf of the simple statements pilots write out when they put in a claim for shooting down a German plane. I copied part of a report by a pilot named Earnhart, who I thought showed a sense of literary style. He had had, according to the intelligence officer, about the same kind of experience as everybody else in the squadron. Earnhart had shot down a Junkers 52, which is a troop-carrier, in the episode he was describing, and then he had been attacked by several enemy fighters. "As I was climbing away from them," he wrote, "a 20-millimetre explosive shell hit the windshield and deflected through the top of the canopy and down on the instrument panel. Three pieces of shell hit me, in the left chest, left arm, and left knee. I dropped my belly tank and, having the ship under control, headed for my home base. On the way I applied a tourniquet to my leg, administered a hypodermic, and took sulfanilamide tablets. I landed the ship at my own base one hour after I had been hit by the shell. The plane was repaired. Claim, one Ju 52 destroyed." The intelligence officer introduced Earnhart to me. He was a calm, slender, dark-haired boy and he persisted in addressing me as sir. He said he came from Lebanon, Ohio, and had gone to Ohio State.

Still another lieutenant I met was named Gustke. He came from Detroit. Gustke had been shot down behind the German lines and had made his way back to the field. He was a tall, gangling type, with a long nose and a prominent Adam's apple. "I crash-landed the plane and stepped out of it wearing my parachute," he told me, "and the first thing I met was some Arabs who looked hostile to me, and as luck would have it I had forgotten to bring along my .45, so I tripped my parachute and threw it to them, and you know how crazy Arabs are about cloth or anything like that. They all got fighting among themselves for the parachute, and while they were doing that I ran like the dickens and got away from them. I got to a place where there were some Frenchmen, and they hid me overnight and the next day put me on a horse and gave me a guide, who brought me back over some mountains to inside the French lines. I had a pretty sore tail from riding the horse."

A pilot from Texas named Ribb, who stood nearby as Gustke and I talked, broke in to tell me that they had a fine bunch of fellows and that when they were in the air they took care of each other and did not leave anybody alone at the end of the formation to be picked off by the enemy. "In this gang we have no butt-end Charlies," he said feelingly.

I asked Lieutenant Hoelle what was in the cards for the afternoon, and he said that eight of the boys, including himself, were going out to strafe some German tanks that had been reported working up into French territory. "We carry a cannon, which the P-40s don't, so we can really puncture a tank the size they use around here," he said. "We expect to meet some P-40s over the target, and they will stay up high and give us cover against any German fighters while we do a job on the tanks. Maybe I had better call the boys together and talk it over."

A couple of pilots had begun a game of blackjack on the top of the packing case, and he told them to quit, so he could spread a map on it. At that moment an enlisted man came in with a lot of mail and some Christmas packages that had been deposited by a courier plane. It was long after Christmas, but that made the things even more welcome, and all the pilots made a rush for their packages and started tearing them open. Earnhart, one of the men who were going on the strafe job, got some National Biscuit crackers and some butterscotch candy and a couple of tubes of shaving cream that he said he couldn't use because he had an electric razor, and the operations officer, a lieutenant named Lusk, got some very rich home-made cookies that an aunt and uncle had sent him from Denver. We were all gobbling butterscotch and cookies as we gathered round the map Hoelle had spread. It was about as formal an affair as looking at a road map to find your way to Washington, Connecticut, from New Milford. "We used to make more fuss over briefings in England," the intelligence officer said, "but when you're flying two or three times a day, what the hell?" He pointed out the place on the map where the tanks were supposed to be, and all the fellows said they knew where it was, having been there before. Hoelle said they would take off at noon. After a while he and the seven other boys went out onto the field to get ready, and I went with them. On the way there was more talk about P-38s and how some Italian prisoners had told their captors that the Italian army could win the war easy if it wasn't for those fork-tailed airplanes coming over and shooting them up, a notion that seemed particularly to amuse the pilots. Then I went to the P-38 squadron mess with Adler, who had just returned from patrol duty and wasn't going out on the strafe job, and Gustke, who was also remaining behind. This mess was relatively luxurious. They had tables with plates and knives and forks on them, so they had no mess tins to wash after every meal. "We live well here," Adler said. "Everything high-class."

"The place the planes are going is not very far away," Gustke said, "so they ought to be back around half past two."

When we had finished lunch, I took another stroll around the post. I was walking toward the P-38 squadron's operations shack when I saw the planes begin to return from the mission. The first one that came in had only the nose wheel of its landing gear down. There was evidently something the matter with the two other wheels. The plane slid in on its belly and stopped in a cloud of dust. Another plane was hovering over the field. I noticed, just after I spotted this one, that a little ambulance was tearing out onto the field. Only one of the two propellers of this plane was turning, but it landed all right, and then I counted one, two, three others, which landed in good shape. Five out of eight. I broke into a jog toward the operations shack. Gustke was standing before the door looking across the field with binoculars. I asked him if he knew whose plane had belly-landed, and he said it was a Lieutenant Moffat's and that a big, rough Texas pilot whom the other fellows called Wolf had been in the plane that had come in with one engine out. "I see Earnhart and Keith and Carlton, too," he said, "but Hoelle and the other two are missing."

A jeep was coming from the field toward the operations shack, and when it got nearer we could see Wolf in it. He looked excited. He was holding his right forearm with his left hand, and when the jeep got up to the shack he jumped out, still holding his arm.

"Is it a bullet hole?" Gustke asked.

"You're a sonofabitch it's a bullet hole!" Wolf shouted. "The sonofabitching P-40s sonofabitching around! As we came in, we saw four fighters coming in the opposite direction and Moffat and I went up to look at them and they were P-40s, coming away. The other fellows was on' the deck and we started to get down nearer them, to about five thousand, and these sonofabitching 190s came out of the sun and hit Moffat and me the first burst and then went down after the others. There was ground fire coming up at us, too, and the sonofabitches said we was going to be over friendly territory. I'm goddam lucky not to be killed."

"Did we get any of them?" Gustke asked.

"I know I didn't get any," Wolf said, "but I saw at least four planes burning on the ground. I don't know who the hell they were."

By that time another jeep had arrived with Earnhart, looking utterly calm, and one of the mechanics from the field. "My plane is all right," Earnhart told Gustke. "All gassed up and ready to go. They can use that for patrol."

The telephone inside the shack rang. It was the post first-aid station calling to say that Moffat was badly cut up by glass from his windshield but would be all right. The mechanic said that the cockpit of Moffat's plane was knee-deep in hydraulic fluid and oil and gas. "No wonder the hydraulic system wouldn't work when he tried to get the wheels down," the mechanic said. The phone rang again. This time it was group operations calling for Earnhart, Keith, and Carlton, all three of them unwounded, to go over there and tell them what had happened. The three pilots went away, and a couple of the men got Wolf back into a jeep and took him off to the first-aid station. Hoelle and the two other pilots were still missing. That left only Gustke and me, and he said in a sad young voice, like a boy whose chum has moved to another city, "Now we have lost our buddies."

A couple of days later I learned that Hoelle had bailed out in disputed territory and made his way back to our lines, but the two other boys are either dead or prisoners.

[May 26, June 2, 1945]

# MOLLIE

*(The Story of a Quest that Began
April 25, 1943, and Ended May 3, 1945)*

A. J. LIEBLING

MOLLIE is a part of the history of La Piste Forestière, and La Piste Forestière is perhaps the most important part of the history of Mollie. La Piste Forestière, or the Foresters' Track, is a dirt road that connects Cap Serrat, on the northern coast of western Tunisia, with Sedjenane, a town twenty miles inland. The country it runs through is covered with small hills, and almost all the hills are coated with a ten-foot growth of tall bushes and short trees, so close together that once you leave the road you can't see fifty feet in front of you. From the top of any hill you can see the top of another hill, but, because of the growth, you can't tell whether there are men on it. This made the country hard to fight in. The hillsides that have no trees are bright with wild flowers in the spring, and two years ago, when some other war correspondents and I travelled back and forth along the Foresters' Track in jeeps, we sometimes used to measure our slow progress by reference to the almost geometrical patterns of color on such slopes. There was, for example, the hill with a rough yellow triangle of buttercups against a reddish-purple background of other blooms; it indicated that you were five miles from the road's junction with the main highway at Sedjenane. With luck you might reach the junction in two hours, but this was extremely unlikely, for the road was just wide enough for one truck—not for a truck and a jeep or even for a truck and a motorcycle. Only a man on foot or on a horse could progress along the margin of the road when there was a vehicle on it, and the horse would often have to scramble by with two feet off the road, like the sidehill bear of eastern Tennessee. When a jeep met a convoy, it sometimes had to back up for hundreds of yards to where there was room to get off the road and wait. Then, when all the heavy vehicles had passed, the jeep would resume its journey, perhaps to meet another convoy before it had recovered the lost yardage. Even when you got in behind trucks going your way, they were packed so closely together that they advanced at a crawl, so you did too. Bits of the war were threaded along the Foresters' Track like beads on a string, and the opportunity to become familiar with them was forced upon you. Mollie, for me, was the gaudiest bead.

The reason the Foresters' Track is such a miserable excuse for a road is that in normal times there is little need for it. There is a lighthouse at Cap Serrat and a forest warden's house about halfway between that and Sedjenane. The few Berbers in the district, who live in brush shelters in the bush, have no vehicles or need of a road. But in late April and early May of 1943, La Piste Forestière was an important military thoroughfare. The Allied armies, facing east, lay in a great arc with their right flank at Sousse, on the Gulf of Tunis, and this little road was the only supply line for twenty miles of front; that is, the extreme left flank of the Allied line. The actual front line ran parallel to the road and only a few hundred yards east of it during the first days of the offensive that was to end the Allies' North African campaign, but because of the hills and the brush, people on the road couldn't see the fighting. However, American artillery placed just west of the road—it would have been an engineering feat to get it any considerable distance into the brush—constantly fired over our heads as our jeeps piddled along. The gunners hoped that some of their shells were falling on the Germans and Italians who were trying to halt our infantry's advance with fire from hidden mortars and machine guns. The Luftwaffe in Africa had predeceased the enemy ground forces; the budget of planes allotted it for the African adventure was exhausted, I suppose, and the German High Command sent no more. This was lucky for us, because one good strafing, at any hour, would have jammed the road with burned-out vehicles and Allied dead. By repeating the strafing once a day, the Germans could have kept the road permanently out of commission. The potential danger from the air did not worry us for long, however. You soon become accustomed to immunity, even when you cannot understand the reason for it.

Trucks left ammunition along the side of the road to be carried up to the fighting lines on the backs of requisitioned mules and horses and little Arab donkeys, a strangely assorted herd conducted by an equally scratch lot of soldiers. The Washington army had decided years before that the war was now one-hundred-per-cent mechanized, so the field army, quite a different organization, had to improvise its animal transport as it went along. The wounded were carried down to the road by stretcher bearers. Ambulances, moving with the same disheartening slowness as everything else, picked up the casualties and took them out to a clearing station near the yellow-triangle hill I have mentioned, where some of the viable ones were patched up for the further slow haul out. Cruder surgical units, strung out along the road, took such cases as they were equipped to handle. These units were always right by the side of the road, since in that claustrophobe's nightmare of a country there was no other place for them to be. The advanced units were French and had women nurses with them. A French doctor I knew used to say that it helped the men bear pain if nurses were looking at them. "Since we have so little anesthesia," he said, "we rely upon vanity." Sometimes I would sit in my jeep and watch that doctor work. He had broken down a few saplings and bushes by the side of the road to clear a space for his ambulance, and next to the ambulance he had set up a camp stool and a folding table with some instruments on it. Once a traffic jam stopped my jeep near his post when he had a tanned giant perched on the camp stool, a second lieutenant in the Corps Franc d'Afrique. The man's breasts were hanging off his chest in a kind of bloody ruff. "A bit of courage now, my son, will save you a great deal of trouble later on," the doctor said as he prepared to do something or other. I assumed, perhaps pessimistically, that he was going to hack off the bits of flesh as you would trim the ragged edges of an ill-cut page. "Go easy, Doctor," the young man said. "I'm such a softie." Then the traffic started to move, so I don't know what the doctor did to him.

The Corps Franc d'Afrique was a unit that had a short and glorious history. Soon after the Allied landings in North Africa, in October, 1942, the Corps Franc organized itself, literally, out of the elements the Darlanists in control of the North African government distrusted too much to incorporate into the regular French Army—Jews, anti-Nazis from concentration camps, de Gaullists, and other Allied sympathizers. A French general named Joseph de Goislard de Montsabert, who had helped plan the landings, had been thrown out by his collaborationist superiors, who, even after Darlan's agreement to play ball with the forces of democracy, had remained his superiors. De Montsabert, because he had a red face and snowy hair, was known to his troops as Strawberry in Cream. There had been among the French in North Africa a number of other professional officers and many reservists who, like the General, were apparently left out of the war because they were suspected of favoring de Gaulle or merely of being hostile to Germany. The Darlan regime had refused to mobilize the Jews because it clung to the Vichy thesis that they were not full citizens, and it did not want them to establish a claim to future consideration, and it was holding thousands of Spanish and German refugees and French Communists in concentration camps.

De Montsabert and a few of his officer friends, talking on the street in Algiers one rainy November day of that year, decided to start a "Free Corps" of men who wanted to fight but whom the government would not allow to. They took over a room in a schoolhouse on the Rue Mogador as headquarters and advertised in the *Echo d'Alger* for volunteers. The ad appeared once and then the Darlanist censorship, which was still operating under the Americans, like every other element of Vichy rule, suppressed it. But scores of volunteers had already appeared at the schoolhouse and de Montsabert sent them out with pieces of schoolroom chalk to write "Join the Corps Franc" on walls all over the city. Hundreds of new volunteers came in. General Giraud, who had arrived in Africa to command all the French but had subsequently accepted a role secondary to Darlan's, heard of the movement and interceded for it.

Giraud, whatever his limitations, considered it natural that anybody in his right mind should want to fight the Germans. Darlan and his Fascist friends began to think of the Corps Franc as a means of getting undesirables out of the way, so the government recognized it but at the same time refused it any equipment. The Corps began life with a miscellany of matériel begged from the British and Americans. Its men wore British battle dress and French insignia of rank, lived on American C rations, and carried any sort of weapons they could lay their hands on. The most characteristic feature of their appearance was a long beard, but even this was not universal, because some of the soldiers were too young to grow one. After the Corps Franc's arrival in Tunisia, it added to its heterogeneous equipment a great deal more stuff it captured from the enemy. The Corps went into the line in February of 1943, in the zone north of Sedjenane, and it remained there into the spring.

Late April in Tunisia is like late June in New York, and heat and dust were great nuisances to our men when they were attacking. In February and March, however, coastal Tunisia is drenched with a cold and constant downpour. The Foresters' Track was two feet deep in water when the Corps Franc began to fight along it. There were two battalions to start with—about twelve hundred men—to cover a sector twenty miles long. A third and fourth battalion had been added by the time the Americans began their offensive. The Corps, in the beginning, had only two ambulances, converted farm trucks owned by a Belgian colonist in Morocco. The Belgian and his son had driven the trucks across North Africa to join the Corps. But the trucks were unable to negotiate the flooded Track, so the men of the Corps carried their wounded out to Sedjenane on their shoulders. I once asked my doctor friend why they had not used mules. "The mules rolled over in the water and crushed the wounded men," he said. "We know. We tried it with wounded prisoners."

Now that the great attack was on, there were other troops along the Track with the Corps—the Sixtieth Infantry of the American Ninth Division, part of the American Ninth Division's artillery, an American tank-destroyer battalion, some Moroccan units, and some American motor-truck and medical outfits. The medics and the artillery made the French feel pampered and their morale got very high. One hot morning, I passed a lean, elderly soldier of the Corps Franc who was burying two of his comrades. He looked about sixty—there was no age limit in the Corps—and had a long, drooping mustache of a faded biscuit color. He had finished one grave and was sitting down to rest and cool off before beginning the other. The two dead men lay with their feet to the road. Blueflies had settled on their faces. I told my jeep driver to stop and asked the gravedigger what men these were. "One stiff was an Arab from Biskra," the old soldier said, "and the other a Spaniard, a nihilist from Oran." I asked him how his work was going. He wiped the sweat from his forehead and said happily, "Monsieur, like on roller skates."

A quarter of the men in the Corps Franc were Jews. A Jewish lieutenant named Rosenberg was its posthumous hero by the time I arrived in the Foresters' Track country. He had commanded a detachment of twenty men covering the retreat of his battalion during a German counterattack in early March. This was a sequel to the counterattack against the Americans at Kasserine Pass in late February, and both assaults were prototypes, on a small scale, of the counter-offensive the Germans were to launch in Belgium at the end of 1944—the last flurry of the hooked and dying fish. Rosenberg, holding one of the innumerable little hills with his men, had decided that it was not fitting for a Jew to retire, even when the Germans looked as though they had surrounded his position. He and his men held on until the rest of the battalion had made its escape. Then he rose, and, intoning the "Marseillaise," led his men in an attack with hand grenades. He and most of his men were, of course, killed.

Besides the Jews, the Corps had hundreds of political prisoners from labor camps in southern Algeria—Spanish Republicans who had fled to Africa in 1939, anti-Nazi Germans who had come even before that, and French "Communists and de Gaullists," to employ the usual Vichy designation for dissidents. The political prisoners had been released upon agreeing to enter the Corps Franc, which they did not consider an onerous condition. There were also hundreds of Frenchmen who had joined because they distrusted the Vichy officers in the regular Army, or because they were "hard heads" who detested any species of regularity, or because they were too old or ill for more conventional fighting units. In the Corps Franc, they were at liberty to march and fight until they dropped. There were also a fair number of Mohammedans, good soldiers who had joined to earn the princely wage of twenty-three francs a day, ten times what they would have got if they had waited to be mobilized in their regular units. Whenever I had a chance, I asked Corps Franc soldiers what they had been in civilian life and why they had enlisted. I remember a former *carabiñero* who had fought in the Spanish Loyalist Army, and a baker of Italian parentage from Bône, in Algeria, who said, "I am a Communist. Rich people are poison to me."

Other members of the Corps who made a special impression on me were a former admiral in the Spanish Republican Navy, who was now a company commander and would not allow junior officers to shout at soldiers; a Hungarian poet who had been studying medicine at the University of Algiers; a sixteen-year-old Alsatian from Strasbourg who had run away from home to avoid being forced to become a German citizen; and a French captain, a shipping broker in civil life, who proclaimed himself a Royalist. The captain's sixteen-year-old son was also in the Corps; the boy was a motorcycle dispatch rider. I also remember two tough Parisians who had not seen each other since one had escaped from jail in Dakar, where they had both been imprisoned for trying to join the Free French in Brazzaville. The other had escaped later. "Say, it's you, old pimp!" one of the men shouted joyously. "And how did you get out of the jug, old rottenness?" the second man shouted back. Once I shared a luncheon of C-ration vegetable hash, scallions, and medlars with a little fifty-three-year-old second lieutenant, one of those Frenchmen with a face like a parakeet, who until 1942 had been vice-president of the Paris Municipal Council, in which he represented the *arrondissement* of the Opéra. He had got out a clandestine paper and had helped Jewish friends smuggle millions of francs out of France. Betrayed to the Gestapo, he had been arrested and put in Cherche-Midi Prison; he had escaped with the aid of a jailer and come to Africa and the Corps Franc. The middle-aged soldier who waited on us spoke French with a farce-comedy Russian accent; he had been a waiter at the Scheherazade, a night club in Montmartre, and had often served the lieutenant when he was a civilian. A handsome young Viennese half-Jew, who had been on the Austrian track team in the last Olympic Games, once asked me for some sulfanilamide. He had been in a labor camp for six months without seeing a woman but had been allowed one night's leave in Oran before being sent on to the front. He wanted the sulfanilamide, he said, so that he could treat himself; he was afraid that a doctor might order him away from the firing line. And in a hospital tent at the clearing station I came across a man with a French flag wrapped around his waist; the medics discovered it when they cut his shirt away. He was a hard-looking, blondish chap with a mouthful of gold teeth and a face adorned by a cross-shaped knife scar—the *croix de vache* with which procurers sometimes mark business rivals. An interesting collection of obscene tattooing showed on the parts of him that the flag did not cover. Outwardly he was not a sentimental type.

"Where are you from?" I asked him.

"Belleville," he said. Belleville is a part of Paris not distinguished for its elegance.

"What did you do in civilian life?" I inquired.

That made him grin. "I lived on my income," he said.

"Why did you choose the Corps Franc?"

"Because I understood," he said.

The American soldiers interspersed with the men of the Corps Franc along the Foresters' Track found them a fantastic lot. Most of the men then in the Ninth Division came from New York, New Jersey, or New England, and their ideas of North Africa and Frenchmen had been acquired from films with Ronald Colman as Beau Geste or Charles Boyer as Charles Boyer. They thought the Frenchmen very reckless. The Ninth had had its first experience in battle on the road to Maknassy, in southern Tunisia, only a few weeks earlier, and it was not yet a polished division. The men of the Ninth in Germany recently took risks as nonchalantly as any Corps Franc soldier used to, but at the time I am speaking of they would sometimes call the Frenchmen "those crazy headhunters." This term reflected a tendency to confuse the

Corps Franc with the Moroccans in the same zone; the Moroccans are not headhunters, either, but there is a popular American belief that they are paid according to how many enemy ears they bring in.

There were two tabors, or battalions, of Moroccans in the zone; a tabor consists of several goums, or companies, and each soldier who is a member of a company is called a goumier. For the sake of simplicity and euphony, Americans called the Moroccan soldiers themselves goums. The goums used to ride along the side of the road on bay mules or gray horses—sure-footed, mountain-bred animals—until they got near the place where they were going to fight. Then they would dismount and go off into the brush on bare feet, and return with their booty when they had finished their business. The goum's sole outer garment is the *djellabah,* which looks like a long brown bathrobe with a hood. It is made of cotton, wool, linen, goats' hair, or camels' hair and usually has vertical black stripes. It sheds water, insulates against heat and cold, is a substitute for a pup tent at night, and serves as a repository for everything the goum gloms, like the capacious garment of a professional shoplifter. In their Moroccan homeland the goums live with their wives and children in their own villages and are supposed to pay themselves with the spoils of tribes that resist the French government. In Tunisia the spoils were pretty well confined to soldiers' gear. As a goum killed or captured more and more enemies, he would put on layer after layer of tunics and trousers, always wearing the *djellabah* over everything. The girth of the goums increased as the campaign wore on. This swollen effect gave a goum an air of prosperity and importance, in his opinion; his standing as a warrior, he thought, was in direct ratio to his circumference. A goum who was doing well often wore, between sorties, one German and one Italian boot and carried a string of extra boots over his saddlebow. The funny part of it was that a goum wearing six men's clothing could slip noiselessly through a thicket that was impassable to a skinny American. The French officers commanding the goums assured me that their men were not paid by the ear; if a goum occasionally had a few dried ears concealed in a fold of his *djellabah,* one officer explained, it was because goums had discovered that such souvenirs had a trade value in G.I. cigarettes and chewing gum. "Far from paying for ears," this officer said, "we have recently been offering a small reward for live prisoners for interrogation. It is evident that a prisoner without ears is not a good subject for interrogation, because he does not hear the questions plainly." To hold the goums' respect, the officers had to be able to march, climb, and fight with them, and a goum is as inexhaustible as a mountain sheep and about as fastidious as a hyena. Most goums come from the Atlas Mountains and few of them speak Arabic, much less French, so the officers have to be fluent in the southern Berber dialects, which are all that the men know. The goums are trying companions in minefields, because, as one officer remarked, "They say, 'If it is the will of God, we go up,' and then they just push forward." Neither they nor the Corps Franc had mine detectors. An American captain named Yankauer, who was the surgeon at the clearing station near the yellow-triangle hill, was once digging scraps of steel out of a goum who had stepped on a mine. The man let out one short squeal—there was no anesthetic—and then began a steady chant. Yankauer asked a goum officer, who was waiting his turn on the table, what the goum was saying. The officer translated, "He chants, 'God forgive me, I am a woman. God forgive me, I am a woman,' because, you see, he has cried aloud, so he is ashamed." The goums' chief weapons were curved knives and long rifles of the vintage of 1871, and one of the supply problems of the campaign for the American G-4 was finding ammunition for these antediluvian small arms. Colonel Pierre Magnan, who had succeeded de Montsabert in command of the Corps Franc, was the senior French officer in the zone. I was with him one day when the commander of a newly arrived tabor presented himself for orders. "How are you fixed for automatic weapons, Major?" Magnan asked. "We have two old machine guns," the goum officer said. Then, when he saw Magnan's glum look, he added cheerily, "But don't worry, my Colonel, we use them only on maneuvers."

Magnan was a trim, rather elegant officer who, before the Allied landings, had commanded a crack infantry regiment in Morocco. On the morning of the American landings, he had arrested General Noguès, the Governor General of Morocco, and then asked him to prevent any fighting between the French and Americans by welcoming the invading forces. Noguès had telephoned to a tank regiment to come and arrest Magnan. Magnan, unwilling to shed French blood, had surrendered to the tankmen and become a prisoner in his turn. The liberated Noguès had then ordered a resistance that cost hundreds of French and American lives. Magnan was kept in prison for several days after Noguès, who was backed by our State Department, had consented to be agreeable to the Allies. Magnan had then been released, but he was deprived of his command and consigned to the Corps Franc. He now commands a division in France, and de Montsabert has a *corps d'armée,* so the scheme to keep them down has not been precisely a success.

The Axis forces north of Sedjenane must have been as hard put to it for supply routes as we were. I don't remember the roads the Intelligence maps showed behind the enemy's lines, but they could not have been numerous or elaborate. The Germans did not seem to have a great deal of artillery, but they occasionally landed shells on our road. Once, I remember, they shot up a couple of tank destroyers shortly after the jeep I was in had pulled out to let them pass. Throughout, it was a stubborn, nasty sort of fighting in the brush, and casualties arrived in a steady trickle rather than any great spurt, because large-scale attacks were impossible. Our men fought their way a few hundred yards further east each day, toward Ferryville and Bizerte. Eventually, when

Rommel's forces crumpled, men of the Corps Franc, in trucks driven by American soldiers, got to Bizerte before any other Allied troops.

On Easter Sunday, which came late in April, I was out along the Track all day, riding in a jeep with Hal Boyle, a correspondent for the Associated Press. At the end of the afternoon we headed home, hoping to get back to the press camp before night so that we wouldn't have to buck a stream of two-and-a-half-ton trucks and armored vehicles in the blackout. Traffic seemed, if anything, heavier than usual along the Foresters' Track, as it always did when you were in a hurry. The jeep stopped for minutes at a time, which gave Boyle the opportunity to climb out and get the names and home addresses of American soldiers for his stories. Sometimes he would stay behind, talking, and catch up with the jeep the next time it was snagged. We could have walked along the Track faster than we rode. Finally we came to a dip in the road. Fifty yards below and to our right there was a shallow stream, and there was almost no brush on the slope from the road down to the water. This, for the Foresters' Track country, was a considerable clearing, and it was being used for a number of activities. Some goums were watering their mounts in the stream, some French and American soldiers were heating rations over brush fires, a number of vehicles were parked there, and Colonel Magnan and some officers were holding a staff meeting. As we approached the clearing, we were stopped again for a moment by the traffic. A dismal American soldier came out of the brush on our left, tugging a gaunt, reluctant white horse. "Come along, Horrible," the soldier said in a tone of intensest loathing. "This goddam horse got me lost three times today," he said to us, looking over his shoulder at the sneering, wall-eyed beast. He evidently thought the horse was supposed to guide him.

We moved downhill a bit and stopped again, this time behind an ambulance that was loading wounded. There was a group of soldiers around the ambulance. Boyle and I got out to look. There were four wounded men, all badly hit. They were breathing hard and probably didn't know what was going on. Shock and heavy doses of morphia were making their move easy, or at least quiet. The four men were all from the Sixtieth Infantry of the Ninth Division. A soldier by the road said that they had been on a patrol and had exchanged shots with a couple of Germans; the Germans had popped up waving white handkerchiefs, the Americans had stood up to take them prisoners, and another German, lying concealed, had opened on them with a machine gun. It was the sort of thing that had happened dozens of times to other units, and that undoubtedly has happened hundreds of times since. Such casualties, a Polish officer once said to me, are an entry fee to battle. That doesn't make them easy to take, however. The soldiers had been told about this particular trick in their training courses, but they had probably thought it was a fable invented to make them hate the enemy. Now the men around the ambulance had really begun to hate the enemy. While Boyle was getting the names and addresses of the men, I saw another American soldier by the side

of the road. This one was dead. A soldier nearby said that the dead man had
been a private known as Mollie.

A blanket covered Mollie's face, so I surmised that it had been shattered,
but there was no blood on the ground, so I judged that he had been killed in
the brush and carried down to the road to await transport. A big, wild-looking
sergeant was standing alongside him—a hawk-nosed, red-necked man with
a couple of front teeth missing—and I asked him if the dead man had been in
the patrol with the four wounded ones. "Jeez, no!" the sergeant said, looking at
me as if I ought to know about the man with the blanket over his face. "That's
Comrade Molotov. The Mayor of Broadway. Didn't you ever hear of him?
Jeez, Mac, he once captured six hundred Eyetalians by himself and brought
them all back along with him. Sniper got him, I guess. I don't know, because
he went out with the French, and he was found dead up there in the hills. He
always liked to do crazy things—go off by himself with a pair of big field
glasses he had and watch the enemy put in minefields, or take off and be an
artillery spotter for a while, or drive a tank. From the minute he seen those
frogs, he was bound to go off with them."

"Was his name really Molotov?" I asked.

"No," said the sergeant, "he just called himself that. The boys mostly
shortened it to Mollie. I don't even know what his real name was—Warren,
I think. Carl Warren. He used to say he was a Broadway big shot. 'Just ask
anybody around Forty-fourth Street,' he used to say. 'They all know me.' Me,
I'm from White Plains—I never heard of him before he joined up."

"I had him with me on a patrol that was to contact the French when
the regiment was moving into this zone last Thursday," a stocky blond corporal said. "The first French patrol we met, Mollie says to me, 'This is too far
back for me. I'm going up in the hills with these frogs and get me some
Lugers.' He was always collecting things he captured off Germans and Italians,
but the one thing he didn't have yet was a Luger. I knew if I didn't let him
go he would take off anyway and get into more trouble with the C.O. He
was always in trouble. So I said, 'All right, but the frogs got to give me a
receipt for you, so I can prove you didn't go A.W.O.L.' One of the soldiers
with me could speak French, so he explained it and the frog noncom give me
a receipt on a piece of toilet paper and Mollie went off with them." The corporal fished in one of the pockets of his field jacket and brought out a sheet
of tissue. On it, the French noncom had written, in pencil, *"Pris avec moi le
soldat américain Molotov, 23 avril, '43, Namin, caporal chef."*

"Mollie couldn't speak French," the American corporal went on, "but he
always got on good with the frogs. It's funny where those big field glasses
went, though. He used to always have them around his neck, but somebody
must have figured they were no more good to him after he was dead, so they

sucked them up. He used to always say that he was a big-shot gambler and that he used to watch the horse races with those glasses."

By now the four wounded men had been loaded into the ambulance. It moved off. Obviously, there was a good story in Mollie, but he was not available for an interview. The driver of the truck behind our jeep was giving us the horn, so I pulled Boyle toward the jeep. He got in, still looking back at Mollie, who said nothing to keep him, and we drove away. When we had gone a little way, at our customary slow pace, a tall lieutenant signalled to us from the roadside that he wanted a hitch and we stopped and indicated that he should hop aboard. He told us his name was Carl Ruff. He was from New York and thought I might know his wife, an advertising woman, but I didn't. Ruff was dog-tired from scrambling through the bush. I said something about Mollie, and Ruff said that he had not known him alive but had been the first American to see his body, on Good Friday morning. The French had led him to it. "He was on the slope of a hill," Ruff said, "and slugs from an automatic rifle had hit him in the right eye and chest. He must have been working his way up the hill, crouching, when the German opened on him and hit him in the chest, and then as he fell, the other bullet probably got him in the eye. He couldn't have lived a minute."

It was a month later, aboard the United States War Shipping Administration steamer Monterey, a luxury liner that had been converted to war service without any needless suppression of comfort, that I next heard of Molotov, the Mayor of Broadway. The Monterey was on her way from Casablanca to New York. On the passenger list were four correspondents besides myself, a thousand German prisoners, five hundred wounded Americans, all of whom would need long hospitalization, and a couple of hundred officers and men who were being transferred or were on various errands. It was one of the advantages of being a correspondent that one could go to America without being a German or wounded, or without being phenomenally lucky, which the unwounded soldiers on our boat considered that they were. The crossing had almost a holiday atmosphere. We were homeward bound after a great victory in the North African campaign, the first the Allies had scored over Germany in a war nearly four years old. The weather was perfect and the Monterey, which was not overcrowded and had wide decks and comfortable lounges, had the aspect and feeling of a cruise ship. The wounded were glad, in their sad way, to be going home. The prisoners were in good spirits, too; they seemed to regard the journey as a Nazi Strength through Joy excursion. They organized vaudeville shows, boxing matches, and art exhibitions with the energetic coöperation of the ship's chaplain, who found much to admire in the Christian cheerfulness with which they endured their increased rations. A couple of anti-Nazi prisoners had announced themselves on the first day out, but the German noncoms had knocked them about and set them to cleaning latrines, so order had soon been restored. "That's an army where they really have some discipline!" one of the American officers on board told me enviously. The prisoners had to put up with some hardships, of course. They complained one evening when ice cream was served to the wounded but not to them, and another time they didn't think the transport surgeon, a Jew, was "sympathetic" enough to a German officer with a stomach ache.

The hospital orderlies would wheel the legless wounded out on the promenade deck in wheelchairs to see the German boxing bouts, and the other wounded would follow them, some swinging along on crutches or hopping on one foot, some with their arms in slings or casts, some with their broken necks held stiffly in casts and harnesses. They had mixed reactions to the bouts. An arm case named Sanderson, a private who wore the Ninth Division shoulder patch, told me one day that he wished he could be turned loose on the prisoners with a tommygun, because he didn't like to see them jumping about in front of his legless pals. Another arm case, named Shapiro, from the same division, always got a lot of amusement out of the show. Shapiro was a rugged-looking boy from the Brownsville part of Brooklyn. He explained how he felt one day after two Afrika Korps heavyweights had gone through a couple of rounds of grunting, posturing, and slapping. "Every time I see them box, I know we can't lose the war," he said. "The Master Race—phooey! Any kid off the street could of took the both of them."

Shapiro and Sanderson, I learned during one ringside conversation with them, had both been in the Sixtieth Infantry, Molotov's old regiment. They had been wounded in the fighting around Maknassy, in southern Tunisia, early in April, the first serious action the regiment had been in. Molotov had been killed late in April, during the drive on Bizerte, and until I told them, the boys hadn't heard he was dead. I asked them if they had known him.

"How could you help it?" Shapiro said. "There will never be anybody in the division as well known as him. In the first place, you couldn't help noticing him on account of his clothes. He looked like a soldier out of some other army, always wearing them twenty-dollar green tailor-made officers' shirts and sometimes riding boots, with a French berrit with a long rooster feather that he got off an Italian prisoner's hat, and a long black-and-red cape that he got off another prisoner for a can of C ration."

"And the officers let him get away with it?" I asked.

"Not in the rear areas, they didn't," Shapiro said. "But in combat, Mollie was an asset. Major Kauffman, his battalion commander, knew it, so he would kind of go along with him. But he would never have him made even a pfc. Mollie couldn't of stood the responsibility. He was the greatest natural-born foul-up in the Army," Shapiro added reverently. "He was court-martialled twenty or thirty times, but the Major always got him out of it. He had the biggest blanket roll in the Ninth Division, with a wall tent inside it and some

Arabian carpets and bronze lamps and a folding washstand and about five changes of uniform, none of them regulation, and he would always manage to get it on a truck when we moved. When he pitched his tent, it looked like a concession at Coney Island. I was with him when he got his first issue of clothing at Camp Dix in 1941. 'I've threw better stuff than this away,' he said. He never liked to wear issue. He was up for court-martial for deserting his post when he was on guard duty at Fort Bragg, but the regiment sailed for Morocco before they could try him, and he did so good in the landing at Port Lyautey that they kind of forgave him. Then he went over the hill again when he was guarding a dock at Oran in the winter, but they moved us up into the combat zone before they could try him then, so he beat that rap, too. He was a very lucky fellow. I can hardly think of him being dead."

"Well, what was so good about him?" I asked.

Sanderson, who was a thin, sharp-faced boy from Michigan, answered me with the embarrassed frankness of a modern mother explaining the facts of life to her offspring. "Sir," he said, "it may not sound nice to say it, and I do not want to knock anyone, but in battle almost everybody is frightened, especially the first couple of times. Once in a while you find a fellow who isn't frightened at all. He goes forward and the other fellows go along with him. So he is very important. Probably he is a popoff, and he kids the other guys, and they all feel better. Mostly those quiet, determined fellows crack up before the popoffs. Mollie was the biggest popoff and the biggest screwball and the biggest foul-up I ever saw, and he wasn't afraid of nothing. Some fellows get brave with experience, I guess, but Mollie never had any fear to begin with. Like one time on the road to Maknassy, the battalion was trying to take some hills and we were getting no place. They were just Italians in front of us, but they had plenty of stuff and they were in cover and we were in the open. Mollie stands right up, wearing the cape and the berrit with the feather, and he says, 'I bet those Italians would surrender if somebody asked them to. What the hell do they want to fight for?' he says. So he walks across the minefield and up the hill to the Italians, waving his arms and making funny motions, and they shoot at him for a while and then stop, thinking he is crazy. He goes up there yelling '*Veni qua!*,' which he says afterward is New York Italian for 'Come here!,' and '*Feeneesh la guerre!*,' which is French, and when he gets to the Italians he finds a soldier who was a barber in Astoria but went home on a visit and got drafted in the Italian Army, so the barber translates for him and the Italians say sure, they would like to surrender, and Mollie comes back to the lines with five hundred and sixty-eight prisoners. He had about ten Italian automatics strapped to his belt and fifteen field glasses hung over his shoulders. So instead of being stopped, we took the position and cleaned up on the enemy. That was good for the morale of the battalion. The next time we got in a fight, we said to ourselves, 'Those guys are just looking for an easy out,' so we got up and chased them the hell away from there. A disciplined soldier would never have did what Mollie done. He was a very unusual guy. He gave the battalion confidence and the battalion gave the regiment confidence, because the other battalions said, 'If the Second can take all those prisoners, we can, too.' And the Thirty-ninth and the Forty-seventh Regiments probably said to themselves, 'If the Sixtieth is winning all them fights, we can also.' So you might say that Mollie made the whole division." I found out afterward that Sanderson had oversimplified the story, but it was essentially true and the tradition endures in the Ninth Division.

"What kind of a looking fellow was Mollie?" I asked.

"He was a good-looking kid," Shapiro said. "Medium-sized, around a hundred and sixty pounds, with long, curly blond hair. They could almost never get him to have his hair cut. Once, when it got too bad, Major Kauffman took him by the hand and said, 'Come along with me. We'll get a haircut together.' So he sat him down and held onto him while the G.I. barber cut both their hair. And everything he wore had to be sharp. I remember that after the French surrendered to us at Port Lyautey, a lot of French officers gave a party and invited a couple of officers from the battalion to it, and when the officers got there they found Mollie was there, and the Frenchmen were all bowing to him and saluting him. He was dressed so sharp they thought he was an officer, too—maybe a colonel."

Another boy, a badly wounded one in a wheelchair, heard us talking about Mollie and rolled his chair over to us. "It was the field glasses I'll always remember," he said. "From the first day we landed on the beach in Morocco, Mollie had those glasses. He told some fellows once he captured them from a French general, but he told some others he brought them all the way from New York. He told them he used to watch horse races with the glasses; he was fit to be tied when he got to Morocco and found there was no scratch sheets. 'Ain't there no way to telegraph a bet on a race?' he said, and then he let out a howl. 'Vot a schvindle!' That was his favorite saying—'Vot a schvindle!' He was always bitching about something. He used to go out scouting with the glasses, all alone, and find the enemy and tip Major Kauffman off where they were. He had a lot of curiosity. He always had plenty of money, but he would never tell where he got it from. He just let people understand he was a big shot—maybe in some racket. When we were down at Fort Bragg, he and another fellow, a sergeant, had a big Buick that he kept outside the camp, and they used to go riding all around the country. They used to get some swell stuff."

"He never shot crap for less than fifty dollars a roll when he had the dice," Shapiro said, "and he never slept with any woman under an actress." The way Shapiro said it, it was as if he had said, "He never saluted anybody under the rank of brigadier general."

During the rest of the voyage, I heard more about Mollie. I found nobody who was sure of his real name, but the majority opinion was that it was something like Carl Warren. "But he wasn't American stock or Irish," Sanderson said one day in a group discussion. "He seemed to me more German-American." Another boy in the conversation said that Mollie had told him he was of Russian descent. Sanderson was sure that Molotov wasn't Russian. "Somebody just called him that because he was a radical, I guess," he said. "He was always hollering he was framed." "He used to have a big map of the eastern front in his tent in Morocco," another soldier said, "and every time the Russians advanced he would mark it with pins and holler, 'Hey, Comrade, howdya like that!'" One boy remembered that Mollie had won fifteen hundred dollars in a crap game at Fort Bragg. "He had it for about three days," he said, "and then lost it to a civilian. When he got cleaned in a game, he would never borrow a buck to play on with. He would just leave. Then the next time he played, he would have a new roll. Right after we landed in Morocco, he was awful flush, even for him, and he told a couple of guys he'd climbed over the wall of an old fort the French had just surrendered and there, in some office, he found a briefcase with fifty thousand francs in it. The next thing he done was hire twelve Arabs to cook and clean and wash dishes for him."

"I was inducted the same time with him, at Grand Central Palace," an armless youngster said, "and him and me and the bunch was marched down to Penn Station to take the train. That was way back in January, 1941," he added, as if referring to a prehistoric event. "He was wearing a blue double-breasted jacket and a dark-blue sport shirt open at the neck and gray flannel trousers and a camel's-hair overcoat. They took us into a restaurant on Thirty-fourth Street to buy us a feed and Mollie started buying beers for the whole crowd. 'Come on, Comrades,' he says. 'Plenty more where this comes from.' Then he led the singing on the train all the way down to Dix. But as soon as he got down there and they took all his fancy clothes away from him, he was licked. 'Vot a schvindle!' he says. He drew K.P. a lot at Dix, but he always paid some other guy to do it for him. The only thing he could ever do good outside of combat was D.R.O.—that's dining-room orderly at the officers' mess. I've seen him carry three stacks of dishes on each arm."

When I told them how Mollie had been killed, Shapiro said that that was just what you'd have expected of Mollie. "He never liked to stay with his own unit," he said. "You could hardly even tell what battalion he was in."

I was not to see the Army's official version of what Mollie had done in the fight against the six hundred Italians until last summer, when I caught up with the Second Battalion of the Sixtieth Infantry near Marigny, in Normandy. Mollie's protector, Major Michael S. Kauffman, by then a lieutenant colonel, was still commanding officer. "Mollie didn't capture the lot by himself," Kauffman said, "but he was instrumental in getting them, and there were about six hundred of them all right. The battalion S-2 got out a mimeographed training pamphlet about that fight, because there were some points in it that we thought instructive. I'll get you a copy." The pamphlet he gave me bears the slightly ambitious title "The Battle of Sened, 23 March, '43, G Co. 60th Infantry Dawn Attack on Sened, Tunisia." The Sened of the title was the village of Sened, in the high *djebel* a couple of miles south of the Sened railroad station. It was country I remembered well: a bare plain with occasional bunch grass, with naked red-rock hills rising above it. The Americans had fought there several times; I had seen the taking of the railroad station by another regiment at the beginning of February, 1943, and it had been lost and retaken between then and March 23rd.

On the first page of the pamphlet there was a map showing the Italian position, on two hills separated by a narrow gorge, and the jump-off position of the Americans, two much smaller hills a couple of miles to the north. Then there was a list of "combat lessons to be learned," some of which were: "A small aggressive force can knock out a large group by determined action," "Individuals, soldiers with initiative, aggressiveness, and courage, can influence a large battle," and "Confusion is normal in combat." I have often since thought that this last one would make a fine title for a book on war. The pamphlet told how an Italian force estimated at from thirty men to three thousand, according to the various persons interviewed in advance of the fight by S-2 ("Question civilians," the pamphlet said. "Don't rely on one estimate of enemy strength. Weigh all information in the light of its source"), had taken refuge in the village of Sened. G Company, about a hundred and fifty men, had been ordered to clean out the Italians. It had artillery support from some guns of the First Armored Division; in fact, a Lieutenant Colonel MacPherson, an artillery battalion commander, was actually the senior American officer in the action. This colonel, acting as his own forward observer, had looked over the situation and at four in the afternoon of March 22nd had ordered the first platoon of the company to attack. It was soon apparent, judging by the defenders' fire, that the lowest estimate of the enemy's strength was very wrong and that there were at least several hundred Italians on the two hills. Then, in the words of the pamphlet, "Private Molotov"—even his officers had long since forgotten his civilian name—"crawls to enemy position with Pfc. De Marco (both are volunteers) and arranges surrender conference. C.O. refuses to surrender and fire fight continues. Individual enemy riflemen begin to throw down their arms. First platoon returns to Sened Station at dark with 147 prisoners, including 3 officers."

"De Marco was a friend of Molotov's," Colonel Kauffman told me. "It was Mollie's idea to go up to the enemy position, and De Marco did the talking. It must have been pretty effective, because all those Italians came back with them."

"G Company," the pamphlet continued, "attacks again at dawn, first and third platoons attacking. Entrance to town is deep narrow gorge between two long ridges. Town lies in continuation of gorge, surrounded on all sides by 1,000-12,000 foot *djebels* as shown in sketch. (Possible enemy escape route was used by Ancient Romans as park for wild animals used in gladiatorial matches.) Approach to gorge entrance is terraced and well concealed by a large olive-tree grove; five (5) or six (6) field pieces in grove have been knocked out by previous day's artillery fire."

Although the pamphlet didn't say so, the olive groves had once covered all the plain. That plain is now given over to bunch grass, but it was carefully irrigated in the days of the Roman Empire. The "wild animals used in gladiatorial matches" were for the arena at the splendid stone city of Capsa, now the sprawling, dried-mud Arab town of Gafsa, fifteen miles from Sened.

"Company attacks as shown on sketch," the pamphlet continued, "third platoon making steep rocky climb around right, first platoon (Molotov's) around left. Light machine guns and mortars follow close behind by bounds, grenadiers move well to front with mission of flushing enemy out of numerous caves where he has taken up defensive positions. Left platoon, commanded by Sergeant Vernon Mugerditchian, moves slowly over ground devoid of concealment, and finally comes to rest. Molotov goes out alone, keeping abreast of faster moving platoon on right, and assists Lt. Col. MacPherson in artillery direction by shouting."

The combined artillery and infantry fire made the Italians quit. The pamphlet says, in closing, "Italian captain leads column of prisoners out of hills, bringing total of 537 (including officers). Total booty includes 2 large trucks, 3 small trucks, several personnel carrier motorcycles, 200 pistols, machine guns, rifles, and ammunition."

"Mollie liked to go out ahead and feel he was running the show," Colonel Kauffman said. "We put him in for a D.S.C. for what he did, but it was turned down. Then we put in for a Silver Star, and that was granted, but he was killed before he ever heard about it. He was a terrible soldier. He and another fellow were to be tried by a general court-martial for quitting their guard posts on the docks at Oran, but we had to go into action before court could be held. The other fellow had his court after the end of the campaign and got five years."

The officers of the battalion, and those at division headquarters, knew that I was going to write a story about Mollie sometime. Whenever I would encounter one of them, in a country tavern or at a corps or Army headquarters, or on a dusty road behind the lines, during our final campaign before Germany's surrender, he would ask me when I was going to "do Mollie." I am doing him now.

Even after I had been back in the States for a while that summer of 1943, I had an intermittent interest in Mollie, although La Piste Forestière assumed a curious unreality after I had been living on lower Fifth Avenue a couple of weeks. I asked a fellow I knew at the *Times* to check back through the casualty lists and see if the death of a soldier with a name like "Carl Warren" had been reported, since I knew the lists gave the addresses of the next of kin and I thought I might be able to find out more about Mollie. The *Times* man found out that there hadn't been any such name but that there was often a long interval between casualties and publication. I took to turning mechanically to the new lists as they came out and looking through the "W"s. One day I saw listed, among the Army dead, "Karl C. Warner, sister Mrs. Ulidjak, 230 E. Eightieth Street, Manhattan." The juxtaposition of "a name like Warren" with one that I took to be Russian or Ukrainian made me suspect that Warner was Molotov, and it turned out that I was right.

A couple of days later, I went uptown to look for Mrs. Ulidjak. No. 230 is between Second and Third Avenues, in a block overshadowed by the great, brute mass of the Manhattan Storage & Warehouse Company's building at the corner of Eightieth. Along the block there were a crumbling, red-brick elementary school of the type Fusion administrations like to keep going so that they can hold the tax rate down, a yellowish, old-fashioned Baptist church, some boys playing ball in the street, and a banner, bearing a number of service stars, hung on a line stretched across the street. As yet, it had no gold stars. No. 230 is what is still called a "new-law tenement," although the law governing this type of construction is fifty years old: a six-story walkup with the apartments built around air shafts. Ulidjak was one of the names on the mail boxes in the vestibule. I pushed the button beside it, and in a minute there was an answering buzz and I walked upstairs. A thin, pale woman with a long, bony face and straight blond hair pulled back into a bun came to the apartment door. She looked under thirty and wore silver-rimmed spectacles. This was Mrs. Ulidjak, Private Warner's sister. Her husband is in the Merchant Marine. She didn't seem startled when I said I was a correspondent; every American expects to be interviewed by a reporter sometime. Mrs. Ulidjak had been notified of her brother's death by the War Department over a week before, but she had no idea how it had happened or where. She said he had been in the Sixtieth Infantry, all right, so I was sure Warner had been Mollie. "Was he fighting the Japs?" she asked me. When I told her no, she seemed slightly disappointed. "And you were there?" she asked. I said I had been. Then, apparently trying to visualize me in the context of war, she asked, "Did you wear a helmet, like Ernie Pyle? Gee, they must be heavy to wear. Did it hurt your head much?" When I had reassured her on this point, she led me into a small sitting room with a window opening on a dark air shaft. A young man and a young woman, who Mrs. Ulidjak said were neighbors, were in the room, but they went into the adjoining kitchen, apparently so that they would not feel obliged to look solemn.

"Was your name Warner, too, before you were married?" I asked Mrs. Ulidjak.

"No," she said, "Karl and I were named Petuskia—that's Russian—but he changed to Warner when he came to New York because he thought it sounded sweller. We were from a little place called Cokesburg, in western Pennsylvania. He hardly ever came up here. He had his own friends."

"Did he go to high school in Cokesburg?" I asked.

The idea amused Mrs. Ulidjak. "No, just grammar school," she said. "He was a pit boy in the coal mines until we came to New York. But he always liked to dress nice. You can ask any of the cops around the Mall in Central Park about him. Curly, they used to call him, or Blondy. He was quite a lady's man."

Then I asked her the question that had puzzled Mollie's Army friends: "What did he do for a living before he went into the Army?"

"He was a bartender down to Jimmy Kelly's, the night club in the Village," Mrs. Ulidjak said.

She then told me that her brother's Christian name really was Karl and that he was twenty-six when he was killed, although he had looked several years younger. Both parents are dead. The parents had never told her, as far as she could remember, what part of Russia they came from. When I said that Mollie had been a hero, she was pleased, and said he had always had an awful crust. She called the young neighbors, who seemed to be of Italian descent, back into the sitting room and made me repeat the story of how Mollie captured the six hundred Italians (I hadn't seen the official version of his exploit yet and naturally I gave him full credit in mine). "Six hundred wops!" Mrs. Ulidjak exclaimed gaily. She got a lot of fun out of Mollie's "big shot" stories, too. She showed me a large, expensive-looking photograph of him "addressing" a golf ball. He was wearing light-colored plus-fours, white stockings, and brogues with tassels, and there was a big, happy grin on his face that made it plain that he was not going to hit the ball but was just posing. He had a wide, plump face with high cheekbones and square white teeth, and the hair about which I had so often heard looked at least six inches long. "He had a room at 456 West Forty-fourth Street, and a little Jewish tailor down in that neighborhood made all those nice things for him special," she said admiringly. She had never heard him called Molotov.

I went over to West Forty-fourth Street a few days later. The 400 block, between Ninth and Tenth Avenues, looks more depressing than the one the Ulidjaks live on. It is mostly shops dealing in the cheap merchandise that is used as premiums, and stores that sell waiters' supplies, and lodging houses favored by waiters and cooks. It was evident from the look of the house at No. 456 that though Mollie had spent a disproportionate share of his income on clothes, he had not wasted anything on his living quarters. No one at No. 456

remembered Mollie. The tenants and the janitor had all come there since his time. I couldn't find the little tailor. But on the north side of Forty-fourth Street, near Ninth Avenue, there is a building occupied by the Warner Brothers' Eastern offices, and I was sure that this had given Mollie the idea of calling himself Warner.

That evening I went down to Jimmy Kelly's, on Sullivan Street. Kelly's is the kind of club that never changes much but that you seldom remember anything specific about unless you have had a fight there. I had been there a few times before I had gone overseas, in 1941, but I couldn't even remember the bartender's face. Kelly's has a dance floor a little bigger than two tablecloths, and there is always a show with young, sometimes pretty girls imitating the specialties that more famous and experienced performers are doing at clubs uptown, and a master of ceremonies making cracks so old that they have been used in Hollywood musicals. The man behind the bar the night I showed up said he had been there several years and had known his predecessor, whose name was not Molotov. He had never heard of a bartender named Molotov or Warner or Mollie or Karl at Kelly's. After I had had a couple of Scotches and had told him the story, he said he wondered if the fellow I meant hadn't been a busboy. The description seemed to fit one who had worked there. "We all used to call this kid Curly," he said, "but Ray, the waiter who is the union delegate, might remember his real name."

Ray was a scholarly-looking man with a high, narrow forehead and shell-rimmed spectacles. "Curly's name *was* Karl C. Warner," he said after he had been told what I wanted to know. "I remember it from his union card. He was a man who would always stand up for his fellow-worker. Waiters and Waitresses Local No. 1 sent him down here in the summer of 1940 and he worked until late the next fall. He was outspoken but a hard worker and strong—he could carry three stacks of dishes on each arm. A busboy has a lot to do in a place like this when there is a rush on—clearing away dishes, setting up for new parties, bringing the waiters their orders—and a stupid boy can spoil the waiters' lives for them. We had another boy here at the same time, an Irish boy, who kidded Curly about the fancy clothes he wore, so they went down in the basement and fought for a couple of hours one afternoon. Nobody won the fight. They just fought until they were tired and then stopped. Curly had wide interests for a busboy," Ray continued. "When there was no rush on, he would sometimes stop by a customer's table, particularly if it was some man who looked important, and talk to him for ten minutes or so. The customers didn't seem to mind. He had a nice way about him. He had a kind of curiosity."

The Army stories about Mollie's wealth made Ray and the bartender laugh. "He used to come back here now and then during the first year he was in the Army," Ray said, "and always he would borrow ten or twenty dollars from one of us waiters. We would lend it to him because we liked him, without expecting to get it back." A busboy at Kelly's is paid only nominal wages, Ray told me—just about enough to cover his laundry bill—but the waiters chip in a percentage of their tips for the boys. "I guess Curly averaged about forty a week here," he said. "If he was anxious to get extra money, he might have had a lunch job someplace else at the same time, but I never heard about it. A tailor like he had probably made those suits for about twenty-five per. What else did he have to spend money on? His night life was here. He used to tell us he had worked at El Morocco, but we used to say, 'What's the difference? Dirty dishes are the same all over.' "

At the union headquarters, which are on the twelfth floor of a loft building on West Fortieth Street, Mollie was also remembered. The serious, chunky young woman in the union secretary's office said, "Warner was always a dissident. He would speak up at every meeting and object to everything. But we all liked him. He stopped paying dues a few months before he went into the Army, but at Christmas time in 1941 he came back here and said he heard that union members in the services were getting a present from the local, so he wanted one, too. So we gave it to him, of course. The secretary will be interested to know he is dead."

The young woman called the secretary, a plump, olive-complexioned man, from his desk in an inner room and said to him, "You remember Karl Warner, the blond boy with curly hair? He has been killed in Africa. He was a hero."

"Is that so?" the secretary said. "Well, get a man to put up a gold paper star on the flag in the members' hall right away and draw up a notice to put on the bulletin board. He is the first member of Local No. 1 to die in this war."

I thought how pleased Mollie would have been at being restored to good standing in the union, without even having paid up his dues. Then I thought of how much fun he would have had on the Mall in Central Park, in the summertime, if he could only have gone up there with his Silver Star ribbon on, and a lot of enemy souvenirs. I also thought of how far La Piste Forestière was from the kitchen in Jimmy Kelly's.

[May 22/29, June 5, 1943]

# THE ESCAPE OF MRS. JEFFRIES

JANET FLANNER

LAST September, Mrs. Ellen Jeffries, an American expatriate who had lived in France for twenty years because she was in love with it, tardily decided to leave Paris. Actually, Mrs. Jeffries is not her name; nor are any of the other names in this narrative the names of the people involved. In 1942, after two years of the German occupation, she was among the dozen or more die-hards, all women, left over from that colony of about five thousand Americans to whom Paris, during the twenties and thirties, had seemed liberty itself. Since Pearl Harbor, however, detention, *résidence forcée,* or even a concentration camp looked like the inevitable expatriate American way. Or there was flight. By finally making up her mind, on September 1st, to leave, and by moving as rapidly, which in the end meant as illegally, as possible, Mrs. Jeffries managed to arrive in New York the second week of April, 1943. All things considered, including the fact that her travel problems included escapes across two French borders and that escapes are slow-moving projects demanding lots of careful talk first, Mrs. Jeffries, who is forty-five, statuesque, unmelodramatic, New Hampshire-born, a seasoned traveller, and nobody's fool, thinks she made fast time.

Certainly, by last September, it was already better, in Paris, to be conquered French than unconquered American, especially if you wanted to leave it. A trickle of Frenchmen, preferably those who were on food or collaboration business, were given German *Ausweise,* the *Kommandantur* exit visas, which allowed them to cross from Occupied into Vichy France. But no American in Paris last summer was given an exit visa for any reason whatever. The Germans had decided that all Americans were dishonorable. As proof, they pointed out that resident Americans, who before Pearl Harbor had been graciously granted passes merely to visit in the Unoccupied Zone, had from there impolitely run for the Spanish border and home. Even before Pearl Harbor, the Nazis, to keep closer tabs on those who were left in Paris and the environs, had ordered them not to set foot outside the Departments of the Seine and the Siene-et-Oise and to report once a week to their local police station to sign an alien ledger that contained their photographs and data on

*175*

them. After Pearl Harbor, the ladies also had to register at the Chambre des Députés, where the Germans, ironically, had set up their alien-enemy *Büro,* and sign a new Nazi alien-enemy questionnaire that included the optimistic inquiry *"Avez-vous un cheval?"* Two entire lines were reserved for this "Have you a horse?" question. There was no need for the Germans to wonder if American men had horses to donate to the Reichswehr, because all male Americans had been crowded into detention barracks at Compiègne a week after America had entered the war.

In the two years that had passed since the Germans had officially cut France in two, the first, wild seepage of refugees, members of separated families, and soldiers' wives and children across the Armistice demarcation line had settled down into an orderly but illicit commuting, organized, for patriotism or pay, by guides who shuttled back and forth two or three times a week with passengers in tow. Right now nobody seems to know if this smuggling of human beings is still going on, since the Nazis occupy both halves of France. All that is known is that early in February, 1943, the Germans, typically, declared that the demarcation line had been erased but that identification papers or passports, which are precisely what some people either do not possess or most want to hide, must still be shown in order to cross what no longer exists. Early in the spring of 1942 the French were still crossing, for fifty or a hundred francs a head, or for nothing, if poor and in trouble. Then, in May, there was a terrible, little-publicized *rafle,* or raid, on the remaining foreign Jews in Paris, which drastically worsened the chances of anyone's crossing the border. The Nazis ordered that non-French Jewish men, women, and children be separated from one another and sent off, in a new, triple form of segregation, to different camps. When the Gestapo arrived in the Belleville Jewish quarter of Paris to enforce the order, some parents threw themselves and their children, or pushed one another, out of the windows of their homes rather than be separated. A new wild flight of Jews from the rest of Occupied France stampeded the border guides. As a result, the guide fees for everybody, Jew or non-Jew, rose in the tragic competition for flight. Also, the Nazi border patrols, an especially venal lot, boosted their bribery rates or refused to coöperate at all. Then, after the Commandos made their first big Continental raid, on August 19th, at Dieppe, the Nazi restrictions on the movements of the population, which had slackened slightly in the course of two years, suddenly tightened. For passing Jews over the line, guides were shot; passing anybody became more difficult; and passing any English-speaking person became dangerous and thus even costlier. Mrs. Jeffries was automatically a bad proposition, from the guides' viewpoint, because, though a Presbyterian, she was a forty-five-year-old American female and therefore regarded as bothersome if everybody should have to cut and run from a Nazi patrol.

To start dickering for one of these crossings, the regular Parisian phrase was *"Connaissez-vous un passage?"* This was usually addressed to any of the ubiquitous, omniscient, and trusted café waiters who, since the German occupation, have performed a patriotic service and earned a little extra by purveying to Parisians certain anti-Nazi necessities, such as black-market food tips, contraband cigarettes, British radio news, and introductions to border guides. On September 1st, Mrs. Jeffries found her waiter. His first offer was an exorbitant demand for eleven thousand francs from a *type* who, upon a refusal, immediately came down to a bargain eight thousand. As was customary, this proposition was offered by a guide's Paris under-cover, or contact, man, who on an every-other-day schedule got together passage parties of a dozen or more people. The guide furnished transportation, exclusive of railroad accommodation, in the shape of hay carts or trucks for long detours on border side roads, and made arrangements for, but didn't pay for, food and lodging en route. For his aid, integrity, organization, and knowledge of the ropes, he charged an over-all service fee. Most of the guides operated in one of five or six topographically convenient crossing points, of which the eastern, being closer to Paris, were the more popular. The Nazis got around, in rotation, to each exit, for a spell methodically watched it like a cat, then went and eyed another place while the mice scurried out through the unplugged holes. During the first week in September, all the eastern passage points were suddenly reported *brûlé,* or hot. The guides got word, through their grapevines, that the Nazi patrols were searching all buses on roads approaching the eastern border crossings; at the same time the Paris Nazis had a temporary fit of checking the identity papers of all travellers leaving by the Gare de Lyon and the Gare d' Austerlitz. Mrs. Jeffries lay low and passed up the eight-thousand bargain.

By the middle of September the coast looked clear again. Through a second and better-connected waiter, Mrs. Jeffries paid a rock-bottom five-thousand-franc fee to a bold, brown-eyed, young de Gaullist named René, the contact man for a guide, a big farm-owner in the district through which she was to cross. She sent her luggage to Lyons, the first city in the Unoccupied Zone she was aiming for, by train; it is one of the anomalies of life under the Nazis that property has more right of way than people. For the crossing, René advised her to travel light, with only a rucksack on her back, in case she had to run. On September 16th, he told her to meet him at a certain railroad station the next morning at six in order to fight for a seat on the eight-o'clock train, and for the love of God not to talk in public, as her American-accented French was *formidable.* At seven o'clock, by which time Mrs. Jeffries had silently struggled into her seat, René appeared and, busy with last-minute details, asked her to find an extra seat for what he called a friend, who was going with them. Largely by sign language, she wangled a seat in the next coach for the friend, who, from the brief view she had of him, looked to be

French, fortyish, pale, and nervous. After the train had started and she had painfully watched the Tour Eiffel fade from her life and view, she began, irresistibly, to enjoy her journey through rural France. She had not been allowed to travel for nearly two years. Also, she had a fine shoe-box lunch with her. A French woman friend who owned a little place outside Paris had brought her, the day before, three precious fresh hard-boiled eggs, two *pâté maison* sandwiches, and a nearly ripe home-grown pear.

Well before noon and well inside the demarcation border, Mrs. Jeffries, according to plan, got off the train at a small town and walked down the main street to the foot of a hill, where René had said she would find a *bistro*. She found five and, being thirsty, chose the nicest and ordered the customary glass of bad beer. René eventually rolled up in an old Citroën, and with him was the guide. When René introduced her to the guide, Joseph, her stomach, which had turned over in terror whenever she thought about making the crossing, was quieted. Joseph was a middle-aged, bull-necked countryman, paternal, polite, and bustling. René, it developed, was in a hurry to get on to Marseille. The two men had a confidential conversation, but she could not help overhearing some of it, and she gathered that René was on a gun-running job for de Gaulle and that Joseph planned to hide him in the back of the Citroën under some vegetables and drive him to a railway station on the other side of the border, where René would get back on the train he had just got off. The train, she knew, would be held up for hours at the border while the French and German police inspected *Ausweise* and civil papers—which René apparently never fussed with—hunted in the toilets and under the seats for refugees, and searched passengers for contraband. Contraband was anything portable, precious, and personal left after two years of German occupation; it could be love letters, family messages, trinkets, old furs, more money than your visa said you possessed, or fine jewels.

René and Joseph left on their mission, Joseph promising to return as soon as possible. As Mrs. Jeffries sat alone, drinking her beer, the pale Frenchman of that morning's journey came up and introduced himself as Monsieur Georges. Then he introduced what seemed to be the rest of Joseph's crossing party—three French provincial matrons who said they were sisters, a Jewish Frenchwoman with a sick-looking little boy, three melancholy young Dutch Jews, and a French sailor in uniform. As if France had never been defeated or divided, the sailor had spent his leave, as usual, visiting his mother in Paris and was now on his way back to his ship in Toulon. Georges begged Mrs. Jeffries, on account of her accent, not to talk, and then invited her to play *belote,* a talkative card game. Since she didn't know how, he told her the story of his recent life. He had wanted to fight on the side of noble-hearted Russia and so had volunteered to be smuggled from Paris across the border near Lyons and thence to London to join the de Gaulle army as a mechanic. She asked in a whisper whether he was an airplane or a tank mechanic. He said he was neither; he was an expert maker of frames for ladies' petit-point handbags, the sort formerly sold to the American and now to the German tourist trade. He proudly said that it cost the de Gaulle movement twenty thousand francs to smuggle a man like him from Paris to London. He had false teeth, limp gray hair, spots on his vest, and delicate, artisan's hands. Because Mrs. Jeffries was polite, she didn't say she thought that the Fighting French had made a poor buy.

Late in the afternoon, Joseph returned and moved his party to a second *bistro,* one farther up the hill and near a church. Four Gestapo agents were drinking beer at the *zinc.* Joseph claimed that he could spot them a mile off, because the Gestapo invariably wore ersatz tweeds of either a bilious brown or an unpleasant gray, apparently the only choice left to the Germans, and they always shaved their necks and carried briefcases, neither of these habits French. The waiter at the new *bistro* warned Joseph's party not to talk over their drinks and then cracked off-color jokes, which made the three Gallic matrons laugh hysterically. At five o'clock, Joseph led Mrs. Jeffries around the corner to a photographer, who took her picture and made out a false French civilian's identification paper that she would get, complete with her picture, the next day on the other side of the border. He told her that the paper was made out in a Gallic version of her name and warned her not to forget that she was to become, temporarily, Madame Hélène Geoffroi.

Shortly afterward, behind the church, Joseph and Mrs. Jeffries joined the rest of the party, who were huddled against the choir door. Joseph hurriedly piled them all into a waiting butcher's camion and pulled a pair of black curtains tight across the back. Inside they found fragments of suet and dried blood and three more Jews. The camion started off. Five minutes later, Joseph, who was driving, was stopped for questioning by two German patrolmen. Behind the black curtains the three new Jews whispered nervously, which made everybody else even more nervous. Then the Germans said, *"Heil Hitler und merci,"* and the truck set off again. After an hour's drive, the truck stopped, Joseph unbuttoned the curtains, and they climbed out. They were in the country, behind a building that will here be described as an old blacksmith's shop. They hurried inside and were put in a new annex, where apparently machine parts were being manufactured. This part of the shop was not yet entirely roofed over, and for the next few hours the party watched the darkening sky and then the stars. As they sat, they could hear an unseen little river frothing against boulders. Joseph had told them that the river, which marked the border, was where they were to cross into the Unoccupied Zone that night and that the rocks were what they were to cross on. No one, not even Monsieur Georges, talked much. It was better not to say anything about where you came from and it was certainly too soon to discuss where you thought you would eventually arrive. Finally they heard two members of the

German night patrol approach the shop on their first round. Over the noise of the water and their own thumping hearts, the hidden party listened to the German voices lifted in puffing, pidgin French. Apparently the two Nazis were hungry only for conversation, though Mrs. Jeffries heard Joseph offer them chocolate. He did not offer them cigarettes or money, the two other things German soldiers have an appetite for.

The party was to cross at nine. At ten minutes to nine, Joseph brought in a young peasant whom he called his nephew. He looked nothing like Joseph. He was big, stalwart, and dressed only in swimming trunks. Joseph explained that the river was no more than four feet deep and that if anyone fell in, not to scream, because his nephew, who would be standing in the middle, would come to the rescue. "We have him here to tranquillize the ladies," Joseph added gravely. Then, less confidently, he said that the Nazi patrol ought to be a quarter of a mile away by then but that one never could tell about those monsters. Everyone was instructed to crouch while crossing the river, in order to be less visible and a smaller target in case the Nazis came back and started to fire. The party was to cross rapidly and one by one.

Everybody filed out of the blacksmith shop and to the edge of the river. Mrs. Jeffries followed the French sailor. Crossing the river, she could see, on the far side, the pompon of his cap silhouetted against the stars. As she stepped, crouching, on the third boulder, she put one foot on the hem of her raincoat and almost fell in. The unlikely nephew, chest-deep in the water, laughed and whispered, *"Courage."* When Mrs. Jeffries got to the other side of the little river, she ran, still crouching, for a quarter of a mile through a field of stubble. Finally she came to a dirt road that led to a village. Then, as already instructed by Joseph, she turned to the right and knocked at the door of the second cottage. A fat, red-faced young woman opened the door. When Mrs. Jeffries asked if she were Joseph's aunt, she nodded indifferently. Falsehoods and the pounding heart of someone who had just run the line meant nothing to her. Fugitives were a business. Without being asked, she said that Mrs. Jeffries could have a bed to herself for fifty francs. Apparently Joseph, like a capitalist carefully splitting up his investments, had distributed his party all over the neighborhood.

Mrs. Jeffries inspected the bed. It looked filthy and stank in memory of other refugees who had lain on it, maybe trembling the way Mrs. Jeffries trembled now. From her rucksack she took out a bottle of perfume and sprinkled the pillow, and then tried, unsuccessfully, to eat one of the hard-boiled eggs. She went to bed with her clothes on. The combination of the bed smell and the perfume made her sick, but there was nothing in the room to be sick in, so she forced herself to go to sleep. In the morning the fat young woman gave her acorn coffee and a slice of sour gray bread. She took the fifty francs agreed upon and absorbed another fifty as tip because she had not asked Madame to sign a lodger's slip, as the law demands. For fugitives, every evasion of the law is a luxury that must be paid for extra, though unofficial kindnesses often come free of charge.

Joseph had told Mrs. Jeffries to go to the local *épicerie* after breakfast and ask the owner for her false French civilian paper. Like a prestidigitator, the grocer obligingly pulled it out of the inside of his old hat. Then he pointed down the empty road and said, "Joseph said to walk that way. You'll meet a truck." After walking a mile in the mild sun, she sat down under a tree to smoke, to wonder what had happened to the truck, and to look at herself, and her new life history, as Madame Hélène Geoffroi. The photograph was nothing like her and the paper said that she had been born in Normandy in a town she had never heard of. A truck rattled by, stopped, and backed up; it contained Joseph and the rest of his party. "You will never get to New York sitting down like that," he called, and they all laughed excitedly. Everyone, even the melancholy Jews, seemed united by a temporary sort of gaiety because of the success of what they had been through together the night before.

At noon they pulled up at one of those modest country inns famed for generations for its cuisine. The black-market luncheon proved to be finer than anything Mrs. Jeffries had sampled since France fell—multiple hors-d'œuvres, delicious local trout (it being Friday), grilled chops, two vegetables, ripe cheese, fruit compote, and a serious Burgundy. Monsieur Georges, who sat beside her, remarked how wise he had been to put his false teeth in his breast pocket before the crossing. He had been afraid that, as he jumped for the rocks, the teeth might fall out of his face. Mrs. Jeffries paid a luncheon check of seven hundred francs, or seven dollars. The waiter had regarded Georges as her husband and had put him on her bill. After the tasty barley coffee, the chef-owner of the place came in to receive compliments on his food. He said that he had run a *fin bec* restaurant at Menton until the Italians came but that he did not like macaroni cooking. Being both an artist and a patriot, he had moved away.

After lunch, Mrs. Jeffries and Georges, who were bound for Lyons, said goodbye to the rest of the party. Where the others were going, or trying to go, they alone knew. On saying goodbye to Joseph, Mrs. Jeffries thanked him with real emotion. He must have been used to that. All he said was *"Ce n'est rien, Madame. A votre service."* He was going back to the *bistro* on the hill and tomorrow night he and another party would be crossing the river. A local guide named Jean, who did odd jobs for Joseph, was detailed to the Lyons contingent, which was joined by an elderly Serb underground worker. They were to sit up in the restaurant until three in the morning, walk to the nearest railway station, and catch an early train for Lyons. There Jean would introduce them to a certain café, where a patriot (as in French Revolutionary times, today all the pals among *le peuple* are patriots) would tip them off to some safe rooms to live in. As Madame Hélène Geoffroi, Mrs. Jeffries tried to show her false paper to the ticket taker at the station next morning. Though under orders from the Vichy police to check up on all travellers, he didn't bother to glance at her forgery, which disappointed her.

Owing to a saboteur's wreck on the main line, their train was four hours late, and they wearily arrived at eleven in the morning at the Lyons café. There a peppery young Fighting Frenchman, Marcel, who had expected only Jean, and him on time, flew into a temper at the sight of an unexpected American woman, an unexplained old Serb, and the unwelcome Georges. As one of the local Fighting French authorities, Marcel ordered Georges back to Paris because he considered him something de Gaulle would not have as a gift. Suspicious and arrogant, Marcel then shut up like a clam, refusing aid to any of them. Apologetically, the Serb offered Mrs. Jeffries the address of a compatriot's boarding house that was reported to have nice food. With her rucksack still on her back, she took three wrong trams to the outskirts of Lyons, walked up four long, wrong streets, and finally managed to arrive, weeping with fatigue, at what turned out to be an ordinary French lodging house for men workers. "Ah, if Madame were only not a woman," the patriot proprietor wailed. He nevertheless offered to give her lunch in his barracklike dining room, where about a hundred workmen were already feeding. However, as the Serb had prophesied, the stew was excellent. While Madame was still reviving herself on it, he walked in. He apologized for intruding and said he had worried about her. It occurred to Mrs. Jeffries at that moment that for the past two years in Paris she had lived her quiet, expatriate, familiar existence without difficulties and also without anyone's help. In Lyons she was a stranger and in a bad way. It was over her stew that she realized that the war had indeed reclassified people; that to those in trouble people had now become very kind or very cruel or as indifferent as stones. At the Serb's kindness she started crying again.

Like friendly homing pigeons, Mrs. Jeffries and the Serb returned to the café. It was closed. From behind the door the owner shouted that the police were expecting an anti-Vichy riot and to get off the streets, quick. Mrs. Jeffries and the Serb ran down the street. At the first hotel they came to, he pushed her in and, still running, disappeared. When she asked for lodging, the woman at the desk calmly offered her a bathroom to sleep in. The city was jammed; the annual commercial fair, the famous Foire de Lyon, was opening that week, just as if war and riots were routine and just as if the fair would show something besides ersatz. When Mrs. Jeffries handed over her false French civilian paper, which, if she spent the night even in a bathroom, would have to be copied on a *fiche* to be presented to the police the next morning, the woman said sharply, "French? With that accent?" Mrs. Jeffries, a poor liar, lamely murmured that she had been brought up in America. "You should say that with more conviction," the woman replied, and put the *fiche* into a desk drawer. Alarmed, Mrs. Jeffries casually strolled out onto the street, then ran back to the café, where, on the deserted sidewalk, the Serb and the angry Marcel were arguing. Marcel became even angrier when she told him of the suspicion that her false French paper had aroused. He declared that since she was an American she hadn't needed such a paper in the first place, that her Parisian *carte d'identité* sufficed in Vichy France, and that if the woman squealed, all of Joseph's papers forged by that particular photographer for foreigners who did need them would become hot. While tearing up her Geoffroi paper, he forbade Mrs. Jeffries to return to the hotel. When she said that she had to sleep somewhere and that she hadn't had her clothes off for two nights, he unexpectedly apologized. Rather grudgingly, he invited her to stay the night with him, explaining that he was sleeping, *sub rosa,* in a collaborationist uncle's flat, and that both he and she would have to be up and out before seven the next morning, when the uncle was returning from a big business trip. Marcel said that his family were bitterly divided; half were de Gaullists like himself and the other half were like the rich, Pétainist, avuncular swine. While they were still talking, the café reopened, and she was able to get a much-needed glass of weak beer. Apparently the riot had been called off.

That evening, after dinner, she took a Saturday-night bath in the collaborationist's luxurious bathtub. Next morning, early, she made both beds, as womanly thanks for the hospitality, and by seven Marcel had installed her in the center of Lyons in what called itself a hotel but was really three floors of furnished rooms over a side-street shop. The hotel did not register its lodgers on any *fiche* and had no breakfasts, hot water, or closets. The clothes cupboard in her room was a length of pink cretonne stretched diagonally across one corner on a string, not nearly big enough to hold her clothes when she picked up her trunk, which had come through more easily than she had. She was to live in this room for the next eight weeks, which was the length of time it would take her to get the solemn, legal papers necessary for her to leave France illegally. The Nazis have upset the law, the logic, and the sense of humor of all Europe.

After the dramas of German occupation that were constantly shaking Paris, Mrs. Jeffries had expected to find life dull in Lyons. However, once she had accepted the difference between the French attitude toward recent history that she had known in Paris and the attitude that she found in Lyons, she had an undeniably stimulating sojourn. In Paris the French had been against the Germans. In Lyons, which the Germans were not to march into until nine days before she left, the French were still enjoying being against other French. Lyons proudly rated itself the most excited and exciting city in Unoccupied France. Certainly bombs in the Royalists' Action Française newspaper offices, in Pétain's Legion headquarters, and in Laval's recruiting stations, where French workmen were being enrolled for labor in Germany, were regarded as commonplaces, and so were street riots and clashes between the silk-mill hands, the brutal Darlan police (modelled on the Gestapo), the Vichy police, and the Lyons police, in all possible combinations, and so, too, were arrests, escapes, denunciations, plots, and counterplots. The Lyonnais subsisted on the violences indigenous to their city, which was the Unoccupied receiving end of whatever was shipped out of Germany on the Mulhouse express and whatever sneaked out of Paris on the P.L.M. *rapide*. For the underground anti-Nazi groups in France, Lyons was the reckless halfway house between northern France and Marseille. In Lyons gun smugglers dictated reports to their confidential secretaries and provided the customary fifty-thousand-franc fees to complacent guards who would wink at a lucky comrade's escape from some Occupied prison, saboteurs held conferences like good businessmen, and draftsmen made blueprints for railway wrecks.

Lyons was the first Unoccupied stop for the escaping Jews, old and young, who never ceased rolling down from the north. The Cathedral's archbishop, Monseigneur Gerlier, boldly adopted a hundred of the foreign Jewish children who had been torn from their parents and sent to concentration camps after a Vichy roundup that had netted ten thousand Jews. French prisoners from Germany who had been wounded by the R.A.F. bombers arrived at the Lyons railway station in coaches which the Germans had carefully labelled *"Blessés par les avions anglais."* One day, in the station, a trainload of returned French war prisoners just arriving from Germany patriotically threw stones, with all their weak strength, at a trainload of French workmen who, with what even the non-collaborationist French at first esteemed equal patriotism, were just starting off to Germany in exchange for the incoming prisoners.

The various patriots' cafés in Lyons functioned as forums, checkrooms, and occasionally dormitories for patriots' out-of-town friends, their suspicious-looking packages, and their girls. In one of the cafés there circulated a young patriot who was, for his underground group, the official killer of members who squealed. He was green-eyed and handsome, had been a gigolo in a well-known Montmartre *boîte* formerly enjoyed by American tourist ladies, had nervous, beautiful hands that itched at the sight of money, and was, his comrades reported, excellent at what they called serious jobs but unreliable at details or organization, which bored him. He dressed in what he thought was the perfect English manner, but he always looked a little too neat. His father was an electrician. The killer dreamed of a France of the future in which, after the Americans had won, he and his father would install expensive American radios in every house in the nation.

In the patriot groups, generosities were fantastic and not uncommon. Among those who were really working for *la patrie,* aid and money were handed around as if both were magnificently uncostly. The traditional French grip on the banknote seemed finally to have been loosed in a gesture of desperate, tardy patriotism. A thousand francs, or five or ten thousand, could always be raised to send some Frenchman on one of the many militant jobs of *les services* (which is what the underground movements are called), in which the success of a man's assignment could often be proved only by his being imprisoned or shot. Because resistance needs equipment, especially scarce in a land where the conqueror has swept the shelves bare, the cash boxes of *les services* had to be kept overflowing. Even to hire a rope long and strong enough to help a comrade escape from the third story of a prison cost twenty thousand francs, or two hundred dollars at the black-market rate of exchange. Wild and naïve schemes flourished among the patriots, and often worked. One morning, Mrs. Jeffries was wakened at her rooming house by a youth who claimed to be an American and said that his father had been a Yankee soldier in the last war. And did the American lady want to go back to New York in a submarine or on a bomber? He could send her free in either one if she could leave in a half hour. She felt that she could not dress so quickly.

When the Americans finally, in the invasion of Africa, on Sunday, November 8th, took their first strategic step toward Europe, Mrs. Jeffries, who had then been in Lyons seven weeks, got the news at breakfast in her favorite patriots' café. The owner came to her table to tell her and offer his felicitations. The clients cheered her. Americans were rare in Lyons and together she and the good news made it a great occasion. "Pétain ordered us to retreat! If we'd only retreated far enough, now we would be in Africa with the Yanks!" one Frenchman shouted to her. When she took out a package of old, bootlegged Lucky Strikes, she was cheered again. To the Lyonnais the Luckies seemed positive proof that the Americans had actually arrived from across the Atlantic.

During the next two days, Lyons seethed with excitement and what turned out to be mistaken preparation for its new role in France's history. The city, in response to a radioed appeal from General de Gaulle in London, busily prepared a reckless Fighting French street demonstration for Wednesday, which was Armistice Day. Instead, on Wednesday, the Germans marched in, en route for Marseille and eventually Toulon. At ten o'clock that morning, when Mrs. Jeffries walked out of her rooming house to have breakfast, she found, instead of a de Gaulle parade on the Place Bellecour, Vichy police circling in a protecting ring around a dozen Germans with machine guns, ready, if necessary, for the sullen crowd that had gathered. All day the Germans poured through in camions with equipment which looked old and used and "nothing like 1940," the Lyonnais jeered with satisfaction. But the Germans continued to pour through the city all night, and what was rushed past after curfew in the dark was, as anyone who dared peer out from behind his window curtains could see, powerfully shining and new. There were miles of unscarred tanks, trucks, and troop carriers packed with jolted, drowsing Nazis, gleaming swarms of buzzing motorcycles, and lumbering contingents of immaculate, stiff-necked guns. By morning, German *Kommissäre* were domiciled in requisitioned hotels, including the town's finest, the Grand-Nouvel. At first the Lyonnais would not believe their eyes and insisted that the Germans were only resting, *de passage*. Then the city realized that it was occupied. No one in Lyons had seen more than one egg a month for half a year. When the news got around that the Germans were really in residence, the black market unfroze, Lyons swarmed to its restaurants, and there was a binge of five-egg omelets which produced a municipal bilious attack. To make sure that the Nazis wouldn't get so much as one yolk, Lyons ate its entire stock of thousands of stale eggs in twenty-four hours flat.

Mrs. Jeffries had left Paris, on September 17th, just in time. On September 24th the Paris Nazis had arrested her remaining American women friends and shipped them for detention to a hotel in the Vosges spa town of Vittel. Now Mrs. Jeffries felt that the Germans, in occupying Lyons, were catching up with her too. On November 18th, a week after they had come, she went with her American passport to the Spanish Consulate and asked for a Spanish visa, the fourth and most difficult of a quartet of permits upon whose accumulation and synchronization a traveller's departure from France depended. These four legal treasures, coming in time, were wings on a refugee's feet, but late, they could be like stones around a refugee's neck, pulling him down to destruction. The first permit was dependent merely upon the possession of a *carte d'identité* and a passport, and each succeeding one upon the one before; the first, third, and fourth were good for only a month; and it could take three months to obtain the whole set, during which time, just as the fourth was granted, the first and third could expire, and the process, through a series of renewals, would have to start all over again. In despair, some refugees killed themselves after a losing race to make their *papiers* come out even, and others, who had enough money to live on through a first lengthy paper-stamping period of hope, became penniless during the second attempt and, unable to escape, eventually rotted in jails or concentration camps. In war-racked, refugee-ridden Europe, people are no longer people, they are their papers.

In the seven weeks she had been in Lyons, Mrs. Jeffries had with diligence accumulated and kept up to date the first three of her permits. The first was her *permis de séjour* from the Rhône prefecture, allowing her to remain in Lyons, where she had no business to be in the first place and where the Vichy police might nab her. Lyons was a refugee bottleneck, so European fugitives were denied *permis* by the hundreds every day, but Mrs. Jeffries, favored as an American by the municipal clerks, some of whom, from the Vichy viewpoint, hadn't yet got into line, obtained her *permis* after only a week of obstinate finagling. Once she had this No. 1 stamp, she could safely go to the Sûreté and ask for her stamp No. 2, a Vichy France *visa de sortie*. Vichy's visa took four weeks. Paper No. 3 was her Portuguese visa, good for only a month, which took two weeks to obtain and on the possession of which her subsequent Spanish visa, also good for only a month, depended. Spain, which is politically worried and physically undernourished, allows no foreigner to enter unless he has stamped proof that he means to hurry right out again, usually to Lisbon and its airport, Europe's last exit. On November 18th, when Mrs. Jeffries asked the Spanish Consulate clerk for her visa, he informed her that (a) Spain had that day mobilized its army, (b) he had heard that the Spanish border was in consequence closed, (c) he had heard that it was open twice a week but that the trains were booked so solidly that no one could get on one for six months, (d) he had heard it was open for one hour every afternoon to pass mail and telegrams only, and (e) he knew it would take ten days for the *señora* to obtain a Spanish visa unless she wished to make him, as she had implied she would, a gracious gift of five hundred francs for the Spanish poor, in which case she could have her visa the day after tomorrow.

Mrs. Jeffries gave him the five hundred francs and two days later he gave her the visa and the official information that the border was indeed closed tighter than a trap. However, he reminded her that in Spain, as in most of contemporary Europe, her visa, paradoxically, would be honored even though she entered the country by stealth. He kindly suggested that she go and look around in the French border city of Pau. Pau, Mrs. Jeffries knew, was the trading center for the mountaineer guides who, for a terrific price, walked their refugee clients over the Pyrenees into Spain.

On November 20th, a little over two months out of Paris, Mrs. Jeffries unhooked her rucksack from underneath the pink cretonne curtains in her rooming house and started for Pau. Her train trip from Lyons to Pau, which would have taken about sixteen hours in peacetime, took the wornout French locomotives twenty-four hours on France's dilapidated railroad tracks. Mrs. Jeffries was lucky; she had a seat for the entire journey. The late November rains, which are southern France's version of early winter, had set in. Her second-class coach was overcrowded, unheated, and damp. Whenever her feet felt congealed in her inadequate, wooden-soled sandals, which are what most women in France now have to wear, she sat on her feet, like Buddha, which most French women have of late learned how to do.

In Pau the only place she could find to sleep was a maid's room under the mansard of a third-class hotel. For two years all the first-class hotels of Pau, the capital of the Basses-Pyrénées, like those of the so-called Unoccupied key cities, had been occupied by the German Gestapo and Armistice Commission. Now, since the Nazis had made the occupation official, the second-class hostelries had been booked for the oncoming German Army *Kommandanturen*. Her first three days in Pau, Mrs. Jeffries found no French face which she wanted to trust with her peculiarly personal question, "Pardon me, but do you know anyone who could smuggle me across the Spanish border?" After the rebellious air of Paris and the violence of Lyons, the sullen atmosphere of bourgeois, once-fashionable Pau was not encouraging. The city seemed indifferent to the war, which had never really touched it; hardened to its Germans, who had come with defeat; and annoyed at America's North African invasion, whose first military achievement, as far as Pau could see, was the cutting off of the city's best black-market green-vegetable supply.

Mrs. Jeffries hoped to avoid walking across the mountains into Spain. She had tried to find in Pau one of the local patriot *cheminots,* who, like thousands of their fellow railroad workers all over France, were helping to resist the Germans by helping anybody who hated them, and by carrying messages for underground *services,* transporting their agents, sidetracking shipments to Germany, chalking tortoises (the symbol of slowdowns) on every piece of freight, sabotaging, passing fugitives in good standing, and the like. Mrs. Jeffries hoped to arrange for a ride across the Pyrenees to Spain in a nice freight car. But the superb, skillful patriotism of the *cheminots,* which everyone in France knew about, had finally become too familiar to the Nazis, and, in a typical, Hydra-headed plan, they had decided to kill the French railroad men's resistance movement, and further paralyze the French people's ability to move about, by inviting twelve thousand French railway workers to go to Germany, since too many German railroad men were on duty in Russia. By the time Mrs. Jeffries began to get her bearings in Pau, dozens of the district's *cheminots* were already in concentration camps for turning down the German invitation to travel, the railroad grapevine was in disorder, and the stowing away of an American woman in a box car was out of the question.

All in all, for the first twelve days Mrs. Jeffries was in Pau, it seemed impossible to find someone to smuggle her out in any way whatever. The smuggling had to be done by guides, arrangements for whom were made by contact men, and no contact man was willing to load a woman onto his unsuspecting mountaineer guide. It was a tough walking trip over the Pyrenees, the Pyrenees' passes being on the whole higher than those in the Alps, and the guides wanted no females, especially one who was forty-five and an American to boot. No one really wanted to smuggle Americans of either sex, because for two years Americans had been as rare as hens' teeth around Pau and so were material for comment. In the first week, after getting a foothold in a good assortment of cafés, high and low, Mrs. Jeffries was refused admittance to over two dozen passage parties she'd heard about. The second week she concentrated on contact men who made appointments only at night; they seemed more responsible, as they usually held respectable office jobs by day. An insurance clerk pessimistically refused to try to pass her or anybody else, because fifty Frenchmen he had helped pass the week before had been caught by the Spaniards and were already back home again and under surveillance; they were white-collar men and students who, since the American invasion, had been eager to go to North Africa, join the French forces, and *"refaire la guerre avec les frères américains."* A kindly, hard-up Swede made a contact for her, and got an offer for an immediate crossing at twenty thousand francs. He thought the fee was too high, and while he was still haggling with the contact man, the party started off for the mountains.

Finally, in a lively café that specialized in B.B.C. news broadcasts, tuned down to a whisper, Mrs. Jeffries discovered a native waiter who had escaped from a prison camp in Germany and who offered not only to seek a contact but, in his enthusiasm, to lend her the money, if necessary, for a passage, which he said ordinarily cost from two to ten thousand francs but for her would be astronomically higher. He was still looking for a passage at any price when, on November 24th, the German Army trucked in and occupied Pau. Three days later the French garrison there was demobilized. That night the waiter told her that after France fell the French soldiers had been mostly anti-British and pro-Vichy. Then, after the Dieppe Commando raid, he said, the men had turned around and wanted to *rejoindre les Alliés*, too late. The American invasion of Africa had added to their fever to fight the Germans again. As an answer to this pro-Allied sentiment, the Germans, in one swift blow delivered everywhere at once in Unoccupied France, in one day demobilized all that was left of what had once been France's army, thus scattering the men and their rebellious hopes and turning what had been men with guns into eighty thousand defenseless unemployed, ripe for shipping to Germany's labor camps. The waiter said that in Pau that morning, while some of the French officers wept, the Germans had simply ordered the French soldiers to fall in line, stack their arms, and fall out as civilians because the French Army no longer existed. Back in their barracks, where they had providently hidden a cache of pistols, the soldiers tied the weapons under their ill-fitting, baggy breeches and got away with them, prepared for the great day when the Yanks would invade France. What uniforms the demobilized soldiers did not have on their backs were gathered up by the Nazis and sent to Germany to add to the Nazi wool pile.

On her twelfth day in Pau, Mrs. Jeffries decided that at least she would be ready and properly dressed for a crossing at a moment's notice, should an offer come. She had shipped her trunk there from Lyons, and it was still at the railway station, waiting baggage-car room on a train to Spain. An amenable porter let her open it and take out the warm clothes she wanted, change into them in the dirty ladies' toilet, and pack the light clothes she had taken off. With her ski boots in her hand, she walked out of the station dressed in a tweed skirt, wool stockings, sweater, scarf, topcoat, and mittens, and nearly roasted en route to a second-hand bookshop, where, it was reported, the proprietress ran a smugglers' travel agency on the side. There she got a too prompt, over-enthusiastic reply. The woman said *"Oui"* and in the same breath demanded fifty thousand francs for a crossing with a group leaving the next morning. She said that the trip would be de luxe, with donkeys to ride up the lower slopes and only two hours of what she called promenading on the peaks. Mrs. Jeffries, who had nearly forty thousand francs left in her pocketbook, declared, with equal airiness, that she had only thirty-five thousand francs on earth, and walked out. When she returned to her hotel, the concierge whispered to her that the Gestapo had called, requesting her to appear at the *Kommissäriat* the next morning. Mrs. Jeffries ran back, sweating, to the bookshop, and the woman big-heartedly accepted the thirty-five thousand francs.

The plan for crossing the Pyrenees into Spain was simple. All Mrs. Jeffries had to do was appear with her rucksack at the bookshop the next morning, pick up a contact man, go with him to the station, and board a certain southbound train, on which, before it started, the bookshop woman's husband, coming in on an earlier northbound train from border business, would find them. The husband would inform the contact man what town they were to get off at, which guide was to take the job, which taxi-man to trust, and other vital details. The husband's train was late. Mrs. Jeffries' train was about to depart and the contact man was hanging nervously out the window when the husband, from the window of his train, arriving on the next track, shouted, "Not now! Tomorrow night!" It was an additional letdown for Mrs. Jeffries to realize that she didn't have a room to spend the next thirty-six hours in. The bookshop woman warned her to keep out of the cafés, as that was where the Gestapo always looked first. She recommended a humble *pension* where no one asked questions or names. Mrs. Jeffries got a room that had a broken window, through which, as special preparation for the crossing, she caught cold.

Mrs. Jeffries and the contact man left Pau by another train the following evening, and in the last vestiges of daylight they got off at a way station and stepped into a waiting taxi and into the company of three men who apparently were to cross with her. All three spoke French with a slight accent and all three immediately protested that she spoke French with a heavy accent and was a woman besides. All three, furthermore, violently agreed that an American woman in the party made the crossing look like a dangerous job. After an hour's quarrelsome ride, the five of them stepped out in the dark into what smelled like a farmyard and fumbled their way into a low building. They were in a sheepfold, together with the warm sheep. The contact man departed. Ten minutes later he returned and said that the coast was clear. He led the party outdoors and, after a brief walk, into a cottage, pleasant and immaculate, which turned out to be the guide's. Their guide, a man named Boniface, who ran a speakeasy in his parlor, where he sold rum by the glass, had just said good night to his last customers. He was big, blond, and dignified. He accepted the surprise of having an American lady with taciturn calm. His young wife served the party a superb supper of black bean soup, an omelet of fresh eggs, a whole roasted baby lamb killed for them that day, goat cheese, strong mountain wine, and a warm loaf of home-made white bread. It was the first white bread Mrs. Jeffries had seen in two years and it tasted like manna.

The bookshop woman had talked of donkeys and a two-hour stroll on the peaks; at the station her husband had mentioned a truck and a four-hour walk. Now Boniface warned them that they would walk on their own legs for fifteen or twenty hours, from the time they left his front door until they slid downhill into Spain, that along the line there was an ascent of seven thousand feet, and that at least one or two nights would be passed in shepherds' huts, unoccupied because of the season of the year. Boniface himself was to take them about three-quarters of the way and then hand them over to a Spanish guide who would meet the party en route. One of the three male travellers, who before supper had formally introduced himself under a fancy French name, angrily declared that he was returning to Pau with the contact man to complain about the American woman, to complain about the distance over the mountains, and to demand his money back. After he had slammed the cottage door on his way out, one of the two remaining men, a dark little fellow, said sadly that his friend would unfortunately be back, that both his fine name and passport were false, that he was really named Fishbein and was a crooked Strasbourg Jew, and that he himself was a Polish Jew named Kowalski.

Kowalski was, he said, a watchmaker; he had become a naturalized Frenchman eighteen years ago and had spent his savings of a hundred thousand francs to get himself and his wife from Paris, via Toulouse, to Pau. Three days ago the Germans had literally kicked the Kowalskis out of their room in Pau, torn him from his wife, and said that she could sleep under the bridges. Madame Kowalski had a weak heart, which would not permit her to walk over the mountains. He could do nothing but leave her there, wondering if he would ever see her again. He was going to try to get to Tunisia and join up as a chauffeur for the American soldiers. The hitherto silent No. 3 of the party, a blond, blue-eyed young man, then said that he would not tell his name or nationality until they reached Spain. When Mrs. Jeffries laughed and said he was a German, he laughed, too, in self-conscious surprise. He said that he planned to tell the American consul at Madrid that he was an American and so get to Casablanca. Then, in broken English, he said to Mrs. Jeffries that his mother's sister lived in Yorkville and gave her name and address. After they had all retired for the night, Mrs. Jeffries was unable to sleep at first because there was only a thin partition between her room and the room occupied by the two men and the German kept her awake with his haranguing.

Next morning breakfast was brought up to the travellers. They ate together in Mrs. Jeffries' room, at her invitation. They were forbidden to go downstairs all day for fear the parlor grog customers, who twice daily were augmented by the Nazi patrol, would see them. Over their hot milk and grain coffee, the blond young man, who had weakened in his resolve at least to the point of calling himself Hans, was still talking. He declared that the whole thing looked like a middle-class swindle to him, that he was an anti-Nazi Socialist who had been in the Foreign Legion, that that cow of a woman in Pau had gypped them all, that he had paid her what she called a bargain price of thirty-five thousand francs because his cousin had paid the same the week before, that the two Jews, because they were Jews, had each had to pay fifty thousand francs, that God alone knew what Madame the American had had to pay, and that out of this fortune the noble Boniface, who did almost all the work and took almost all the risk, received only two thousand francs for the whole job. At noon the noble Boniface brought up a dozen fried eggs, with ham, and said that the other *monsieur*—Fishbein, or whatever his name was —had better return from Pau that day if he expected to cross into Spain before spring. A shepherd down from the uplands had just reported that snow was expected in two days; when it arrived, the pass would be closed for the winter. Fishbein, arrayed in a brand-new mountain-climbing outfit of glossy brown corduroy, turned up for a cold lamb supper.

On the following day, the party set off in the blackness just before dawn. The slopes of the foothills were steep, slippery with dried grass, and tiring. Mrs. Jeffries, who hadn't eaten as well in two years as she had during the past two days, was short of breath. Boniface vainly kept urging speed; until they reached their first stop, at a shepherd's hut, a few hours up, they would be in danger of encountering the French customs guard, a neighbor of Boniface and a law-abiding man. They came to the hut just before noon. Boniface forbade them to kindle a fire for fear his *douanier* would see the smoke. In the confused haste of departure, no one had remembered to take along water. A lunch of cheese and chocolate made them thirstier. While they rested, Boniface, who had to meet a rum-smuggling friend, walked off into the panorama of soaring granite slopes like a man going to keep a business engagement just around the corner. It was nearly dusk when he returned with a jug of icy mountain-torrent water and bad news. The Spanish guide, who was to meet them the next day, was *brûlé;* the Nazi patrol was after him and anyone else loose on the mountains. Boniface ordered the party to lie low and spend the night where it was. The hut contained a shelf on which the shepherd, when he was with his flock in the summer, slept on a pallet of bracken. It was too late in the year for bracken, so Mrs. Jeffries slept on the bare boards. The four men slept on the floor.

Daybreak was magnificent in the circus-shaped valleys below, but Boniface was too familiar with the view to waste time on it and was impatient to start the big climb. That day they walked nine hours single file, stopping twice to eat chocolate and bread. All morning the men begged Mrs. Jeffries not to hold them back but to walk faster. By noon only Boniface was still striding along easily. They had left the fan-ribbed plateaus for the Pyrenees' upper reaches and were ascending the gullies that marked the next portion of their route. Once Mrs. Jeffries lit a cigarette, but she quickly found that she was too busy walking to smoke. The gullies, which were the beds of torrents in spring, became rougher and steeper and the stones they walked on rolled in little avalanches underfoot. To maintain her balance, she had to keep her eyes on the toes of her boots and on the heels of the boots in front of her; this gave her something to concentrate on and steadied her. Like a man showing off the local sights to a visiting lady, Boniface politely pointed out to her evidences of his rum runners—the charred wood of a fire under a sheltering rock and later, in a gulch, a broken cask, which it made her thirsty to look at.

A soft rain started and then turned to sleet. Fishbein, who was hung about with small luggage, entreated Mrs. Jeffries to shelter under her topcoat a card-board box that he said contained noodles, though it felt heavier to her. By four they entered the pass, seventy-five hundred feet above sea level, which Boniface had been aiming for. On the boulders beside a waterfall at which they stopped to drink, they found whiskers of ice that were refreshing to the throat. Here Fishbein emitted a series of questions he had apparently been storing up during the plodding, single-file silence of the day. Did Boniface know if you could get good prices for Moroccan food in the black market in Marseille? How much could you get for English gold sovereigns in Lisbon? Was it true that saccharine was selling for two thousand pesetas a kilo in Madrid, and did he know anybody on the other side of the border who had ever heard of the stuff? "We have heard enough, Monsieur," said Boniface, "to know that saccharine is so scarce in Pau that the cafés serve it already dissolved in bottles, like sugar water. Here in the mountains, when war comes, we use honey. From father to son we have smuggled rum. *Ça, c'est notre droit.* But we never smuggled dirty things like drugs, even sweet ones." He turned to Mrs. Jeffries. "Give him back his package," he ordered. She handed it over, saying she supposed that Fishbein, after all, was not fool enough to ask her to lug noodles over the Pyrenees and that the box was too light for gold but probably heavy enough for saccharine. Fishbein didn't look at the other men, but he laughed at her and took back his box with alacrity.

At sundown, an increasingly cold wind revived Mrs. Jeffries' New Hampshire blood and gave her second strength, but it seemed to exhaust the already weary men, who begged Boniface, at whose heels she was sturdily treading, to slow down, for the lady's sake. Just before nightfall they reached a second shepherd's hut, also vacant. It proved to be comfortably large; its shelf was big enough for all four travellers to throw themselves down together to rest, close, indifferent, exhausted. A while later, after cheese and chocolate, Mrs. Jeffries uncorked a flask of armagnac she had brought with her, Hans produced a jar of jam, and Kowalski passed around a box of biscuits. There was a spring by the hut but no bucket, so they leaned over the pool and drank from their dirty hands.

At four the next morning the Spanish guide arrived with his dog and a Basque friend. The three had walked all night in contempt of the Nazi patrols, who didn't know their way around in the dark. The Spaniard, who looked like an American Indian and was a taciturn man, grunted what little he had to say in a very limited French. The dog was affectionate. The Basque spoke fluent French and carried a hunting gun, forbidden in France since the armistice. He said that he had brought it along for any game birds he might encounter but that he preferred to shoot at the Nazi patrols; in the mountains their corpses were never found. In the dark and another rainstorm, they started off on their two ways, big Boniface to go alone back home and the crossing party on toward invisible Spain. The party now included two mountaineers, but in the damp darkness Mrs. Jeffries' real guide was whatever light neck scarf was visible in front of her. The Spaniard, who led the way, was nervous and stopped to listen a lot. Just before dawn they walked past a big stone house, inside which a dog barked. No one, however, came outdoors to see what was up. Long after sunup the gullies still gleamed with the ice that had formed in the night. By noon Mrs. Jeffries' pack—her rucksack and a small overnight case strapped to it with her belt—seemed so heavy that she could scarcely breathe in the thin mountain air. Apologetically she offered the mountaineers a thousand francs if they would carry her luggage. The Spaniard reluctantly took the money. The Basque refused at first to accept her banknote; *tout de même,* he said, he was only a friend, not a guide entitled to pay. Then he gave in.

By two o'clock the party had almost reached the Spanish border. The Spaniard then thought he heard a Nazi patrol and hastily ordered the travellers to slide down a series of gulches. The stones, as Mrs. Jeffries' skirt rolled up, cut her bare thighs. It took the party two more hours to zigzag their way up the side of a mountain to get back on the trail again. Just before they came to the border, their route was strewn with morsels of torn paper. These were the fragments of passports that escaping Frenchmen, who probably aimed to pass themselves off as French-Canadians, had destroyed, as the last proof of their national identity. Hans was not surprised to find a piece of his cousin's forged French passport behind a rock. A tall, impressive stone monument, with "France" carved on the north side and "España" on the south, marked the border line. The party rushed a few feet into Spain and started laughing. They had arrived and felt safe. Hysterically, the German, the Pole, and the Alsatian began asking the American Mrs. Jeffries' advice and shouting their immediate plans. Hans asked if he might become her brother in Spain, since he was going to be American anyhow. It seemed to her a good idea. Fishbein and Kowalski said that they would declare themselves French-Canadians, since they spoke no English. Fishbein said that Quebec was the popular birthplace these days and Kowalski was enthusiastic, though he couldn't remember the name and kept asking Mrs. Jeffries, "Where was it that I was born?"

Their gaiety vanished when their escorts refused to go any farther. The Spaniard and his friend had walked all night, they lived over on the next ridge, and they had to bring another party across the next day, if the snow held off. Mrs. Jeffries, Kowalski, and Hans each offered first the Spaniard and then his friend a thousand francs to continue, but Fishbein wouldn't offer anything. Both escorts haughtily refused to accept any more money, but they nevertheless accompanied the party another mile to the brow of the mountain. There the guide pointed to a settlement far below. He told his party to go to a house with a wire fence and ask for the friend of José. The two mountaineers and the dog then turned on their heels toward home.

In the scattered settlement, which the crossing party reached before dusk, no one had heard of José or his friend, and the first three dwellings Mrs. Jeffries and the men came upon all had wire fences. At the third, a tall, elderly Spanish shepherd with two tall young sons hospitably took them in. His cottage consisted of a single room, without illumination except for two resin torches stuck in iron rings beside the fireplace. The room opened into a haymow. While the sons stared in embarrassment, Mrs. Jeffries took off her sweater and skirt by the fire and changed to a rumpled flannel dress. The father gave the visitors bread and two bottles of dark wine, for which he would take no money. He and his sons then sat down at a small table and ate their frugal supper of cabbage soup from one pitifully small pot. There was apparently no other food in the house. The hungry party slept in the haymow and next morning washed in a brook.

By eight o'clock, Hans and Kowalski, who had gone forth to see what sort of hamlet they were in and how they could get out of it, had already been arrested. Fishbein came running into the cottage with the news, plucked his precious cardboard box and bags from the corner in which he had placed them, and plunged into the haymow. For a few minutes Mrs. Jeffries heard him burrowing. She never laid eyes on him again.

Two youthful, smiling members of the *guardia civil,* wearing cocked hats, walked in, quite sociably, with the arrested men. Mrs. Jeffries was not arrested, because she had a passport, but she was detained for questioning. She heard Hans, in Foreign Legion Spanish, tell the police that he was her *hermano,* Frank Jeffries, of Nuevo Hampshire. Kowalski said nothing; he merely looked sad and fatalistic. Neither of them had papers to prove or disprove anything they might say. Hans claimed that their papers had been stolen. Both believed the popular French legend that there were British and American consuls at the big, nearby town of X and that these officials had the magic power of transmuting men, willingly without a country, into British and

American soldiers and transporting them to fight on the North African front. There was some discussion between the young policemen of whether it would be correct to let the three foreigners hire a cart to take them to the nearest village jail, ten kilometres distant, or whether they should walk. Kowalski, the only one who had any Spanish money, paid a hundred pesetas for the use of their host's cart. They reached the jail at four.

At the jail the two men were searched for dangerous instruments and Hans's nailfile was taken from him. He stuck to his story that he was Mrs. Jeffries' brother, young Jeffries; neither he nor Mrs. Jeffries had stopped to think, though the village police chief thought of it right away, that as a Jeffries he could at best be only her brother-in-law. The chief, who seemed to be in a dither, said that he had been swamped by ninety so-called French-Canadians in five days and that his jail was full. *Sotto voce,* the two members of the *guardia civil* suggested to the *americana,* whose pocketbook they had just searched for forbidden foreign monies, that, if she wanted to rid herself of her two thousand illegal French francs, accommodations could perhaps be had in the village's crowded hotel for the night for her relative, friend, and self, and how many rooms would they want? Hans and Kowalski humbly whispered, "One room for us all would be fine." Mrs. Jeffries said oh, for the love of God, could she room alone for a change?

Mrs. Jeffries was granted the luxury of solitude. Her room contained an enlarged photograph of a young man whom the proprietress bitterly described as her last and littlest brother, shot by Franco. Three others, she said, had died as Loyalist soldiers during the Civil War. She advised Kowalski and Hans to write that night to the British and American consuls in Madrid and say that if they never turned up to look for them in the stinkhole jail in the town of X.

The bus to X the next morning contained Mrs. Jeffries, Hans, Kowalski, and eighteen arrested Frenchmen who still hoped to get to North Africa to fight alongside the Americans. Most of the eighteen were advance-guard men and had groups of followers waiting in France to start if and when the chiefs got safely through. An ex-Army officer on the seat beside Mrs. Jeffries was a de Gaullist volunteer who had been arrested in Dakar and sent to a prison camp in Pétain's France, where he had learned English and Spanish from other prisoners and, like them, lived on carrot tops. Thirteen of his comrades there had starved to death. When some food packages from home finally came through, five of the men gained enough strength to escape from the concentration camp. He said that the friends of the American lady were lucky not to have been arrested till morning; he and twelve of the others in the bus had spent the night in the village calaboose in a room with a privy in it; the room was so small that five men took turns standing up while eight men lay on the floor. They had been given no food for twenty-four hours. When the French officer discovered that Mrs. Jeffries was that rare traveller, one whose passport and papers were actually in order, she instantly became, in his eyes, a sort of emissary extraordinary. The unreasonable European conviction in a crisis that Americans are saviors who can think of everything and get anything done swept through the bus when the prisoners saw the officer start scribbling on bits of paper. As fugitives, and experienced rebels, they guessed' what that meant; he was trusting her with the names and addresses of Spanish friends who might intercede for him if he was imprisoned. Immediately all the men tried to crowd around her in an eager, swaying mass, to give her their own touchstone addresses or their mothers' names. Would she write *Maman,* would she even write President Roosevelt? Most of the men were fliers. One ex-captain had five hundred pilots back in France waiting a chance to fly American fighting planes; the group in the bus included everything from two frightened students who didn't want to be sent to work in Germany to a retired artillery colonel. All the Frenchmen implicitly believed that the British and American consulates could get them through Axis Spain and over to Allied North Africa, which they admitted would be a miracle if it came off but a disgrace if it didn't.

The two amiable members of the *guardia civil* had told Mrs. Jeffries, probably to please a lady, that she was *en libertad* and that there was an American consul at X. At the X police station, which, Spanish fashion, reopened for business at ten o'clock at night, she learned that the nearest British and American consulates were at Madrid and that she certainly was not at liberty. Furthermore, as the police department's problem child, she was put at the end of the night's docket for special questioning, not because she had entered Spain illegally but because her papers were suspiciously O.K. She sat in the station-house till midnight, helplessly watching and hearing Hans and Kowalski and all eighteen militant Frenchmen from the bus interrogated into jail. Seventeen of the eighteen declared, while the Spanish roared with laughter, that they were born in Quebec. The retired artillery colonel, who wanted to be different, said he had been born in Winnipeg. Mrs. Jeffries felt very sad when she said good night to Kowalski, whom she promised to visit in jail next day, and to Hans, whom she kissed on both cheeks to strengthen the brother-and-sister story. The police, after studying her papers and questioning her, told her to return in the morning and sent her to a hotel, where a housekeeper was assigned to watch her closely. At 1 A.M. she took off all her clothes for the first time in four days. Her feet had bled when she was crossing the mountains and her thighs were still lacerated from sliding down gullies. Then she took her first bath since leaving Lyons.

The next morning Mrs. Jeffries discovered that though she was in Spain physically she was not there officially and that though she had money in her pocket she was penniless. She had crossed the border with exactly fifty dollars in American currency and a Banque de France draft for two hundred pesetas. No one in X would touch her greenbacks, American money being too illegal in provincial Spain even for the black market. No bank would cash her draft, which was drawn on a bank in the Spanish border town of Canfranc, across the Pyrenees from Pau. The Spanish police refused to admit that she was in Spain at all, because Canfranc, and not X, had also been put on her passport as her Spanish port of entry by the accommodating Lyons Spanish Consulate clerk, who was obliged to write down some entrance town and knew that she was planning to smuggle herself across somewhere in the neighborhood of Canfranc. This clerk had also told her that her draft would be good anywhere in Spain and that she need never set foot in Canfranc. Now it looked as if she wouldn't even be allowed to, since, on top of everything else, her hotel refused to let her leave town unless she paid her bill. The police, on the other hand, wouldn't let her stay in town unless her entry visa was stamped at Canfranc first. The police unsentimentally advised her to raise some cash by selling her wedding ring, which she still wore. That noon, in the hotel corridor, a courtly, middle-aged Spaniard made her a remarkable speech in French which began, "I am not very rich." In it, he explained that he had heard of her sad case and would she permit him to lend her the money for her hotel bill and her journey to Canfranc? When, in her gratitude, she offered him her ring as security to cover his fantastic offer, he refused it. His only request was that the American *señora* post from Lisbon a love letter to his fiancée, aged thirty-five, who for ten years had lived in Rio de Janeiro. At that moment he seemed to Mrs. Jeffries the most quixotic, romantic, and kind man in the world.

Spanish trains, because of a shortage of equipment, run into a terminal point one day and out of it the next. X was such a point and this was X's out day, so Mrs. Jeffries left that night at six for the town of Saragossa, which was south, and there she had to wait from midnight till six the next morning for a train to Canfranc, which was north. Two other hotel guests, who also had port-of-entry and money complications at Canfranc, made the trip with her. They were a German-Jewish couple travelling as Catholics on false French passports, which were nothing but sheets of typewriter paper stamped with visas for which, being Jews, they had been forced to pay ten times what Mrs. Jeffries had paid. The couple were desperate because their Portuguese visas, without which their entry visas into Spain were not valid, had just lapsed and they feared, with justification, that they would be sent back to the Nazis in France. By the time Mrs. Jeffries cashed her draft and arrived at the police station in Canfranc to get her passport stamped, the couple's Spanish visas had, indeed, been invalidated and they were speechless with terror. In this state they numbly refused to act as interpreters for an even more tragic female compatriot, just picked up by the police, who could not figure her out. Through Mrs. Jeffries' questionings in halting, high-school German, it was revealed that this woman was Jewish, from Frankfort, and sixty, and had four American dollars and thirty French francs to her name, plus a sister in New Jersey and a ticket

to Palestine on a ship that had sailed from Barcelona the month before. The
police had temporarily saved her life by arresting her in the border hills; she
was in a daze, her feet were frozen, her luggage consisted of a string shopping
bag, and she claimed that she had crossed the Pyrenees alone. Her mind was
still wandering. She thought that Canfranc, which is in the mountains, was
Barcelona, which is on the sea. Mrs. Jeffries took her to a restaurant and fed
her. In the midst of the meal she whispered reproachfully, "I have never eaten
any but kosher food," and hid some morsels of broken bread in her shopping
bag. After coffee she tried to pay her half of the check. Later the police said
that they had no choice but to return her to France, though Mrs. Jeffries
cajoled, stormed, made a scene, and prophesied that they were sending the
old woman back to a very disagreeable death.

From Canfranc, Mrs. Jeffries wearily took the train back to Saragossa. That
evening, at the Saragossa station, where she was to catch the express for
Madrid, she again met, to her surprise, the Jewish couple, shaken but hopeful.
They had been able to "arrange things" with the Canfranc police. To pay for
their tickets to Madrid, they were selling a heavy gold chain to the station
lunch-counter woman, who really did not want to buy it; she said that this
sort of jewelry only reminded her of the troubles everybody had been through.

Mrs. Jeffries, at least, was fortunate enough to have three pesetas left when
she arrived in Madrid, so she was able to take a tram to the American consulate. There she found a comforting letter of credit, a Clipper reservation,
and loving, questioning letters from her worried New Hampshire family.
Then the troubles of the world at large and of the Spaniards in particular,
with civil war behind them and poverty ahead; the nightmare, somnambulistic
existence of refugees, all trying to wake up outside of the continent of Europe;
the xenophobia of embittered, hungry Madrileños; the Puerta del Sol prison
across the street from one of the nicest cafés in town, and the fourteen other
city prisons with anxious crowds hovering nervously at the gates; the sick
faces and shabby clothes of the city's poor—the whole costly, cruel Fascist
pattern of life began closing in on her again. In Madrid the penniless political
prisoners were dying in rocky cells underground and up on the streets life
was even more expensive than it had been under the German occupation in
Paris. She spent a hundred and thirty dollars in eight days in Madrid, though
all she did was pay her debt to the Quixote in the hotel in X, buy one necessary pair of bad stockings for $3.50, live *en pension* with poor meals and no
butter at the second-class Hotel Nacional, and purchase food packages for the
now-imprisoned middle-aged Jewish couple, who, whatever they had arranged
for themselves in Canfranc, had not been able to make it stick in Madrid. She
received a pathetic postal card from Hans, in a concentration camp with
Kowalski at Campo de Miranda de Ebro, in the mountains. Like a man of the
modern world, he said that it was not a bad concentration camp, as camps
went, and that the American consul had sent him neither passport, uniform,

nor food. In a faint, pencilled postscript in English he added, "I am kold. Write soonly. Your brother, Frank J."

It took a full eight days and ceaseless scurrying for Mrs. Jeffries to renew her Portuguese visa, which had lapsed, and to obtain a precious temporary extension of her Spanish visa until the new Portuguese stamp was obtained. The complications of special police papers, which the Franco administration had built up like a towering wall against foreigners, whom it was supposed to keep from staying in the country, in the end merely made it more difficult for them to leave. For forty-eight hours she stayed in her hotel because the Madrid police had taken and held her passport. In the Europe of today, to walk around without your passport buttoned in your pocket is as abnormal as it would be to walk around without your heart beating in your body.

Ignorance, revenge, and bureaucracy in all their contemporary European forms made Mrs. Jeffries' days in Madrid a seesaw of uncertainty. Until her last hour there she did not know when she would leave or why it could not have been sooner. No one in any country in Europe knows what is going on in the country next to it; international trains, whose movement formerly seemed as sure as the sun's, are now spoken of as if they could disappear off the face of the earth once they crossed a border. Officials themselves, who have people's lives, documents, and plans in their hands, know little that is exact, except that whatever they know can change by breakfast tomorrow. In place of certainty there is only a vast, tangled ball of rumor. In place of sensible, humane procedure, now destroyed by wars, revenge, suspicion, and power politics, petty official strictures have been built up against which the individual is as helpless as a caged animal. Because Mrs. Jeffries had lived in so-called Communistic France under the Front Populaire, which favored the Spanish Loyalists, a high-up Spanish Fascist official spitefully delayed signing one of her papers, which made her miss the night express she was scheduled to take to Lisbon. Because she had lived in non-interventionist France under the Radical Socialists, who had imprisoned refugee Loyalists, a lower-down Spanish Republican concierge maliciously made her miss the next night's train.

Mrs. Jeffries had been officially told that the Madrid-Lisbon sleeping compartments cost seventy pesetas and could be arranged for only with the porter on the train; rumor told her that the compartments actually cost thirty pesetas at the railway station but were sold there only to Spaniards. She got on the train Monday, December 21, 1942, with seventy-five pesetas in her pocket and discovered that the porter demanded eighty for a berth. Fortunately, an Englishman in the crowded day coach had the eighty and was willing to spend it, so at least she was able to get his seat. She had been officially told that she could take a hundred pesetas from Spain into Portugal. Next morning, at the Portuguese border, a Spanish customs inspector told her she could not take even her seventy-five pesetas out, that all of it had to be left behind for the poor of Spain. A jovial Spanish policeman advised her to spend her money for breakfast in the station. She spent her pesetas for her breakfast and for his, too. The policeman drank a cup of coffee and a bottle of anisette.

After the harshness of Madrid, Lisbon seemed soft. After the acute astringencies of the rest of Europe, Portugal seemed only pinched. The hotels and bars of Lisbon, the last diplomatic freehold on the Continent's all-important Atlantic coastline, were full of Turks, Americans, English, Poles, French, Germans, Scandinavians, Swiss, Iranians, South Americans, and a medley of decorated buttonholes, uniforms, medals, spies, oil men, ambassadors, black-market agents, legation attachés, political secretaries, and Berlin *Damen* who, if they had any chic at all, were sized up as tarts doubling as *agents provocateurs*. Mrs. Jeffries passed Christmas Day in bed, reading a second-hand copy of Voltaire's "Candide," which is now having a popular revival among Lisbon's international, war-worn misanthropes, possibly because it cynically describes the city's calamitous earthquake of nearly two hundred years back as being (like Europe's new disasters?) something that was "all for the best in the best of all possible worlds."

Mrs. Jeffries had supposed that she would leave Lisbon, and all Europe, shortly after New Year's Day. However, an early January Clipper reservation was cancelled, owing to the priorities of diplomats and generals. As the weeks went by, she was squeezed out again and again by diplomats' secretaries, lend-lease agents, and the military. Along with a growing crowd of patient, unimportant civilians, Mrs. Jeffries, awaiting her turn, saw the winter out and spring established in Lisbon before she was at last lucky enough to get another Clipper passage for the first week in April. Seven months after Mrs. Jeffries had left Paris, she left Europe and started flying, roundabout, toward the United States. To get to New York from Lisbon she flew to Portuguese Guinea, and from there to Fisherman's Lake in Liberia, where the passengers lunched on fried pork chops a few steps from the equator. From there she flew the South Atlantic to Natal in Brazil, then to Belém in the same country, then north to Port of Spain in Trinidad, on to San Juan in Puerto Rico, to Bermuda, and, on her fourth day in the air, to LaGuardia Field, wet but welcome in an April shower. She had never flown home before. It didn't seem quite right to land in New York without first sighting the Statue of Liberty.

[August 21/28, September 4, 1943]

# EIGHTY-THREE DAYS

MARK MURPHY

ABOUT four-thirty in the afternoon of November 2, 1942, a certain fast Dutch luxury liner with clean, handsome lines was torpedoed and sunk several hundred miles off Recife, on the coast of Brazil. Only a few of the more than four hundred persons aboard this ship survived. Three of them were Basil Dominick Izzi, a second-class seaman of the United States Navy, and Cornelius van der Slot and Nicko Hoogendam, both Dutch merchant seamen, who together drifted on a raft until January 24, 1943, a day short of twelve weeks after the sinking, before they were picked up by a Navy PC boat. In the months that followed the rescue, Seaman Izzi, a small, husky Italian-American boy of twenty, whose home is in South Barre, Massachusetts, first went through a long period of convalescence and then made a speaking tour around the country, telling workers in factories about his adventure. I spent a good deal of time with him during this tour, and out of the many talks we had I was able to piece together the story of his remarkable eighty-three days.

Izzi was a member of the United States Navy armed guard assigned to the Dutch ship. The guard, made up of young men from all parts of the United States, was an efficient and slightly obstreperous one and was under the command of Ensign James Shaw Maddox, a former college instructor. Izzi was the pointer on a four-inch gun, a responsible job. The ship, loaded with ammunition, food, and Army officers, put out from Brooklyn in July. She stopped at Recife to pick up water and food and set out for Cape Town. Off Cape Town, she joined a British convoy. The convoy put in at Cape Town for a couple of days and then set out for the Red Sea. It broke up there, and the Dutch ship made a run to Ismailia, on the Suez Canal, alone. She unloaded and came back to Cape Town, where she stayed for three days to load cargo. Izzi and a few friends got leave there. Izzi shopped for presents for his family. He bought some painted silk pillow cases for his mother, ivory bracelets for his four sisters, ivory-handled knives for his two younger brothers, and a huge-bowled English pipe for his father.

On October 18th, Izzi's ship, having loaded ore, hemp, and flax, took on

202

more than two hundred passengers. Most of them were survivors of torpedoed ships—Navy and merchant-marine officers, members of Navy armed guards, and merchant seamen. On November 1st, Izzi and some of his pals reckoned that they were thirteen days from New York, and they began to talk about shore leave. That day an airplane circled high above the ship. The boys in the armed guard couldn't identify it but thought that it was a friendly one and that the next day they would probably meet and join a convoy. The following day, a bright, pleasant one, the boys spent cleaning and painting the ship's guns. "I was on a detail on the port side painting our thirty-seven millimetres," Izzi recalls. "Me and three other fellows got finished painting them about three-thirty in the afternoon and we thought we'd go aft where another detail was working on our four-inch gun. They had got the gun scraped and were putting red lead on her when we went to look at them. We razzed them for a while, and they threw a wrench at us, and so me and Jensen, Joudy, Labe, and Satterwhite, fellows in my detail, went back to our quarters to play some five-hundred rummy before we went to chow. Joudy went to take a shower, and Labe, a kid from Fall River, and myself were partners against Jensen and Satterwhite. Labe wasn't much good, but we weren't playing for money and so it didn't matter much. We played about three hands and a radio man named Lorenz came in. He said we were three or four hundred miles off the coast of Brazil and then he lit a cigarette and started talking about things in general. We told him to scram, that we didn't want to listen to his stuff while we were trying to play cards. Now it's about four-fifteen or four-thirty, and so he walks out, and we play a few hands more. Jensen is dealing, and bam! we get hit. I holler, 'Jeez, right under us!'

"We all rushed out of the cabin, leaving Joudy in the shower. We forgot all about him. It was just around the corner from our quarters to the main deck, and the first fellow I bump into has his hands over his head, and I looked up and water and wreckage was falling down over him and us. The hallway filled with water and wreckage and we couldn't get out. So we hollered, 'Everybody back and through the lounge.' There were about five of us and we shoved through to get to the guns. Some people on the ship were hollering and screaming, scared as hell, but most of them were calm. The whole place had a horrible smell and it filled up with smoke. We got outside and were running to the guns, and I noticed the ship's crew letting go the rafts over the side, but the ship was still going, making headway, and that's how we lost a lot of our rafts.

"We got to the guns. They were in order. I went to my cabin to get my life jacket. When I got there, I looked and found that Joudy had got out, so I grabbed my jacket and went back to the gun. Our room was a wreck—chairs broken, pictures down, everything in pieces.

"Ensign Maddox, our gunnery officer, was on the bridge, and he gave us a range of two thousand yards, figuring, I suppose, that that would be about where a submarine would fire from. The gun crew were working. I was at my position, and the talker—he's the fellow with the things on his head who talks to the bridge—said to Maddox, 'Loaded and ready, sir.' We were loaded and ready and I was set to pull the trigger, but there wasn't any submarine that we could see. Then bam! another torpedo hit us, hit us again right on the port side. This knocked out the communications between the gun and Maddox, on the bridge. That second one shook hell out of us. Men were trying to get the lifeboats loose, and they did get the ones on the starboard side down, but the ones on the port side were damaged by the explosions. A ship's officer came by and said, 'Don't get nervous, boys.' That sounded funny to me, and I had to laugh."

The four-inch-gun platform was high above the deck at the stern of the ship. Izzi and his companions stayed there for a while as the ship, her superstructure twisted and awry, began to sink, bow first. As the bow sank, the stern lifted, and soon the gun was useless, pointing up in the air. One of the boys said, "Let's get out of here," and they dropped down to the deck.

Izzi had on only a pair of dungarees, so he ducked into the ship's laundry, which was right below the gun deck, and grabbed the first shirt he saw. He put the shirt on, not bothering to tuck it in under his trousers. "Jensen and Joudy, my best pals," Izzi said, "were standing on the deck at the stern, and it was raising up higher all the time. Men and wreckage were in the water, and now and then you could hear a fellow scream. I couldn't figure whether to jump from right where I was or move thirty or forty feet forward and *walk* right into the water. I decided I'd better get out of there quick, and I looked down and yelled to some fellows swimming below me to get out of the way. They cleared a space, and I grabbed the top of my life jacket with both hands so when I hit the water it wouldn't come up and break my neck, and I jumped. A fellow came right behind me and landed on top of me, and I thought I never would come up.

"The old ship was going fast, so I swam as hard as I could to get away from her in order not to be sucked under. The last thing I ever saw of her was her twin screws sticking out of the water. There was a lifeboat right near me. When the ship went under, bow first like she was diving, she made a noise like a waterfall, and there was a great big wave. The wave lifted the lifeboat up against the sky and I could see her and everybody in her.

"The sea was choppy. There were a lot of little bamboo rafts floating around, and pieces of hatch covers that had been blown out in the water by the explosions, and people were hanging on to the rafts, which were built to give a man some support but not to carry him, and to the hatch covers and to any piece of wreckage they could find. I came across Jensen in the water and we grabbed one of the bamboo rafts and began to kick it along in the water." Two of the three lifeboats on the starboard side of the ship got safely into the water. The third capsized but was finally righted. All of them were overloaded. "It was kind of tough to see the lifeboats put up sail and go away," Izzi told me, "but they were jammed as it was and they couldn't have done anything for us. You couldn't help but think, though, about how with a little luck you might have been one of the guys in those boats that were going some-place."

Jensen and Izzi clung to their bamboo raft. Ensign Maddox floated by, hanging on to another raft, and Izzi and Jensen yelled to him. He reached out and grabbed the boys' raft. The three of them tried to tie the two rafts together with pieces of rope on them but couldn't manage it because of the choppy sea. Maddox asked Izzi and Jensen if they had seen the other boys of the gun crew, and they gave him the names of a few men they had seen drift-ing on wreckage. The open and swelling sea makes for loneliness, for a man in the water might be ten feet from another and not see him. If he calls, he is likely to swallow salt water, and even someone floating near him cannot tell which direction he is shouting from. Hundreds of men were struggling and dying in the water that warm afternoon, and yet only a few saw anyone else.

After a while, Jensen swam away toward a piece of wreckage that looked a little safer than the raft, but Izzi and Maddox stayed together. They later drifted near a larger bamboo raft on which lay two men who said that they were unable to swim. They had no life jackets and were frightened. Maddox and Izzi let go of the smaller raft and clung to the side of the larger one. Then four other gunners, Joudy, Labe, Satterwhite, and Autripp, swam up to the big raft and clung to it, too. Soon they were joined by three or four other men. Desperately, the men tried to gather other wreckage and tie things together to make themselves a haven for the approaching night. The two men who were lying on the raft would not move from their positions, because they were sure that if they fell into the water they would drown. Izzi borrowed a clasp knife with a single, long blade from one of them, to cut rope to bind the sev-eral rafts together. After he had finished, he kept the knife. "It started to get dark," Izzi said, "and then you began to hear the hollering and the cries again. A fellow would yell, 'I'm over here,' and another would cry back, 'I can't see you.' It was not so cold, not so warm, and the sunset was red in the sky, and then a wave would lift you high and you could see the sun setting on the horizon."

The few pitifully mismated pieces of wreckage—the flimsy bamboo rafts and ungainly hatch covers—the men had been able to lash together constantly broke apart, and the men had a hard time bringing them together again. The men were not too well protected from the elements, for many of them, includ-ing Izzi, had taken off their shoes and dungarees in the water. All had swal-lowed at least a little salt water in the rough sea and that made them feel ill. Most of the men wore life jackets, which were hard and uncomfortable, and now and then a wave would drive one against a man's neck or chin and add a sharp pain to his weariness and sickness. "Once in a while," Izzi said, "a guy would drift away. Maybe he thought of a better place to go, or maybe he got tired and quit, or maybe he just went to sleep. Then you would hear guys hollering for help, screaming that sharks were attacking them, and there was nothing you could do, and then maybe they would stop screaming, and you wouldn't hear them after that, or maybe a guy would stop right in the middle of a yell and you would know that something certainly got him. Pretty soon there was left just me, Joudy, Satterwhite, Autripp, Labe, the two men on top of the raft, and Mr. Maddox. Those of us who were in the water struggled, hanging on to the big bamboo raft. Then about midnight, things began to happen to me.

"I was hanging on to the raft, and I looked over to the left and there was a wall, a fairly tall stone wall, and I could hear the water lapping against it. I *knew* that if there was a wall over there, there was sure to be land behind it, so I started to swim over to it. Joudy left the raft and pulled me back, and I hung on for a while longer. Then about half an hour later I looked over to the left again, and there was the wall and behind it were some big towers for high-tension wires, and I knew that this must be near civilization, so I started for the wall again and Joudy brought me back again, although I could hear the water lapping against the wall and I knew that it was there. The way it seemed to me, it really *was* there. I could see the wall and the waves hit against it and bounce right back. And each time I started out for it, Joudy brought me back."

Then Izzi began thinking about Coca-Cola, and he began talking about it, and then he could feel it going down his throat. "I thought I was on a motor-boat," he said, "going a mile a minute, it was so fast. There was a driver up front and I asked him, 'Where are you taking me?' He didn't say anything but just kept driving fast, and pretty soon I got the idea of where we were going. We were going to a night club across the lake. The stars were big and close and they looked like the lights on a ship, and they blinked like the lights on a ship, and I was sure there were ships around us. Then I smelled some smoke and I noticed a big hole near me, where guys were going down for a cigarette. I felt like a cigarette, and I said to Joudy, 'Johnny, I'm going down for a smoke, down to where all those guys are coming up from smoking.' Joudy hauled me back to the raft again."

Then Izzi saw the wall once more, and behind it were the high electric towers, just like the ones that run through the woods behind his home in South Barre, and this time there was a lunchroom behind the wall, too. It was a white one, the sort of place that sells mainly hamburgers, pie, doughnuts, and coffee. Izzi could see fellows going in and out of the lunchroom, and now and then a truck would stop and the driver would get out, go in, and sit on a stool. Izzi wanted some coffee and he set out for the stand. Joudy hauled him back. "You can't go there now," Joudy said. "You got to stay here. It's orders. We'll all go over there in the morning."

Then Izzi saw the stern of the torpedoed ship, clearly outlined in the bright, starry tropical night, rise out of the sea. The whole after half of the ship rose out of the water and levelled nicely. As Izzi watched, he saw men swim over to the ship and climb a ladder up to her deck, where the cook gave them bacon and eggs. "I thought we were on a detail," Izzi said. "I thought we were out here in the water doing some sort of a job, and I could see these other fellows going in and getting something to eat. I saw the bread on the mess tables and the cook and the messmen handing out the food and fellows going and sitting down. So I called over to Mr. Maddox, who was still hanging on to the raft, and asked him if we all couldn't go in and get something to eat, and change our clothes, smoke a cigarette, and then we would all come back out here. He said he didn't think we would all come back out here. He said he didn't think we had better go, and then I asked him how about my cup of coffee. Couldn't we have some messman bring us out one, the way he would do if we were out a cold night on watch? Mr. Maddox said, 'Tomorrow morning, Izzi, we will all have eggs and coffee.' I couldn't see why we shouldn't all go in and get some rest and come back tomorrow and finish the job. Joudy kept me at the raft, holding on to the top of my life jacket and pulling me back whenever I started to leave."

Throughout the night, Izzi kept seeing his wall, riding in the motorboat, and pleading to be allowed to go back to the ship for some coffee. He was not the only one to suffer from hallucinations. Satterwhite, a North Carolina boy who once had auctioned tobacco, thought he saw a hill. "Satterwhite got to talking," Izzi said, "about this hill. The swells really made you think there were hills nearby. He said, 'Come on, we'll go over that hill, and I know some German spies who have a place over there. I know them pretty well, and they'll treat us swell. We'll get us plenty to eat from them, all fixed up.' He convinced Autripp that there was something over the hill and they both started to leave. I yelled at Satterwhite and Autripp, 'Are you crazy?' That made Satterwhite mad, and he swore at me, and he and Autripp swam away. Nobody had the strength to try and stop them."

Izzi began to talk to Joudy about Coca-Cola, and the wall, the motorboat, the power lines, the lunchroom, and the ship. Joudy, holding firmly to Izzi's life jacket, would reply, "Stick with us and tomorrow we'll get all we want." Then Izzi heard a man yell, "Balance it, balance it!" over and over. This might have been a man on a raft yelling instructions to a companion, but to Izzi it sounded as if it was addressed to him and it had an authoritative, uncanny tone. He couldn't understand what the voice meant, what he was supposed to do when the man told him to balance it, whatever it was. After a while he saw a man writing figures in a book, and he was puzzled. "This sort of thing went on all night," Izzi said. "The wall, and then the power lines, and then the hamburger stand, and then the ship, and then this guy writing the figures down, two columns, fast as hell, in that book he had. Once in a while the other guys would see a ship or a fellow would yell for coffee and butts. Now and then a guy floating around on a hatch cover would bump into you and stick around for a while. A small moon came up, and the phosphorus in the water was like stars, and the stars in the sky were beating down on you, all different colors, like spotlights, and that's what happened all that night. Sometime toward the end of the night, I came to and I was all right again."

Shortly before dawn a star fell, looking like a flare shot from a ship, and some men near Izzi's raft yelled that a vessel had come and was going to save them. Off in the distance, a few men were raving and wailing. "Just before the sun came up," Izzi said, "we bumped into another gun-crew officer, Ensign Fawks, who had been torpedoed in the Red Sea and was coming home on our ship as a passenger. He was sitting on a hatch cover, riding it like a horse. He had a bamboo pole in his hand and he stayed close to us. If we started to drift apart, one of us would grab the pole and pull him along, or he'd pull us along, I don't know which. Then the sharks began coming around, and Fawks would watch for them, and when one got close he would give it a whack on the nose with his pole and drive it away. He'd say, 'Look out, here comes one! Watch!,' and then he'd whack it. The sharks would go off for a while and then they'd come back, and Mr. Fawks would hit them with his pole and drive them away again.

"All that day the sun was very strong. It was cloudy, but every few minutes the sun would come out and burn you. I was hungry as the devil, and sleepy, and thirsty, and all around us was wreckage and guys, hardly alive, doubled up over pieces of wood. We kept trying to pull in wreckage that we could tie together into a raft, but waves would take it away from us. Once in a while we could see a bird. And the day seemed to go like that. We were awfully tired, and it was hard hanging on to the bamboo raft, and the two fellows who were on top wouldn't get off, and we kept asking them to get off and hang on a while, so one of us could rest, but they were too scared.

"Then night came, and the moon was high, and the waves were choppy, and a wave would hit you, and you would swallow salt water and vomit. I would doze off and then wake up and I would still be hanging on to the raft, and the life jacket was getting so hard around the edges it cut into my belly."

Shortly before sunrise, Ensign Maddox began having hallucinations, which he described so eloquently that the men with him were inclined to believe him. "Mr. Maddox," Izzi told me, "said he had noticed a hatch cover near us with some beer in it. All we had to do was find this particular cover, lift it up, and there were three or four cases of beer. Well, Labe and Joudy and Mr. Maddox and me, all separate, leave the bamboo raft and go looking for the beer. Jeez, there I was, swimming around, vomiting once in a while, and trying to find this hatch cover where you could go down below and get some beer.

"Then daylight came, and I could see that wall again, and the high-tension wires, and I heard a cry, 'Help, help! I can't make it!' I saw a sailor trying to make the raft. He was off another crew, one of the torpedoed fellows who had been a passenger." Izzi swam over to him and took him by an arm. The man had cramps, and Izzi told him to kick, and somehow they made the raft. The two men on top of the raft were still lying there; Ensign Fawks was riding his hatch cover, staying as near the raft as he could, and another member of Izzi's gun crew, named Kacevitch, had swum to the raft. Maddox and Labe were gone, Izzi didn't know where. "And there we were, busy hanging on to the raft again," Izzi continued. "Kacevitch was pretty bad, and he kept saying, 'I got to get it back to my father. I got a book with me and I can't let it sink because I got to get it back to my father.' *We* couldn't see any book. Joudy and I got Kacevitch between us and tried to help him. We tried to get the guys on the raft to come over the side and hang on, so we could get Kacevitch up on it so he could rest, but they wouldn't get off."

Then Izzi spied a raft, a substantial wooden one with four men on it. "I thought I saw Lorenz, our radio man, on it," Izzi said, "and I told Joudy I would swim over there and get them to come back and help Kacevitch and the rest of them. I started out, and jeez, it felt like a year. At first I swam directly toward it, and saw I couldn't make it, because it was drifting. Then I swam to get in front of it, and figured the current would bring it down to me. There were sharks around, and my legs ached, and my life jacket was heavy and hard and giving me cramps, and I thought I would never make it."

The raft finally drifted past Izzi, who by then was just bobbing in the water. Izzi climbed unaided onto the raft and fell across it. On the raft were Ensign Maddox, two Dutch seamen, Cornelius van der Slot and Nicko Hoogendam, and an American sailor named George Beasley. Hoogendam and Beasley had been torpedoed once before and had been passengers on the Dutch ship. Van der Slot had been an oiler in the ship's crew. Izzi was to spend a good long time with these four men on the wooden raft.

Izzi explained the plight of the men he had left on the bamboo raft, and for a few minutes the men on the wooden raft tried to paddle toward them, but the current they were in carried them farther away. Soon the men whom Izzi had left in an attempt to get help for them were out of sight, among them Joudy, who many times had saved Izzi's life, and Ensign Fawks, who, riding a hatch cover as if it were a horse and wielding a bamboo pole like a lance, had driven the sharks away.

The five men who found themselves together on the raft were an oddly assorted group. Izzi was an intelligent, athletic boy of nineteen who had worked, along with most of the other Italian-Americans in the community, in a South Barre, Massachusetts, wool-combing mill before joining the Navy; Ensign Maddox was a sensitive, scholarly man of twenty-nine who had been an instructor in public speaking at Purdue University; Beasley was a rough-and-tumble thirty-two-year-old American sailor from Hannibal, Missouri; van der Slot was an experienced Dutch merchant seaman of thirty-seven; and Hoogendam was a seventeen-year-old Dutch boy who had been a fisherman from the time he was thirteen or fourteen and had only recently escaped from the Nazis and become a merchant seaman.

Maddox had been dragged up on the raft shortly before Izzi had reached it. The three other men had been aboard for more than a day and were therefore in better shape than either Maddox or Izzi, who for the first few hours had lain in a half-sleep of exhaustion. After they had rested, the two of them talked quietly for a while. Maddox, who couldn't clearly remember the events of the night before, asked Izzi, "Where were you all night?" Izzi was startled by the question, because he had been right with Maddox, hanging on to the bamboo raft. Izzi reminded him of his hallucination. "I was out looking for that beer you were telling us about," Izzi said.

The raft, which was eight feet wide and nine feet long, was about as navigable as a washtub, yet it was seaworthy and durable and well suited to the purpose for which it had been built. It consisted of a slatted platform, or deck, four feet wide and nine feet long, hung between two pairs of watertight steel drums, fastened end to end, which ran along the sides. These drums, which had a diameter of two feet, extended a foot above the platform and a foot below it. Rafts so constructed are usable either side up, and the idea is that whichever side is up after the raft goes overboard remains the top side. The drums were boxed in by slats, which formed ledges, a foot and a half high and two feet wide, upon which the men could sit or lie when the sea was calm. At either end of the platform there was a board a foot and a half high, which, like the ledges, was intended to keep the men from being washed overboard. The raft rode fairly well in any kind of sea, and the water came to just below the level of the platform. The men could reach down between the slats into the water. They soon cut a large hole at the center of the platform, and through that they could fish or put their feet in the water. In each of the wide ledges there was a hatch, opening into a watertight compartment that ran through the drum beneath and ended in a corresponding hatch on the opposite side, thus making it usable from that side, too. One compartment contained water and the other contained food.

A checkup of the stores aboard the raft revealed that there were a can of flares, two cans of matches, two small flashlights, a larger electric light that could be used for a running light, a life preserver, some rope, two paddles, a bundle of small sticks to support the flares when they were shot off, a big canvas tarpaulin, a smaller piece of yellow sailcloth, a drinking cup, a Dutch flag; a medical kit containing bandages, a bottle of iodine, a pair of tweezers, and a pair of scissors; nine cans of milk, a few dozen hardtack biscuits, about ten gallons of water, and a two-pound can of chocolate. The chocolate was in inch-and-a-half squares. A conference was held, presided over by Maddox, the only commissioned officer aboard (a point still important with the men), and it was decided what each man's daily ration would be: a cup of water and a piece of cracker in the morning; a half cup of water, a little milk, and a piece of cracker in the afternoon; and, for supper, a cup of water, a piece of hard-tack, and a fifth of a piece of chocolate, which was about the size of a thumb-nail.

"We decided to stand watches day and night to make sure we'd sight any ship that came into view," Izzi told me in one of our numerous talks. "During the day, about fifteen or twenty minutes was all a man could stand looking into the water and sun; then he'd have to look down at the deck or close his eyes. At night the watch was one to two hours; we didn't have any way of telling what time it was, so we figured that as long as a fellow could keep looking around at night, that was two hours. After three or four days we got so we weren't too particular about how we stood watches, but we kept it up one way or another just the same for about a month and a half before we stopped altogether. At night the fellow on watch, about every hour or so, would make a couple of swings with one of the flashlights, so that if any ship was around the people on it could see the light.

"At first it didn't seem so bad, especially after those days in the water. You know what it was like when you were a kid and you used to think about float-ing down a river or out to sea, all alone on a raft? It seemed kind of like that, with beautiful days, wonderful sunsets, and nights with the stars close. There were hundreds of birds, most of them black with white spots on their head. These were a little smaller than robins. The second day, we fed them cracker crumbs, we were that sure of being picked up soon. We thought we were close to land, or else why should all the birds be out there? Especially the little birds. Other birds were white, like small sea gulls. Sometimes a bird would rest on the raft and we wouldn't even bother it. Mr. Maddox thought it would bring us bad luck if we killed and ate a bird."

Except for Maddox, the men on the raft had all been workmen before the war, and they observed the courtesies that men on ships and in road gangs and factories show one another. They were helpful and coöperative, and any curiosity they may have felt about each other they kept to themselves. It was several days before Izzi knew the names of all of his companions. Names caused the five men a little trouble. "Like with van der Slot," Izzi said. "He told us finally that his name was Cornelius van der Slot. You couldn't call a fellow Cornelius all the time. Van der Slot didn't speak English as well as the kid Hoogendam, and so we asked Hoogendam to ask van der Slot what to call him. The kid talked to Cornelius, and he said we should call van der Slot Case, which is the name the Dutch use for Cornelius.

"Then there was the kid. His name was Nicko Hoogendam. You couldn't call him Nicko; it sounded funny. Beasley started calling him Junior, and that stuck for a while, but Hoogendam didn't like it. He got the idea of it and he didn't like it. One day he said, 'Why do you always call me Junior? I've got a name, haven't I?' We asked him what he wanted us to call him, and he said 'Nick,' and that's what it was. The rest of us—Maddox, Beasley, and me—went by our last names. I'm always called Izzi anyway. Somebody asks me my name and I say 'Izzi' and they usually say 'Izzi what?' and I have to go through explaining how Izzi is my last name."

For the first three or four weeks of their stay on the raft, Izzi addressed Maddox as "Sir." When the watches were abandoned, that led to further informality. Izzi began to address Maddox as Maddox, which made the ensign feel more comfortable. Eventually, as a real friendship developed between the two men, Izzi called Maddox Jimmy. At first van der Slot, Beasley, and Hoogendam called Maddox Mr. Maddox, but later they, too, called him Maddox.

The sun beat brutally upon the raft. Izzi is naturally dark and a man who normally doesn't burn. However, he had soaked in the water for days and his skin had been softened and bleached. He wore only a shirt. Van der Slot had a shirt, dungarees, and shorts. Hoogendam had a shirt, a pair of civilian trousers, socks, and shoes. Beasley wore a shirt, shorts, and dungarees. Maddox wore only shorts and a shirt. Izzi, Maddox, and van der Slot also had life jackets.

"The afternoons felt like a year," Izzi said. "Holes got burned in our legs and feet. We started bandaging the worst parts of our skins. My legs and feet were open sores from the sun and bumping, and when we'd take the bandages off after a couple of days they would take holes out of our skin. We put iodine on the worst parts, and then one day I spilled the iodine and it was gone. Our skin kept peeling and peeling. That peeling lasted a month and a half until we just sort of fried up." Izzi and van der Slot suffered most from sunburn. Maddox, who had had pneumonia twice and had a horror of dampness, had appropriated the smaller of the two pieces of canvas that were on the raft, and it was large enough to cover most of him, so he was burned less severely; Beasley, Hoogendam, and van der Slot were fully clothed. Maddox thought he had a right to the cloth because of his pneumonia and came to feel that it belonged to him. This was a constant source of irritation to the other men on the raft, especially to van der Slot.

"And there was the kid's shoes," Izzi said. "Hoogendam bought a pair of shoes in Cape Town for seven bucks, and they dried all out and hurt the hell out of him. He'd wear them anyway, and we'd tell him to throw them away. He'd say, 'These are a good pair of shoes; cost seven bucks. I can wear them in New York.' Then he would move around the raft and step on your feet and it would hurt you so much it would make you cry. It was two weeks before we got rid of those shoes for him. We threw them overboard."

The raft was not built for comfort. The ledges made it impossible to stretch out all the way when lying down on the deck, and at night the five men had to huddle together in an elaborate fashion to make room for everyone. One man would sit down with his back and neck against the ledge on one side and his feet against the ledge on the opposite side; the space was so small that his knees would be in the air. The second man would get in a corresponding position facing him, and so on. If one man moved in the night, everyone was disturbed. As each man took his turn standing watch, he merely kept awake; he didn't change his position.

The first few weeks on the raft were days of great hunger and pain for the men. Although van der Slot and Izzi suffered more than the others from sunburn, they all suffered considerably. Hoogendam had been injured when the ship was torpedoed. He had been on the main deck watching some men playing shuffleboard when the first torpedo struck, and it knocked him clear into the water. Somehow he got a deep gash in one knee. He bandaged it once a day, but still it festered. Every day each of the men took a dip in the water, but they advised Hoogendam not to. One day he did anyway, and after that the knee began to heal. They had all forgotten, if they ever knew, that salt water usually has a healing effect on open wounds.

"The days were funny," Izzi said. "The mornings went by quick, and the afternoons like years. Each day we made a notch on one of our paddles to mark the passing of time. We all waited for night to come so we could get our little piece of chocolate. When mealtime came around, we would act as if we were having a big meal, and we would try to make it last a long time, but it was usually over in two minutes." At night the men covered themselves with the tarpaulin, putting half of it under them to secure it. The last man to lie down had the duty of lashing it down, a task that soon became painful, because each movement of a limb cracked blisters and tortured unused muscles. Izzi and Maddox ripped open their life jackets and made pillows out of the kapok stuffing. Izzi, with the help of van der Slot, made a pair of shorts out of the canvas of his life jacket.

There were two knives aboard the raft—the single-blade one Izzi had borrowed while hanging onto the bamboo raft, and a jackknife belonging to Beasley. "By God, it pays to carry a jackknife," Beasley would sometimes say proudly. "On my other torpedoing, I was the only fellow to carry a knife, and it sure came in handy." The men saved the milk cans after they were emptied so that everyone would have his own drinking cup.

By a coincidence, both the food and the water ran out on November 18th, the sixteenth day after the sinking, and the men began looking wistfully at the birds which flew over them. Maddox still insisted that it was bad luck to kill sea birds. "Wait until tomorrow," he would say whenever anyone spoke hungrily of eating fowl. Maddox's aversion to killing birds led him to try an unusual stunt. Sharks were always around the raft. When each man took his daily dip in the water, a rope was tied around him and held by the others. The men holding the rope kept a sharp lookout for sharks, and when they saw a gray fin approaching, they jerked their companion back on the raft. Often the shark went right under the raft and came out on the other side. Maddox thought of making a lasso with the rope, dangling the noose in the water, and attempting to catch a shark with it. "He tried it and we watched him for a couple of hours," Izzi said. "We told him, 'You won't get a shark that way.' Then I dangled my feet over the side of the raft and a shark came by, and Maddox got him with the lasso. I hadn't intended using my feet as bait. It just happened that way. How we got that shark was a miracle. It was three feet long at least, and Maddox pulled the rope tight around his fins. It took all five of us to bring him in. We were scared he would bite one of us, and we shoved the handle of a paddle in his mouth. He flopped and fought, and we couldn't get a knife into him. His back was like rock. Finally we turned him over and ripped him open with a knife, down the soft white belly he had. When we took the paddle out of his mouth, he had bitten off the end of it.

"Mr. Maddox said, 'I caught the shark. How about letting me have the heart?' We said O.K., and took it out and gave it to him, and we took the liver out for ourselves because we had heard somewhere that it was good for you. It didn't look good, and we didn't know whether to eat it or not, but finally we cut it up, and some of the white meat in the liver was all right—tough but not so bad. Maddox held the heart for a long time. It was still beating. He said he had read somewhere of a man eating a heart while it was beating, but he couldn't quite bring himself to do it. Finally he did. Then we cut off two big chunks of meat from the sides and put them in our food container for the next day, and left the rest of the shark on the deck. The next day there was a *beautiful* aroma. We opened the hatch and the meat had turned color and the smell was awful. We tossed the stuff overboard, and other fish came along and grabbed the meat like cannibals."

The men went without water entirely on the seventeenth and eighteenth days. Then it rained, and they sopped up as much rain water as they could in the sailcloth and their shirts, which they wrung out into the water container. After that they returned to the same water rations they had established at the beginning. They were always thirsty, but they didn't suffer as much from thirst as from hunger. The rains kept them reasonably well supplied, but they never relaxed their rigid rationing. Whenever it rained and their supply was replenished, they figured that it might be their last rainfall.

Of all the men on the raft, Maddox seems to have been emotionally affected the most by their predicament. He continually watched the horizon, and now and then he nervously struck the ledge of the raft with his fist, like a man who had been waiting a long time for a telephone call. The spoiling of the shark meat seemed to heighten his impatience. That day he sat with his yellow cloth wrapped about him, his hand slapping rhythmically at the ledge. Then he stood up suddenly, stared at the horizon for almost a full minute, turned to the other men, and asked, "Am I going crazy, fellows? I think I see something." The others looked. In the distance was a ship. Maddox waved the yellow cloth. He tired, and another man took over the job, and when that one tired another stood and waved the cloth. Although it was daylight, they burned some flares, hoping that the smoke and the red light would catch the eye of the lookout on the ship.

"It looked as though it was turning around as if to come toward us," Izzi said. "A guy would wave the flag, get tired, sit down, and begin to cry. We were sure for a while that the ship was turning around, but it went on and on, and we could see it was a big freighter, and then it disappeared. It didn't make us feel so terribly bad, though, because we figured then that we were in a shipping lane. Maybe, we said, the ship will radio and a plane will come out and pick us up. We felt good and we prayed and talked about how if that ship had picked us up, why right now we'd be warm and all dressed up." The men hopefully watched the sea and sky the rest of that day, and as the five of them crammed themselves into a space smaller than a double bed that night, they talked of how they would soon be in New York.

The following day, all the men kept watch. They had been on the raft over three weeks and had eaten no food in two days. They were weak and yet buoyed up by a hope that kept them restlessly moving. "Late that afternoon Maddox saw something else and again it was a ship," Izzi said. "We brought out flares and the yellow cloth and our Dutch flag and waved. 'Take it easy, take it easy, don't get nervous,' we'd tell each other. This one didn't come as close as the other one, but we could see big boxes on the deck and parts of the ship painted with red lead. Just like the other one, she kept right on going, and we sat down and cried. 'How can they miss us?' we asked. 'If they had a good watch on that ship, they certainly would see us. What the hell kind of a crew have they got on that ship?' One of the guys said, 'Maybe they think we're a submarine.' Someone answered, 'What the hell, does *this* look like a submarine?' "

The next day was the one before Thanksgiving. "We talked about Thanksgiving in the States," Izzi said. "Our water supply was gone again and we prayed at least that we get rain or something to eat. Thanksgiving Day itself we couldn't keep our mind off of it. At noon we talked about people in the States sitting down for some turkey and some fruit. And then at about two o'clock we talked about how *now* the people in the States have finished eating and are sitting around, all full of food, and smoking and talking.

"Then—I was the first to notice it—a big bird came flying around the raft.

I grabbed for it and missed, and then it rested in the water right near us. The kid Hoogendam wanted to dive over after it, but we were afraid sharks would get him. He kept talking about it, and so we held him by the ankles, and he threw himself forward and grabbed it, and he fell halfway out of the raft. It made a squawk, but he had it. It pecked at his hands, but he held on, and we dragged him and the bird onto the raft. It was about the size of a chicken. It was a gray bird. We wrung its neck, pulled the feathers out, and divided it up in five parts. It was the biggest bird we ever did get, and it came on Thanksgiving. The bird had dark meat, just like a chicken, and it tasted wonderful. We felt a lot better after that.

"We caught birds other times, but none of them as big as that first one. They were usually about the size of sparrows. Most of the birds would fish all day, and at night they would be tired, and sometimes they would rest in the water, and sometimes they'd even make a noise—wrack, wrack—just like a duck. At night, sometimes, a bird would light on the canvas and the fellow on the outside would whisper, 'There's a bird.' He'd sneak out from under the canvas and crawl across the rest of us, reach out, and wham! he'd usually have him. The most we got that way was three one night, and we got about twenty-five in all. Each one was divided five ways, even if it meant that the piece you got was about the size of a quarter. If we got the bird at night, we'd save him for breakfast, and if we got it in the daytime we'd usually divide it up and eat it right then."

At Izzi's suggestion, they saved intestines from the birds and used them, without hook or line, for bait. One man would dangle an innard at the end of his fingers until a fish had swallowed part of it, then he would jerk it and bring the fish onto the raft. Most of them were about the size of sardines. One day Izzi and Hoogendam got nearly eighty of them that way. Occasionally sharks would chase schools of tiny fish under the raft, and the men would reach through the hole they had cut in the deck and snatch the fish. "Me and the two Dutchmen," Izzi said, "got so we ate the fish bones and all, but Beasley and Mr. Maddox wouldn't eat the bones, and sometimes they would give the bones to us and we would chew on them at night. That was my idea, and I found that when I couldn't sleep, it felt kind of good to chew on the bones; made my mouth watery. It was something like the peanuts and pretzels they give you in a beer parlor."

The days went on. The chronology of the men's adventure became vague and confused. Izzi speaks of certain events as happening "a couple of weeks before we were picked up" or "about a month and a half after we got on the raft." Much of the time the men sat silently, looking at the bottom of the raft or out to sea. Izzi said there was much to admire in the South Atlantic. "Sometimes you would see fish fighting, big green fish that looked like dragons, and it was wonderful to watch. Once a great big blue fish jumped twenty feet out of the water. I'll never forget, either, a bird on a piece of cork that drifted along in the current with us for a while. This bird, about the size of a bluejay, landed on the piece of cork about the second week and tagged along with us for a couple of days. The cork would bob up and down and the bird with it. A shark got its eye on the bird, and would come up after it, flipping over on his back and his mouth open. The bird would just flutter up a couple of feet and after the shark was gone would come down on the cork again. I watched it for a hell of a time. It was fun to watch, and it made me laugh right out loud. Every once in a while out there something made one or two of us laugh. Silly things like the bird on the cork. The sunsets and sunrises were the most beautiful you have ever seen, red and purple and all the colors in the world. I never did get tired of those sunsets, even if it did mean night and cold was coming. When it got dark, there'd be phosphorescent fish around us, making streaks and flashes."

At night the men looked at the stars, and it seemed to Izzi that they were able to recognize one especially big star most of the time. None of the men knew much about stars, and Maddox kept saying that when he got back on shore he was going to study astronomy. "We always tried to head west, or toward what we thought was west," Izzi said, "although you couldn't head that raft much of anyplace. We had a sort of sail, that smaller piece of yellow cloth, and sometimes we'd put it up on the sticks, but Mr. Maddox would take it down and wrap up in it. A lot of the time we would argue about where we were and where we were heading, and one fellow would say we were going into the South American shore and another would say we were headed for the Caribbean, but I usually didn't give a damn. I just wanted to get picked up."

At the beginning of the second month, the rainy season began. Squalls and storms would strike them, toss the raft about, and reduce the men to sodden misery. The men would huddle, jammed together, under the canvas and argue bitterly about who had the driest spot. "During this period it was pitiful how much it rained on us," Izzi said. "We had to go under the canvas to keep dry. Once we had to stay under, in the dark, for two whole days. Of course, the rains helped us, too, with our water supply, but I kept saying to myself: God, it doesn't rain this much." The rain brought on more arguments about what part of the ocean they were in. All Izzi cared about was being rescued, wherever he was, and anyway he wanted to keep to himself his slightly cynical belief that they were heading back toward Africa. Actually, they were drifting northeast, a few hundred miles off the coast of South America. At one time or another they quite possibly drifted across the outflux of the Amazon, which carries fresh water hundreds of miles to sea. If they did, they did not know it. Not one of the men ever made an attempt to drink sea water.

Seeing what appeared to be land birds often made the men optimistic. A tiny bird, whose feet were not webbed, would come twittering along, dipping after microscopic fish, and Izzi and his friends would for the moment be positive they were near shore. "The birds would come out in the morning opposite from the sun," Izzi said, "and they would go back with the sun at night, the same way they came from, you see. We used to say to each other, 'How can a *little* bird like that fly very far? We must be near land,' and we would kill ourselves trying to paddle after them. You can't really paddle a raft. You put one leg on the ledge, one leg in the water, and paddle it like it was a canoe, but it doesn't get you anywhere.

"Even a medium-sized bird, once you get the feathers off, is a little bit of a thing. Once we caught a bird the size of a robin, and we all got pieces out of it. Maddox got an idea. We had matches, and he never liked the idea of eating things raw, so he decided to cook his piece. He took a match, and we were all interested. The old man, van der Slot, shielded him so the match wouldn't go out, and Maddox lit one. It went out, and then another. He lit another match and it stayed lit, and he held it under the little piece of bird he had until the meat was black. Then he nibbled at it. 'How is it?' we asked him. 'Pretty good,' he said, taking a little bite. 'Let's have some of it,' we asked him. We had already eaten our shares raw. 'It's so little,' he said, and ate it. He never tried it again."

The two watertight tins of matches among the provisions under the hatch had been the cause, on one of the early days on the raft, of a great disappointment, since they had led the men to believe that another watertight tin, which had an almost irremovable cover, contained cigarettes. "Else why would they put matches on the raft?" Izzi said. "The cover on this can had one of those little tiny handles that you can only get two fingers on. Our hands were soft and weak from the water, and we hit the handle with sticks and everything we could find to force the top off. We finally get it open, and what do we find? Flares. I suppose we needed flares, but we sure were disappointed there wasn't any cigarettes."

For some time the scissors in the first-aid kit were used to trim the beards that the men naturally began to grow. Hoogendam acted as barber. Van der Slot had a luxuriant beard, of which he was proud, but Maddox had the handsomest one on the raft. One of the reasons they finally gave up barbering was that they needed the scissors for a more important use. It was decided to break the scissors apart, tie each of the blades to one of the sticks provided to support the flares, and use them to spear fish. This idea was Maddox's, like most of the other good ones. Hoogendam was the best man with a spear, and, weak as he was, he caught eight or ten flat fish in the remaining weeks the men were on the raft. "The kid was damn good at spearing fish," Izzi said, "but he couldn't tell us much about them, even though he had been a fisherman."

The men on the raft talked a lot about their past and especially about the things they had eaten at one time or another. Sometimes the discussion had a rapt quality and sometimes it became argumentative, mostly when a man was describing what he was going to eat when he got ashore. Sometimes, too, it became lyrical. Beasley used to talk about Hannibal, Missouri, his home town. It seems that there the hardier boys carried on the tradition of the town's great citizens, Tom Sawyer and Huckleberry Finn. Beasley would tell of sneaking out of school, robbing a garden, sliding down to a thicket along the Mississippi, dropping into a rowboat, and going off on an excursion. Sometimes he did this alone, but quite often he had companions of about his own age, twelve or thirteen. They would row out into the river, drop lines, and try for channel catfish. Sometimes, after catching a measly pickerel, Beasley and his friends would come ashore, find a chicken, boil it in a pot with vegetables, and have a meal. That, Beasley would say, was life in Missouri, and it was a fine life. However, he supposed that if he were put ashore the next day, he would walk into a good restaurant and get some Southern fried chicken. Or maybe he would find himself a Chinese joint, say in San Francisco, and have chow mein. Beasley changed his mind often—chow mein one day, fried chicken the next.

Van der Slot and Hoogendam, perhaps with perverse Dutch humor, talked of horsemeat. Horsemeat, van der Slot told Izzi, was the finest dish a man could get in Holland. Beef was all right, and so were lamb and pork, but horsemeat was really delicious. They agreed that the meal they wanted would consist mostly of meat and potatoes, and they'd settle for any kind of meat, even beef. Maddox chose to talk about *Smörgåsbord*. "He told me," Izzi said, "that there is fish, all kinds, and cheese, all kinds, and all kinds of meat, like salami, liverwurst, and bologna, and you keep going back to it until you got all you want, and you heap your plate high—bread and stuff, even salads." Izzi, whose tastes were Italian, gave his companions a really moving description of what a good spaghetti dish should be. Izzi's description was so eloquent that on one occasion the four other men agreed that the first thing they would have when they got ashore was a spaghetti party and that Izzi should tell the cook how to prepare the food. Then they decided, after listening to Maddox, that the second night ashore they would find a *Smörgåsbord* place and end up that meal with filet mignon; the third night they would have either chicken or chow mein, and next night they'd go to someplace where there was good meat and potatoes. The exact order in which they would do the rounds was arrived at after weeks of discussion, and before it was made final the matter was put to a vote.

Izzi usually makes a distinction between the talks the men had of meals and of things to eat. The men's descriptions of the meals they hoped to eat someday were academic, philosophic exercises, as distinguished from burning issues. Izzi defines the latter as "The thing I would like to have right now." Beasley, speaking of his immediate desire, usually said he would like to have an Oh Henry! candy bar. Maddox, one of the two married men aboard, wanted chocolate cake, precisely as his young wife baked it, and preferably by her hand. Van der Slot, the other husband, dreamed of apple pie or chocolate cream pie. Sometimes he would talk for almost an hour without stopping about the cookies which were made in Holland. Hoogendam wanted any kind of candy. Izzi wanted a Milky Way candy bar. All of these men, even young Hoogendam and the rather intellectual Maddox, were convivial fellows, yet their dreams were not of beer and whiskey but of sweets. "That talking about food was good," Izzi said. "You talk about it, and you think about it, and your mouth gets watery, and jeez, it helps!

"I talked to the kid one day about éclairs. He didn't know what an éclair was. I explained it to him—an éclair is a great long bun, and on top of it is all chocolate and inside of it is all cream. He didn't get what I meant by cream, so I explained to him it was custard. Then I tell him about my folks taking me into town, say on a Saturday, when I was a kid, and they give me a dime and I spend it on two éclairs. Well, Hoogendam challenged me to a race after he figured out what I meant. We go into New York, and we see who can eat the most éclairs. Whoever loses would pay. I said when we got to New York we would go into a five-and-dime and get some fig squares. In a five-and-dime they are always most fresh, and we will walk down Broadway, I said, and eat them in front of everybody. Mr. Maddox couldn't quite figure what fig squares were, but after a while he said they called them Newtons out where he used to live in Indiana.

"We didn't talk much about drinks. Once in a while we did, though. I said once that when I get to my home town I am going over to my cousin's barroom and line up all the drinks I would ever want, from water down to whiskey, and drink them all. We didn't talk much about girls, either. I thought a lot about my sisters, and Mr. Maddox talked a lot about his wife, but that wasn't the same as talking about women in general. The one thing I resolved on that raft was that if I ever got back I never would be without a chocolate bar."

Izzi's twentieth birthday fell on December 3rd, the thirty-first day after the sinking, and he kept thinking about it for a week beforehand. "I told them I never had been missing from home on my birthday, and here I am out on a raft," Izzi said. "I used to always get a cake and gifts, and people would drop into the house and my old man would serve wine and beer, and my mom would always have a big feed. The four other men tried to cheer me up. They put their hands on my shoulder and said, 'Never worry, Izzi, we'll be in New York or Brazil for your birthday, and you can send a telegram home, or maybe even make a phone call.' 'How are we going to be picked up that soon?' I'd say, and they would tell me, 'Never forget, it takes a ship only half an hour to cross over the horizon and come over and pick us up.' We were always saying that it takes only half an hour for a boat to cross the horizon and find us. They kept cheering me up. 'When the boat rescues us tomorrow,' they'd say, 'we'll tell the ship's cook it's your birthday and he'll bake you a cake. If they pick us up today, we'll tell him tomorrow's your birthday and he'll bake you a cake anyway.'

"We were in the rainy season, and next day, my birthday, it was dark and cloudy and cold and it started raining. We all went under the canvas, and I took the outside position so I could watch out and see if a ship was coming. Hours went by and we still talked about my birthday, and it rained and rained. It rained harder on my birthday than it ever did any other time we were out there. They tried to cheer me, and late in the day van der Slot said, 'We'll be picked up tomorrow, and we'll tell the ship's cook that *yesterday* was your birthday.' It rained so hard I couldn't see more than a few feet in front of me, and I cried, and the tears rolled down out of my eyes because I knew that if a ship came by they couldn't see us."

The day after Izzi's birthday, Ensign Maddox announced to his four companions on the raft that December 12th, their fortieth day adrift, would be his own birthday. He was going to be thirty. "Mr. Maddox said to van der Slot," Izzi told me, "that if we got picked up on his birthday and that if van der Slot smoked a pipe, he would go out and buy him the most expensive pipe he could find. I told Hoogendam that if we got picked up that day I would buy him a ring and he said he would buy me a ring, too.

"December twelfth came," Izzi continued, "and we were still on the raft. It was pouring rain, not quite as hard as on my birthday, but pouring just the same. Mr. Maddox said that, like me, he had never missed a birthday with either his family or with his wife. His wife always give him something, some kind of a present that day, he said. We tried to cheer him up, but he felt very bad about it, and a lot of the time he would just look out to sea and hit his hand against the ledge of the raft like he was waiting for something. Then, when we were still trying to cheer him up, he kind of laughed, and said that before he sailed he had gone to a fortuneteller and she had told him that he would never live to see his thirtieth birthday. 'When I get back,' he told us, 'I'm going to go and see that old witch and tell her how wrong she was.' Mr. Maddox was so discouraged that day that we had to sit beside him all the time and pat him on the shoulder and say how nice it would be if we were picked up tomorrow. At least, we told him, we got *water*."

It rained almost every day in December, and though the weather was fairly warm, the men were chilled all the time. Three of them had bad colds and Beasley was becoming very ill. The canvas tarpaulin began to rot because of the rain, and when the men huddled under it in a storm, water soaked through on them. Toward the end of the month they rigged up the tarpaulin so that the rain drained off it into the water container, but, even when the container was full, they continued their water rationing, because they feared that the rain might stop any day. The men were gaunt and their bones ached and stuck out grotesquely. They tried giving one another rubdowns to keep their muscles conditioned. There were days when a man might spend hours feeling the muscles of his legs. When the men gave each other rubdowns, they had to do it in shifts, because no man was strong enough to use his hands for more than a minute or two.

It was about the middle of December when they spotted a third ship. "It was a cloudy day and Mr. Maddox saw it first," Izzi said. "He was always first to see the ships. We saw smoke at first and then the ship. It must have been an old coal burner. We had only one flare left, and it was wet, so we couldn't use it. We waved our flag, but they didn't see us. We took turns waving the flag, and we were so weak that when a guy stood up it took two of us to hold him, and the guy would only wave the flag two or three times and then he would have to sit down again. When that third ship disappeared, it was awful. We all slumped down and cried. We had always said that the *third* ship wouldn't pass us up, and here this one had gone right on by, away out there in the distance. We didn't talk much about it. We just cried and sobbed, and we were very discouraged."

As Christmas approached, Izzi grew particularly depressed. He had grown up in a pleasant New England countryside of Colonial architecture and woods and hills. Izzi led a fine life in South Barre. He hunted in the hills, played shortstop on the town baseball team, got in fights, was nicknamed Tuffy, had dates with girls, and often sneaked out nights with his father's car. "When I thought of Christmas, I was very sad," he said. "We always had a big celebration at our house on Christmas. The table would be piled with food, and there would be wine, beer, cordials, and whiskey, and no matter what time of night you came in on Christmas Eve, there would be my dad and mom at the table, talking to each other. They would talk to each other all through the night, and people would drop in and talk, and there would be presents for me and my six brothers and sisters. I could see this Christmas at home. It would be different. There hadn't been any deaths in our family around Barre for years, and with Italian people a death in the family is a very sad thing. They seem to feel it awfully deep. I could see there wouldn't be any celebration at home. Everybody would be in black, and the kids would be quiet, and my mom would be crying. The Ciccones and the Falcos and the Martones would be all trying to comfort them, and I could see my family, all in black."

Izzi thought about a lot of things on Christmas Eve, the fifty-second day adrift. "I thought of that pipe I had got my dad in Cape Town before we sailed," he said, "and those pillow cases for Mother, and the bracelets for my sisters, and the knives for my brothers. Christmas Eve we all got to talking about Christmas, and I told about how for a couple of weeks before Christmas every year we'd roam all over the hills looking for just the right tree to put up, and then how either Dad or I would cut it down, bring it into the house, and the whole family would help decorate the tree, and eat big bowls of figs and dates and nuts that Mom would put on the living-room table. Mr. Maddox led Christmas carols that night. He knew all the words, and Beasley and I knew most of them. The two Dutchmen knew the tunes, and sometimes they would use the Dutch words. We sang 'Silent Night,' 'Little Town of Bethlehem,' and 'Adeste Fidelis.' It sounded kind of nice, with the stars shining bright as hell and the water so calm that it reflected back the stars. Nick and the old Dutchman told us about Christmas in Holland, where they celebrate two days. We thought that was a swell idea, and we said that if we were picked up Christmas Day we sure would celebrate both the twenty-fifth and the twenty-sixth.

"Christmas Day was all right, although it rained a little and all of us were sad and pretty quiet. Mr. Maddox just looked out toward the horizon and now and then he'd hit the ledge with his hand. The next holiday would be New Year's, and we prayed we would be picked up by then."

All the men prayed a good deal during their weeks on the raft. Maddox had studied for the ministry for a while before deciding to become a teacher, and when the other men found it out they asked him to lead prayers. He prayed aloud every evening for several weeks, in a sort of formal prayer service, and then gave it up. He explained that he didn't like to lead prayers, and everyone else seemed somewhat relieved. After that, however, each man prayed in his own way. Sometimes a man would say aloud, "O God, help us tomorrow." Izzi would say an "Our Father" and two or three "Hail Marys" every evening.

For a few evenings, Maddox also conducted a rather odd story hour for Hoogendam. Hoogendam had said idly that he liked bedtime stories, so Maddox told him "The Three Bears," "The Three Little Pigs," "Little Red Riding Hood," and several others. Hoogendam wanted to hear more, but finally Maddox said he didn't want to keep on, and the story hour came to an abrupt end.

Hoogendam and van der Slot often talked to each other in Dutch. Sometimes they quarrelled bitterly. The others of course had no way of telling exactly what the pair were arguing about. Izzi said he thought that one argument arose over Nick's saying that he wished he was an American and that he was going to be one after the war. This hurt van der Slot, a proud Hollander. The Dutchmen also debated the respective merits of their home towns.

All the men except Izzi talked at one time or another about dying. Izzi tried not to acknowledge even to himself that he might die. Around the end of the first month, Maddox had proposed that all the men on the raft write their names on the outside of the flare can, and the date they were torpedoed, November 2nd. "He said that then in case we died," Izzi recalled, "our names would be on the can, and if the raft was ever found or if it drifted ashore someplace, why, then our names would be there and our families would know what became of us. Mr. Maddox put his name and address down, Hoogendam put his name and address down, and Beasley put his down. Then only me and Case van der Slot was left. The men were scratching the names on the can with a knife, and Beasley handed the knife to me, and I handed it to Case. I didn't want to write my name down on that flare can. I wasn't going to die. I didn't want to die and I didn't want to think of dying. I wanted to live and I wanted to think about that. I didn't want these other guys to see how I felt, though. I didn't want to admit to them that I was afraid to admit I might be going to die. Well, van der Slot sliced his name on the can, and when he finished I said, 'There isn't any more room,' and I never did write my name down on that can. I was always glad my name wasn't there."

Beasley, the first man to become seriously ill, had begun weakening the fourth week on the raft. The raw birds and fish they had had to eat after their rations gave out seemed to upset him—he and Maddox were the only ones who were squeamish about raw food—and he would gag and vainly try to vomit. Then he would hiccup and retch for a whole day. Sometimes he would lie in one cramped position for days. Then he would rally and speak feebly to his companions. A couple of weeks later he became blind in one eye. Then he began to lose his hearing and the sight of the other eye. "We would hold up four fingers in front of him," Izzi told me, "and say, 'How many fingers I got up, Beasley?,' and he'd say, 'Two.' During the day he tried to keep his eyes covered all the time, and it hurt him terribly to open them. He had high cheekbones, and his face sunk in until it looked awful. When the third ship didn't stop, he began to just fall away. If we caught a bird or a fish and gave him a piece, he would spit it out. Then it got so he wouldn't move at all, and at night, when we wanted to put him under the canvas, we would have to pick him up, and we were weak, too. It gave him awful pain. We'd say, 'Come on, Beasley, let's get under the canvas.' He'd scream, 'Don't touch me! You're trying to hurt me! Let me alone, please! What are you trying to do, kill me?'

"It went on like that, and then he was almost blind and deaf, and he started talking about people we didn't know and asking for cigarettes and candy. He'd say, 'I *know* there're some Lucky Strikes on the shelf and you guys are hiding them from me.' And then he'd go on about Harry and other people we didn't know. 'Why don't you help me, Harry?' Or he'd say, 'Please, Alice, why don't you help me? I'm over here.' And then he'd say he didn't want to die, he didn't want to die.

"On the sixty-sixth morning, when we woke up, the old Dutchman asked

me how Beasley was. He'd been groaning all day before and most of the night
—mmmm mmmm, like that. Beasley was next to me, and I looked at him,
and his hands were out in front of him, clutched like he was grabbing for
something, and his teeth were all showing, and the whites of his eyes. We
knew he was dead, but we watched him for a couple of hours, kind of hoping,
I guess, that maybe he would move, and then we were sure he was dead. We
wanted to wait until night to bury him, but then after looking at him just lying there for a few more hours, we decided not to wait. I said prayers to myself and the others said some prayers aloud. Mr. Maddox said the main prayer.
He said, 'He is probably going to a better spot. May he rest in peace.' And
we buried him at sea. It took the four of us to roll him overboard, and after
he had splashed in, we didn't look at him but just sat and waited and looked
out to sea the other way."

Izzi took Beasley's wallet to return to his family, and a cameo ring his girl
had given him. In the wallet were some American paper money, a few foreign
coins, and Beasley's dog tag. All of this Izzi put in the flare can, so that it
wouldn't be washed overboard.

For weeks Maddox and van der Slot argued about the piece of cloth Maddox had taken possession of. Sometimes van der Slot would sit and glare at
Maddox for hours, and occasionally van der Slot told Maddox that he should
either give up the cloth or sleep on one of the ledges along the sides of the
raft, completely exposed to the weather and sea, so that there'd be more room
under the tarpaulin for the rest of the men. Maddox always chose to sleep on
a ledge. Another source of bitterness was the positions the men took when
they lay down at night to sleep. They were supposed to rotate, so that no man
would have the same place two nights in a row. They numbered the positions
from one to five, and Number 1, being the driest, was the favored position.
One day after the rainy season had started, Izzi and Hoogendam got into a
fight about it. "The kid said it was his turn to have the dry spot," Izzi told
me, "and I said it was my turn and that he had had it the night before. He
said I was lying and that he wouldn't move from it. I drew back to hit
him, but Mr. Maddox and the old man grabbed me, and so the kid and I said
we would fight it out the first thing when we got on land."

Beasley, during the two months before he sank into unconsciousness, got
on Izzi's nerves more than anyone else. Beasley had an annoying habit of
speech. "He said 'thataway' all the time," Izzi recalled, "until I thought I'd
go nuts. He would say something was 'over thataway' or he'd say, 'Don't
shove me thataway,' and I got so I could hardly stand it."

The organization of life aboard the raft was gradually simplified. No one
tried to exert any authority over the others, nor did any one man turn out to
be a leader. That was probably just as well. The five men were more or less
helpless, for the raft could not be sailed or guided; it could only drift with the

wind and the ocean currents, and in such circumstances a too forceful character might have driven his companions insane from sheer irritation. For a while, Maddox was looked upon as boss, but in time he came to be regarded as just one of the group, not because of any slackness on his part or any lack of discipline in the others but merely because there was no real need for a leader.

Beasley, Hoogendam, and van der Slot spent so much time arguing about who had first found the raft that Izzi is not sure who actually did. The feeling among the men seemed to be that if anyone could prove that he had first found the raft he would have a little more authority than the rest. Izzi thinks that Hoogendam, van der Slot, and Beasley were together in the water and that Beasley swam to the raft and held on to it while the others climbed on and then was helped aboard by them. The fact that Beasley, van der Slot, and Hoogendam had been on the raft before Maddox and Izzi gave them a vague sort of prestige and authority. However, for a long time Maddox was a dominant figure in the group because of his alertness and his ideas. It was he who thought of lassoing the shark, of making a trough in the tarpaulin so that rain water would run into the water container, and of making fish spears from the blades of the pair of scissors.

There were two knives on board when the journey on the raft began. There were also two flashlights and the light that could be used as a running light. Beasley dropped one flashlight overboard. He didn't know quite how he did it; it just slipped out of his hand. "We didn't bawl him out," Izzi said. The battery of the running light gave out and eventually the second flashlight gave out. However, the men kept both of them, thinking they would be useful someday for something or other. One day, toward the end of the second month, Hoogendam and van der Slot were sitting on one of the ledges of the raft, pulling the feathers out of a bird, when they saw a large wave coming. They got down to the deck and pulled the canvas over them just as the wave struck. One of the knives, which was lying on the ledge, was washed overboard. "Then, a few weeks later," Izzi said, "Hoogendam and I were reaching down after some little fish through the hole in the center of the deck. As we caught them, we threw them to Mr. Maddox and van der Slot, who were cutting the heads off and cleaning them. Beasley was too sick to do anything. He couldn't even wash a fish, he was so sick. The second knife was lying on the canvas. The kid and I were so anxious to get the fish we were grabbing them and throwing them, splashing sort of careless, I guess, and van der Slot said, 'Take it easy.' Beasley was watching and he said, 'Why don't you push the tarpaulin back so you won't get it wet with your splashing?' Hoogendam didn't know the knife was on the tarpaulin, and he pushed it back and the knife fell between the slats into the water."

The men on the raft caught a fair number of fish with the two spears they had made out of the scissors. One day, as Hoogendam stabbed at a fish, the blade of his spear broke. The second spear was washed overboard not long afterward. The men then removed the glass from the burnt-out flashlight and tried to break it so that they would have something with which to cut up any birds and fish they caught. They tried for hours and finally Hoogendam succeeded by slamming the glass against the edge of a slat. The glass broke cleanly, however, and the edges weren't sharp enough to cut anything, so the men removed the reflector and bent it into the shape of a cookie cutter and sliced fish with that.

Only for one short period did the men play any kind of game. "Hoogendam and Mr. Maddox started a checker game," Izzi said. "I don't think Hoogendam had ever played checkers, but he was more interested in playing than the rest of us, and Mr. Maddox said he would teach him. 'Get the first-aid kit,' Mr. Maddox told him, 'and scratch some squares on it with a knife.' We had a hell of a time explaining to Hoogendam what he meant by squares, but the kid finally got it. They didn't have room for a full board—only about four squares one way and five squares another. They took some matches, broke them in two, and used the ends with the heads for red checkers and the other ends for black ones. Nick and Mr. Maddox played for a while, and Nick beat Mr. Maddox, and Mr. Maddox didn't want to play any more. Mr. Maddox told me to play with Nick, and Nick kept asking me, and finally I played, but I didn't like it. You couldn't tell which match was which, and you moved twice and you were on his side. I got fed up. It was silly. It just lasted for a couple of days.

"As far as entertaining ourselves went, Beasley and Mr. Maddox used to sing a lot at first. They were from the West, you know—Indiana and Missouri—and they knew a lot of the same kind of songs, slow songs, like cowboy songs. They had good voices, and sometimes they would hum. I never sang much. I wasn't in the mood."

Shortly after Beasley's death, Maddox, who had been growing weaker and weaker, became ill. "After we buried Beasley at sea," Izzi recalls, "Mr. Maddox said to me, 'Izzi, I think I'm going next.' I told him nobody is going next, and that if anyone was going to die we'd all go together. He patted me on the shoulder and said, 'Izzi, you're a brave man.' He always was saying I was a brave man. I didn't get it. Mr. Maddox used to tell me about how his mother had wanted him to be a minister and how his father had wanted him to be a lawyer, and finally how he had become a teacher. He was a good-looking, very sociable guy. He had gotten married and he built a little house on a hill in Lafayette, Indiana, and he would talk about that, and how when we all got back he wanted me to come visit him and we would go horseback riding. His family had been over here for a long, long time, and whenever there was a war some of his family would be in the cavalry. His family couldn't understand why he didn't join the cavalry and why he had picked the Navy. He was just stubborn, I guess. He talked a lot about books. He used to read all the time on shipboard. I can remember going out on watch and coming back at two in the morning, and he would still be in his cabin, reading. Some nights he must have got only three or four hours' sleep, he read so much."

Maddox began to pound the ledges of the raft more and more. He would also twist the gold wedding ring on his finger and talk to Izzi about it. "My wife," Maddox said, "told me not to come back without this ring. It's good luck." Like Beasley, Maddox began to lose his sight and hearing. He became nervous, and the three other men tried to calm him. Finally, on the seventieth day, Maddox had the same trouble with his eyes that Beasley had had. The other men would hold up four fingers and ask, "How many fingers am I holding up, Jimmy?," and Maddox would reply, "Two."

A dry spell set in, and on the seventy-sixth day they ran out of water. They had run out of water several times before, but now, when everyone was so weak he was hardly able to move, the situation was much more serious. Maddox was having long spells of delirium; he talked of his wife, of fellow-instructors at Purdue, of his family, of horses, of books, and of people he had known in his childhood. Sometimes his talk became merely a mutter and the men could not understand him. The men wrapped him in the yellow cloth and laid him on a ledge, where he could lie stretched out and more comfortably than he could in the cramped confines of the deck. The sea was calm and there was a hot sun. "He would keep asking for a drink," Izzi said. "He'd insist we had water but were keeping it from him. He couldn't see and he could hardly hear, and he would beg us for water, and we would say, 'But, Jimmy, there *isn't* any water. We haven't got any water either.' On the seventy-sixth night, he was groaning away all night—ooooh, ooooh, like that. The next morning, when I woke up, Nick said to me, 'You'd better look at your gunnery officer.' I felt his pulse and I found out he was dead. I bawled. The other men tried to comfort me. They crawled over the canvas and put their hands on my shoulder, and van der Slot said, 'Have courage.'

"I remembered Mr. Maddox saying his wife had told him to be sure he came back with that ring. I took it off his hand and put it in Beasley's wallet with the other stuff. We said some prayers about may he rest in peace. I said, 'If there is anybody else going to die, let the Lord take all three of us.' The Dutchmen agreed to that, and they prayed and I prayed. We said another prayer for Mr. Maddox and we rolled him over the side and buried him at sea. This time we watched. His hair was long, and it floated out in the water. We saw him drift away, his hair floating out in the water.

"We sat back, and van der Slot said, 'Well, that's two out of five, three left.' Hoogendam said, 'Well, now we're the Three Musketeers.' Then I remembered there used to be a Three Musketeers chocolate bar in the States, and I told them about that, and said, 'When we get back, I'll buy you a case of them.' But most of that day I cried."

"Right after Mr. Maddox's death," said Izzi, "something happened *for* us. Back weeks before, we had put the remains of that first shark in the food container, and it had spoiled and made a terrible, rotten stink, and we had dumped the stuff out and never used the food container again. Well, the day after Mr. Maddox died, the old Dutchman put his hand in the container for no reason at all and felt water. He put his fingers to his lips, and it was sweet water. He jumped up and shook our hands. 'I've found water, I've found water!' he said. We had been without water for two days. We strained it through a handkerchief and there were two cupfuls, and we each had a sip. It lasted for three days and saved us, I think. I don't know how it got there."

In the days after Maddox's death, there was little talking. The men lay on the bottom of the raft and tried to catch fish with their hands. Sometimes, too, two of them would tie a rope around the third man and let him over the side into the water, and, weak as he was, he would work his way under the raft and hunt for snails. They took turns at going under. It was van der Slot who discovered the snails. He was taking a bath one day when he saw a snail on the bottom of the raft. He pried it off with his fingers, brought it on board, picked it out of its shell, tasted it gingerly, and announced that it was good to eat. Finally, all the men were eating snails.

On the eighty-first day it rained, and the men soaked up some water in Maddox's piece of yellow cloth and in what remained of the leaky tarpaulin, then carefully squeezed them out into the water container after each man had taken a sip as his ration. "On the eighty-second night, just before we got under the canvas," Izzi said, "we heard a rumble, and there above us, very high, was an airplane. I held my right arm up with my left arm and waved it. The other two fellows waved, too. The plane, way up there, went right across the sky above us. It didn't slow down or circle, but it made us feel good to know we were someplace near where airplanes were. We went to sleep happy and I thought of the things we were going to do when we got picked up.

"The next day van der Slot heard another rumble early in the morning. He shook us and woke us up, and said, 'Look.' We looked up and there was some sort of a plane, a big four-motor job, went past us, and after a while it came back from the way it went. Each time we waved. Then after that a seaplane flew by and it looked like it was scouting, not looking for us but just scouting. Then early in the afternoon, van der Slot saw some smoke. He rubbed his eyes and said, 'I don't know, but I think I see something on the horizon.' We couldn't see anything then, but later on we did. We saw one ship, then two ships, then four ships—a convoy. We hardly dared to say anything to each other. We just looked, and then van der Slot said, 'If this misses us today, I'm going to jump overboard.'

"The convoy didn't come toward us but just went along the horizon. There were planes flying around the convoy, and the first ship was a destroyer. We tried to stand up, but we were too weak and we would fall down. Then we

noticed some smaller ships, some PC boats. Then one PC boat seemed headed
right for us.

"We told van der Slot to stand up and wave our Dutch flag, and me and
the kid would hold him. We each held him by the ankle with one hand and
braced his knees with our other hands. We were lying down holding him and
we couldn't see what was going on. 'They're coming closer,' he told us. The
kid and I were awfully nervous and scared. 'What are they doing? What are
they doing?' we'd keep yelling at van der Slot. And he'd say, 'Shut up! Shut
up!' And we'd get more nervous and try to lift our heads to see what was
happening, and we'd forget and let go of the old man and he would start to
fall down, and we'd grab him again, and it would start all over. 'What's happening? What's happening?' we'd ask, and he was just as nervous and scared
as we were, and he'd say, 'Shut up! Shut up! They're coming closer!' Then
the boat came right over toward us at full speed, and even the kid and I could
see it. The first man I saw was a fellow on the bow beside a three-inch gun
that was pointed right at us. He had a shell in his hand, and I said, 'Holy
mackerel, are they going to shoot us?' Then I saw the American flag on the
boat, but still I was scared the way that guy was looking at us that had the
three-inch shell in his hands." Once van der Slot and Hoogendam saw that
they were about to be rescued, they rushed for the water container and started
drinking the last of their water. They asked Izzi to join them, but he said he'd
wait until he got on board.

The PC boat came alongside the raft and the crew dropped rope ladders
down onto it. The three men tried to climb up by themselves. Izzi's and
Hoogendam's knees buckled. Van der Slot, however, somehow managed to
make it. The other men finally had to be lifted up to the PC's deck. Van der
Slot took the Dutch flag along with him and Izzi took the flare can containing
Maddox's and Beasley's things. The crew of the PC asked the three men how
long they had been out and they said, "Eighty-two days." They were only one
day off in their count. They thought it was a Saturday instead of a Sunday.
They had kept no definite record of time after the forty-fifth day; the marks
they had been putting on the paddle had begun to discourage them. "Just the
same, it was easy to keep track of the days after that," Izzi explained. "You
know, today's Monday, tomorrow's Tuesday."

The men on the PC boat wrapped the rescued men in blankets and gave
them each a bowl of peach juice. Izzi asked for a cigarette. It tasted bad. As
the three men lay on the deck, wrapped in blankets, they watched the crew
of the PC boat try to sink the raft, which, if left to drift, might attract the
attention of other American ships and needlessly draw them off their course.
"They put a lot of twenty-millimetre shells into our raft before they gave up
trying," Izzi said, "but they missed it most of the time and the shells that did
hit her wouldn't sink her. I was kind of glad of it. She was a pretty good old
raft."

# SEALED SHIP

GEORGE SESSIONS PERRY

OUR ship, a transport loaded with United States amphibious troops and anchored off the coast of Algeria, was sealed today. Between now and the time we set out to invade Axis territory, no one except the officer messenger who delivers and picks up mail may board or leave the ship. I am aboard merely as a correspondent, but the rest of the men are here to fight. When you read this, you will know what some of us will never know—whether we won or lost. Many of the men on this ship feel that the operation will determine whether this war will end in a stalemate or whether it will be fought to a clear-cut decision. Up to now in this war, no one has been able to bring off a full-scale amphibious operation against the home shores of a major power. The only fair test was at Dieppe, and you know what happened there. Neither North Africa nor Attu nor Guadalcanal was a proper test of amphibious assault. All three were surprise attacks, something no large-scale assault by one nation upon another of equal strength could possibly be under modern conditions. In none of these three was heavy and determined resistance met at the beach. In the impending attack, however, the enemy knows that we are coming and that the best place to kill an opponent is when he is waist-deep in the water. So far we haven't been told what our objective is to be. Perhaps it is Sicily.

Our invasion force has jammed the ports on the mountainous, ochreous coast of Algeria. The combat flotilla I am in is made up of troop transports, destroyers, PCs, minesweepers, and minelayers. Naturally, it does not include the freighters that are standing by to form our baggage train—the tankers, repair ships, refrigerated meat and vegetable ships, and so on. So much for the American delegation. The British have provided small, fast carriers and some destroyers and battleships. Just up the coast is a nest of British assault landing craft. These vessels joined us the other night in a practice landing maneuver that involved the entire Allied task force. Above the port off which we ourselves lie, the bright, clear North African air is dotted with still brighter pellets, the barrage balloons that lace the sky with slender steel cables.

Aboard my ship there are roughly two thousand men. (My figures are purposely inexact.) About fifteen hundred of them are the soldiers of what is

*231*

known as a reinforced battalion; all sorts of specialists required for the operation have been added. Three hundred and fifty of the men are the regular
ship's company. The rest are the young amphibious naval officers and crews
who will man the landing craft that cover our decks—the small boats that will
put the troops and their supplies ashore. In addition to personnel, we also carry
all the vehicles, weapons (including anti-tank and anti-aircraft guns), food,
ammunition, and gasoline the troops will require during the first week or so
they are ashore. The troops belong to a Southwestern division. They aren't
hand-picked, but they are good. They have a gangling toughness about them.
They have been in the Army for quite a while. They have been trained on
mountains, in deserts, and in ship-to-shore operations. When I asked one of
them how he felt about this trip, he said, "If the ship was to turn back to the
States, we'd all be disappointed."

The officer in command of this battalion, and the only West Pointer aboard,
is Lieutenant Colonel C. D. Wiegand, a short, stocky man who knows his
trade, is a hard-working and intelligent officer, and is completely lacking in
brass-hattery. Most of the ship's officers have been drawn from the Naval
Reserve or the Merchant Marine. The main difference between these men
and the officers on a man-of-war is that there is less talk of gunnery, which is
the breath of life to a ship of the line. Only our skipper, Captain L. B. Schulten,
is an Academy man. He is very quiet, apparently conscious of every detail of
the ship's life and operation, and tough. So long as the young amphibs, or
small-boat men, remain aboard this ship, he is their commanding officer too.
Almost none of the landing-craft men are more than twenty-five years old.
The officers among them are almost entirely ensigns. When they entered the
service, they were lawyers, schoolteachers, accountants, college athletes. Until
now many of them have felt they were getting a raw deal. They were attached
to no ship, and usually they were stationed at this or that shore base for only
short periods. For that reason, there was a certain ambiguity in their position.
They seemed to belong to neither the shore Navy nor the sea Navy. It was as
if they were poor relations on a perennial round of visits. Moreover, since almost all their training was in shallow-draught craft, they knew little about sea-
faring and were regarded as ignoramuses by any bluejacket who had made
even one trip across the ocean. There had been jokes back in training school:
"If you don't do better, we'll see that you get assigned to amphibious duty.
See how you like bouncing around on the surf on one of those ensign eliminators." All of that is forgotten now. We are poised on the lip of the Mediterranean, on the eve of a job that is perhaps the most difficult type of warfare. If
Naval guns have long odds against them in an engagement with shore batteries, the ensign eliminators bouncing around on the surf have much longer
odds.

Inasmuch as this landing operation is not going to work perfectly, I will try to tell you why perfection is out of the question and how the thing would work if it were perfectly executed. The operation will be imperfect not because of faulty planning, equipment, or personnel, but because of the innate difficulties of this kind of fighting and because every advantage, except the selection of the time and place of battle, will rest with the enemy. First, we must run the gantlet of the enemy's surface craft, submarines, aircraft, and coastal-defense batteries in order to bring our transports into the debarkation area. Then, the sea must be fairly smooth for us to launch our landing craft successfully. Then, in the blackness of night, those hundreds of small craft must rendezvous in an orderly group. That sounds easy, but it is almost inexpressibly difficult. Darkness and radio silence must be maintained. The air will be filled with the noise of hundreds of motors, so it will be impossible to shout from boat to boat. The eye will be everywhere befuddled by the green, ghastly flow of phosphorus. Boats will be lunging at you from out of the night. To become disoriented and utterly lost will be more than easy. At the same time, the enemy will be throwing everything he has at you. The difficulty and confusion inherent in this phase of the operation will be extreme.

Once approximate order has been established, the landing craft will come out of their formations and run under the debarkation nets hanging down the sides of the transports. Down these wood-rung chain ladders the troops will climb with their equipment, feeling with their feet and whatever sixth sense they possess for the right moment to step or jump into the landing craft, which may on a sudden whim leap sideways, pin a descending man against his ship, and break his legs. Once the boats are loaded, they will return to their formations, array themselves into waves (how easy it is to tell!), and set out in that order for the shore, where, if the enemy is on his toes, we'll leap out of our craft into water filled with barbed wire, while the star shells and the cold, blue beams of searchlights illuminate us so that we may be raked with rapid-fire weapons as we struggle to make our way up a beach studded with land mines and bayonets.

As for the feelings of the amphibs about the enemy, I have not heard one, in the time I have lived with them, give the slightest indication of ill will toward the Italian people or their army and navy. They know that many of their own men will be killed in combat with the Italian forces, and they plan to slaughter those forces as rapidly and as efficiently as possible, which they'll do with no hatred at all. As often as not, the individual destruction of the enemy will actually be accomplished with a tinge of regret.

The young officers, far from being brutalized, seem almost gentle. They are eager to play fair and they are touched by anyone else's hard luck, even the enemy's. They are still like civilians in uniform. I got talking to one landing-boat officer the other night. He told me that he had a law degree from one of the state universities. He had gone with the same girl for three years before we got into the war. They had meant to marry as soon as he finished school. After Pearl Harbor, he joined the Navy and there were so many transfers and other complications that the wedding had been delayed until two days before he had been ordered to report to this ship. As it turned out, they had one whole uninterrupted day together. However, he doesn't complain. He keeps busy and tries not to think how his wife must be feeling.

The last tiny details are being arranged in preparation for putting to sea. The last conferences are being held, the last gimmicks issued and cleaned, or stowed and lashed in place. The Protestant and Jewish boys are at their last religious services. The Catholics were confessed last night. As a few of us sit around drinking coffee, the senior medical officer, preoccupied with germs and infections, warns us that we must put by one complete outfit of freshly laundered battle dress. The "hour," he says in his tender, almost fatherly way, must find us all freshly scrubbed and in clean clothes for battle.

# THE TAKING OF FICARRA

WALTER BERNSTEIN

THE town of Ficarra, in Sicily, rests on top of a mountain, some eight miles from the north coast and about halfway between Palermo and Messina. It is a small and ancient town, so small that it doesn't appear in the atlases, but it was militarily important because of its position. The American Army, moving toward Messina, had to take Ficarra before it could move on along the coast road. However, before doing anything conclusive about Ficarra, such as sending in foot troops, it was necessary to know what was in the town. Air reconnaissance had reported nothing at all, but a division patrol that had explored the neighborhood had reported seeing what looked like a couple of Germans hanging around the outskirts. The definitive mission of exploration was assigned to a regimental intelligence detachment to which I belonged. This detachment consisted of two squads and a lieutenant to lead them, a total of seventeen men, including myself, each of whom carried either a rifle or a tommy gun. The purpose of the mission was simply to discover what was in the town; we were not to pick any fights.

We set out from regimental headquarters in four jeeps at 1400 hours, which is a civilian two o'clock in the afternoon. I rode in the forward jeep, together with the lieutenant and his driver. The lieutenant was a young, blond Texan named Riley. He was a salesman before the war, but he intended, after it was over, to return to the University of Texas, which he had left before graduating, and take up painting. He was only a second lieutenant, although the kind of job he had called for a first lieutenant, but that didn't bother him much. He had been recommended for the D.S.C. because of bravery displayed on the push up to Palermo, and even that didn't bother him. All Riley wanted to do was finish the war and go back to the University of Texas. His driver was a corporal named Johns, a Mormon from California who wore a fringe of beard around his face and drove as if he were a midget-auto racer on a dirt track. Johns had been recommended for the Silver Star, also because of bravery in the Palermo push, but that was of less interest to him than the news he had recently received that a ranch he had had his eye on for three years had at last been offered for sale.

The road to Ficarra led up into the mountains that began about half a mile from headquarters. It was a dirt road and it climbed in hairpin turns all the way. A battle on the preceding day had been fought about halfway up the road. The grass all along the sides was burned in little patches where shells had landed. Once we passed a German tank that had been knocked out. It had been set on fire and was all black now, the cross on it barely visible, and lying beside it in a ditch was a corpse covered by a blanket. Farther on we passed an abandoned Italian truck that had been knocked over on its back. The road was terribly quiet. It was littered here and there with documents and equipment dropped by the Germans in their rush to escape. There were no soldiers anywhere and no sign of activity. There was only the hot, midday stillness and the Mediterranean stretching out behind us, flat and glassy.

After we had gone about six miles up the road, Riley motioned Johns to pull over to one side, against a cliff. As the other jeeps came up, he motioned them to do the same. Then Riley called for everyone except the drivers to start up the road on foot. The men piled out of the jeeps and followed him, slinging their guns over their shoulders. I followed too. When Riley got up the road a little way, he turned off into a grove of lemon trees. There he unslung his rifle and sat down under one of the trees, took a map out of his pocket, and began to study it. The rest of the men came up and either leaned against the trees or sat down around Riley. None of them said anything. They had gone through other missions like this one before and were waiting now without worry, certain of their ability to bring it off. They thought only up to the minute at a time like this. They waited quietly, nerves buried under their professionalism, the thin, always present edge of their impatience now hardly noticeable. They looked at Riley or back at the sea; one of them started to pick a lemon off a tree, then stopped. The Germans have a habit of booby-trapping fruit trees.

After a while, Riley put the map back in his pocket, took off his helmet, and scratched his head. He had thin, white hair that lay flat on his head. "There's no sense in going straight up the road," he said. "We'll split into two squad columns and move up the mountain, then flank the town from below." He paused and looked out over the mountains. "Probably there's nothing there," he said. No one questioned him. He sighed and stood up. "Billerbeck," he said.

"Yes, sir," a sergeant said. Billerbeck was a good-looking farm boy from Illinois.

"You take your squad along the road and I'll lead the other one farther down," Riley said.

"Yes, *sir*," Billerbeck said.

Riley put on his helmet and slung his rifle over his shoulder again. "Let's go," he said.

Riley led the squad I was in, which was headed by a Sergeant Sheehan, to a path that wound its way up the mountain more or less parallel to the road and about thirty yards below. We took this path while Billerbeck and his men walked along the road above us. Riley was in the lead, followed by Sergeant Sheehan, a tall, thin Irishman from New Haven who used to sell magazine subscriptions. I came behind Sheehan. Each man walked twenty feet or so behind the one ahead of him. Nothing had been said about land mines, but each of us made an almost unnoticeable effort to walk in the footsteps of the men before us. The most popular anti-personnel mine the Germans use is called the S mine. This makes a little pop when you step on it and shoots a container five feet into the air, where it explodes with terrific force and scatters several hundred steel balls. We walked along slowly, listening all the time.

In twenty minutes we were almost at the top of our mountain and we cut back to the road again. There Riley dropped to his knees and wriggled the rest of the way up, motioning back to the rest of us to stop where we were. Then he took out his field glasses and peered over the crest. The rest of us sat down. Riley motioned to Sheehan and me to join him, and we crept up to where he was. He handed the glasses to Sheehan and said, "Take a look." We could see the edge of the town from where we lay. It was up the road about half a mile, huddled on the top of the mountain. The road dipped into a hollow ahead of us and then rose to the town. All we could see without the glasses were a few buildings and the road curving into town. There was no sign of life. Sheehan peered a moment, then said, "You mean those two people in the shadow?" Riley nodded, took the glasses from Sheehan, and gave them to me. He said, "Right under that red barn closest to us." I looked and saw two men standing next to the barn. They seemed to be talking. I couldn't tell whether or not they wore uniforms. "I think they're civilians," Riley said. I looked again through the glasses and saw the two men, who clearly were wearing white shirts, come out of the shadow and start to walk down the road toward us. I returned the glasses to Riley and he watched the two men until they disappeared into the hollow. Then he wriggled back to where he could stand up without being seen from above. "Caruso," he called. One of the men down the slope said, "Here I am." Riley waved for him to come up. "A job for you," he said.

"Yes, sir," Caruso said. He was a small and very dark Italian with a big nose, who used to work for Bloomingdale's.

"There are two civilians coming down the road," Riley said. "I want you to ask them what plays in the town."

"Sure," Caruso said.

"They should be here in a minute," Riley said. He went back up the slope and looked over the crest. "They're coming now," he said. He turned around and waved for the other men to come up to the ridge. They moved up carefully and Riley dispersed them with hand signals until they were spread out along the edge of the road and had it covered with their guns. Then he concealed himself.

I looked over the crest and saw the two men coming along the road. They were civilians, all right, and Italians. They were talking and gesturing with their hands. When they were thirty yards from us, Caruso stepped out into the road. The men stopped short. They looked around, and two of our men stepped out on the road behind them. The Italians seemed very frightened. They were short, middle-aged men, and their hands continued to flutter after they had stopped talking. Caruso said something in Italian. The men looked around them again and the taller of them said, *"Americano?"* Caruso nodded. "Ha!" the Italian said, and then he and his companion smiled broadly, moved up to shake hands with Caruso, and began to talk very rapidly. Caruso answered with equal rapidity and soon they were having a great conversation, the taller Italian talking in long stretches, Caruso interrupting every now and then with what sounded like questions. Caruso finally turned back to Riley. "He says the people are waiting for us in the village," Caruso said. "They have wine ready for us."

"The hell with the wine," Riley said. "Are there any Germans?"

"He says there are some Germans waiting to give themselves up at the edge of town," said Caruso.

Riley walked out on the road and looked at the two Italians. "You think they're telling the truth?" he asked Caruso.

"I think so," Caruso said.

"How many Germans are there?" Riley asked.

"He doesn't know how many," Caruso said. "He says there are more Germans in the town, but some of them are in a building at the edge of town and want to give themselves up. He says most of them pulled out this morning. They were told we would cut their throats if we caught them." Riley didn't say anything. The taller Italian spoke again to Caruso. "He says he'll show us where the Germans are hiding," Caruso said. Riley didn't say anything. He took out his glasses again and swept the town with them. Then he said, "All right." He put away his glasses and turned to the Italians. "God help you if this isn't on the level," he said. He turned to Caruso and said, "You go with them along the road to town. We'll cover you from the sides." "You bet," Caruso said. He spoke to the Italians, motioning toward the town, and they nodded. "They go first," Riley said. "Sure," Caruso said. He started up the road, the rifle now off his shoulder and in his hands, the two Italians walking in front of him. "Take it easy!" Riley called after him.

We got off the road again, reassembled in formation some yards below it, and started ahead. We stayed closer to the road than before. Caruso was moving slowly, but on the mountainside we had to cover twice as much ground to travel the same distance, and it was hard going. When we got within two hundred yards of the town, Riley called to Caruso to stop. He called to Biller-beck, too, and told him to take his squad, cross the road, and enter the town from the upper side. Billerbeck and his squad crossed over and Riley led our squad up onto the road, where we strung out on both sides about twenty paces apart. We waited there until Billerbeck and his men disappeared around the edge of town; they went along carefully, taking advantage of the conceal-ment offered by a large clump of trees. Then Riley told Caruso to move for-ward.

We walked even more slowly now. It was very quiet and hot, and our woollen shirts were black with sweat. The silence was oppressive; it had a heavy, malignant quality. We dipped into the hollow of the road and the town disappeared from sight. When we came up the hill on the other side, the red barn was immediately ahead. The two Italians stopped. They said some-thing to Caruso and pointed into the town. "They say it's the third house," Caruso said. The road went around a bend into town and we could not see past the barn. The Italians spoke again to Caruso, who said to Riley, "They tell me the Germans are just waiting for us to come." "I'll bet they are," Riley said. He motioned back for us to separate a little more, then said, "Let's go," and we moved up the road again.

The bend in the road was not sharp, and the third house came into view gradually. Riley led the way, with Sheehan on the opposite side of the road a little behind him. I was behind Sheehan. Opposite me was a young private named Taylor. Caruso had dropped back to the end of our line with the Italians, who were beginning to look frightened again. Suddenly Riley stopped. He dropped to one knee and brought up his rifle. I couldn't see why for a moment. Then I saw a machine gun parked by the third house, pointing down the road at us. That was the first thing I saw, and then I saw a man coming out of the cellar of the house. He was wearing a German uniform and he held his hands high in the air. I got down on one knee and so did Sheehan and Taylor, and we all covered the German. Riley put down his gun and shouted, "Come on! Come on!," his voice harsh and commanding. The Ger-man walked out onto the road. Three other Germans followed him, all with their hands up. They stood uncertainly in the road and Riley shouted, "Come over here!" He motioned to them and they came down the road. Riley said, "Take them, Sheehan," his eyes still on the house and the road beyond. The Germans came up to us and Sheehan moved to meet them. Taylor slipped across the road to take Sheehan's place and I stood up to cover the prisoners. They were three privates and a sergeant. The privates were maybe thirty-seven or thirty-eight, and the sergeant looked about twenty-five. They were all trying very hard to smile, but none of them could quite make it. Sheehan and I walked backward as they came on, until we were around the bend again, and then we stopped. "Send them back," Riley called to Sheehan. "Send a man back with them to the jeeps." Sheehan called down to one of our men to take the prisoners. The Germans had been looking from one of us to the other, waiting to see what we would do with them. When a soldier came up to take them back, he raised his tommy gun to cover them, and one of the Germans said, *"Nicht, nicht."*

"We're not going to shoot you," Sheehan said.

*"Nicht,"* the German said. He was one of the older men and very much afraid. He spoke in a low, pleading voice, holding out his hands to us.

"For God's sake," Sheehan said. *"Nicht."*

The German understood and tried to smile, but nothing came out. Sheehan motioned them down the road and they shuffled off, followed by the soldier with the tommy gun.

Sheehan and I rounded the bend again. Riley was still on one knee, watching the house. He stood up when we took our places. "O.K.?" he asked Sheehan. "O.K.," Sheehan said. Riley looked back to see that the rest of the men were there and then led the way slowly forward, staying close to one side of the road. He didn't stop when we came to the third house. The machine gun was there and so were two rifles, but we didn't touch them. After the third house there was a gap of perhaps fifty yards and then the town really began, with a church that had a stone tower and four broad steps leading up to its doors. The road turned at the church, plunging suddenly into the town and becoming a narrow, cobblestoned street flanked by stone houses crowded one against the other. The air was cool and almost dank, the sun shut out by the narrowness of the street. At first sight everything looked dirty, but then you realized that it was just old. The houses hung over the street in two long, weatherbeaten rows. "How can they live in a place like this?" Taylor whispered. We were walking very slowly now, hugging the sides of the buildings, each man watching the doors and windows and roofs across the street. But there was nothing to see; there were no people around. The only sound was of our heels on the pavement. The town was dead; there was no breath of life in it at all. There was not even a Fascist slogan on a wall. There was only the ancient, narrow, dead town, and we made our way through it gingerly, guns held loosely and at the ready.

The street began to go downhill. It ran into a little square with a fountain in the center. Halfway down was an alley leading off the street. We waited there for a moment while Riley and Sheehan peered down it. No one was in it, but nevertheless we ran past it bent low. At the bottom of the street, Riley stepped off the curb to go past the fountain. The silence was blasted by two shots that sounded louder than anything in the world ever had before. A man was on one knee behind the fountain, with a gun at his shoulder. I dove for a doorway. There were two more shots, close together, and then I was in the doorway, pressing back as far as I could go. I got down on one knee, resting my gun against the side of the doorway, and looked down the street. All I could see at first was a thin spiral of dust settling in the middle of the square. Then I spotted Riley in a doorway across the street and Taylor flat on his belly against the side of a building. The echo of the shots was still very loud in my ears. There was a long silence, and then Riley called softly, "Is anyone hurt?" There was no answer and he repeated the question, his voice soft but urgent.

"I'm all right," Sheehan's voice said.

"He missed me," Taylor said. "I don't know how, but he missed me."

I said I was all right, and the men echoed this answer down the line.

"Where'd he go?" Sheehan asked.

"I don't know," Riley said. "I was too busy ducking."

"I think he went down the street," Taylor said.

No one said anything for a while. Then Riley stepped out of his doorway and started down the street again. Sheehan stepped out of a doorway ahead of me, and I stepped out of mine. I looked back and saw that the rest of the men were coming. Riley led the way around one side of the square, giving the fountain plenty of room and sticking close to the doorways. Sheehan went around the square on the other side the same way. We had just got around to the far side and were starting down the street that led out of it when another shot was fired. I hit the ground and rolled against the side of a building. There was a blur of movement at the end of the street and I fired twice at it, resting my elbows on the stones of the sidewalk. Riley was also on the ground nearby and I could see his shoulder kick back as he fired. Then he put his gun down. "Son of a bitch," he said. He got to his feet. "I saw him that time," he said. I stood up and saw Taylor come out of a doorway across the street.

"Did you hit him?" Riley asked me.

I said I didn't think so.

"I didn't get a chance," Sheehan said.

"He ran like hell," Riley said. "I got a quick bead on the bastard and he was gone."

We stood there and then we heard the quick burst of a tommy gun to our left. "That's Billerbeck," Sheehan said.

"You *hope* it's Billerbeck," Riley said.

We listened, but there was no other sound. Riley bent over and rubbed his knee. "Those stones are hard," he said. He moved forward and we followed him. It was all quiet again, but my ears were still ringing from the shots. The air was different, though; it had the burnt smell of shooting. It was a faint smell but very noticeable, and it made the town seem suddenly familiar, linking it with all the other towns in Sicily which had had that smell. We followed Riley down the street, walking easier now, knowing finally what we had got ourselves in for. I looked across the street at Taylor and he smiled. "Isn't this like the movies?" he said. "Isn't this just like the movies?"

We came to an intersection and Riley stopped before crossing it. He peered around the corner and then pulled his head back in a hurry. He peered around again, took a good look up the cross street, and then stepped out into the intersection. "It's Billerbeck," he said. In a few seconds Billerbeck came walking down to join Riley. His men were strung out along their street the way we were on ours. "Was that you firing?" Riley asked. Billerbeck nodded. "They were running up the street and we only had time to turn the tommy gun on them," he said. "Don't think we hit anything." Riley asked Billerbeck if his squad had been fired on and Billerbeck said no. He said that they had skirted the edge of the town and were cutting down to meet us when they saw five Germans running up the street. They were gone before Billerbeck could do more than fire a few rounds at them. "I think they're still running," he said.

"Well, I wish they'd make up their mind," Riley said.

Riley told Billerbeck to have his men fall in behind us, and we all started down the street our squad had been on. The town was thinning out now. We could see the houses beginning to space out ahead of us and some trees at the far end of the street. The street curved and suddenly we were out in the sun again. There were houses only on our left; the other side was the mountainside, stretching down in a series of plowed terraces, the earth black and fertile. The road curved again and the houses thinned out still further. As we came around this curve, we saw two civilians running from a house that stood off by itself. They disappeared before we could do anything. We all stopped and looked at the closed door of the house. The house was a two-story affair, with a large wooden door and no windows. Riley dropped to one knee, aiming his rifle at the door. Sheehan aimed his tommy gun. No one talked. I moved quietly up to the door and stood at one side of it, with my back against the house. Taylor moved over to take my place and covered the door. As soon as all the men were in position, I reached over and slowly tried the knob. The door was locked. I pressed against it very slowly, but it wouldn't give. I looked back at Riley, who nodded, and then I banged the door very hard with my gun. Almost immediately a woman began to cry inside. I banged again and she cried louder, and then she began to yell and shriek. I couldn't understand a word she said. She was yelling at the top of her lungs and all I could tell was that she was speaking Italian. *"Tedeschi?"* I asked, giving the Italian name for the Germans.

*"No,"* the woman screamed. *"No! No!"*

I looked over at Riley and he shrugged. He stood up and called for Caruso, who came running up. He motioned Caruso to the house and Caruso came over and stood at the other side of the door. The woman was still screaming and Caruso had to shout to make himself heard. Finally he yelled something in Italian that sounded very fierce and the woman shut up. For a moment there was no sound. Then the knob turned and the door slowly opened. A thin, middle-aged woman with stringy black hair stuck her head out. She looked first at me, then at Caruso. *"Americano?"* she asked. We nodded and Caruso said something in Italian. The woman looked at us again and then at the other soldiers in the street. She began to cry. She held her hands to her face and cried, and then she went over to Caruso and threw her arms around him and kissed him on both cheeks. She came over and kissed me and went down the road and kissed the other men, every one of them, even Lieutenant Riley. She was crying all the time. After she had finished kissing everyone, she came back to Caruso and kissed him again. I couldn't tell now whether she was laughing or crying. She went into the house and came out with a huge plate of grapes. She handed them around until Riley finally told Caruso to tell her that we had some work to do and would see her later. Caruso told her and the woman smiled and nodded happily. She went into the house, leaving the door open, and we moved on down the road.

The road curved twice again. After the first curve, it went downhill and there were no more houses. Riley stopped there and gazed down the road. It was very quiet. We were in the country again and there was a hot, summer stillness over everything, no longer oppressive but still good and hot. The countryside looked very peaceful. The mountains were hazy in the˙distance and olive trees lined the road. "They moved a lot of vehicles out of here," Riley said, studying the road. He took off his helmet. His hair was matted on his head in little flat ringlets. As we stood there, an Italian came around the next curve toward us. He was a very old man in patched overalls and he was carrying a jug. He looked at us without interest and was going past us into the town when Riley stopped him. "What's down there?" Riley asked. The old man looked at him blankly. *"Tedeschi?"* Riley asked, pointing down the road. The old man nodded, still without interest. He had very bright little eyes set in a deeply lined face. He must have been eighty years old. *"Tede-schi,"* the old man said. He waved both hands down the road. "O.K.," Riley said. He stepped aside and the old man walked on, paying no attention to us as he passed. "I guess they beat it out of here in a hurry," Sheehan said. Riley scratched his head, then put on his helmet. "We'd better go back," he said. He sounded regretful. "All we were supposed to do was find out what was in town," he said. "There's no sense going any further without more men." I asked him if he thought there were any more of the enemy in town and he shook his head. "They ran," he said.

We all turned around and walked slowly back to town, keeping the same formation but not being as careful as before. When we got back into the narrow street and the buildings closed in on us, Riley stopped and waved us into the proper intervals. "Let's not get careless," he said. We still hugged the sides of the buildings, but there was less tension. When we came to the center of town, we heard voices. In the square there was a group of civilians standing around the fountain. There were men and women and children and even young girls. We hadn't seen a young girl in five weeks. As soon as we came up, they began to laugh and cheer. They made a path for us and then, as we walked along the street, the whole town came to life. Windows and doors opened and people came out from everywhere. They stood on the street and on the balconies and leaned out of windows, and they all cheered us. It was a regular parade. They even threw flowers at us. The kids ran alongside, looking at our uniforms and guns. The word had been passed around that Caruso was a countryman and he was immediately surrounded. Everyone was laughing, even the babies. One woman ran up with a bottle of wine, which she gave to Riley. Sheehan already had two, one under each arm. Taylor had his rifle slung over his shoulder and was walking along with his hands clasped over his head, like a boxer acknowledging a crowd.

When we got back to the other edge of the town, by the church, Riley stopped and made sure we were all there. Then we started down the road to the jeeps, leaving the townspeople waving at us from the steps of the church. We passed the house with the machine gun in front but didn't stop. We didn't bother cutting around the mountain but went straight down the road. On the way, we passed an old German bivouac area, with neatly dug foxholes and empty cases of ammunition lying around. There were also several empty S-mine boxes and we stopped to look at them. "The dirty bastards," Taylor said.

When we got to the jeeps, we found the prisoners sitting on the bank of the road, surrounded by the drivers. Riley asked Johns if he had heard any shots and Johns said that he hadn't. The prisoners seemed happier now and were smoking American cigarettes. They looked seedy, anxious to please, and very human. They smiled at us when we came up. Sheehan said, "Smile, you sons of bitches." None of them did any talking, not even to each other. They just smiled at us with an apologetic air. "I'd like to shoot the four of them," one of our men said. I think that was what we all felt, but nobody did anything about it. There would have been no satisfaction in killing them now. There was no satisfaction in doing anything to them once you had them. There was only the impotent hatred, the inability even to say, "See where you are now." So all we did was look at them. Finally, we put them into our four jeeps, one man into each. Then the rest of us climbed in and we drove slowly back down the road.

[October 16, 1943]

# BUSY MORNING

WALTER BERNSTEIN

W E MOVED into the new regimental Command Post at eight o'clock in
the morning. A command post, better known as a C.P., is a field headquarters. I was a member of the regimental reconnaissance platoon attached to
the headquarters. We were thirty miles out of Messina in Sicily, working our
way slowly along the north coast toward the Italian mainland. Usually the
regimental C.P. is several miles back of the lines, but the colonel commanding
this regiment believed in getting as close to the front as he could without
actually outstripping his infantry. Right then the C.P. was only a mile and a
half from the enemy, or was believed to be only that far. There was still some
uncertainty about just where the front was. The C.P. was hidden in a fairly
dense grove of trees between a road and the sea. The trees were no protection
against anything serious, but they were good concealment. On the other side
of the road was a series of ridges running at right angles to it, and the gullies
between the ridges offered cover. It was about two hundred yards from the
C.P. to these gullies.

The C.P. area had been an enemy motor park and it was full of abandoned
Italian trucks with their tires removed. There were also a few damaged motorcycles. It didn't look as though the area had been used for troops, because there
were no foxholes. The Germans and Italians always dug foxholes, even when
they knew they were stopping for only a short time. The Germans dug good
foxholes, and they came in handy when we took over, but the Italian foxholes
were works of art. You could put an army into an Italian foxhole dug for one
man. All they lacked was running water. You had to be careful getting into
them, however. Often the Italians would booby-trap the holes before they left.
I reached the area in a jeep driven by Lieutenant Samuel, the officer in charge
of the reconnaissance platoon. Samuel was an easygoing young man from
Colorado who was in real estate before the war. He drove our jeep skillfully
down a steep embankment, through a bramblebush, and into the shade of a
large elm tree in the grove. All around us trucks and other jeeps were being
parked. A captain was walking around yelling, "Fifty feet between vehicles!
Fifty feet between vehicles!" Samuel got out of our jeep. He had to see the
regimental intelligence officer to get his assignment, he said. He walked off

245

between the trees and I leaned back in my seat and took it easy. The day promised to be hot and muggy.

The parking area gradually filled up. As soon as the drivers had parked their vehicles, they started camouflaging them with the special camouflage nets they carried with them in their machines. Over in one corner of the area, at the edge of the grove, was a medical tent with a large red cross on it. Back of our jeep was a supply truck from which a mess sergeant was unloading boxes of rations and five-gallon cans of water. Everybody was working. The scene might just have been maneuvers in Louisiana or North Carolina.

After a while, Samuel returned with one of his men, a private named Keith. "Keith and I are going up front," Samuel said. "Just the two of us." He told Keith to take the jeep away, fill it with gas, and meet him up on the road. The Lieutenant and I walked up there to wait for the jeep, and he explained the situation. It seemed that the enemy was directly ahead and close, but no one knew how close or in how much strength. The road crossed a dry river bed about two miles ahead and the colonel thought that perhaps the enemy had withdrawn across it. One company of the regiment was already advancing across the ridges on the river. That was Z Company. Two more were on their way up from behind the C.P. Samuel's job was to set up an observation post overlooking the river and see what he could see. As we reached the road, we saw another company—X Company—coming up from the rear. The men were strung out on both sides of the road at five-yard intervals. A tall, handsome lieutenant was leading them. Samuel waved to him. "Where are you headed, Johnny?" Samuel called.

"Where do you think we're headed?" Johnny said. He didn't stop walking, but he turned his head as he passed so that he could keep talking to Samuel. He looked a little like Gary Cooper, only younger, and very healthy. He had two rifles slung over one shoulder and I noticed that the soldier walking behind him didn't have any.

"I hear there's trouble up front," Samuel said.

"That's no skin off me," Johnny said. "I got orders."

"You shouldn't go up there without a reconnaissance," Samuel said. "Whose orders are they?"

"How should I know?" Johnny said. "All I know is that I got orders." He laughed and waved his hand. "See you later, Sam," he said.

"See you later," Samuel said, and, turning back to me, he added, "Johnny's a good boy. We went to O.C.S. together." He shook his head and said, "But he shouldn't go up there without a reconnaissance."

A little later, Keith drove up with the jeep. Samuel climbed in and they drove off. The company was still coming down the road, marching slowly, with the heavy, pushing step of men who are dead tired. The regiment had been in the line for a week now and most of that time had been spent hiking over the sheer, Sicilian mountains, carrying rifles and machine guns and mortars, chasing the enemy and never quite catching him. That had been the whole pattern of the war along this north coast: the Germans retreating, blowing up bridges, laying mines, blasting the road with artillery as they retreated, rarely making a stand unless they were sure of taking a heavy toll before they retreated again. They had made a stand two days before on top of a mountain, and this company marching down the road had climbed the mountain and taken it. First, though, these men had lain at the foot of the mountain for twelve hours while the Germans tried to blow them out with cannon. The company had had just six hours' sleep since then, and you could see it on the soldiers' faces and in the way they walked.

After X Company was out of sight, I went back to my reconnaissance platoon, which was waiting for orders. There wasn't anything to do, so I decided to shave. I hadn't had a chance to shave for three days and some general had issued orders that we were to shave every two days. My musette bag was in one of the other jeeps and I went to get it. Sitting in the jeep, reading a two-month-old copy of *PM,* was the platoon sergeant, a New York boy named Vrana. He was a commercial artist who had joined the Regular Army five years ago because he thought the war was imminent and he wanted to get into it. He was a Czechoslovakian who had come to the United States when he was very young and he still spoke with a faint accent. I got my shaving stuff and propped the mirror up on the hood of the jeep. Then I filled my helmet from a can of water from the back of the jeep. I was just preparing to lather my face when there was a whining noise overhead. I put down my brush. Vrana put down his paper, and we both listened. There was a faint crash that sounded as if it were a mile back of us. "Now I wonder what *that* was," Vrana said. We knew what it was. It was an enemy artillery shell that had overshot us. But maybe if we were skeptical, it would go away. Then there was another whine, and the next crash sounded closer. "He's shortening the range," Vrana said. I rinsed off the brush, dried it carefully, and put it back in my bag. I emptied my helmet and put it on. There was another whine far off, but closer, and we both hit the ground as a shell crashed a hundred yards down the road. "This is not for me," Vrana said. He was reading his newspaper on the ground, half under the jeep.

All around the area, men were picking themselves up and looking at each other. Work had stopped. We were all waiting for the next one. It came. It started with the whine and grew into the sudden rush of air that meant it was very near. I was on my face when it hit, fifty yards away. I could see the dust rising at the back of the C.P., where it hit. "The gullies for us," Vrana said. We started for the nearest gully, two hundred yards away, at a slow trot. Everyone seemed to be heading in the same direction. Then there was another whine, and still another, the low whistle rising until it became the violent, sucked-in whine that meant it was coming very close, and we were flat on the ground, trying to crawl right inside. "They got it," said Vrana. He meant the range. We stood up and started to run. Everybody was running. There was the whine again and I dove as though off a diving board and belly-flopped on the ground. The dirt was dry and gritty in my mouth. The whine grew louder and louder, coming straight at me, and I opened my mouth against it. There was a crash like the sky falling in, and the ground heaved and something whistled viciously over my head, and then dirt was dropping quietly around, like rain.

There was another whine, and another, and another. They came like death. There was nothing to do but press into the ground and wait. Three more came, one after the other. I put my face in the dirt and tried to dig deeper with my knees. There were three more. It was like trying to hold on to the rail of a ship in a storm, only there was nothing to hang on to, nothing. I thought of a leather handbag my wife and I had once seen in the window of John-Frederics in New York. It was the most beautiful bag we had ever seen, simple and wonderfully worked, but it was too expensive, and I thought now, the shells falling like the end of the world: We should have bought the bag, we should have bought the bag. Another three came. It must have been a whole battery firing at us. Through the noise I could hear someone shouting, "Medics! Medics!" There was a pause and I got to my feet and ran for the gully again, my breath coming short and painful. I didn't know where Vrana was. Out of the corner of one eye, I could see another soldier running beside me, but I didn't know who he was. Everybody was running for the gully. It was the longest two hundred yards I have ever covered. I finally reached the road and started across it. There was a captain on the road, directing everyone into the gullies. It was the same captain who had ordered the jeeps fifty feet apart, but now he was wearing only one legging. I wondered what had happened to the other legging. The other soldier was ahead of me now. I followed him up a bank and down a little path. I thought I was going fast, but he was really travelling. Then we were in the gully, the protecting walls of the ridges rising on either side, and the soldier slowed up. "Son of a bitch," I heard him say, and then I saw the two stars on his collar. My God, I said to myself, it's a general.

I followed the general along the gully until I came upon Vrana, sitting with his back against one side of it. I sat down next to him. He was reading his newspaper. The gully was full of men from the C.P., most of them sitting or lying on the ground, waiting out the barrage. The shells were still coming and we could hear them whistle over our heads and crash in the C.P. area. They were coming about one every thirty seconds. A lot of the men were still breathing hard from the run; the rest were just sitting and talking. Next to me was a lieutenant with artillery insignia on his collar. He looked disgusted, and explained that he was supposed to be back with his battery and had just come up to headquarters on a liaison mission when the shelling began. "They're going to wonder what happened to me," he said gloomily. "They're

going to think I went over to the goddam infantry." The men around him
didn't take too kindly to this and began asking him where was this artillery
support they had been hearing so much about. "Don't worry," the lieutenant
said. "Don't worry."

"Who's worrying?" said a small, grimy private. "Am I worrying? Do I look
like I'm worrying?" His face was smeared with dirt, which he had probably
picked up when he hit the ground. "I'm not the worrying type," he went on.
"I'm just curious. I'm the curious type. I just want to know when the hell I'm
getting out of this hole."

Another shell whined overhead and crashed in the C.P. "They must have
beautiful observation," the artillery lieutenant said, with professional admiration.

"Please!" the small private said. "How about *our* beautiful observation?"

There was a loud boom to our rear and everyone jumped. The artillery
lieutenant just leaned back and smiled.

"Well, it's about time," the private said.

There was another boom and then a whole salvo. It was a highly reassuring sound. Our own artillery was firing back. Our observers must have spotted
a target, because the guns let off two more salvos. We could hear the shells
crackle overhead, going the other way. The enemy guns had stopped firing,
and after the third salvo our guns stopped too. For a moment all was peace
and quiet. Then there was another whine and a shell burst in the C.P. This
was immediately answered by another salvo from our guns. "Battery salvo,"
the artillery lieutenant said. "They must have spotted something." There was
no answer from the enemy guns, and very gradually everyone relaxed.

When five minutes had gone by without any enemy fire, some of the men
began climbing back to the road. The artillery lieutenant stood up and sighed.
"Hope they didn't hit my jeep," he said. "I got five bottles of wine in it."

He moved off and Vrana and I stood up to follow him. "Might as well go
back," Vrana said. We started toward the road. "Heigh ho, heigh ho," Vrana
said. "Now off to work we go." He was still carrying his newspaper. "I wish
they'd give me time to finish this damned thing," he said.

When Vrana and I got back to the road, we found Keith in Lieutenant
Samuel's jeep, parked at the entrance to the C.P. "Where the hell have you
been?" he asked Vrana.

"I've been getting my nails done," Vrana said. "Where the hell do you think
I've been?"

"Well, the Lieutenant wants two more men up there," Keith said. "We've
got an O.P. on top of a hill and he wants another observer and someone to
work a radio." Vrana told me to go as the observer. "I'll get Verele for the
radio," Vrana said, and walked back into the C.P.

The men were still streaming out from the gullies and the captain with only one legging came over and told Keith to move the jeep out of the way. I got into the jeep and Keith drove fifty yards back up the road. I asked him where he had been when the shelling was on and he said he had been on his way back from the hill overlooking the river. "They're having trouble up front," he said. "I think X Company marched right into an 88." I asked if anyone had been hurt and Keith shrugged. "The ambulance came up," he said. I told him what had happened to us at the C.P. He shook his head sadly. "This is no way to make a living," he said.

After a few minutes, Vrana came down the road with Sergeant Verele, a quiet, slow-talking farmer from Illinois. Verele was carrying a hand radio set, the kind that has a collapsible aerial. I asked Vrana if much damage had been done to the C.P. "They hit the medic's tent," he said. "Was anyone there?" Keith asked. Vrana nodded. None of us said anything. We all knew that the C.P. was a legitimate military objective and that you couldn't call your shots on the nose at seven miles, but it wasn't right for the medic's tent to be hit. "A couple of other guys were hit by shrapnel," Vrana said. He mentioned their names. There was nothing else to say, so Keith started the jeep's motor and Verele climbed into the back. "Your call is Item Roger One," Vrana said to Verele. "I'll be Item Roger."

"Check," Verele said.

Vrana stepped back and Keith turned the jeep around carefully, trying to keep off the dirt shoulder of the road in case it had been mined. He moved past the C.P. in second and then whipped into high. The jeep jumped forward and Keith pushed the accelerator to the floor. "Excuse the speed!" he yelled to me above the noise. "I think they got the road under observation."

We swept along the road. I held on grimly. The road was full of curves, and Keith slowed down before each curve and then gunned the car as soon as he was around it. The idea was to cover the straightaways as fast as possible, before anyone could draw a bead on you. I crouched in my seat, trying to stick with the car and make myself as inconspicuous as possible. After a few minutes we sped past a lot of infantrymen, seated on the bank of the road. Some of them waved at us. Ahead of us the road ran down almost to the sea and then there was a long straightaway with what looked like a very sharp curve at the end of it. We came into this stretch and some soldiers seated by the road yelled as we went past. "What did they say?" Keith shouted. I hadn't understood either, but Verele leaned forward and shouted, "They said there's an 88 trained on that curve up there!"

The road now was straight and flat, and I felt very naked. On our right there were fields running up to the ridges and on the left was a stretch of beach along the sea. Up ahead, past the curve, there was an old barge aground on the beach. There was no sign of life, but I knew how much that meant. We were nearing the curve and I tried to sink a little lower in my seat. Keith jammed on the brakes and pulled over to one side. "This is where we get off," he said. He hopped out of the jeep and started to walk up the road. Verele and I followed him. "Keep your eye on that barge," he said. "We think maybe they're directing fire from there."

We were almost up to the curve now. The fields on our right had become a grove of trees. There was a path going off the road into the wood. Keith started up it. It felt good to get some concealment. When we got into the grove, Keith stopped and took out his pistol. I· took out mine too. I had my doubts about the effectiveness of a .45 against an 88-millimetre cannon, but it was nice to have something in your hand. I only wished I knew what the hell was going on. Keith led the way slowly through the trees. Soon I saw why he had drawn his gun. There was a small house ahead of us. Keith made a wide circle around the house, always facing it. Once he stopped and we all froze, but nothing happened. The house sat there, dappled by the sunlight through the trees, looking quiet and innocent. We got past the house, and the hill became steeper. We passed over a burned spot where a shell had hit. The earth was blackened and raw. Then there was another house, but Keith led the way right past this time. Outside it were a table and a large easy chair. The Germans had evidently had a C.P. or an observation post there. There were three mattresses on the ground and papers scattered around the table. There was also a large foxhole, practically a dugout. We walked past them all without touching anything. The hill was steeper now and it was hard climbing. There were onion skins and tomatoes all around; the enemy must have eaten well.

When we were almost at the crest, Keith stopped and whistled softly. There was a movement at the top and Lieutenant Samuel came sliding down. He was smiling. The first thing he asked was whether we had had a pleasant trip. His helmet was covered with twigs and leaves were stuck into the helmet net. "I feel like a woman with all this greenery on my head," he said. I wondered what he was so happy about. We all sat down on the hillside. Samuel took off his helmet and laid it beside him. Verele already had his aerial up and was trying to make contact with Vrana. "Item Roger," he called, his mouth close to the speaker. "Item Roger. This is Item Roger One." He pronounced the words very carefully, exaggerating each syllable. He had no success the first few times, then Vrana's voice suddenly came back, thin and metallic: "This is Item Roger."

"Ask him if there are any messages," Samuel said.

Verele relayed the question. There was a pause and then Vrana's voice said, "Artillery wants to know where they're hitting."

"O.K.," Samuel said.

"This is Item Roger One," Verele said over the radio. "Roger. Wilco. Over and out." He was saying he had heard the message, would coöperate, and was now closing his set.

Samuel put on his helmet and stood up. "You stay here," he said to Verele. He started back up the hill and motioned to Keith and me to follow him.

When he got near the top, he dropped down on his stomach and began to crawl, motioning us to do the same. We crawled to the crest of the hill and looked over.

We were looking almost straight down on the bed of the river, which was dry and rocky. There were two bridges across it, a wooden railroad bridge to our left and a stone highway bridge almost directly beneath us. Both of them had been blown up. The stone bridge gaped in the middle. The railroad bridge had also been blasted at the center and the two ends leaned down toward the river bed. Across the river was a ridge like ours, dropping down to the sea in a series of hills, each a little lower than the one before, and there was a town on top of one of the hills. The highway disappeared over the ridge on the other side of the river. We couldn't see the road at all on our side.

There was nothing stirring, no sign of life anywhere, not even in the town. It was a little surprising after the violence of the shelling we had undergone and the reports of trouble with an 88 along the road. You expected more than a quiet, normal countryside. Samuel pointed to the bit of road we could see across the river. "That's where they had the 88," he said. "Right out in the middle of the road." I asked if he had seen it. "Sure I saw it," he said. The trouble with the 88 had happened just as Samuel and Keith had come up to the crest. They had seen the enemy gun sitting out in the road, across the blown-up highway bridge, waiting for X Company to come around that last curve, but there hadn't been time for them to do anything about it. The Company had started to march around the curve before Samuel could get word down. Luckily, the enemy had been too anxious and had fired when only the first few men had come into view. Samuel didn't think many had been hurt. The 88 had fired only twice; then it had been pulled out of sight. "I think they were the rear guard," Samuel said. "They just wanted to get one last lick."

We lay there about five minutes and then we heard the whistle of a shell over our heads. It was going toward the enemy. We watched to see where it would land. We heard the dull crump as it hit, but we couldn't see where. Three more shells came over, crackling through the air, but it was the same with them. "They're shooting over the ridge," said Samuel, who was looking through field glasses. He turned to Keith and told him to relay the information back to Vrana. Keith slithered away and we tried again to see where the shells were landing. Finally, we gave up and Samuel turned his glasses on the town, looking for signs of life or gun emplacements. The town still seemed dead to me. I lay down beside a rock and looked around. It was warm and lazy on top of the hill. Off to our left the Mediterranean glittered in the haze. I heard a cowbell ringing, very faintly. I picked up some dirt and let it sift through my fingers. A tiny lizard ran out from under the rock and stopped; his tongue flickered in and out. I threw the dirt at him and he fled back under the rock. I put my head on my arms. The civilian sun was hot and pleasant. I closed my eyes and Samuel said, "I can't see a damned thing. If you ask me, I think they pulled out."

There was a whine through the air and a shell crashed off to our left. I opened my eyes. A cloud of dust drifted up from the beach beside the grounded barge. There was another whine and crash, and this time the shell hit the water about twenty feet from the barge. I asked Samuel if it was our side or the other side firing and he shook his head. "Damned if I know," he said. "I think maybe they had an O.P. there and they had to leave some stuff they don't want us to get." I wondered if somewhere there was someone who always knew exactly what was going on. Shells were being put all around the barge, but none of them were hitting. Then one hit right on the bow. The whole barge shook and pieces of wood flew every which way. Another shell landed in the water and then one hit square in the middle of the barge. Half the vessel went flying into the air. "Give the gentleman a cigar," Samuel said.

There was no more shooting after that. Samuel and I turned our attention once more to the ridge opposite us, but there was nothing doing there, either. "I'm sure they pulled out," Samuel said. He looked hard at the town. "Wait a minute," he said. He handed me the glasses and told me to look where a dirt road, winding down the ridge, entered the lower part of the town. People were walking up that road. "They look like doggies to me," Samuel said. It was hard to tell. They walked like Americans. "I'll bet it's Z Company, that came across the ridges," Samuel said. Once we had spotted the men, we could see them without field glasses. There were six of them, walking up the road. "They're our boys," Samuel said positively. "That means the Jerries *have* cleared out." He began to wriggle back down the hill. I followed him. We stood up when we got far enough down, then slid on our feet to where Keith and Verele were sitting. Samuel told Verele to get Vrana on the radio and have him tell the colonel that Z Company had entered the town across the river. Verele tried, but this time there was no answer. Samuel thought for a minute and then told Verele to drive back to the C.P. and tell the colonel himself. Verele pulled in his aerial and started down the hill toward our jeep.

After a while, Samuel said to Keith and me, "We may as well go back, too. We're not doing any good up here." He led the way down the hill, not using the course we had taken coming up. We passed more mattresses and Keith said, "They must have had officers sleeping here." We cut across a field at the foot of the hill, fifty yards down the road from where we had entered. A gate in a stone fence opened onto the road. Samuel started for it and then stopped. "That's a bad idea," he said. He hopped over the stone fence onto the road. No one was around. We had just started back to the C.P. when a jeep came toward us. In it was a very young lieutenant from regimental headquarters who was in charge of the wire section, which had the task of laying wires for our field telephones. He couldn't have been more than twenty. He stopped alongside us. "How's it going up there, Sam?" he asked. Samuel told him the highway bridge was blown up. "That means we won't be able to lay wire until the engineers have cleared," the lieutenant said. He was just growing a mustache; the little hairs were blond and fuzzy. "Nothing to do but wait," he said. He backed up the jeep and turned it around. He put it into gear to start off, then stopped. "You hear about Johnny?" he said to Samuel.

"What about him?" Samuel said.

"He was killed leading X Company around that curve," the lieutenant said. "An 88 got him."

The young lieutenant started off, clashing the gears as he went into second. "He's going to strip those gears," Samuel said absently. Samuel, Keith, and I silently started along the road again. Presently Samuel said, "I told him there was trouble up here." The road was still deserted. On our right, the beach dropped off to the sea, sparkling in the sun, waiting for the bathers. "He never should have gone up without a reconnaissance," Samuel said. He shook his head. "I wonder whose orders they were."

We walked around a curve and there were the infantrymen, still sitting along the road. They were eating now, cooking cans of meat over other cans filled with burning gasoline. They looked at us expressionlessly as we went by. I figured this must have been the company that got it. We passed a soldier sitting by himself, with a bandage on his forehead, and he asked us what was doing up front. Samuel said that the Jerries had retreated.

"I thought they'd *fight* here," the soldier said. His face was lined with sweat and dirt and he looked very tired.

"No," Samuel said. "They retreated."

The soldier lay back and closed his eyes. "Good," he said softly.

We began to encounter a lot of activity, and before long we had to walk along the edge of the road. Vehicles were coming past us, going toward the river. The rest of the regiment was moving up, following the enemy. We passed some engineers who were clearing mines off the sides of the road. They were futuristic men, with the strange mechanical apparatus fastened to their chests and the long detector rods stretched out before them, looking like shuffleboard poles. They were using the poles like divining rods, working carefully and silently, so carefully that it looked like a slow-motion movie. The only sound was the sudden hum of one of the contraptions when it located a mine. We walked past the engineers and past an artillery battery setting up beside the road. "I guess they'll send me to that town this afternoon to set up another O.P.," Samuel said to Keith and me.

More vehicles rushed past us—the engineers to restore the blown-up bridge, the sappers to clear the road of mines, the anti-aircraft guns to protect the men. I asked Samuel what time it was. "Eleven o'clock," he said. I asked him if he was sure, and he nodded. "It seems like four in the afternoon," Keith said, and sighed. "I feel I've done a day's work already." A truck roared past, pulling a howitzer. "I would like to sleep for two years," Keith said.

There was the sound of a plane and we stopped, suddenly wary, but the sound went away. "I wonder what we have for chow today," Samuel said. I said I didn't know. I wasn't very hungry; I was just tired. We walked along and suddenly there was a loud explosion back of us. We stopped. It was a sound we had all heard too often. "It's a mine," Keith said. "Some poor bastard stepped on a mine." We started to walk again, but now it was different. Keith was walking beside me, his jaw tight, shaking his head a little from side to side.

An ambulance passed us, racing toward the scene of the explosion. "God damn them," Keith finally said. "God *damn* them." We were almost to the C.P. now. I could see the men packing the stuff back on the trucks to move up again. "I hope we have time to get something to eat," Samuel said.

# ANZIO, FEBRUARY 10TH

JOHN LARDNER

TENEMENT life is no more congested than life on a beachhead. We took the Germans by surprise when we landed around Anzio, and we quickly collected a wedge of Lebensraum ten miles wide along the seacoast and six miles long at its apex up the road toward Rome. Then the Germans reacted with their customary speed, skill, and sureness of touch, and our boundaries became quite firm. Our ships, shuttling up from Naples, kept putting stuff ashore—troops, vehicles, food, fuel, and other supplies—but it was like cramming a month's needs into an overnight bag. The unit I travelled with as a correspondent found an empty farmhouse to its liking the sixth day after we landed, and set up housekeeping there. The next thing we knew, it was like Broadway and Forty-second Street on a Sunday afternoon. Some Army longshoremen from the Pier 80 neighborhood of Hell's Kitchen moved into a lane behind us. Their ship had been shot from under them in the Anzio harbor by a German dive-bomber pilot whom the boys described as "a Colin Kelly with a kraut accent." It seems that the German, his plane set afire by an antiaircraft shell, picked out this ship as the handiest and dove into it, plane, bomb, and all. Four of the longshoremen came in to pass the time of day with us and borrow magazines. "I used to take a drink now and then at Duffy's Tavern on Fortieth Street," said Francis Jay Cronin, a private from Fortieth and Tenth Avenue. "How we coming? Are we anywheres near Rome yet?"

We also had a dozen Italians for close neighbors. One, a straight-backed old lady, came over from the farm next door to barter for bully beef and biscuits. Our unit was British, and biscuits and bully beef were what we had the most of. She gave us home-grown scallions in exchange, which helped make our own bully edible. "Have nothing to do with those two girls," the old lady said. She was speaking of two young women who lived with their father on another farm nearby. They paid occasional social calls on the enlisted men in our unit and traded for food on the same basis as the old lady. One was plump, good-looking, and, by her own genial account, six months pregnant. The other was tall, slim, vehement, and lightly mustached. "They are very bad, *molto cattivi*," said their neighbor. "They were fond of the Germans who lived in the house where you are now, and wept a great deal when they left." These remarks

256

were delivered, in Italian, to Captain Geoffrey Mason, who commanded our British Army public-relations detail. Mason, tall and deep-voiced, was a schoolmaster before the war, and I suspect he was regarded as something of a character by the boys he instructed in biology and zoology in Wiltshire. He took a somewhat rigid but fatherly attitude toward all Italians. Convinced—I think mistakenly—that it would be easier for him to master Italian than for them to make sense in English, he worked hard at their language and boomed at them in forceful infinitives, upbraiding them for their light-hearted approach to sanitation, encouraging them to tell him their needs, and asking kindly questions about their home life. "These peasants are really damned good people, aren't they?" the Captain would roar out thoughtfully at supper.

Peasants were the people the Captain liked best. About Americans he was undecided, though he admitted he had found good types among them. The two types who had made the deepest impression on him before the war were Walter Hagen, whose golf swing and competitive disposition he admired, and Damon Runyon, in the roll call of whose characters he took great relish— particularly Harry the Horse and Nicely Nicely. "Whatcha know, boy?" Captain Mason sometimes bawled gaily at me. "Is it true all you newspaper guys make plenty of potatoes?"

The American longshoremen down the lane had come ashore with rich crops of whiskers and they remained bearded till they had their foxholes dug. This convinced Mason that they never shaved, and this in turn persuaded him of their guilt when the old lady from the farm next door reported six chickens missing. A day or two later, a British journalist found one of the Hell's Kitchen men shaving in the bushes, with traces of genuine lather still on his face. The Captain was reluctant to accept this report at first, but in view of the journalist's more or less unbroken record of veracity, he reconsidered. "Do you suppose those chaps down there really didn't take those birds?" the Captain wondered aloud, in powerful tones. As a matter of fact, they hadn't. Two of the chickens reappeared, alive and in fairly good spirits, and the rest were traced by a dockworker named Shea to a party of foragers some distance away.

A couple of days after we moved into the farmhouse, a prisoner-of-war cage was set up on a sandy field a few hundred yards from us. A barbed-wire fence was strung around the field and raised platforms for the guards were built at the four corners. German prisoners with long green overcoats and inquisitive eyes came down the main Rome road steadily, in batches of fifty or a hundred. They were from both the British fighting zone, which was ten minutes away from us by jeep, and the American front, twenty minutes away. The Germans casually lay around the field, awaiting transportation from the beachhead. Occasionally we heard the rattle of small-arms fire by night, when a guard warned prisoners away from the fence with his gun or a German attempted to make a break.

Small-arms fire was the only sound effect we hadn't already had. Every proper fold or corner in the woody plain around us, from the Rome road to the sea, was a nest of anti-aircraft guns. That's a thing which adds strongly to your sense of congestion on a beachhead: all known types of gun, shell, and bomb are going off more or less continuously in an area smaller—in this case, at least—than Manhattan Island. Every window in our house was broken within a week. Shells flew over the house by night. The Germans had a lot of guns around us, including some 210-millimetre weapons mounted on railway cars. These threw an eight-inch shell twenty miles and outranged more than slightly our own long toms, or 155-millimetre, rifled guns. But our side moved the long toms as close as we could and whacked back at the Germans with great regularity, and the naval guns offshore joined the ensemble.

Our flak was always busy, because the German planes were always busy above us. Sinister is the word for some of the German raids on our shipping off Anzio and the adjoining town of Nettuno (Allied map spelling) or Nettunia (local chamber-of-commerce spelling). In what were still considered, as I wrote some of the above, to be their death throes, the Germans here toyed extensively with a superman gadget—the glider bomb or radio-controlled torpedo bomb, which more or less stalks its target and is believed by some impressionable observers on the ground to be able to go into a hotel, ascend the elevator shaft, unlock the victim's door, and follow him into the bathroom.

"Hell, it carries a lunch pail," said an anti-aircraft corporal I met on the Anzio beach, a man named Larry Arbogast.

"It's got a belt in the back," said a colleague of his named John Chambers.

I was told by informal strategists, as we watched this bomb turn corners like a purple imp on an invisible motorcycle, that it lifts the fringe of the curtain behind which robot warfare lurks. Happily, however, these same informants tell me that other nations have also read *Popular Science* faithfully and are ready with measures of their own to release the cosmos through a trapdoor by pushing buttons. If anyone at all survives the next war, some butterfingered robot is going to catch hell for it.

As we lay on our cots and bedrolls on the stone floor of the farmhouse, we could count the German shells passing overhead and assess the duds among them. Sometimes as many as three out of four would lose the shrill, rich flavor of their whistling and go scratchy dry and impotent. In the dawn hours there was generally at least one air raid, and then all the ack-ack in the region broke loose. Another pane of glass would fall out of one of our windows, enemy planes would whine as they dive-bombed, smoke would rise in billows from the coastline beyond the trees in our front yard, and, as the racket subsided, the dawn talkers would pick up the threads of their discussions. "What do you mean, hillbilly?" Private Clyde Foster, a jeep driver, was saying from his bed, as the bark of the Bofors next door died away. "Canada is the North, isn't it? Cleveland, where I come from, is only sixty miles from Canada." Foster, who is barely twenty and made ninety dollars a week in a war plant before his induction, added that he knew a fellow in a camp in Kentucky with a wife ·and child who had had gonorrhea nine times. "What do you think of that?" asked Foster.

Corporal Brown, a British dispatch rider in the next bed, reached, simultaneously with this question, the climax of his imitation of the comedian Lou Costello and sang "Rose Marie" in a high falsetto. Private First Class John Moore, another jeep driver, from Pennsylvania, denied that Americans ever mixed apricots and bacon in one dish for breakfast. Smith, a British cook, was sure he had seen it done in American messes. Yielding on this point, he insisted that the British field ration of tinned steak-and-kidney pie was the best single field ration in the Allied repertory. To my way of thinking, he was right.

These men had got over the beachhead jumps, the lonely, haunted feeling that touches everybody at first after landing. The front-line troops were over them, too, and were back slogging and crawling and killing and dying in the old ritual they had just followed for four months around Naples. Others—the staff officers and reporters, who were paid to think about the situation—had entered a new phase of the jumps, the second or slightly inland phase, which contemplates counterattack.

There was a lot of comedy, none of it very good, about sleeping in your life belt or buying shares in the Italian canoes we found in the yards or cellars of seaside farms and summer villas. The Germans whooped up counterattack over their radio and pushed at us whenever we stopped pushing at them or paused to wipe the blood off our noses. One day, when six newspaper correspondents left the beachhead for Naples for sound professional reasons involving the dispatching of copy, the American public-relations officer complained that it was affecting the morale of his enlisted men. There did not seem to be anything about this condition, however, which a change of unit would not cure. The enlisted men had merely been too long in contact with counterattack thinkers and were overexposed.

We got our mail quickly, which is the best bulwark of morale. Then, there was a certain amount of wine to be had from a merchant who slid back into the deserted village of Nettunia shortly after we landed and unearthed his stock, which the Germans had failed to find. In connection with it I had my most discouraging experience since the night twelve small Arab boys conspired, with sensational success, to pick my pocket of five hundred dollars in Algiers. Captain Mason wanted wine because other units on the beachhead had wine and he felt he owed it to us. Besides, there was little water to spare from washing and cooking, and the field-ration, or "compo," tea was poor stuff. He loaded two vast, empty demijohns into the back seat of a jeep. These

vessels were laced stoutly in straw and each accommodated sixty litres. I drove
the jeep into town, because the deal was one that had to be made through
American channels, in an American beachhead area. Negotiations were concluded for twenty-four hundred lire, or twenty-four dollars, cash down. I
tipped the loaders three Chelsea, or front-line, cigarettes apiece and drove back·
with a high heart. Ten yards from home I hit a sharp ditch in the yard, which
caused the starboard demijohn to disintegrate with a noise like the crack of a
rifle. The floor of the jeep was immediately four inches deep in wine, and the
tipple of the country shot through gaps in the sides like a cataract. The other
correspondents and the enlisted men came out of our farmhouse and stood
around in a circle, taking a lively interest in the plight of four fat, white earth-
worms beside the car, who stiffened, after stubborn resistance, and passed out.
Captain Mason also appeared, and I cast an uneasy glance at him. The Captain
looked things over silently. The wine supply was close to his heart, but there
was something about my position, apparently, which put him in mind of
Harry the Horse or Nicely Nicely, if not both, for he scratched his chin and
burst out laughing. "This is one of the droll episodes of the war," he announced. He then supervised the unloading of the remaining demijohn, taking
care to see that I kept some distance away from the operation.

On nights when the shells fell close around us and rocked the house like
a cradle, and German infantry movements brought the enemy eight minutes
away from us by car instead of ten, the Captain took his rifle to bed with him
·on the stone terrace outdoors and lay awake till dawn keeping guard over us.
No paratroopers landed, but it was a ghostly time and reminded me of our
first two days on the beachhead.

The haunted properties of a beachhead can work two ways if the landing
force takes the enemy by surprise. I'm sure we took the enemy by surprise,
though an Italian nobleman in the area told us later that he considered the
absence of German forces on the Anzio beaches on D Day to be a deliberate
ruse and stratagem. It sounds oversubtle. At any rate, the enemy had only
one company here when we landed, and the first Germans we found were not
expecting guests. Three of them were asleep in a house, with a cowshed at-
tachment, about a mile inland from the beach where the British came in on
the left wing of the landing. This twofold building is my favorite landmark of
the campaign, because I found it sketched out, even to the cowshed, on the
large-scale topographical map given me aboard ship before we went ashore and
I was able to match the sketch up with its original fifteen minutes after landing. Put a map like that in the hands of an amateur tactician and he begins to
remind himself of Stonewall Jackson in the valley.

The three Germans were sleeping in metal camp beds, surrounded by
souvenir bottles of Italian perfume, hand lotion, and nail polish, and snapshots
of their families at home, which ran as a rule to three generations of about

two women apiece. The British, galloping up the beach ahead of me, practically overran the house, so rapid was their pace through the flat brown fields and pinewoods. Two of the Germans pulled on their pants, got out by a back way, and disappeared up the coast road in an armored car, shooting petulantly as they went at a sea that was suddenly full of ships that had not been there when they went to bed. The third was taken in his underwear. I slept that night under one of the fugitives' blankets, my own being still at sea.

It was eerie sleeping—six of us in a row in the cowshed, with nothing inland of us, as far as we knew, but empty country, or Germans, or both. Toward one o'clock in the morning, Captain Mason and his bed groaned simultaneously. Then the Captain sat up and challenged a shadow in the doorway of the shed. "Who is that?" he thundered. "Speak up, speak up!"

The shadow did not reply, but it conveyed an impression of discomfort and started kicking at some straw.

"I insist upon knowing," said the Captain, throwing one leg out of bed.

The rest of us listened intently. We were not, as they say in the British Army, quite happy. Mason, however, perhaps through some sense developed in the schoolroom, felt that the situation had passed into his control and he advanced relentlessly upon his prey and cornered it just outside the door, where it identified itself as an American private in search of a stolen jeep.

"You expected to find it under our straw?" asked the Captain sternly.

"God only knows," said the private, with a desperate show of spirit. "Who knows anything around here? I'm just eight hours off the boat and my jeep is gone."

"Ah, well, it's very unfortunate," said Mason, mellowing. "I hope you find it. But you are very lucky in a way, old chap, because under the circumstances, and with this howling wilderness full of Boche scouts and prisoners, if I'd had my gun in my hand, I would certainly have shot you through the eye. I was quite a first-class shot on the test range," he added as he got back into bed.

After our first couple of days on the beachhead, the Germans suddenly appeared from all directions and fixed our borders, as I said before, very firmly. There were indications that some came from as far away as France. Whatever was the truth of this trivial detail, they brought a great many guns with them. The British soldiers, who had gone through the two stages, both unsatisfactory, of wild surmise before landing and anticlimax afterward, now began to bleed very freely.

One of the British brigades—a brigade approximates an American regiment—was led by a tall, ingratiating officer who had landed on the beach from the same stubby craft that had brought me in. I remembered him as he was at sea before dawn on D Day, brushing his teeth so intensely that he seemed to be lashing himself back and forth in an arc, ten feet long, at the end of a bullwhip. At the front the Brigadier was always mild and charming, and, to me, always unintelligible. He spoke rapidly, in a low voice, and at the end of each burst he cocked his head to left or right with a brilliant smile. It was hard to tell how to react. I decided that when the Brig cocked his head to the left he had made a joke and expected laughter, and when he bobbed to the right he ought to be answered yes or no. Either answer seemed to work out fine. One thing I did hear him say, from time to time, was, "It was a bit sticky last night, you know, but now we are quite happy." All the officers in the brigade said this over and over. The brigade was drawn from units that assay a high content of blood of various shades of blue. The brigade major was the son of a headmaster of Harrow. One battalion was commanded by a member of the Royal Family. The enlisted men of these regiments stamp their feet very loudly on parade or in drill and fight very well in action. They never said they were quite happy on this beachhead, since it would have been flagrantly untrue. I talked with one who had just survived a hard machine-gun attack. He was recuperating over a book of cartoons about Jane, a British comic-strip character. "That's the kind of war I'd like to be fighting," he said. The notable thing about Jane is that she is always undressed or being undressed. She spends eight out of each ten newspaper panels of her existence stripped down to a brassière, lace drawers, silk stockings, and a pair of high-heeled shoes. In the cartoon the soldier showed me, Jane had just been defrocked by a German with a bayonet and was replying by stabbing the Boche with a long knife she had drawn from the top of one stocking. For my taste, Jane is so tall, fair, and lean as to suggest a poster warning against the perils of pneumonia rather than authentic cheesecake. However, she is part of the standard ration of the British submarine fleet and is doled out to sailors on a mission, at the rate of a strip a day, from a sealed package in custody of the commanding officer. And in the Army she is fully as important.

In trying to find a good place from which to cover this front—and the American front to our right, which was bleeding as freely and fighting as strongly as the British—the other press people and I shopped all over the beachhead before settling, with the troops, in the farmhouse. There was flying metal and rush-hour traffic everywhere. On the waterfront, in the summer villas owned by rich Romans, you were only a couple of rings away from the shipping, the bull's-eye of the bomb target and the heart's desire of German long-range shells. The masonry peeled off the villas like sunburned skin, water pipes burst, and every bomb sounded as though it were headed down your chimney. Corporal Brown, the dispatch rider, won his letter in life while motorcycling briskly through Anzio on his way to deliver our copy to the censors. As he rode by, a shell splashed against a wall, killing one Army photographer on the spot and wounding three others. Brown got transportation organized and saw two of the wounded to the hospital in time to save their lives. He came home feeling depressed about a dog whose belly had been

ripped out in the same shelling. This particular casualty was just another example of beachhead congestion under fire. The peril extended even to birds. I
never actually saw a bird hit in the air by shellfire, but often it seemed unlikely
that they could all avoid it. I did see one small black bird pinned down, as
the military phrase goes, by anti-aircraft fire during a bombing. Each time he
tried to take off from a crevice of sea wall, another gun opened fire from another direction and the bird dropped back to his shelter.

The unit I was with suffered its only casualty when an engineer for the
British Broadcasting Corporation, named Walden, got a glancing blow on the
head from a spent fragment of flak. "I have a very thick head of hair," Walden explained. "I was hanging blankets on the line to dry when I felt a slight
sting, you might say. Not until I looked into my bit of a mirror in my truck
did I know my head was bleeding. I straightway applied iodine."

We had a new development in our third week on the beachhead. Shells
landing in the field beside the house sent plaster showering gently from the
walls, and this patter on your head in bed made a strangely romantic impression, as though a beautiful girl outside the window were pelting you with bits
of earth to catch your attention. At least, that was one way of looking at it.

A United States Army lieutenant named Wilson, who censored press copy
on the beachhead, published from time to time a typewritten newspaper of his
own called the *Beachhead Bugle*. It contained a comical column of travel
notes on the movements of outbound reporters ("The following rats deserted
the sinking ship yesterday") and news of various kinds of casualties. When a
soldier down the line, hearing of the paper, appeared with a story of a shell
explosion he had just seen, Wilson turned it down firmly. "I only handle
disasters that occur within fifty yards of my office," he said.

[May 27, 1944]

# THE MAYOR OF FUTANI

JOHN LARDNER

ALLIED progress in the war in Italy began to freeze some months ago, but by then the campaign had left Tony Cuda far behind, and I can say things about Tony and his hospitality now that were better left unsaid at the time I knew him. Mainly, however, it isn't the way his grapevine system nursed us through German outpost lines in the wild Salerno hill country, smelling of bandits and light opera, that makes me remember Tony. It is that to me, at least, he is Exhibit A in what might be called the "Peetsborgh" phase of the war. This phase began in Sicily, but it came of age on the Italian mainland. It's hard to see how anything exactly like it can have occurred in war before or will occur again. The ingredients are rare. American soldiers, most of them on their first campaign abroad and going into foreign lands, into Europe, into the cradle of Europe, with a good deal of spiritual diffidence, in spite of the guns in their hands, were suddenly hailed in every village by characters of various ages who brandished passports, snapshots, letters, or all three, and said loudly and happily, "Hello, I'm glad you come. I used to live in the States. My family, she's in Peetsborgh now." This delighted the Americans—even the ones from Iowa, Oklahoma, and Texas, to whom it seemed strangest, though they quickly learned to take it in stride. It's a tendency of American soldiers overseas to revert to nonchalance with the least possible delay, and before long they were slapping Italian peasants on the back with fatherly encouragement and saying, "You from Peetsborgh, Giuseppe?"

"Peetsborgh" was a watchword in the Army, but the range of American habitat of the Italians-from-the-States had been wide and their distribution in Italy was patchy. For instance, Tony Cuda, the Mayor of Futani, a hill town where I happened to spend some time in the course of my work as a war correspondent, had lived in Philadelphia and Williamsport, Pennsylvania, and in his town there was a woman from Hazleton, Pennsylvania, and one man from Allentown and another from Wilkes-Barre. On the Sorrento peninsula, the representation was largely New York—New York City and upstate places like Corning and Amsterdam. In Caiazzo, a village north of Naples, I found a Connecticut colony. At the sight of American troops, these pilgrims overflowed with American memories, at the expense of the life around them, however sensational. "I ran a goddam nice restaurant in New Haven; lotsa college boys come to my place," said John J. Pannone, of Caiazzo, as soon as he made himself known, and it was another ten minutes before I found that he had been practically an eyewitness, the day before, of a German atrocity we were on the trail of. "I seen things here yesterday you wouldn't believe them, you couldn't sleep," Pannone said finally. "You could get drinks in my place in New Haven, you understand, besides eats. Good beer."

The British soldiers in Italy accepted this species of Italian tolerantly, but at first they were surprised to meet it, being as unfamiliar with Italian emigration to America as they were with a naval battle that was fought, as they now sometimes heard it alleged, on a sort of American mere or sluice called Lake Erie in 1813. When they cared to, the British could argue with justice' that most of the Italians we liberated jointly were more deeply aware of England as a power and an influence than of America. But the Peetsborgh variety is something else again. He is explosive and single-track in his rapture for America, and I was flattered, for no good reason, because Tony Cuda could never understand English as rendered by Englishmen and always called on me to interpret. This inability to understand worked both ways. The British unit with whom I travelled could not understand Tony worth a damn. He spoke the English of Tom Daly and Henry Armetta, strictly a stage guinea dialect. Captain Mike Davis, of the London Irish Regiment, leading our party of three war correspondents—a Scotsman, an Australian, and myself—was anxious to know the disposition of the Germans in the hills and towns around Futani, which lay in No Man's Land, on the path that the four of us hoped to cover between the Eighth British Army and the Fifth American Army. Tony Cuda did not see us as correspondents with a sort of B-picture Hollywood stunt for a mission, which was what we were. To him we were Allied avengers pursuing the grand strategy, as well as his own ends, and he addressed Captain Davis with overwhelming power and affection.

"I can't make out a word the bugger is saying," said Davis.

"What's the troub', Mister John?" said the Mayor of Futani earnestly, clutching me by the shoulder. "I don't understand him good. You I understand good forcause you *americano.*"

The Mayor thereafter was polite and gentle, but resolute, in his determination to pursue negotiations in three styles of English, with me as the pivot man. When a Scottish reporter named McDowell, speaking more clearly and neutrally, it seemed to me, than any of the rest of us, insisted on addressing Cuda directly, Tony beamed on him for a moment, then gave him the brushoff and turned back to me. It was flattering, as I say, but I could not conceal from myself that the fact of the Mayor of Futani's having three thousand dollars in the Fourth National Bank of Williamsport slightly colored his attitude toward the two Allied forces.

Nearly all the characteristics of the Italians-from-the-States were united in Tony: the stage dialect, the craving for American cigarettes or cigars, the survival of a few emphatic American profanities, the record of service in the American Army in the last war, the violent tirades against Fascism. "That sonum-a-beetch *Fascismo,* she's keep me, she don't let me go," said Tony.

The chart of Tony's international movements followed a pattern familiar all over Sicily and the mainland of Italy. He went to America as a young man, worked, made money, and then gave way to the standard instinct to visit Italy again and marry there and prove—very briefly—the pleasures that a little American capital could buy in the threadbare provinces of the south. As all Italians agree, that way you could live like a king. Kingly living is soporific, and Cuda and many unnaturalized Italians like him overstayed their leaves and voided their reëntry permits. The year of Tony's pilgrimage was 1922, the Year I of Fascism. The Italian government expressed a wish that Tony remain in Futani, and the American consul at Salerno, the provincial capital, could not do much about it.

I met an Italian named Cimini in Positano, a little resort town near Amalfi, who said that he was glad to leave America, that he had to, that for medical reasons he could not afford to go back. "I was sick to my stomach all the time there," he said. I asked him why. "I drank too much," explained the fugitive.

Signor Cimini's case was unique in my experience. Other Italians with American pasts felt a honing to go back that became urgent when Italy went to war in 1940. Tony Cuda's feeling was the sharper because he had made, in the States, a leap most unusual among immigrants unable to read or write English: he had passed from the ranks of labor into the capitalist class. This came about romantically, as a result of the first World War, and Tony has been romantically disposed toward that war ever since. When he showed us a photograph of his Army company at Camp Lee, Virginia, and another of himself in puttees and broad-brimmed hat, his patriotic emotions were sweetened by the memory of a wand that had touched him in France and transformed him economically. Cuda had migrated from Futani to Philadelphia in 1906, at the age of fifteen, and straightway gone to work with his hands, in the steps of the man in the song who pooshed on the Delaware Lackawan'. He had reached the grade of locomotive fireman when he entered the Army. His division, the Fourth Infantry, was sent to France, and while Tony did not see combat there, his company was maneuvered around a good deal and asked to build its share of bivouacs and dig its share of holes. This was up the alley of Private Cuda. "I could dig a big hole in four, five minutes," he said. "And that's how Tony got rich," he added tenderly, "just like a story in the newspapers." Another enlisted man in his company, George Dayton, dug poorly, not being in the way of it. Tony dug Dayton's holes as well as his own and lent him a hand with other chores. Dayton, as Frances Hodgson Burnett or any other student of the formula could have told you, turned out to be wealthy and full of gratitude. "He told to me, 'Tony, you never have to work again,'" said Cuda, and whether the quote is exact or not, the meaning of those words was clear. Once the war had ended, Cuda ceased to work with his hands and became a merchant and a saver. As soon as the division was demobilized, Dayton's father, head of the Dayton Shoe Company, set Tony up with a store of his own, selling shoes to workmen in Williamsport. In three years he saved ten thousand dollars. The better part of this sum was on his body—he left, however, three thousand dollars in the bank—when he sailed home to Italy to marry and to live like a king within the terms of his contract with the U. S. Government, which gave him six months to do it in.

It was twenty-one years later when we drove into Futani in a jeep and a tired British staff car, just as the sun was setting. It was a shabby town and desperately poor. Perched high, like all Italian towns in mountain country, it made a yellow-gray patch on the green of its hilltop. The road and the hills were lonely and mysterious. The stone village, bunched around a public fountain where women waited their turn to fill bottles, jugs, and pails with water, was yelling and crawling with life. Tony's house—at any rate, a house built and owned by Tony, of which he and his family occupied the top floor—was the only clean one in town, the only one less than twenty years old. It stood near the fountain, on the right side of the highway, which climbed steeply through the village to the crest, just beyond.

Futani was in a state of siege, more or less voluntary. Cuda, as mayor, had forbidden his nine hundred constituents to leave the village, because of German patrols in the hills around it. Now and then, in the preceding ten days, a German scout car had driven through town, but its passengers never stopped to talk and nobody talked to them. Five days before we arrived, Futani's electricity had been shut off. This was happening all over the province, as the result of sabotage of the main supply sources by the German Army, withdrawing northward, but Futani did not know the reason. Tony, owner of the only radio in town, a handsome cabinet set, had not received any news since the electricity had been cut off and knew no more than anyone else. His state of mind when we found him, therefore, was a nice blend of excitement and confusion, bordering at moments on hysteria. While the radio worked, he and his secretary, a studious young man in spectacles, son of a shopkeeper, had huddled over the set every evening trying gamely to follow the campaign by means of London broadcasts beamed to Italy. They had been interrupted at the point when Italy seemed to be free but not quite free and Germans, British, and Americans were maneuvering vaguely all over the countryside, from Reggio, in the toe of the boot, to Salerno, on the coast above Futani.

Food was running low in Tony's village. Besides, the Allied invasion had raised his yearning for Williamsport to fever level. At the sight of us, the first people in Allied uniforms to reach Futani, he charged like a buffalo to the place where we had stopped our cars, near the fountain. "How glad I am to see you!" yelled Tony, who is a broad, stocky, full-faced man with operatic chest tones. "We waited so long, so long. I want to shake hands. I am *podestà,* mayor, of the town."

In his apartment, to which he led us by an outdoor stairway up the back of his neat yellow stone house, we parleyed in three-way English about the Germans. Actually, Futani lay in no one's line of advance or retreat. The British Eighth Army, with which I had landed in Italy, was clambering northward as fast as blown-up bridges would permit, but its line of movement was northeast, on the Adriatic coast, and the road through Futani was an offshoot, leading northwest toward Salerno, where the American Fifth Army had made its separate landing a few days after we came in. The Allied command had no intention of hooking up the two armies just yet. The Fifth, facing most of the Germans in Italy, had a fight on its hands, but the command expected it to win this and push on through Naples toward Rome by itself, as it eventually did. The Eighth Army at the moment constituted a sort of general threat to the Germans' rear and flank, sufficient by its mere existence to make the German position around Salerno and Naples untenable in the long run. We did not then know the details of the plan, naturally, nor did most of the men in the two Allied armies. The well-bruised troops and officers of the Fifth were expecting Montgomery's Eighth Army to come to its support. We knew that there were no Germans in the fifty miles of mountain and coast between the armies except for outposts and roving patrols. It seemed like a good idea, and not especially perilous, to try to bridge the gap by car. Three or four squads of correspondents set out from different points, each so ignorant of the other's movements that during the journey one party mistook another for German reconnaissance and ducked off the road to hide.

Captain Davis was conducting officer for our squad. He combined the functions of governess and forager, as prescribed by the British Army for the care and feeding of the press. By the time we got to Futani and talked awhile with its mayor, the Captain's temper was drawing in. He did not think it would look good to lose correspondents to the Germans, and at the same time information in a pitch that did not club the eardrums or in a form that he could decode seemed hard to come by.

"*Dove tedeschi? Où* are the *Allemands?* Where the hell are the Germans?" snarled Captain Davis.

"No understand," said Tony helplessly.

Three of the Mayor's followers came at Davis from the starboard quarter with advice in Italian.

"Shut up, shut up," said the Captain, and dashed down to our staff car to soothe himself by inspecting our rations and planning a meal.

Through me, Tony reported that five German armored cars had been seen that afternoon in Vallo, the next town ahead on our road. "I getta good informash'," said Tony. "Tomorrow morning I getta more."

Tony's wife, a plump, dark, shy woman, and his two dark, shy daughters, helped us fix our supper, and we ate it on Tony's table, in the main room of his apartment. It was a clean room, with a well-brushed balcony overlooking the road through the village. There was a desk where Cuda and his secretary conducted civic affairs and had listened to the radio. On the walls were a picture of the Virgin, Tony's American Army photographs, and a lurid poster of the sinking of the Lusitania. After supper we sat on a sofa drinking wine made by Tony on his farm, outside town, and talking with neighbors who had come to see us, including the village doctor, Rocco Zaino, a second exile from the States. Tony and Zaino tried to remember the names of all the cigars, cigarettes, toothpastes, and laxatives they had known in America. Speaking of his passion for Camels, Zaino became excited and turned to tell his fellow-townsmen about them, but he forgot in his excitement to switch from English to Italian. They listened to him for a moment with reproachful stares and then began to shake their heads violently as they broke into a chorus of *"No, no, no."* Zaino, bewildered, went on more loudly in English. It was some time before they derailed him.

We slept in the open that night, in a woods beyond the village, in spite of the Mayor's pressing offers of lodging. Late that evening, as I stood in the moonlight in my underwear, unfolding a blanket, there was a sudden stampede of men, women, and children to my side, led by Zaino, carrying a bottle of wine. Perceiving that I was ready for bed, Zaino scolded the sightseers away. He and I exchanged a couple of friendly toasts and then he returned to the village with his following. It looked as though the arrival of the Allied force had lifted the Mayor's ban on leaving town.

Tony and Zaino came to round us up for breakfast in the morning, and we had it at the Mayor's house—fresh eggs, stiff brown bread, cheese, homemade salami, and wine.

"How you lika the eggs cook'?" asked the Mayor, rubbing his hands with pleasure.

I said fried.

"I'm having them scrambled. We're in a great rush. D'you mind?" said Captain Davis, who was in the kitchen with Signora Cuda, getting the meal ready.

I didn't mind, but I thought Tony's feelings might be wounded. However, he had a great capacity for sliding with the Captain's punches.

"Now, how about those Germans, old boy, right away?" said Davis to Tony as we gobbled the breakfast down.

"What he say?" asked Tony tolerantly.

I translated the request into my own English, which sounded approximately the same as Davis's to me.

"Oh, shoe, shoe," said the Mayor. "You drink a little *vino,* little wine, and by and by we go see my telegraph. Boy, Jesus, I'm a certainly glad see you fellas come here."

"What's the delay?" said Captain Davis.

I told him.

"My God!" said the Captain.

The Futani telegraph office was a hundred yards up the road from the Mayor's house. The Mayor, standing outside and leaning through an open window, told the telegrapher to check the situation with his colleagues in nearby towns. The key clicked with messages outbound and incoming. The five German armored cars, it appeared, were still prowling the vicinity of Vallo. There were even more Germans in Laurito, on an alternate road north. "You better stay here little more," said Tony. "Them sonum-a-beetches, you better not meet them." Captain Davis reached the same conclusion about meeting them, though not about staying there. He steered his brood of correspondents, arguing fretfully, into the cars, and we went off the way we had come, after promising Tony to return before nightfall. Davis reported his findings to a British brigade headquarters. When we started back for Futani in the afternoon, we had a file of Bren gun carriers, light mobile armed vehicles running on tracks, for company. Their purpose was to clean out any German patrols they could find, but the mission turned out to be impractical. On the steep, winding mountain road, the carriers dropped out one by one with track or engine trouble, and when we came to Futani, at dusk, we were alone again, a jeep and a British staff car.

Davis and the Mayor jockeyed for position. Tony wanted us to stay in his town house, pending tomorrow morning's informash'; Davis wanted us to stay at Tony's farm. The farm was away from the main roads and out of the way of any Germans who might drop in to scout Futani. "Well, come on, come on, hasn't he got a farm?" said the Captain, clawing at his hair after five minutes of debate. He was high-strung, and Cuda was a strong and tireless talker. Tony's trouble was that he did not understand why Davis wanted to go to the farm, and Davis saw no reason for explaining. The Mayor's mind, like most Italian minds, hungered for logic. It did not occur to him that Davis was ordering, not suggesting, and I hesitated to explain this as directly as the Captain would have liked. Also, I was bashful about stating the Captain's motive to a man whose life, property, country, and parish we were redeeming from the enemy up the road.

The Mayor, luckily, had come in the last twenty-four hours to consider Davis a hopeless and irreclaimable nut. After paying logic the duty he owed it, he climbed into one of the cars and pointed down the road. "O.K., Mister John, I show," he said. "But my farm, she's a no good shape for company right now. I like give you fellas best I got."

Tony's farm, and three houses he had bought in its neighborhood, had cost him five thousand dollars of his Williamsport shoe fortune. The farm was six hundred acres. He had bought it as soon as he got back home, even before marrying, and the position it gave him in Futani must have had something to do with his overstaying his leave from the States. He automatically became the town's leading citizen. Leading, that is, in a financial sense. Politically, Tony had remained passive and without rank for twenty years. Toward the end of 1942, the anti-Fascist prefect of the district uprooted Futani's Fascist government and inserted Tony as *podestà*. That is one way of putting it. Alternately, it can be said that the prefect was not actually a blackshirt or charter marcher on Rome, that he disliked the village administration for personal reasons, and that in 1942 he felt the state of national and world affairs justified his putting his rich and popular friend Cuda, from America, into office. The neighboring town of Centola underwent a similar upheaval at the same time, and a man named Louis, a former travelling salesman for an American wholesale house, was made mayor. Having so much in common, he and Tony became friends. "He got a radio too, Louis the mayor of Centola," said Tony. "He's fine, smart fella, I like you should meet. You oughta stay awhile."

Tony, Zaino, and I sat on the front steps of the farmhouse under the moon, and Tony talked about his farm while Zaino sat below us smoking English Players cigarettes one after another and dreaming of Camels. Both he and the Mayor had trouble from time to time remembering the English words for things they wanted to say—"truck," for instance, and "wheat," and "cow."

"How you say for *vacca* in America?" asked Tony frowning. "I no remember. Oh shoe, shoe, shoe—cow."

Tony's thirty-five head of cattle were in charge of a cowhand. Fifty-five other hands worked on the farm, tending the Mayor's horse, mules, pigs, sheep, apples, figs, olives, grapes, wheat, and corn. The grapes yielded two hundred to five hundred gallons of wine a year. The newest feature of the farm was a belly fuel tank dropped in a field by an American bomber plane on its way home from a mission. Tony had had it set up as a sort of monument in his barnyard.

"Theesa pipe, she's come from Williamsport," he said, pulling a straight yellow pipe from his pocket. "I bought for seventy-five cents. Six bits. Remember six bits, Rocco?"

"Yeah, six bits, two bits, four bits, a dime, a nickel," said Rocco rapidly. "You goddam right."

"Rocco, he's a got son in New York States. He's lonesome, only got six children here," said Tony laughing. We got up from the steps and went into the house. "I move you' bed away from there," the Mayor added, pointing to some wheat sacks on the floor. "You sleep there, you get itch. There's you' bed over there, lotsa pillows. Good night, sleep good."

It was pleasant sleeping at the farm, and the gray gravel highway to the northwest looked rough and unappetizing in the morning. But the man at the telegraph key admitted, reluctantly, that the enemy cars had gone from Vallo, headed east. The way to the Americans would be clear, especially if we took a couple of subsidiary roads that Tony described to us, looping around the larger towns and cutting over to the Tyrrhenian coast south of Salerno. Davis, in high spirits, patted the Mayor's back and told me to write out a chit endorsing Tony's loyalty to whom it might concern. Tony watched this operation eagerly over my shoulder. "You please remember put I was in American Army," he said.

"He's a good old boy," said Davis, growing more genial as our cars climbed the road from the village and the strong voices of Futani faded behind him. "It's a bloody remarkable thing, you know, the way these blokes have all been to the States and talk American or whatever it is. Bloody remarkable country, this."

One of the other reporters suggested that it might be the same campaigning through Ireland, home of Davis's ancestors.

"God stone the bleeding rocks, you're wrong," said the Captain. "They never come back to Ireland."

[February 5, 1944]

# DUMPLINGS IN OUR SOUP

BRENDAN GILL

O F THE five thousand British children who were brought to this country for safekeeping soon after the outbreak of war in 1939, about a thousand have already gone back home. A large number of those who have returned are boys who, upon reaching the age of seventeen, became liable for service in the British armed forces. The fact is that the war has gone on so long that many youngsters who were hurried out of England to escape the heavy bombings of 1940 are now engaged, as members of the R. A. F., in a fifty-times-heavier bombing of Germany. In recent months a few boys have been given the privilege of sailing home aboard British warships. There is, of course, a severe shortage of passenger space to England, but the remainder of the children here look forward with increasing excitement to rejoining their families by midsummer or fall of this year. By then they will have been separated from their fathers and mothers for four years, a period that is, in some cases, more than half their remembered lifetimes.

I had lunch a while ago with a group of young British refugees who have been living in Tuxedo Park since late in 1940. Their stay in that well-groomed and exclusive wilderness has been made possible by residents of the Park under the leadership of Mrs. H. C. Sonne, who has not only provided the house in which the children, their two supervisors, and two servants live, but has raised the funds necessary to supply them with food, clothing, and schooling. While Mrs. Sonne, who had met me at the Tuxedo station, drove me over the suicidally winding roads of the Park to the mansion known as Children's House, she gave me a brief outline of the undertaking.

"Like almost everyone else in that summer of 1940," she said, "we in Tuxedo were anxious to do what we could for refugee children. We formed a committee in June and offered to take a total of forty children into our various homes. On October fifth, with almost no advance notice, eighteen children arrived. Seven of these had already arranged to stay with relatives or close friends of their families. We brought the rest of them to Children's House." Mrs. Sonne hesitated. "Perhaps you don't know the history of this place," she said. "The house formerly belonged to—you know—Charles E. Mitchell, and my husband picked it up at auction a short while before. There

273

were no furnishings in the house, but I called on all the neighbors to contribute what they could find in their attics, and, as you will see, we got together a strange but fairly serviceable collection of odds and ends. We had barely installed beds and chairs when the children descended on us."

While I clung to the side of the car, Mrs. Sonne rounded a terrifying curve between a cliff and a pond. Perched on every bluff and towering out of every valley were immense nineteenth-century castles of brick, stucco, and faded cedar shingles. One of them, identified by Mrs. Sonne as the Stillman place, was falling into ruin, with a gaping roof, broken windows, and soiled white draperies blowing in the wind. A few boys and girls were skating on the pond beside the road. "The committee was faced," Mrs. Sonne went on, "with a choice of placing the children in foster homes or of leaving them together at Children's House, which we had meant at first to use as a sort of dispatching center. A number of people had already agreed to pay a minimum of three hundred and seventy-five dollars a year for the duration to care for a child in a foster home, and we realized that if we could persuade them to let the committee do so, it would be possible to keep all the children right there in Children's House. Though this was bound to be more expensive than putting them in foster homes, there were, it seemed to us, several reasons it might be better to do it. In the first place, ideal foster homes are pretty hard to find. Secondly, if we closed Children's House, we would be shutting off a refuge for any children who found life uncongenial in their foster homes or whose foster homes were being broken up for one reason or another. Furthermore, we felt that these children deserved as good schooling as our own children were getting and we knew that we could arrange to send them to the private school here in Tuxedo.

"The people who had pledged the money agreed that it would be best to keep the children together, and they have since fulfilled their annual pledges one hundred per cent. Though the cost of feeding a child has risen from about forty-five cents a day to nearly sixty-five, by carefully cutting corners here and there we've kept costs steady at just under a thousand dollars a year a child. The neighborhood stores have given us a large discount on everything we buy, and doctors and dentists have contributed their services free of charge. Up to now, the committee has cared for a total of thirty children. Six of these have been lucky enough to be picked up by their parents here and to return with them to England, while several of the older boys have recently gone home to enter the services. At the moment, therefore, we have only ten children. They seem to us like a very small family indeed."

As we swung up the driveway to a rambling, stucco-covered house, Mrs. Sonne pointed out, over the doorway, a graceful "V" made of evergreen, and explained that this had been put there by the children. A minute later she led me into a stone-paved and rather baronial-looking hall. I noted that a stuffed turtle, undoubtedly a contribution from some sober Tuxedo attic, was a part of the hall's furnishings. We were met at the head of a flight of steps by Mrs. Suffern, who, with an assistant, supervises the running of the house. Mrs. Sonne left me with Mrs. Suffern. After all, she said, it was lunchtime and she had four children of her own to look after.

Mrs. Suffern, a short, middle-aged woman with bright eyes and an agreeable presence, invited me into her office, just off the hall. The unnatural silence in the house, Mrs. Suffern said, was due to the fact that the children were all upstairs washing their hands before lunch. I asked Mrs. Suffern how they had reacted to the shock of their removal from England, and she said that I might be able to get an idea of their feelings by reading one or two of the letters that she and the children's parents have exchanged. Opening a small filing cabinet and selecting at random, Mrs. Suffern picked out a letter written by the mother of eight children, the four youngest of whom—ranging in age from eight to twelve—had been among the first arrivals at Children's House. The letter, dated October 30, 1940, read:

"Thank you very much indeed for your very kind letter this morning. We *were* so glad to have it and to hear about the children from you. Their own dear little letters cannot tell us very much and we do miss them so much, bless their hearts! We are indeed grateful to you and the committee for all that you are doing for our family. It is simply wonderful to feel that they are safe and away from this horrible war and in such lovely surroundings. The air raids have been getting worse around here recently, but I have not told the children anything about them. We are so thankful they are not here to know anything about them. . . .

"Now, about the children. Faith is a dear child, but *very* sensitive, and has always been a good little elder sister to the little ones and a child one can trust absolutely. *Quite* in confidence, I had a very 'homesick' letter from her this morning, but as it was written a fortnight ago I hope by now she will be feeling more settled and less strange. She seemed to think that we had not sent her and the other children with as many clothes or as much money as the other children in her group, and I *do* feel so horribly unhappy about it. We thought we had given them enough clothes, but I will try to send them some more in a few days when I can find out what we may send. We did not give them very much money, as they have never been used to very much, and I did not think they would need a lot. But I feel so distressed to think that they are suffering from an 'inferiority complex,' poor darlings! They have always *loved* their own home and it has always been such a happy one (in spite of our not being a bit well off—one *can't* be with eight children!).

"Philip is the most sunny-tempered and helpful of all our children. I love his nice wide grin, don't you? I *think* the way Phil holds things close to his eyes is more habit than anything else, but he started reading at an early age and may need watching. Tony's eyes are much better than when he first had to wear glasses two years ago. Our oculist hopes the squint may disappear completely by the time he is nine, if he does not do too much reading. He is a sharp little fellow, and I think his occasional fits of temper are probably partly due to his eyes. I do hope he is not being troublesome; he can be very naughty!

"Little Peggy is easily managed, as she is so very loving and affectionate. She was rather a delicate baby, as she had scarlet fever so badly at two years old and it left her with ear trouble for some time afterwards. Thank you for writing so charmingly about the children. I hope you won't mind such a long letter in return! My husband has been on sick leave from the Army for a year, but has been pronounced fit, so I think I shall be losing him before very long now, and I shall feel more solitary than ever. Thank you again a thousand times for all your kindness."

A note from Mrs. Suffern's assistant reassured Faith's mother:

". . . Faith seems to be over her homesickness to a large extent. She cried a bit one night, but I think she was more tired than anything else, and an extra hug seemed to pretty well set her straight. She talks about home a great deal, and quite happily of the places you went and the adventures you had. She is very proud that her father is with the Army now, and when other children say to her that they do not understand how she can be so glad because his work is dangerous, she says simply, 'I know. But it is what he wanted, and I am happy for him.' I get the impression that Fay is very close to her father.

"She has grown so that some of her clothes were better fitted to Peggy, and so Fay has several new frocks. She is utterly delighted with herself, and you should certainly feel at ease about her needs. Both she and Peggy are amply outfitted, and have more things than they can very well wear out. Faith must have told you about her 'fancy skates' and how she is practicing different jumps and turns. Your two boys skate without any attention to form, since both are more interested in playing ice hockey. Peggy on skates looks like an old man bent over with a perpetual crook in his back, but her speed is remarkable. She can outrace almost anyone on the lake.

"Philip and Tony had dinner at Mrs. Parker's on Sunday, and reported a fine time. Philip knows a good deal about the progress of the war and the legislation that is under discussion in this country for increased aid to England. He is at present contenting himself with composing imaginary insulting cables to Hitler! . . . Tony is a thoroughly lovable little boy, and we do not find him at all naughty. It is generally Tony who plays the elaborate host when we have visitors, making great efforts to entertain them and set them at ease. Peggy is very sweet and even-tempered, with none of Fay's moodiness. She has written some really nice poetry; her ideas are highly imaginative, and the words seem to tumble out and into place almost without her volition. She is experimenting with different rhythms and shows real talent. Philip has that poetic streak in him, too. One day we lay resting on our sleds looking at the clouds.

He asked the direction of one great fast sailing cloud and we decided that it might have come from England. Philip said, 'Lovely cloud! I wish you would open and pour some English rain on me.'"

As I finished reading this note, Mrs. Suffern said, "You can see, I think, that we've kept in close touch with one another. We write at least once every two weeks, and the children write every Sunday. They haven't lost the sense of having parents, the sense of what their parents are like, and we, for our part, try to keep the parents aware of the fact that their children are bound to change as they grow. Four years is an awfully long time, but letters and snapshots help to bridge the gap. You'll find that the children are still English children. Even their accents, which they think they've lost, have remained intact."

Mrs. Suffern stood up as a bell rang at the other end of the hall and what sounded like a regiment began charging down the stairs. "Lunch," she explained. "The children are always absolutely starved." She led me into a large, sunny dining room. From the long French windows, facing east and south, there was a fine view of the pond and the bare, cold hills beyond. There were two maple tables, one presided over by Mrs. Suffern, the other by her assistant. The children at Mrs. Suffern's table were standing at their places, waiting to be introduced to me. They all smiled and said, "How d'you do?" The group at the other table were already seated and eating, and we soon set to work ourselves. Mrs. Suffern served what struck me as gigantic portions of roast lamb and gravy, carrots, potatoes, and peas. As we ate, we spoke casually of Tuxedo, school, the weather, and then, more and more, of England.

Faith sat at my right, and, knowing about her only what I had read in her mother's letter, I was interested to see that she was by now a strikingly good-looking girl of fifteen, with ash-blond hair and blue eyes. Two sisters, Fiona and Maggie, aged thirteen and eleven, and a sister and brother, Penelope and Nicky, aged fourteen and ten, made up the rest of our group. I asked Faith if she had been skating, and she said, "Oh, yes! It was super! We've been having the most super time on the pond."

"I've been skating, too," Nicky said. "No wonder I'm a bit hungry." By some miracle of application, he had already finished everything on his plate, which he now passed soberly to Mrs. Suffern for a second helping.

"We don't have much skating in England, you know," Fiona said, to help me along with making conversation. "Sometimes a shallow pond will freeze over for a few days, but nothing like here at Tuxedo."

"Once, I remember," Penelope said, "we went skating in a flooded meadow at home, and the grass stuck right up through the ice, and it caught in our skates. How we laughed, Mother and Daddy and me!"

"I couldn't skate at all when I came over," Nicky said. "That was ages ago, of course. I was only a child."

"You consider yourself an old man now, do you?" Faith asked. She too passed her plate to Mrs. Suffern, who filled it again with lamb, carrots, and peas. Maggie, a bright-faced little girl, likewise held out her plate for a second helping. "The food here," she said to me, "isn't a bit like the food we used to have in England." I figured that Maggie had been under eight when she left England and Nicky had been six and a half; it at first seemed unlikely that they could remember things so accurately, but apparently they did. Maggie said, "For instance, at home we used to have porridge all the time. It was icky stuff. Cook here tried to give it to us once or twice, but we—we discouraged her. We haven't had porridge for ages."

"But we had nice things at home, too. We used to have dumplings in our soup," Fiona said.

"Oh, they *were* wonderful!" Nicky said. "I remember having dumplings in our soup."

"Nobody in America ever has dumplings in his soup," Maggie said, while Penelope and Fiona passed their plates for a second helping. "And there was something else we always ate in England that we don't eat here—something we called dripping toast."

"Really, Maggie!" Faith said, shaking her head in disapproval. I gathered that dripping toast had been a plebeian pleasure at best, and one not mentioned among the better families. "*I* never ate dripping toast," Faith said.

"It was toast dipped in hot fat, and it was simply delicious," Maggie said, determined to have her way. "I used to eat it and eat it and eat it."

Fiona looked up from her plate. "And spotted-dog pudding," she said. "Don't forget spotted-dog pudding."

Penelope said, "*We* used to call it schoolgirl pudding, but I expect it was the same thing."

It wasn't long before Nicky cleared his throat, apparently preparing to ask for a third helping. Mrs. Suffern anticipated him. "Would anyone like a little more?" she asked, and everyone promptly said, "Yes, please." The third helping emptied the platter of meat and the serving dishes of carrots, peas, and potatoes. While the plates were being taken away by Fiona and Nicky, Faith brought from her pocket a letter she had just received from her brother Tony. Both Tony and Faith's other brother, Philip, who had come with her and her sister Peggy to Children's House in the fall of 1940, went back home a few weeks ago. Mrs. Suffern suggested that Faith read Tony's letter aloud so that everyone would be able to hear about the boy's journey home. Faith began to read it in a clear, serious voice, looking up now and then and smiling at one of Tony's lighter remarks.

"Darling Fay," the letter said, "here we are back again at home. Mookie is very well; in fact, if he stands up on his hind legs he would probably be taller than Hugh! By the way, Hugh has a new way of sliding down the stairs. He goes much faster than one would ordinarily go. We came across on an aircraft carrier, a new one, American-made, that was being lent to the British Navy for the duration. One of the boys called it a 'tub made of tin cans and stuck together with waterproofed chewing gum,' but I thought it was quite a decent ship. It rocked and pitched as though it were a destroyer, though, and that was pretty bad. We had quite rough weather, but Phil and I were lucky and we didn't get sick at all during the trip. The trip took ten days. In that time I learnt an awful lot about recognizing airplanes and also I learned how to work a five-inch gun. The ship had a shop canteen and I bought a lot of truck (sugar, lemons, tobacco, razor blades, also candy) for the family. Well, after we got off the ship, we stayed at a rest home for a day. Then we trained down to Birm. We found Ted on the platform there. Gosh, he looked so different there—six feet tall and all! Ted took us to where we had lunch and afterwards we all had our hair cut. We travelled to Droitwich, where everyone except Chris was. When I first looked at the house, it seemed so different."

Faith hesitated, then went on reading in a strangely grown-up voice. "Next day Phil, Ted, and I went to Worcester to meet Chris. We had quite a time finding him, but we 'dood' it. Chris is almost six feet now. Phil is going to play Grampa in chess sometimes. We are all looking forward to going to church together tomorrow."

Faith began to crumple the letter into a ball. Then she smoothed it out and read, "P. S. You might tell the other children at Children's House that I know how to work a five-inch gun." She stood up and said, "Excuse me, please," and walked out of the dining room. No one else said anything. At that moment, luckily, Nicky brought in a bowlful of ice cream for our dessert. Maggie grinned across the table at me and said, "We have ice cream in England, too, but not like this. It's ice cream, but it doesn't taste like ice cream, but it tastes good, do you see what I mean?" I told Maggie that I saw what she meant.

[August 12, 1944]

# YOUNG MAN BEHIND PLEXIGLAS

### BRENDAN GILL

JOSEPH THEODORE HALLOCK, who has light-blue eyes and an engaging smile and is usually called Ted, is a first lieutenant in the United States Army Air Forces. Two years ago he was an undergraduate at the University of Oregon; today he is a veteran bombardier who has completed thirty missions in a B-17 over Germany and Occupied Europe. Eighteen months ago he fainted when an Army doctor examining him pricked his finger to get a sample of blood; today he wears the Purple Heart for wounds received in a raid on Augsburg, the Air Medal with three oak-leaf clusters, and the Distinguished Flying Cross. Before he got into the Air Forces, he had been rejected by the Navy and Marines because of insufficient chest expansion; he still weighs less than a hundred and thirty pounds, and this gives him an air of tempered, high-strung fragility. When he relaxes, which is not often, he looks younger than his twenty-two years, but he doesn't think of himself as being young. "Sometimes I feel as if I'd never had a chance to live at all," he says flatly, "but most of the time I feel as if I'd lived forever."

Hallock and his wife, Muriel, recently spent a three-week leave in New York, and I met him through friends. I took him aside one morning and talked with him for an hour or two about his part in the war. I was naturally curious to know what it felt like to complete thirty missions in a Flying Fortress, but I also saw, or thought I saw, that he was eager to speak to someone of his experiences. Apparently he considers himself typical of thousands of young men in the armed forces, and he rejects any suggestion that he has done more than was specifically demanded of him. "Whatever I tell you," he said, "boils down to this: I'm a cog in one hell of a big machine. The more I think about it, and I've thought about it a lot lately, the more it looks as if I've been a cog in one thing or another since the day I was born. Whenever I get set to do what I want to do, something a whole lot bigger than me comes along and shoves me back into place. It's not especially pleasant, but there it is.

"As a matter of fact, my father had about the same deal. He'd graduated from Oregon State and was just starting in business when we got mixed up in the first World War. He joined the Navy, and from what he says I guess he disliked the war but liked his job. He'd been trained as a radio engineer, and that was the sort of work they gave him to do, so he got to be a C.P.O. and kept on working for the Navy for quite a while after the war was over. He and Mother moved around from Mare Island to Portland, down to Los Angeles and San Diego, and so on, and they seem to have had a good enough time. Like Muriel and me, they probably didn't try to figure what was going to happen to them next. I was their only child, and I was born on October twenty-fifth, 1921." Hallock shrugged. "In a way, it's funny my being born then. I was arguing about the war with a fellow the other night, and he kept telling me what Wilson should have done and what Wilson shouldn't have done. I got sore finally. Why, hell's bells, I hadn't even been born when Wilson was president! I don't give a hoot about Wilson, I told this guy, Wilson's been dead for years; it's 1944 I'm worrying about.

"Things must have been pretty unsettled when I was a baby, just as they've been ever since I grew up. Whatever that boom was I've heard about, I doubt if it meant anything ritzy for the Hallocks. My father helped found a company that manufactured radios—he was in on the ground floor in radio, from crystal pickup sets to those big old-fashioned jobs with all the knobs and dials— but he figured the fad wouldn't last. That was what he used to say—'Radio won't last.' Those early sets cost too much for the average guy, Dad thought, and it didn't occur to him that the prices were bound to come down someday. So he drifted into one job or another, some good and some bad, up to the time of the crash.

"Naturally, I don't remember anything about Harding and Coolidge. One of my earliest memories is of betting marbles with the kids at school about who was going to win the election, Hoover or Roosevelt. I bet on Roosevelt. I suppose my mother and father had been talking about him at home—about how bad things were and about how the country needed a change. While I don't remember good times, I'd hear Mother and Dad talking about what they'd had once and didn't have any more—nothing like yachts or fur coats, just something like security, whatever that is. It's the same thing Muriel and I talk about sometimes, wondering what the hell it looks and tastes like. Most of the other guys in the Army who grew up when I did feel the same way. We keep trying to figure out what it was our parents had before we grew up, or what our grandparents had. There must have been something back there someplace, or we wouldn't miss it so much.

"Moving around the country during those bad times, I had plenty of trouble with schools, and I guess it's a wonder I managed to learn anything at all. In California, for instance, I'd have to take French but not Latin, and in Maryland I'd have to take Latin but not French. I finally graduated from a Portland, Oregon, high school in 1939. I wasn't very popular at school, partly because I never was in a place long enough to know anybody well, but mostly because I spent my time reading books and listening to good jazz, which can be a lonely thing to do. I was a pretty serious character in those days, and I boned up a lot on the first World War. I listened to my father talk and I read about the munitions kings and I felt sure I'd never be willing to fight in any war about anything. I delivered the commencement address when I graduated from high school, and I called it 'Cannon Fodder?' You can bet I made that question mark a big one.

"Then I began to grow confused. I was disgusted when the League of Nations gave in to Mussolini on the Ethiopian grab, and even before that, when the Spanish War broke out, I saw that that was a war the Loyalists had to fight, and I also saw that it was a war the Loyalists had to win. I was only fifteen or sixteen at the time, but I wanted them to win more than anything else in the world. Besides, there was the Jap attack on China. Naturally, I sided with the Chinese right from the start. What it came down to was that I believed in other people's wars but I didn't believe in any American war. I guess I was as bad as a lot of people in that respect, like the other kids who were brought up on Senator Nye and the Veterans of Future Wars.

"I wanted to go to Reed College, in Portland, so after I got out of high school I spent a year working as busboy, dishwasher, and things like that to make some money. I also got a job at a radio station, where I had charge of the record library and helped out the announcers on the night shift, and I played drums in a local band. Being on the air when the flash announcing the second World War came through, I remember the time exactly: it was 2:17 A.M., on September third, 1939. As soon as I got home that morning, I asked my father if he thought we'd ever get into the war, and he said, 'No, of course not.' But I suspected we might, and I hated the thought of it. My father had already taken the Civil Service exams for a job with the Federal Communications Commission and passed them, and at about that time he was sent to an F.C.C. job in Texas. I found out that I couldn't afford to go to Reed College unless I was able to live board-free at home, so I had to plan on going to the University of Oregon instead. My family and I got separated back there in 1940, and I've been away from them pretty steadily ever since. There were only the three of us, and we miss each other." Hallock smiled without embarrassment and said, "Damn it, we miss each other a lot."

Hallock and I talked about his family for a while, then got back to the war. "All the time up to Pearl Harbor, I kept trying to pretend that the war wasn't really happening," he said. "I kept telling myself that this was a different kind of war from the Chinese and Spanish wars. When my roommate at college woke me up on Sunday morning, December seventh, 1941, and told me that the Japs had attacked Pearl Harbor, I didn't believe it. It sounded like Warner Brothers stuff to me, so I went back to sleep. Later on I was listening to the André Kostelanetz program when the announcer cut in with some news flashes, and this time I believed it. I guess it's typical of me that as far as I was concerned the war started in the middle of the Coca-Cola program, 'the pause that refreshes on the air.'

"Nearly everybody at college got drunk and burned his books. My roommate and I killed a bottle of kümmel between us and I painted our windows with black enamel as an air-raid precaution. I spent the next two weeks scraping off the enamel with a razor. Undergraduate guards were posted on the library roof, and when the rumor got around that San Francisco had been bombed, twenty-two-calibre rifles started showing up around the campus. Everybody else seemed to be doing something, so I wired my father that I wanted to enlist in the Signal Corps. My father wired back for me to sit tight until the Army told me what to do. In spite of him, I tried enlisting as a cadet in the Navy and Marines, but they said I had insufficient chest expansion and too few college credits. I didn't mind terribly when they turned me down. I had no real convictions about the war in Europe, and I was more or less willing to wait my turn at taking a crack at the Japs. I'd started an orchestra at college called Ted Hallock's Band, which played at sorority and fraternity dances, and during the year I'd had an article on jazz published in *Downbeat*. I'd even made a quick trip to New York and haunted all the night clubs that had good bands. I'd had to hock my Speed Graphic camera to do it, but it was worth it. I felt I was really on my way.

"Besides all that, and a lot more important than all that, I had Muriel, back in Portland. That is, I'd fallen in love with her and I wanted to marry her, but she didn't give me much encouragement. She just wouldn't say anything when I'd ask her to marry me, and I figured that if I got into the Army I might never have a chance to see her again. I wanted time to see her. I wanted time to do a lot of things I hadn't been able to do, and every day outside the Army was worth weeks and months in terms of Muriel and jazz and reading and ordinary living. Finally, in June, 1942, thinking I was bound to be drafted soon, I enlisted as an aviation cadet in the Army Air Forces. I was underweight the first time I took my physical, but I ate fifteen bananas, drank three quarts of milk, passed a second physical, and was sick as a pup for a couple of days afterward.

"The Air Forces told me they'd notify me when to report for training. I didn't feel like going back to college, and I was sore at Muriel because she wouldn't say she'd marry me, so I went down to Galveston to visit my mother and father. I got a job there as a pipe-fitter's apprentice—a fine fate for someone who thought of himself as a rising young authority on jazz and other fine arts. When I couldn't stand not hearing from Muriel, I returned to Portland and got a job in a record shop in a department store. Later, I set up a pitch as a disc jockey at the radio station, playing jazz records and ad-libbing from midnight to eight A.M. I managed to pick up sixty-five or seventy dollars a week, and Muriel and I had some fine times. It seemed as if for once I wasn't just a cog in something bigger than me; I was doing what I wanted to do. But of course that feeling was too good to last. I was ordered to report for duty on February second, 1943, at the A.A.F. base at Santa Ana, California, where I received my pre-flight training.

"That training was really rugged. We had two and a half months of calisthenics led by Fred Perry and Joe DiMaggio, obstacle races, drill, and studies. The saying there was that the discipline was so tough you'd be gigged if they found air under your bed. We took enough mathematics in six weeks to go from two plus two makes four to trig and calculus. I suspected I might be washed out as pilot material, so to keep from getting a broken heart like a lot of other fellows, I applied to be sent to bombardier school. That was just good strategy on my part, but apparently the officers liked it. We—the bombardier candidates—were sent on to Deming, New Mexico. We arrived there and lined up in one hell of a sandstorm, in terrible heat, feeling a million miles from anywhere. I can still remember the C.O. yelling, as the sand blew down his throat and blinded his eyes, 'Welcome to Deming, men!'

"There were a thousand men at the base and two bars in the town, and things were about as unpleasant as that sounds. We had three months of training with the Norden bomb sight at Deming. The men who had been trained before us had not even been allowed to take notes on what they learned. We could take notes, but we had to burn them as soon as we finished memorizing them. We used to take our notes out to the latrines at night after lights out and study them there. We had to learn how to strip and assemble a bomb sight, a job that became sort of a religious ritual with me. The more I found out about the bomb sight, the more ingenious and inhuman it seemed. It was something bigger, I kept thinking, than any one man was intended to comprehend. I ended up with a conviction, which I still have, that a bombardier can't help feeling inferior to his bomb sight—at least, this bombardier can't. It's not a good feeling to have; it doesn't help you very much when you're over Germany and going into your run to realize that everything depends on your control of something you'll never fully understand, but the feeling is there.

"In July, 1943, I finished the course at Deming and got my wings as a second lieutenant. Muriel had stopped corresponding with me for the umptieth time by then, and I had got so sore that I had written her that I would never see her again. At the last minute, though, I hopped on a train and stood up all the way back to Portland. As soon as I saw Muriel, I told her, 'You know you're going to marry me, don't you?' She said, 'Well, maybe,' which was the greatest encouragement she'd ever given me. I wasted a lot of time—three whole days—making up her mind for her, which left us only three days of my leave in which to get married and have a honeymoon. We spent our honeymoon in a hotel in Portland. Then we took a train to Ephrata, Washington, the training center for B-17s to which I'd been ordered to report.

"Muriel stayed at a hotel in Wenatchee, several miles away. That meant that I was A.W.O.L. a good deal of the time. But I guess I learned something. I didn't like the first pilot to whom I was assigned, so the C.O. assigned me to another pilot, a fellow just my age, with whom I got along fine. It's literally a matter of life and death for everybody in the crew of a Fort to get on well; the ship just won't fly otherwise. There are ten men in a Fort crew—the pilot, co-pilot, navigator, bombardier, and six gunners, and there's more than enough responsibility to go around. The bombardier, for example, is also gunnery officer and in charge of fire control, first aid, and oxygen. Most of those jobs are theoretical in practice flights, but they can all need you at once in a hot raid.

"After a couple of months at Ephrata, where we got the hang of flying a Fort, we were sent on to Rapid City, South Dakota, for some bomb practice on the target ranges there. Muriel and I felt really married for the first time in Rapid City, because we rented a bungalow and Muriel, who'd never cooked before, practiced her cooking on me. As it turned out, we lived on spaghetti most of the time. Muriel and I had a lot of scraps at Rapid City. I'd come down from a flight looking for trouble, looking for someone to pick on, and Muriel was always the easiest to hurt. That kind of irritability seems to be a characteristic of high flying. I blame it mostly on using oxygen, but, oxygen or no oxygen, there's no doubt the sky does something to you. There it is around you, and it's so damn big, and yet you have a false feeling of having mastered it. And when you come down out of it you feel like elbowing all the civilians you see into the streets that from above looked like little trickles of nothing. The difficulty is, you have to try to live in two different scales of worlds, the one up there and the one down here, and it's not a natural thing to do.

"Muriel must have understood what was going on inside me, because in spite of the way I behaved we had a good time in that cheap little bungalow. As soon as I finished the course at Rapid City, we went to Washington, so I could say goodbye to my parents. My father had been made chief of the Facility Security Division of the F.C.C. when the war broke out, and he and Mother had had to move to Washington. Later, we came up here to New York for a day or two before I went across. We spent most of our time at Nick's in the Village, getting a last fill of good music. In November, 1943, I shipped out to England, and Muriel went back to Portland and got a job at an advertising agency there."

I asked Hallock a few questions about Muriel, and then he took up his story again. "Right from the start, I liked England. That helped me to stand my separation from Muriel and the fact that I was fighting in a war I'd never particularly believed in fighting. England was so much older physically and spiritually than I had expected that I felt shocked. I understood for the first time that there were people in the world who looked the same as us but thought differently from us, and I began to wonder if the Germans were maybe as much different from the English and us as a lot of writers and politicians claimed. After a day or two in an indoctrination pool, our crew was assigned to an old and well-established operational base south of London and given our Fort, which our pilot christened Ginger. None of us ever found out why he named the ship Ginger, but it's the pilot's privilege to choose any name he likes; probably ginger was the color of his girl's hair or the name of his dog—something like that. We never painted the name on our Fort, because the Forts with names seemed to get shot up more than the ones without.

"My first raid was on December thirty-first, over Ludwigshaven. Naturally, not knowing what it was going to be like, I didn't feel scared. A little sick, maybe, but not scared. That comes later, when you begin to understand what your chances of survival are. Once we'd crossed into Germany, we spotted some flak, but it was a good long distance below us and looked pretty and not dangerous: different-colored puffs making a soft, cushiony-looking pattern under our plane. A bombardier sits right in the plexiglas nose of a Fort, so he sees everything neatly laid out in front of him, like a living-room rug. It seemed to me at first that I'd simply moved in on a wonderful show. I got over feeling sick, there was so much to watch. We made our run over the target, got our bombs away, and apparently did a good job. Maybe it was the auto-pilot and bomb sight that saw to that, but I'm sure I was cool enough on that first raid to do my job without thinking too much about it. Then, on the way home, some Focke-Wulfs showed up, armed with rockets, and I saw three B-17s in the different groups around us suddenly blow up and drop through the sky. Just simply blow up and drop through the sky. Nowadays, if you come across something awful happening, you always think, 'My God, it's just like a movie,' and that's what I thought. I had a feeling that the planes weren't really falling and burning, the men inside them weren't really dying, and everything would turn out happily in the end. Then, very quietly through the interphone, our tail gunner said, 'I'm sorry, sir, I've been hit.'

"I crawled back to him and found that he'd been wounded in the side of the head—not deeply but enough so he was bleeding pretty bad. Also, he'd got a lot of the plexiglas dust from his shattered turret in his eyes, so he was, at least for the time being, blind. The blood that would have bothered me back in California a few months before didn't bother me at all then. The Army had trained me in a given job and I went ahead and did what I was trained to do, bandaging the gunner well enough to last him back to our base. Though he was blind, he was still able to use his hands, and I ordered him to fire his guns whenever he heard from me. I figured that a few bursts every so often from his fifties would keep the Germans off our tail, and I also figured that it would give the kid something to think about besides the fact that he'd been hit. When I got back to the nose, the pilot told me that our No. 4 engine had been shot out. Gradually we lost our place in the formation and flew nearly alone over France. That's about the most dangerous thing that can happen to a lame Fort, but the German fighters had luckily given up and we skimmed over the top of the flak all the way to the Channel.

"Our second raid was on Lille, and it was an easy one. Our third was on Frankfort. France was the milk run, Germany the bad news. On the day of a raid, we'd get up in the morning, eat breakfast, be briefed, check our equipment, crawl into the plane, maybe catch some more sleep. Then the raid, easy or tough, and we'd come back bushed, everybody sore and excited, everybody talking, hashing over the raid. Then we'd take lighted candles and write the date and place of the raid in smoke on our barracks ceiling. Maybe we wouldn't go out again for a week or ten days. Then we'd go out for four or five days in a row, taking chances, waiting for the Germans to come up and give us hell. They have a saying that nobody's afraid on his first five raids, and he's only moderately afraid on his next ten raids, but that he really sweats out all the rest of them, and that's the way it worked with me and the men I knew.

"When we started our missions, we were told that after twenty-five we would probably be sent home for a rest, so that was how we kept figuring things—so many missions accomplished, so many missions still to go. We worked it all out on a mathematical basis, or on what we pretended was a mathematical basis—how many months it would take us to finish our stint, how many missions we'd have to make over Germany proper, what our chances of getting shot down were. Then, at about the halfway mark, the number of missions we would have to make was raised from twenty-five to thirty. That was one hell of a heartbreaker. Supposedly, they changed the rules of the game because flying had got that much safer, but you couldn't make us think in terms of being safer. Those five extra raids might as well have been fifty.

"The pressure kept building up from raid to raid more than ever after that. The nearer we got to the end of the thirty missions, the narrower we made our odds on surviving. Those odds acted on different guys in different ways. One fellow I knew never once mentioned any member of his family, never wore a trinket, never showed us any pictures, and when he got a letter from home he read it through once and tore it up. He said he didn't trust himself to do anything else, but still it took guts. Most of the rest of us would lug a letter around and read it over and over, and show our family pictures to each other until they got cracked and dirty. There was also a difference in the way we faked our feelings. Some of the guys would say, 'Well, if I managed to get through that raid, it stands to reason they'll never get me,' but they didn't mean it. They were knocking on wood. Some of the other guys would say, 'I'm getting it this time. I'll be meeting you in Stalag Luft tonight,' but they were knocking on wood, too. We were all about equally scared all the time.

"My best friend over there was an ardent Catholic. He used to pray and go to confession and Mass whenever he could. I kept telling him, 'What's the use? The whole business is written down in a book someplace. Praying won't make any difference.' But whenever I got caught in a tight spot over Germany, I'd find myself whispering, 'God, you gotta. You gotta get me back. God, listen, you gotta.' Some of the guys prayed harder than that. They promised God a lot of stuff, like swearing off liquor and women, if He'd pull them through. I never tried to promise Him anything, because I figured that if God was really God he'd be bound to understand how men feel about liquor and women. I was lucky, anyhow, because I had something to fall back on, and that was music. I went up to London several times between missions and visited some of those Rhythm Clubs that are scattered all over the country. I listened to some good hot records and a few times I even delivered lectures on jazz. The nearest town to our base had its own Rhythm Club, and I spoke there to about a hundred and fifty people on Duke Ellington and Louis Armstrong. Now and then I got a chance to play drums in a band. That helped a lot and made it seem less like a million years ago that I'd been leading Ted Hallock's Band out at Oregon."

Hallock got onto the subject of jazz, then abruptly switched back to his story again. "The missions went on and on," he said, "and the pressure kept on building. Guys I knew and liked would disappear. Somebody I'd be playing ping-pong with one day would be dead the next. It began to look as if I didn't have a chance of getting through, but I tried to take it easy. The worst raid we were ever on was one over Augsburg. That was our twenty-sixth, the one after what we expected to be our last mission. When we were briefed that morning and warned that we might be heading for trouble, I couldn't help thinking, 'By God, I'm getting rooked, I ought to be heading home to Muriel and New York and Nick's this very minute.'

"There was never any predicting which targets the Germans would come up to fight for. I was over Berlin five times, over Frankfurt four times, over Saarbrücken, Hamm, Münster, Leipzig, Wilhelmshaven, and I had it both ways, easy and hard. We had a feeling, though, that this Augsburg show was bound to be tough, and it was. We made our runs and got off our bombs in the midst of one hell of a dogfight. Our group leader was shot down and about a hundred and fifty or two hundred German fighters swarmed over us as we headed for home. Then, screaming in from someplace, a twenty-millimetre cannon shell exploded in the nose of our Fort. It shattered the plexiglas, broke my interphone and oxygen connections, and a fragment of it cut through my heated suit and flak suit. I could feel it burning into my right shoulder and arm. My first reaction was to disconnect my heated suit. I had some idea that I might get electrocuted if I didn't.

"I crawled back in the plane, wondering if anyone else needed first aid. I couldn't communicate with them, you see, with my phone dead. I found that two shells had hit in the waist of the plane, exploding the cartridge belts stored there, and that one waist gunner had been hit in the forehead and the other in the jugular vein. I thought, 'I'm wounded, but I'm the only man on the ship who can do this job right.' I placed my finger against the gunner's jugular vein, applied pressure bandages, and injected morphine into him. Then I sprinkled the other man's wound with sulfa powder. We had no plasma aboard, so there wasn't much of anything else I could do. When I told the pilot that my head set had been blown off, the tail gunner thought he'd heard someone say that my head had been blown off, and he yelled that he wanted to jump. The pilot assured him that I was only wounded. Then I crawled back to the nose of the ship to handle my gun, fussing with my wounds when I could and making use of an emergency bottle of oxygen.

"The German fighters chased us for about forty-five minutes. They came so close that I could see the pilots' faces, and I fired so fast that my gun jammed. I went back to the left nose gun and fired that gun till *it* jammed. By that time we'd fallen behind the rest of the group, but the Germans were beginning to slack off. It was turning into a question of whether we could sneak home without having to bail out. The plane was pretty well shot up and the whole oxygen system had been cut to pieces. The pilot told us we had the choice of trying to get back to England, which would be next to impossible, or of flying to Switzerland and being interned, which would be fairly easy. He asked us what we wanted to do. I would have voted for Switzerland, but I was so busy handing out bottles of oxygen that before I had a chance to say anything the other men said, 'What the hell, let's try for England.' After a while, with the emergency oxygen running out, we had to come down to ten thousand feet, which is dangerously low. We saw four fighters dead ahead of us, somewhere over France, and we thought we were licked. After a minute or two we discovered that they were P-47s, more beautiful than any woman who ever lived. I said, 'I think now's the time for a short prayer, men. Thanks, God, for what you've done for us.'

"When we got back to our base, I found a batch of nineteen letters waiting for me, but I couldn't read a single one of them. I just walked up and down babbling and shaking and listening to the other guys babble. I had my wounds looked at, but they weren't serious. The scars are already beginning to fade a little, and the wounds didn't hurt me much at the time. Still, I never wanted to go up again. I felt sure I couldn't go up again. On the day after the raid, I didn't feel any better, and on the second day after the raid I went to my squadron commander and told him that I had better be sent up at once or I'd never be of any use to him again. So he sent me up in another plane on what he must have known would be a fairly easy raid over France, the milk run, and that helped.

"That was my twenty-seventh mission. The twenty-eighth was on Berlin, and I was scared damn near to death. It was getting close to the end and my luck was bound to be running out faster and faster. The raid wasn't too bad, though, and we got back safe. The twenty-ninth mission was to Thionville, in

France, and all I thought about on that run was 'One more, one more, one more.' My last mission was to Saarbrücken. One of the waist gunners was new, a young kid like the kid I'd been six months before. He wasn't a bit scared—just cocky and excited. Over Saarbrücken he was wounded in the foot by a shell, and I had to give him first aid. He acted more surprised than hurt. He had a look on his face like a child who's been cheated by grownups.

"That was only the beginning for him, but it was the end for me. I couldn't believe it when I got back to the base. I kept thinking, 'Maybe they'll change the rules again, maybe I won't be going home, maybe I'll be going up with that kid again, maybe I'll have another five missions, another ten, another twenty.' I kept thinking those things, but I wasn't especially bitter about them. I knew then, even when I was most scared, that fliers have to be expendable, that that's what Eaker and Doolittle had us trained for. That's what war is. The hell with pampering us. We're supposed to be used up. If the Army worried one way or another about our feelings, it'd never get any of us out of Santa Ana or Deming."

I asked Hallock how long he had to wait before he was ordered back to the States. "In just a few days," he said, "the word came through that I could go home for a three-week leave. I cabled Muriel and she met me here in New York. I must have looked a lot different to her, and acted different, but she looked and acted the same to me. She brought along whatever money she'd managed to save out of what I'd sent her, so we could shoot it all on a good time. I'd been made a first lieutenant, and I get good pay, but saving any of it is something else again. Muriel and I both figure we'd better spend it while we're here to spend it. After a couple of days in Washington with my mother and father, we settled ourselves here in New York. We've just been eating and sleeping and listening to jazz and wandering around the town in a nice daze. I don't care if things are booming, if the civilians are all pulling down big dough, if no one seems to know there's a war on. For the moment, I don't care about any other damn thing in the world except that I'm here in New York with Muriel.

"We haven't made any plans. Hell's bells, I've *never* been able to make any plans. As soon as my leave's up, I have to report to a rehabilitation center in Miami, and I suppose I'll be sent on from there to another post. Frankly, I'd like to land a job somewhere on the ground. I don't care where. Even Deming sounds beautiful to me. I don't particularly want to fly again. Pilots and navigators seem to feel different about the flying end of it; they don't seem to get that feeling of never wanting to go up again. Maybe that's because they're really flying the ship. When you're only one of the hired hands, who's being carried along to do the dirty work, to drop the bombs and do the killing, you don't feel so good about it.

"As for after the war, we don't dare to think too much about that. We're not ready to settle down and have kids and all that stuff. We feel as if we'd been cheated out of a good big chunk of our lives, and we want to make it up. I want to go back to college. Damn it, I want to play drums in a band again, in Ted Hallock's Band. I want to feel that maybe I can look two days ahead without getting scared. I want to feel *good* about things. You know what I mean. It seems to me that sooner or later I'm going to be entitled to say to myself, 'O.K., kid, relax. Take it easy. You and Muriel got a lifetime in front of you. Do what you damn please with it.' I want to be able to tell myself, 'Listen, Hallock, all that cannon-fodder stuff never happened. You're safe. You're fine. Things are going to be different for Muriel and you. Things are going to be great. You're not a damn little cog any more. You're on your way.'"

# SURVIVAL

JOHN HERSEY

OUR men in the South Pacific fight nature, when they are pitted against her, with a greater fierceness than they could ever expend on a human enemy. Lieutenant John F. Kennedy, the ex-Ambassador's son and lately a PT skipper in the Solomons, came through town the other day and told me the story of his survival in the South Pacific. I asked Kennedy if I might write the story down. He asked me if I wouldn't talk first with some of his crew, so I went up to the Motor Torpedo Boat Training Center at Melville, Rhode Island, and there, under the curving iron of a Quonset hut, three enlisted men named Johnston, McMahon, and McGuire filled in the gaps.

It seems that Kennedy's PT, the 109, was out one night with a squadron patrolling Blackett Strait, in mid-Solomons. Blackett Strait is a patch of water bounded on the northeast by the volcano called Kolombangara, on the west by the island of Vella Lavella, on the south by the island of Gizo and a string of coral-fringed islets, and on the east by the bulk of New Georgia. The boats were working about forty miles away from their base on the island of Rendova, on the south side of New Georgia. They had entered Blackett Strait, as was their habit, through Ferguson Passage, between the coral islets and New Georgia.

The night was a starless black and Japanese destroyers were around. It was about two-thirty. The 109, with three officers and ten enlisted men aboard, was leading three boats on a sweep for a target. An officer named George Ross was up on the bow, magnifying the void with binoculars. Kennedy was at the wheel and he saw Ross turn and point into the darkness. The man in the forward machine-gun turret shouted, "Ship at two o'clock!" Kennedy saw a shape and spun the wheel to turn for an attack, but the 109 answered sluggishly. She was running slowly on only one of her three engines, so as to make a minimum wake and avoid detection from the air. The shape became a Japanese destroyer, cutting through the night at forty knots and heading straight for the 109. The thirteen men on the PT hardly had time to brace themselves. Those who saw the Japanese ship coming were paralyzed by fear in a curious way: they could move their hands but not their feet. Kennedy whirled the wheel to the left, but again the 109 did not respond. Ross went through

292

the gallant but futile motions of slamming a shell into the breach of the 37-millimetre anti-tank gun which had been temporarily mounted that very day, wheels and all, on the foredeck. The urge to bolt and dive over the side was terribly strong, but still no one was able to move; all hands froze to their battle stations. Then the Japanese crashed into the 109 and cut her right in two. The sharp enemy forefoot struck the PT on the starboard side about fifteen feet from the bow and crunched diagonally across with a racking noise. The PT's wooden hull hardly even delayed the destroyer. Kennedy was thrown hard to the left in the cockpit, and he thought, "This is how it feels to be killed." In a moment he found himself on his back on the deck, looking up at the destroyer as it passed through his boat. There was another loud noise and a huge flash of yellow-red light, and the destroyer glowed. Its peculiar, raked, inverted-Y stack stood out in the brilliant light and, later, in Kennedy's memory.

There was only one man below decks at the moment of collision. That was McMahon, engineer. He had no idea what was up. He was just reaching forward to slam the starboard engine into gear when a ship came into his engine room. He was lifted from the narrow passage between two of the engines and thrown painfully against the starboard bulkhead aft of the boat's auxiliary generator. He landed in a sitting position. A tremendous burst of flame came back at him from the day room, where some of the gas tanks were. He put his hands over his face, drew his legs up tight, and waited to die. But he felt water hit him after the fire, and he was sucked far downward as his half of the PT sank. He began to struggle upward through the water. He had held his breath since the impact, so his lungs were tight and they hurt. He looked up through the water. Over his head he saw a yellow glow—gasoline burning on the water. He broke the surface and was in fire again. He splashed hard to keep a little island of water around him.

Johnston, another engineer, had been asleep on deck when the collision came. It lifted him and dropped him overboard. He saw the flame and the destroyer for a moment. Then a huge propeller pounded by near him and the awful turbulence of the destroyer's wake took him down, turned him over and over, held him down, shook him, and drubbed on his ribs. He hung on and came up in water that was like a river rapids. The next day his body turned black and blue from the beating.

Kennedy's half of the PT stayed afloat. The bulkheads were sealed, so the undamaged watertight compartments up forward kept the half hull floating. The destroyer rushed off into the dark. There was an awful quiet: only the sound of gasoline burning.

Kennedy shouted, "Who's aboard?"

Feeble answers came from three of the enlisted men, McGuire, Mauer, and Albert; and from one of the officers, Thom.

Kennedy saw the fire only ten feet from the boat. He thought it might reach her and explode the remaining gas tanks, so he shouted, "Over the side!"

The five men slid into the water. But the wake of the destroyer swept the fire away from the PT, so after a few minutes, Kennedy and the others crawled back aboard. Kennedy shouted for survivors in the water. One by one they answered: Ross, the third officer; Harris, McMahon, Johnston, Zinsser, Starkey, enlisted men. Two did not answer: Kirksey and Marney, enlisted men. Since the last bombing at base, Kirksey had been sure he would die. He had huddled at his battle station by the fantail gun, with his kapok life jacket tied tight up to his cheeks. No one knows what happened to him or to Marney.

Harris shouted from the darkness, "Mr. Kennedy! Mr. Kennedy! McMahon is badly hurt." Kennedy took his shoes, his shirt, and his sidearms off, told Mauer to blink a light so that the men in the water would know where the half hull was, then dived in and swam toward the voice. The survivors were widely scattered. McMahon and Harris were a hundred yards away.

When Kennedy reached McMahon, he asked, "How are you, Mac?"

McMahon said, "I'm all right. I'm kind of burnt."

Kennedy shouted out, "How are the others?"

Harris said softly, "I hurt my leg."

Kennedy, who had been on the Harvard swimming team five years before, took McMahon in tow and headed for the PT. A gentle breeze kept blowing the boat away from the swimmers. It took forty-five minutes to make what had been an easy hundred yards. On the way in, Harris said, "I can't go any farther." Kennedy, of the Boston Kennedys, said to Harris, of the same home town, "For a guy from Boston, you're certainly putting up a great exhibition out here, Harris." Harris made it all right and didn't complain any more. Then Kennedy swam from man to man, to see how they were doing. All who had survived the crash were able to stay afloat, since they were wearing life preservers—kapok jackets shaped like overstuffed vests, aviators' yellow Mae Wests, or air-filled belts like small inner tubes. But those who couldn't swim had to be towed back to the wreckage by those who could. One of the men screamed for help. When Ross reached him, he found that the screaming man had two life jackets on. Johnston was treading water in a film of gasoline which did not catch fire. The fumes filled his lungs and he fainted. Thom towed him in. The others got in under their own power. It was now after 5 A.M., but still dark. It had taken nearly three hours to get everyone aboard.

The men stretched out on the tilted deck of the PT. Johnston, McMahon, and Ross collapsed into sleep. The men talked about how wonderful it was to be alive and speculated on when the other PTs would come back to rescue them. Mauer kept blinking the light to point their way. But the other boats had no idea of coming back. They had seen a collision, a sheet of flame, and a slow burning on the water. When the skipper of one of the boats saw the sight, he put his hands over his face and sobbed, "My God! My God!" He and the others turned away. Back at the base, after a couple of days, the squadron held services for the souls of the thirteen men, and one of the officers wrote his mother, "George Ross lost his life for a cause that he believed in stronger than any one of us, because he was an idealist in the purest sense. Jack Kennedy, the Ambassador's son, was on the same boat and also lost his life. The man that said the cream of a nation is lost in war can never be accused of making an overstatement of a very cruel fact. . . ."

When day broke, the men on the remains of the 109 stirred and looked around. To the northeast, three miles off, they saw the monumental cone of Kolombangara; there, the men knew, ten thousand Japanese swarmed. To the west, five miles away, they saw Vella Lavella; more Japs. To the south, only a mile or so away, they actually could see a Japanese camp on Gizo. Kennedy ordered his men to keep as low as possible, so that no moving silhouettes would show against the sky. The listing hulk was gurgling and gradually settling. Kennedy said, "What do you want to do if the Japs come out? Fight or surrender?" One said, "Fight with what?" So they took an inventory of their armament. The 37-millimetre gun had flopped over the side and was hanging there by a chain. They had one tommy gun, six 45-calibre automatics, and one .38. Not much.

"Well," Kennedy said, "what do you want to do?"

One said, "Anything you say, Mr. Kennedy. You're the boss."

Kennedy said, "There's nothing in the book about a situation like this. Seems to me we're not a military organization any more. Let's just talk this over."

They talked it over, and pretty soon they argued, and Kennedy could see that they would never survive in anarchy. So he took command again.

It was vital that McMahon and Johnston should have room to lie down. McMahon's face, neck, hands, wrists, and feet were horribly burned. Johnston was pale and he coughed continually. There was scarcely space for everyone, so Kennedy ordered the other men into the water to make room, and went in himself. All morning they clung to the hulk and talked about how incredible it was that no one had come to rescue them. All morning they watched for the plane which they thought would be looking for them. They cursed war in general and PTs in particular. At about ten o'clock the hulk heaved a moist sigh and turned turtle. McMahon and Johnston had to hang on as best they could. It was clear that the remains of the 109 would soon sink. When the sun had passed the meridian, Kennedy said, "We will swim to that small island," pointing to one of a group three miles to the southeast. "We have less chance of making it than some of these other islands here, but there'll be less chance of Japs, too." Those who could not swim well grouped themselves around a long two-by-six timber with which carpenters had braced the 37-millimetre cannon on deck and which had been knocked overboard by the force of the collision. They tied several pairs of shoes to the timber, as well as the ship's lantern, wrapped in a life jacket to keep it afloat. Thom took charge of this unwieldy group. Kennedy took McMahon in tow again. He cut loose one end of a long strap on McMahon's Mae West and took the end in his teeth. He swam breast stroke, pulling the helpless McMahon along on his back. It took over five hours to reach the island. Water lapped into Kennedy's mouth through his clenched teeth, and he swallowed a lot. The salt water cut into McMahon's awful burns, but he did not complain. Every few minutes, when Kennedy stopped to rest, taking the strap out of his mouth and holding it in his hand, McMahon would simply say, "How far do we have to go?"

Kennedy would reply, "We're going good." Then he would ask, "How do you feel, Mac?"

McMahon always answered, "I'm O.K., Mr. Kennedy. How about you?"

In spite of his burden, Kennedy beat the other men to the reef that surrounded the island. He left McMahon on the reef and told him to keep low, so as not to be spotted by Japs. Kennedy went ahead and explored the island. It was only a hundred yards in diameter; coconuts on the trees but none on the ground; no visible Japs. Just as the others reached the island, one of them spotted a Japanese barge chugging along close to shore. They all lay low. The barge went on. Johnston, who was very pale and weak and who was still coughing a lot, said, "They wouldn't come here. What'd they be walking around here for? It's too small." Kennedy lay in some bushes, exhausted by his effort, his stomach heavy with the water he had swallowed. He had been in the sea, except for short intervals on the hulk, for fifteen and a half hours. Now he started thinking. Every night for several nights the PTs had cut through Ferguson Passage on their way to action. Ferguson Passage was just beyond the next little island. Maybe . . .

He stood up. He took one of the pairs of shoes. He put one of the rubber life belts around his waist. He hung the .38 around his neck on a lanyard. He took his pants off. He picked up the ship's lantern, a heavy battery affair ten inches by ten inches, still wrapped in the kapok jacket. He said, "If I find a boat, I'll flash the lantern twice. The password will be 'Roger,' the answer will be 'Wilco.'" He walked toward the water. After fifteen paces he was dizzy, but in the water he felt all right.

It was early evening. It took half an hour to swim to the reef around the next island. Just as he planted his feet on the reef, which lay about four feet under the surface, he saw the shape of a very big fish in the clear water. He flashed the light at it and splashed hard. The fish went away. Kennedy remembered what one of his men had said a few days before, "These barracuda will come up under a swimming man and eat his testicles." He had many occasions to think of that remark in the next few hours.

Now it was dark. Kennedy blundered along the uneven reef in water up to his waist. Sometimes he would reach forward with his leg and cut one of his shins or ankles on sharp coral. Other times he would step forward onto emptiness. He made his way like a slow-motion drunk, hugging the lantern. At about nine o'clock he came to the end of the reef, alongside Ferguson Passage. He took his shoes off and tied them to the life jacket, then struck out into open water. He swam about an hour, until he felt he was far enough out to intercept the PTs. Treading water, he listened for the muffled roar of motors, getting chilled, waiting, holding the lamp. Once he looked west and saw flares and the false gaiety of an action. The lights were far beyond the little islands, even beyond Gizo, ten miles away. Kennedy realized that the PT boats had chosen, for the first night in many, to go around Gizo instead of through Ferguson Passage. There was no hope. He started back. He made the same painful promenade of the reef and struck out for the tiny island where his friends were. But this swim was different. He was very tired and now the current was running fast, carrying him to the right. He saw that he could not make the island, so he flashed the light once and shouted "Roger! Roger!" to identify himself.

On the beach the men were hopefully vigilant. They saw the light and heard the shouts. They were very happy, because they thought that Kennedy had found a PT. They walked out onto the reef, sometimes up to their waists in water, and waited. It was very painful for those who had no shoes. The men shouted, but not much, because they were afraid of Japanese.

One said, "There's another flash."

A few minutes later a second said, "There's a light over there."

A third said, "We're seeing things in this dark."

They waited a long time, but they saw nothing except phosphorescence and heard nothing but the sound of waves. They went back, very discouraged.

One said despairingly, "We're going to die."

Johnston said, "Aw, shut up. You can't die. Only the good die young."

Kennedy had drifted right by the little island. He thought he had never known such deep trouble, but something he did shows that unconsciously he had not given up hope. He dropped his shoes, but he held onto the heavy lantern, his symbol of contact with his fellows. He stopped trying to swim. He seemed to stop caring. His body drifted through the wet hours, and he was very cold. His mind was a jumble. A few hours before, he had wanted desperately to get to the base at Rendova. Now he only wanted to get back to the little island he had left that night, but he didn't try to get there; he just wanted to. His mind seemed to float away from his body. Darkness and time took the place of a mind in his skull. For a long time he slept, or was crazy, or floated in a chill trance.

The currents of the Solomon Islands are queer. The tide shoves and sucks through the islands and makes the currents curl in odd patterns. It was a fateful pattern into which Jack Kennedy drifted. He drifted in it all night. His mind was blank, but his fist was tightly clenched on the kapok around the lantern. The current moved in a huge circle—west past Gizo, then north and east past Kolombangara, then south into Ferguson Passage. Early in the morning the sky turned from black to gray, and so did Kennedy's mind. Light came to both at about six. Kennedy looked around and saw that he was exactly where he had been the night before when he saw the flares beyond Gizo. For a second time, he started home. He thought for a while that he had lost his mind and that he only imagined that he was repeating his attempt to reach the island. But the chill of the water was real enough, the lantern was real, his progress was measurable. He made the reef, crossed the lagoon, and got to the first island. He lay on the beach awhile. He found that his lantern did not work any more, so he left it and started back to the next island, where his men were. This time the trip along the reef was awful. He had discarded his shoes, and every step on the coral was painful. This time the swim across the gap where the current had caught him the night before seemed endless. But the current had changed; he made the island. He crawled up on the beach. He was vomiting when his men came up to him. He said, "Ross, you try it tonight." Then he passed out.

Ross, seeing Kennedy so sick, did not look forward to the execution of the order. He distracted himself by complaining about his hunger. There were a few coconuts on the trees, but the men were too weak to climb up for them. One of the men thought of sea food, stirred his tired body, and found a snail on the beach. He said, "If we were desperate, we could eat these." Ross said, "Desperate, hell. Give me that. I'll eat that." He took it in his hand and looked at it. The snail put its head out and looked at him. Ross was startled, but he shelled the snail and ate it, making faces because it was bitter.

In the afternoon, Ross swam across to the next island. He took a pistol to signal with, and he spent the night watching Ferguson Passage from the reef around the island. Nothing came through. Kennedy slept badly that night; he was cold and sick.

The next morning everyone felt wretched. Planes that the men were unable to identify flew overhead and there were dogfights. That meant Japs as well as friends, so the men dragged themselves into the bushes and lay low. Some prayed. Johnston said, "You guys make me sore. You didn't spend ten cents in church in ten years, then all of a sudden you're in trouble and you see the light." Kennedy felt a little better now. When Ross came back, Kennedy decided that the group should move to another, larger island to the southeast, where there seemed to be more coconut trees and where the party would be nearer Ferguson Passage. Again Kennedy took McMahon in tow with the strap in his teeth, and the nine others grouped themselves around the timber.

This swim took three hours. The nine around the timber were caught by the current and barely made the far tip of the island. Kennedy found walking the quarter mile across to them much harder than the three-hour swim. The cuts on his bare feet were festered and looked like small balloons. The men were suffering most from thirst, and they broke open some coconuts lying on the ground and avidly drank the milk. Kennedy and McMahon, the first to drink, were sickened, and Thom told the others to drink sparingly. In the middle of the night it rained, and someone suggested moving into the underbrush and licking water off the leaves. Ross and McMahon kept contact at first by touching feet as they licked. Somehow they got separated, and, being uncertain whether there were any Japs on the island, they became frightened. McMahon, trying to make his way back to the beach, bumped into someone and froze. It turned out to be Johnston, licking leaves on his own. In the morning the group saw that all the leaves were covered with droppings. Bitterly, they named the place Bird Island.

On this fourth day, the men were low. Even Johnston was low. He had changed his mind about praying. McGuire had a rosary around his neck, and Johnston said, "McGuire, give that necklace a working over." McGuire said quietly, "Yes, I'll take care of all you fellows." Kennedy was still unwilling to admit that things were hopeless. He asked Ross if he would swim with him to an island called Nauru, to the southeast and even nearer Ferguson Passage. They were very weak indeed by now, but after an hour's swim they made it.

They walked painfully across Nauru to the Ferguson Passage side, where they saw a Japanese barge aground on the reef. There were two men by the barge—possibly Japs. They apparently spotted Kennedy and Ross, for they got into a dugout canoe and hurriedly paddled to the other side of the island. Kennedy and Ross moved up the beach. They came upon an unopened rope-bound box and, back in the trees, a little shelter containing a keg of water, a Japanese gas mask, and a crude wooden fetish shaped like a fish. There were Japanese hardtack and candy in the box and the two had a wary feast. Down by the water they found a one-man canoe. They hid from imagined Japs all day. When night fell, Kennedy left Ross and took the canoe, with some hardtack and a can of water from the keg, out into Ferguson Passage. But no PTs came, so he paddled to Bird Island. The men there told him that the two men he had spotted by the barge that morning were natives, who had paddled to Bird Island. The natives had said that there were Japs on Nauru and the men had given Kennedy and Ross up for lost. Then the natives had gone away. Kennedy gave out small rations of crackers and water, and the  men went to sleep. During the night, one man, who kept himself awake until the rest were asleep, drank all the water in the can Kennedy had brought back. In the morning the others figured out that he was the guilty one. They swore at him and found it hard to forgive him.

Before dawn, Kennedy started out in the canoe to rejoin Ross on Nauru, but when day broke a wind arose and the canoe was swamped. Some natives appeared from nowhere in a canoe, rescued Kennedy, and took him to Nauru. There they showed him where a two-man canoe was cached. Kennedy picked up a coconut with a smooth shell and scratched a message on it with a jack-knife: "ELEVEN ALIVE NATIVE KNOWS POSIT AND REEFS NAURU ISLAND KENNEDY." Then he said to the natives, "Rendova, Rendova."

One of the natives seemed to understand. They took the coconut and paddled off.

Ross and Kennedy lay in a sickly daze all day. Toward evening it rained and they crawled under a bush. When it got dark, conscience took hold of Kennedy and he persuaded Ross to go out into Ferguson Passage with him in the two-man canoe. Ross argued against it. Kennedy insisted. The two started out in the canoe. They had shaped paddles from the boards of the Japanese box, and they took a coconut shell to bail with. As they got out into the Passage, the wind rose again and the water became choppy. The canoe began to fill. Ross bailed and Kennedy kept the bow into the wind. The waves grew until they were five or six feet high. Kennedy shouted, "Better turn around and go back!" As soon as the canoe was broadside to the waves, the water poured in and the dugout was swamped. The two clung to it, Kennedy at the bow, Ross at the stern. The tide carried them southward toward the open sea, so they kicked and tugged the canoe, aiming northwest. They struggled that way for two hours, not knowing whether they would hit the small island or drift into the endless open.

The weather got worse; rain poured down and they couldn't see more than ten feet. Kennedy shouted, "Sorry I got you out here, Barney!" Ross shouted back, "This would be a great time to say I told you so, but I won't!"

Soon the two could see a white line ahead and could hear a frightening roar—waves crashing on a reef. They had got out of the tidal current and were approaching the island all right, but now they realized that the wind and the waves were carrying them toward the reef. But it was too late to do anything, now that their canoe was swamped, except hang on and wait.

When they were near the reef, a wave broke Kennedy's hold, ripped him away from the canoe, turned him head over heels, and spun him in a violent rush. His ears roared and his eyes pinwheeled, and for the third time since the collision he thought he was dying. Somehow he was not thrown against the coral but floated into a kind of eddy. Suddenly he felt the reef under his feet. Steadying himself so that he would not be swept off it, he shouted, "Barney!" There was no reply. Kennedy thought of how he had insisted on going out in the canoe, and he screamed, "Barney!" This time Ross answered. He, too, had been thrown on the reef. He had not been as lucky as Kennedy; his right arm and shoulder had been cruelly lacerated by the coral, and his feet, which were already infected from earlier wounds, were cut some more.

The procession of Kennedy and Ross from reef to beach was a crazy one. Ross's feet hurt so much that Kennedy would hold one paddle on the bottom while Ross put a foot on it, then the other paddle forward for another step, then the first paddle forward again, until they reached sand. They fell on the beach and slept.

Kennedy and Ross were wakened early in the morning by a noise. They looked up and saw four husky natives. One walked up to them and said in an excellent English accent, "I have a letter for you, sir." Kennedy tore the note open. It said, "On His Majesty's Service. To the Senior Officer, Nauru Island. I have just learned of your presence on Nauru Is. I am in command of a New Zealand infantry patrol operating in conjunction with U. S. Army troops on New Georgia. I strongly advise that you come with these natives to me. Meanwhile I shall be in radio communication with your authorities at Rendova, and we can finalize plans to collect balance of your party. Lt. Wincote. P.S. Will warn aviation of your crossing Ferguson Passage."

Everyone shook hands and the four natives took Ross and Kennedy in their war canoe across to Bird Island to tell the others the good news. There the natives broke out a spirit stove and cooked a feast of yams and C ration. Then they built a leanto for McMahon, whose burns had begun to rot and stink, and for Ross, whose arm had swelled to the size of a thigh because of the coral cuts. The natives put Kennedy in the bottom of their canoe and covered him with sacking and palm fronds, in case Japanese planes should buzz them. The long trip was fun for the natives. They stopped once to try to grab a turtle, and laughed at the sport they were having. Thirty Japanese planes went over low toward Rendova, and the natives waved and shouted gaily. They rowed with a strange rhythm, pounding paddles on the gunwales between strokes. At last they reached a censored place. Lieutenant Wincote came to the water's edge and said formally, "How do you do. Leftenant Wincote."

Kennedy said, "Hello. I'm Kennedy."

Wincote said, "Come up to my tent and have a cup of tea."

In the middle of the night, after several radio conversations between Wincote's outfit and the PT base, Kennedy sat in the war canoe waiting at an arranged rendezvous for a PT. The moon went down at eleven-twenty. Shortly afterward, Kennedy heard the signal he was waiting for—four shots. Kennedy fired four answering shots.

A voice shouted to him, "Hey, Jack!"

Kennedy said, "Where the hell you been?"

The voice said, "We got some food for you."

Kennedy said bitterly, "No, thanks, I just had a coconut."

A moment later a PT came alongside. Kennedy jumped onto it and hugged the men aboard—his friends. In the American tradition, Kennedy held under his arm a couple of souvenirs: one of the improvised paddles and the Japanese gas mask.

With the help of the natives, the PT made its way to Bird Island. A skiff went in and picked up the men. In the deep of the night, the PT and its happy cargo roared back toward base. The squadron medic had sent some brandy along to revive the weakened men. Johnston felt the need of a little revival. In fact, he felt he needed quite a bit of revival. After taking care of that, he retired topside and sat with his arms around a couple of roly-poly, mission-trained natives. And in the fresh breeze on the way home they sang together a hymn all three happened to know:

> *Jesus loves me, this I know,*
> *For the Bible tells me so;*
> *Little ones to Him belong,*
> *They are weak, but He is strong.*
> *Yes, Jesus loves me; yes, Jesus loves me . . .*

# LETTER FROM LONDON

MOLLIE PANTER-DOWNES

*May 7, 1944*

A VISITOR to this city who had managed to get in before the last pre-invasion drawbridge was hauled up would probably be able to deduce nothing much from its appearance. Londoners, whatever they feel is coming in the near future, are getting on with their day-to-day existence in an almost ostentatiously normal way. After the tense chattiness of the past few weeks, most people have settled down to a calm, quiet wait, and even speculations on likely invasion dates and places have mercifully petered out. Now there appears to be a conspiracy to pretend that this is just another spring, instead of the spring everybody has been waiting for since Dunkirk. Although no one knows if he'll be able to keep them, private and public engagements are imperturbably being made for the next few weeks. The Royal Academy's private preview, which in peacetime opens the London social season, went off much as usual last week. Women are cheering themselves up with uncouponed new spring hats at dizzy prices that the Board of Trade, whose members are possibly husbands as well as officials, have promised to bring under control. The grass around the display of tulips in Hyde Park has been worn bald by the feet of garden lovers, who are taking advantage of their lunch hour to forget the war for five minutes and revive their memories of the Chelsea flower show. Traffic on the streets seems thicker than usual, most of its liveliness being contributed by American jeeps and glossy staff cars. Cinema managers report ruefully that there has been a sharp drop in business, something that is not entirely attributable to the longer spring days. While waiting in a deceptively placid way for events to occur, the public apparently does not want its mind taken off them. The mood of the moment here resembles the trusting calm that descends on a man in the hospital for an operation who, after months of anxiety, realizes all at once that there is nothing for him to do but lie back and leave everything to the professionals.

The cinema and theatre managers, incidentally, were among the people most gratified by Sir John Anderson's "no change" budget, which many Britons had expected would call for a more severe tax on entertainment. On the night Sir John's new budget was announced, the bars were full of tax-payers gratefully ordering a drink of Scotch to celebrate its not being upped, as they had nervously anticipated, to thirty bob a bottle. The news that there was no news in the way of financial shocks was naturally a big relief to the man in the street, "who," the Manchester *Guardian* observed, "in West London now is usually an American soldier." The satisfaction of the genuine local article, however, resulted in the unusual phenomenon of a Chancellor of the Exchequer's being discussed with affectionate enthusiasm. The excellent impression produced by Sir John's first budget has possibly strengthened the feeling that he might make a good Prime Minister, but this view, it should be added, seems to be held by a fairly select few in high places. A newspaper poll held the other day to decide who would best fill out the folds in the ample Churchillian mantle overwhelmingly gave the popular vote to Anthony Eden, with Sir Stafford Cripps an exceedingly poor second. Though Sir John didn't even place in this trial heat, he has received plenty of complimentary bouquets from economists and businessmen who feel that all in all he has thrown them several important postwar life belts and from just plain people who are glad to be left with their heads still above water.

After having been given such a pleasing financial blueprint for the next year, Londoners were last week introduced to an architectural blueprint of what large areas of Britain are going to look like after the war. The first of Mr. Churchill's promised prefabricated steel houses for newlyweds has, like a squat mushroom, suddenly sprung up in the shadow of the Tate Gallery. While its aesthetic appeal is limited, lots of housewives who go to see it will think its labor-saving devices are much better-looking than anything in the Tate. It is being emphasized that such houses represent only a temporary solution of the postwar housing problem, which, on this bombed island, will certainly be acute—a reassuring guarantee to those apprehensive lovers of rural England who were beginning to visualize bungaloid growths sprawling all over the green countryside.

The Royal Academy show, like the budget, was comfortably free of shocks, and, in this most critical of problem years, free of problem pictures, too. At the preview, the greatest crowds seemed to collect around Augustus John's portrait of General Montgomery, a work that didn't flatter either John or Montgomery, and around Dame Laura Knight's detailed interiors of bombers and aircraft factories. A popular subject picture, in the good old Academy tradition, entitled "The Week's Ration," showed a good-humored butcher quizzically regarding two mutton chops and somebody's weekly one-and-tuppence meat allowance. This struck an almost painfully topical note in a week in which news of the letup on meat rationing in the United States had caught Britons trying not to look too envious, and at the same time becomingly grateful for their one-and-tuppence worth of frozen lend-lease pork.

# LETTER FROM LONDON

### MOLLIE PANTER-DOWNES

*May 21, 1944*

LIVING on this little island just now uncomfortably resembles living on a vast combination of an aircraft carrier, a floating dock jammed with men, and a warehouse stacked to the ceiling with material labelled "Europe." It's not at all difficult for one to imagine that England's coastline can actually be seen bulging and trembling like the walls of a Silly Symphony house in which a terrific fight is going on. The fight everybody is waiting for hasn't started yet, but all over England, from the big cities to the tiniest hamlet, the people, at least in spirit, seem already to have begun it. There is a curious new something in their expressions which recalls the way people looked when the blitz was on. It's an air of responsibility, as though they had shouldered the job of being back in the civilian front line once again. It's evident in the faces of women looking up thoughtfully from their gardens at the gliders passing overhead, in the unguarded faces of businessmen wearily cat-napping on trams on their way home to all-night Home Guard duty, in the faces of everybody except the young fighting men themselves. The troops look unfailingly cheerful and lighthearted, as though they didn't know that anything unusual was afoot, and it is obvious that they are in wonderful physical shape.

Life is reminiscent of the blitz in other ways, too, for now, as then, people are keyed up to withstand something which they have often imagined but never experienced, and there is the same element of uncertainty about what is coming. The ordinary citizen seems far less worried, however, about possible bombs, long-distance shelling, or gas attacks than about such problems as how the dickens he is going to get to and from work if transport is seriously curtailed. It has already been announced that trains may be suddenly cancelled without warning, but there is a vague promise that motorbuses for essential workers will take their place whenever possible. Stay-at-home Britons seem resigned to the probability that their second front will consist mainly of humdrum hardships, including more inconvenience, fatigue, and doing without. The idea that London, during the invasion, will come in for heavy air attacks seems to have faded away, oddly, and there is even less worrying over any secret weapon that may be up the German sleeve for D Day. It is plausible to

*305*

lots of English that the Germans may stage a token invasion or series of parachute raids. This would mean that, since the Army's attention would be engaged elsewhere, the Home Guard would be expected to take charge of the situation.

Already, in the country, the milk and the mail arrive late, delivered by a somewhat bleary-eyed milkman or postman who explains that he has just finished standing his watch with the all-night guard, which once more has been established. The shadow of the second front falls across day-to-day happenings in even the smallest community. One country-dwelling lady who recently decided that she must have some urgent plumbing repairs done in her home was warned by the contractor that he and his plumber's mates were all Home Guards. He pointed out that if anything happened (there isn't a village in England which doesn't proudly imagine that it's all-important to the Nazis), the boys would just drop her new water tank smack on the lawn and she would be left bathless until the fighting was over. It is often in just such a ridiculous way that English families begin to realize what it may be like to have the battle of Europe right on their doorsteps, involving not only big and historic issues but also small and homely ones like baths, trains, the morning paper, and the day's milk.

There has been, so far as can be judged, no panic buying of food. The authorities have announced reassuringly that the situation is in good enough order to make anything but temporary local shortages unlikely. Moreover, in case any village gets cut off from its source of food supply, it has its own iron rations stored away in barns and other places, with plans for their distribution already organized by the squire, the vicar, and the schoolmaster. Villagers may not be hungry this summer, but they are likely to be thirsty for their traditional pint at the end of the day's work. In many rural districts, beer is so scarce already that pubs only open certain days of the week. This is due in part to the labor shortage and second-front traffic priorities and in part to the presence everywhere of troops who cheerfully drink the place dry before the locals can put on their clean corduroys and toddle round to the Dog and Pheasant.

Whether or not the High Command hopes to confuse the enemy with constant troop movements, they are certainly succeeding in confusing the village know-it-alls. The pretty girls hardly have time to get excited over the news that the Yanks have moved in before the Yanks are succeeded by the Canadians. When word gets around that the Canadians are leaving, too, there is much head-wagging over the rumor that something is really starting this time, but by next afternoon the English troops have arrived.

The peaceful charm of the English countryside is now mostly something that the English, too, read about in books. Like the phrase "weather permitting," the unspoken phrase "second front permitting" is, more and more, tacked on to all minor plans for the future, from a lunch date for next week to a village flower-show announcement that a regimental band will play—if the regiment is still there, that is.

In this dreamlike pause, the big London railway stations, crowded with men in uniform who have rushed up for a few hours' leave, are the only places where the invasion seems real and pressing and dramatic. The women who have come to see their men off nearly always walk to the very end of the platform to wave their elaborately smiling goodbyes as the train pulls out. Sometimes they look to one as though they're standing on the extreme tip of England itself, fluttering their gay, undeceiving handkerchiefs, and possibly they look that way to the boys hanging out of the windows to wave back at them.

[June 10, 1944]


# LETTER FROM LONDON

MOLLIE PANTER-DOWNES

*June 4, 1944*

ALTHOUGH the British have had the news from Rome to cheer them and the recent Churchill speech to puzzle them, the really big news for them is the fact that it's still C Day and not yet D Day. In the curious hush of the moment—a hush that is not merely figurative, since Londoners haven't been awakened by sirens for a month—it seems as though everyone is existing merely from one ordinary day to the next, waiting for the great, extraordinary one. Until the invasion begins, even the most momentous domestic happenings are bound to fall flat. For example, Lord Woolton's first important offering as Minister of Reconstruction, his White Paper dealing with the problem of maintaining full employment after the war, created as little stir as if it had described plans for preventing unemployment among the Hottentots rather than among the men who will be coming back from the invasion. In contrast to the enormous interest the public showed in the Beveridge plan, the lack of excitement over Lord Woolton's plan was remarkable.

There was, of course, a certain amount of heated discussion of the Prime Minister's latest speech. It was, as everyone knows, largely concerned with foreign policy, but exactly what policy emerged from it, the patient, bewildered public couldn't seem to decide. The average man wasn't able to make head or tail of the injunction to be nice to General Franco, who apparently wasn't the same kind of Fascist one's sons were fighting outside Rome. The Left press was naturally outraged by Mr. Churchill's rather disconcerting politeness toward Spain, and even the Right press seemed perplexed, as though trying to think what to think. The middle-of-the-road chap, too, was worried by what Mr. Churchill had to say about the nonrecognition of the French National Committee, a policy which, to most English, looks like writing "Not Welcome" on the mat before anyone has arrived. No Churchill speech could fail to be an event, but thousands of Britons conspicuously didn't cheer this one.

Civilians have already had a foretaste of the interruptions in the routine of existence which the invasion will bring, for the railways, as was threatened, have been quietly withdrawing services here and there under the very noses of commuters, who frequently arrive at the station in their city clothes only to find that there are no trains to take them to the city. Furthermore, over the recent Whitsun weekend, many of the determined holiday-makers who went to look for trains to take them out of London were disappointed. Among the successful ones were those who headed up the Thames, which suddenly had a prewar boom in punts, or went to see the horses run at Ascot. Few of Ascot's traditional frills remain, and the Bank Holiday crowd in the formerly exclusive Royal Enclosure munched sandwiches like any cheerful tripper party on Hampstead Heath.

Other Londoners spent what they felt to be their last breather for some time to come watching the Australians play cricket at Lord's, where a record crowd enjoyed what the weather bulletin described as a heat wave. Newspapers aren't allowed to comment on the weather, at least until the information is too dated to help the enemy, but as a conversational topic in the countryside its behavior has recently run a close second to the invasion. Dismayed rural folk have been bewailing a series of disastrous May frosts, which wiped out the famous Vale of Evesham berry and plum crops and blackened the blossoms of what promised to be a record yield in Kentish orchards. The fruit growers regret that the official secrecy on weather conditions was not relaxed for once to give them a warning that might have helped save some of the fruit. The loss in this particular year, when all England is crowded out of both house and larder, is a serious one. Then, to add to the joys of a rollicking farmer's life, the drought has damaged the hay crop, and this, in turn, will affect the milk yield. Although these headaches naturally figure in a good many of the discussions after opening time in the village pub, the one unfailing topic, as much there as in London clubs and bars, is the invasion.

In coastal hamlets, where one can see the Channel simply by toiling up a chalk track to the downs, the coming invasion is felt to be very much a local affair. So, in a way, is the fighting in Italy. Gaffers who have taken Sunday strolls to the local Roman villa or earthworks all their lives have seemed to accept, with a cozy sense of familiarity, the fact that their grandsons were now slogging up the Appian Way. All the little churches will be open for prayers and improvised services when the invasion signal is given. The local folk, especially in southern parts, think that they will get a hint of what is afoot long before those slow London chaps read it in their newspapers. It's true that the peace of the countryside is rent day and night with every variety of loud noise, but they nevertheless expect to recognize the real thing when it comes. Any particularly heavy coastal barrage put up against the German reconnaissance raids these nights has wives excitedly jabbing sleeping husbands in the ribs and saying, "Wake up, Dad! It's started!" Tiny coastal communities, where cars never even bothered to stop in peacetime, proudly expect that when it does start they will find themselves in the front line, just as they have always been in the hundreds of years that Englishmen, in one pattern of warfare or another, have been slipping away across the Channel on other D Days.

# LETTER FROM LONDON

MOLLIE PANTER-DOWNES

*June 11, 1944*

FOR the English, D Day might well have stood for Dunkirk Day. The tremendous news that British soldiers were back on French soil seemed suddenly to reveal exactly how much it had rankled when they were beaten off it four years ago. As the great fleets of planes roared toward the coast all day long, people glancing up at them said, "Now they'll know how our boys felt on the beaches of Dunkirk." And as the people went soberly back to their jobs, they had a satisfied look, as though this return trip to France had in itself been worth waiting four impatient, interminable years for. There was also a slightly bemused expression on most D Day faces, because the event wasn't working out quite the way anybody had expected. Londoners seemed to imagine that there would be some immediate, miraculous change, that the heavens would open, that something like the last trumpet would sound. What they definitely hadn't expected was that the greatest day of our times would be just the same old London day, with men and women going to the office, queuing up for fish, getting haircuts, and scrambling for lunch.

D Day sneaked up on people so quietly that half the crowds flocking to business on Tuesday morning didn't know it was anything but Tuesday, and then it fooled them by going right on being Tuesday. The principal impression one got on the streets was that nobody was smiling. The un-English urge to talk to strangers which came over Londoners during the blitzes, and in other recent times of crisis, was noticeably absent. Everybody seemed to be existing wholly in a preoccupied silence of his own, a silence that had something almost frantic about it, as if the effort of punching bus tickets, or shopping for kitchen pans, or whatever the day's chore might be, was, in its quiet way, harder to bear than a bombardment. Later in the day, the people who patiently waited in the queues at each newsstand for the vans to turn up with the latest editions were still enclosed in their individual silences. In the queer hush, one could sense the strain of a city trying to project itself across the intervening English orchards and cornfields, across the strip of water, to the men already beginning to die in the French orchards and cornfields that once more had become "over there." Flag sellers for a Red Cross drive were on the streets, and many people looked thoughtfully at the little red paper symbol before pinning it to their lapels, for it was yet another reminder of the personal loss that D Day was bringing closer for thousands of them.

In Westminster Abbey, typists in summer dresses and the usual elderly visitors in country-looking clothes came in to pray beside the tomb of the last war's Unknown Soldier, or to gaze rather vacantly at the tattered colors and the marble heroes of battles which no longer seemed remote. The top-hatted old warrior who is gatekeeper at Marlborough House, where King George V was born, pinned on all his medals in honor of the day, and hawkers selling cornflowers and red and white peonies had hastily concocted little patriotic floral arrangements, but there was no rush to put out flags, no cheers, no out-ward emotion. In the shops, since people aren't specially interested in spending money when they are anxious, business was extremely bad. Streets that normally are crowded had the deserted look of a small provincial town on a wet Sunday afternoon. Taxi-drivers, incredulously cruising about for cus-tomers, said that it was their worst day in months. Even after the King's broad-cast was over, Londoners stayed home. Everybody seemed to feel that this was one night you wanted your own thoughts in your own chair. Theatre and cinema receipts slumped, despite the movie houses' attempt to attract audiences by broadcasting the King's speech and the invasion bulletins. Even the pubs didn't draw the usual cronies. At midnight, London was utterly quiet, the Civil Defense people were standing by for a half-expected alert that didn't come, and D Day had passed into history.

It is in the country districts just back of the sealed south coast that one gets a real and urgent sense of what is happening only a few minutes' flying time away. Pheasants whir their alarm at the distant rumble of guns, just as they did when Dunkirk's guns were booming. On Tuesday evening, villagers hoe-ing weeds in the wheat fields watched the gliders passing in an almost unend-ing string toward Normandy. And always there are the planes. When the big American bombers sail overhead, moving with a sinister drowsiness in their perfect formations, people who have not bothered to glance up at the familiar drone for months rush out of their houses to stare. Everything is different now that the second front has opened, and every truck on the road, every piece of gear on the railways, every jeep and half-track that is heading toward the front has become a thing of passionate concern. The dry weather, which coun-try folk a week ago were hoping would end, has now become a matter for worry the other way round. Farmers who wanted gray skies for their hay's sake now want blue ones for the sake of their sons, fighting in the skies and on the earth across the Channel. Finally, there are the trainloads of wounded, which are already beginning to pass through summer England, festooned with its dog roses and honeysuckle. The red symbol which Londoners were pin-ning to their lapels on Tuesday now shines on the side of trains going past crossings where the waiting women, shopping baskets on their arms, don't know whether to wave or cheer or cry. Sometimes they do all three.

# CROSS-CHANNEL TRIP

A.  J.  LIEBLING

THREE days after the first Allied landing in France, I was in the ward-room of an LCIL (Landing Craft, Infantry, Large) that was bobbing in the lee of the French cruiser Montcalm off the Normandy coast. The word "large" in landing-craft designation is purely relative; the wardroom of the one I was on is seven by seven feet and contains two officers' bunks and a table with four places at it. She carries a complement of four officers, but since one of them must always be on watch there is room for a guest at the ward-room table, which is how I fitted in. The Montcalm was loosing salvos, each of which rocked our ship; she was firing at a German pocket of resistance a couple of miles from the shoreline. The suave voice of a B.B.C. announcer came over the wardroom radio: "Next in our series of impressions from the front will be a recording of an artillery barrage." The French ship loosed off again, drowning out the recording. It was this same announcer, I think—I'm not sure, because all B.B.C. announcers sound alike—who said, a little while later, "We are now in a position to say the landings came off with surprising ease. The Air Force and the big guns of the Navy smashed coastal defenses, and the Army occupied them." Lieutenant Henry Rigg, United States Coast Guard Reserve, the skipper of our landing craft, looked at Long, her engineer-ing officer, and they both began to laugh. Kavanaugh, the ship's communica-tions officer, said, "Now, what do you think of that?" I called briefly upon God. Aboard the LCIL, D Day hadn't seemed like that to us. There is nothing like a broadcasting studio in London to give a chap perspective.

I went aboard our LCIL on Thursday evening, June 1st. The little ship was one of a long double file that lay along the dock in a certain British port. She was fast to the dock, with another LCIL lashed to her on the other side. An LCIL is a hundred and fifty-five feet long and about three hundred dead-weight tons. A destroyer is a big ship indeed by comparison; even an LST (Landing Ship, Tanks) looms over an LCIL like a monster. The LCIL has a flat bottom and draws only five feet of water, so she can go right up on a beach. Her hull is a box for carrying men; she can sleep two hundred soldiers belowdecks or can carry five hundred on a short ferrying trip, when men stand both below and topside. An LCIL has a stern anchor that she drops just before she goes aground and two forward ramps that she runs out as she touches bottom. As troops go down the ramps, the ship naturally lightens, and she rises a few inches in the water; she then winches herself off by the stern anchor, in much the same way a monkey pulls himself back on a limb by his tail. Troop space is about all there is to an LCIL, except for a compact engine room and a few indispensable sundries like navigation instruments and anti-aircraft guns. LCILs are the smallest ocean-crossing landing craft, and all those now in the European theatre arrived under their own power. The crews probably would have found it more comfortable sailing on the Santa María. Most LCILs are operated by the Navy, but several score of them have Coast Guard crews. Ours was one of the latter. The name "Coast Guard" has always reminded me of the little cutters plying out to ocean liners from the barge office at the Battery in New York, and the association gave me a definite pleasure. Before boarding the landing craft, I had been briefed, along with twenty other correspondents, on the flagship of Rear Admiral John L. Hall, Jr., who commanded the task force of which our craft formed a minute part, so I knew where we were going and approximately when. Since that morning I had been sealed off from the civilian world, in the marshalling area, and when I went aboard our landing craft I knew that I would not be permitted even to set foot on the dock except in the company of a commissioned officer.

It was warm and the air felt soporific when I arrived. The scene somehow reminded me more of the Sheepshead Bay channel, with its fishing boats, than of the jumping-off place for an invasion. A young naval officer who had brought me ashore from the flagship took me over the landing craft's gangplank and introduced me to Lieutenant Rigg. Rigg, familiarly known as Bunny, was a big man, thirty-three years old, with clear, light-blue eyes and a fleshy, good-tempered face. He was a yacht broker in civilian life and often wrote articles about boats. Rigg welcomed me aboard as if we were going for a cruise to Block Island, and invited me into the wardroom to have a cup of coffee. There was standing room only, because Rigg's three junior officers and a Navy commander were already drinking coffee at the table. The junior officers—Long, Kavanaugh, and Williams—were all lieutenants (j.g.). Long, a small, jolly man with an upturned nose, was a Coast Guard regular with twenty years' service, mostly as a chief petty officer. He came from Baltimore. Kavanaugh, tall and straight-featured, was from Crary, North Dakota, and Williams, a very polite, blond boy, came from White Deer, Texas. Kavanaugh and Williams were both in their extremely early twenties. The three-striper, a handsome, slender man with prematurely white hair and black eyebrows, was introduced to me by Rigg as the C.O. of a naval beach battalion that would go in to organize boat traffic on a stretch of beach as soon as the first waves of Infantry had taken it over. He was going to travel to the invasion coast aboard our landing craft, and since he disliked life ashore in the marshalling area, he had come aboard ship early. The commander,· who had a drawl hard to match north of Georgia, was in fact a Washingtonian. He was an Annapolis man, he soon told me, but had left the Navy for several years to practice law in the District of Columbia and then returned to it for the war. His battalion was divided for the crossing among six LCILs, which would go in in pairs on adjacent beaches, so naturally he had much more detailed dope on the coming operation than normally would come to, say, the skipper of a landing craft, and this was to make conversations in the tiny wardroom more interesting than they otherwise would have been.

Even before I had finished my second cup of coffee, I realized that I had been assigned to a prize LCIL; our ship was to beach at H Hour plus sixty-five, which means one hour and five minutes after the first assault soldier gets ashore. "This ship and No. X will be the first LCILs on the beach," Rigg said complacently. "The first men will go in in small boats, because of mines and underwater obstacles, and Navy demolition men with them will blow us a lane through element C—that's sunken concrete and iron obstacles. They will also sweep the lane of mines, we hope. We just have to stay in the lane."

"These things move pretty fast and they make a fairly small target bow on," Long added cheerfully.

The others had eaten, but I had not, so Williams went out to tell the cook to get me up some chow. While it was being prepared, I went out on deck to look around.

Our landing craft, built in 1942, is one of the first class of LCILs, which have a rectangular superstructure and a narrow strip of open deck on each side of it. Painted on one side of the superstructure I noted a neat Italian flag, with the legend "Italy" underneath so that there would be no mistake, and beside the flag a blue shield with white vertical stripes and the word "Sicily." There was also a swastika and the outline of an airplane, which could only mean that the ship had shot down a German plane in a landing either in Sicily or Italy. Under Britain's double summer time, it was still light, and there were several groups of sailors on deck, most of them rubbing "impregnating grease" into shoes to make them impervious to mustard gas. There had been a great last-minute furore about the possibility that the Germans might use gas against the invasion, and everybody had been fitted with impregnated gear and two kinds of protective ointment. Our ship's rails were topped with rows of drying shoes.

"This is the first time I ever tried to get a pair of shoes pregnant, sir," one of the sailors called out sociably as I was watching him.

"No doubt you tried it on about everything else, I guess," another sailor yelled as he, too, worked on his shoes.

I could see I would not be troubled by any of that formality which has occasionally oppressed me aboard flagships. Most of the sailors had their names stencilled in white on the backs of their jumpers, so there was no need for introductions. One sailor I encountered was in the middle of a complaint about a shore officer who had "eaten him out" because of the way he was dressed on the dock, and he continued after I arrived. "They treat us like children," he said. "You'd think we was the pea-jacket navy instead of the ambiguous farce." The first term is one that landing-craft sailors apply to those on big ships, who keep so dry that they can afford to dress the part. "The ambiguous farce" is their pet name for the amphibious forces. A chief petty officer, who wore a khaki cap with his blue coveralls, said, "You don't want to mind them, sir. This isn't a regular ship and doesn't even pretend to be. But it's a good working ship. You ought to see our engine room."

A little sailor with a Levantine face asked me where I came from. When I told him New York, he said, "Me too—Hundred twenty-second and First." The name stencilled on his back was Landini. "I made up a song about this deal," he said, breaking into a kind of Off to Buffalo. "I'm going over to France and I'm shaking in my pants."

Through the open door of the galley, I could watch the cook, a fattish man with wavy hair and a narrow mustache, getting my supper ready. His name was Fassy, and he was the commissary steward. He appeared to have a prejudice against utensils; he slapped frankfurters and beans down on the hot stove top, rolled them around, and flipped them onto the plate with a spatula. I thought the routine looked familiar and I found out later that in his civilian days Fassy had worked in Shanty restaurants in New York.

While I was standing there, a young seaman stencilled Sitnitsky popped his head into the galley to ask for some soap powder so he could wash his clothes. Fassy poured some out of a vast carton into a pail of hot water the boy held. " 'Not recommended for delicate fabrics,' " the steward read from the carton, then roared, "So don't use it on your dainty lingerie!"

Since the frankfurters and beans were ready, I returned to the wardroom. There the board of strategy was again in session. The beach we were headed for was near the American line, only a mile or two from Port-en-Bessin, where the British area began. Eighteen years before, I had walked along the tops of the same cliffs the Americans would be fighting under. In those days I had thought of it as holiday country, not sufficiently spectacular to attract *le grand tourisme* but beautiful in a reasonable, Norman way. This illogically made the whole operation seem less sinister to me. Two pillboxes showed plainly on photographs we had, and, in addition, there were two houses that looked suspiciously like shells built around other pillboxes. Our intelligence people had furnished us with extraordinarily detailed charts of gradients in the beach and correlated tide tables. The charts later proved to be extraordinarily accurate, too.

"What worries me about landing is the bomb holes the Air Forces may leave in the beach before we hit," the commander was saying when I entered. "The chart may show three feet of water, but the men may step into a ten-foot hole anywhere. I'd rather the Air Forces left the beach alone and just let the naval guns knock out the beach defenses. They're accurate."

The general plan, I knew, was for planes and big guns of the fleet to put on an intensive bombardment before the landing. A couple of weeks earlier, I had heard a Marine colonel on the planning staff tell how the guns would hammer the pillboxes, leaving only a few stunned defenders for the Infantry to gather up on their way through to positions inland.

"We're lucky," the commander said. "This beach looks like a soft one."

His opinion, in conjunction with frankfurters and beans, made me happy.

We didn't get our passengers aboard until Saturday. On Friday I spent my time in alternate stretches of talk with the men on deck and the officers in the wardroom. Back in Sicily, the ship had been unable to get off after grounding at Licata, a boatswain's mate named Pendleton told me. "She got hit so bad we had to leave her," he said, "and for three days we had to live in foxholes, just like Infantrymen. Didn't feel safe a minute. We was sure glad to get back on the ship. Guess she had all her bad luck that trip."

Pendleton, a large, fair-haired fellow who was known to his shipmates as the Little Admiral, came from Neodesha, Kansas. "They never heard of the Coast Guard out there," he said. "Nobody but me. I knew I would have to go in some kind of service and I was reading in a Kansas City paper one day that the Coast Guard would send a station wagon to your house to get you if it was within a day's drive of their recruiting station. So I wrote 'em. Never did like to walk."

Sitnitsky was washing underclothes at a sink aft of the galley once when I came upon him. When he saw me, he said, "The fois' ting I'm gonna do when I get home is buy my mudder a Washington machine. I never realize what the old lady was up against."

Our neighbor LCIL, tied alongside us, got her soldier passengers late Friday night. The tide was low and the plank leading down to our ship from the dock was at a steep angle as men came aboard grumbling and filed across our deck to the other LCIL. "Didjever see a goddam gangplank in the right place?" one man called over his shoulder as he eased himself down with his load. I could identify a part of a mortar on his back, in addition to a full pack. "All aboard for the second Oran," another soldier yelled, and a third man, passing by the emblems painted on the bridge, as he crossed our ship, yelled, "Sicily! *They* been there, too." So I knew these men were part of the First Division, which landed at Oran in Africa in 1942 and later fought in Sicily. I think I would have known anyway by the beefing. The First Division is always beefing about something, which adds to its effectiveness as a fighting unit.

The next day the soldiers were spread all over the LCIL next door, most of them reading paper-cover, armed-services editions of books. They were just going on one more trip, and they didn't seem excited about it. I overheard a bit of technical conversation when I leaned over the rail to visit with a few of them. "Me, I like a bar [Browning automatic rifle]," a sergeant was saying to a private. "You can punch a lot of tickets with one of them."

The private, a rangy middleweight with a small, close-cropped head and a rectangular profile, said, "I'm going into this one with a pickaxe and a block of TNT. It's an interesting assignment. I'm going to work on each pillbox individually," he added, carefully pronouncing each syllable.

When I spoke to them, the sergeant said, "Huh! A correspondent! Why don't they give the First Division some credit?"

"I guess you don't read much if you say that, Sarge," a tall blond boy with a Southern accent said. "There's a whole book of funnies called 'Terry Allen and the First Division at El Guettar.'"

All three men were part of an Infantry regiment. The soldier who was going to work on pillboxes asked if I was from New York, and said that he was from the Bensonhurst section of Brooklyn. "I am only sorry my brother-in-law is not here," he said. "My brother-in-law is an M.P. He is six inches bigger than me. He gets an assignment in New York. I would like to see him here. He would be apprehensive." He went on to say that the company he was with had been captured near the end of the African campaign, when, after being cut off by the Germans, it had expended all its ammunition. He had been a prisoner in Tunis for a few hours, until the British arrived and set him free. "There are some nice broads in Tunis," he said. "I had a hell of a time." He nodded toward the book he was holding. "These little books are a great thing," he said. "They take you away. I remember when my battalion was cut off on top of a hill at El Guettar, I read a whole book in one day. It was called 'Knight Without Armor.' This one I am reading now is called 'Candide.' It is kind of unusual, but I like it. I think the fellow who wrote it, Voltaire, used the same gag too often, though. The characters are always getting killed and then turning out not to have been killed after all, and they tell their friends what happened to them in the meantime. I like the character in it called Pangloss."

Fassy was lounging near the rail and I called him over to meet a brother Brooklynite. "Brooklyn is a beautiful place to live in," Fassy said. "I have bush Number Three at Prospect Park."

"I used to have bush Number Four," the soldier said.

"You remind me of a fellow named Sidney Wetzelbaum," Fassy said. "Are you by any chance related?"

I left them talking.

Our own passengers came aboard later in the day. There were two groups

—a platoon of the commander's beach battalion and a platoon of amphibious engineers. The beach-battalion men were sailors dressed like soldiers, except that they wore black jerseys under their field jackets; among them were a medical unit and a hydrographic unit. The engineers included an M.P. detachment, a chemical-warfare unit, and some demolition men. A beach battalion is a part of the Navy that goes ashore; amphibious engineers are a part of the Army that seldom has its feet dry. Together they form a link between the land and sea forces. These two detachments had rehearsed together in landing exercises, during which they had travelled aboard our LCIL. Unlike the Coastguardsmen or the Infantry on the next boat, they had never been in the real thing before and were not so offhand about it. Among them were a fair number of men in their thirties. I noticed one chief petty officer with the Navy crowd who looked about fifty. It was hard to realize that these older men had important and potentially dangerous assignments that called for a good deal of specialized skill; they seemed to me more out of place than the Infantry kids. Some sailors carried carbines and most of the engineers had rifles packed in oilskin cases. There were about a hundred and forty men in all. The old chief, Joe Smith, who was the first of the lot I got to know, said he had been on battleships in the last war and had been recalled from the fleet reserves at the beginning of this. He took considerable comfort from the fact that several aged battleships would lay down a barrage for us before we went in. You could see that he was glad to be aboard a ship again, even if it was a small one and he would be on it for only a couple of days. He was a stout, red-faced, merry man whose home town was Spring Lake, New Jersey. "I'm a tomato squeezer," he told me. "Just a country boy."

Cases of rations had been stacked against the superstructure for the passengers' use. The galley wasn't big enough to provide complete hot meals for them, but it did provide coffee, and their own cook warmed up canned stew and corned beef for them for one meal. The rest of the time they seemed simply to rummage among the cans until they found something they liked and then ate it. They ate pretty steadily, because there wasn't much else for them to do.

Our landing craft had four sleeping compartments belowdecks. The two forward ones, which were given over to passengers, contained about eighty bunks apiece. Most of the crew slept in the third compartment, amidships, and a number of petty officers and noncoms slept in the fourth, the smallest one, aft. I had been sleeping in this last one myself since coming aboard, because there was only one extra bunk for an officer and the commander had that. Four officers who came aboard with the troops joined me in this compartment. There were two sittings at the wardroom table for meals, but we managed to wedge eight men in there at one time for a poker game.

There was no sign of a move Saturday night, and on Sunday morning everybody aboard began asking when we were going to shove off. The morning sun was strong and the crew mingled with the beach-battalion men and the soldiers on deck. It was the same on board every other LCIL in the long double row. The port didn't look like Sheepshead Bay now, for every narrow boat was covered with men in drab-green field jackets, many of them wearing tin hats, because the easiest way not to lose a tin hat in a crowd is to wear it. The small ships and helmets pointed up the analogy to a crusade and made the term seem less threadbare than it usually does. We were waiting for weather, as many times the crusaders, too, had waited, but nobody thought of praying for it, not even the chaplain who came aboard in mid-morning to conduct services. He was a captain attached to the amphibious engineers, a husky man I had noticed throwing a football around on the dock the previous day. He took his text from Romans: "If God be for us, who can be against us?" He didn't seem to want the men to get the idea that we were depending entirely on faith, however. "Give us that dynamic, that drive, which, coupled with our matchless super-modern weapons, will ensure victory," he prayed. After that, he read aloud General Eisenhower's message to the Allied Expeditionary Force.

After the services, printed copies of Eisenhower's message were distributed to all hands on board. Members of our ship's crew went about getting autographs of their shipmates on their "Eisenhowers," which they apparently intended to keep as souvenirs of the invasion. Among the fellows who came to me for my signature was the ship's coxswain, a long-legged, serious-looking young man, from a little town in Mississippi, who had talked to me several times before because he wanted to be a newspaperman after the war. He had had one year at Tulane, in New Orleans, before joining up with the Coast Guard, and he hoped he could finish up later. The coxswain, I knew, would be the first man out of the ship when she grounded, even though he was a member of the crew. It was his task to run a guideline ashore in front of the disembarking soldiers. Then, when he had arrived in water only a foot or two deep, he would pull on the line and bring an anchor floating in after him, the anchor being a light one tied in a life jacket so that it would float. He would then fix the anchor—without the life jacket, of course—and return to the ship. This procedure had been worked out after a number of soldiers had been drowned on landing exercises by stepping into unexpected depressions in the beach after they had left the landing craft. Soldiers, loaded down with gear, had simply disappeared. With a guideline to hold onto, they could have struggled past bad spots. I asked the boy what he was going to wear when he went into the water with the line and he said just swimming trunks and a tin hat. He said he was a fair swimmer.

The rumor got about that we would sail that evening, but late in the afternoon the skipper told me we weren't going to. I learned that the first elements of the invasion fleet, the slowest ones, had gone out but had met rough weather in the Channel and had returned, because they couldn't have arrived at their destination in time. Admiral Hall had told correspondents that there would be three successive days when tide conditions on the Norman beaches would be right and that if we missed them the expedition might have to be put off, so I knew that we now had one strike on us, with only two more chances.

That evening, in the wardroom, we had a long session of a wild, distant derivative of poker called "high low rollem." Some young officers who had come aboard with the troops introduced it. We used what they called "funny money" for chips—five-franc notes printed in America and issued to the troops for use after they got ashore. It was the first time I had seen these notes, which reminded me of old-time cigar-store coupons. There was nothing on them to indicate who authorized them or would pay off on them—just *"Emis en France"* on one side and on the other side the tricolor and *"Liberté, Egalité, Fraternité."* In the game were three beach-battalion officers, a medical lieutenant (j.g.) named Davey, from Philadelphia, and two ensigns—a big, ham-handed college football player from Danbury, Connecticut, named Vaghi, and a blocky, placid youngster from Chicago named Reich. The commander of the engineer detachment, the only Army officer aboard, was a first lieutenant named Miller, a sallow, apparently nervous boy who had started to grow an ambitious black beard.

Next morning the first copy of the *Stars and Stripes* to arrive on board gave us something new to talk about. It carried the story of the premature invasion report by the Associated Press in America. In an atmosphere heavy with una-vowed anxiety, the story hit a sour note. "Maybe they let out more than *Stars and Stripes* says," somebody in the wardroom said. "Maybe they not only an-nounced the invasion but told where we had landed. I mean, where we *planned* to land. Maybe the whole deal will be called off now." The com-mander, who had spent so much time pondering element C, said, "Add ob-stacles—element A.P." A report got about among the more pessimistic crew members that the Germans had been tipped off and would be ready for us. The Allied high command evidently did not read the *Stars and Stripes,* how-ever, for Rigg, after going ashore for a brief conference, returned with the information that we were shoving off at five o'clock. I said to myself, in the great cliché of the second World War, "This is it," and so, I suppose, did every other man in our fleet of little ships when he heard the news.

Peace or war, the boat trip across the English Channel always begins with the passengers in the same mood: everybody hopes he won't get seasick. On the whole, this is a favorable morale factor at the outset of an invasion. A sol-dier cannot fret about possible attacks by the Luftwaffe or E-boats while he is preoccupied with himself, and the vague fear of secret weapons on the far shore is balanced by the fervent desire to get the far shore under his feet. Few of the hundred and forty passengers on the LCIL I was on were actively sick the night before D Day, but they were all busy thinking about it. The four officers and twenty-nine men of the United States Coast Guard who made up her complement were not even queasy, but they had work to do, which was just as good. The rough weather, about which the papers have talked so much since D Day and which in fact interfered with the landing, was not the kind that tosses about transatlantic liners or even Channel packets; it was just a bit too rough for the smaller types of landing craft we employed. Aboard our LCIL, the Channel didn't seem especially bad that night. There was a ground swell for an hour after we left port, but then the going became better than I had anticipated. LCTs (Landing Craft, Tanks), built like open troughs a hundred feet long, to carry armored vehicles, had a much worse time, particularly since, being slow, they had had to start hours before us. Fifty-foot LCMs (Landing Craft, Mechanized) and fifty-foot and thirty-six-foot LCVPs (Landing Craft, Vehicles and Personnel), swarms of which crossed the Channel under their own power, had still more trouble. The setting out of our group of LCILs was unimpressive—just a double file of ships, each a hundred and fifty-five feet long, bound for a rendezvous with a great many other ships at three in the morning ten or fifteen miles off a spot on the coast of lower Normandy. Most of the troops travelled in large transports, from which the smaller craft transferred them to shore. The LCILs carried specially packaged units for early delivery on the Continent doorstep.

Rigg turned in early that evening because he wanted to be fresh for a hard day's work by the time we arrived at the rendezvous, which was to take place in what was known as the transport area. So did the commander of the naval beach battalion. I stood on deck for a while. As soon as I felt sleepy, I went down to my bunk and got to sleep—with my clothes on, naturally. There didn't seem to be anything else to do. That was at about eight. I woke three hours later and saw a fellow next to me being sick in a paper bag and I went up to the galley and had a cup of coffee. Then I went back to my bunk and slept until a change in motion and in the noise of the motors woke me again.

The ship was wallowing slowly now, and I judged that we had arrived at the transport area and were loafing about. I looked at my wristwatch and saw that we were on time. It was about three. So we hadn't been torpedoed by an E-boat. A good thing. Drowsily, I wondered a little at the fact that the enemy had made no attempt to intercept the fleet and hoped there would be good air cover, because I felt sure that the Luftwaffe couldn't possibly pass up the biggest target of history. My opinion of the Luftwaffe was still strongly influenced by what I remembered from June, 1940, in France, and even from January and February, 1943, in Tunisia. I decided to stay in my bunk until daylight, dozed, woke again, and then decided I couldn't make it. I went up on deck in the gray pre-dawn light sometime before five. I drew myself a cup of coffee from an electric urn in the galley and stood by the door drinking it and looking at the big ships around us. They made me feel proletarian. They would stay out in the Channel and send in their troops in small craft, while working-class vessels like us went right up on the beach. I pictured them in-

habited by officers in dress blues and shiny brass buttons, all scented like the
World's Most Distinguished After-Shave Club. The admiral's command ship
lay nearby. I imagined it to be gaffed with ingenious gimmicks that would
record the developments of the operation. I could imagine a terse report coming in of the annihilation of a flotilla of LCILs, including us, and hear
some Annapolis man saying, "After all, that sort of thing is to be expected."
Then I felt that everything was going to be all right, because it always had
been. A boatswain's mate, second class, named Barrett, from Rich Square,
North Carolina, stopped next to me to drink his coffee and said, "I bet Findley
a pound that we'd be hit this time. We most always is. Even money."

We wouldn't start to move, I knew, until about six-thirty, the time when the
very first man was scheduled to walk onto the beach. Then we would leave the
transport area so that we could beach and perform our particular chore—landing one platoon of the naval beach battalion and a platoon of Army amphibious engineers—at seven-thirty-five. A preliminary bombardment of the beach
defenses by the Navy was due to begin at dawn. "Ought to be hearing the
guns soon," I said to Barrett, and climbed the ladder to the upper deck. Rigg
was on the bridge drinking coffee, and with him was Long, the ship's engineering officer. It grew lighter and the guns began between us and the shore. The
sound made us all cheerful and Long said, "I'd hate to be in under that." Before
dawn the transports had begun putting men into small craft that headed for
the line of departure, a line nearer shore from which the first assault wave
would be launched.

Time didn't drag now. We got under way sooner than I had somehow
expected. The first troops were on the beaches. The battleship Arkansas and
the French cruisers Montcalm and Georges Leygues were pounding away on
our starboard as we moved in. They were firing over the heads of troops, at
targets farther inland. Clouds of yellow cordite smoke billowed up. There
was something leonine in their tint as well as in the roar that followed, after
that lapse of time which never fails to disconcert me. We went on past the big
ships, like a little boy with the paternal blessing. In this region the Germans
evidently had no long-range coastal guns, like the ones near Calais, for the
warships' fire was not returned. This made me feel good. The absence of
resistance always increases my confidence. The commander of the naval beach
battalion had now come on deck, accoutred like a soldier, in greenish coveralls
and tin hat. I said to him cheerfully, "Well, it looks as though the biggest
difficulty you're going to have is getting your feet in cold water."

He stood there for a minute and said, "What are you thinking of?"

I said, "I don't know why, but I'm thinking of the garden restaurant behind
the Museum of Modern Art in New York." He laughed, and I gave him a
pair of binoculars I had, because I knew that he didn't have any and that he
had important use for them.

Our passengers—the beach-battalion platoon and the amphibious engineers—were now forming two single lines on the main deck, each group facing the ramp by which it would leave the ship. Vaghi and Reich, the beach-battalion ensigns, were lining up their men on the port side and Miller, the Army lieutenant with the new beard, was arranging his men on the starboard side. I wished the commander good luck and went up on the bridge, which was small and crowded but afforded the best view.

An LCIL has two ramps, one on each side of her bow, which she lowers and thrusts out ahead of her when she beaches. Each ramp is handled by means of a winch worked by two men; the two winches stand side by side deep in an open-well deck just aft of the bow. If the ramps don't work, the whole operation is fouled up, so an LCIL skipper always assigns reliable men to operate them. Two seamen named Findley and Lechich were on the port winch, and two whom I knew as Rocky and Bill were on the other. Williams, the ship's executive officer, was down in the well deck with the four of them.

We had been in sight of shore for a long while, and now I could recognize our strip of beach from our intelligence photographs. There was the house with the tower on top of the cliff on our starboard as we went in. We had been warned that preliminary bombardment might remove it, so we should not count too much upon it as a landmark; however, there it was and it gave me the pleasure of recognition. A path was to have been blasted and swept for us through element C and the mines, and the entrance to it was to have been marked with colored buoys. The buoys were there, so evidently the operation was going all right. Our LCIL made a turn and headed for the opening like a halfback going into a hole in the line. I don't know whether Rigg suddenly became solicitous for my safety or whether he simply didn't want me underfoot on the bridge, where two officers and two signalmen had trouble getting around even without me. He said, "Mr. Liebling will take his station on the upper deck during action." This was formal language from the young man I had learned to call Bunny, especially since the action did not seem violent as yet, but I climbed down the short ladder from the bridge to the deck, a move that put the wheelhouse between me and the bow. The upper deck was also the station for a pharmacist's mate named Kallam, who was our reserve first-aid man. A landing craft carries no doctor, the theory being that a pharmacist's mate will make temporary repairs until the patient can be transferred to a larger ship. We had two men with this rating aboard. The other, a fellow named Barry, was up in the bow. Kallam was a sallow, long-faced North Carolinian who once told me he had gone into the peacetime Navy as a youth and had never been good for anything else since. This was his first action, except for a couple of landings in Nicaragua around 1930.

The shore curved out toward us on the port side of the ship, and when I looked out in that direction I could see a lot of smoke from what appeared to be shells bursting on the beach. There was also an LCT, grounded and burn-

ing. "Looks as if there's opposition," I said to Kallam, without much originality. At about the same time something splashed in the water off our
starboard quarter, sending up a high spray. We were moving in fast now. I
could visualize, from the plan I had seen so often in the last few days, the
straight, narrow lane in which we had to stay. "On a straight line—like a rope
ferry," I thought. The view on both sides changed rapidly. The LCT that
had been on our port bow was now on our port quarter, and another LCT,
also grounded, was now visible. A number of men, who had evidently just
left her, were in the water, some up to their necks and others up to their
armpits, and they didn't look as if they were trying to get ashore. Tracer
bullets were skipping around them and they seemed perplexed. What I hate
most about tracers is that every time you see one, you know there are four
more bullets that you don't see, because only one tracer to five bullets is loaded in
a machine-gun belt. Just about then, it seems in retrospect, I felt the ship ground.

I looked down at the main deck, and the beach-battalion men were already
moving ahead, so I knew that the ramps must be down. I could hear Long
shouting, "Move along now! Move along!," as if he were unloading an excursion boat at Coney Island. But the men needed no urging; they were moving
without a sign of flinching. You didn't have to look far for tracers now, and
Kallam and I flattened our backs against the pilot house and pulled in our
stomachs, as if to give a possible bullet an extra couple of inches clearance. Something tickled the back of my neck. I slapped at it and discovered that I had
most of the ship's rigging draped around my neck and shoulders, like a
character in an old slapstick movie about a spaghetti factory, or like Captain
Horatio Hornblower. The rigging had been cut away by bullets. As Kallam
and I looked toward the stern, we could see a tableau that was like a recruiting poster. There was a twenty-millimetre rapid-firing gun on the upper deck.
Since it couldn't bear forward because of the pilot house and since there was
nothing to shoot at on either side, it was pointed straight up at the sky in readi-
ness for a possible dive-bombing attack. It had a crew of three men, and they
were kneeling about it, one on each side and one behind the gun barrel, all
looking up at the sky in an extremely earnest manner, and getting all the
protection they could out of the gunshield. As a background to the men's
heads, an American flag at the ship's stern streamed across the field of vision.
It was a new flag, which Rigg had ordered hoisted for the first time for the
invasion, and its colors were brilliant in the sun. To make the poster motif
perfect, one of the three men was a Negro, William Jackson, from New Orleans, a wardroom steward, who, like everybody else on the LCIL, had multiple duties.

The last passenger was off the ship now, and I could hear the stern anchor
cable rattling on the drum as it came up. An LCIL drops a stern anchor just
before it grounds, and pays out fifty to a hundred fathoms of chain cable as
it slowly slides the last couple of ship's lengths toward shore. To get under

way again, it takes up the cable, pulling itself afloat. I had not known until that minute how eager I was to hear the sound of the cable that follows the order "Take in on stern anchor." Almost as soon as the cable began to come in, something hit the ship with the solid clunk of metal against metal—not as hard as a collision or a bomb blast; just "clink." Long yelled down, "Pharmacist's mate go forward. Somebody's hurt." Kallam scrambled down the ladder to the main deck with his kit. Then Long yelled to a man at the stern anchor winch, "Give it hell!" An LCIL has to pull itself out and get the anchor up before it can use its motors, because otherwise the propeller might foul in the cable. The little engine that supplies power for the winch is built by a farm-machinery company in Waukesha, Wisconsin, and every drop of gasoline that went into the one on our ship was filtered through chamois skin first. That engine is the ship's insurance policy. A sailor now came running up the stairway from the cabin. He grabbed me and shouted, "Two casualties in bow!" I passed this information on to the bridge for whatever good it might do; both pharmacist's mates were forward already and there was really nothing else to be done. Our craft had now swung clear, the anchor was up, and the engines went into play. She turned about and shot forward like a destroyer. The chief machinist's mate said afterward that the engines did seven hundred revolutions a minute instead of the six hundred that was normal top speed. Shells were kicking up waterspouts around us as we went; the water they raised looked black. Rigg said afterward, "Funny thing. When I was going in, I had my whole attention fixed on two mines attached to sunken concrete blocks on either side of the place where we went in. I knew they hadn't been cleared away—just a path between them. They were spider mines, those things with a lot of loose cables. Touch one cable and you detonate the mine. When I was going out, I was so excited that I forgot all about the damn mines and didn't think of them until I was two miles past them."

A sailor came by and Shorty, one of the men in the gun crew, said to him, "Who was it?" The sailor said, "Rocky and Bill. They're all tore up. A shell got the winch and ramps and all." I went forward to the well deck, which was sticky with a mixture of blood and condensed milk. Soldiers had left cases of rations lying all about the ship, and a fragment of the shell that hit the boys had torn into a carton of cans of milk. Rocky and Bill had been moved below-decks into one of the large forward compartments. Rocky was dead beyond possible doubt, somebody told me, but the pharmacist's mates had given Bill blood plasma and thought he might still be alive. I remembered Bill, a big, baby-faced kid from the District of Columbia, built like a wrestler. He was about twenty, and the other boys used to kid him about a girl he was always writing letters to. A third wounded man, a soldier dressed in khaki, lay on a stretcher on deck breathing hard through his mouth. His long, triangular face looked like a dirty drumhead; his skin was white and drawn tight over his high cheekbones. He wasn't making much noise. There was a shooting-gallery smell over everything and when we passed close under the Arkansas and she let off a salvo, a couple of our men who had their backs to her quivered and had to be reassured. Long and Kavanaugh, the communications officer, were already going about the ship trying to get things ticking again, but they had little success at first.

Halfway out to the transport area, another LCIL hailed us and asked us to take a wounded man aboard. They had got him from some smaller craft, but they had to complete a mission before they could go back to the big ships. We went alongside and took him over the rail. He was wrapped in khaki blankets and strapped into a wire basket litter. After we had sheered away, a man aboard the other LCIL yelled at us to come back so that he could hand over a half-empty bottle of plasma with a long rubber tube attached. "This goes with him," he said. We went alongside again and he handed the bottle to one of our fellows. It was trouble for nothing, because the man by then had stopped breathing.

We made our way out to a transport called the Dorothea Dix, which had a hospital ward fitted out. We went alongside and Rigg yelled that we had four casualties aboard. A young naval doctor climbed down the grapple net hanging on the Dix's side and came aboard. After he had looked at our soldier, he called for a breeches buoy and the soldier was hoisted up sitting in that. He had been hit in one shoulder and one leg, and the doctor said he had a good chance. The three others had to be sent up in wire baskets, vertically, like Indian papooses. A couple of Negroes on the upper deck of the Dix dropped a line, which our men made fast to the top of one basket after another. Then the man would be jerked up in the air by the Negroes as if he were going to heaven. Now that we carried no passengers and were lighter, the sea seemed rough. We bobbled under the towering transport and the wounded men swung wildly on the end of the line, a few times almost striking against the ship. A Coastguardsman reached up for the bottom of one basket so that he could steady it on its way up. At least a quart of blood ran down on him, covering his tin hat, his upturned face, and his blue overalls. He stood motionless for an instant, as if he didn't know what had happened, seeing the world through a film of red, because he wore eyeglasses and blood had covered the lenses. The basket, swaying eccentrically, went up the side. After a couple of seconds, the Coastguardsman turned and ran to a sink aft of the galley, where he turned on the water and began washing himself. A couple of minutes after the last litter had been hoisted aboard, an officer on the Dix leaned over her rail and shouted down, "Medical officer in charge says two of these men are dead! He says you should take them back to the beach and bury them." Out there, fifteen miles off shore, they evidently thought that this was just another landing exercise. A sailor on deck said, "The son of a bitch ought to see that beach."

Rigg explained to the officer that it would be impossible to return to the beach and ordered the men to cast off the lines, and we went away from the Dix. Now that the dead and wounded were gone, I saw Kallam sneak to the far rail and be sicker than I have ever seen a man at sea. We passed close by the command ship and signalled that we had completed our mission. We received a signal, "Wait for orders," and for the rest of the day we loafed, while we tried to reconstruct what had happened to us. Almost everybody on the ship had a battle headache.

"What hurts me worst," Lechich said, "is thinking what happened to those poor guys we landed. That beach was hot with Jerries. And they didn't have nothing to fight with—only carbines and rifles. They weren't even supposed to be combat troops."

"I don't think any of them could be alive now," another man said.

As the hours went by and we weren't ordered to do anything, it became evident that our bit of beach wasn't doing well, for we had expected, after delivering our first load on shore, to be employed in ferrying other troops from transports to the beach, which the beach-battalion boys and engineers would in the meantime have been helping to clear. Other LCILs of our flotilla were also lying idle. We saw one of them being towed, and then we saw her capsize. Three others, we heard, were lying up on one strip of beach, burned. Landing craft are reckoned expendable. Rigg came down from the bridge and, seeing me, said, "The beach is closed to LCILs now. Only small boats going in. Wish they'd thought of that earlier. We lost three good men."

"Which three?" I asked. "I know about Rocky and Bill."

"The coxswain is gone," Bunny said. I remembered the coxswain, the earnest young fellow who wanted to be a newspaperman, who, dressed in swimming trunks, was going to go overboard ahead of everyone else and run a guideline into shore.

"Couldn't he get back?" I asked.

"He couldn't get anywhere," Rigg answered. "He had just stepped off the ramp when he disintegrated. He must have stepped right into an H. E. shell. Cox was a good lad. We'd recommended him for officers' school." Rigg walked away for the inevitable cup of coffee, shaking his big tawny head. I knew he had a battle headache, too.

A while afterward, I asked Rigg what he had been thinking as we neared the coast and he said he had been angry because the men we were going to put ashore hadn't had any coffee. "The poor guys had stayed in the sack as late as they could instead," he said. "Going ashore without any coffee!"

Long was having a look at the damage the shell had done to our ship, and I joined him in tracing its course. It had entered the starboard bow well above the waterline, about the level of the ship's number, then had hit the forward anchor winch, had been deflected toward the stern of the boat, had torn through the bulkhead and up through the cover of the escape hatch, then had smashed the ramp winch and Rocky and Bill. It had been a seventy-five-millimetre anti-tank shell with a solid-armor-piercing head, which had broken into several pieces after it hit the ramp winch. The boys kept finding chunks of it around, but enough of it stayed in one piece to show what it had been. "They had us crisscrossed with guns in all those pillboxes that were supposed to have been knocked off," Long said. "Something must have gone wrong. We gave them a perfect landing, though," he added with professional pride. "I promised the commander we would land him dry tail and we did." Long has been in the Coast Guard twenty years and nothing surprises him; he has survived prohibition, Miami and Fire Island hurricanes, and three landings. He is a cheerful soul who has an original theory about fear. "I always tell my boys that fear is a passion like any other passion," he had once told me. "Now, if you see a beautiful dame walking down the street, you feel passion but you control it, don't you? Well, if you begin to get frightened, which is natural, just control yourself also, I tell them." Long said that he had seen the commander start off from the ship at a good clip, run well until he got up near the first line of sand dunes, then stagger. "The commander was at the head of the line about to leave the ship when young Vaghi, that big ensign, came up and must have asked him for the honor of going first," Long said. "They went off that way, Vaghi out ahead, running as if he was running out on a field with a football under his arm. Miller led the soldiers off the other ramp, and he stepped out like a little gentleman, too." The space where the starboard ramp had once been gave the same effect as an empty sleeve or eye socket.

It was Frankel, a signalman who had been on the bridge, who told me sometime that afternoon about how the wounded soldier had come to be on board. Frankel, whose family lives on East Eighteenth Street in Brooklyn, was a slender, restless fellow who used to be a cutter in the garment center. He played in dance bands before he got his garment-union card, he once told me, and on the ship he occasionally played hot licks on the bugle slung on the bridge. "A shell hit just as we were beginning to pull out," Frankel said, "and we had begun to raise the ramps. It cut all but about one strand of the cable that was holding the starboard ramp and the ramp was wobbling in the air when I saw a guy holding on to the end of it. I guess a lot of us saw him at the same time. He was just clutching the ramp with his left arm, because he had been shot in the other shoulder. I'll never forget his eyes. They seemed to say, 'Don't leave me behind.' He must have been hit just as he stepped off the ramp leaving the ship. It was this soldier. So Ryan and Landini went out and got him. Ryan worked along the rail inside the ramp and Landini worked along the outside edge of the ramp and they got him and carried him back into the ship. There was plenty of stuff flying around, too, and the ramp came away almost as soon as they got back. That's one guy saved, anyway." Ryan was a seaman cook who helped Fassy in the galley, and Landini was the little First Avenue Italian who had made up the special song for himself.

Along about noon, an LCVP, a troughlike fifty-footer, hailed us and asked if we could take care of five soldiers. Rigg said we could. The craft came along-side and passed over five drenched and shivering tank soldiers who had been found floating on a rubber raft. They were the crew of a tank that had been going in on a very small craft and they had been swamped by a wave. The tank had gone to the bottom and the soldiers had just managed to make it to the raft. The pharmacist's mates covered them with piles of blankets and put them to bed in one of our large compartments. By evening they were in the galley drinking coffee with the rest of us. They were to stay on the ship for nearly a week, as it turned out, because nobody would tell us what to do with them. They got to be pretty amphibious themselves. The sergeant in command was a fellow from Cleveland named Angelatti. He was especially happy about being saved, apparently because he liked his wife. He would keep repeating, "Gee, to think it's my second anniversary—I guess it's my lucky day!" But when he heard about what we thought had happened to the men we put ashore, he grew gloomy. The tanks had been headed for that beach and should have helped knock out the pillboxes. It hadn't been the tankmen's fault that the waves had swamped them, but the sergeant said disconsolately, "If we hadn't got bitched up, maybe those other guys wouldn't have been killed." He had a soldier's heart.

On the morning of D Day-plus-one, our LCIL was like a ship with a hang-over. Her deck was littered with cartons of tinned rations. There was a gap where the starboard ramp had been and there were various holes in the hull and hatches to mark the path of the anti-tank shell. Everybody aboard was nursing a headache. We hung around in the Channel, waiting for orders and talking over the things that had happened to us. The men in the engine room, which was so clean that it looked like the model dairy exhibit at the World's Fair—all white paint and aluminum trim—had sweated it out at their posts during the excitement on deck and the engine-room log had been punctiliously kept. On the morning of D-plus-one, Cope, the chief machinist's mate, a tall, quiet chap from Philadelphia, told somebody that from the order "Drop stern anchor" to the order "Take in on stern anchor," which included all the time we had spent aground, exactly four minutes had elapsed. Most of us on deck would have put it at half an hour. During those four minutes all the hundred and forty passengers we carried had run off the ramps into three feet of water, three members of our Coast Guard complement of thirty-three had been killed, and two others had rescued a wounded soldier clinging to the end of the star-board ramp. The experience had left us without appetite. I remember, on the afternoon of D Day, sitting on a ration case on the pitching deck and being tempted by the rosy picture on the label of a roast-beef can. I opened it, but I could only pick at the jellied juice, which reminded me too much of the blood I had seen that morning, and I threw the tin over the rail.

By D-plus-one we were beginning to eat again. That morning I was on the upper deck talking to Barrett, when we saw a German mine go off. It threw a column of water high into the air and damaged a ship near it. German planes had been fiddling around above our anchorage during the night, without bombing us; evidently they had been dropping mines. We had seen three of the planes shot down. Barrett looked at the water spout and said, "If we ever hit a mine like that, we'll go up in the air like an arrow." It was Barrett who had bet a pound, even money, that we would be hit during the action. I asked him if he had collected the bet and he said, "Sure. As long as we got hit whether I take the money or not, I might as well take it." In the wardroom, Kavanaugh, the communications officer, talked to me about Bill, one of the Coast Guard boys who had been hit. Kavanaugh, who had censored Bill's letters, said, "Bill began every letter he ever wrote, 'Well, honey, here I am again.'" Long, the engineering officer, told me about a patch he had devised that would expand in water and would close up any underwater holes in the hull, and seemed rather to regret that he had had no chance to try it out. Rigg kept repeating a tag line he had picked up from Sid Fields, a comedian in a London revue: "What a performance! What a performance!" But the most frequent subject of conversation among both officers and men was the fate of the fellows we had put on the beach. We had left them splashing through shallow water, with tracer bullets flying around them and only a nearly level, coverless beach immediately in front of them and with a beach pillbox and more of the enemy on a cliff inshore blazing away with everything they had. We had decided that hardly any of our men could have survived.

Late that afternoon our landing craft got an order to help unload soldiers from a big troopship several miles off the French shore. We were to carry the men almost as far as the beach and then transfer them to Higgins boats. One of our ramps was gone and the other one was not usable, and it would have been superfluous cruelty to drop a soldier with a full pack into five feet of water, our minimum draught. We gathered from the order that the Germans were no longer shooting on the beach; this, at least, represented progress.

The soldiers who lined the decks of the transport, all eager to get ashore at once, belonged to the Second Division; they wore a white star and an Indian head on their shoulder flashes. A scramble net hung down the port side of the vessel, and soldiers with full equipment strapped to their backs climbed down it one by one and stepped backward onto our landing craft. As each man made the step, two seamen grabbed him and helped him aboard. It often took as much time to unload the soldiers from a big ship as it did for the ship itself to get from Britain to the Norman coast, and it seemed to me that a small expenditure on gangplanks of various lengths and furnished with grapples, like the ones used in boarding operations in ancient naval battles, would have sped these transfers more than a comparable outlay for any other device could possibly have done. While we were loading the men, a thirty-six-foot craft approached us on the other side. There were two other thirty-six-footers there

side by side already. The newest thirty-six-footer got alongside the outer one
of the pair of earlier arrivals and the crew boosted up a man who had been
standing in the stern of the boat and helped him on to the other craft. The
man made his way unsteadily across both of the intervening thirty-six-footers
to us, and men on the boats passed his gear, consisting of a typewriter and a
gas mask, along after him. He was in a field jacket and long khaki trousers without leggings. The clothes were obviously fresh out of a quartermaster's stores.
He wore the war correspondent's green shoulder patch on his field jacket.
His face and form indicated that he had led a long and comfortable life, and
his eyes betrayed astonishment that he should be there at all, but he was smiling.
Some of our Coastguardsmen helped him over our rail. He said that he was
Richard Stokes of the St. Louis *Post-Dispatch,* that he had been a Washington
correspondent and a music critic for many years, that he had wanted to go overseas when we got into the war, and that he had finally induced his paper to send
him over. He had got airplane passage to Britain, where he had arrived two
weeks before, and had been sent to the invasion coast on a Liberty ship that was
to land men on D-plus-one. "It seems just wonderful to be here," Stokes said.
"I can hardly believe it." He had been very much disappointed when he found
out that because of the violence of the German resistance, the Liberty ship was
not going to land her passengers for a couple of days. The ship's captain had said
to him, "There's another crowd going ashore. Why don't you go with them?"
Then the skipper had hailed a boat for him. "And here I am," said Stokes. "It's
too good to be true." He was sixty-one years old, and the world seemed mar-
vellous to him. He said he had never been in a battle and he wanted to see
what it was like.

We got all our soldiers—about four hundred of them—aboard and started
in toward the same stretch of shore we had left in such haste thirty-six hours
before. The way in looked familiar and yet devoid of the character it had once
had for us, like the scene of an old assignation revisited. The house with the
tower on top of the cliff was now gone, I noticed. The naval bombardment,
although tardy, had been thorough. Scattered along the shore were the wrecked
and burned-out landing craft that had been less lucky than ours. Several of our
men told me they had seen the LCT that had been burning off our port quarter on D Day pull out, still aflame, and extinguish the fire as she put to sea,
but plenty of others remained. Small craft came out to us from the shore that
had so recently been hostile, and soldiers started climbing into them, a less
complicated process than the transfer from the troopship because the highest
points of the small craft were nearly on a level with our main deck. I could see
occasional puffs of smoke well up on the beach. They looked as if they might
be the bursts of German shells coming from behind the cliff, and I felt protective toward Stokes. "Mr. Stokes," I said, "it seems to be pretty rough in
there." He didn't even have a blanket to sleep on, and he didn't have the
slightest idea whom he was going to look for when he got in; he was just

going ahead like a good city reporter on an ordinary assignment. He watched two boats load up with soldiers and then, as a third came alongside—I remember that the name painted inside her ramp was "Impatient Virgin"—he said, "Mr. Liebling, I have made up my mind," and went down and scrambled aboard, assisted by everybody who could get a hand on him. He got ashore all right and did some fine stories. A couple of weeks afterward he told me, "I couldn't stand being within sight of the promised land and then coming back."

There was nothing for us to do during the daylight hours of D-plus-two, but toward eight o'clock in the evening we got an order to go out to another troopship and unload more Second Division soldiers, who were to be taken to a beach next to the one where we had landed on D Day. The ship was an American Export liner. Several other LCILs were also assigned to the job of emptying her. I was on our bridge with Rigg when we came under her towering side, and the smell of fresh bread, which her cooks had evidently been baking, drove all other thoughts from our minds. Rigg hailed a young deck officer who was looking down at us and asked him if he could spare some bread. The officer said sure, and a few minutes later a steward pushed six long loaves across to our bridge from a porthole at approximately our level. They were an inestimable treasure to us. Everything is relative in an amphibious operation; to the four-man crews who operate the thirty-six-foot LCVPs, which are open to the weather and have no cooking facilities, an LCIL seems a floating palace. They would often come alongside us and beg tinned fruit, which they would receive with the same doglike gratitude we felt toward the merchantman for our bread.

The soldiers came aboard us along a single narrow plank, which was put over from the port side of the troopship to our rail, sloping at an angle of forty-five degrees. We pitched continuously in the rough water, and the soldiers, burdened with rifles and about fifty pounds of equipment apiece, slid rather than ran down the plank. Our crew had arranged a pile of ration cases at the rail, right where the gangplank was fastened, and the soldiers stepped from the end of the plank to the top case and then jumped down. We made two trips between the merchantman and the small boats that night, and only one soldier fell, and was lost, between the ships during the whole operation. That, I suppose, was a good percentage, but it still seemed to me an unnecessary loss. On our first trip from ship to shore, while we were unloading soldiers into small boats a couple of hundred yards off the beach, there was an air raid. The soldiers standing on our narrow deck, with their backs to the deckhouse walls, had never been under real fire before, but they remained impassive amid the cascade of Bofors shells that rose from hundreds of ships. Much of the barrage had a low trajectory and almost scraped the paint off our bridge. On one ship some gunners who knew their business would hit a plane, and then, as it fell, less intelligent gun crews would start after it and follow it down, forgetting that when a plane hits the water it is at the waterline. An anti-aircraft shell travelling upward at an angle of not more than twenty degrees wounded a good friend of mine sleeping in a dugout on the side of a cliff ashore a couple of nights later.

A beach-battalion sailor came out to us on one of the first small boats from the shore. He was a big, smiling fellow whom we had brought from England on our first trip to the invasion coast, one of "those poor bastards" we had all assumed were dead. The cooks hauled him into the galley for sandwiches and coffee, and within a couple of minutes officers as well as men were crowding about him. Nearly everybody we asked him about turned out to be alive—the commander of the beach battalion; Miller, the Army lieutenant; little Dr. Davey; Vaghi and Reich, the poker-playing ensigns; Smith, the beach battalion's veteran chief petty officer; and others whom we had got to know on the ship. They had had a rough time, the sailor said. They had lain for five hours in holes they had scooped in the sand when they went ashore, while one or two American tanks that had landed shot at pillboxes and the pillboxes shot back. Then some infantrymen who had landed in small boats at H Hour worked their way up the beach and took the German positions, releasing our friends from the position in which they were pinned down. They were living on the side of a hill now and getting on with their work of organizing traffic between ship and shore. It was very pleasant news for us aboard the landing craft. We worked all night unloading soldiers, but the Coast Guard crew didn't mind; they were in a good mood.

Early the next day, D-plus-three, I thumbed a ride ashore to go visiting. I hailed a passing assault craft, a rocket-firing speedboat, which took me part of the way and then transferred me to an LCVP that was headed inshore. The LCVP ran up onto the beach, dropped her bow ramp, and I walked onto French soil without even wetting my feet. This was the moment I had looked forward to for four years minus nine days, since the day I had crossed the Spanish frontier at Irún after the fall of France. Then the words of de Gaulle —"France has lost a battle but not the war"—were ringing in my ears, for I had just heard his first radio speech from London, but I had not dared hope that the wheel would turn almost full circle so soon. There was the noise of cannonading a couple of miles or so beyond the cliffs, where the First Division was pushing on from the fingerhold it had made good on D Day, but on the beach everything was calm. Troops and sailors of the amphibious forces had cleared away much of the wreckage, so that landing craft coming in would not foul their hulls or anchor chains; metal road strips led up from the water's edge to the road parallel with the shore. Men were going about their work as if there were no enemy within a hundred miles, and this was understandable, because no German planes ever arrived to molest them as they unloaded vehicles and munitions for the troops up ahead. To men who had been in other campaigns, when a solitary jeep couldn't pass down a road without three Messerschmitts' having a pass at it, this lack of interference seemed eerie, but it was true all the same. During the first week after the invasion began, I didn't see one German plane by daylight. Almost in front of me, as I stepped off the boat, were the ruins of the concrete blockhouse that had fired at us as we ran in on D Day. The concrete had been masked by a simulated house, but the disguise had been shot away and the place gaped white and roofless. I had more a sense of coming home to the United States Army than to France, for the first M.P. of whom I inquired the way to the command post of the beach battalion said he didn't know. This is S.O.P., or standard operating procedure, because a soldier figures that if he tells you he knows, he will, at best, have trouble directing you, and if the directions turn out to be wrong you may come back and complain. He has nothing to lose by denying knowledge.

I walked along the beach and met a beach-battalion sailor. He was equally unknowledgeable until I convinced him that I was a friend of the commander. Then he led me two hundred yards up a cliff to the place I had asked about. The commander was not there, but a Lieutenant Commander Watts and a Lieutenant Reardon, both New Yorkers, were. They had gone ashore on another landing craft, but I had met them both while we were in port in Britain awaiting sailing orders. They had landed five hundred yards up the beach from us and had, of course, got the same reception we got. The command post was installed in a row of burrows in the face of the cliff from which the Germans had fired down on the incoming boats and the beach on D Day; now it was we who overlooked the beach. In the side of another cliff, which was almost at a right angle to this one, the Germans had had two sunken concrete pillboxes enfilading the beach, and I realized that the crossfire had centered on our landing craft and the others nearby. Meeting these men reminded me of what the First Division soldier had said to me a few days earlier about "Candide": "Voltaire used the same gag too often. The characters are always getting killed and then turning out not to have been killed at all, and they tell their friends what happened to them in the meantime." Watts said that after they had left their landing craft, they had run forward like hell and then had thrown themselves down on the beach because there was nothing else to do. The forepart of the beach was covered with large, round pebbles about the size, I imagine, of the one David used on Goliath, and when the German machine-gun bullets skittered among them the stones became a secondary form of ammunition themselves and went flying among the men. "We had infantry up ahead of us, but at first they were pinned down too," Watts said. "A couple of tanks had landed and one of them knocked out a seventy-five up on the side of the hill, but in a short while the Germans either replaced it or got it going again. Then, after a couple of hours, two destroyers came and worked close in to shore, although there were plenty of mines still in there, and really plastered the pillboxes. The infantry went up the hill in the face of machine-gun fire and drove the Germans out of the trench system they had on the crown of the hill. I'll show it to you in a couple of minutes. It's a regular young Maginot Line. By nightfall we felt fairly safe. We found out later from prisoners that the Three Hundred and Fifty-second German Field Division had been holding anti-invasion exercises here the day before we attacked. They had been scheduled to go back to their barracks D Day morning, but when scouts told them about the big fleet on the way in, they decided to stay and give us a good time. They did." It wasn't until a week later, in London, that I found out that because of this untoward circumstance our beach and those on either side of it had been the toughest spots encountered in the landings, and that the losses there had not been at all typical of the operation.

I was delighted to discover Smith, the old chief petty officer, reclining in a nearby slit trench. He was looking very fit. He was forty-seven, and I had wondered how he would do in the scramble to the beach. He had not only made it but had gathered a large new repertory of anecdotes on the way. "A guy in front of me got it through the throat," Smitty said. "Another guy in front of me got it through the heart. I run on. I heard a shell coming and I threw myself face down. There was an Army colonel on one side of me, a Navy captain on the other. The shell hit. I was all right. I looked up and the captain and the colonel was gone, blown to pieces. I grabbed for my tommy gun, which I had dropped next to me. It had been twisted into a complete circle. I was disarmed, so I just laid there."

While I was listening to Smitty, Reardon, talking over a field telephone, had located the commander somewhere on top of the cliff, along the German trench system, which had been taken over by the amphibious engineers as billets. Watts and I decided to walk up and find him. We made our way along the face of the cliff, on a narrow path that led past clusters of slit trenches in which soldiers were sleeping, and got up to the crest at a point where some Negro soldiers had made their bivouac in a thicket. We followed another path through a tangled, scrubby wood. The Germans had left numbers of wooden skull-and-crossbones signs on the tree trunks. These signs said *"Achtung Minen"* and *"Attention aux Mines."* Whether they indicated that we had taken the enemy by surprise and that he had not had time to remove the signs put up for the protection of his own and civilian personnel, or whether the signs were put there for psychological purposes, like dummy guns, was a question for the engineers to determine. Watts and I took care to stay in the path.

We found the commander, who was in good form. He said that he had lost only a couple of the forty-five beach-battalion men who had been on the landing craft with us but that in the battalion as a whole the casualties had been fairly heavy. "Not nearly what I thought they would be when I left that boat, though," he said.

The trench system was a fine monument to the infantrymen of the First

Division who had taken it. I couldn't help thinking, as I looked it over, that the German soldiers of 1939-41 would not have been driven from it in one day, even by heroes, and the thought encouraged me. Maybe they were beginning to understand that they were beaten. There were no indications that the position had been under artillery fire and I could see only one trace of the use of a flamethrower. As I reconstructed the action, our fellows must have climbed the hill and outflanked the position, and the Germans, rather than fight it out in their holes, had cleared out to avoid being cut off. They had probably stayed in and continued firing just as long as they still had a chance to kill without taking losses. As the French say, they had not insisted. The trenches were deep, narrow, and so convoluted that an attacking force at any point could be fired on from several directions. Important knots in the system, like the command post and mortar emplacements, were of concrete. The command post was sunk at least twenty-five feet into the ground and was faced with brick on the inside. The garrison had slept in underground bombproofs, with timbered ceilings and wooden floors. In one of them, probably the officers' quarters, there was rustic furniture, a magnificent French radio, and flowers, still fresh, in vases. On the walls were cheap French prints of the innocuous sort one used to see in speakeasies: the little boy and the little girl, and the coyly equivocal captions.

An engineer sergeant who showed us through the place said that the Americans had found hairnets and hairpins in this bombproof. I could imagine an *Oberstleutnant* and his mistress, perhaps the daughter of a French collaborationist, living uneventfully here and waiting for something in which the *Oberstleutnant* had unconsciously ceased to believe, something that he wished so strongly would never happen that he had convinced himself it would happen, if anywhere, on some distant part of the coast. I thought of the Frenchmen I had known in 1939, waiting in a similar mood in the Maginot Line. The sergeant, a straight-featured Jewish fellow in his late thirties, said, "Those infantrymen were like angels. I tell you, I laid there on the beach and prayed for them while they went up that hill with nothing—with bayonets and hand grenades. They did it with nothing. It was a miracle." That made me feel good, because the infantry regiment involved had long been my favorite outfit. The commander was sardonic about one thing. "You remember how I used to worry about how my men would fall into bomb holes and drown on the way in because the Air Forces had laid down such a terrific bombardment?" he asked. "Well, I defy you to find one bomb hole on this whole beach for a mile each way."

The commander and Watts accompanied me back to the shore. On the way, we stopped at a field hospital that had been set up under canvas. There I talked to some Italian prisoners who were digging shelter trenches. They were fine, rugged specimens, as they should have been, because since the Italian surrender they had undoubtedly had plenty of exercise swinging pickaxes for the Todt organization. Their regiment of bridge-building engineers had been disarmed by the Germans in Greece and the men had been given the choice of enrolling in Fascist combat units or in labor service, they told me. They had all chosen labor service. They seemed to expect to be commended for their choice. They had built many of the trenches in the district. "We wouldn't fight for Hitler," they assured me. I thought that the point had been pretty well proved. Now they were digging for us. They said that all Germans were cowards.

We went down to the shore, and the commander, who, being beachmaster, was in charge of all traffic alongshore, hailed a Duck for me. The Duck put me on an LCVP, which took me back to my ship. On the way out, I realized that I had not seen a single French civilian the entire time ashore.

When I came aboard our landing craft, Long, the engineering officer, grinned at me.

"Did you notice a slight list, sometimes on one side, sometimes on the other, the last two days?" he asked.

I said, "You mean the one you said must be on account of the crew's all turning over in their sleep at the same time?"

"Yes," he said. "Well, today we found an open seam down in the stern. She started to list that night the big bomb dropped next to us, but you were sleeping too sound to get up. So maybe we'll go back to port. She has no ramps, the forward anchor winch is sheered in half, and she may as well go into the yard for a couple of days."

The morning of D-plus-four, Rigg signalled the command ship for permission to put back to Britain. As soon as the signalman blinked out the message, every man on board knew there was a chance we would go back, and even fellows who had expressed a low opinion of the British port at which our flotilla had been stationed looked extremely happy. While we were waiting for an answer to our request, an LCIL that acted as a group leader, a kind of straw boss among the little ships, passed near us, and the lieutenant on her bridge ordered us over to help tow a barge of ammunition. We were to be paired with another LCIL on this job. The barge, a two-hundred-and-fifty-tonner, was loaded with TNT, and the idea was for one LCIL to make fast on each side of her and shove her in to shore. The Diesel motors of an LCIL, although they can move their craft along at a fair speed, haven't the towing power of a tug. The two LCILs bounced about in the choppy sea for quite a while as we tried to get towing lines aboard the big barge that would hold. Even after we finally got started, every now and then the lines would snap; and we would bounce against the side of the barge, as we put more lines aboard her, with a crash that disquieted us, even though we had been told many times that the explosive was packed so carefully that no jouncing would possibly set it off. We were very happy when the barge grounded on the beach according to plan and we could cast off and leave her. Just before we had finished, the group leader came along again and an officer on her bridge shouted over to us through a megaphone, "Report to control-ship shuttle service!" This meant that we were going back to Britain; control ships organize cross-Channel convoys. We were not sorry to go.

By Sunday, D-plus-five, when we at last got started, the water had smoothed out so much that the Channel was like the Hyde Park Serpentine. The flat-bottomed LCIL will bounce about in the slightest sea, but today our craft moved along like a swanboat. The water was full of ration cartons, life jackets, and shell cases, and on the way over we picked up one corpse, of a soldier wearing a life jacket, which indicated that he had never got ashore. Since German planes were dropping mines every night, the lookout was instructed to keep a sharp watch for suspicious objects in the water, and this was almost the only thing it was necessary to think about as we loafed along. A seaman from Florida named Hurwitz was lookout on the bow in the early morning. "Suspicious object off port bow!" he would bawl, and then, "Suspicious object off starboard quarter!" Most of the suspicious objects turned out to be shell cases. Finally, Hurwitz yelled, "Bridge! The water is just full of suspicious objects!"

The main interest aboard now was whether we would get to port before the pubs closed, at ten o'clock in the evening. Long was getting unheard-of speed out of his motors and it seemed that we would make the pubs easily. Then we happened upon a British LCT that was all alone and was having engine trouble. She asked us to stand by in case her motors conked out altogether. We proceeded at four knots. When the British skipper signalled to us, "Doing my utmost, can make no more," which meant that our chance of beer had gone glimmering, Rigg made a gesture that for delicacy and regard for international relations must have few parallels in naval history. He ordered a signal that may someday be in schoolbooks along with Nelson's "England expects every man to do his duty." "Never mind," he signalled the crippled LCT. "We would have been too late for pub-closing time anyway."

[August 19, 1944]

# SECOND MAN OUT

GUY REMINGTON

THE parachute infantry regiment to which I was attached spent the eight days before D Day confined in a marshalling area in England, where we stored up food and sleep and so much knowledge of Normandy that we began to feel as though we knew the country at first hand. On Monday, June 5th, D Day-minus-one, after several hours spent in sharpening knives, cleaning guns, being issued grenades, and adjusting our equipment, we had an early supper and heard a final lecture. Then we blackened our faces, collected our gear, and marched off to our planes. As we passed a railroad crossing, the watchwoman on duty caught my arm and squeezed it impulsively. "Give it to them, Lieutenant," she said. There were tears in her eyes, and, for all I know, in mine.

At the airfield, we were directed to the planes that were to carry us over the Channel. I had seen some action before, so I had at least an idea of what to expect. Not many of the other men were so fortunate. The only thing that worried me, as we sat in the dark waiting for the takeoff, was the thought that I might break a leg in my jump. I tried not to think about that. We took off at ten-thirty, just as the moon was coming up. There appeared to be very little ground wind, and the weather seemed ideal for a night jump. Through the open door of my plane, I watched the other transports lifting heavily off the ground. They looked like huge, black bats as they skimmed slowly over the treetops and fell into formation. Before long, we took off too. Presently, near the coast of England, a squadron of fighters appeared below us. They flashed their lights on and off, and then wheeled away. That was *adiós*.

We had a two-hour run ahead of us, so I settled down in my seat. A major, sitting directly across from me, smiled, his teeth startlingly white in the dark. I smiled back. The noise of the plane made it impossible to talk. Suddenly the jump master shouted, "Stand up and hook up!" I realized that I had been asleep, hard as it was to believe. The plane was rocking and bucking, trying to dodge the occasional bursts of flak from the dark, anonymous countryside below. A small red light gleamed in the panel by the door. We hooked up

339

our parachutes, lined up close together, and waited. Then we stood there, waiting, for twelve and a half minutes. It seemed a long and terrible time.

The green light flashed on at seven minutes past midnight. The jump master shouted, "Go!" I was the second man out. The black Normandy pastures tilted and turned far beneath me. The first German flare came arching up, and instantly machine guns and forty-millimetre guns began firing from the corners of the fields, striping the night with yellow, green, blue, and red tracers. I pitched down through a wild Fourth of July. Fire licked through the sky and blazed around the transports heaving high overhead. I saw some of them go plunging down in flames. One of them came down with a trooper, whose parachute had become caught on the tailpiece, streaming out behind. I heard a loud gush of air: a man went hurtling past, only a few yards away, his parachute collapsed and burning. Other parachutes, with men whose legs had been shot off slumped in the harness, floated gently toward the earth.

I was caught in a machine-gun cross fire as I approached the ground. It seemed impossible that they could miss me. One of the guns, hidden in a building, was firing at my parachute, which was already badly torn; the other aimed at my body. I reached up, caught the left risers of my parachute, and pulled on them. I went into a fast slip, but the tracers followed me down. I held the slip until I was about twenty-five feet from the ground and then let go the risers. I landed up against a hedge in a little garden at the rear of a German barracks. There were four tracer holes through one of my pants legs, two through the other, and another bullet had ripped off both my breast pockets, but I hadn't a scratch.

I fought behind the German lines for eight days before I was relieved by our seaborne troops.

# LETTER FROM ROME

DANIEL LANG

*July 7, 1944*

THE Romans, a people with a talent for historical perspective, already are beginning to discuss the German occupation as if it were something as remote as the Caesars and the Borgias. They have not yet attained complete detachment, probably because of the continuing shortage of food and housing, and their recollections are apt to include a lot of operatic talk about their own exploits during the Germans' nine-month stay. However, they are objective enough to give one a fairly clear idea of what went on here during that period.

When the armistice was signed, on September 8th, the Germans had very few troops in Rome, and the Italian radio, announcing the capitulation at seven-forty-five that evening, suggested, without making any specific recommendations, that any German aggression should be met with resistance. The Germans, with their usual tact, did not immediately commit any public aggression. Instead, they put their Fifth Columnists, most of them German-Italians from the Tyrol, to work inside the city. The agents moved fast. They went to all the Italian Army bureaus, where, at the point of a pistol, they disarmed the commandants, took over their offices, and dispatched orders disbanding whatever troops were under their jurisdiction. They cut telephone wires at vital points in the city, seized the radio stations, and broadcast misinformation. They posed as Italian officers and openhandedly distributed furloughs among the enlisted men. In crews of ten, armed with tommy guns, they went to Army barracks and, assuring the regiments quartered there that no aggression was intended, methodically frisked the dazed, uninstructed *soldati* for small arms and grenades. Simultaneously, an intentional or unintentional defection was occurring within high Italian Army circles. Badoglio, who had replaced Mussolini as head of the government, charged General Carboni, the Rome area commandant, with the defense of the city, and departed for southern Italy. When Carboni saw his chief getting out of town, he decided to skip, too. Other members of the Stato Maggiore followed. This wanderlust filtered down through the ranks until it reached the enlisted men. Thousands left their posts, made for their homes, and disappeared into mufti.

The Germans, with two or three divisions deployed to the north and south

*341*

of Rome, were now in a position to take the city. The only opposition they encountered came from small, scattered detachments of soldiers, from civilian patriots, and from gangs of tough kids in their teens. These irregulars met the enemy at Tivoli, Monte Rotondo, Porta San Paolo, and several other towns outside Rome. They kept up their fight until the afternoon of September 10th, by which time the Reichswehr had completely surrounded the city. Kesselring then offered his terms: If opposition ceased immediately, Rome would be an open city, would not be attacked by the Germans, and would be occupied only by Italian soldiers; otherwise the city would be bombed and the water supply would be cut off. A Marshal Caviglia, who was in the city but had nothing to do officially with its defense, was pressed into service as the Italian negotiator. In the circumstances, he and other high officers thought, the German offer looked good: the wounded Italian defenders were streaming back into the city muttering *"Un finimondo,"* supplies were low, and the unarmed city and its populace were at the mercy of German artillery. The Marshal accepted. A half hour later, the Germans blandly tore up another scrap of paper and moved, unopposed, into the city.

During the first few weeks of the occupation, the Nazis, possibly because the Allied landing at Salerno made them think that they might not be there much longer, went in for looting. They stopped civilians in the streets and took away their watches and money, they swept shops clean of cameras and jewelry. Then, in what appeared to be a conciliatory gesture, they opened the doors of the Mercati Generali, the city's main food market, near the Ostia railroad station, and invited the crowds of hungry Romans to step inside and help themselves. Mounted on the roof of a truck nearby, a Nazi newsreel crew went to work as the Italians emerged, joyously carrying cheese and sacks of flour. As soon as the cameramen had all the pictures they wanted, the laden Romans were arrested on a charge of looting. For German and other non-Italian audiences, the films were used to illustrate the essentially irresponsible Italian character, which, of course, now that the Germans were on the scene, would be reformed. For Italian audiences outside Rome, the commentary accompanying the newsreel played up German bountifulness. In Rome itself, where the film wasn't shown at all, the stunt increased the confusion among civilians and thus strengthened the German grip on the city.

By late December, the Germans, growing calmer as Allied progress in the south was stalled, decided to make an attempt to win over the Romans. The first thing they did was to flex their muscles. Over and over they showed their newsreels of Mussolini's rescue from the Allies, as proof that the Germans could do anything once they set their minds to it. Then they staged parades of heavily armed soldiers. Meanwhile, they went around reminding people of German victories and telling everybody that the Allies were not invincible. Shortly before Christmas, they started a lively whispering campaign to the effect that Churchill had said that the Allies would be in Rome on Christmas and that they themselves thought Churchill was probably right. Then, at one o'clock on the afternoon of Christmas Day, a hundred Allied prisoners of war were led into the Excelsior Hotel and fed a sumptuous meal. While the captured men were gorging themselves on their unexpected feast, Nazi representatives, posted outside the windows of the hotel dining room, kept saying owlishly to passersby, "Churchill was right, wasn't he?"

The Germans even tried to appeal to the Romans' Italianism by reviving the militaristic clichés of the Fascist regime. "National Honor," "The Country's Glorious Past," "The Dignity of Italy," and "Fascist Redemption" reappeared in the press. Graziani and Mussolini, from their Republican Fascist headquarters in northern Italy, sent reassuring messages, which were prominently displayed in the newspapers. Just to show how relaxed and confident of victory they were, the Germans permitted Bruno Spampanato, the Fascist editor of *Il Messagero,* to run a letters-to-the-editor column in which nearly all the mail turned out to be anti-Fascist. Spampanato had an introvert's reaction to his disappointment; he decided to write letters to himself, letters that could be crisply and decisively answered. One synthetic reader wrote in, "Why is there freedom of the press in southern Italy and not here?" Editor: "There is freedom of the press here. Your letter was printed, was it not?" Some of his replies were less theoretical in content. The day the damaged water pipes in the Quartiere Prenestino, a residential neighborhood, were finally repaired, he printed an exchange of letters on the subject. Reader: "Why is there no water in the Quartiere Prenestino?" Editor: "There is. All you need do is turn on the faucet." Finally, the Germans, still determined to persuade the Italians that life was again normal, opened all the movie theatres and the Royal Opera House, with Gigli as leading tenor, and put back the curfew they had imposed from six o'clock to nine-thirty.

Soon after the first of the year, the Nazis became convinced that they had sold themselves to the Romans and they began asking for what they wanted. They announced that both soldiers and workers were needed and that conscription of men between eighteen and thirty-eight was now in effect. Of course, the announcement continued amiably, everybody would voluntarily answer the call. For anyone who refused, it added, the penalty could be death. An elaborate registration system was set up and Fascist Party members were assigned to act as clerks. They had little work to do, for less than ten per cent of the prospective conscriptees showed up. Most men thenceforth concentrated on dodging the draft. Half of Rome, is has been said, hid the other half. Friends swapped apartments. Concierges were bribed to say that the newcomers were old tenants of many years' standing. People changed their names. To stop this moving around, the Germans decided to take a census and to require that everyone must stay put at the address he gave on the census blank he was handed to fill out. Everybody put down a phony name or a phony address, or both. For good measure, the Italian partisans printed up, filled out, and mailed to the census bureau over a million forms, all containing nothing but false information. After a few days of checking up on what seemed to be largely a mythical population, the Germans gave up and threw away their voluminous data.

The Nazis persevered for a while longer at trying to make friends with the Romans and at the same time to force them into the army or into labor battalions, but when the Allies landed at Anzio the Germans' ambivalence came to an end. They were undoubtedly angered by the Romans' behavior after the landing. Earlier that week, they had seen seven German divisions moving northward, and they expected the Allies to enter Rome in two or three days. On the day of the landing there were a few fist fights with Nazis and some impetuous parades, and several dozen Allied flags were unfurled over balconies. Every English dictionary in town was bought up, and bands of armed partisans moved south and occupied a number of road junctions.

After the Nazis managed to contain the beachhead, they gave their full attention once more to Rome. They began by marching long columns of prisoners of war through the streets, the theme this time being "Here are the men you expected." They threatened a purge of "Communists." They picked up men off the streets and shipped them to Anzio and Cassino to build fortifications. When the people got the idea and began to stay off the streets, the Germans employed what the Italians call the *retata,* a tactic that consisted of suddenly roping off whole blocks, searching all the buildings in them, assembling all the people they found, and then marching off the likely-looking technicians, laborers, and soldiers in the collection. When anyone complained around this time about the shortage of transportation facilities, the standard retort was "Don't worry, the S.S. will come for you soon in a nice big truck." It was in a *retata* that Colonel Montezemolo, the sixty-five-year-old head of the partisans, was picked up by German counter-espionage agents. He was taken to a torture chamber in the jail on the Via Tasso, where German police stuffed wads of cotton into his ears and set fire to them, and pulled out his nails and teeth one by one, in an effort to get information from him. Montezemolo died after he had been in the jail only a short time, having disclosed nothing.

As the German defensive successes at Cassino and Anzio continued, the Nazis stepped up their activities in Rome. Mussolini sent down a man called Caruso, an ex-gangster, to act as chief of the Italian police. Himmler assigned a super-S.S. unit, the Security Defense, to the Rome area. On March 23rd, one of a group of Italians threw a bomb at a detachment of German soldiers on the Via Rasella, killing thirty-two of them. The next day, the Nazis took three hundred and twenty prisoners, ten times the number of their own dead, out of their cells and drove them off in trucks to the Viale Ardeatine, near the San Sebastiano catacombs. There the hostages were herded into a quarry and shot down by machine guns. The walls of the quarry were then blown in to make a grave for the bodies.

Three days after Easter, Count Ottino Caracciolo, a young man who had been doing good work for the partisans' intelligence unit, was arrested as a suspect and taken to the Regina Coeli jail. The Germans asked him many questions. Was he harboring escaped Allied prisoners of war? (The night before, he had helped deliver a British prisoner of war, stricken with appendicitis, to the Policlinico, where a partisan doctor had operated on the man.) Had he been throwing nails on highways to puncture German tires? (He had helped devise the four-spiked nail the underground was using.) Caracciolo could tell by the nature of the questioning that the police had nothing specific on him, and he answered accordingly. His wife went to Major Boehm, the German chief of staff for the Rome area, and begged for his release. After six days in prison, he was set free. Before he returned to his underground work, he looked up Boehm, expressed his gratitude, and said that someday he hoped he would be able to repay the Nazi officer. As it turned out, he didn't have to wait long.

When the Allies started their big offensive in the middle of May, the Nazis relaxed their repressive measures. If things went badly to the south, they knew, hostile action by the citizens of Rome could disrupt an orderly retreat northward. The frequency of the *retate* decreased sharply. Gestapo visits to people's homes diminished. The "Communists" were suddenly considered less dangerous. General Maeltzer, the German commandant of the Rome area, went so far as to visit a residential section and hand out free rice. There were no arrests for looting this time, but the inevitable newsreel crew was on hand to record the General's charitable action. The Germans did, however, decide to arrest the partisans' chief of staff, General Oddone, and on May 20th he was taken to the Via Tasso prison. This was a strategic move, for the underground had already been hard hit by the loss of Montezemolo. There were plenty of courageous men in its ranks, but professional soldiers like Montezemolo and Oddone were scarce. The partisans knew that as the Allies approached the city, their own group might be called upon to harass the Nazis from the rear, and in this task Oddone's military experience would be invaluable. The partisan leaders worried about the problem for some time, but the only plan they could think of, storming the jail, might well have cost Oddone his life. Finally, they made up their minds to ask the Germans straight out for Oddone's freedom.

Two weeks after the arrest of the chief of staff, Caracciolo entered the German headquarters, on the Corso d'Italia, and walked into Boehm's office. Discussing the visit not long ago, Caracciolo said that Boehm was surprisingly unoccupied the afternoon he saw him, considering that the Fifth Army was just outside Rome. The partisan reminded Boehm of their last meeting and said that he was prepared to repay the German for his kindness. He had heard, he said, that General Oddone had been arrested. In his opinion, he went on, the Nazis had made a dangerous mistake. General Oddone was one of the few steadying influences inside the partisan organization. Since his arrest, a faction of hotheads were in control of the underground and had decided to shoot at the German soldiers as they retreated before the Allies. They had noted the condition of the Reichswehr units returning to the city from the southern fronts and they felt sure that if they entrenched themselves inside good, solid buildings they could carry out their plan. Only Oddone could stay their hand. Caracciolo added that he had information that Oddone, in exchange for his freedom, would pledge his word that no partisan would fire at the Nazis. Boehm asked him to wait and walked out of the room. "While he was gone," Caracciolo recalls, "I couldn't help comparing Kesselring's offer and our own. Kesselring said he wouldn't come into Rome, but he did. Oddone knew that the partisans had strict orders to do no fighting inside the city, so if he gave his word he was going to be able to keep it. I do believe our offer was the fairer of the two." Boehm returned in a few minutes with General Maeltzer, the German commandant, who questioned Caracciolo closely. Caracciolo repeated his story. The German officers listened attentively, for they knew the partisans' skill in sabotage. The underground's nails had punctured the tires of hundreds of Nazi lorries. Dozens of small bridges outside Rome had been wrecked. German engineers had spent days hiding munitions dumps beneath superb camouflage, but Allied planes had known exactly where to drop their bombs. Maeltzer's intelligence reports had often mentioned the partisans' secret caches of arms and the General knew that the German troops wanted to use Rome as an escape route, not as a battlefield. When Caracciolo finished, Maeltzer considered the offer briefly, then said that he would have Oddone brought to his office later that day and if the underground leader gave him the promise Caracciolo had outlined, he would be released. "They seemed very tired," Caracciolo recently said. "I don't suppose they'd had an easy time of it with their jobs." Before Caracciolo departed, Boehm looked at him and laughed. "Don't you worry," he said. "Someday we'll have a cell for you in the Regina Coeli, but since you've been so kind to us we'll let you listen to the B.B.C. every evening."

A Roman bookkeeper, like a good many other people here, claims to have seen the last little clump of Germans leaving the city. He says that among them were two soldiers, a sergeant and a private, who were leading two donkeys through the Corso Umberto at eleven o'clock at night. A twenty-millimetre machine gun was slung between the donkeys, but the soldiers, probably in too big a hurry to get away, hadn't secured the ropes well. The gun slipped off and fell to the pavement. The Germans, startled, ran into a nearby doorway—just why, the bookkeeper couldn't guess. After a few minutes, they came out again and stared at the gun. They looked depressed. Presently, a *Volkswagen* roared up the street and the sergeant flagged it. He and his comrade started to hitch the donkeys to the rear of the car. The bookkeeper says that there was a long argument between the driver and the two soldiers, in which the driver obviously maintained that the animals could hardly keep pace with his machine. Finally, the two soldiers gave up, lifted the gun, threw it into the car, and got in themselves. The *Volkswagen* drove off, leaving the donkeys behind. One of them started to bray and the other just walked around in circles.

[July 22, 1944]

# LETTER FROM FRANCE

A. J. LIEBLING

*July 14, 1944*

FOR a year before the Allied landings here, Germans occupied a large, moated, Norman farmhouse near which I now live. Sixty of them were billeted in it, sleeping in great, pine-panelled living rooms on mattresses they had stolen from a nearby summer hotel and in the fetid warmth that is a German soldier's ideal of comfort. This atmosphere is customarily maintained by keeping all windows and doors closed tight. The owners of the farmhouse, who moved into the kitchen wing when their guests took over, listened regularly to the B.B.C. broadcasts and always harbored from two to six young men who were evading forced labor in Germany. In the evening, Mme. H., the matriarch who rules the family, clipped certain items bearing on the war from the German-controlled French newspapers, or, when there was nothing worth clipping, reread old items in the collection she was gathering. A couple of nights ago, while I was drinking warm milk in the kitchen, which, because Americans are billeted in the house now, is still the family living room, Madame showed me her clippings. The first one was dated August 17, 1941. Each of them had to do either with a proclamation by a German *Komman-dantur* or with a Vichy official threatening reprisal for some act of sabotage committed in northwestern France or with an announcement of the execution of hostages, invariably described as "Jews and Communists." Mme. H., who had no direct contact with the resistance movement and knew nothing first-hand about the victims named in the newspapers, felt certain from the first that they were on the only decent side. Collaborationist cant never deceived her for a moment, and yet she is of the type most susceptible to Pétainolatry—rich, intensely Catholic, and in considerable fear of "Reds." Her son, a blond, broad-headed chap with a decided limp, was a prisoner of war in Germany for three years. He had served in Alsace in a French engineering regiment and right after his capture was set to work with other prisoners digging up French mines. A mine exploded, killing six of his comrades and shattering one of his feet. Even after that, he was sent into forced labor, first in Alsace and then in Germany. Officials of the local *Kommandantur* approached Mme. H. some time after the armistice with an offer to have her son sent home if she would persuade him to be an informer against farmers who were with-

348

holding cattle and fats from the Germans. She said she would prefer not to have her son home. Eventually the Germans released him anyway, along with a few thousand other crippled or tubercular prisoners, when, in 1943, Vichy put on a great drive to induce young Frenchmen to volunteer for labor in Germany to "relieve" prisoners of war who had been there since 1940. These incapacitated prisoners were supposed to be the advance guard of a great mass of returning Frenchmen; actually, they were the only ones ever released. Young H., as he will be known in the countryside as long as his mother lives, although he is now over forty, came home with a great admiration for the Alsatians, who, he says, are the most patriotic French he ever met, and with an almost patronizing view of Germans. " A German is either a bandit or a decent fellow," he says. "There are no in-between Germans. The bandits run the rest. I have seen the Germans in air raids, and individually they are shameless cowards, but fantastic discipline keeps them going." He says there was enough food, but it was all starchy, and that few German workmen, even at the time he left the country, seemed to believe that Germany could win the war, whereas most French prisoners were confident even in the worst days that Germany would lose.

When H. returned to Normandy and saw what the German Army had become by then, he grew optimistic too, like most of the Normans who had stayed home. The athletes in uniform who had invaded western France in 1940 had given place to a mixed lot of Georgians, Russians, Poles, and adolescent and middle-aged Germans, and the motorized equipment that had amazed the French in the blitzkrieg days had been shipped away to active fronts and had been supplanted in great part by horse-drawn vehicles. The soldiers of the polyglot regiments seemed resigned to defeat and stuffed themselves in quiet desperation, consuming Norman butter and milk as if they were trying to eat enough to last them through the black years they saw ahead of them. The arrogance of the invaders had given way to the alternate fits of meekness and ill manners of the garrison troops. The Germans were so short of motor vehicles that they commandeered farmers' carriages for their officers and sometimes drafted farmers to drive them. A substantial farmer, a neighbor of Mme. H., often tells about the time he drove a German major to a railroad station three miles from the officers' billet; he managed to take an hour getting to the station, pretending first that he didn't know the way and then that the horse had gone lame. The German missed his train and was furious about it, but the Norman pretended not to understand anything he said. This was the sort of thing that kept the Germans miserable; they had the feeling that they were constantly being tricked and laughed at. The German authorities knew that they were getting only a fraction of the cattle and dairy produce available, but they couldn't confiscate the herds without putting a stop to production, since they had no agricultural personnel of their own to put on the farms.

Few of the country people in Normandy expected a landing there. The majority, in fact, thought that there would be no landing at all but that the Allies would wear Germany down by bombing. They were perhaps persuaded to this way of thinking by a hope that their land would not be fought upon. But the landings, when they came, delighted them. The discomfiture of the Germans was particularly pleasing, and peasants, offering their best bottled cider to Americans, suddenly burst into laughter as they remember how the supermen scuttled off. During the first days of the invasion, there was a bit of foolish talk in British newspapers, and probably also in American papers, which I have not seen, about the Normans' lack of enthusiasm, stories evidently written by correspondents who acquired their ideas of Frenchmen from music-hall turns and comic drawings. One might as well expect public demonstrations of emotion in Contoocook, New Hampshire, or in Burrillville, Rhode Island, as in Normandy, where the people are more like New Englanders than they are like, for instance, Charles Boyer. Young men of the resistance groups did invaluable service both before and after the landing; they drew plans for us of German fortifications before we landed and went through the German lines repeatedly during the fighting in order to get information about enemy movements. Not one report of a French civilian's sniping at Allied troops has been authenticated, and relations between our soldiers and the country people are excellent everywhere, now that the inevitable misunderstandings of the early days have passed.

A common cause of misunderstanding was the farmers' habit of loitering about fields that had been requisitioned for Allied tank parks. One Armored Forces colonel was thinking of having the *maire* of a certain village shot as an obvious spy when a French-speaking American officer interrogated the *maire* and found that he was just waiting around for a chance to milk his cows. "There may perhaps be a war and you may perhaps be beating Boches," said the *maire,* with traditional Norman crypticism, raising his voice occasionally as the sound of guns threatened to drown his words, "but what I am sure of is that my horned beasts must be milked." Even the farmers who were happiest to see the Allied tanks arrive are now beginning to ask wistfully when they are going to get their pastures back again.

The French sometimes misinterpreted American actions, too. There was, for example, the *maire* of a small *commune* just outside Cherbourg who came into Army Civil Affairs headquarters there five days after we took the city and complained to a French liaison officer that American troops had put him out of the *mairie* and that now he had no place in which to carry on the affairs of the *commune.* The French liaison officer, Captain Gérard Lambert, an energetic Gaulliste, replied emphatically, "But that is against all the policy set on high levels! They have no right to commandeer a French Government building unless for extreme military necessity," and he and the *maire* immediately drove off to the *mairie.* There were no American troops there, but a sign on the door said, "Keep Out—U. S. Military Police." As Captain Lambert and the *maire,* who must have been around seventy-five, climbed the stairs to the first floor, the captain said, "This is curious. Why did they order you out?"

The old man answered indignantly, "Because they said there were mines in the cellar."

The captain said with dignity, "You are an idiot. If it amuses you to go up with a mine, remain."

"However, my captain," the old man said, "it is not certain there are mines in the cellar." So he did remain.

All sorts of difficulties were referred to our Civil Affairs officers during the first few days following the liberation of any city. The manager of the Cherbourg branch of the Banque de France requested Lieutenant Colonel Frank Howley, Cherbourg Civil Affairs Chief, to have a guard posted over a certain heap of rubble in Valognes, a town that had been almost completely flattened by artillery fire. The bank manager explained that he had sent a hundred million francs to the Valognes branch for safekeeping, because he had expected the bombardment of Cherbourg. A shell had demolished the Valognes branch and two adjoining buildings had collapsed on top of it, so the hundred million francs were now buried under all three. The manager seemed to fear that some casual looter might shove the ruins out of the way and unearth the money, a feat which, actually, a steam shovel will probably accomplish in about two weeks.

Cherbourg, the nearest thing to a big city we have yet captured, was the first testing ground in France for the Allies' Army Civil Affairs Branch. When the Americans took over, on June 27th, the city had no water, electricity, gas, transportation, or government. The Vichy *sous-préfet* had fled and so had twenty-five thousand of Cherbourg's civilian population of forty thousand. The Civil Affairs team, headed by Colonel Howley, an American, and including both British and American officers, moved in before the street sniping had ended, and immediately started in on the job of resuscitation. The Civil Affairs men's task, as Howley saw it, was to get the city government functioning normally again. The Civil Affairs Branch had no enlisted personnel it could put to work policing the streets or making repairs. Cherbourg had had a fairly modern water system; water was pumped from the little Divette River to a purifying plant, from which it was distributed through mains. Bombs had broken the pipeline from the river to the plant. Major John C. Diggs, a former sanitary engineer for the State of Indiana, is Public-Works Officer in the Howley team. He got together the staff of the Cherbourg water system, who told him that the Germans had taken away all the reserve pipe. He got piping from the Army Engineers, the French installed it with their own workmen, and on July 1st the city had water again. "All they needed was a little encouragement," Major Diggs told me. "I've seen several floods and hurricanes in Indiana and the effect on local governments is always the same—they're a bit stunned, like a man suffering from battle shock. A little shove gets them going again." When it was time to turn the water on, a new problem presented itself, one that it is safe to say nobody in Washington or London had foreseen. There were hundreds of empty buildings in Cherbourg, many of them partly wrecked. The hastily departing owners had left the taps open. When the water was turned on, thousands of gallons would not only be wasted but would do further damage to the structures. Men with loudspeakers borrowed from the local American Psychological Warfare Unit were sent through the streets to warn people to turn off their taps. This expedient did not, of course, take care of the empty houses, so the British Major Palfrey, Police Officer of the team, the American Lieutenant Colonel Hensel, who is its Civil Defense Expert, and the American Lieutenant Davis, who is a former battalion chief in the Columbus, Ohio, fire department, got in touch with the French police, the Défense Passive, and the local fire department, respectively, and members of all three services went, just to be sure, to every house in the city and turned off the open taps. Two other officers, Lieutenant Robertson and Captain Westervelt, who were utilities and telephone men in civilian life, got the electric-power and telephone system restored to service in much the same thoroughgoing fashion.

On June 29th, M. Coulet, General de Gaulle's Normandy delegate, installed in office, as the new *sous-préfet* of Cherbourg, M. Le Viander, who had been chief engineer of the municipality and active in the resistance movement. He had been absent from the city when the invasion came but had made his way to the Allied lines a couple of days after the landings. Police and civil servants fell into line and took orders from the new *sous-préfet,* who was, after all, a colleague who had been in civil service a long time, more readily, in most cases, than they had taken them from his Vichy predecessor. He knew precisely which of his subordinates had collaborated beyond absolute necessity, and he sacked them. They were not numerous. After that, the *sous-préfecture* and the Civil Affairs men worked smoothly together. The same thing had already happened in Bayeux, where M. Coulet had his headquarters and where he had installed another resistance *sous-préfet.* The Civil Affairs team in the much smaller but architecturally more interesting Bayeux is headed by an Englishman, and includes both American and British officers.

Coulet, a tall, thin-lipped, smooth-shaven man of slightly sombre elegance, speaks English well. He has no army behind him, but he has the prestige, in a Norman's eyes, of representing the only French government the Normans recognize, the Gouvernement Provisoire, and he proceeds with complete assurance, making contact with the resistance group in each district as soon as the Allied forces enter it, and organizing the district with the assistance he receives from local resistance leaders. It is a program which up to now has worked smoothly and bloodlessly. So far, there have been neither legal nor unofficial executions.

[July 29, 1944]

# LETTER FROM FRANCE

A. J. LIEBLING

*July 20, 1944*

THE contrast that existed in the first World War between the front and behind the lines has returned with the present Allied campaign in Normandy. Staff officers drive toward the front along roads upon which the shadow of a strafing plane never falls and, leaving it, return to an area in which traffic and sanitation are as well organized as in Westchester. Nobody worries about the possibility of a flanking movement or a breakthrough by the enemy because our flanks rest on the sea and the enemy has shown no signs of having real striking power. Even within a couple of miles of the front there is only slight danger, because the Germans have disclosed little artillery. The arrival of a shell on a road near a command post is something to talk about for the next three days. The last few hundred yards make all the difference; the fighting is a nasty business in which hedgerows, drainage ditches, and apple trees have assumed the same lethal associations as Tunisian *djebels*. This struggle for orchards and pastures is disheartening because it is so repetitious. There is, as Army men say, no observation in this country, which means that you can't see an enemy position until you have taken the one in front of it. Even then you don't know that it really is an enemy position until a machine gun opens fire on you from a hedge or a mortar in the next field ahead starts dropping stuff in the one you have just taken. It is not safe to assume that any corner of any field you are attacking is undefended. The property sense of the Norman is so strong that no bit of useful land is without its surrounding hedge and ditch. The Germans dig in behind the hedges like moles—moles with excellent eyesight—and the pattern of the fields frequently gives them a fine opportunity for cross fire, which happens to be one of their specialties. The business of rooting them out of these fields is both dangerous and tedious, and it is one phase of war in which air power is of almost no help, because foliage conceals the defenders from strafing planes and because bombing entire fields on speculation is likely to pay extremely small dividends in dead Germans. Our artillery is useful in inducing machine gunners to keep their heads down, but foot soldiers have to make the actual kills.

After each few days of this hedgerow fighting, one of our divisions comes to a small town, which it takes. The towns, except for their names, are as much alike as the orchards: always the main street that is merely a stretch of the motor highway; the austere gray stone church that had survived eight centuries and then been shattered the week before; the trepanned, amputated houses with glassless windows; and, if there is one café still ungutted, the sign upon it that says "Off limits to military personnel." A unit takes a mild pride in the catalogue of the towns it has captured—such as St. Jean de Daye, known to the troops as Saint John D Day, and La Haye du Puits, called Hooey da Pooey—but that's about all. There are usually several dead Germans in the buildings of these towns, snipers left behind by their retreating comrades and killed by incoming Americans. Our soldiers, preoccupied with the possibility of surviving snipers and with the mortar fire that the enemy is sure to drop back into any town he has abandoned, hurry past the bodies with only perfunctory interest. There is more affinity between a wax dummy and a corpse than between a corpse and a live man. Some of the corpses wear fairly good gray-green uniforms, and others wear nondescript rags. The most impressive corpses seldom come from the best regiments; the most effective German troops here are the starveling adolescents of the new Nazi formations. Older, more fully developed men give up sooner. The Russians, Georgians, and Poles who were starved into enlisting in German coastal regiments are naturally the easiest game of all. Unfortunately, we have liquidated most of these "static" troops and are now meeting a higher percentage of Germans. For all their stubbornness in defense, the Germans have not been making any counterattacks in force. This has led to a certain optimism, particularly in the zone beginning a thousand yards to the rear of the line. Some officers are saying that the situation reminds them of Tunisia late in April, 1943, when the Germans, though still hanging on to good defensive positions, were about to collapse rather suddenly.

Many peasants remain in their homes in the battle areas, despite the efforts of both Germans and Americans to move them out. The Germans have been trying to evacuate people and their livestock before them as they retreat, but the peasants hide themselves and their beasts. When American troops start fighting around their farmhouses, our Civil Affairs officers attempt to get the peasants to move back of our lines, for their own protection, but they usually say that they won't go unless they can take their cattle with them, and since they can't take their pasture along with the cattle this is not practical. A crop farmer can leave his land for a time and find it there when he comes back, but herds will stray or starve or sicken or wander into machine-gun fire if left to themselves, and the Normans stick to their cows. Near St. Lô, a refugee camp has been established for people whose homes have been destroyed. It is an unusual refugee camp, because it does not receive any supplies from the Army; the French authorities provide the food and the farmers of the district donate clothing and furniture. The refugees have organized themselves into a self-governing community and have succeeded in making themselves more comfortable than the American soldiers of the local Civil Affairs detachment, who are now taking French lessons from the refugee children. Almost every family has deaths to mourn, but the tragic aspect of the situation is naturally not comprehended by the children, who consider the affair a sort of large-scale picnic and are not disturbed by the racket of the American medium artillery immediately behind their temporary home. The subway-train noise the shells make as they go over the children's heads merely provokes them to imitative whistles. Very old people are similarly unmoved by the war. A well-to-do farmer's widow, crippled with rheumatism, and her *bonne* were the only inhabitants left in the village of St. André de L'Epine after two days of heavy fighting. When our Civil Affairs detachment got there, it evacuated them in an ambulance. The mistress was seventy-seven and the maid seventy-two, and the thing that had made the greatest impression on them was the fact that they hadn't been able to get any milk or vegetables for several days and had had to eat their pet rabbit. Their house had been badly damaged and every other one in the village had been flattened.

The Fourteenth of July apparently found everybody in the liberated zone happy. Tricolors that had not seen the light since the Pétain armistice fluttered over houses and draped window sills everywhere, usually along with homemade American flags and often with signs saying "Vive l'Amérique" or "Merci à Nos Libérateurs." The understanding recently reached between de Gaulle and the United States Government seemed to have removed the last suspicion entertained by the French, and the crowds that gathered for the ceremonies in front of the *mairies* were unaffectedly joyous. As one thick-waisted old farmer, an ex-cuirassier, said, "An armored formation has cut up my best pasture, a promising heifer has gone up with a mine, and a bomb has removed most of the tiles from the roof of my house, but, Monsieur, I assure you, I was never so happy in my life." And Mme. R., the proprietress of a fine farm near Isigny, said, as she put on her red-white-and-blue rosette (an extra-large one), "Last year I wore a blue dress, my daughter a white one, and my daughter-in-law a red one, and we walked down the street arm in arm, because it was forbidden to wear the tricolor. Now it is different." However, it would be a mistake to assume, because things have gone so smoothly in the part of France liberated up to now, that there will be no serious problems, especially of relief, in *départements* that either are less self-sufficient or that the Germans have had more time to loot. It is also too soon to be able to say that in the big cities the change of regime will be effected with as little violence as it has in the essentially reasonable, rural Normandy. Still, there is every justification for being satisfied with the way things have gone so far.

There was one ceremony on Bastille Day that had not been foreseen—the burial of Brigadier General Theodore Roosevelt, who had died of a heart attack after surviving more front-line perils than any other general officer in this theatre of operations. Nearly all of Roosevelt's scrapes were of his own seeking; he was as nearly fearless as it is given to man to be. The name "Rough Rider," in white letters on his jeep, was a familiar sight just behind the lines in four campaigns of this war. It had been painted out by the time of the funeral and the vehicle had been returned to the motor pool and anonymity, and there was no other charger to lead behind the scout car that carried this flamboyant little man's body to the grave, but nothing else was missing from the solemnities. The man who used to tell his friends in New York how as a small boy he had put on the shoes of his father, the former President, and walked ecstatically about his bedroom at Sagamore Hill was never a sufficiently acute politician to fill them, but he found his métier in 1940, when he took up his reserve commission in the Army. Old Teddy was a dilettante soldier and a first-class politician; his son was a dilettante politician and a first-class soldier. After serving with the First Division in Africa and Sicily and with the French in Italy, he was assigned to a new unit, as assistant division commander, a couple of months before D Day. It was the Fourth Division, which had never fought before, and, by his own example, he gave it much of the lift that took it across the beaches and all the way to Cherbourg. It is no longer a run-of-the-mill division but one of the best in the Army, and his death has endowed it with a tradition. In the circumstances, it was easy to condone his indiscriminate passion for reciting poems, which he rolled out with the large facility of a juke box full of quarters. He was a man you had to see fight to believe in.

The taking of St. Lô was the climax of the hedgerow phase of our campaign. St. Lô, at the juncture of several major highways, is a larger version of the rural crossroads that are the prizes of smaller operations. The correspondents, going out every day in jeeps to the St. Lô sector of the front, got to know every turning in the lanes, bordered by the omnipresent hedges, that led to the suburbs where the final attack was to be made. Troops fanned out from these lanes to fight their way through the fields. Each day it was possible for vehicles to get past one or two more turnings in the lanes; one remembered these new turnings by the burned-out half-tracks or by groups of dead cows. The jeeps that carried the correspondents breasted a seemingly regular stream of other jeeps with litters, each bearing two seriously wounded men, strapped to their hoods. The stream was regular because the casualties in this sort of war, though they vary from field to field, don't vary from day to day. You lose a few more men in one hedge-fenced pasture and one or two less in another; there is never a spate of casualties, but the stream never dries up, either. There were about as many German as American wounded on the litters, but we seemed to see many more German than American dead on the ground, probably because we were advancing over terrain that had been hammered by

American artillery, whereas the enemy had employed comparatively little artillery. We also got to know every sizable gap in the ragged seven- to ten-foot-high hedges along the lanes, for the gaps enabled enemy snipers and mortar crews to see and to shoot accurately. A rapidly moving jeep raised a cloud of dust that might bring down mortar fire even when there was no gap; a jeep creeping at the ten miles an hour that is prescribed in the area seemed to the occupants to be minutes getting past each gap. When, by the evening of July 18th, the Americans had fought themselves out of the turnings and hedgerows, they rushed into the town of St. Lô with all the joy of a band of claustrophobes released from a maze.

The Germans, as expected, broke out what artillery they had and bombarded St. Lô as soon as our troops came in, and our tired infantrymen, lying face down in the streets at the foot of the buildings, realized that life is just a succession of frying pans and fires. The correspondents, flat on their faces like the rest, wondered whether the Pulitzer Prize was worth all this trouble. They were further depressed by the magnificent aplomb of the brigadier general who walked erect down the center of the street, directing troop movements with a cane. When a sniper's bullet went through his right arm, he transferred the cane to his left hand. That gesture will be hard for us to match in our autobiographies.

# LETTER FROM FRANCE

A .  J .  L I E B L I N G

*August 4, 1944*

RIDING, last week, down the road that led to Coutances, Avranches, and beyond evoked memories of the tragic June of 1940, when refugees streamed down the one route left open for civilians between Paris and Tours. Last week, as four years ago, the road was choked with vehicles moving as slowly as a trickle of water through dust, but this time, instead of autobuses and pitiful automobiles loaded with civilians, the traffic was half-tracks, empty ambulances, tank destroyers, two-and-a-half-ton trucks, the small, tracked carriers (called weasels) that take ammunition across country, and, scattered through all the heavy stuff, jeeps. The procession was heading toward the Germans instead of away from them. One would never have believed, in peacetime, that the mere act of riding slowly down a road in an uncomfortably crowded vehicle on two separate occasions could produce such antithetical emotions. In 1940, the unfortunates on the road stared apprehensively at the sky every time the procession stopped because of a jam. In 1944, soldiers in trucks grinned every time they heard an airplane motor. The Luftwaffe had lost its terror; the Ninth Air Force was patrolling the skies of France with absolute authority. The men moving forward had a hunch that no serious battle awaited them. It turned out that they were mostly right. There were some sharp local actions, which were less counterattacks than group attempts to escape, but in general the parallel with the end of the Tunisian campaign held good: German resistance, disconcertingly stiff in the earlier phase of the Normandy fighting, crumbled suddenly and swiftly, and American units heading toward their objectives unexpectedly found themselves racing other units that had progressed farther and faster than anyone had anticipated. It was a disturbing experience for the artillery officers, who soon found that there was no place that their shells would not be likely to fall among Americans advancing from other points of the compass.

I watched the air bombardment that preceded the breakthrough from an upstairs window of a Normandy farmhouse. The dwelling looked south, toward the area, five miles away, which was to be bombed. There were three ridges, the first two crowned with poplars, the third with pines, between the farmhouse and the target area. One stream of bombers came in to the left of the farmhouse, turned behind the third ridge, dropped its bombs, and came away to my right; another stream came in over my right, turned, and went off to the left. For two hours the air was filled with the hum of motors, and the concussions of the bombs, even though they were falling five miles away, kept my sleeves fluttering. I was living with a headquarters battery of divisional artillery, and some of the men in it, watching the bombardment from the sloping ground under my window, rolled on the grass with unsportsmanlike glee. One man yelled, "I'm glad my father was born in Ireland!" Their emotion was crude but understandable. "The more bombs we drop, the less fight there'll be left in them," another soldier said, and, remembering the first bombs on Paris in 1940 and all the bombings I have seen decent people undergo since then, I could not feel ashamed of the men's reaction.

The only residents of the farm who seemed uncomfortable were a great, long-barrelled sow and her litter of six shoats, who walked about uneasily, shaking their ears as if the concussions hurt them. At brief intervals, they would lie down in a circle, all their snouts pointing toward center. Then they would get up again, perhaps because the earth quivering against their bellies frightened them. Puffs of black flak smoke dotted the sky under the first two waves of bombers; one plane came swirling down, on fire and trailing smoke, and crashed behind the second ridge of poplars. White parachutes flashed in the sun as the plane fell. A great cloud of slate-gray smoke rose from behind the trees where it had gone down. Soon after that the flak puffs disappeared; the German gunners either had been killed or, as one artillerist suggested, had simply run out of ammunition. The succeeding waves of planes did their bombing unopposed. It was rather horrifying, at that.

After the bombardment, we waited all afternoon for the order to advance. We had heard that the divisional artillery headquarters and the division's battalion of medium howitzers, which throw their shells about seven miles, were to be moved up that night to positions beyond the line the Germans had held that morning. As it happened, the breakthrough wasn't quite as abrupt as all that. We didn't move until the evening, and then we moved only a couple of miles, to a hollow behind the first ridge of poplars, territory that infantry of another division had won from the enemy a couple of days before. When night fell, neither our own infantry division, which the Germans have been good enough to refer to as a *corps d'élite,* nor our armor had even gone into battle. The infantry divisions ahead of us had been expected to move forward hard on the tail of the air bombardment and make an opening through which we and the armor would pass, but they had not advanced appreciably. Discouraging rumors, such as frequently attend the opening of offensives, cropped up in the small, exclusive mess of the divisional artillery that night. One was that the Germans had not been shaken by the bombardment, another that they had been annihilated but that bomb craters had made all the roads impassable. The favorite explanation of the delay, I am afraid, was that the divisions ahead of us had snarled things up as usual.

Next morning, at seven o'clock, a combat team of infantry from the division I was with went into action. By nine o'clock, the news came that the men had advanced thousands of yards in the first hour, and all day they kept on moving forward, against slight opposition. Parts of two armored divisions, engaged at other points, also made rapid advances. The early discouragement around our headquarters disappeared. The mess even made generous allowances for the shortcomings of other infantry divisions. (It turned out afterward that they had run into an abortive German offensive just beyond the bombed area and had not done badly at all.) The artillery prepared to move up behind the infantry, in order to shoot it out of trouble when it ran up against the inevitable tough going. But the tough going that had developed at some point in every other operation the division had participated in, whether in the Mediterranean campaign or in France, did not develop in this curious advance.

"The dough," as officers of divisional artillery call the infantry, flowed forward for five days; the artillery followed, but it was hardly ever called upon to shoot. Whenever the Germans looked as though they might make a stand, some other American unit got behind them. By the fifth evening, the gunners found themselves in the impasse I have already described. It was an artillerist's nightmare: there was no place they *could* shoot without fear of hitting some of our own people. Army Corps headquarters had marked on a map what were called "no fire" lines; these lines completely hemmed our guns in. On that fifth night, the division stretched out toward Coutances like a long finger. There were—theoretically, at least—Germans in front of us and on both flanks, but there was part of an American armored division behind the Germans in front of us and there were other American troops behind the Germans on our right. Still other American troops were supposed to be getting around to the rear of the Germans on our left, too, and all the Germans in the area were trying to get out at once. The chief danger we faced was being trampled to death by escaping supermen while we slept.

Divarty, the familiar term for divisional artillery headquarters, is under ordinary conditions an ideal place to follow the progress of a battle, or at least one division's part in it, because Divarty controls the small spotter planes, usually Piper Cubs, which serve as the division's eyes. The pilots and observers in these craft, known to "the dough" as Maytag Messerschmitts, are not Air Forces men but artillery officers. They report not only on targets and the effect of the division's artillery fire but on all enemy troop and vehicle movements they observe. This information is channelized through Divarty to Division, which is short for division headquarters. When ground observation is available, Divarty has the best of that, too, for the artillery has its observers at points of vantage up in the line with advanced elements of the infantry. These observers have telephone lines to their battalions, and the battalions in turn have direct lines to Divarty. The infantry is served by a parallel but separate telephone network. Communications between the infantry and the artillery go through a division switchboard. The infantry and artillery of a division live like a sensible married couple—in the same house but in separate beds.

There is a detached, academic atmosphere about Divarty that is lacking in the larger, more bustling Division, and artillerists in general view war with the objectivity of men who seldom see their victims. The headquarters battery of Divarty has no guns, it merely has a switchboard, a set of maps, and a lot of telephone wires. Divarty is a small, itinerant brain trust that moves quietly with the front-line troops and calls down upon distant Germans the thunder of the division's battalions of artillery. It sets up its command post in a farmhouse or barn within the division area, lays its wires to the battalions, and blacks out windows and chinks through which light might escape. Then, after nightfall, when the Cubs come down, its higher officers sit around a long row of tables—in an atmosphere that recalls a newspaper copy desk during the slack hours—drinking strong coffee and playing cribbage while they wait for telephone calls. A call comes in, and an executive officer engages in a brief conversation, rings off, then remarks, "Infantry patrols report some sort of Jerry movement at that road junction at 4124. Mediums can reach it." He picks up the telephone again, makes a call, and returns to his cribbage game, and outside, in the night, twelve hundred pounds of high explosive scream toward the dark crossroad twenty-five times, at short, irregular intervals. In this particular engagement, however, we simply ran out of crossroads to shoot at.

# MY DEAR LITTLE LOUISE

A. J. LIEBLING

DURING our breaking-out offensive in Normandy, the division artillery headquarters I was travelling with occupied four command posts in five days. A French family was living in one wing of the first house we used, although most of the roof was gone and a couple of the bedrooms had only three walls, but the farmhouses in which we had our second and third command posts were deserted. The Germans had forced all the inhabitants to leave. In our fourth one, we found civilians again. The Germans, not expecting so quick an advance, had not evacuated people from what they still considered the rear area. In the barnyard of that place, we found a dead Panzer Grenadier of a Schutzstaffel division. His pay book said that he had been born in Essen, and on his body there was a typewritten form that he had filled out but obviously had not had time to hand in to his company commander, asking for what we would call an emergency leave to go home. His reason was "Bombing deaths in family—urgent telegram from wife." He had been hit by a fragment of shell, but it had not torn him up much. A detail of our fellows buried him in back of the barn.

The dead cows were more of a problem. Now that we have moved on to Brittany, one of the things that make us happy is that we are out of dead-cattle country. The war moves more swiftly and it isn't necessary to drop artillery shells on every field and crossroad. Besides, the cattle in Brittany are fewer and more scattered than in Normandy, where every pasture was full of them. You need a bulldozer to bury cows properly, unless you are going to take all day about it, and nobody had men to spare for a large-scale interment detail. They lay in the fields with their four legs pointing stiffly in the air, like wooden cows discarded from a child's Noah's Ark, and their smell hung over the land as the dust hung over the roads. Men are smaller than cattle and they are always buried first; we lived in the stench of innocent death. At our fourth command post, there were more dead cows than usual, because, the people on the farm told us, eighteen extra cows had arrived with the Germans a couple of weeks before. There had been two sets of Germans in the farm buildings—ten paratroopers who had showed up driving eight cows, and forty S.S. men who had appeared driving ten cows. The paratroopers, one of whom

362

was a captain, had got there first and taken up quarters in the farmhouse. The S.S. men, arriving later, had billeted themselves in the outbuildings, but only after a noisy argument, in which they had failed to get the paratroopers out of the big house. The captain had too much rank for them. The paratroopers had been fighting a long time and were very down in the mouth, the people of the house said. A soldier who served as interpreter had told the French family that the war was over, that Germany was beaten. But the S.S. fellows, who had come from soft berths in Warsaw and Brno, were still *gonflés en bloc* (blown up hard) and talked as if they owned the earth. That was less than two weeks ago, but even the S.S. men, to judge by those taken prisoner, have changed now. The S.S. soldiers had brought a refugee family with them to milk the cows, the people on the farm said. Every day the paratroopers drank the cream from their eight cows and threw the milk away. Both sets of Germans had departed abruptly, but the S.S. had left one man to guard the cows, presumably in case the reports of the Allied attack proved exaggerated. A shell had killed the cowtender.

I am sure that I will remember our two deserted command posts longer and more vividly than the two that were inhabited. Perhaps that is because you think more about people when they aren't there, and because you can be your own Sherlock Holmes and reconstruct them in accordance with your own hypothesis. The first deserted farm was a solid rectangle of stone and stucco buildings with walls nearly a foot thick. The farmyard, on which all the buildings fronted, could be reached only by narrow lanes that pierced the solid row of buildings at the front and at the back. It would have been a tough defensive position to crack if there had been any tactical reason to defend it. The farmhouse was very old and must have belonged to an aged, rich, crippled, bigoted woman or to a crippled man who had a fat old woman for a housekeeper. There was a crutch in the farmyard, lying as if it had fallen off a departing wagon, and in two of the bedrooms there was a pair of old, mended crutches that must have been discarded for newer ones. In the kitchen, by the great open hearth, there was a reclining chair with an extension on which to rest your legs, and in one bedroom there were several old and dirty corsets, whose whalebones, despite the garments' immense girth, had all sprung because of the continual effort to encompass a bulging body. There was a tall Norman clock in every room. Clocks of this sort are made in little towns, like Périers and Colombières and Marigny, which nobody outside Normandy ever heard of before this summer. Every crossroads seems to have had its clockmaker as well as its baker and its harness maker. The wooden cases of these timepieces are generally rather austere, but the dials are framed by hammered gilt sculpture; sheaves, golden apples, plows, and peasants in donkey carts are favorite motifs. The pendulums are vast, and they too are encrusted with ornament. A bride, I imagine, although no one has told me so, brings a clock as part of her dowry, and a house where there are many clocks has been ruled in turn by many women. This house was full of hideous modern religious images and of wax fruits and flowers under glass bells. There were no books except devotional ones and those that gave quick ways of making the computations a farmer must make in doing business with wholesalers. There were many of each kind.

The farmsteaders had left the place in a great hurry, and some soldiers, either German or American, had been there afterward and rummaged through the house, littering the floors with things, useless to them, that they had pulled from the cupboards—women's high-collared blouses, skirt hoops, dingy photographs of family outings and one of a man in a cuirassier's uniform, with breastplate and horsetail helmet, and three or four parchment manuscripts. One, dated 1779, was the deed of sale of a farm, another was a marriage contract dated the Year 3 of the First Republic. The contract enumerated the items the bride was to bring in her dowry, which included six pillowcases, one canopy for a bed, and ten handkerchiefs; the whole thing was to come to a thousand and fifty-seven francs. If the husband died before the wife, she was to be allowed to withdraw that much from the estate in consideration of her dowry. If the wife died first, the widower was to keep the pillowcases, handkerchiefs, and all the rest, probably to bestow on his next choice. I wondered, naturally, which of them had survived the other. There were canopies over the beds in all the bedrooms; one must have been the canopy listed in the contract. The house had stone floors that did not shake even when some guns just across the road were being fired, which happened for one entire night we spent there.

The guns were only three thousand yards behind the front line, but they were firing at a target—a railroad station or road junction—eleven miles away. They belonged not to division artillery but to a remote, unfamiliar entity called Corps. The battery commander, a harassed-looking little captain, called on our artillery general as soon as we moved in and said he hoped the general did not mind guns; there were a lot of generals who couldn't sleep on account of the noise and he had had to move twice already. He was like a man apologizing to his new neighbors for having noisy children; he was sensitive. Our general said that the guns were music to his ears, and we all smiled mechanically and obediently. The captain said, "I'm sure glad to hear that, because I feel I have an ideal setup here."

Across the yard from the house, in a small storeroom, lived a donkey so old that he had a gray beard. His hoofs were long and misshapen, like the nails of an old dog who gets no exercise, and he stayed in his gloomy cell, blinking out at the world, without enough energy to walk into the adjoining barn and eat the hay, although he would accept cabbages if they were brought to him.

From the crippled woman's, or man's, house we moved into a region that

had been heavily bombed on the first day of the offensive and was completely
deserted except for the surviving animals. An officer who had done some
reconnoitering had found a hamlet, Chapelle en Litige (Chapel in Litigation),
which was intact. Bombs had fallen into all the adjoining fields and bomb
craters had made the roads into it almost impassable, but its half-dozen houses
and the dependent barns stood untouched. One officer, who considers the Air
Forces a form of artillery totally lacking in professional direction, said, "If
they had dropped hundred-pound bombs instead of five-hundred, they'd have
killed just as many cows without spoiling the roads." The façade of the granite
house in which we set up shop was hidden by pear trees *en espalier,* laden
with fruit and lush with leaves. An old hen had made a nest in a branch under the hayloft window and was rearing her chicks there; they were hard to
find, buried among the pears, and produced a noise that was inexplicable to us
until we discovered them. Some of the soldiers with us took up quarters in
smaller houses, and once they had found niches for themselves, we all strolled
about the village looking over the interiors of the houses. The owners had
evacuated them in an orderly fashion, taking most of their belongings with
them. There was not much left except furniture.

I found a pile of letters, most of them old, a few recent, lying on a dressing
table in one of the houses. In a nearby cupboard was a long row of schoolboys'
notebooks filled with exercises in drawing, arithmetic, and composition. All
the books bore the inscription, written in a hand that became progressively
less slack, "Cahier d'Albert Hédouin." A couple of recent business letters were
addressed to Veuve Hédouin, and I assumed that Albert was the widow's son.
There were also in the cupboard a number of the usual breviaries and cheap
books of devotion, including a pamphlet of prayers for prisoners of war. Idly,
because as a camp follower I had nothing else at the moment to do, I took
some of the letters and, sitting down on the threshold of the plain little house
I was in, started to read them.

One was dated September 25, 1914. It began, "My dear little Louise: I
utilize a little moment to send you news of me. I am in good health and hope
my letter finds you the same. I'd rather be at Chapelle en Litige than where I
am, for it isn't nice to sleep outdoors. If this thing ends soon, I won't be sorry.
I am with Anatole and Désiré, and they are in good health, too. Probably the
buckwheat has been harvested, if the weather is as good there as it is here.
I'd like to help thresh it and drink a big bowl of cider instead of being here,
but it's useless to think about it. When you geld the little colt, leave him in
the barn for two days, then turn him into the fields of broom, where the
donkey is. Put some branches on top of the gate, so he won't try to jump over
it. When you get this letter, send me some news of what goes on at home.
Have you made a barrel of cider for Pannel yet and have the cows turned
out well? Excuse me for being brief, my dear little Louise and cherished
babies. I write this letter in the open air, sitting on my knapsack, and now I

must go. Your husband, who loves you and kisses you again and again, Louis Hédouin, 336th Infantry. P.S. Put the donkey in Fernand's field."

The next letter was dated in November, 1914, and began, "My dear little Louise: It is with great pleasure I learn that you are in good health. I too am in good health. Dear little Louise, I think you should make at least three barrels of cider, although I know it will give you a lot of trouble. Considering the price of apples and the price of cider, it pays better to make cider than to sell apples. And make a good barrel for us, so that we can have the pleasure of drinking it together when I come home." ("Come home," I thought. "That war had four years to go then.") "My dear little Louise, you tell me that you have planted some wheat. Good. Prices are going up. I hope you have sowed oats, dear one. Dear little Louise, I hope you are well. Also the cows and calves. Butter is selling at a pretty good price, if it can only continue. I was glad to hear you had someone help you thresh the buckwheat. Dear little Louise, I wish I could have been there, but it's useless to think about it. Here one is and here one stays—until when, nobody knows. Your husband, who loves and will never cease to love you and the dear little children, Louis."

Looking up, I saw that four or five cows, probably wanting to be milked, were staring hopefully at me, and I wondered how Louis Hédouin would have felt if he had known that in thirty years not even a woman would be left to care for the cattle in Chapelle en Litige. There was another letter, also written in 1914, in which he said he had been to Mass and then eaten some ham dear little Louise had sent him; he would rather have attended Mass at home, but it was "useless to think of it."

"Dear little Louise," he went on, "you say you have had a card from Aimable and he is in good health. So much the better, for you can't imagine how unhealthy it is where he finds himself. I couldn't either, unless I had been there, but don't worry, I'm all right. Dear little Louise, you say that Marie has had a letter from Pierre and he is a prisoner. So much the better. That way he is sure to survive. I know that threshing must be a lot of trouble to you. I am sorry you are alone and have so much work to do. Do you remember, on that evening before I went away, Enée said that this business wouldn't be over before Easter? I am afraid he was right. It is sad when I think of it. Days are indeed long. Louis."

And on March 15, 1915, he wrote that he was sorry to hear that Louise was suffering but hoped she would soon be delivered—the first indication I had had that he knew she was pregnant. "My dear little Louise," he continued, "I had a letter from Papa the same time as yours. He says he has sold the old cow for three hundred and forty-five francs. It's not bad, when you think that she only had four teeth left. What about the black cow you thought was going to calve March 8th and what are you doing with the Jersey? Tell me in your next letter. Dear little Louise, you say you have threshed the oats. Good. There must have been some loss, but you did the best you could. The worst of it is we probably won't be home in time for the haying this season. Excuse me for not having written. We were taking ammunition up to the front lines. Lately things go badly. The regiment has refused to march to an attack. Everybody is sick of this business, and we lose courage and ask for an end of this terrible war. A sweet kiss from your husband, Louis."

Then, on the twenty-second of March, the latest date I found on any of his letters, Hédouin wrote, "My dear little Louise: I have received with great pleasure your letter of the eighteenth. Your mother writes to me that you have had a nine-pound boy and are doing well, and the boy, too. My dear little Louise, you did well to have a midwife from Remilly, and she didn't charge much, either—eight francs. My dear little Louise, I'd like to be with you, but it's useless to think of it. Distance keeps us apart. I hope God will help you in your troubles. My parents write me that at home people are saying this will end soon. So much the better. Dear little Louise, the boy will be called Albert. Before telling you, I waited to see whether you would have a boy or a girl. Your husband, who loves you, Louis. P.S. What about the black cow?"

Nineteen-fifteen. I did a bit of subtraction. Albert would have been twenty-four in 1939—just the right age. I thought of the graded notebooks and the pamphlet of prayers for prisoners of war.

# LETTER FROM PARIS

A. J. LIEBLING

*September 1, 1944*

FOR the first time in my life and probably the last, I have lived for a week in a great city where everybody is happy. Moreover, since this city is Paris, everybody makes this euphoria manifest. To drive along the boulevards in a jeep is like walking into some as yet unmade René Clair film, with hundreds of bicyclists coming toward you in a stream that divides before the jeep just when you feel sure that a collision is imminent. Among the bicyclists there are pretty girls, their hair dressed high on their heads in what seems to be the current mode here. These girls show legs of a length and slimness and firmness and brownness never associated with French womanhood. Food restrictions and the amount of bicycling that is necessary in getting around in a big city without any other means of transportation have endowed these girls with the best figures in the world, which they will doubtless be glad to trade in for three square meals, plentiful supplies of chocolate, and a seat in the family Citroën as soon as the situation becomes more normal. There are handsome young matrons with children mounted behind them on their bikes, and there are husky young workmen, stubby little *employés de bureau* in striped pants, and old professors in wing collars and chin whiskers, all of them smiling and all of them lifting their right hands from the handlebars to wave as they go past. The most frequently repeated phrase of the week is *"Enfin on respire."*

Happiest of all, in the French film manner, are the police, who stand at street intersections with their thumbs in their belts and beam paternally at everybody instead of looking stern and important, as they used to. Cyclists wave to them appreciatively. When, occasionally, a truck passes through a street, taking policemen to their beats, people standing on the café *terrasses* applaud and shout *"Vive la police!"* For Paris, where the street cry has always been *"A bas les flics!* [Down with the cops!],"* this is behavior so unprecedented that the cops sometimes look as though they think it is all a dream. There is good reason for the change of heart; for the first time since Etienne Marcel led a street mob against the royal court in about 1350, the police and the people have been on the same side of the barricades. It was the police who, on August 15th, gave the signal for a mass disregard of the Ger-

368

mans by going on strike. It was also the police who, four days later, began the street fighting by seizing the Prefecture of the Seine, their headquarters, across the square from Notre Dame on the Ile de la Cité. Three thousand of them, in plain clothes and armed with carbines, revolvers, and a few sub-machine guns, took the place over and defended it successfully for six days before being relieved by the arrival of the French armored division of General Leclerc. This was the largest center of patriot resistance during the struggle. Because it is in the middle of the city, it was the knot that kept the network of patriot strongpoints together. The Germans held fortresses in the Place de la Concorde, the Place St. Michel, the Luxembourg Gardens, and along the Rue de Rivoli. Von Choltitz, the German military governor of the city, was finally captured by soldiers of the armored division in the Hôtel Meurice, and the Crillon was fought for as though it were a blockhouse. During the five days of fighting before the first elements of Allied troops began to penetrate the city, the Germans sallied from their strongpoints in tanks and systematically shot up the town. The Forces Françaises de l'Intérieur had erected barricades to stop the tanks, and boys fourteen or fifteen years old, with courage that was more than a riposte to the fanaticism of the Hitler Jugend, often destroyed tanks by throwing bottles of incendiary fluid through their ports. The bottles were usually filled with mixtures prepared by neighborhood druggists. The youngsters who did the fighting were not always of the type that is ordinarily on good terms with the police. They included the problem children of every neighborhood as well as students and factory workers. So the oldest of all Paris feuds has ended.

It has perhaps already been hinted in the New York press that our Army had not expected to take Paris quite so soon. The city was to be bypassed and encircled to save it from street fighting, on the theory that the last elements of the German garrison would withdraw just before being cut off. Thus a certain amount of damage to the city's buildings would be prevented, unless, of course, the Germans mined them before departing. As it turned out, the Germans laid mines, all right, but they didn't set them off because they were caught sitting on them. There were ten tons of explosives in the vaults under the Senate alone. But none of this is so important for the future of the world as the fact that the French saved their self-respect forever by going into the streets and fighting. The F.F.I.s were already in control of the city when the regular troops arrived, they like to tell you when you talk with them in the cafés. And, with a fine bit of military courtesy, the Allied Command, when it was informed that conditions in Paris called for an immediate move, sent in Leclerc's division first. Frenchmen had begun the liberation of Paris; other Frenchmen completed it. As a result, the Parisians are happy not only because of the liberation but because they feel they earned it.

The gratitude toward Americans is immense and sometimes embarrassing in its manifestations. People are always stopping one in the street, pumping one's hand, and saying "Thank you." It is useless to protest. To the Parisians, and especially to the children, all Americans are now *héros du cinéma*. This is particularly disconcerting to sensitive war correspondents, if any, aware, as they are, that these innocent thanks belong to those American combat troops who won the beachhead and then made the breakthrough. There are few such men in Paris. Young women, the first day or two after the Allies arrived, were as enthusiastic as children; they covered the cheeks of French and American soldiers alike with lipstick. This stage of Franco-American relations is approaching an end. Children, however, still follow the American soldiers everywhere, singing the "Marseillaise" and hopefully eying pockets from which they think gum might emerge. And it is still hard for an American who speaks French to pay for a drink in a bar.

The city is resuming normal life with a speed I would never have believed possible. The noise of battle has receded and the only visible reminders of the recent fighting are some damaged buildings, holes in a few streets, and a considerable number of captured German automobiles dashing about loaded with F.F.I.s and their girls, all wearing tricolor brassards and festooned with German machine pistols, Lugers, and grenades. French adolescents have for years been deprived of the simple pleasure of riding about on four wheels, and if they seem to find an excessive number of military missions for themselves, all of which involve riding down the boulevards and cheering, nobody can blame them. Until very recently they seemed to have great difficulty in resisting the equally natural temptation to shoot off their new weapons, and every day sounded like the Fourth of July, but the F.F.I., whose officers are serious soldiers, is now being absorbed into the French Army and the promiscuous shooting has come to an end. On a shattered concrete pillbox in the Place de la Concorde, some playful fellow has printed, in chalk, "Liquidation. To rent, forty thousand francs." And as I write a painter is relettering "Guaranty Trust of New York" on the building next to the Crillon, which the bank occupied before we went to war.

The physical conditions of life here are not too bad. Paris was spared the most uncomfortable experience a big modern city can have, for the water system has continued to work, a very important factor not only in sanitation but morale. Only a limited quantity of electricity is available; the power plants and distributing system are in good shape, but the hydroelectric power from central France is no longer coming in and there is a very small supply of fuel. Consequently, lights are on for only about two hours every evening, except in government offices. There is as yet no gas for cooking, but it has been promised that there soon will be. For that matter, there is not very much to cook; the city had no more than a two weeks' supply of strictly necessary foods when the liberators entered it, and though the American and French authorities have been steadily pumping food into the town, there is not yet enough for the reëstablishment of good eating at home, let alone good restaurant life. Only a few small black-market restaurants still exist. The price of *petit salé* (a kind of New England boiled dinner), one pear, and a half bottle of Bordeaux is seven hundred francs. This is the best fare you can get, and seven hundred francs, just to remind you, is fourteen dollars. Butter is four hundred francs a pound. However, the day of the black-market people is ending, because there are great quantities of butter, meat, and vegetables in Normandy, Brittany, and Anjou at about an eighth of Paris prices, and bringing them here is now simply a matter of transportation. Considering that all this food is only fifty to a hundred and fifty miles away, there is little reason to doubt that the problem will soon be solved. A decent pair of leather shoes costs a hundred dollars, a man's suit three hundred, and a portable typewriter five hundred and sixty. My advice to the Frenchman who wants any of these things is to do without for a few weeks, because such a situation can last only under the rule of the Germans, who drain a country dry of everything except grace, beauty, and good sense. The German occupation gave the black-market a sort of moral sanction here. In Britain the feeling has been, ever since the blitz days, that a man who bought in the black market deprived other Britons of their share. Here people said, truthfully enough, that if you had money and didn't buy in the black market, what you wanted to buy would simply go to Germany. The black-market operators themselves are an unprepossessing lot, however, and a visit to a black-market restaurant will quickly convince anyone that a fair proportion of the patrons are engaged in other branches of the same racket.

The question of what is to be done with all this group is receiving considerable attention in the new French press. There are already eleven dailies in Paris, all almost direct offshoots of the clandestine resistance papers. Only three bear names well known before the war—the conservative *Figaro*, the Communist *L'Humanité*, and the Socialist *Le Populaire*. These three had been suppressed by Vichy, but *Le Populaire* and *L'Humanité* became as powerful as ever in their clandestine editions. Others, like *Combat, Libération*, and *Franc-Tireur*, are resistance papers appearing for the first time above ground and in full size. The editorial offices and printing plants of the big collaborationist papers have been handed over to the newcomers. *Le Populaire*, for example, is now published in the plant of *Le Matin*, on the Boulevard Poissonnière. The new papers have from the beginning taken divergent political lines; in the cases of *Figaro, L'Humanité*, and *Le Populaire*, it would perhaps be better to say that they have resumed them. They are in complete accord, however, on the prestige and position of General de Gaulle and his provisional government. So is every man, woman, and child I have heard speak of de Gaulle or his government in Paris. The man's prestige is so vast that it is slightly nauseating now to think of the "opposition" to him that rich Frenchmen were still telling credulous friends about in London and Washington only a few months ago. He put the seal on a personal legend last Saturday, when, on foot and towering above a couple of million compatriots, he led a parade down the Champs-Elysées and as far as Notre Dame, where he listened to the Te Deum while snipers and F.F.I.s exchanged shots around him. Such overwhelming popularity may in time prove to be a handicap to him; he must eventually disappoint some of the people who now expect irreconcilable things of him. His hold on the public could not possibly be greater. A united France has crystallized around him.

# THE YELLOW FLOUR

DANIEL LANG

IT DOESN'T take more than one brief look to see how the war has affected San Pietro, Cisterna, Terracina, or any of the other towns that had the ill luck to lie along the main highways followed by the Allies in their arduous Italian campaign. The bombs and shells crumpled the houses and shops, set disease loose, killed or wounded a number of townspeople, and drove a few of them insane. The impact of the war on these towns has been quick and violent. Even if the inhabitants decide to rebuild their towns, the marks of battle may be visible for years; if they decide to take up life elsewhere, they will leave behind them twentieth-century ruins that may remain for generations. There are, however, Italian towns in which no fighting has taken place and which look just as they always have. Letino, a mountain village in the province of Campobasso, is such a place. Since the third century before Christ, its dwellings have stood along the slopes of a mountain deep in the Matese range. There, thirty-six hundred feet above sea level, people have kept to their agricultural life and tried to have as little as possible to do with the rest of the world. Their isolationist tradition runs deep and they are remarkably clannish. The citizens of Letino detest their nearest neighbors, the citizens of Gallo, three miles away on the road down to the plains. The reasons, all of which are considered excellent by the Letinese, are many. To begin with, Gallo was settled by Bulgars; Letino, on the other hand, owes its development largely to the Greeks. Besides, Gallo is a thousand feet lower. Moreover, the Gallese can't grow potatoes in their soil and must come to Letino for their supply. There are any number of other charges of which Gallo has also been found guilty.

I first heard of Letino while I was billeted with a Canadian Army field detachment near Venafro. A lieutenant had been sent out in a jeep one morning to find more space for their bivouac. When he returned, much later than he was expected, he announced that he hadn't found what he was looking for but had found something else. "All I did was discover Shangri-La," he said modestly. In the course of his mission, he explained, he had misread his map and become so sore about it that, having got on the wrong road, he had ordered his driver to stay on it and find out where the damn thing led to. The two men had gone winding up into the Matese Mountains. A short distance past Gallo, the mountains suddenly closed in on the valley the jeep was ascending. Pushing on, the soldiers soon came to Letino, at the end of the valley and the end of the road. "It was a most unusual spot," the lieutenant said. "They seem to be living in another time." He said he had learned that the Greeks, during their expansionist period, had occupied the town for two hundred and fifty years. The inhabitants were of Italian stock, but the women still wore Greek costumes. Their clothes, from headdress down to stockings, were in three colors: red for married women, green for single girls, and black for widows. "I'm not really sure if they know up there that a war is going on," he said. I decided that I'd like to run up to Letino myself to see what it *did* know. The next morning, the Canadians let me have a jeep and the driver who knew the way, and I set out for the village.

It took an hour's driving up a bumpy dirt road to reach the dead end at which Letino lay. I got out of the jeep, thanked the driver, and walked up the town's single street. It was narrow and cobblestoned, and it slanted up the mountainside to the summit. There, I discovered later on, the town's cemetery was laid out around the ruins of a thirteenth-century castle. The low stone houses that lined the street were obviously extremely old. On their fronts were dark weather splotches. There was no one on the street. I was just beginning to think that the town was deserted when, after I had walked a hundred feet or so, the row of houses on my left came to an end and the street widened into a plaza no bigger than a back yard in the East Seventies, and I saw, sitting on the steps of a small church, a dozen women carding wool, a couple of them holding infants in their laps, and others watching some older children play. Most of the women wore brilliant red skirts, two of them wore green ones, and two others, a very old woman and a young girl, were dressed in black. On one side of the plaza, eight middle-aged men were playing *pezzucchi,* a form of lawn bowling, in front of a combination tailor shop and general store. The wooden balls they were using rolled erratically over the uneven cobbles. The men seemed to be enjoying themselves immensely. They played together a half hour or so almost every day, I found out later. It was a gay, bright spot, and the thin mountain air smelled sweet.

My appearance, of course, was an event. The women stopped chattering and stared at me. The men halted their game long enough to smile and wave. The children came running toward me and, before I knew it, I was surrounded by about forty of them. Anywhere else in Italy all of them would probably have shouted, *"Caramèlle!"* Here only one, a little girl with braided black hair, came up to me and asked, shyly, for candy. Most of the other children laughed self-consciously, and two of them reached forward and pulled her back. One of the women sitting on the church steps called out shrilly, "Popolizio, *chiamate* Popolizio!" Half a dozen children ran into the shop and led a short man in his thirties, dressed in a loosely hanging G.I. uniform, toward me. When he reached me, he clicked his heels, saluted, and said, "Antonio Popolizio, American citizen." He put his hand into a pocket and pulled out an American passport, which he gave me. He was the village miller, he said. He had been born in the States and had been brought to Italy when he was still an infant. In 1929 he had returned and spent seven years there, half of them as a truck driver on a C.C.C. project in Schenectady. Except for the fact that his clothes and curly black hair were powdered with the flour he had been grinding, he was the Italian that Chico Marx has always been trying to look like, but his English sounded more like Jimmy Durante's. I told him I had come up to find out something about Letino, and he said that he would be glad to tell me what he could but that he knew someone who could help me much more. "Dis guy and his wife is educated," Popolizio said. "Dis guy is a doctor. He studied in college. He lives with his wife and two boys not far away. Dis guy and his wife both speak English, too."

We walked to the doctor's residence, an old stone house a short distance below the square. Popolizio banged on the door as though he had a case of acute appendicitis. It was opened by a stooped man of about fifty with reddish-brown hair. "Dr. Emilio Pitucco," Popolizio said, as he introduced us. The Doctor shook hands enthusiastically. "Come sit on the balcony," he said. "It is cooler than in the house." He led us through a large living room and onto the balcony, which was actually a small terrace with a wrought-iron railing. From it we could see the valley and the surrounding mountains. It was a magnificent view, and I said so. "I will be ready to die when I grow tired of it," Dr. Pitucco said.

He held out his arms to the southeast. "Monte Ianara, sixteen hundred metres high," he said. "Beyond it lies the city of Piedimonte d'Alife. To the east, Monte Miletto, two thousand and fifty metres high, always with snow on it. To the south, Monte Cappello, thirteen hundred and seventy-five metres. And below, our fields." The village farmland was perhaps a mile in length and half as wide. Every bit of it was under cultivation. The intensely green fields swept upward from the valley floor to the gray, rocky barrenness of the Matese. I could see a man and the red skirts of six women moving through a patch where they were planting something. "My mill," Popolizio said, pointing to a low white wooden building to the east of the fields. "See de river? I get my power dere. It's full of trout."

"The Greeks called the river the Lethos," the Doctor said. "It means 'oblivion' in their language. Now it is known as the Lete. The river disappears into the mountains not far beyond the mill. That's where the oblivion begins. When it gets out of the mountains, it flows into the Volturno."

An extremely handsome woman joined us on the balcony. "My wife, Luisa," the Doctor said. She was taller and much younger than her husband. She had a long, V-shaped face, an olive complexion, jet-black hair and eyes, and a full, rather musical voice. "Emilio," she said, "there are chairs here. Ask the visitors to sit down. I will make coffee at once." I asked her not to bother, and explained why I'd come up to Letino. She laughed. "Why, of *course* the war has come to us," she said as she walked away. "It began with the yellow flour. But why can't we have coffee?"

In a little while she returned with a pot of coffee and four globular glasses with beaten egg yolk in them. I was a little surprised when she poured the coffee into the glasses. "Drink it," she said, handing me a glass. "It is very good. We call it *uova battute col caffè*. Two egg yolks whipped with sugar, and then the coffee." It had a nice texture and flavor. "Tell him what he wants to know," Signora Pitucco said to her husband, almost as if she, too, was eager to hear what he had to say.

"It is a healthy village," Dr. Pitucco began. "Mostly I deliver babies. There are colds and backaches, too. A few weeks ago, Anna Chiodi died. She was ninety-nine. It is common for people of eighty here to have their teeth. That man working in the wheat field below is eighty-five. The Matese air is pure and the people go to sleep soon after supper. They sleep well and long and by seven-thirty next morning they are in the fields. There are only six men here who do not farm—the shoemaker, the carpenter, the blacksmith, the tailor, who is also the general storekeeper, Popolizio, and myself. We grow potatoes and wheat. Our cheese and milk come from our goats and cows. We get our wood from the mountains. Most of our meat we get from our pigs and goats. We hunt gray partridge and rabbits in the mountains. We are lacking in wine and olive oil and soap, and sometimes in tools for our farming. We use money here, but mostly we exchange goods. Before the war a pig was worth ten kilos of flour; for seventy eggs one would receive five kilos of sugar. We have no bank here."

"There are two policemen," Signora Pitucco broke in. "Pasquale del Giudice and Luigi Tomasone. They are both farmers as well as policemen. Neither has ever arrested anyone and each thinks he is the police chief."

"Most families own their own land," the Doctor said. "It is nearly always inherited by the sons. Some sons, when the father is still able to work hard, get married and then go to the United States or Canada for six, seven years to make money. They send it back to their wives. The wife cannot touch the money. She must work while the husband is away. The men always return, and when they do they join their money with the land by buying sheep and cows and whatever is needed."

"I got de electric generator for my father's mill de same way," Popolizio said.

The village pasturage, Dr. Pitucco told me, is common property and so is its electric-power plant. "The richest man is Michele Vaccaro," the Doctor said. "He owns sixty sheep, eight cows, and twenty-five hectares of land. The rest of us have less, but enough. Those who do not always have what they need are remembered." He explained that the mayor of Letino levied taxes, such as six lire for a sheep, twenty for a mule, thirty for a cow, and four on a light bulb. "Half of what I earn comes from this money," Dr. Pitucco said. "The other half comes from those who can pay me themselves." Tax money is also used to buy half the Doctor's medicines, to pay the two policemen, and to fix the road. After every harvest, before the surplus crop is bartered in the lowlands, a check is made to see if any of the villagers are short of food; if they are, part of the surplus is given to them.

"It is only fitting," the Doctor said. "With the children, of which there are many, we are only thirteen hundred. Most of us are related. There are seven main names among us—Orsi, Tomasone, Fortini, di Cecco, Saccone, Mancini, and my own. Besides, it snows six months a year and often the snow is two metres deep, and the people have the time to visit each other then. It would be impossible for people not to feel friendly toward one another. At that time, too, many of the men take the cattle down to pasturage in the lowlands around Capriati and Venafro. They build themselves straw huts there and see to it that the cattle are fed and do not freeze. They also trade our crops for what we need."

"We learned from these men that the war was coming," Signora Pitucco said.

"Yes," her husband said. "Every two weeks a few of them come back from the lowlands for provisions. From them we find out how our crops are selling and how the cattle are, and what is happening in the large towns. But in 1939 —the pasturage was near Capriati that year—when they came back, they talked of only one thing: how motorcycles and guns and trucks full of soldiers were going by on the roads day and night."

"A few months later, in the spring, came the yellow flour," Signora Pitucco said. "It was so foolish, the entire affair." She explained that every year the government had sent Letino a consignment of flour, which was placed on sale in the general store. When the Letinese were unusually busy with their farming, they bought some of it. Ordinarily, however, they turned their own wheat over to Popolizio, who ground it and delivered the flour to the housewives, who baked their own bread. That spring, Signora Pitucco said, the flour sent by the government was yellow. "It was mixed with corn, that's why," she said angrily, as though it had happened yesterday. "How dared they send us inferior flour!" I asked her if, since the townspeople had their own grain, it had made much difference. "No," she said, "but now everybody said they wouldn't even *think* of buying the government flour."

Several weeks after that, the government had informed the villagers that thereafter students and farmers were restricted to three hundred and fifty grams of bread daily and that children and those with sedentary jobs were to have one hundred grams less than that. All the grain not used for this bread was to be turned over to the government. Dr. Pitucco nodded reflectively. "We did what we wanted," he said. "Still, the rationing was an impressive formality. Up to then, all we knew of the government was that one *impiegato*—civil servant, that is—would come up once a month in the spring. He didn't like to come. He had a motorcycle and we are high up and the roads are rough. He would say that the Fascist commissioner at Campobasso, the capital of our province, wanted this or that and we would give it to him and he would go away and leave us alone. I remember the first time he came, many years ago. He spoke severely to us. He said that unless one were a Fascist one would eventually not be able to work for a living in Italy. He puzzled us. We knew we would always go on farming. We had been farming long before this *impiegato* was born. We never knew if we were Fascists or anti-Fascists or perhaps something else."

I asked Dr. Pitucco how well the government's rationing order had been observed.

"To begin with," he replied, "we told the *impiegato* not to expect too much grain from us because here in the mountains the soil is rocky."

"Only we didn't tell him how hard we work," Popolizio said.

"The people filled out the slips wrong," Dr. Pitucco said. "If someone put down he had ten *quintali,* then he had fifteen."

"During the day," Signora Pitucco said, "Antonio here ground the flour that the *impiegato* knew about. At night he made the flour that we knew about."

"In charge of all this," Dr. Pitucco said, "was the secretary of the mayor of Letino. The Fascist commissioner at Campobasso appointed him."

I asked if the secretary had caught anyone evading the regulations. Signora Pitucco laughed and the two men smiled broadly.

"The secretary of the mayor," Dr. Pitucco said, "was my father."

Toward the end of 1940, the effect of the war on Letino began to go beyond the hardships of yellow flour that no one bought and rationing regulations that everyone evaded. The town was severely hit by conscription. The classes from 1917 through 1920 were called up, and the younger boys already undergoing compulsory military service were told that they would not be released at the end of their two-year term. Dr. Pitucco seemed to feel that there was something especially impertinent about conscripting Letinese. He explained that before the war the youngsters of the town always served their time in the Army but had regarded the training as more or less of a lark. A few of them had fought in Abyssinia, but none had been killed or wounded. Most of them had trained in Libya and had enjoyed their adventures. "When they came back," Signora Pitucco said, "they would tell what they saw far away from Letino over and over again. The only man in Letino who has not married is a young farmer whom the Army would not accept. He was regarded as an undesirable husband because he never had any stories to tell."

This time, Dr. Pitucco said, the men's departure was not taken lightly. "Too many of them were leaving. We didn't know how long they would be gone and we didn't know when those who were already with the Army would come back."

"We lost Ottavio Cristino that year," Signora Pitucco said. "A very intelligent boy. People had talked of sending him to the University at Naples. That autumn the old men and very young boys took the cattle to the winter pasturage. Their news from the lowlands was not interesting. The old men only complained of their backaches and the young boys talked about nothing but the war."

Next year the government ordered the classes from 1916 through 1907 to report to the Army, and seventy of Letino's older farmers went off. Some of the men, Dr. Pitucco said, discussed hiding in the mountains, but they did nothing about it because they knew that the Army would retaliate by punishing their families.

In the spring of 1942, word came to the village that five of its men had been killed in action. "In Libya, too—where the boys used to like to go in peacetime," Signora Pitucco said. Twenty other Letinese soldiers had been captured and sent to prison camps in Kenya Colony and Canada. "That was a very hard year," the Doctor said. "People began to sell some of their sheep and cows. There were not enough men left to take care of all the cattle. The crops were less, too." He shrugged. "But whatever was happening, we were alone. There were still no outsiders in Letino."

By the middle of 1943, the drone of Allied airplanes could be heard occasionally in the valley. Once, Dr. Pitucco said, they flew directly over it. In September came the Italian capitulation. Thousands of soldiers tramped through the countryside in all directions, trying to get to their homes. "They reached the towns below," Signora Pitucco said. "Many of us went down to look at them and see if they were ours. None of them were. It was foolish of us. Our men would know the way to Letino well."

"No, none of our boys came here," Dr. Pitucco said. "Only the South Africans. Antonio, tell about them."

Late in September, it seemed, around nine in the morning, six worn-out, hungry men appeared at the mill. They were British airmen who had escaped from a German prison camp in the Abruzzi. Popolizio took them to his home, fed them, and gave them blankets. Then he led them to a hut in the woods where they could hide. After that he went back to Letino to consult with his friends. "Dere was a big argument," Popolizio said. "Some guys say I do right and others say I'm crazy, I'm going to get Letino in trouble."

"We didn't know what to think," Dr. Pitucco remarked. "These men were strangers."

"Den I tell everybody dese fellers is hungry," Popolizio continued. "Everybody says, 'Feed dem and get dem de hell outa here to where dey belong.'" Popolizio took care of them for four days. They stayed in the hut by day and came to his house at night. Popolizio went to Venafro, and found out where the Allied armies were. He returned and led the airmen through German lines, delivering them, after two days and nights, into American hands at Benevento, eighty kilometres to the southeast. "I got dese clothes from dere," Popolizio said, indicating his G.I. uniform. "Dey gave me cigarettes and dis, too, to get back wid." He pulled a torn piece of paper out of his shirt pocket. It read, "The bearer of this note, Antonio Popolizio, is an American citizen and we would deem it a great honour if you would give him any immediate assistance you can." The six soldiers' signatures, ranks, and serial numbers followed. They were all South Africans except a lance bombardier from Tunbridge Wells in Kent.

No one spoke for a moment after Popolizio had finished. Then the Doctor suddenly got up, went into the house, and came back with a map of the region surrounding the valley. "Tell me," he said, handing me the map, "why, last October, would the Americans want to come over the mountains to here?" The Americans, I recalled, were then in the Piedimonte d'Alife region and were trying to push on to Isernia, an important road junction, which would enable the Allied armies to regroup their forces for an offensive against Cassino. I could see on the map that the Americans, by coming over the mountains in a straight line instead of using the highway, could have cut the distance to Isernia almost in half. I said as much to Dr. Pitucco. "I have asked you a very important question," he said. "Now I know what the Germans feared when they came here. It was on October eighteenth."

At three o'clock on the morning of that day, the Doctor said, the town was startled out of its sleep by the roar of motorcycles and armored cars. There were sixty soldiers in the detachment. They parked their vehicles at the end of the road and then walked into the village—its first invaders, Dr. Pitucco said, since 1125, when a neighboring mountain settlement had made war on Letino. The Germans billeted themselves in a number of houses. "My wife, our two sons, and I spent the early hours of the morning packing. We did not want to live among intruders," Dr. Pitucco said. There was no chance of armed resistance; the Italian government had by then requisitioned what hunting rifles the Letinese owned.

Around seven o'clock, the Pituccos, looking out of their windows, saw that their neighbors had also been preparing to leave. Most of the Germans, the Doctor said, had gone up into the mountains to the southeast on patrols. The few Nazis who had stayed behind in the village did not interfere with the inhabitants' exodus. "They told us we could stay or go, as we pleased. Raffaelle

Orsi—he is eighty-one—asked the officer in charge if he and his men intended to farm. The officer laughed. Then we left the village."

The villagers banded themselves into groups of twenty-five or more and set off for various places in the mountains. Their herds of mules and donkeys were divided up so that everyone would have a chance to take away at least a part of his possessions. During the early morning hours they had hidden their grain and oil in caves. The trousseaus that Letino mothers work on from the birth of an infant daughter to her wedding day had been buried in boxes in the ground and their bulky feather mattresses had been concealed in haystacks. The men and women carried baskets and sacks of food on their heads; the donkeys and mules bore blankets, pots, and trunks of clothes. The people corralled what goats and sheep they could and drove them ahead of the mule trains. Fortunately, nearly all of the cattle had already been driven off to winter pasturage. Most of the villagers, Dr. Pitucco said, started off for some hills in Benevento Province, where the cattle had been sent that autumn, because there they could join the Letinese herdsmen. Only a few old men, too feeble to travel, remained in the town.

"I can tell you what happened to me," Dr. Pitucco said. "My wife and two boys and I took only my medical equipment, some blankets, some food, and the family clock. We were with forty friends. We went by a mule path to Giuditta Tomasone's house, which lies near some woods below Letino on the other side of this mountain. In all, seventy-seven people stayed with Giuditta. In the room in which we slept, on straw, there were twenty others. Others slept in the kitchen, and some were in the barn with the animals. When our food was used up, Giuditta used up much of the food she had stored for the winter and also killed a calf. We said we would do work for her after the Germans left, but she laughed. She said she would rather we came back when her husband, Filioberto, returned from the Army, and then she would give us better food and wine."

Mornings, when nearly all the Germans were known to be on patrol, Dr. Pitucco continued, the young men went on reconnoitering trips back to Letino, to see what the Germans were doing to the village and, when they could, go to the caches in the caves and bring food to their families. The Germans, they reported, were eating all the chickens and pigs they could find and were doing petty looting, such as stealing a phonograph here and blankets there. They were not, however, planting mines in the village. On one trip, five lads spied a pig the Germans had killed near Popolizio's mill. The boys made for the pig, with the idea of taking it away with them. A couple of Germans spotted them, and the soldiers opened up with a machine gun and killed all five. The old men who had stayed in the village heard the shots and discovered what had happened. One of them went to the nearest hideout, from which messengers were dispatched to tell the boys' mothers what had happened. The fathers of the dead boys were either in the Army or tending their cattle. The boys' mothers, accompanied by their other children, went to Letino and asked the German commandant if they could bury their boys. He consented, and the women, watched by a guard, went down to the mill and, with the help of their children, carried their sons up the street that led through the village and buried them in the cemetery.

Two days later, on October 27th, another reconnoitering group discovered that the Letinese no longer had to worry about intruders; the Germans had gone. They raced back to the hideaways and reported the good news. In a few hours the Letinese had returned with their mules and donkeys.

"At two o'clock that afternoon some other outsiders came to Letino," Dr. Pitucco said. Two hundred American soldiers had entered the valley from above the town by following a path around Monte Cappello. This was the reason the smaller enemy force in Letino had withdrawn. It was now in Gallo, where it was trying to dig in. The Americans went down the road, opened fire on the Germans, and then rushed the town. The Germans, leaving fifteen dead in Gallo, retreated down the valley with the Americans in pursuit. "It lasted only an hour," the Doctor said. "Hardly enough time for us to leave again."

"Only Raffaelle Orsi went away," Signora Pitucco said.

"I was uncertain if I wanted to go a second time," Dr. Pitucco said. He raised his hands expressively. "South Africans, Germans, Americans," he said. "We might as well have been in the lowlands." I found myself thinking that even in the Matese Mountains, even in Shangri-La, people were being forced to learn the painful and hopeful lesson of our time: that this is indeed one world. A man in Letino could not have the privilege of ignoring the Fascists in Rome or of making no distinction between South Africans, Germans, and Americans.

Since that skirmish, which was soon followed by the Allies' capture of the territory surrounding the valley, the village has seen no more fighting. Its isolation, however, has frequently been violated. Not long after the Allies had taken over the district, a Polish tank unit began training down in the valley. Sometimes the drivers ran their tanks clear to Letino. The sound of their tank treads, Dr. Pitucco said, was harsh. Some French engineers were also below, not far from the Poles. Nearly every day they blew up something or other, and the villagers had had to accustom themselves to the sound of the explosions. Groups of Canadians and Americans, stationed near Venafro, began to appear. "We bargain with the soldiers for such strange things now," Signora Pitucco said. "We give them eggs and they give us small boxes with chewing gum and cigarettes and cocoa powder and candy."

As for the village, the Doctor said, it could be in better shape. A hundred and seventy of its men had not yet returned. Fifteen were known to be dead, four were missing in action, and fifty were in prison camps. Some were in the German-held part of Italy. "Two weeks ago," Signora Pitucco said, "Giuditta Tomasone received word of her husband. He is in India—a prisoner."

"If only the men were here to work," Dr. Pitucco said, "we would not have to keep selling our cattle. People who used to have thirty sheep now have two, those who had ten cows now can take care of only one."

"And the girls," Signora Pitucco added apprehensively. "Only four marriages in the last five years. There used to be twenty a year."

"Dey'll be too old to get married when de men get back," Popolizio said.

"Ah, no," Signora Pitucco replied, smiling. "So many of the men will be coming back at the same time, they'll have to take what they can get." The three of them laughed.

A red-skirted woman leading a donkey was coming up the road toward the village. A little green-skirted girl was seated on the animal. "The sheep, the crops, the marriages are hard," Dr. Pitucco said, "but they are not impossible to solve. Yet I wonder what the men will think of the village when they return. The children did not beg for *caramèlle* when they left."

"I think I go to America," Popolizio said. "It's noisy, but it's supposed to be noisy."

The woman on the road stopped her donkey and leaned against him for a moment. Then, apparently refreshed, she started up the road again. Dr. Pitucco turned to the miller and looked at him thoughtfully. "I think I shall stay," he said.

# LETTER FROM FLORENCE

DANIEL LANG

*August 25, 1944*

FLORENCE, being at once a treasury of art and a city rather too close to the Gothic Line, has been going through one of the most protracted, nerve-racking liberations the war is likely to produce. Since August 11th, the official date of the liberation, according to an Allied communiqué, enough untoward incidents have taken place to leave the Florentines in some doubt that the great event has actually happened. The Germans, ignoring the fact that they had proclaimed Florence an open city, have been shelling the center of the town. One of their hits killed forty parishioners and wounded more than a hundred as they were emerging from Sunday Mass at the Church of San Lorenzo. The Germans have been pushed back beyond the Mugnone Canal, in the northern part of the city, but there are still certain neighborhoods—hushed places with only a few women pedestrians on the sidewalks—where the sight of an Allied uniform or the red, white, and green partisan armband is likely to draw an Italian Fascist bullet from behind a shuttered window. Bomb-disposal squads are still busy taking care of unexploded shells and mines. All day long, too, shells from Allied artillery on the heights to the south of the city pass high overhead en route to Nazi emplacements, and their whooshing sound is hardly likely to give one that old liberated feeling.

During the earlier days of the so-called liberation, the Florentines saw a good deal of fighting in their streets between the black-shirted Republican Fascists and the partisans, who belong to the Comitato di Liberazione Nazionale of Tuscany. When the Allies entered the southern outskirts of the town, on August 3rd, they did not cross the Arno into the main part of Florence, for fear that the Germans would respond by doing further damage to the city. The Nazis, pretending to follow the Allies' example, supposedly withdrew from the city. Actually, they hid tanks in the Cascine, the wooded public park in western Florence, mounted machine guns near the principal railroad station, and issued arms to the Fascists inside the city. For a time it looked as though the British Eighth Army and the Reichswehr, who had been pounding each other ever since the desert campaigns in North Africa, would permit the fate of a major Italian prize to be decided by a sort of vendetta between

384

two local bands. The Allies, wisely or unwisely, continued to keep their troops out of the city. The Nazis, however, seeing that the partisans were making headway against the Fascists, began showing up in the streets in their tanks and cutting loose with their machine guns. At a terrible cost to themselves, the Tuscan patriots, possibly the best guerrilla fighters in Italy, finally rid the city of its enemies. While this was going on, the inhabitants of Florence became acquainted with warfare at its most fluid. German tanks, hot after a band of partisans, would penetrate the city as far as the great cathedral in the Piazza del Duomo and then lumber back into the Cascine. Later, the partisans, reinforced, would go through the Piazza hunting for the tanks. Such signs of liberation as there were consisted of jeeploads of A.M.G. officers, who are not accustomed to finding themselves advance elements, and war correspondents. The Florentines would crowd around the jeeps and inquire ingenuously, "Are we liberated?" The usual answer was "Yes, but we don't want to fight in your beautiful city, so we are letting the partisans kill the enemy." The Florentines would nod their heads uncomprehendingly and move on.

A British correspondent who dared to venture into one of the hushed neighborhoods—one in which an English convent was situated—returned to press headquarters intact and said that he had got himself a fair story. He was disturbed, however, by the bad manners he was sure he had exhibited at the convent. The nuns, he said, had greeted him with worldly shouts of joy and had pressed rosaries and medals into his hands, but he had been so preoccupied that he hadn't thanked them. "All I did was just stand there and stare at their feet," he said unhappily. "I was looking to see if any of them were wearing hobnailed boots."

The German treatment of Florence amounts to an atrocity story. Most of the city is still standing, but, thanks to the enemy's well-placed demolitions, many of the most beloved parts are gone. According to Lieutenant Frederick Hartt, a former Yale art instructor, now serving as the A.M.G.'s Fine Arts and Monuments Officer for this region, about a third of medieval Florence has been destroyed or damaged beyond repair. Much of the section that was always considered most characteristic of old Florence—the walk along the Arno, where the thirteenth- and fourteenth-century houses, with their bell towers and enclosed balconies, lined the river's bank—is now rubble. After the war, there may be an attempt to put up facsimiles of these houses, but there is certainly reason to doubt that it will be possible to recapture the atmosphere of these buildings that Dante and Petrarch and other immortals once knew. With these buildings disappeared their contents—irreplaceable furnishings, invaluable libraries and collections, among them the books and photographs assembled by the late Raimond van Marle, the noted Dutch art historian.

All this destruction can be ascribed to what appears to have been one of the rare attempts of the Germans to preserve *Kultur* outside their own country.

As the Allies moved toward the city, the Nazis, using understandable military tactics, decided to destroy the bridges across the Arno to delay our advance. Although they had no hesitation about blowing up the Ponte Santa Trinità, one of the finest of all Renaissance bridges (it resisted three charges of explosives before it fell), they felt that the shop-encrusted Ponte Vecchio, which is somewhat reminiscent of Nuremberg architecture, ought to be spared. They were not, however, prepared to cede any military advantages to the Allies. They therefore set demolition charges in the houses at both ends of the bridge, to block it with huge mounds of rubble. To keep the partisans from learning of their plans and possibly deactivating the mines, the Germans gave the occupants of the houses no warning. After the explosions, an uncounted number of corpses lay buried under the ruins, and parts of the Via de' Bardi, the Via de' Guicciardini, the Borgo San Jacopo, the Via Por Santa Maria, and several other streets—the heart of Giotto's Florence—were wrecked. Among the more heavily damaged buildings were the Churches of Santo Stefano and Santa Trinità and the Palazzo di Parte Guelfa, all particularly fine structures. Several of the Uffizi Gallery's sixteenth-century frescoed ceilings fell and the north end of the Pitti Palace is scarred and windowless. Now that the Nazis have begun shelling the city, there will be further destruction. So far, the Strozzi Palace has been struck thirty times. Brunelleschi's Church of San Lorenzo has suffered seven hits and the Churches of the Santo Spirito and Santa Croce have gaping holes in their roofs. Just the other day the Germans damaged a new military objective, the Duomo's Baptistry.

The real battle for this region is being decided in the mountains to the north and west of the city, and even those Allied officers who think solely in military terms and look upon Florence as just another town can see no purpose in the enemy's shelling. The general feeling is that the Germans are firing out of sheer maliciousness, because of their reversals elsewhere, or else that some Nazi officers are going down to defeat in a blaze of hatred.

For the past four years, Florence has been richer than ever in art. In 1940, when the Mussolini government held an immense exhibition of sixteenth-century Italian art here, Tuscan churches and museums throughout the country sent their finest possessions on loan. By the time the show was over, Italy was at war and the problems of transportation had become difficult, so the paintings were not returned. No one thought then that Italy would ever be invaded, but it was realized that Italian cities might be bombed, so these pictures and others in Florence were stored for safekeeping in the villas and castles just outside the city. When the Allied officers arrived, a few weeks ago, they found the pictures still scattered about the suburban houses as if they were wastepaper. Lippo Lippi's fifteenth-century "Annunciation" was discovered, without a case or frame, in a wine cellar. Uncrated Del Sartos, Raphaels, Fra Angelicos, and Giottos were strewn about on floors, in closets, and in stables. There are now several patches of bare canvas in Botticelli's "Spring." The Allies also found, as might be expected, that the Germans, continuing their art collecting, had made off with a number of paintings, mostly Dutch and Flemish. Inventories of the missing works are being made for presentation at the peace conference, where the Germans will presumably be told to return the stolen goods. The villas and castles are still serving as repositories, and detachments of American soldiers have been assigned to guard the paintings inside them. The men are thoroughly impressed by the importance of their duties, but they are sometimes hazy about what it is they are watching. That doesn't prevent them from making appraisals of the paintings. When a friend of mine and I reached the castle in which we were to be billeted, a sergeant, a diligent fellow from Bensonhurst, stopped us.

"Where yuh goin'?" he asked.

We showed him our billet orders.

"O.K.," he said reluctantly. "But watch your step. There's a million bucks' wortha nice pictures in there."

"A million and a half bucks," a soldier standing nearby said.

The sergeant turned back to us. "D'ja hear that?" he asked. "A million and a half bucks."

During these unhappy yet stirring days in Florence, several figures have emerged whose names may or may not be remembered but whose heroic contributions were made when they counted. There is the partisan commander who, to protect his family, in German-held territory north of Florence, was called simply Il Potente (the powerful one). After he was killed by German mortar fire, his casket was covered with an Italian flag on which a picture of Garibaldi had been sewn over the House of Savoy's emblem. There is also Lieutenant Tinto (the sunburned one), who served under him and was seriously wounded in the same action. And there is the rest of the partisans' Arno Division, three thousand brave men who provided abundant evidence that Italians can fight when they feel like it. Although they lost nearly half their number in dead and wounded, they finally managed to drive the Germans and the Fascists from Florence (the Allied soldiers didn't suffer a single combat casualty in the city), and then turned the town over to the Allies in a formal ceremony on August 15th. The Frati della Misericordia, a humanitarian order founded in medieval times, has also done useful work, picking up the wounded in the streets and taking them to hospitals. Day and night its members, who wear black, hooded robes while performing their voluntary duties, can be seen pulling, like rickshaw boys, the hand-drawn carts they have been using as ambulances for generations.

So far the A.M.G., whose members deliberate on garbage-disposal, rationing, and health problems in the elegant rooms in which the Medici used to close big business deals and hatch cabals, have made a good impression on the

Florentines. The going was particularly tough in the beginning, when the
A.M.G. had to bring supplies across the almost bridgeless Arno to the northern part of the city, where they were often fired on by snipers. Once they
found that they were maintaining headquarters only four hundred yards from
a German position. The mainspring of the A.M.G. in this province is a thirty-
year-old Englishman, Lieutenant Colonel Ralph Rolph, the youngest provincial commissioner in Italy. There is no telling what may happen to him once
the higher-echelon boys of the Allied Control Commission move in and start
running things with complicated shrewdness, but at the moment he has a
free hand and he seems to have a clear idea of what he wants to do. "Why,
of course I'm recognizing the local Comitato," he recently told a correspondent. "They've certainly shed enough blood to deserve it." He went on to say
that he planned to give his province a form of government based on the pre-
Fascist constitution of 1915. He was sorry that, because no electoral machinery
was available, the representatives to the Deputazione Provinciale couldn't be
elected now, but he said that he would try to find out from the people whom
they would have elected had they been able to cast a ballot. "Even if it means
picking a man who is not so intelligent," he said. "If we don't do such things
now, there'll be an incredible free-for-all when we leave."

The commissioner, when I questioned him, admitted a certain disappointment in the Italian aristocracy in this region. He said that the one aristocrat on
the Comitato, a descendant of the Medici, had been so embarrassed by the
behavior of his old friends that he was asking people not to address him any
longer as Marchese. Members of the nobility, Rolph explained, kept coming
to the A.M.G. with requests for permission to go to one of their country estates
or to use their automobiles again. "They never seem to talk about a plan for
feeding ten thousand of their fellow-men," Rolph said. A few days ago, a
Count Duccio Marsichi-Lensi had come in with a proposal to reopen the race
track in the Cascine. "He was a member of the Florence Jockey Club," Rolph
said, "and he told me he had good news—Jerry had forgotten to steal the race
horses. The Count knew where to get feed for the horses and all that, and he
considered that five weeks from now would be a proper time for beginning
the races. He was sitting right there in that chair where you are now and he
had on a white linen suit and a blue shirt and a boutonnière." The commissioner shook his head incredulously. "Actually, old chap," he said, "I'd say
that he looked just like an Italian count who wanted to start a race track in
1944."

[September 23, 1944]

# SEARCH FOR A BATTLE

## WALTER BERNSTEIN

THE attack was to jump off at nine in the morning. The objective of my infantry regiment was a long, steep ridge that stood like a door at the head of the valley we occupied. The pattern of attack was familiar and orthodox: first an hour of dive-bombing to soften the objective, then a half hour of artillery, and finally the infantry to do the dirty work. It was a pattern that had been followed ever since we had landed in Italy. Everyone was getting tired of it. Our regiment had fought through Sicily and all the way up from Salerno, and the men were particularly tired of walking. They were not tired of fighting, if fighting meant that they would get home sooner, but they were very weary of long night marches and then hours of fancy mountain climbing in the face of enemy fire. This struck them as a hell of a way to fight a war that was supposed to be so mechanized and motorized, and they frequently said so. My job in this operation was going to be with the headquarters of one of the attacking battalions. I was now on duty at regimental headquarters, which was in a one-room farmhouse by the side of a dirt road, and the plan was for me to join the battalion as it marched past the regimental command post during the night on its way to the jump-off point. The battalion was scheduled to come by at two in the morning, and someone was supposed to wake me. No one did. When the guard was changed at midnight, the old guard forgot to tell the new guard. At four-thirty the regimental C.P. moved out, leaving me behind. I was asleep in a haystack and they could have moved the whole Fifth Army without my hearing them. A horse nibbling at the hay was what finally woke me. It was six o'clock.

There was no one around the place when I slid out of the hay, and the road was deserted. It was just getting light. Fog lay like chalk over the valley, twisting at the bottom as it began to rise. The air was cold and damp. The only living thing in sight seemed to be the horse, and he was no bargain. I dressed, put on my helmet and pistol belt, then went up to the farmhouse and looked in. There was nothing inside but guttered candles, torn and empty K-ration boxes, and piles of straw on which the officers had slept. I returned to the haystack and made up my bedding roll. Most of the line troops carried only a raincoat and half a blanket. At night they wrapped the half blanket around

*389*

their head and shoulders, put the raincoat over that, and lay on the ground. I had a whole blanket and a shelter half, a combination which, by comparison, was equal to an inner-spring mattress. After making up the roll, I ate a bar of K-ration chocolate. As the fog lifted, it revealed the mountains along the valley. At the end of the valley was the ridge we were going to take, looming black and forbidding through the mist. I finished the chocolate, slung the bedding roll over one shoulder, and started along the road toward the front.

There was no activity at all on the road, which seemed strange, considering that an attack was coming off. The valley was completely quiet. There were not even the ordinary morning-in-the-country noises. I walked for about a mile without seeing anyone and then passed an artillery battery dug in beside the road. The guns were camouflaged with nets. The men sat beside them, eating out of C-ration cans. No one looked up as I passed. Ahead of me, growing larger, was the high ridge. Before it were a few small hills. Between these hills and the ridge was another, smaller valley, running at right angles to the one I was following. Our men would have to cross it under fire. It was seven o'clock now, and there was still no sound of gunfire.

I had gone half a mile past the artillery when I heard a car behind me. A jeep was coming up the road. It stopped when I thumbed it. A colonel was sitting next to the driver, and he said, "Hop in." I climbed into the back and sat on my bedding roll. "We're going to the regimental C.P.," the colonel said. That suited me; I could find out there where my battalion was. The colonel must have been important, because the driver, a staff sergeant, drove very carefully, as if he were driving a sedan instead of a jeep. The road was full of holes, and he actually went into second for some of them, which is a rare thing to do with a jeep. I kept my eye out for planes. The ceiling was still very low, but you never could tell. The road curved to the right, when we came to the first of the little hills, and then headed straight for the ridge. The colonel told the driver to slow down. We caught up to a young lieutenant walking along the road, and the colonel leaned out and asked him where the regimental C.P. was. "Damned if I know," the lieutenant said. He needed a shave and looked tired. "Well, what outfit are you?" the colonel asked. "Support battalion," the lieutenant said. He turned off the road and started across a field toward some vehicles parked under a tree. The colonel looked as though he were going to call him back, but finally he ordered the driver to go ahead. A hundred yards beyond, we came to a crossroads, and there was an M.P. here. The colonel shouted his question about the regimental C.P. at him and the M.P. waved us to the left. We took the road he had indicated, but it soon turned into a cow path and finally petered out altogether in front of an old farmhouse. Another M.P. was standing there, scratching his head. We stopped beside him and the colonel asked directions again. The M.P. kept scratching his head, but he pointed across a field to a wooded hill.

The driver started off again. The M.P. called, "Hey!" We stopped, and the M.P. said mildly, "You better be careful crossing that field. It's supposed to be mined." None of us said anything for a moment; then the colonel sighed and told the driver to go ahead.

The driver went slowly across the field, following what he probably hoped were wheel tracks. I shifted around so that I was sitting on the side of the jeep with my feet on the back seat. I wondered briefly whether I shouldn't sit on my helmet, but decided that it wasn't really necessary. We didn't hit any mines, but we thought about them and it seemed like a long time before we got across that field. There was a dirt road on the other side and we followed it as we ascended the hill. Halfway up the hill we reached the C.P., which was in a grove of trees. I saw the regimental commander and his executive officer standing in a large excavation; the C.O. was talking over a telephone. The drivers and other headquarters-company men were digging foxholes and putting up a blackout tent. We parked under a tree. I thanked the colonel for the lift and went off to see if I could find someone I knew. I finally found the sergeant in charge of the intelligence platoon, a New Yorker named Vrana, whom I had been with in Sicily. He was sitting in a ditch by the side of the road, fooling around with a hand radio. I asked him where the battle was and he said it hadn't started yet. "We got observation on top of this hill," he said. "I was just talking to them. They said they couldn't see a damned thing." Vrana thought that the best way to find the battalion was to go up to the observation post and try to spot it from there. I could climb to the crest of the hill and walk along it until I found the post. He thought it was safe. He said that there had been only a little shelling, and that the enemy had settled down to throwing one shell into the C.P. every twenty minutes. "But on the nose," Vrana said. "You can set your watch by those bastards."

I said goodbye and started up the hill. It was easy climbing and I got to the top without much trouble. I came across a telephone wire there and followed it along the crest. The hill dipped into a saddle. I went down into it and was halfway up the other side when I heard the sound of men descending above me. They turned out to be two infantrymen, looking very dirty and completely bushed. One carried a rifle and the other had the base plate of a mortar. The rifleman said wearily, "How do you get out of this damned place?" I told them to follow the wire.

"You know where C Company is?" the mortar man asked me.

I asked him what outfit.

"Second battalion," he said.

"We just got relieved," the rifleman said. "Only nobody knows where we're supposed to go."

"I ain't even sure we been relieved," the mortar man said.

"I'm sure," the rifleman said. "The lieutenant come by and said we were relieved. That's good enough for me."

"The lieutenant got killed," the other man said.

"So what?" the rifleman said. "He relieved us before he got killed."

I said that I didn't know where C Company was but that they could probably find out at the C.P., and then it developed that they weren't even from our regiment. Their outfit had been in the line for eight days, and had held the hill we were on against four counterattacks; they had been spread all over the place and when our regiment had moved through, the night before, they had got mixed up. Now all they wanted was some hot chow and a place to sleep for a few days. Finally they decided to go down to the C.P., and moved off, cursing with the mechanical passion that everyone picks up in the Army.

I continued to follow the wire. It led up the slope to the top of the hill, which I suddenly realized was now flat and grassy. I felt very conspicuous. I ducked low and was creeping along beside the wire when a voice called my name. In a hollow between some rocks were three members of our regiment's intelligence platoon. The man who had called me was a private named Caruso, a small, dark man whom I had also known in Sicily. I crawled down to them. They said that they were the observation post. The two others were a lieutenant named Bixby and a private named Rich. You couldn't see anything from the hollow, but they said it was more comfortable there. "It's also healthier," Caruso explained. At that moment we heard the whine of a shell, growing steadily louder, and then a great swish, as though someone were cutting the tops of the trees with a giant scythe.

"See what I mean?" Caruso said.

"They throw one like that every twenty minutes," Lieutenant Bixby said. "You can set a clock by it."

I said I had heard about that before; the shells were landing below, in the C.P.

Caruso laughed. "I bet they're sweating down there," he said.

The fact that the shells were aimed at the C.P. and not at them seemed to make them happy. Caruso reached behind a rock and drew out a cardboard box full of rations. "How about something to eat?" he said.

"You just finished breakfast," Rich said.

"I got something better to do?" Caruso asked. He rummaged around in the box and came up with a can of meat balls and spaghetti. He opened it with a trench knife and ate the whole can, using the knife as a spoon.

While Caruso was eating, the lieutenant kept looking at his watch. Finally he said, "Listen." Very far away there was the faint cough of a gun, and then a rising whine and a sudden heavy rush of air as another shell passed over our heads. "See?" the lieutenant said, looking very pleased with himself. "Twenty minutes on the nose."

When Caruso had finished his meal, we climbed out of the hollow and up to the crest of the hill, where we lay on our stomachs, looking across the smaller valley toward the ridge. The lieutenant had a pair of field glasses. He looked through them and said, "There's fighting on the side of the ridge." He handed me the glasses. Through them I could see faint puffs of smoke half-way up the ridge and movement among the trees and rocks. "That's for me," I said. I was greatly tempted just to stay at the observation post. Sitting in the hollow was safe and secret, and no shell in the world would find me there. The air was getting warmer and the grass was soft and only a little wet. I could sleep. But I had to find the battalion, so I stood up, shouldered my roll, said goodbye, and started off again.

Lieutenant Bixby had said to follow the wire, which he thought led to the ridge. There was not even a suggestion of a path, and if you didn't know regimental wire teams you wouldn't think the wire could possibly lead any-where. Finally, halfway down the hill, the wire brought me onto a muddy path that ran diagonally down the hill. The path was screened by trees and seemed insulated from the rest of the world. The air was cold down there. The only sound was the squish of my shoes in the mud, and even that was a cold, clammy sound. It was easy going, but there was nothing pleasant about it. It was like walking in a cold jungle. But I soon lost myself in the rhythm of walking. It wasn't until I was almost at the foot of the hill that I discovered that I had also lost the wire. I walked back a few yards, then decided that it wasn't worth going all the way back up the hill. I had no idea where the path led, but if the fighting was halfway up the ridge the valley was probably safe. If it wasn't safe, I was just out of luck. I started to descend again, only slower. It was very quiet. The path straightened out near the bottom of the hill and the trees became sparser. Then it dipped suddenly and I began to walk fast.

The path turned abruptly. Ahead of me was a group of men. I went for the ground, but it was unnecessary—they were Americans. There were four of them, carrying a blanket stretched out between them. Lying on the blanket was another soldier. His feet were drawn up and his face was buried in his arms. He lay very still. The men came slowly toward me, carrying the blanket with great care. They all had rifles slung over their shoulders; their faces were drawn and their eyes were deep in their sockets. They stopped when they reached me and one of the two front men said, "You know where the medics are?" His voice was too tired to have any expression; it seemed to come from a great distance. I said I didn't know. "We got to find the medics," the soldier said. "We got a man hurt bad." I said they would have to climb the hill and then maybe they could send down from the observation post for one of the first-aid men at the C.P. The soldier was silent for a while, then he said again, "We got to find the medics." The three other men stood silent, looking at the one who was talking. The blanket was stiff with caked blood. The wounded man was scarcely breathing. Once in a while his fingers twitched and tapped weakly on the blanket. I said that they would pick up a wire farther along and that it would take them to the observation post. "Thank you," the man who had spoken to me said. He shifted his feet, moving very gently so as not to disturb the wounded man. "All right," he said to the others. "Left foot." They began to walk again, synchronizing their steps so that they wouldn't shake the blanket. As they passed, I stepped aside, but not quickly enough to avoid brushing against one of the rear men. He said, "Excuse me." They moved up the path slowly, like sleepwalkers, and I watched until they turned the corner and were out of sight. Then I went on along the path, following the tiny trail of blood they had left.

The path broadened at the foot of the hill and before I knew it I was in the valley. It was wider than I had thought, looking at it from above; the ridge seemed a couple of miles away. The path ended at a dirt road running through the valley, but I decided to cut straight across and head for the ridge. The ground was soft and grassy; it felt good to be walking on the level again. There was a lovely tranquillity in the valley, and the ridge was quiet again. I had walked about two hundred yards from the foot of the hill when there was a rush of air and a clap of thunder, and I fell flat on my face. When the ground had settled down, I lifted my head and looked around. A thin cloud of smoke and dust hung peacefully in the air a hundred feet to my left. There was nothing else to be seen. I lay there until I began to feel a little foolish, then stood up and began walking toward the ridge again. This time I got about twenty yards before there was the flat wham of something going very fast and another thunderclap. This time the smoke was closer. Then, while I was still lying on the ground, another shell hit only thirty feet away, throwing dirt all over the place. I stood up, bent low, and ran like hell. Another shell landed somewhere behind me, but I didn't stop until I got back to the foot of the hill. The first thing I saw was a ditch, and I hopped into that. It was full of water, but it was deep. It could have been full of hydrochloric acid as long as it was deep.

I lay in the ditch perhaps twenty minutes. There was no more shelling. The echoes still rang in my ears, but the valley was quiet again. Finally I climbed out of the ditch and started along the base of the hill, keeping under cover as much as I could. The road through the valley curved toward me, and I found myself walking on it. I went slowly, trying to look all around me at once. My clothes were wet and I began to shiver. The valley was deathly quiet. I couldn't stop shivering, and then I felt afraid. I wasn't afraid of snipers, or even of mines, which can irritate you so much that eventually you say the hell with them, just to be able to walk freely and with dignity again. But there is something about heavy artillery that is inhuman and terribly frightening. You never know whether you are running away from it or into it. It is like the finger of God. I felt cowardly and small at the base of this tremendous hill, walking alone on the floor of this enormous valley. I felt like a fly about to be swatted. It was a lousy feeling. I was very angry until I realized that there was nothing I could do about it. Then I began to wish I were somewhere else.

The road hugged the base of the hill and then swung out into the valley again. I stayed on it, partly from inertia and partly to assert myself. All of a sudden I heard an automobile horn. I looked up and down the road, but nothing was in sight. The horn blew again. It was a nice, raucous city horn; I thought I was imagining things. The horn blew again and a voice called out, "You dumb son of a bitch, where do you think *you're* going?" The voice came from the hill. I looked over and saw a soldier standing above me near some bushes, waving. "Come back here!" he yelled. "You want your goddam head blown off?" I started toward him. I had almost reached him when he yelled "Run!" and jumped in among the bushes. I started to run, and then there was the whistle of a shell and a loud crack and a piece of the hill flew into the air. I hit the ground, digging with my nose, and the soldier stuck his head out of the bushes and yelled, "Here! In here!" I got up and ran toward him and he pulled me through the bushes. There was a shallow cleft in the hill, hidden by foliage, and parked in the cleft was a jeep. In the jeep was another soldier and on the back was a reel of telephone wire. "I hope you got insurance," the soldier in the jeep said, "because the way you travel around this country you're sure going to need it." As soon as I got my breath, I asked him what he meant, and the first soldier took me by the arm and pulled me back to the bushes. He held them apart and asked me what I saw. I couldn't see anything. "Over there by the foot of the ridge," he said. I looked again. "You see it?" he said. I saw it. A German tank was sitting in a field below the ridge. It was far away, but you could see that it was a heavy tank and you could see the black cross on the side. "Get a load of that kraut bastard," the soldier said. "He nearly blew us off the road."

We went back to the jeep and he explained that they and another man had come around the other side of the hill along a wide trail, stringing wire for the battalion, and the tank had opened fire, forcing them to take cover in the cleft. The tank was apparently afraid to come down into the valley, since we had covering fire on it, but it would fire on anything that moved. The one who had yelled to me was short and red-faced; his name was Jenkins. The other was tall, with a long, sad face and huge hands, and Jenkins called him Tex. "He really comes from Oklahoma," Jenkins said, "but he served two years at Fort Sam Houston, so everyone calls him Tex." I asked if they had done anything about the tank. Jenkins said they had sent the third man up to the artillery observation post to put some fire on it. He said we had men working their way up the ridge; he didn't think they were meeting much opposition, since all the firing he had heard had been light and sporadic. There seemed to be nothing to do but wait, so I sat down in the jeep and relaxed. The two other men went into what was apparently a running argument about the relative attractions of French women in Algiers and Italian women in Italy. Jenkins was upholding the French.

"They got more class," he kept saying to Tex.

"Maybe so," Tex said, unimpressed, "but what good is it if you can't get anywhere?"

"That's just what I mean," Jenkins said triumphantly. "That's *class*."

Just then there was the crackle of a shell overhead. "That's it!" Jenkins said. He rushed to the bushes and held them apart so that he could look across the valley. Tex and I followed him. "It's our goddam artillery," Tex said. "They finally realized there's a war on." The shell had hit a hundred yards or so from the tank. The tank began to move, obviously trying to retreat, but something must have been wrong, because it turned only part way around. Another shell landed closer, and Jenkins whispered, "You kraut bastard, stay there, stay there!" The tank looked like a huge bug, twitching as it strained to get away. Another shell came over, but this one was farther off, and then two more, closer.

"How can you hit a tank from that distance?" Tex asked. "It'd be a miracle."

"Shut your face!" Jenkins said, without looking at him. He was whispering to the artillery, "Hit the bastard, hit him, *hit* him!"

But the next shell was off the target and the two after that were even farther off, and then the tank spun around, wobbled for a second, and lumbered out of sight. Two more shells went over, but it was too late. The tank was hidden now.

"God *damn!*" Jenkins said, turning back to us. He looked as if he were going to cry.

"Listen," Tex said. "Them guns have been firing since Salerno. I bet right now they got bores as smooth as a baby's bottom. You're lucky they get as close as two hundred yards to what they're aiming at."

Jenkins got into the driver's seat of the jeep and started the motor. "That tank ain't going to stick his nose out no more," he said. "We might as well get this wire laid." Tex went around behind the jeep, so that he could follow it and see that the wire didn't get tangled as it reeled out, and I got into the front seat. We drove out through the bushes and headed across the valley toward the ridge but bearing away from the part of the ridge where the tank had disappeared. "He ain't going to bother us," Jenkins said, "but there ain't no sense giving him the chance." We drove across the valley in second, Tex walking behind, paying out the wire. Once we heard the crackle of a shell going over. Jenkins slammed on the brakes and we both spilled out, but the shell kept going and we heard it hit on the other side of the ridge. When we got to the base of the ridge, Jenkins parked the car and said he'd be damned if he was going to lug that wire up a mountain; he was going to wait for the man they had sent to the artillery observation post. I offered to help them, but he said they'd better wait for him. I said I thought I'd be on my way then. I got my bedding roll and thanked them for saving my life. "Hell," Tex said. "He might have missed you." Jenkins warned me to watch out for trip wires on the way up; while they had been pinned down by the tank, they had heard some explosions on the ridge that sounded like mines, and trip wires were the favorite German method of mining a mountain. I thanked them again and started off.

There was no path up the ridge here, so I went straight up. It wasn't hard going at first; the ground was soft and I had to fight my way through bushes, but they weren't too thick. Then the soft ground ended and rocks began. They were big rocks, with thickets growing between them, and I had to hop from one to another. Even this wasn't too bad, but then the rocks ended and there was nothing but thickets, which I had to claw my way through. They were full of thistles, and after a few minutes my hands and face were bleeding. Finally I stopped and looked back. The valley was just the same, calm and green and peaceful. In the distance I could see dust on the road, which meant that trucks were moving up. Then I heard the sharp sounds of small-arms fire above me and to the right, so I headed that way. The sounds grew louder and distinguishable: the crack of a rifle and the riveting-machine burst of a German machine pistol, and then the slower, measured answer of our machine guns. I stopped to get my breath, and when I started again my legs felt very heavy. My pistol dragged at my side and the bedding roll felt as heavy as a sack of flour. But as I approached the firing, I began to feel life-size. The valley fear and sense of insignificance disappeared and I felt human, and very important. I didn't know how close I was to the top of the ridge, but that didn't matter now.

The ridge grew steeper; the rocks appeared again, and then the bushes. I ripped my way through. My uniform was soaked with sweat and my helmet bounced up and down on my head and slid over my eyes. At last I got on a trail which went uphill. The firing was very near now, but it had slackened. Alongside the path, I saw, ahead of me, three soldiers with red crosses on their arms, standing over another soldier on the ground. They paid no attention to me. When I got closer, I saw that two of them were working on the man on the ground, cutting away his uniform around a lumpy brown stain on his side. The third man was standing a little apart. He was a medical captain. I asked him where the battalion C.P. was and he pointed up the trail without speaking. I kept on the trail and began to encounter signs that there had been a fight. There was a German machine-gun emplacement dug in between two trees, the gun still pointing down the mountain, and two dead Germans lying beside the gun. Farther up, cases of German ammunition were scattered around. The trail widened. It mounted a little farther and then ran for a while along the side of the ridge, hidden from the top by an overhanging cliff. I came upon the mouth of a cave in the cliff. Two officers were sitting before it, looking at a map. One was the battalion commander, a young, tough colonel with a mustache. The other was the regimental intelligence officer, a child lieutenant who looked about eighteen when he was shaved. He was one of the people I was supposed to have gone with. When he saw me, all he said was, "You're a little late, aren't you?" I told him what had happened. "You missed all the fun," he said. "We've already chased the krauts off the hill." I asked what the shooting was, and he said it was just some isolated snipers the boys were cleaning up. "You can go on up to the top of the hill if you want," he said. "Just keep your head down."

I said I'd take a quick look and continued up the trail. There were infantrymen scattered along it, opening packages of K ration or sleeping or just sitting and smoking. None of them were talking. There were also several men lying on the ground with blankets over their faces. The path grew steeper and then dribbled out among some rocks. I started to climb up over the rocks and a voice said, "Keep your head down." A soldier was sitting behind a large rock at the top. I kept low and climbed up to him. "This is the end of the line," he said. "Unless you want your head handed to you." I dropped my bedding roll, climbed the rock, and looked over. Everything was exactly the same. There was the other side of the ridge dropping off beneath me and at the bottom was a green little valley, and then another ridge. Beyond that were more ridges, rising and falling in the same pattern. There seemed to be no end; it was like being in an airplane over a sea of clouds that stretched forever into space. It was very quiet on top of the ridge. There was no more firing and the air was warm and motionless. Then there was the sound of planes and two of our dive-bombers appeared, flying very high and fast, heading for the next ridge. When they were over it, they gunned their motors and then heeled over and went down with terrific directness in a long, plummeting dive, the motor sound lost in the screaming of the wings; and when it seemed that they would never pull out, they pulled out, and from the bottom of the planes, like droppings from a bird, the bombs fell beautifully down and hit and exploded. Then the planes flattened out and climbed and sped swiftly back toward their field.

I lay there for a while longer and then climbed down to the soldier behind the rock. "How does it look?" he asked.

"It looks familiar," I said.

# LETTER FROM LUXEMBOURG

DAVID LARDNER

*October 10, 1944*

JUST before the American Fifth Armored Division moved into the city of Luxembourg, capital of the grand duchy of the same name, a despondent German officer jumped off the Pont Adolphe, which is near the center of town, and landed in the suburbs, dying instantly. That is to say, he landed in what the citizens of Luxembourg call the suburbs, which happen to be in the middle of the city and two hundred feet below it instead of on the outskirts. They lie at the grassy bottom of the gorge formed by the rivers Alzette and Pétrusse, which meet at right angles and flow into the capital from, respectively, the north and the west. This underslung suburban district is picturesque, but it is neither wealthy nor very lively, and although the people up in the metropolis cross over it every day on one bridge or another, they are inclined to forget that it's there—at least they are, now that the Germans have gone. During the German occupation—or, rather, annexation—quite a bit of attention was focussed downward on the Alzette section of the suburbs, where the city prison stands. Every morning at eleven, the inmates, who were nearly all anti-Nazis, would come out in the yard for their exercise. The prison has a high wall, but the townspeople, by gathering above, on the ruined buttress of a castle built by a Count Siegfried in 963, were able to pick out their friends and relatives through binoculars. Now the inmates are collaborationists, whom nobody comes to look at, even with the naked eye.

This castle of Siegfried's and the fourteen miles of underground passages that reach out from beneath it are the principal scenic wonders of the city. The passages have served handily as air-raid shelters in both World Wars and could probably hold the city's whole population, which is fifty thousand. A couple of blocks from the castle are the Chamber of Deputies and the Grand Ducal Palace. The royal family, a large one, is not yet in residence again. Since a certain number of isolated Germans are still plaguing the countryside, the Grand Duchess Charlotte and five of her children—Princess Elisabeth, Princess Marie-Adélaïde, Princess Marie-Gabrielle, Prince Charles, and Princess Alix—have not returned from England. Prince Félix, who is the Prince Consort, and Crown Prince Jean came in with the Americans last month, but they have since gone elsewhere on a diplomatic mission. At the time of the liberation, the *Luxemburger Wort,* the only newspaper then being published in the city, carried a picture of Prince Félix and an American general who the caption said was Patton but who was actually Oliver of the Fifth Armored Division. The *Wort* had simply figured that since it wasn't Eisenhower it must be Patton.

The *Wort* is the paper of the Catholic Party. The Duchy is Catholic from top to bottom, but there are two non-church political parties, the Liberal and the Socialist. The *Luxemburger Zeitung,* the Liberal paper, hasn't resumed publication yet, but the Socialists, who don't seem to be any more radical than some of the French Socialists of prewar days, are once more printing the *Escher Tageblatt* down in Esch-sur-Alzette, a big steel town to the south. *Le Luxembourg,* the capital's French-language paper, will presumably be published again soon, and then the language situation around here will be the wonderful shambles it used to be. Left to itself, the Duchy is trilingual. It uses French, German, and Luxembourgeois, which is the French name that has been given to the highly Teutonic patois of the Duchy as well as to the people themselves. Both the *Zeitung* and the *Tageblatt* are German-language. The *Luxemburger Wort* prints stories in German, French, or Luxembourgeois, more or less at random. The Germans outlawed French altogether, which entailed renaming most of the streets in the city of Luxembourg. Now the old street signs are gradually going back up, and what was for four years the Adolf Hitler Strasse is once more the Avenue de la Liberté. Incidentally, the Pont Adolphe is named after Adolphe I, Grand Duke from 1890 to 1905, and nobody else.

The currency situation isn't much fun, except for the merchant class. When the Germans came in, they tossed out the Luxembourg franc, and it hasn't been restored yet. There are, however, the French franc, imported by the American soldiers, and the German mark, which the Germans left behind. We have pegged the French franc at fifty to the dollar. The Germans long ago announced, in a fit of fantasy, that the mark was worth twenty francs, which is the latest word the Luxembourg merchant has had on the subject. Consequently, for something priced at a mark he demands forty cents' worth of francs, which is murder. There has been some Allied talk of knocking the mark down to ten cents, but nothing has come of it yet.

Except at the Army messes, food is scarce in town, and so is about everything to drink, including Moselle, the wine of the Duchy. When the Germans had retreated as far as the Moselle, they paused to take revenge on the fairly effective Luxembourg resistance forces by squashing the grape crop and overturning all the barrels of Moselle they could find (and also by blowing up a few houses with the dynamite left over from bridge demolitions). The citizens have been realistic about the food shortage. The German rationing system, which seems to work as well as any, is still in force, and not only do shoppers go on surrendering the same old German coupons but natives who patronize hotels give up the same old tickets for so many grams of meat, bread, and fat when they eat a meal in the dining room. American and British guests don't have to give up tickets, but they aren't apt to get a great many grams, either. A hotel widely mentioned as the best in town is the Brasseur, which was called the Brauer when it was occupied by the German commanding officer and his staff. This is the hotel to which the returning Luxembourg cabinet officers were going for a welcome-home party last month when their automobiles were fired on by persons as yet unidentified. The Brasseur features shiny, green-tiled bathrooms and a back yard containing a chicken house and a rabbit hutch.

The Grand Duchy of Luxembourg is meant to be a buffer state, but there is no doubt that as such it was something of a bust in 1939. However, its subsequent war record is pretty good. The Ligue Patriotique de Luxembourg, or L.P.L., was formed soon after the annexation and went right to work forging papers and getting Luxembourgeois refugees into Belgium, whence they might escape to England. It was broken up in 1942, but it managed to get itself together again. By the time the American Third Army got here, the L.P.L. and several other resistance groups were combined in an organization called the Union. The Duchy wasn't exactly a moil of sabotage and guerrilla action, however; the simple fact is that there were too many Germans here—something like seventy thousand, which made them one-fifth of the total population, and even more than one-fifth after the deportation of Luxembourgeois to Germany began. That was in September, 1942, and the deportation was a reprisal for the general strike of September 10th, which in turn was a protest over the formal annexation of the Duchy to Greater Germany and over the projected conscription of Luxembourg boys of twenty to twenty-five into the German Army. Some ten thousand were conscripted and some fifty thousand of their elders were deported to work for the Reich.

It was something of an achievement on the part of the Duchy that after four and a half years of Nazi pressure it had to be only liberated and not amputated. The people spoke German and looked German, to begin with, and the Germans pointed this out to them until they could spell it backwards. School children were compelled to join the Hitler Youth Movement and boys were encouraged to go to German universities. The Germans must have felt that this country would be the easiest indoctrinating job on their schedule. At the end, though, they and the people of Luxembourg were still wrangling with each other and there were some angry words at parting. The Germans said to look out because they were coming back in a couple of weeks, and then went off to the Moselle to kick the grapes around. The Luxembourgeois went on muttering a slogan of theirs which goes, in their language, *"Letzeburg de Letzeburger"* and means "Luxembourg for you know who."

There is one young matron here in the city, though, who sounds a little discouraged about living in a grand duchy. She and her husband have Americans in for dinner sometimes and she always asks them, "Did you know this place was here before you came?"

# THE FIRES ON SAIPAN

EUGENE KINKEAD

TWO days before our troops landed on the island of Saipan, in the Marianas, the United States Navy made a rather boisterous appearance offshore. It was my good luck to be along. I was aboard one of a number of new battleships that were part of a task force, including aircraft carriers, that had been assigned by the Navy to assist in the operation. The duties of the force were to smash Saipan's defenses by bomb and shellfire, to give the soldiers air support as they landed, and to engage the Japanese fleet (assuming there is one) if it should try to interfere. On the fourth and third days before our landings, our armada, a hundred miles off Saipan's east coast, cruised up and down while carrier planes flew in and attacked the island's fortifications and airfields. Two days before the landing, the battleships, accompanied by some cruisers and a comforting screen of destroyers, parted company with the rest of the fleet and approached the island to shell it. These new battleships, as any reader of a naval manual can discover, are armed with a main battery of nine sixteen-inch guns, set three to a turret, two turrets forward of the foremast and one aft. In addition to light anti-aircraft weapons, they carry, amidships, a secondary armament of twenty five-inch rifles, which can be useful for bombarding a shore at close range. A naval bombardment is, of course, an extremely important part of an amphibious assault. Our orders that day were to destroy Saipan's larger gun emplacements, to wreck its supply depots and barracks, and to protect a fleet of minesweepers that were to clear the mined waters inshore so that our troop transports could later pass through.

It was not yet dawn as our battleships, under the command of an admiral aboard the flagship, steamed toward Saipan in formation at a speed of twenty knots. The plan was for us to circle Saipan at the north, then turn south and shell the western coast, where most of the important defense works were and where our main landings would be made. Every hatch and passageway in the ship I was on had been closed to reduce the fire hazard and to provide what the Navy calls watertight integrity. All our officers and men manned their battle stations in helmets and life belts. My own battle station—also manned in helmet and life belt—was with the captain in the conning tower. This is on the navigating bridge, where the commanding officer remains throughout an operation, eating and sleeping in quarters called his sea cabin and spending the rest of the time either at his battle station or on the open platform that runs around the conning tower. Our skipper was a lean, terse, auburn-haired fellow in his fifties, with an Irish name. Like the rest of us, he was moderately tense as we headed toward our objective. Everyone aboard had been at battle stations much of the night, during which Japanese aircraft had kept us on our feet, and we badly needed sleep. An hour before dawn, we could just see the outline of an island on our starboard bow. "Japanese-held territory," the captain said to me. "It gives me a very definite bang whenever I see it." It was the island of Anatahan, north of Saipan. We changed our course not long afterward, and the captain ordered battle stations unmanned and the ship's passageways opened. This gave the crew a chance to have breakfast. After that, they were told, over the ship's loudspeaker system, to go about their regular duties until further notice. I went below to my cabin, took off my helmet and life belt, had breakfast, and then, leaving my helmet and life belt, returned to the navigating bridge.

We caught sight of Saipan from the northwest around nine in the morning. It is twenty miles long and five and a half miles wide, and fairly hilly in the middle. As we got nearer, I looked through some binoculars I had and could see the broad, cultivated green fields on the slopes, and here and there smoke, which I presumed came from fires started by our planes. The targets for the battleships in our division lay on the water or inland along the southern half of the western shore. Among them were a number of coastal-defense batteries and some military installations in Charan-Kanoa, a town a few hundred yards back from the beach. Our ships were under orders to start firing at a distance of twelve miles at 11 A.M. The operation was divided into six one-hour phases, and during the fifth there was to be no firing. Since we were off Saipan at 9 A.M., we cruised outside the bombardment range, with the destroyers forming an anti-submarine defense around us. As for the guns on the island, even the largest would probably be unable to reach our ships at that distance. A little after nine, the crew was ordered to secure objects that might be shaken loose when we began firing. The officers, I noticed, now wore small cases, containing morphine syrettes, attached to their belts. These would come in handy if there were any long delay in getting a wounded man through the battened-down ship to a dressing station.

All significant developments aboard and around the ship were noted by our communication service and reported to the captain. Since I was standing near him, I naturally picked up considerable information. A number of our carrier planes were operating over the island, and at nine-fifteen one of them radioed a request to all ships in our neighborhood to keep a watch for one of our fliers, who had been shot down into the sea by anti-aircraft fire. The captain ordered that the lookouts be informed. A few minutes later a destroyer some miles away sent out a message that it had spotted fourteen Japanese on life rafts. They were evidently survivors of a merchantman sunk by one of our carrier planes; the water around them was full of boxes. The destroyer asked the flagship for permission to rescue the men and was told to pick them up. Shortly before ten o'clock, one of our air patrols let the ships know that there didn't seem to be a single enemy plane over the island. Our planes had presumably downed or driven off all the opposition. Shortly afterward, the lookouts on our ship reported a series of splashes in the water made by shells from enemy shore batteries. The shells were falling far short, but the firing kept up for quite some time. I asked the captain why the Japanese continued to shoot when they could see that they were not reaching us. "You know the Japanese as well as I do," he said.

At 10:20 A.M. word came over the ship's loudspeaker system to man battle stations for the bombardment. I went below to my cabin, got my life belt and helmet, and returned to the navigating bridge. Since our firing was not to start for more than half an hour, the captain didn't go at once into the conning tower but stayed outside on the platform. I stood there with him. As we steamed in closer, he studied Saipan through his binoculars. A column of smoke was rising from the island. "It's white smoke. I prefer the thick, black kind," he said. At 10:30 A.M. the catapult officer, astern, asked the captain's permission to launch two of our seaplanes. One machine was to act as spotter for our gunnery control and the other was to take over if the first was shot down. The planes were hurtled off, one after the other, circled the ship, gained altitude, and started for the island. A minute later loud hisses came from the sixteen-inch gun barrels fore and aft as compressed air was shot through them to clean the bores. Since there would be no hot midday meal aboard, the cooks had prepared hundreds of sandwiches, and a tray of them, together with a thermos bucket of water, was taken into the conning tower by an enlisted man. At 10:41 A.M. the captain was informed that all battle stations were manned and that all hatches and passageways in the ship were again closed. Shortly afterward we received a message from one of our planes that the anti-aircraft fire over the island was light and the visibility good.

At 10:53 A.M. the captain entered the conning tower, which was heavily armored, through one of a pair of electrically operated doors set in its port and starboard sides. I followed him. The interior, roughly oval in shape, had slits in the thick walls affording a good view in every direction but astern. Red bulbs supplied what little illumination there was. The room was fairly crowded. In addition to the captain and myself, there were the navigator, the communications officer, the helmsman, and a dozen other officers and men, called "talkers," who wore telephone headsets. Through these men information passed between the captain and important stations on the vessel. Any department head could reach him immediately on one of the lines. The conning tower is the brain of the battleship. An enlisted man handed the captain and me some cotton to plug our ears. It decreased but did not entirely eliminate sound, so conversation was still possible. I sat on a stool near one of the several periscopes in the tower. I found that I usually hit my head on it whenever I made a sudden move. The captain had warned me that this was one of the hazards peculiar to the conning tower. Occasionally he hit his head on a periscope himself.

At 10:56 A.M. a lookout reported a box, apparently flotsam from a sunken Jap merchantman, in the water near the ship. His intelligence was quickly followed by news of the same sort from another quarter. The captain ordered all lookouts to cease reporting boxes. Then he instructed an enlisted man to open one door in the conning tower—the one, happily, opposite the side from which we were to fire our guns—to let in more light and air. I was told that before we did any firing a salvo buzzer would go "dit dit" to prepare us for the coming explosion.

Promptly at 11 A.M. our battleship division started shelling the island, the sound of the big guns reverberating over the water with a deep boom, boom, boom. Our ship didn't join in immediately. For the first ten minutes we were assigned to counter-battery fire; that is, we were supposed to reply only to shore artillery that revealed itself by shooting at us. None did. We began to maneuver into position off our first target, Agingan Point, near Saipan's southern tip, where there was believed to be an emplacement of coast-defense guns. We were to shell it with our sixteen-inch guns. At exactly 11:10 A.M. the gunnery officer telephoned the conning tower that the range of our objective was twenty thousand yards. He said that the three guns of Turret One, on the forward deck, which was to begin our bombardment, were ready, and he asked authority to open fire, which the captain granted. The salvo buzzer went "dit dit," the guns were fired, a lemon-colored light flashed through the slits of the conning tower, and the concussion slammed against my chest. Powder fumes, smelling of hydrogen sulphide, drifted through the slits. Through an overhead loudspeaker in the conning tower the voice of our plane spotter began to come in, telling us the results of our fire. A few seconds after each salvo, from then on, he would tell us the results and give us corrections, using a code. We also got reports from the gunnery officer. As salvo followed salvo, he announced each time whether it was coming from a single turret, from one gun from each turret, or from the full main battery. I discovered that the shock of a discharge from Turret Three, astern, was mild compared with what happened when Turret One, forward, was fired. A discharge from Turret Two, right under the conning tower, or a single-gun salvo from all three mounts, was worse than either of these, and the effect of a full salvo was like being hit in the chest with a baseball bat. The captain kept an eye to his periscope, watching the shoreline. It wasn't long before our spotter ended a message with "No change. So sorry!" This meant, in the perverse code we were using, that we had made a direct hit. The captain lifted his head from the periscope and smiled. "That sounds like sleigh bells on Christmas Eve," he said. Then he quickly ordered a full salvo.

When our allotted time off Agingan Point was up, we turned our attention to our next objective, Afetna Point, which was slightly to the north. Afetna Point had some coast-defense guns and an airstrip with a hangar. We bombarded these and did quite well, according to our spotter. At 12:30 P.M. the captain asked that the sandwiches in the conning tower be passed and each of us took a couple. Peanut butter, I found, was preferable to lamb, because it went down easier under concussion. As we ate, our minesweepers, which were converted over-age destroyers, steamed into view. Through the conning-tower slits, I watched them as they began to work over the waters between us and the shore. Shortly after they appeared, the flagship signalled us to hold our fire until further notice; some planes were going over the island to unload a few bombs. The lull lasted for ten minutes. At the end of nine and a half minutes we got a testy message from our plane spotter. He said that if we were going to continue to hold our fire, would we be kind enough to let him know, so that he could leave Afetna Point, where the anti-aircraft fire was brisk. It seemed a reasonable request. We explained the circumstances, and told him that we had just received a resume-fire order and would comply with it in thirty seconds.

From 1 to 3 P.M. we bombarded, for an hour each, our third and fourth objectives. These were: first, some barracks, storehouses, and gun emplacements around the town of Charan-Kanoa and, second, the shoreline north of the town. While we were concentrating on the military installations of the town, one of our lookouts reported that three aircraft near shore off our port bow were laying a smoke screen. The captain instantly ordered our port five-inch batteries trained on the smoke, then dashed out of the conning tower. When he got outside, he must have decided that our five-inch rifles were not bearing on the smoke, for he came back in and rather heatedly ordered the talker whose line led to the gunnery department to take off his headset and hand it to him. Then he asked whoever was at the other end of the line to put the gunnery officer on. When the gunnery officer got on, the captain gave him a stiff talking-to for not having the five-inch guns trained on the smoke, and he also tossed in a few sharp words for the anti-aircraft spotters aloft in the ship, in what is called sky control, for permitting a lookout somewhere else on the ship to spot the screen first. For all anyone knew, he said, it was an enemy maneuver to conceal approaching torpedo planes and it should be so regarded until proved otherwise. "Sky control, I hope you're listening," he said. Then he handed the headset back to the talker. "The whole business was far from bright," he said, to no one in particular. Later, it was assumed that the screen had been laid down by our own planes, but we never did find out the reason for it. Within the next five minutes one of our salvos struck what was apparently a cache of inflammable supplies in a storehouse in Charan-Kanoa. Our aerial spotter, informing us of this, ended his announcement with an uncoded "Good shooting. You have started a brilliant fire." The captain turned to the gunnery talker. "Give my congratulations to the gunnery officer," he said.

At 3 P.M., according to plan, a signal was received to cease firing for an hour. Our battleship division stood away from the island and the captain ordered our two planes to return for fuelling. They landed on the water astern of the ship and were hoisted aboard by a crane, one at a time, twenty minutes later. The final phase of the bombardment was scheduled to run from 4 to 5 P.M., or until the ammunition allotted for this bombardment had been used up. It was to be devoted to "targets of opportunity," as pointed out by our planes. As soon as our pilots got aboard, they came up to the navigating bridge, where they discussed the remaining objectives with the captain and officers of the gunnery department. It was decided, after all the possibilities had been considered, to concentrate our sixteen-inch guns on a coast-defense battery, which had not yet been put out of action, on Afetna Point, and on some store-houses and barracks areas. It was also decided that we should go in close enough to let the five-inch pieces shell some trenches and machine-gun nests along the shore. These decisions were radioed to the flagship and were approved. A little before four our two planes were catapulted again and we started back toward Saipan. Our big guns opened up first. When we got close enough, the five-inchers were brought to bear. They snapped sharply, several salvos to the minute. Our plane spotters were both working now and they said we were doing well with our big and small guns. At one point, back from the beach, we started quite a fire, which gave off the thick, black smoke the captain liked. As I peered through the slits, I noticed that the destroyers, which were on our shoreward side, were shooting too; they had got near enough to the island for their guns to be effective. Occasionally, through my periscope, I could see where our sixteen-inch missiles struck on the shore, raising fountains of debris from what I hoped were military installations.

At 5 P.M. our ship and others of the force reported to the flagship that they still had ammunition, so the firing continued. At 5:10 P.M. the minesweepers signalled that they had completed their task and they steamed away. At 5:30 P.M. the flagship, after checking with all vessels, issued an order to cease fire. We called our planes home and started away from Saipan. Before long we stopped to pick up the planes, we unmanned the battle stations, and we opened the hatches. The deck divisions of our crew wet down the decks and swept up in dustpans the litter of unexploded splinters of powder, which look like pieces of yellow-green straw, that had been blown onto the decks from the muzzles of the guns. The men threw these scraps over the side. Dinner, we knew, would be a couple of hours late that night, and we were all a little groggy from concussion, but everybody was in high spirits. As our force set off to join the carriers, we could see behind us, in the dusk, a number of fires on Saipan. The men aboard our battleship had the satisfaction of knowing that they had started their share of them.

[November 18, 1944]

# LOVELY AMERICANS

ROBERT SHAPLEN

FOR nearly two and a half years the American troops in General Douglas MacArthur's Southwest Pacific Command fought in some of the world's most uncivilized territory. As they made their way along the New Guinea coast and invaded New Britain, the Admiralty Islands, Biak, Morotai, and other places with strange names, they experienced none of the satisfaction of the Allied troops in Europe, who have been marching through town after town on triumphant crusades of liberation. The only towns the men in the Pacific saw were the native *kampongs* and the only welcome they received from the not visibly overjoyed inhabitants was an unintelligible chatter. With the invasion of the Philippines, MacArthur's men finally got their reward. Ever since Bataan, as the world knew, MacArthur had had one aspiration: to return to the Islands. For him the invasion of Leyte was a personal triumph, the end of a long, complicated battle. But for the men, weary of jungles, it was something more; it was like coming out of darkness into the light.

I landed on Leyte the morning of October 20th as a correspondent attached to the Seventh Regiment of the First Cavalry Division, which was dismounted when it left the United States, soon after Pearl Harbor, with the objective, even then, of helping recapture the Philippines. Under cover of violent naval gunfire, capped by a cascade of rockets that literally tore our landing beach apart, we got ashore successfully, with less opposition than we had expected. A few bomb-happy Japanese snipers were still in the trees and a few others were still in the concrete pillboxes along the shore, but these were quickly disposed of. The snipers were picked off their perches by sharpshooters with carbines and Garands and the pillboxes were dynamited. Three divisions to the south of us, particularly the Twenty-fourth Division, on our left flank, ran into much heavier opposition. We were able to push rapidly north toward the town of Tacloban, four miles from our landing point. It turned out that the troops of the notorious Sixteenth Imperial Japanese Division, whom our division had expected to encounter in the Tacloban area, had been moved south just before the invasion. In the village of San José, some four hundred yards from where we landed, we found several Japanese automobiles, a large quantity of Japanese beer (bottled in Manila), and some new guns the enemy had not taken the time to destroy in his flight. San José was deserted. All but a few of the houses, which had been bombed for days from the air before the landing and shelled for hours from the sea that morning, were rubble, and even those that were standing looked as if they were ready to fall down. The cavalrymen didn't stay in San José very long. They pushed on toward the Barayan River, a narrow stream a little less than a mile ahead. Here the Japs had, conveniently, left a bridge intact, so the cavalry kept moving. By dusk we had reached what was supposed to be our second-day objective, a road junction a mile or so from Tacloban. Here we established a perimeter defense for the night, and here began the magnificent reception we got in the Philippines. This, it seemed to me, was what all the men had been waiting for during the long, malarial months in the jungles.

Hundreds of soldiers will always remember the white-clad figure of the Filipino who came walking toward us (running was more like it), wheeling a bicycle, at four o'clock that afternoon. It had been raining and the road was too slippery to ride on. The advance troops spied him several hundred yards ahead through the trees and held their fire when they saw him waving frantically, taking off and putting on his broad-brimmed hat again and again. As he approached, his face appeared to be composed entirely of smile. It was impossible to understand what he was saying, but it was easy to see that he was filled with an almost hysterical happiness. He grabbed the hand of every soldier he could reach and shook it ecstatically. When he had quieted down, we were able, with the help of one of the Filipino soldiers with us, to learn that his name was Isaios Budlong and that he had formerly been a telegraph operator in Tacloban. To him went the honor of being the first liberated Filipino. He had left the town that morning and made his way through whatever was left of the Japanese lines to reach us.

Having liberated Budlong, the troops began digging foxholes and setting up mortars and machine guns in preparation for a possible Jap counterattack. As they dug in, more Filipinos came running down the two roads leading to the junction. In half an hour there were a hundred of them milling around us. There were men, one of whom brought a large box of Japanese hard crackers and gave it to Lieutenant Colonel Robert P. Kirk, our squadron commander; and there were young girls, mothers carrying crying infants in their arms, and old women, their faces wrinkled, their skin hanging loosely. One old woman stood at the side of the road, her hands outstretched. Like Budlong, she reached out at the soldiers near her, but whereas his hands had darted eagerly, hers moved through the air with a gentle, swinging motion, touching a man only now and then, as a woman would fondle a piece of silk. She looked as if she were dreaming and couldn't believe her dream, and she had as beatific a smile on her worn, brown face as I have ever seen.

Most of the men and women who came toward us were in rags. After a few minutes, those of them that lived nearby ran home to change into the clothes they had been saving for the day of liberation. Before it was dark, they were back again, the girls in bright cotton dresses, the men in white or blue trousers and shirts. The young men were exuberant. They wanted, even before food—which they obviously needed badly—guns, so that they could join in the fight against the Japs. Most of them spoke English, but haltingly. A twenty-one-year-old lad named Guillermo Peñaranda asked us, "Where is our president?" We were glad to be able to tell him that President Sergio Osmeña was with General MacArthur and would be in Tacloban in a day or two. Restituta Jarohohon, a pretty twenty-year-old girl with her first child in her arms, shook hands with everyone and said, "We are very glad to meet you." The Filipinos told us that the Japanese had fled into the hills beyond Tacloban. Despite the artillery and mortar fire from the beach behind us, and the mosquitoes that swarmed into our foxholes, we slept peacefully that night.

In the morning, we went on north toward Tacloban. On the outskirts, we ran into some opposition. Two hundred Japs were well entrenched on a low hill on the southeast side. It took us three hours to clean them out with artillery and mortar fire. While we were stalled, the Filipinos once again came to us before we could get to them. A long-legged, loosely put-together figure who looked as if he had been drawn by Thomas Benton came running up the road to Colonel Walter E. Finnegan, our regimental commander, and said that he was Governor Bernardo Torres. He wore lavender pants, a yellow shirt, and a broad yellow hat. He told us that he had been the Governor of Leyte Province before the Japs came to Tacloban, in May, 1942, and that the Japs had kept him on as Governor until they had become dissatisfied with him in that job. Then they had appointed him Director of Agriculture for the Philippines and put him in charge of food production for the Visayan island group, of which Leyte is one. Torres seemed more than eager to tell us what he could about the Japs—where they were and what they had done to the civilians of the town. He said that the hated Kempeitai, the Jap military police, had had a large force in Tacloban and had maltreated the natives.

The case of Torres is a queer one and a good example of the ticklish question: when is a collaborationist not a collaborationist? Torres was so eager to tell everything he knew that he was suspect. Three days later, when Colonel Ruperto Kangleon, the guerrilla chief on Leyte, was made military governor of the island, one of his first actions was to have Torres put in jail, together with about two hundred other suspected collaborationists. Kangleon had for nearly three years led an armed revolt in the hills, and his forces had killed thirty-eight hundred Japanese soldiers since February. This was a case of a bitter, fighting opponent of the Japs showing his contempt for a man who had stayed behind and tried to compromise. Yet there may well be something to be said for Torres, and if there is, it will be said at the trial that he and others like him will get before the Philippine and American authorities.

Townspeople whose loyalty to the Americans cannot be doubted thought highly of Torres and trusted him. He got for them what little food the Japs did not steal and maintained as amicable relations as possible with an entrenched enemy through the difficult months. He was no Pétain, like the Japanese puppet Governor Pastor Salazar, but he was not a Tito, like Kangleon, either.

While we were talking to Torres in front of the command post, we could hear shots in the center of the town. From the windows of the houses, Jap sharpshooters were trying to pick off the Americans in the streets. Before the war, Tacloban was a town of eighteen thousand. It had a movie theatre, an ice plant, an athletic field, several restaurants, and a sizable business district near the wharves. The Japs had occupied practically all the business buildings and the best dwellings, and when several other correspondents and I reached the town, the remains of their paraphernalia of war were scattered everywhere.

We correspondents walked into town behind the troops and were directed to the two-story house of Mayor Vicente Quintero, a small, bespectacled man, who was looking very happy. He set up some Jap beer for us and also brought out a bottle of whiskey he said he had been saving for the great day. His home had beautiful, polished floors of narra and molave, Philippine hardwoods. Quintero has been Mayor for twelve years. "We are very glad to see you," he said. "It has been a long time. Things have been very hard under the Japanese." Until three months before, he said, most families had managed to get enough rice and *camotes,* or yams. Since then, the Japanese had pressed more and more Filipinos into the labor battalions, and there had been few left to work the fields. The Japanese had needed the additional forced labor for a series of airstrips they were feverishly building on the island. Children as young as ten, as well as old men and women, had been conscripted, Quintero told us. As we left his house, toward evening, we encountered fifty Formosans, used by the Japs as laborers, who had been taken prisoner by our forces and were being brought through town to division headquarters. They looked scared and frazzled as they stumbled by, their thin arms upraised.

That night I slept, along with many of the cavalrymen, on the floor of the Leyte Intermediate School for Girls. In the morning I walked to the market place, where there was to be a meeting of the citizens at ten o'clock. There I met young Bob Price, the son of Tacloban's most celebrated citizen, Walter Price, an American. The elder Price went to the Philippines as an infantry captain in the Spanish-American War and stayed there when the war was over, married a Filipino, and raised a family of seventeen. Price was the founder and owner of the Leyte Transportation Company, and probably the wealthiest man on the island, and he and his family lived in a luxurious concrete house that has six bathrooms. He is now a prisoner of the Japanese in Manila. Bob and his brother Joe, who were beaten and imprisoned three times—once for seventy-seven days, on a charge of working with the guerrillas—were allowed to remain in Tacloban. They both look more like Filipinos than Americans.

The ten-o'clock meeting was the principal event of the liberation of Tacloban. One purpose of the gathering was to welcome the American troops and another was to recruit native labor to work for the Philippine Civil Affairs Unit, an organization set up in Australia a year ago to control civilian affairs on the Islands when we got there. The meeting was opened by Caesar Sotto, a former Davao assemblyman and Labor Commissioner of Leyte Province, who had been forced by the Japs to recruit the workers for the airstrips. Sotto was dressed in an immaculate white suit. He mounted a platform that had been set up in the center of the market place and, in a brief speech in Visayan, introduced Saturino Gonzales, a member of the Provincial Board, who spoke in English. "The Americans have arrived to redeem us from slavery," Gonzales said. "We had to obey the Japanese to save our necks, but there was never any doubt, as you know, what our feelings were beneath. I ask you to consider now what the policies of the American government were like before the Japanese came and how they are to be compared to the Japanese administration. You will now understand the famous democratic ways of the United States."

Sotto spoke again, and a man next to me in the crowd explained that he was comparing the food policies of the Japanese and Americans as an argument to round up labor volunteers. As Sotto waved a K-ration container to emphasize his point, the crowd roared, in English, "Long live the Americans! Lovely Americans!" Mr. Sotto went on to say that ten thousand tons of rice would be brought in shortly by the Americans and that President Osmeña was already on Leyte. The rice and their president being the two things the Filipinos most wanted, this statement brought forth further cries of "Lovely Americans!"

The next speaker was Captain Abner Pickering, one of the American Civil Affairs officers. Pickering has been in the Philippines off and on for twenty-five years and before the war was in business in Manila. "My friends," he said, in English, after the applause died down, "when I landed in Leyte the day before yesterday, it was the first time in three years that I had been in the Philippines. The Japanese will never come back to Tacloban. It took us several years to get organized, to get the ships, to get the bases for us to return, but now we're here to stay. The Philippines are yours. Your Commonwealth Government will be set up under your own president, President Osmeña. We are going to see that you get food and clothing. We want you to be patient. We need labor. You will get paid for the work you do in Philippine currency and with it you will be able to buy the rice and the other products we will bring. But, by God, you'll do it as free men!" It is doubtful whether most of the audience understood everything Captain Pickering said. Whether they did or not, the important fact to them was that here, on the platform in front of them, an American was talking; that was enough. When he finished, the applause lasted several minutes.

Vicente Delacruz, ex-Governor of Leyte Province and the last speaker, touched upon more spiritual matters. "We all need to be rebaptized in our churches," he said. "The first sin was committed by Adam and Eve. The second sin was committed by Germany and Japan. When the Japanese were here, our mouths were talking for them but our hearts were one-hundred-per-cent American. For the Americans we will work not three, not four days a week but three hundred and sixty-five days a year, and we will work for nothing." Captain Pickering waved a hand in protest, but the gesture was ignored. "Lovely Americans!" the crowd shouted. "We will work, we will work!"

[December 16, 1944]

# THE NICEST FELLOWS
# YOU EVER MET

ROBERT LEWIS TAYLOR

AT BOUGAINVILLE, where I was on duty with the Navy not long ago, nearly everybody felt that the best fighters in those parts were the Fijians, who do much of our jungle scouting in the Solomons. The Fijians are tall and black and bushy-haired, and most of their time at home is spent at water sports of one kind and another. Consequently, the majority of the men are built along the lines of Johnny Weissmuller, only more rugged. The wonderful enlarged photograph that hangs in the lobby of the Grand Pacific Hotel in Suva, the Fiji capital, called "Oliva, a Fisherman of Fiji," depicts perhaps the typical Fiji male—graceful and muscular but not overdeveloped like some of our bar-bell addicts. A funny thing about the Fijians is that they are thicker than first seems apparent; they weigh more than you would think. For example, a man whose erect carriage gives an impression of slimness often turns out to weigh something like two hundred and thirty pounds, which the Japs find runs a little high for hand-to-hand fighting.

I have visited Fiji two or three times. In 1936, I was in Suva for a while and had a chance to watch the Fijians play Rugby. They generally play Rugby intramurally; that is, just among themselves. Their style of play is considered too vigorous for the English colonials there, or for anyone else, for that matter. A team from an Australian cruiser took them on one Sunday afternoon but played only one game. Owing to a brisk run on the ship's doctor, who treated about fifteen crewmen for assorted abrasions and contusions, the cruiser was tied up in port an extra four days. The Fijians don't play Rugby viciously; in fact, they play it happily and in the friendliest spirit. But they try very hard to win and they bowl over everything in their way.

The traffic policemen are one of the greatest sights of Suva. In the old days, tourists from the Matson ships would collect on the street corners and watch them, and nowadays the American troops who pass through find them a curiosity. Fiji policemen are chosen partly for their looks and physique. There is a mixture of races and some poverty in Fiji, but crime is no problem. The sunny, uninhibited policemen often have a dull time, so when an opportunity

*415*

comes to nab a felon, they sometimes forget and imagine they are playing Rugby. A half-caste, say, warmed up by native beer, may snatch a string of cat's-eye beads from a sidewalk merchant and go sprinting off down the street. With many a joyous leap and wild cry, the cops will string out in pursuit. When they catch up, as they always do, they will try to bring him down in various ways. The policeman in the lead may elect to smack him from the side with a body block. If this happens, the others may dive or jump on the pair, landing head downward or in a sitting position. Again, the leading officer may just swing his bolo, or native billy. In this case, the delinquency authorities seldom find a regeneration program necessary. The offender has learned his lesson; if he ever gets out of the hospital, he goes straight.

All the Fiji police wear a blue serge skirt, a bright-red sash, and a white blouse, and go barefoot, and the traffic cops usually provide themselves with an extra fillip, such as gold earrings or gardenias in their hair. Standing on a little podium and under a huge umbrella, they go through amazing contortions. No symphony conductor fired by the genius of Beethoven has ever risen to greater muscular heights. At the approach of a two-wheeled cart pulled by a sick donkey, a Fiji traffic cop is likely to raise his left hand slowly, palm inward, then swing his right hand up in a beautiful arc and lay his head straight back, nose pointed to the sky. The gesture presumably means "Come ahead, if your donkey can make it," but an onlooker from the Western world is apt to find himself listening for the opening strains of the "Pastoral" or "Till Eulenspiegel." The Fiji traffic cops love their work. They get equal pleasure from a Chinese rickshaw and the limousine of the governor general, and they have been known to do some of their best work on a perfectly empty street. Just practicing.

From birth, the Fijians are in and out of the jungle. They understand the tangled greenery that covers the South Pacific islands the way a New Yorker understands Times Square. Their senses are sharper than the white man's and their strength and endurance are greater. There is very little left for them to learn about the jungle. Certainly the news, a year or so ago, that they were to be "trained for jungle fighting" by the Allies must have struck them as comical, though none of them ever said so. In fact, I was recently told by a New Zealand captain stationed at the Fiji camp on Bougainville that the men there had been unfailingly deferential and kind to their white tutors. They are a people with an extraordinary sense of humor, but they have an almost pathological aversion to hurting the feelings of a friend. However, at the end of their training, which took place in the Fijis, they allowed their sense of humor a fairly free hand. The company of white soldiers who had trained them arranged to fight a mock battle with them in the bush. After dark, each side was to try to penetrate as far as possible into the other's lines. The main idea was to see how well the new Fiji scouts had learned their lessons. It turned out that they had learned them pretty well. During the night some of the white scouts worked thirty or forty feet into the Fiji lines, and figured they had the battle won, since they hadn't caught any Fijians behind *their* lines. When they came to check up at daylight, it developed that most of the Fijians had apparently spent the night in the white headquarters. They had chalked huge crosses on the tents and the furniture and had left one of the most distinct crosses on the seat of the commanding officer's trousers, which he had thrown over a chair around 4 A.M.

After the mock battle, it was felt that the Fijians were ready for the jungle. They were shipped up to Bougainville, several hundred strong, and introduced to the Japanese. At that time, as now, the Americans and New Zealanders held only a pinpoint of land on the big island. In this area we had several airstrips and from them we bombed Rabaul every day. The Japs occupied the rest of Bougainville; all around the perimeter of our small territory they were thick in the jungle, fanatically fighting to throw us out. There were times when it was touch and go with the Allied troops, who were generally outnumbered and frequently unskilled in bush warfare. The fighting on the perimeter went on continuously. In the daytime it was often limited to guerrilla-like skirmishes and sniper activity, but before dawn every morning there was always a lively exchange of artillery. For a while the booming of the big guns woke up all the aviation people, but eventually they got used to the racket and slept right through it. "Quite a morning out on the perimeter" was a common breakfast observation back during the early artillery duels. The situation, though not desperate, called for experts in jungle reconnaissance, who could sift through the enemy's lines and keep us posted on what he was up to. The Fiji scouts rose hilariously to the occasion. It seemed that they were homesick for the wildwood after their dreary ocean voyage and, besides, they had never liked Japs.

The jungle on Bougainville, and throughout the South Pacific, is a dark, unwholesome, hostile thing. Great, stifling webs of vegetation spread over the ground and crawl up the giant banyan and eucalyptus trees, forming big cones that look like green circus tents. Men unfamiliar with the jungle have burrowed fifty yards into it and been lost for a week. When airplanes crash in the jungle, even within sight of the ground units, a party of natives usually takes two or three days to find them. The planes penetrate the top layer of foliage and are swallowed up. Into this colorful natural hell the Fijians plunged with fine high spirits. Primarily they were after information, but they never neglected any stray Japs that were handy. In a very short time the enemy on Bougainville came to know the Fiji scouts and to regard them with terror. American and New Zealand troops emphatically verified this on several occasions.

Once, during my stay on Bougainville, a report came in from the perimeter that a pocket of two hundred American soldiers had been cut off. Gloom was heavy throughout the Allied camps; the men had many friends. That evening word got around that the Fijians were going out to have a look at the trouble. I walked along the road past their camp and stared through the high wire fence that surrounded it. There was no use going in, since at that time the New Zealanders in charge of the Fijians were a little reluctant to discuss them. The huge black men appeared to be in a rollicking mood, joking and laughing as they strapped on knives and made other preparations for the bush. Their assignment seemed to me particularly dismal—facing a heavily armed and numerous enemy in a cheerless jungle on a night as black as ebony—and I wondered how they could be looking forward to it so gaily. The next morning, however, when the news came in about the night's outing, their good humor seemed perfectly justified. The Americans, it appeared, had been rescued, all two hundred of them, and the Fijians were back in camp and sleeping soundly. Just how this miracle was accomplished was never announced, but later in the day I stopped the New Zealand captain I knew and asked him if there had been much trouble. "Why, yes," he replied, "the boys said they had to rough up the little bastards a bit." That was all the information I ever got out of him.

Some time after that I was quartered in a Quonset hut with an American Army photographer who had just had a singular and nerve-racking experience. He had been out in the bush for two weeks with a party of Fijians, having put in a request to take some motion pictures behind the enemy lines. Someone, he said almost bitterly, had taken him up on it. He had lost about twenty-five pounds and figured that he had aged somewhere between ten and fifteen years. It was not that the Fijians had treated him badly. On the contrary, they had been most solicitous, in their own way. But the photographer had nevertheless found the pace quite trying. His escorts carried all his photographic gear, but most of the time he had to run to stay with them. And he was always getting tangled in creepers and vines and tripping up. "They didn't seem to use any paths," he told me. "They kept disappearing into walls of stuff that a snake couldn't have got through with a bush knife." The disappearing was, in fact, one of the worst aspects of the trip, and the photographer couldn't explain it. "They must have been pulling my leg," he said over and over to me. "And yet, why would they? They were the nicest fellows you ever met. I don't understand it. We would be going along, me hardly daring to breathe—we'd run across two Jap patrols the first hour out—and all of a sudden I'd look around and I'd be alone, completely damned horribly alone, not a sign of them anywhere, no leaf stirring, no sound, nothing. I'd just stand there, thinking, 'O.K., sniper, let's have it, I'm right out in front of you and no place to go. Let's have it.' And then in a minute, all of those big black guys would be around again, and pretty soon my heart would start back up and things were all right. I don't know where they went and I don't know where they came from, but most of all I don't know why they did it. They *must* have been pulling my leg." He really seemed very concerned about it.

On the second day, the photographer said, the Fijians spotted a group of Japs in a clearing in a valley below them. He explained to them in some excitement that he wanted to take pictures, and started fitting a telescopic lens to his camera. The Fiji corporal in charge of the group gave an amiable nod; then he and his men disappeared again. It was ten minutes before the photographer was ready to shoot. When he got set up and had a look at the clearing, there were no Japs in sight. The Fijians reappeared shortly. "Where'd they go, fellows?" the photographer kept asking. "What about the patrol?" His questions seemed to amuse the scouts. "They laughed and laughed," he said to me. "Some of them slapped their knees. I began to get the general idea. There had been some misunderstanding. The Jap patrol had quit patrolling—for good."

The Fijians, the photographer told me, carried no food. They ate herbs and roots and wild fruits and vegetables. Sometimes they cooked their meal, squatting over a quick, small fire, and sometimes they didn't. The photographer lived on some field rations he had started out with, and when they gave out he tried the Fiji diet, but it disagreed with him. Their sleeping habits distressed him, too. Several times they made camp in what seemed to the photographer the middle of the most populous Jap territory. He would roll up in a blanket, feeling exposed and uneasy, and perhaps a couple of hours later he would wake up and look around. The Fijians would be missing. "Not one left," he told me. "All gone—God knows where and God knows why. And me surrounded by the Japanese South Pacific Army. It was great." On none of these occasions did he see any of them return. They were always on hand early in the morning, though, always fresh and ready to move. In camp the Fiji scouts wear khaki clothing similar to that of other jungle troops, but they cached it soon after they left on this trip and proceeded almost naked. They had their own methods of camouflage, the photographer said a little ruefully, adding, "Not that they had been getting in my way as it was." By a skillful use of berry juices and miscellaneous greenery, they were able to surpass their customary efforts to become one with the jungle. They usually did this, I gathered, when they were going to be operating within a few feet of the enemy.

The photographer took a lot of pictures of Japs in action during the two weeks. The Fijians wove back and forth behind the Jap front, counting the troops, noting what kind of equipment they had and how it was brought in, and in general taking inventory. It was the photographer's impression that his colleagues were spending their mysterious nights visiting the Jap camps. In view of what we learned from various sources later, the visits must have been lively. The Fijians had side arms, but the photographer never saw any of them fire one. The scouts apparently depended on the knives and small hardwood bludgeons they carried. Also, he thought, they must frequently have used only their hands at close quarters. "You know," he told me, "I think everybody down here feels grateful to the Fijis. Soldiers watching them come in from a mission seem to be saying to themselves, 'Fine. Nice work, boys. We wouldn't be down here if it weren't for those nasty little Japs, and a lot more of us would be alive today. We don't know what you've been up to, and we're not especially bloodthirsty, but we hope there's quite a little group of ex-supermen lying around somewhere nearby. They got better than they deserved. A nice clean death in the dark is too damn good for them.'"

Before I left Bougainville, I dropped into the Fijians' camp. The secrecy about them had been relaxed by then. Most of the scouts were sitting on the front steps of their huts, quietly talking and laughing. As soon as I got near enough for them to see that I was a lieutenant, they sprang to their feet and froze to attention. "Freeze" seems to be the only word that describes the stance they take in the presence of an officer. There is nothing in our services like it as a symbol of discipline; a Marine guard saluting a Marine general comes close. At the headquarters shack, I asked the Fiji guard on duty if the commanding officer was in. He saluted and answered promptly. He said, "Him fella go get lawnmower belong'm head." I thanked him, returned his salute, and struck out briskly down the path, headed for no place in particular. Some of the Fijians speak good English, some can't speak any, and most of them speak pidgin. I worked on the guard's reply for a while, then finally went over to the barbershop and asked for the commanding officer. He had already got a haircut and left for the perimeter.

On the way out of the camp, I stopped to talk to a Fiji sergeant. He was at least six feet five, he was wearing a skin-tight blouse and a pair of khaki shorts, and he had what appeared to be an orchid behind his left ear. I looked again; it was an orchid. "How have things been out in the bush lately?" I asked, not much impressed with my opening.

"It has been quiet of late, sir," he said, in a cultured voice.

"Not much doing, hey?" I asked.

"By and large, I should say quiet, sir," the sergeant answered.

I had a question in mind and I decided to come out with it. "I suppose you fellows have a lot of casualties out there, don't you?" I asked.

It seemed to be an ill-advised question. His attitude changed abruptly. His posture stiffened and his face took on an unmistakable look of pain.

"I'm sorry," I said. "They must be terribly high, of course."

"Sir," said the sergeant, "we have no casualties."

I muttered something polite and waited.

"We have no casualties," he repeated. "Sir, we are not seen by the enemy. It is a point of pride."

His feelings were plainly hurt. I felt very bad about it, and I have ever since.

[January 27, 1945]

# THE SUSPENDED DRAWING ROOM

S. N. BEHRMAN

TO ARRIVE in London in a Saturday twilight late in 1944, after having been away since before the war began, was to experience a sinking of the heart for which even the destruction in the suburbs, visible from the windows of the train, had not prepared me. The suburban wash, hung amply across the gaps made by the bombs in the rows of workers' houses, stirred a quick, sympathetic awareness of human adaptability, and so did the window curtains and flowerpots in the truncated dwellings that remained—the persistent, vivid, still-life ameliorations. But these things I somewhat expected, though even here there was a shocking discrepancy between what one has written off as history and what was actually still contemporary. I accepted the neat erasures in the long rows of houses, and even the vestiges of normality in the partially demolished ones. And I wondered about the displaced inhabitants of the houses that were gone. Where, on that darkening afternoon, were they warming their feet and how were they going to kill the unpromising evening?

London was something else again. Nothing in the outworks had quite suggested the lowered atmosphere in the citadel itself. It was not merely the almost deserted railway station. I had arrived late in the day, and the British government official who met me remarked casually that the first V-2s had fallen earlier. They had made deep craters, my host said, but had been far less destructive than had been anticipated. There were no instructions about how to behave if you were out walking when the V-2s came, he said, because there were no alerts. You just strolled along, daydreaming, till you were hit. The instructions about what to do when you heard the sirens for the V-1s were very simple: fall flat on your face. My host, who was going to give me a lift to Claridge's, where I was to stay, asked me if I'd mind detouring to the Savoy to drop two other visitors who had arrived on the same train. In the curved areaway of the Savoy, off the Strand, I got out for a few minutes while the others went in to register and I walked into the Strand. It was very still. For reassurance, I sought the entrance to the Savoy Grill. Sandbags were piled up against it. I peeped inside. There were a few people sitting around having tea. If, in the old days, there was a vivacious room in Europe, it was the Savoy Grill. It was the nerve center of bohemian and artistic London. I remembered

*421*

an evening there: Paderewski, Yvonne Printemps, Sacha Guitry; Chaliapin blowing kisses at large. (On the plane coming over, I had heard an anecdote about Guitry. When, recently, he arrived in a French prison for collaborationists, he was told, to cheer him up, that his first wife was there. Guitry threw up his hands. "Everything I can endure," he groaned, "but this!") That evening was millennially far away. What had made me feel that the Savoy Grill would keep up its tempo forever, I did not know, but I must have felt that, because I was so struck by the change. My Englishman came back and we resumed our drive to Claridge's. He asked about America. He had been an Oxford debater and had travelled through forty-seven of our states. He was wistful about that forty-eighth state, one of the Dakotas. He wanted me to tell him about it. As I had never been in it either, I couldn't help him much. With a careful detachment, he asked about "the election." In the ensuing eight weeks of my stay, I was to observe that no matter where a conversation started, it always ended up with speculation about the forthcoming election. I may add that I never heard a word against Dewey from any Englishman. That all came from the Americans.

Down the Strand, past the Admiralty Arch, and across Piccadilly Circus, with its boxed-up Eros, I kept my eyes—while I consoled my companion for having missed North or South Dakota—at the windows, watching the familiar streets and the people on the sidewalks. The streets, with distressing elisions, were still there, but they were subdued and very shabby, and so were the pedestrians. There was an air about the buildings and the people of being on the defensive. London, it was apparent at once, had endured unbelievably and was still enduring unbelievably. Thirty-six hours before, I had left an America simmering with the exhilaration of a boom; England was tense in the paroxysm of a death struggle. When I left New York, the end of the war was imminent—"in the bag," as people said—but here it was being fought out.

An English editor I met on the plane had told me that the day after I arrived would provide one of the biggest news stories of the war: London, for the first time in five years, was to have light. That night, however, the blackout was still to be on, and I deposited my fifty-five pounds of luggage in Claridge's and went for a walk while there was still some daylight. I made for Berkeley Square. Soldiers and sailors, English and American, were walking with their girls in a faint, intermittent drizzle. Most of the women wore no stockings. I had been seeing this all summer in New York. But the American legs were tanned and agreeable, whereas these English ones were muddy and streaked bluish and red with the cold. (A young woman later told me that she was embarrassed at having to go without stockings. "I hate the unusual," she said. As she had been going barelegged for five years, I wondered how long it took for the unusual to become the usual.) The façades of the houses leading into the square have a strangely quiet look; at a casual glance, you might think the houses were shut up for the weekend, but a closer inspection shows you that they have been shut up for longer than that. I peered in through a grimy, narrow, leaded window at the side of a fine oaken street door. Behind it was a great, obscene shambles of shattered brick and mortar and twisted iron. A huge sheet of what had been a fluted ceiling lay against a section of stairway, as if propped up on one elbow. I looked down the row. Several places in the long vista of wreckage had been cleared for the pools—for emergency use against incendiaries—which are now a common feature of the London scene. These dark, liquid oblongs, fine-meshed in the rain, reflected jagged back walls and gargoyles of contorted pipes. I remembered going out to the set in Hollywood where Leslie Howard was making the motion picture of "Berkeley Square." Those reproductions of eighteenth-century façades had not much less behind them than this one had.

I looked up. On the third story of a house on the corner, following accurately the theatrical convention of the missing fourth wall, was an exquisite, suspended drawing room: delicately tinted blue walls, molded cornices, the curved, rifted ceiling, with a beautifully shaped oval where the center chandelier had been. All but the framework of the rest of the house was gone, but there it hung, this upstairs drawing room, elegant and aloof. I thought of Henry James. Here was his Mayfair, crisply anatomized. What would he have done with this room? With what malevolent ghosts would he have peopled it? What seedlings of social casuistry would have sprouted beneath that nonexistent chandelier, simmered along those pastel walls? An acute English critic speaks of James as the harbinger of decay and says that he described the final throes of a society he knew was done with. But James did not, I am sure, anticipate quite this finale. He must have visualized a long, slow inanition— the inhabitants of these drawing rooms giving up eventually because of their inability to sustain their own attitudes, to save face before their own pretensions. Certainly he could not have anticipated such rude visitations as there have been, cutting short the tortuous inhibitions, freezing the slow molds of refinement. Inescapably the Cassandra wails of our prophets, who are fond of reminding us that our civilization, like earlier ones, may disappear, somehow become very plausible. Ordinarily, when we become aware of moral rifts, we believe we can surmount them. Here disintegration was a physical actuality.

Later, I was to have this same feeling in drawing rooms still intact. I visited an august Englishman who has had a career of the highest distinction in English public life. He took me upstairs to show me his books—some of which he had written—and then into his shrouded drawing room. The long salon was musty and denuded. He lifted a linen hood from the head of a lovely statuette of a young girl. The girl smiled ravishingly, as if in sudden relief at her unveiling. He had bought her in Spain years ago. "We cannot, of course," he said, "keep these rooms open any longer." He walked about, uncovering other precious objects. "England," he said in the standard summary, "will never be the same again." He then made a rueful acknowledgment that there would be another England, but he felt that his had vanished. Fashionable London, upper-class London, is a vast, urban Cherry Orchard.

While I was still staring up at the Jamesian drawing room, I was gradually swallowed up by darkness. Before I knew it, the suspended drawing room had disappeared, together with the framework which suspended it. Suddenly there were no buildings, no streets, no squares. There was darkness. I started back to the hotel in something of a panic, knowing that a sense of direction was not my strong point. A few taxis went by and I hailed them, because I had not yet learned that it was no use whatever to hail a taxi in a London street. I was told afterward that in a poll taken to discover what people considered the greatest hardship of the war, the blackout won hands down. I didn't wonder. This blackout was inhuman; it was too literal; it couldn't take a joke. We had had a blackout in New York that gave you a break. I remembered it, on that perilous walk back to Claridge's, as a flaming incandescence, a pillar of fire by night, a civic bonfire. Cars passed by—little points of blue light dragging darkness after them but leaving blackness behind. I made it finally, but I had aged. When I did get to Claridge's, I didn't know it for a minute—not till the doorman flashed his torch to light a guest across the sidewalk. When I got through the swinging door into the lighted lobby, I gasped with relief.

The next night was no better, or any night thereafter. The promised illumination did not come. The government didn't go through with the moderation of the blackout, nor did it make an explanation. About this there was much grumbling. Why, since the bombs that were coming over were pilotless, was the blackout necessary at all? The common explanation, that it was necessary to save fuel, did not silence the grousing, which went on all the time I was in London, as did the blackout—profound, terrifying, impenetrable. The girl at Paddington police station who made out my ration card told me that she hadn't been out in the evening in five years. She would rather stay in than face the blackout. I must say, however, that one night several weeks later the blackout yielded some compensation: for once a full moon overcame it and London lay bathed in silver. Looking back at the Palace from St. James's Street, one saw its turrets against the clear sky as they must have looked at night in the unlit centuries. A companion pointed up to the turret where King Charles had spent his last night before his execution. "He complained," my friend said, "that his feet were cold." I could understand how he felt; it was still nippy. But the walk that night was breath-taking; never had I seen London so unimaginably beautiful. The skeletons of buildings filtered the sky, the ubiquitous pools shimmered, the grayness of the London masonry took kindly to this soft light. I realized that this was the first time I had ever really seen London by moonlight.

Back in my room the first night, I rang for the floor waiter. There he was, my old friend James, flourishing a greatly abbreviated dinner card. He was in tails, as always (the waiters are the only ones left in London who dress for dinner), but he had thinned out a bit and his clothes, quite shiny and threadbare, almost hung on him. Still, he wore them with an air, and his smile of welcome was the only thing in London so far that had not changed. There wasn't much on the menu: a no-man's land of mousses and pilaffs, with nothing really definable. I ventured several choices. "I wouldn't have that, sir," James cautioned each time. Finally I ordered a chicken cutlet, which turned out to have a mealy neutrality. It inexorably filled you up, and that was all that could be said for it. I diverted my attention from it by talking to James.

"Well, James," I began, "quite a lot you've gone through in these five years!"

"Bit rough 'ere and there, sir."

"I'm sure it must have been."

"Worst was in the blitz of '40-'41, when I used to have to walk 'ome at night to Maida Vale, ducking into areaways every second, dodging shrapnel."

"Why did you have to walk?"

"Well, sir, during the worst of the blitz the buses would just draw up at the curb and stay there all night. Had to walk. Pretty thick it was some nights, coming down so fast. Why, sir, would you believe it, one night it took me an hour and a half to walk one hundred yards from this 'otel!"

I was indignant. "Why," I demanded, "wouldn't they let you sleep here, in the hotel?"

James was shocked. "Oh, sir, I wouldn't sleep in this 'otel."

"Why not, James?"

"Far too 'ot. Don't care for the central 'eating. I'm a countryman—like open air, open windows!"

Feeling terribly effete for having proposed sleeping in Claridge's, I finished my dinner quickly and said good night to James. Then I started to go to bed. While I was undressing, the sirens began—a long ululation rising in piercing crescendo. I sat down with a shoe in one hand. There was a deafening crash. A buzz bomb had fallen, and seemingly dreadfully close. I hadn't been so acutely aware, till that moment, that I was in the South of England. I looked at the thick, drawn curtains. Flying glass couldn't very well get through those. Or could it? I put out the light and quickly got under the covers.

"The next war," said a keen-minded Anglicized Hungarian at a dinner party a few nights later, "will start with someone pressing a push button in some underground electric works in Central Europe, which will send robot bombs to Detroit." It is generally agreed that London escaped complete destruction last summer by only a hair's breadth, that had the invasion not taken place when it did, the enemy installations in France would have sent across twenty-five hundred robots a day. This they were equipped to do. Even allowing for the admitted imprecision of aim, this would have meant the total extinction of the capital. "The robot is a very clever weapon," a distinguished physicist in the British Civil Service told me. "It is, of course, in the early stages of its development, but it has great possibilities." From a Mephistophelean point of view, it has done pretty well already. I arrived after the V-1s had, presumably, done their worst. They were now sporadic but always impending. And when they fell, they and the V-2s, they did something more than show their possibilities. As I was going to dinner one night in Kensington Palace Gardens, the great park flared suddenly into brilliant illumination. The trees became alive with light and dredged from my memory the awful scene in Arthur Machen's novel "The Terror." For a moment I thought it was a thunderstorm. The air shuddered, as well as the car in which I sat. With the blackness that followed there came the sound of an immense explosion. Then everything was as before, at least where I was. Nothing daunts the London chauffeur. Mine had stopped the car; now he started it again, chuckling to himself. I didn't ask him what he found funny. I arrived at dinner fifteen minutes late. "I thought," said my hostess as she rose to greet me, "that we should have to revise the dinner table." That was the only reference to the explosion. Next day the same chauffeur drove me somewhere else. The London taxi-drivers and chauffeurs know everything. Late at night, in some mysterious rendezvous, they check up on every bomb, every explosion. This man was able to give me precise information about last night's bomb. It had killed many people and destroyed or partially demolished several hundred houses.

The nonchalance about bombs is general throughout England. A lady who drives a lorry to blitzed areas told me that she is never in the least frightened, no matter what happens, while she is driving, nor does she flinch no matter what gruesome charges she has to carry. It is only when she is lying in bed at night that she is frightened, and then more at the sirens than at the explosions, because, she imagines, the former are anticipation, the latter *faits accomplis*. If you are alive to hear the explosion, you are all right. On the opening night of John Gielgud's revival of the "The Circle," there was an alert during the last act. The bedraggled and bedizened Lady Kitty was sitting down front on a sofa, admonishing the young Elizabeth to profit by her example and not run away with a married man. The sirens began. In front of the footlights a square transparency lit up to reveal the word "ALERT" in huge black letters—quite unnecessarily, it seemed to me, as the sirens were distinctly audible. Lady Kitty had been describing the shabbier social aspects of life in Monte Carlo. I half expected Yvonne Arnaud, playing Lady Kitty, to say, "My dear Elizabeth, go to the nearest shelter at once." But Lady Kitty didn't. She went on fervently imploring Elizabeth to avoid scandal. No one in the audience stirred, except to strain forward a bit to hear Yvonne Arnaud better.

William Wyler, the director of the motion picture "Mrs. Miniver," once told me that he wants to do a scene in a film of people having lunch or dinner during an alert, with the conversation proceeding completely undeflected by

the bombing. (He says that he'll shoot the scene without telling the actors anything about it and add the sound effects afterward.) In the two months I was
in England, I encountered this sort of thing five times. To get a change from
the inedible food at Claridge's, I used to go out for the inedible food at several
little restaurants I knew. One day I was lunching in one of these with Chaim
Weizmann and a number of his friends. Everybody was enchanted with the
quietly ironic utterances of this extraordinary man. An alert began, screaming
in crescendo over the very roof of the restaurant. Weizmann lifted his voice
slightly—the only time I have ever known him to lift it. The conversation
went on to its end without a reference to the alert. Not long before, a bomb
had fallen on a restaurant in this neighborhood during the lunch hour, killing
hundreds of people, but no one said a word about the incident. I never discussed an air raid with anyone in London except taxi-drivers and chauffeurs.
No one else will talk about them. Three or four lines in the papers will tell
you that several bombs fell the day before in Southern England, but that is all.
Beyond the casual remark that was made the day I arrived, the V-2s were
never spoken of. Presumably it has been different since Churchill's speech
about them.

This nonchalance has affected Americans, too. There is the story the
Lunts tell. Alfred Lunt was standing in the wings one night ready to make
his entrance in the second act of "There Shall Be No Night." The sirens
sounded, and a bomb exploded, quite close. Lynn Fontanne, who was
onstage, turned to address the young man playing her son and found him
not there. He had obeyed a conditioned reflex and run off the stage
to the doubtful shelter of his dressing room. Disregarding this, Lunt made
his entrance. His first line was to Miss Fontanne: "Darling, are you
all right?" The audience applauded when she said she was all right. "Do
you know," Lunt told me, "what Lynn's first remark to me was when we left
the stage after the curtain was down? She turned on me accusingly and said,
'That's the first time, Alfred—that's the first time in the years we've been doing this play—that's the very first time you ever read it properly!' " I remarked
that I had always suspected that the only really effective director for Lunt was
Himmler. This consoled Miss Fontanne.

The country's absorption in the war is complete, but the peculiar anomalies
of English life and English character, political and otherwise, persist. The taxi-
driver who took me to see Harold Laski knew about him. "Oh, yes, Professor
Laski," he said possessively. "I am Labour and I think we'll get in at the next
election. Clever man, Professor Laski. Churchill likes him." Laski was amused
by this when I told him, as well as by another remark I quoted to him, made
by an American when the New York *Times* carried a story that the Laski
home had been blitzed during the night. Laski, the *Times* related, had been

knocked out of bed, had fallen down several flights of stairs, and waked up. "He must be a light sleeper," said the American.

Then, on a four-hour trip to Cardiff, on a train on which there was no food, no heat, no seats, I stood in a corridor talking to a young instructor in the Home Defense. He was full of gruesome details of the work performed in London by his Home Defense volunteers, one of them a man well over seventy. "Unsparing," he said. "They work sometimes for days with no sleep at all." The most unbearable part of his work, he said, was finding the bodies of children. Only the week before, he had pulled out of the wreckage of a bombed building the body of a little girl about the same age as his own, who was, he thanked God, evacuated to Gloucester and whom he was now on his way to visit. "It isn't all unrelieved gloom, though," he said. "Sometimes funny things happen." I encouraged him to tell me a funny thing. "Well," he said, "one day we were clearing out a badly blitzed house. We found a decapitated man. We looked and looked for his head but couldn't find it. Finally we gave up. As we were carrying the torso through what used to be the garden into the van, we heard a chicken clucking. Hello, I thought, what's that chicken clucking about? There's certainly nothing left for him in the garden. We went back and followed the clucking till we found the chicken. It wasn't in the garden at all but in part of the rubble and it was clucking at the missing head." I was happy to find that there was a lighter side to this man's work.

At the station in Cardiff, I was met by Jack Jones, the novelist and playwright and the biographer of Lloyd George. Cardiff, I had been told in London, was hell even in peacetime. Jones took me to a sing in a local tabernacle. A banker in the town had organized a series of Sunday-night sings for service men. The place was packed, the mood warm and informal, and the singing, in Welsh and English, magnificent. The phenomenon of a great crowd spending the evening just singing struck me as extraordinary; in America it wouldn't occur to people to sing en masse without being paid for it. Jones walked me back to my hotel afterward. It was obvious, once we were on the street, that only a few of the American service men in the vicinity had gone to the tabernacle. The rest appeared to be walking the streets with girls, many of them almost children. The atmosphere was high-pitched, like an American college town on a football night. In the few blocks between the tabernacle and the hotel, I must have seen twenty pickups. "The girls like the American approach," said Jones. "Your boys dispense with preliminaries. Result: high illegitimacy." It was obvious that the blackout was a help. Long after I went to bed, I could hear the boys and girls tramping the streets, laughing and singing. I heard a boy teaching a Welsh girl "I Can't Give You Anything but Love, Baby." She seemed apt. I was eavesdropping on the active permutation of cultures; I could almost feel the graph of illegitimacy soaring. The process sounded gay.

During a trip to the Valleys, as the mining areas in Wales are called, Jones and I stopped at Merthyr Tydfil, his birthplace and the cradle of the Industrial

Revolution. Jones showed me the hut in which he was born. It was one of a whole block of identical huts. He pointed out, at the corner, the privy that served the entire block. Fifty yards from these dwellings is a bronze plaque commemorating the fact that from here the world's first steam locomotive made a run of twenty-seven miles. In the middle of the nineteenth century, Jones told me, Merthyr Tydfil was one of the busiest industrial cities in the world; the products of the surrounding valleys went to every part of the globe. All one can say is that the Industrial Revolution hasn't done well by its birthplace—the eroded hills, the rows of boarded-up buildings, the squalid artifacts left by succeeding generations make one wonder who got the benefits of all this. A few London mansions occupied by absentee mine owners could scarcely compensate for the scars, topographical and human, on the landscape. These hovels are the shelters of the Industrial Revolution, and they are not much better than those of the current one; they're aboveground, and that's about all you can say for them. We went through village after village with shops boarded up, their districts all mined out. The inhabitants go by bus to work in war plants some distance away. What they will do after the war, Jones didn't know. It was through one of these villages that the Duke of Windsor made a tour when he was King. As the vistas of misery opened up before him, he muttered, "Something has to be done about this." For this mutter the people are grateful to this day. The Duke is popular in the district. " 'E was done in by the 'igher-ups," a taxi-driver in Cardiff said to me. There is a decided impression, even in other parts of England, that it was not so much Mrs. Simpson as a program of social improvement, forming slowly in the Duke's conscience, that cost him his crown.

Having been in London's shelters, I can see readily why most people—at least, those who have some alternative—will take their chance on being hit rather than go into them. There are three main types: surface shelters, which look like enlarged Nissen huts; shallow shelters, which vary in size and depth and are only fairly safe; and the deep shelters, of which there are five in London. Each of the last can accommodate eight thousand people. Then, of course, there are the subways, which are still favored by many. On the concrete platforms of the stations are built tiers of steel shelves somewhat like the ones used in American railway stations for checking baggage. On them you see men, women, and small children asleep with their clothes on. As a concession to light sleepers, the trains do not run after eleven-thirty at night, but no alarm clock is needed in the early morning. One morning, while I was waiting in a station for a train, I saw a little boy rather younger than my own, who is seven, lying asleep, his arm curved up over his eyes as if to shield them from the light. The train roared in. Just as I was caught in the crowd that sucked me aboard, quite in the New York fashion, I looked back at this child. The noise of the milling crowd must have penetrated the planes of sleep; he turned abruptly, huddling himself and his blanket against the glazed brick wall behind his bunk.

When I asked why people used the subways when they could use the regular shelters, which at least didn't have trains rushing through them, I was told that the subways appeal to many simply because of their safety; several of the regular shelters—that is, the surface and shallow ones—have been hit and their occupants killed. What I found most trying in all the shelters, though for the habitués it is probably a solace, was the constant blaring, through loudspeakers, of ancient records of American popular tunes: "Whispering," "Avalon," "Blue Skies." These nostalgic idyls, dinned out in incessant fortissimo, impart an atmosphere of phantasmagoria to scenes that might otherwise be merely abysmally depressing. This public music is a wartime phenomenon; the railway stations, too, have acquired the habit of playing American, or mainlyAmerican, jazz records to speed the departing trains. The raucous evocation of the melodies of the seven fat years makes the prevailing dreariness macabre; the orchestrations of "This Side of Paradise" somehow fail in their efforts to diminish the electrified gloom of the urban foxholes.

There are children who have never known any homes but shelters. A pretty young woman sat in one of them beside her baby, which was in a pram. I asked her whether she couldn't be evacuated. She said she had been but hadn't liked the place where they had sent her. "It was the noise," she said. "The place was near a bomber command and I couldn't stand the racket of the bombers making off for France." An apple-cheeked old lady smiled cheerfully at the young woman and me. Someone asked her whether she had had dinner. "Yes," she said, "I went home and cooked it in my own kitchen." "But weren't you bombed out?" "Oh, yes," she said. "The rest of the house is gone, but Jerry didn't get the kitchen." Obviously she was proud of having put one over on Jerry.

The deep shelters are amazing. They are cities hundreds of feet underground. A companion and I timed the descent to one in the lift; it took several minutes. It is planned, after the war, to use them for stations in a projected express subway system. The interminable, brightly lit corridors curving beside the endless shelves of bunks have the antiseptic horror of the German film "Metropolis." These shelters are really safe. The one we visited has a long bar-canteen which serves cocoa, milk, and sandwiches at nominal prices. There is a fully equipped hospital with nurses and doctors in attendance. We walked miles on concrete platforms while the loudspeakers blared "Dardanella" and "Tea for Two." We went to a lower level and visited the power room, which might serve as a sizzling, violet-lit shrine to the God Dynamo. The girl in charge manipulated switches; the immense electric bulb in the heart of an intestinal coil of lighted glass tubing changed its complexion from violet to magenta to lemon. We went to the telephone control. The operator there told us that she could instantly get in communication with the four other deep shelters.

We went up again and walked around the corridors. A good-looking, very neatly dressed man of forty was sitting on a bunk beside a boy who must have been his son, about twelve and also nicely dressed. The boy's hair was brushed smooth and he looked as if he had got himself up to visit a rich aunt. I talked to the man. He said he had lost every possession he had in the world except the clothes he and his son were wearing. They had been living in this shelter for eight months. In the morning he went to his work and the boy went to school. The problem in the shelter was to get up early enough, before six-thirty, because after that hour lift service, except for the aged and crippled, stopped, and there were seven hundred stairs.

We finally left the deep shelter. My companion wanted me to see still another type of shelter. I begged off. I simply couldn't stand one more. I was aware that the people in them had been standing them for over five years.

"Perhaps," an Englishwoman in the Civil Service said to me of the shelter residents, "you would have been less shocked by what you have seen if you were familiar with the peacetime homes of these people." This, of course, is a devastating comment on the civilization the war is implacably destroying. The transfer of great populations underground has been accomplished, but its accomplishment divides your feelings when you walk the surface of the city. At the end of their day's work, the miners in Wales, emerging with blackened faces, have their cottages to look forward to for the evening, far though they may be from the idyllic interiors of the film version of "How Green Was My Valley." The Londoners submerge.

The Londoners submerge and sit and listen to the loudspeakers and huddle around the stoves and are patient. Their patience is rather appalling. Nor are they vindictive. They are humorous about "the Jerries." I had been told that the robot raids had changed all that, but I saw nothing to prove it. They have got used to the robots, too. The people I saw do not seem to comprehend that human beings have done this to them. They take it as they might a flood or an earthquake. The bitterness against the Germans is almost entirely confined to the articulate classes, and even among them many think that Vansittart is a crank with a "fixed idea." Compared to the English, we Americans are a very violent people indeed.

It is somehow a misstatement to say that the British are indomitable. It is rather that capitulation is a concept with which they are not equipped. Perhaps it is precisely because they depersonalize the enemy that the idea of a negotiated peace is also foreign to them. After all, you can't negotiate with a flood or an earthquake. The conditions of their life are stringent to an extent which we cannot imagine. For more than five years they have been underfed, underclothed, moving in a darkness lit only by bomb flashes and the venomous streaks of robot bombs. An American congressman from a Western state made a hasty trip to England. He stayed four days. He clamored to go to France, where he stayed four more. He went back to New York, bearing the nimbus of one who has stood his ground within the sound of the guns. Upon his return, he gave a statement to the press in which he said that the English were well off, that the shop windows were full of things. One wonders what would have satisfied this congressman, exactly what deprivations he would have liked to see. For myself, I can only say that a case might be made for sending over to England our civilians instead of our soldiers. The war would last longer, but so might the peace.

[March 3/10, 1945]

# THE DUGGANS OF WAPPING

MOLLIE PANTER-DOWNS

THE borough of Stepney, in London's East End, holds a record that it would probably just as soon do without, although the people who live there speak of it with a certain amount of pride. Stepney, eighteen hundred acres in all, takes in, among other districts, Wapping, Shadwell, and a bit of Limehouse, and of its thirty-five thousand houses, nearly twenty-five thousand have been hit in the bombing attacks on London. Of these, twelve thousand either have been totally destroyed or will have to be torn down. The damage is terribly evident. Sometimes only occasional houses are gone in a block, but here and there whole neighborhoods have disappeared and grass has already sprung up in the quiet clearings, so that old Stepney residents coming back after a long time away find it hard to get their bearings. The people living in the borough have got so conditioned to being bombed out that it is regarded as an unpleasant accident that might happen to anyone, not much more extraordinary than slipping on a wet pavement or falling downstairs. The Duggans, a Stepney family whom I met recently, do not think their bombing history is anything special, and it is certainly not anything special measured against the uncomfortable local average. When I asked Mr. John Duggan, who is a dustman employed by the Stepney Borough Council, to tell me how many times the several houses he has lived in since the war began had been blasted, he thought for a minute or two and then said that he didn't remember. "Little bits of blast was 'appenin' all the time," he said. "A window 'ere and a bit of plaster there—well, we didn't take no notice of it. Nobody in Wapping took no notice of it."

Mr. Duggan, his wife, and their thirteen children have lived all their lives in Wapping, which is a dockside section of Stepney. In what Londoners call "the old blitz," and in the more recent V-bomb raids, they have been bombed out three times and have had to leave two houses because of conditions caused by bombings. The most recent incident to cost them a home also seriously injured Mrs. Duggan, a woman of sixty, who is still in the hospital with head and eye injuries that may result in her losing the sight of one eye, if not both. This time, three of the Duggans' married sons, Timmy and Patsy and Joey, have divided up the homeless members of the family—several of the children

*433*

were still living with their parents—between them. Patsy is away from home, though still in England, serving as a driver with the Royal Signals, and his wife and small son Denis live in a three-room flat, facing a big warehouse, in a grimy block of old buildings. Ic was there that I went to see some of the Duggans not long ago.

Wapping is a district with a flavor of its own. Not far away is Commercial Road, one of the East End's principal arteries, where little tailors sit bent over treadle sewing-machines behind unpronounceable shop names, where cheerful fat women preside over jellied-eel-and-whelk stalls, and where shopping house-wives favor slacks, a fur coat, and elaborate, frizzy pompadours. But in Wapping the air blows salty off the river and the cranes peer over the housetops like giraffes looking out of a zoo enclosure. Here and there small eighteenth-century churches, some of them gutted by incendiary bombs, face eerie grave-yards—they make you think of illustrations for "Bleak House"—crowded with sooty tombs that are toppling drunkenly, as though the last trumpet had already sounded. Each of the several warehouses in the district scents the air with its special commodity, so you walk from spices into linseed, from linseed into tea, and so on. Mr. Duggan told me that a great number of Wapping residents are, like himself, descended from Irish emigrants who came over looking for work on the wharves so long ago that nobody remembers the date. "I was born and bred 'ere sixty years ago," he said. "But my father's family was from Cork. When I was a kid, they was all Irish in our court—the O'Sul-livans, the O'Reillys, the Hallahans, the Callahans, and a lot more beside. We're all Catholics, of course. You can go to our church, St. Patrick's, any mass you like, and you'll find it packed with men, women, and kids. Then pop over to the English church and you'll be lucky if you find a dozen. But they're all decent, Wapping people are; it don't signify where they goes to church." Mr. Duggan's pride in his neighborhood is so intense that when I spoke of some bomb damage I had noticed along the way, he said reproachfully that it was in Shadwell. "We don't 'ave nothing to do with Shadwell in Wapping," he explained. Mr. Duggan is also extremely proud of his family. "Everybody knows me in Wapping," he said. "Ask anyone you meet, and they'll say, 'What, Jack Duggan? 'Im with all the kids?' And then they'll send you up to my place. They know me partly because we've been 'ere so long and partly because I'm shelter marshal of the air-raid shelter under the Colo-nial Warehouse. All us Duggans sleep there nights, and so does all the neigh-bors. Four 'undred of them I 'ave to look after, and some of them been unluckier than we 'ave through the bombings. Father gone, or mother gone, or kids gone. Of course we've been unlucky, too, no denying it—lost our 'ouse, our furniture, and all our duds, and now my old woman in 'ospital—but we're all alive so far, thank God. I always used to say to the old woman, 'Well,' I says, 'the Jerries 'aven't been able to write off none of the Duggans yet, though they've tried. And that's all that matters,' I says."

On my first visit to the Duggans, Mr. Duggan was out making his round with his dust van. After I had toiled up the stone staircase, along which cheerful "V"s were chalked on the walls, I was asked into a small kitchen that seemed packed with people, although there were actually only four. They were presently sorted out for me into Mrs. Patsy Duggan, an amiable young woman of twenty-eight; her son, Denis, a child with a dirty face around which long corkscrew ringlets dangled; Eileen Duggan, who is twenty; and her sister Peggy, a year or two younger. There was also a friendly dog of collie tendencies called Sally. A peculiar squeaking noise came from under the kitchen table, and it turned out that it was coming from a squirming mass of nine puppies which Sally, a true Duggan, had added to the household in the already congested flat. "She don't like being left alone since the bombs," said Mrs. Patsy, whom the others called Maggie. "If she 'ears a siren, she whines dreadful. It's 'ard on dumb animals. They don't understand the same as we do."

Peggy had been doing some washing. She put away the tub and came and sat down with us. She had a beautiful Irish face, a mass of dark chestnut hair, and a nasty jagged scar running down one arm below the short sleeve of her pink-spotted blouse. "I got that from the flying bomb which got Mum," she said. The girls told me that they had been down the day before to see their mother, who had been evacuated to a hospital in Essex. "She wasn't so good this time," Peggy said sadly. " 'Er 'ead aches terrible all the time and she don't eat. 'Try to eat, Mum,' I says. 'It'll do you good.' Someone give us three eggs to take down to 'er, and I thought she might fancy them, but she lies there all the time worrying about us at 'ome. She's been used to being active all 'er life, see—she used to do office cleaning besides looking after us all—and it comes difficult to lie there all bandaged round the eyes with nothing to do but worry. She always tells us girls to 'urry along 'ome in case of a siren. She don't bother about 'erself—Mum was never one to think of 'erself."

"She didn't deserve to 'ave this 'appen to 'er, Mum didn't," said Eileen, shaking her head.

I looked around the room, which was decorated with photographs of Duggans in uniform. Eileen volunteered to list the members of the family for me. She is a handsome, sturdily built girl with a husky East End voice, and she seemed a lot more self-assured than her sister Peggy. She wore an extremely short gray pinafore dress over a flimsy white blouse, she had fixed her chestnut hair in an elaborate Hollywood style, and tiny gold earrings shaped like anchors dangled from her ears. With promptings from the two other girls, she finally got the numerous Duggans straightened out into some sort of order in my mind. "Ellen's the eldest," she said. "She's thirty-nine and married to a chap who works at one of the wharves. Then comes my brother Johnnie—he's thirty-eight and in the merchant navy. Maggie's next—not this Maggie but my sister Maggie. She's thirty-seven, married, and doing cooking for the A.R.P. people. Then there's Timmy, thirty-four, and working where they makes invasion craft. After 'im comes our Joey, thirty-two, married and living in Wisbech, and working in a garage, and then Patsy, married to Maggie 'ere."

"Patsy's thirty," said Maggie. "They 'aven't sent 'im overseas yet, thank God. 'E's coming 'ome Saturday on leave. Daddy's coming 'ome, eh, Denis?" Denis, who was exploring the coal scuttle, gave an excited yip.

"After Patsy comes—let me see, now—Teddy, isn't it?" Eileen continued. They all argued for a moment and then agreed on Teddy. " 'E's overseas in the Ambulance Corps because 'e got malaria in the Middle East and couldn't go on in the regular Army," Eileen said. "Then there's Frankie, twenty-two and working on demolition. Then me, and then Peggy. I was 'elping my boy Leslie's mother to run a teashop for all the chaps working on demolition round 'ere—plenty of that, as you may 'ave noticed. But the last bomb—the one that got us—got the teashop, too, so I'm out of work at present. My boy was killed after D Day. 'E was in the Army, see, and 'e stopped one at the battle of Falaise—one of 'is pals writes to me and tells me about it. 'E was a good boy, Leslie was." She took a photograph of a young man in uniform off a dresser and almost truculently pushed it toward me. "That's 'im," she said. After a minute, she put the photograph back and went on with her chronicle. "Peg works in a tools factory," she said, "but since our last bomb she's been 'elping Maggie at 'ome, because she's not well enough to go back yet. Sheila's seventeen, and she works packing tea—that's a photo of *er* boy there, 'im in the sailor's uniform. Maureen's fifteen, and she nails up packing cases in the pepper-and-spice warehouse. It's a regular boy's job, which suits 'er to a T. She's so 'andy in a barge, the boatmen round 'ere call 'er Wapping's Grace Darling. After we was bombed out last, we went round to the W.V.S. to get some clothes, because we 'ad nothing but what we stood up in. 'Now a dress for Maureen,' says the lady there. 'Dress!' 'ollers Maureen. 'I don't want no dress! Gimme some trousers, can't you?' 'I'm afraid we 'ave no ladies' trousers,' says the lady, so Maureen says, 'Give us a pair of men's, then.' So they give 'er a pair and Maureen was pleased as Punch."

Peggy chipped in to say that Terry, aged eight, completed the rota of the Duggan family. Terry is also something of a local character; he established an impressive record as an infant weight-lifter by picking up three-quarters of a hundredweight at the age of five before an admiring audience at Mr. Duggan's social club. After the bomb demolished the Duggans' last house, Terry was evacuated to the home of his married brother Joey. " 'E didn't want to go," Peggy said. "Terry's all for Mum, see, and 'e wanted to stay with us and go down and see 'er in 'ospital when we did. But we're too much of a crowd since we split up, so 'e 'ad to go. Me and Eileen and Sheila and Dad live 'ere with Maggie—leastways, we live 'ere all day and sleep nights in the shelter." Maggie, who apparently didn't feel that this arrangement was a strain on her hospitality, nodded and smiled. "Maureen and Frankie are staying with my brother Timmy," Peggy went on. " 'Is wife's away being confined, so one of my married sisters does their cooking. They're a big crowd there, with Timmy's kids. They live just round the corner. Our family all stick round in Wapping."

When the war broke out, the Duggans were living in an eight-room house, No. 45 Hermitage Wall. They have lived at various numbers in that street for thirty-five years. "The only time we ever moved away is to Sampson Street, just round the corner," said Eileen. "We're a proper 'Ermitage Wall family. I don't know why they call it that. Perhaps there was a wall there ever such a long time ago. Anyway, there we was when the war comes. Peggy and me were only kids at school then, and lots of the boys 'adn't married yet, so we was a monstrous great bunch at 'ome. The cooking and the washing and the mending Mum 'ad to do! Honest, it was like a regiment, and as though it wasn't enough, she goes and adopts a friend of one of my brothers, called Billy, because 'e didn't 'ave no family of 'is own. 'One more or less won't make no difference,' she says, so Billy moves in with us. 'E's in the Army now, and 'e thinks the world of Mum. 'E wasn't 'alf upset when 'e heard what 'ad 'appened to her. All the neighborhood boys used to pop in and tell Mother Duggan about it if they was in trouble. When the blitz started, and we used to go to the shelter under Watson's Warehouse every night, they used to call the shelter Mother Duggan's Cabin."

Maggie handed round cups of very strong sweet tea and Eileen produced a package of cigarettes. "Before we come up out of Watson's in the mornings, one of the boys would always make us a cup of tea," Eileen said. "They'd kid us, after we'd drunk it, that they'd stirred it up with the broom 'andle, but it tasted lovely. The nights was awful in 1940, because the Jerries was trying to knock out the poor old East End because of the docks being so important, see. My brother Patsy wasn't in the Army then; 'e was at 'ome, working down at the docks, and 'e got together a bunch of the boys round 'Ermitage Wall and started training them for fire spotting. They was all ages, from nineteen to thirteen—all boys except Maureen, and they let 'er in because she's always round with their gang, and as nippy as any of them. They called themselves the Dead End Kids, and pretty soon they wasn't only spotting fires, they was fighting them. When the Jerries really made it 'ot for us, there was more fires than the proper fire services could put out, so the Dead End Kids often saved the 'ole of Wapping from going up in cinders. They clubbed together and bought 'atchets and 'oses, and the A.R.P. people give them tin 'ats, and when an incendiary drops anywhere in our district, off they go to it with all their fireman's stuff piled up on a barrow—an ordinary coster's barrow, it was. Patsy drilled and drilled them, and they wasn't afraid of nothing, those kids wasn't. All of us in 'Ermitage Wall who used to go down into Watson's shelter every night, we felt as 'appy as kings and safe as 'ouses, though there was nothing but a couple of flimsy floors over us, if we'd only thought. But we 'ad confidence in my brother Patsy and the Dead End Kids. Oh, they was good boys, they was. My boy Leslie, the one that was killed, 'e was one of them. They kept the shelter wonderful—fixed it up with little green curtains for the cubicles, and we called them all different West End names. One was No. 10 Downing Street, and we 'ad the Ritz and the Dorchester and all the toff restaurant names. Oh, we was 'appy down in old Watson's! Even people who were snobby and wouldn't 'ave smiled at you and said 'Cheerio' if you met them in the street warmed up when they got down there."

At Christmas time, in 1940, Patsy and his Dead End Kids decided that since they had to spend the holiday in the shelter, they'd give Watson's a Christmas to remember. They bought a big tree and everyone in the neighborhood gave something toward presents and refreshments. For two or three nights before the twenty-fifth, the boys worked down in the shelter fixing up electric fairy lights, and they blew the fuses of the shelter lights now and then, so everybody had to grope about with torches. They kept the tree carefully covered with sacking so that the children shouldn't see it beforehand, but on the twenty-fourth someone wobbling in late from a seasonable evening in the pubs kicked it over and ecstatic squeals came from the bunks where the kids were lying wide awake with excitement. On Christmas Day, Maggie Duggan, who is a fine cook, finished making the jellies and blancmanges for the party, and the spread, Eileen said, was fixed up a treat. "All the kids come up three times for presents," she said. "Everyone said it was the best Christmas they ever 'ad, Jerries or no Jerries. And the Jerries never come over that night—they left us in peace and quiet for once, the blighters."

As soon as the season of peace and good will was officially over, the Luftwaffe resumed operations in businesslike fashion. By the spring of 1941, the Duggan family was having plenty of noisy nights down in Watson's, and the Dead End Kids were having plenty of dangerous ones up on top. Two of the Kids, Ronnie Ayres and Bert Eden, were killed during the raids while tackling blazes with the gang. On May 10th, a date most Londoners remember uncomfortably well, Stepney had one of the worst nights of the blitz. The ack-ack was deafening, and the bombers, droning above the cones made by the searchlights, unloaded seemingly endless packets of high explosives and incendiaries. Patsy and his squad, black with grime, were hampered by a water shortage. Several times they had to stand by helplessly while a building burned down. In the middle of the night, one of the boys burst into Watson's yelling, "Get out! The shelter's on fire!" Everybody, down to the smallest kid, trooped out as quiet as you please, Eileen remembered. "We felt that my brother and the boys would look after us," she said. "When we got out, you never saw such a sight in your life. Fires! It was ever so pretty, really, just like fairyland, but the boys wouldn't let us stop to gape at it. They 'ustled us along to other shelters, leaving poor old Watson's burning. They come back after they'd settled us, and 'elped get the fire out, but by that time it was morning, and they was so tired that they went down into the shelter and just dropped into their bunks and slept so sound that it would take a raft of Jerries to wake them. They didn't care if the warehouse was still smoldering on top of them or not. There was a lot of 'orses screaming in a burning warehouse. Some of the bridges were on fire, and they 'ad to take people away up the river in barges. All us family got separated in the scrum—they'd found room for some of us in one shelter and some in another, see. Coo, what a night! When we all got together again in the morning, you never see such a mess. Most of the neighborhood 'ad copped it one way or another, and our 'ouse was one of the ones which 'ad."

A high-explosive bomb had landed not far from the Duggans' house, beside a burning building that six firemen were trying to save. The firemen simply disappeared. The Duggans' place, while not completely flat, was temporarily uninhabitable, with holes in its roof, windows out, doors off, and ceilings sagging. Most of their furniture was all right, but it was covered with dust and plaster. The blast had broken lots of stuff like the china and some curtains had been ruined. Some of the family's clothes had been messed up, too. The Duggans, after looking the wreckage over, went to the local rest center to have the cup of tea that inevitably accompanies British disasters and to get their wind while they decided what to do next. The morning after a district has had a bad raid, all the relief organizations start functioning. The rest center's main job is implied by its name: bombed-out persons are invited to take a hot bath, handed clean nightwear, and given a comfortable bunk in which they can sleep until their nervous systems have recovered from the shock sufficiently for them to see about finding a billet, salvaging their belongings, and so on. This usually takes a day. The next step is to go to the administrative center, in the town hall. The billeting officer and the salvage officer are there, aided by the hard-working ladies of the W.V.S. and the Citizens' Advice Bureau, who hand out clothes (lots of them are gifts from America), arrange for issues of bedding and pots and pans, provide transportation for families who are going to billets in the country, and supply emergency identity cards and ration books to replace those lost in the raid. The officers of the Assistance Board are also there, to dole out cash to anybody who has lost his home and clothing. This money is really an advance on the compensation, to be fixed by the district valuer, which will be paid to the bombed-out householder at the end of the war.

The Duggans didn't spend much time at the rest center. "Dad went round to the Assistance Board and they give 'im twelve pounds," Eileen said. "Six pounds for furniture and six for the clothes we'd lost. They fixed up for our stuff to be carted off and stored free—they always do that if you're bombed out. Of course, they didn't do that for quite a bit—they 'ad their 'ands full in Stepney just then, I can tell you." I asked if the family had got any free clothes from the W.V.S. to replace what they had lost, and Eileen said they hadn't.

I began to suspect what was later confirmed by an official who supplied me with some facts on the Stepney bombings. "The Wapping bunch are as independent as the devil," the official said with a blend of pride, affection, and despair. "It's often quite a job to get them to come and apply for the relief they're entitled to." Eileen said that they hadn't tried to get themselves fixed up with temporary billets, either. They liked being together and they had no intention of being split up if they could help it. For the next few weeks they spent their nights in another shelter and their days leading what sounded like a hideously uncomfortable camping-out existence in their damaged home. The raid had cut off the gas, electricity, and water, but the boys built a little brick oven in the back yard and Mrs. Duggan cooked for the family there.

"There was plenty of communal kitchens and such like going," said Eileen, "but my dad don't like that kind of thing, so Mum cooks in the open like we were 'opping. Every summer before the war, we all used to go off and make a bit of extra cash 'op-picking near Canterbury. Oh, it was lovely there! So we were used to roughing it, you might say, and would you believe it, the very first morning after the bomb got us, we found the leg of mutton we'd been going to 'ave for dinner. 'Alf a ceiling 'ad fallen on it, but it was good as new and only a little gritty like. 'Bit of luck,' Mum says, and she turns to and cooks it for our dinner just as she'd planned. A little while later, a couple of the boys found a cake Mum had baked, and they just dusted it off and eat it on the quiet. They always did love Mother Duggan's cakes."

The girls laughed. Viewed from a distance, what happened after their first bombing-out apparently seemed as cheerful as a prolonged hopping party. The worst part, they agreed, was being without water in the house, for the air was never free of smoke from the fires and dust from the demolitions. However, the borough authorities sent around a water cart every day, and the Duggans, with the rest of Hermitage Wall, would run out with their buckets and jugs. Eileen said that they were black most of the time, though. Stepney suffered terrible damage in that raid, and it was obviously better to look about for a new house than to wait for the harassed authorities to get around to repairing the old one. In July, Mr. Duggan found a house, No. 7 Sampson Street, to which the family moved its furniture, new dishes, and new curtains. They had been there only a couple of months when the ceilings, weakened by the bombings, fell, and they moved again. Their belongings weren't damaged that time—only dusty. Their next house, which was No. 24, back in Hermitage Wall, wasn't entirely satisfactory, either. "Smells," said Peggy. She explained that something, probably because of the bombs, had gone wrong with the drainage system. None of the family was sorry when they moved to another and less fragrant address in Hermitage Wall early in 1942.

In the next couple of years, the Duggan family began to split up. Several of the older children married and set up homes of their own. Patsy, along with other Dead End Kids, went into the Army. Eileen deserted Wapping for a brief spell in the Women's Land Army, and the little gold anchors jigged violently on her ears as she described the curious attitude of the farmer for whom she went to work. " 'You cockneys don't know nothing about the war,' 'e'd say to us," Eileen told me. " 'I'd like old 'Itler to come and learn you a thing or two,' 'e'd say, and 'im sleeping in 'is nice warm bed all those nights us cockneys 'ad been sleeping down in the shelters. So I wasn't really sorry, though I liked the work, when I chucked it and come back to Wapping and took the job in the teashop I was telling you about."

The raids slackened, started up again, and finally slackened to the point where the Duggans didn't bother to go and sleep in the shelter. They got to believe that the Jerries wouldn't be able to put on any more blitzes. In the summer of 1944, when they were as confident about that as most other Londoners, they had come to rest in No. 37, their last address in Hermitage Wall. It was over a pub, the Old Sugar Loaf, which was something of a landmark in Wapping. "Dad used to say, 'Why don't you take the doors off their 'inges and 'ave done with it?' " said Eileen. "For some one of us was always tramp, tramping upstairs and slamming those old doors until you'd think the place would come down on your ears—us Duggans, or else Peggy's boy, or Sheila's boy, or one of the tough kids our Maureen larks around with. We'd settled in real cozy over the Old Sugar Loaf when the Jerries started sending over those doodlebugs, and back we 'ad to go to the shelter nights. Only not old Watson's, of course. We all started going under the Colonial Warehouse, where my Dad is shelter marshal now."

Peggy took up the story from there. She told it very quietly, and she laughed several times, but nevertheless she seemed edgy. On the evening of July 8th, she said, they were blasted out by a robot that fell on an A.R.P. post in the street next to Hermitage Wall, killing seven A.R.P. workers and a man who happened to be passing. "It was ten in the evening when the doodle come down, and there was nobody but me and my brother Joey and Mum in the 'ouse," she said. "Dad 'ad gone off on duty fire watching, and Eileen was visiting 'er boy's mother. The rest 'ad gone off to the shelter. I'd been saying for a long time to Mum that I'd give the rooms a lick of paint when I 'ad the time from the factory, because what with all the shakings the place 'ad taken in the last few years, it looked terrible. So I bought a tin of green paint, and I thought I'd start on one of the bedrooms, freshening up the doors and the skirting and that. It was a lovely bright green, a sort of emerald. Someone was in visiting us when I brought it back, and they says, 'Green's unlucky.' 'Not for us—we're Irish,' says Mum. My brother Joey came round that evening, and 'e says 'e'll 'elp me, so we set at it and kept on painting long after the others 'ad gone to the shelter. It was ten by the time we finished, and the siren 'ad gone, but we didn't take no notice. They was always going with those doodlebugs coming over all the blessed day and night, and then you might not even 'ear the doodlebug—it might crash miles and miles away. Mum was still in the 'ouse with us. She was in the kitchen, shelling peas for tomorrow's dinner—she always likes to be a day ahead with the work, Mum does. Well, we finished the painting and it looked smashing. I could 'ear a doodlebug somewhere, but I didn't bother. My mind was on the painting, see. 'Come and look, Mum,' I calls to 'er, joking. 'It may be your last chance.' After that, I don't remember what 'appens, except that the ceiling comes down on me and Joey and all that lovely new paint. I was sitting on the floor with all the plaster and stuff over my legs, and I suppose they felt a bit numb, because I got it into my 'ead that they'd been blown off, and I began yelling, 'My legs is gone! Bring 'em back! Bring 'em back!' Joey'd been standing by a jug full of water, which of course breaks and soaks 'is legs and backside, so 'e imagines that 'is backside's gone and the water trickling down is the blood. 'E was white as a sheet, 'olding 'imself and not daring to look. I suppose we were both a bit dazed. Mum was all right, thank God, but the place looked as though it 'ad been 'it by a tank—all the tiles gone off the roof, and glass and plaster everywhere. When I saw all that smashing green paint covered with muck, I burst out crying. We'd cleaned all the windows the day before. They'd been looking a treat, and now they wasn't there. Dad didn't know our place 'ad caught it until 'e come 'ome next morning, though 'e'd been worrying that a doodle 'ad come down near 'Ermitage Wall."

The A.R.P. post the robot had landed on was next door to the Old Sugar Loaf's rival pub. Patsy Duggan, who was back on leave, was playing the piano there while a few soldiers and sailors and dockers danced with their girls. Maggie, his wife, was there with him. Patsy was playing a tune called "It Can't Be Wrong, It Must Be Right" when the doodlebug came down, and the air was immediately full of suffocating fumes, thick gray dust, and murderous slivers of glass.

"Patsy was all right," Maggie said, taking up the story. " 'E jumped out of the wreckage through one of the window frames and began 'elping to get the people out. There was an awful lot of casualties. At first I thought everybody in the place was dead but me—I see these gray shapes lying about—but then they began to get up, looking like ghosts. They was covered in dust so that you couldn't 'ave recognized your own mother. Women came rushing out of the 'ouses which 'adn't been badly 'it, tearing up sheets and their own clothes and anything which comes 'andy for bandages. Our Eileen 'ere, she sees a man with his nose covered with blood and she sticks a great bit of plaster across it. But 'e takes it off a couple of days later and finds that there's nothing on 'is nose but a patch of dried blood, what 'ad splashed up on 'im from one of the real casualties, and there's our Eileen sticking the poor fellow up with a plaster as big as a mustard poultice."

"The warehouse where Maureen works, packing spices and pepper, got it too," Eileen said. "Pepper was blowing round like one of them sandstorms in the movies. The neighborhood smelt like a blooming Christmas pudding. Sheila'd been in the pub too, 'aving a drink with 'er boy, who's a sailor. 'E was just back on leave, and 'e was saying to Sheila that 'e 'adn't 'eard one of these flying bombs yet. You know 'ow natty sailors always are, so clean-looking and all, and Sheila's boy is a blond, too. After the doodle comes down, 'e looks like an African sweep. When 'e comes round to see what 'e could do to 'elp at our place, Mum says, 'Oo are you?' Come to that, we all looked awful, with faces as black as your 'at, and anyway we'd been black round the eyes already through not 'aving slept much the last few nights. Honest, we 'ad to laugh, though there wasn't much to laugh about, with our place messed up again and nowhere to lay our 'eads that wasn't glass and muck except the shelter."

Sheila had to go to the hospital to be treated for shock, and Peggy and the others were cut, bruised, and badly shaken. "But we're lucky compared with some," said Peggy. "We're all alive, not like others in our street. The bomb that got the Old Sugar Loaf 'ouse after we moved back into it was the nearest, but even that didn't kill us, though it got Mum so bad. I don't know why it 'ad to 'appen to 'er instead of one of us young ones."

Down in the street, the motor of a lorry outside one of the warehouses started up with a roar, and Peggy stiffened convulsively in her chair. "It's only a lorry, Peg," said her sister-in-law. Peggy relaxed, laughing a bit self-consciously. "Ever since our last bomb, bangs make me jump," she said. "It makes you feel stupid."

The second time I called on the Duggans, the father, John Duggan, a short, stocky, pugnacious-looking man of sixty, was home having his midday dinner. As he and I talked, you could hear tugs on the river going wham-wham and the sound of hammers in a wrecked building some workmen were demolishing. There were workmen in the Patsy Duggan flat, too, while I was there. The bombings must have loosened a lot of the chimneys in Wapping. At any rate, quite a nice little fire had started the evening before in the ceiling above the kitchen range and done a sizable amount of damage before it was discovered. The family had had to contract their already cramped living quarters to one bedroom, and with Sally, the Patsy Duggans' bitch, and her nine puppies crammed into a box in one corner, the general effect was somewhat jumbled. Mr. Duggan, however, was calm about it. "That's nothing," he said. "We don't take no notice of that sort of thing." Just then his daughter-in-law set a vast plate of meat stew and Brussels sprouts on the oilcloth-covered table before him and he began to eat. He was dressed in a dustman's uniform, and he said, "I'm not very fresh. Some of the stuff we 'ave to 'andle on this job don't leave you very fresh *or* nice. But you'd be surprised if you saw the swill after it's gone through the factory—it comes out like a clean green powder, so they tell me. No," he went on, jerking his head toward the hammerings in the kitchen, "after you had your place and things messed up three times from bombings, this sort of thing seems a flea bite, you might say. I wish you'd been to see us when I was in my own place. It wasn't like this. *This* isn't my style at all." He waved his hand disparagingly at the furniture, which was sparse and somewhat shabby. His daughter-in-law, who had fetched two more plates of stew for herself and Denis, didn't seem to resent the remark. "*My* things were very different," Mr. Duggan observed gloomily. "Solid ma'ogany, most of it, stuff you couldn't get today. It took me and two of my sons to lift the back of my sideboard in place. I wish you'd seen us of a Sunday dinner before the war. It was worth seeing, I can tell you. My old lady at the top, dishing out the grub, me at the other end, and all the sons and daughters round. It would 'ave put you in mind of one of those paintings of the Last Supper. Now it's all gone, and I don't suppose I'll ever get it back as it was. But I don't worry about that. I worry about getting us all together again and the old woman out of 'ospital."

When a salvage squad got around to fishing out the Duggans' furniture after the first bombing of the Old Sugar Loaf house, in July, most of it was found to be in fairly good shape. "Though it wasn't what it 'ad been, naturally," Mr. Duggan said. "It don't improve stuff to 'ave ceilings come down on it and 'undreds of little bits of window glass whirling in the air. The curtains was cut to ribbons. You never seen such a mess. I'd been fire watching that night, and when I come in, what an 'ome to get back to! But the old woman kept saying, 'We're safe and sound, thank God, and what's furniture?' My solid-ma'ogany sideboard was bust up too. Oh, a proper mess! *Oh,* yes!"

A couple of days afterward, Mrs. Duggan went to the Assistance Board to put in a claim at the administrative center, for a cash grant and coupons to replace their damaged clothing. The Assistance Board came across with sixteen pounds in cash and a hundred and sixty coupons to replace the clothes and the curtains. (The blackout makes the last item a particularly urgent part of refurnishing.) Later, Eileen, who had lost the most, was given another six pounds and sixty more coupons. They could all have been fitted out free from top to toe by the W.V.S., but they preferred not to be. Wapping is actually an island, connected by two bridges with the mainland, and its residents appear to have the islander's characteristic qualities of pride and somewhat thorny independence. In the course of the conversation, I said something about the big dock fire one night in 1941, when, I had been told, people had had to be evacuated up the river by barge. Mr. Duggan put down his knife and fork and looked at me belligerently. "Not Wapping people," he said. "Don't get the idea that it was anybody from Wapping. You wouldn't catch Wapping people being pushed into no boats and carted off like a lot of cattle. They wouldn't stand for it. *Oh,* no!"

Peggy and Sheila had come in while we were talking. Sheila, dressed in the shirt and slacks she wore in the tea warehouse, supplied another reason the girls had preferred to buy new clothes themselves rather than take a handout.

"At the relief place they give you combinations which come right down to 'ere," she said with a giggle, indicating her elbows and her calves. Both girls got themselves plates of dinner from the kitchen and sat down at the table.

I said that I didn't see how the cash grant covered what they had lost in the July incident, and Mr. Duggan said testily that it didn't. "My old lady sees to that sort of thing," he said. "I leave it all to 'er. She gets coupons and some money for the girls' clothes, and I bought some new stuff out of my own pocket. The old woman says that all that matters is to get the roof on and all of us back sitting round the same table again, and that's 'ow I feel about it. I don't want to be give anything. But I goes along to the Borough and asks them to patch up the 'ouse as quick as they could. The Borough knows me well, as well they ought to. I've worked for 'em in this line of business for thirty years, and I've lived in Wapping sixty years. So they gets the ceilings patched up, and the tiles and windows put in again, and we move back in. This time, I thought, the Jerries will 'ave 'ad enough of bombing Jack Duggan and 'is kids. But it seems I was wrong. Peggy will tell you about the third time we got it, because a funny thing—I 'appened to be on fire watch again that night, too. The first I 'ear is when one of my pals grabs me and says, 'Jack, your place is 'it, and your old woman and kids took to 'ospital.'"

Maggie got up and fetched us all cups of tea. She put her father-in-law's down before him without a word, and he picked it up in silence. Denis, who apparently regarded Mr. Duggan with awe, alternately pushed Brussels sprouts into his mouth with his knife and stared with round, fascinated blue eyes at his grandfather. I asked Peggy if she would mind telling me about that last bombing out. Her voice was soft and Irish, in spite of the local accent that flavored it, and she told the story gently and sometimes rather humorously, which seemed to make it all much worse. The second robot to come the Duggans' way glided in one evening not many weeks after the family had moved home again; the exact date cannot be given. "We didn't 'ear it coming," Peggy said, "though we knew that the warning 'ad gone. Maybe it glided in for miles and miles. If I 'ad 'eard it, I'd 'ave got down under the table—since our first, I wasn't feeling so brave about doodles. But I'll tell you a queer thing. I'd a feeling we were going to get something that night. You know 'ow you get feelings, and you think it's silly, but it keeps on? The others were out, everybody except me and Mum and Terry, my little brother. Some of 'em 'ad gone to the pictures. We liked to get Mum to the shelter early, see—we'd take 'er there, fix 'er up with a bit of something to eat and a cup of tea, then us girls would nip back 'ome and clear up. Well, that evening I kept on saying to Mum, 'Do go over to the shelter, Mum. Go on, do—I can finish up.' 'All right, I'm going in a minute,' she says, but she didn't, and suddenly down it come."

Peggy took a deep breath. "This one was nearer than our last. It was right at the back of the 'ouse. You could chuck a stone into the crater from our

windows. That is, if there were still any windows to chuck it from. I don't
remember 'earing any bang. When they're as close as that to you, you don't.
I don't remember clearly what 'appened, either, except that I was sort of
knocked across the room and everything collapsed in dust and splinters and
bits of glass. The blast went rushing through the place, hot and sucking the
insides right out of you. I thought, 'My stomach's clean gone—I'm dead.'
What saves me is knowing that I'd got our mum there, see, and I couldn't
give up until I see what's 'appened to 'er; otherwise maybe I'd 'ave fainted.
My mouth was full of dust, and everything seemed so quiet, except for the
ringing in my 'ead. I suppose I was sort of knocked out. Well, I got the dust
out of my throat, and I calls, 'ardly daring to ask, 'Are you there, Mum?'
Thank God, she calls back, 'Yes, Peg.' 'Are you bleeding, Mum?' I says. I
knew I'd been 'it myself, because I could feel the blood running down my back,
and my shoulder and arm felt so queer—like they 'ad 'ot pins and needles
stuck in them. 'Yes, I'm bleeding,' she says. But she's full of pluck. 'Don't
bother about me,' she says. 'Where's Terry?' What 'ad 'appened was, the bomb
'ad blown the great 'eavy stone coping off the big warehouse out back of our
'ouse, and a bit 'ad come busting through the air and through the wall, easy as
though it was cheese, and caught Mum on the 'ead. Thank God she'd been
turned away talking to me, for if it 'ad caught 'er sideways, she'd 'ave lost both
eyes for sure. She was torn open, and the blood pouring down 'er eyes, but I
didn't know it then. I began calling, 'Terry! Are you all right, Terry?,' and I
'eard 'im saying, 'I'm all right, Peg.' 'We've got to get out of 'ere,' I says.

"The light 'ad gone out when the bomb fell, so I 'ad to feel my way round,
but I could tell that the place was smashed up and no mistake. The 'ouse
seemed to 'ave sort of settled sideways, with all the 'ouses in the row up against
it like a pack of cards, but of course I couldn't see that until the men came
and got me out. All I could think was that we must get down to the next floor
—we was up on the top, see. I crawled along to Mum, with Terry behind me.
'E didn't make no fuss—'e was a good boy, 'e was. I found a box of matches,
by a bit of luck, in the mess in our kitchen, and when I struck one, I could
see that Mum was bad. 'Try not to pass out yet, Mum,' I says, because if
she did I couldn't think 'ow I was going to get 'er out. 'I won't,' she says. But
I think she must 'ave, a bit later. We got down to the next floor somehow,
crawling and dragging Mum over the great lumps of stuff that was lying
everywhere. The stairs was cracking, and I was praying they wouldn't go in,
and after the first floor I see that they'd disappeared altogether. Our dog was
with us—a lovely big Alsatian. One of my brothers 'as 'im now. I was wearing
slacks, and 'e kept on whining and putting 'is paw in my pocket as though 'e
was saying, like a 'uman, 'Don't forget I'm with you, don't forget to get me
out of this, too.' And when they did get that dog out, you'd 'ave laughed—'e
streaked off round the corner and dived down into the air-raid shelter like a
mad thing.

"Well, I got to the window, or what 'ad been the window—it was just an 'ole in the wall now. I'd left Mum propped up on something. I could 'ear men shouting up the street. I suppose they was A.R.P. chaps beginning to get people out of the 'ouses. I leant out and shouted as loud as I could. It was pretty dark by now, so I struck a match and lighted a bit of newspaper to show them where we was. 'Get Mum out quick—she's bad,' I says to the first chap who climbed up to us. The window wasn't far off the ground and the A.R.P. men and the ambulance chaps lower Mum down very carefully to the men underneath, see. First they catch 'old of 'er ankles, then 'er legs, and she's down. They took 'er to our 'ospital for the night, and next day they evacuated 'er down to an 'ospital in Essex. That's where she is now. I told them that my sisters and my brother Frankie were at the cinema, so they flash a notice on the screen, 'Will any Duggans in the audience go to the box office quick?' They come rushing 'ome in a terrible state. Terry and me 'ad been taken to 'ospital, too, for my shoulder and arm 'ad to be dressed and Terry was cut about, and we was both suffering from shock. They only kept us about a week or so, though, and Terry's all right now. 'E was mad at 'aving to go to my married brother's, but we thought it best to get 'im out of the way until we got somewhere new to live. I'm all right too, except that I don't like the nights now until I get down in the shelter. Days is all right, but when it gets dark— well, I like to be in the shelter." Peggy laughed apologetically.

Mr. Duggan pushed aside his teacup and cleared his throat. "It's the old lady I'm worrying about," he said. "Losing my place don't matter so long as I get 'er 'ome all right. They don't know at the 'ospital when that'll be. There's a good eye specialist there, and she's being took nice care of. I clean up and go down and see 'er Sundays, and one or other of the girls pops down on visiting days in the week. She's full of pluck, the old woman is. When I goes to see 'er, she jokes about 'er 'air being off. It always was in a bun at the back of 'er 'ead, but they shaved it all off the front so as they could dress the wound, and now all she's got is a couple of skinny little pigtails at the back. When my son Patsy, who's in the Army, goes down to see 'er, she makes jokes to 'im. 'You'll 'ave to lend me your soldier's cap,' she says, 'to perch on the front of my old billiard ball.' "

"Last time I see 'er," Peggy said, "she says to me, 'I lie 'ere worrying, Peg, in case when I get out I get mistook for one of those there women who collaborated with the Jerries.' "

"Well," said Mr. Duggan, "when she does get out, we won't be in this no longer." He again waved his hand disparagingly at the room. His daughter-in-law kept on stirring her tea without changing her calm expression. "The Borough 'ave found me a new 'ouse," Mr. Duggan said then. "They know I've got a big family, so they give me first call. It's a nice 'ouse, right down on the river, one of the old-fashioned ones. Parts of Wapping are very old, you know. You've 'eard of Wapping Old Stairs, I daresay? Well, the 'ouse is right by there. It's got nine rooms and a bath and a decent scullery. I shan't feel right until we're all together again. We've 'ad enough of living all split up, some 'ere, some there. We're not used to it, any of us." He glared at the table, as though accusing it of being a small, paltry affair instead of a stout family board lined on either side with rows of healthy, handsome Duggan faces.

I asked how one went about furnishing a nine-room house when all one's belongings had been destroyed. Mr. Duggan said that he didn't quite know yet but that it would be all right. This time the calamity had been so complete that the family had been obliged to ask for help from both the Assistance Board and the W.V.S. Mr. Duggan had filled out a claim for his furniture and sent it to the Assistance Board. Although in most cases this money will not be paid until the end of the war, in a case such as the Duggans' it is advanced immediately, along with a permit to buy some of the inexpensive, well-designed utility furniture reserved for newly married couples and bombed-out families. There is also a system for lending the minimum requirements of utility furniture to bombed-out people for three months, at the end of which, if they still need the stuff, they can buy it very cheaply. The Assistance Board also grants temporary allowances to people who cannot work because of injuries received during raids. This grant amounts to twenty-four shillings sixpence a week while patients are in the hospital and thirty shillings a week after they come out. Since housewives are eligible for this compensation, Mrs. Duggan was entitled to an allowance just as much as Peggy was, and if Mrs. Duggan's injuries turn out to be a permanent handicap, she can later put in a claim for a pension.

Mr. Duggan said that he didn't know what the Assistance Board was going to give him toward replacing his furniture. They had already let him have forty pounds and had allotted over four hundred clothing coupons for himself and his two youngest children, Maureen and Terry. (The yearly allotment for the ordinary, unbombed British citizen is forty-eight coupons.) The other Duggans who lived at home—Frank, Peggy, Sheila, and Eileen—had had an average of fifteen pounds and a hundred and fifty coupons apiece. Since they had lost everything but the clothes they were wearing, they had been forced to pocket their Wapping independence and get from the W.V.S. a minimum wardrobe to keep them going. Mr. Duggan got a shirt, trunks, undershirt, and socks; the boys, Frank and Terry, got the same and, in addition, trousers, shoes, jackets, and jerseys. The girls got the equivalent—skirt, underclothes, stockings, nightdress, and second-hand jumpers. Maureen had been given, by the slightly startled W.V.S., two pairs of men's trousers, shirts, pajamas, and some mannish underwear.

"I figure out that I lost 'undreds of pounds' worth of furniture at my place," said Mr. Duggan sadly, "but I shan't get the full value of it, that's certain. My stuff wasn't none of this utility furniture. Why, that solid-ma'ogany sideboard I mentioned just now—it would be forty or fifty pounds, shouldn't wonder, at today's prices. It's the same with clothes. 'Ow far does fifteen quid go now? Not far, is the answer. And men's clothes take a lot of coupons, too. I reckon that you want two suits, an everyday and a walking-out suit to change into Sundays and suchlike. 'Ow can that be done, I ask you? When you've got everything else to replace, it can't be. Of course, these working clothes I've got on now are provided free by the Borough. But can you go to a cinema in these? *Oh,* no! Leastways, if you did, you'd very soon 'ave the seats clear for miles all round you. One thing, while we're all sleeping down in the shelter, we don't need to buy no beds. All we've got left out of our old 'ouse is a table, a chest of drawers, and some cups without 'andles. But we've got enough to be getting on with, and as soon as I 'ear from the Assistance Board, I shall buy a bit of new stuff and we'll move in. I've known young couples with worse starts, and I've still got my strength, thank God, and all the kids except Terry are working. Our church is very good to us, too. All through the blitzes, the priest is there working day and night, looking after us Wapping people."

Mr. Duggan suggested that I go with him when he went back to work and see the shelter under the Colonial Warehouse and what was left of the Duggans' old street, Hermitage Wall, so when he was ready I said goodbye to the girls and Denis and we started off. The sunny streets were full of men going back to the dockside warehouses after the dinner hour. As they passed us, many of them jerked their heads toward Mr. Duggan and said, "Cheerio, Jack." "They all know me," he said proudly, leading the way up a flight of stone steps into the Colonial Warehouse. He brought a lot of keys out of a pocket and unlocked a door on which a handwritten notice was nailed. "Dear friends and neighbours," it began, and went on to convey thanks to everybody for "the floral tribute and cash collection totalling £4 18s." "That was the same bomb got us," Mr. Duggan explained. "Four killed in the one family."

Inside, he led me through a series of stone basements lined with bunks, running the whole length of the big warehouse. Everything seemed clean and shipshape. "I'm very particular about everybody airing their bedding," Mr. Duggan said sternly. "I allow them lights until eleven, then off they go, *and* no disturbances after that. Four 'undred people there every night, and I keep order like it was in the Army. When I say 'ush to the kids, they 'ush without a murmur. It's nice and deep down 'ere—an old building with good thick walls—and I reckon they're as safe as anywhere. The rescue-squad party told me that why our place over the Old Sugar Loaf didn't fall right down flat when we was bombed last, and kill Peggy and Terry and their mother right out, was because it was a sturdy, old-fashioned building. It 'ad nice deep cellars, too. Matter of fact, they'd been thinking of making those

cellars into an air-raid shelter, and they'd started shoring them up with timber supports. So when the bomb comes, the 'ouse could take it better than some
of these trashy modern 'ouses could."

Mr. Duggan showed me the corner of the shelter where his family now
spent a considerable portion of their lives. The Duggan section seemed to
take up a large area of floor and bunk space. It was right by a door, which
Mr. Duggan opened to point out a fine view of the river, with a row of sea
gulls bobbing gently up and down on an anchored coal barge. "I picked this
corner by the door because we all like air," he said. "When we first started
sleeping in shelters, the girls felt the stuffiness terrible, but we got fans fixed
up down 'ere and it's not so bad. In fact, it's a pretty good shelter." He regarded the family lair keenly yet with satisfaction, like a young matron showing off her new guest room but keeping an eye open for dust on the bureau
top. It looked a fairly grim setting for domestic evenings, but Mr. Duggan
apparently didn't think so. "I'd like you to see us of a night when we're all in
bed," he said with patriarchal pride as we walked on. "It's quite a sight—Duggans as far as you can see. I couldn't tell you off 'and 'ow many of us are down
'ere, but there are a lot. Know 'ow many grandchildren I've got? Between
thirty and forty—I 'aven't counted lately, but I think it's thirty-eight. Not all
'ere, of course, by no means. Some of the older grandsons are great big lads
in the forces, some serving in India, some in France and 'Olland. They 'ave
to call my nipper, Terry, who's only eight, Uncle Terry, which of course is
somewhat awkward for all concerned."

He locked the shelter up and we set off for Hermitage Wall. It wasn't very
far from the warehouse. Mr. Duggan showed me where the robot that bombed
them out last summer had fallen. In the middle of the debris of what had
been an A.R.P. post stood the rusting skeletons of two motor cars. "There was
people sitting in them at the time," Mr. Duggan said. We turned a corner
into Hermitage Wall. It was desolate. What wasn't already flattened out,
which was very little, was being pulled down by demolition squads. It had
rained heavily the night before, and the ground, as pockmarked as the surface of the moon, was all deep mud. Men were making bonfires of stuff that
wasn't worth salvaging, and where there was an upstairs to a house, rubble
was pouring dustily down chutes into trucks. Mr. Duggan pointed to the
remnants of a reddish-brick building—simply some arches and a sketchy
suggestion of upper floors—which looked rather bigger and stood up more
boldly than any of the dingy, ruined houses around it. "That's my place,"
he said. "That's the Old Sugar Loaf."

We stood and looked in silence at the place. The demolition men, who
seemed to recognize Mr. Duggan, stood and watched us silently, too. They
had cleaned up inside the shell of the Duggans' home, so that you could look
down into the foundations and up into the sky. Only the strips of faded, sodden wallpaper peeling off the walls indicated that people had ever lived there,

and it was difficult to believe that anybody had been taken out of it alive. Twirling his watch chain, a chunky figure in his dustman's clothes, Mr. Duggan looked away, down the street. He didn't seem either sad or angry as he said, "I remember when I was a little kid, there was apple trees growing in some of the back yards. Me and the old woman 'ave lived in one 'ouse or another on this street the best part of our married lives."

As we walked away, he went on talking, but it sounded as though it were to himself as much as to me. "What I've got to do is to get my old woman 'ome," he said. "The rest don't matter. She's been a wonderful wife to me. When I was away in the last war, in the Royal Engineers, I didn't worry my 'ead like some men, because I knew she was looking after everything proper for me. She's never been in a pub in 'er life, my old woman 'asn't. I don't know why it 'ad to be 'er copped it, when she's worked 'ard all 'er life and entitled to a rest. So long as I get my old woman 'ome, everything will be all right. I don't worry about nothing else."

[February 17, 1945]

# PERSIAN GULF COMMAND
## THE HEAT

JOEL SAYRE

THOUGH I have no hope of being completely successful, I want to try to give an idea of how hot the summers were in Major General Donald H. Connolly's Persian Gulf Command, where, from December, 1942, to December, 1944, his officers and men ran American supplies up the western side of Iran from the Persian Gulf to the Red Army and the Russian people. Even the natives thought there was something unusual about their summers; in a sort of inverted chamber-of-commerce spirit, three towns in southern Iran claimed to be the Hottest Place on Earth. I spent nearly a year with the P.G.C. and discovered that when the sun was operating wide open, hardly anybody there discussed the heat; you needed all your breath to fight it. Nobody ever said, "Well, looks like another scorcher today." That it would be another scorcher went without saying. A letter I received from a friend of mine in the P.G.C. was mailed last August from a town called Ahwaz, and in the upper right-hand corner he had written, "Temperature today 149." That was the temperature in the sun, of course. At the top of the Persian Gulf, on the island of Abadan, where the Anglo-Iranian Oil Company has its colossal refinery and we have one or two knickknacks of our own, they will show you a record of a temperature of 189. Personally, I think that thermometers turn a little crazy themselves if left in the Iranian kind of heat too long, but what are a few lousy degrees one way or the other when your brains are baking? The boys had to do a lot of their work in the sun, and wonderful work it was—some of the most important in the whole American war effort.

Naturally, the boys did as much of the work as possible in the shade, and that helped, as you will realize when you compare 189 or 149 to 120, which was the average summer shade temperature in the Iranian south. The south was heat-stroke country. All over it you saw signs pointing to Army heat-stroke centers. Some of them, in the early days, were just canvas flies pitched over a cot or two; others, built later, were fancy caverns sunk in stone, as comfortable as the Pentagon Building. When somebody was stricken, the Medics would immediately whizz him off to a center and throw him on a cot and slosh him down with ice water and pour cold drinks into him and fan him. Thomas

452

Mann's daughter Erika visited the Command, as a correspondent. Later, in Cairo, she was interviewed by an Egypto-French periodical, which attributed to her the statement that the P.G.C.'s cure for heat-stroke victims was to freeze them in blocks of ice. It was hot in the P.G.C., but never quite that hot. If some Medic gave Miss Mann this ice gag, he must have been at the vodka beforehand. Recalling Iranian vodka, I am surprised he did not make it solid blocks of aspic they froze them in.

The Medics used to play a joke with the clinical thermometers. They would hand one that hadn't been kept on ice to a doctor newly arrived in the Command, then follow him into a ward and watch him take his first temperature. The new doc would shake the thermometer down, glance at it, and slip it into the patient's mouth, but even before it got there its mercury would have zipped up to ward temperature, probably 104 or 105, which is what the heat in the wards used to hit until they were air-conditioned. The doc's reactions when he took his next look at the thermometer were always good for a laugh. One night last May, in the town of Andimeshk (a claimant to the Hottest on Earth title), three thousand officers and men were waiting under the stars to hear Lily Pons, while backstage Miss Pons was announcing that she couldn't go on. It turned out that she had taken her temperature with her own thermometer and found that it was 103. A properly chilled thermometer was rushed to Miss Pons' dressing room and it was quickly determined that she was still a long way from the mortician's. Colonel Francis Dryden, the district commander, explained the workings of thermometers in Iran. Reassured, Miss Pons went to town with "Lo! Here the Gentle Lark" and other favorites.

The sun killed a few of the boys during the P.G.C.'s first summer; it wounded, so to speak, a larger number. The Medics worked hard to keep the heat casualties down, raising hell with everybody they caught not taking precautions. Whenever a Medic found one of the crazier kids in the open without his lion-tamer hat, or trying to take a sun bath, he would bawl him out and chase him. Once the sun had really taken hold, it was easier to get coöperation. For instance, some of the men were contemptuous of salt tablets until their own salt began coming out on their shirts in great white stains. The Medics arranged for as many men as could be spared to knock off work and siesta in the afternoons of the bad months, which are May, June, July, August, and September. The time lost was made up on night shifts. On the whole, the Medics in the P.G.C. did a good job in every phase of their work. It is an axiom of military medicine that even in a non-combat zone, such as the Persian Gulf Command, ten per cent of your troops will always be in the hospital. In the P.G.C. the hospitalization was never higher than five or six per cent, which was gratifying in a locale saturated with malaria, dysentery, smallpox, sandfly fever, trachoma, and all the social ailments.

Many of the men were convinced that there would be a big heat slaughter that first summer. During the previous winter somebody had asked a native what the summer weather was like. "July, flies die," the native answered. "August, Johnny die." "Johnny" was local Basic Pidgin for "American soldier," and the remark swept the Command. It was repeated as a joke, but it caused quite a little worry, especially when July came and it was noticed that the flies were fulfilling their part of the prophecy. But by the end of August most of the boys were still on their feet. Though they had suffered horribly from the sun, they were very glad that the native seer had been right about the flies. Middle East flies seem to have been crossed with bulldogs: brush them off your face and there they are again.

In the years to come, no veteran of the Persian Gulf Command will ever be able to listen unbemused when his home folks complain about the sticky spells. Down in the Iranian south, some buglers used to keep their mouthpieces in glasses of water between calls. When a man was working in the sun, he would have to sponge any metal tools he needed before he picked them up, and if he was smart he always had his work gloves on when he took hold of a grab-iron to climb into the cab of a locomotive or seized the propeller of a plane to give it a whip or started to unscrew the radiator cap of a vehicle. It was really something to put in a full day's work in the cab of a truck, with extra heat coming up through the floor from the motor, or over a rolling asphalt cooker as a member of a road gang, or at the Ordnance Depot's tire factory, or down in the hold of a ship, where it could sometimes be 140 at midnight. In the bad months, even working at an office desk could be fierce. Because your dogtags burned your flesh when you worked in the open, you took them from around your neck and put them in your pocket, although you could get in trouble for it if you were caught not wearing them. You did the same with your scapular, if you were a Catholic. You also put away your ring, which you had probably bought from one of the native silversmiths, who guaranteed that it was solid silver and had made it out of an old hub cap. Some of the boys even stopped wearing belts, insisting that the buckles were roasting their navels. God knows how they kept their pants up; with the heat working on them day in and day out, they were all as straight up and down as tent poles. You almost never saw a fat man in the south. Of those who arrived fat, the sun policed up the overwhelming majority.

The soldiers in the south didn't have to worry about pressing their clothes. If you wanted to slick up before going on a date, you merely put on your suntan pants and shirt and walked under the shower in them. After letting them soak thoroughly, you smoothed them with the palms of your hands, then stepped from under the shower and swiftly squeezed in the desired creases with the thumb and forefinger. By the time you had combed your hair, the shirt and pants would be as crisp as a new shavetail's. In the south you never bothered to take a towel to the shower with you. The only time you used towels was when you soaked them and spread them over your body when you went to bed.

Everybody agreed that the most intolerable post in the command was the port of Bandar Shahpur, a tiny island off the Gulf's tidal salt flats, entirely surrounded by poisonous water snakes. Yard engines charged back and forth across it day and night, and when you were eating you were sure they would be coming down the mess-hall table any minute. Shade temperature at Bandar Shahpur was seldom higher than 116; what made duty there so tough was the humidity that came rolling up the Gulf out of the Indian Ocean. It was really murder. After you had been in Bandar an hour, the dear old 140-degree desert oven you had left, with its nice, fresh, unadulterated heat, seemed like Sun Valley and you longed to flee back to it.

Elsewhere in the P.G.C., Bandar Shahpur was always considered a place of exile, but its morale was nevertheless as high as it was anywhere in the Command. For a while, with fewer men and fewer berths for the ships, it unloaded more tonnage than either of the two other ports in the Command did. The outfit there was proud and defiant. In the early days, they held a Perspiration Handicap once a week. Each entry would roll up a sleeve, crook an elbow, and, timed by a stopwatch, see how fast he could fill an empty C-ration can. Eight minutes, forty-one and two-fifths seconds was the record, achieved by a fat but fading major. There was always a heavy play on the entries. Finally, this fixture had to be discontinued. "The boys are just plumb sweat out," one of the officers told me. You could always spot a newcomer to Bandar Shahpur. After ten minutes in the place, he looked as though he had fallen off one of the jetties.

The heat was everybody's headache, the greatest common denominator. Even in the seasons when it was not grinding away, everyone was thinking about it, worrying over it, preparing for it, bracing himself against it, wondering what it would do to him when it returned. Western man has always thought of the sun as a giver of life, a lifter of the spirit, a bringer of hope. But this sun that burned down on the Persian Gulf Command was a different and truly odious thing, malevolent, totally dispiriting. After a while it made you numb to the roots of your brain; you really felt that you had been lowered down to hell and left there and you didn't much care any more how things turned out. There was a story that in a caravan that had struggled its way over the desert, the travellers fell on each other's necks and wept for joy when the sun went down. Nobody in the P.G.C. doubted that story.

When the Command's first summer ended, nearly everybody in the south swore he couldn't take a second and live. But by the second summer the work was rolling on ball bearings, the food was much better, and the equipment for living had been improved enormously. Besides, it is astonishing what the human body can do. One Sunday morning last June I saw a ball game between two ordnance companies in Andimeshk when it was 140. Every player kept giving it the old college try, the umpire was continually threatened with braining, one man stole home, and the game went into extra innings. I was watching from a jeep whose top had been raised. My sleeves were rolled up, and every now and then I would forget and rest my forearm on some metal part; by the end of the game it was a mass of nasty welts. But the men on the field didn't even know it was hot. Then I remember a Red Cross girl's telling about the afternoon she and several colleagues landed in Basra, which is in Iraq but nevertheless part of the P.G.C. It was 135 in the shade, but at the news that genuine American girls had arrived everybody abandoned his siesta. Nobody had jitterbugged with a white woman for a long time, and since one of the Red Cross's functions is to improve morale, there was jitterbugging until the girls begged for mercy.

The Persian Gulf Command's first sizable detachment—nine thousand officers and men—landed at Khorramshahr on December 11, 1942, after a look at Rio from the roadstead and a brief stopover at Bombay. The congestion on the Army transport which carried all these early settlers was like that on the tubs their ancestors reached America in. Had heraldic devices representing the spirit of the voyage been contrived, a bare foot couchant on a soldier's face would have got the most votes. Until the transport reached Bombay, few on board her knew their destination or mission, but there the word got around. The news that the outfit was going to run American supplies to the Red Army produced great cheer. The invasion of North Africa had begun while the boys were still at sea, and they were disappointed that they hadn't been in on it. However, ahead of them now was an even bigger show, with the Russians engaging the main body of the German Army and seemingly in their worst trouble at a place called Stalingrad. The men and their officers were, in the main, engineering, railroading, trucking, stevedoring, or communications professionals. They knew how mightily the Russians were helping us and they were eager to help them all they could in return. They also looked forward to showing them some stuff. "Just leave us know where you want it, Stalin" was the spirit.

A bonus was added to this cheering news when it was discovered on the way up the Gulf that Iran is merely an alias for Persia. Probably everybody, except the chaplains, perhaps, retained in his memory a Persian sequence in some motion picture, and in a pleasant, Technicolor way the sequence was provoking to the imagination. I once asked a representative P.G.C. corporal for his own pre-debarkation concept. "The way I seen Persia," he said, "was a swell big marble layout in the moonlight with a built-in pool. Birds was singing, but not too loud, and everything smelt wonderful. Some guys with turbans was taking it easy on cushions. They had whiskers and they was having a smoke out of one of them jars with the hose on them and they was smothered in wonderful-looking broads, all of them wearing them long peek-aboo pants. Setting on the floor was a three-piece orchestra playing midway music. Standing out front was the best-looking broad of them all doing bumps and boy, was she built! Did she have hermanns! Up here you'd think she was gonna explode! Yes, sir, that was Persia."

[April 7, 1945]

# PERSIAN GULF COMMAND
## YOU DON'T FOOL AROUND
## WITH A RAILROAD

JOEL SAYRE

DURING the first year of the existence of the U. S. Army's Persian Gulf Command, the supplies never ceased to flow from the ports in the Gulf across the desert and over the mountains to their destinations, and the boys never once failed to top their monthly tonnage quotas, which were called "targets" and were always being increased. The hauling was done over the Iranian State Railway, run by the Army's Military Railway Service, and over a roughly parallel truck route run by the Army's Motor Transport Service. This double flow was sound logistics; if the railroad had ever been bombed out of action —which seemed more than a possibility when blueprints for the Command were being drawn up four months after Pearl Harbor—the Motor Transport Service could have kept at least some of the stuff rolling. However, the railroad never was bombed. The P.G.C.'s railroaders got a terrific jump on its truckers at the start, because the road the truckers had to use was then in frightful shape. Altogether, the railroad outhauled the trucks about four to one. Indeed, there were guardhouse Eisenhowers who would show you how the work could have been done entirely by its railroaders and dockwallopers, thus eliminating the whole Motor Transport Service and the elaborate layout with which the Ordnance maintenanced it and all the painful labor the Engineers had had to put in on seven hundred-odd miles of desert and mountain highway. But then there are guardhouse Eisenhowers who will show you how the Normandy beachheads could have been established by the Finance Department. Once the truckers got rolling, they did wonderful work, particularly last summer, and, in all, they accomplished more than ninety-seven million route miles of hauling. Nevertheless, the P.G.C.'s railroaders—almost a hundred per cent of whom were professionals—would have told you before they left home that they would haul rings around any competing truck lines that might be set up. With the possible exception of big-time circus people, American railroaders, from board chairmen to wheeltappers, are probably the proudest and most self-assured group in our national life. Deep down in their hearts, real railroaders believe that any man worthy of the name who does

458

not work for a railroad must be cursed by Fate, and that any man who would not care to work for a railroad, given the chance, is a man by courtesy only. A sergeant engineer named Bill Leppert, whose run with his ninety-ton MacArthur locomotive was between Teheran and the holy city of Qum, once tried to explain to me the feelings that true, working railroaders have. "Many a time at grade crossings on the B. & O.," he said, "I've seen millionaires look up at me from their limousines with envy in their eyes."

With no disrespect for the Eagle of the Pacific, all railroaders call MacArthur locomotives "Mikes," because the type was originally designed for Hirohito's grandfather and was called the Mikado. Hence "Mick," hence "Mike," and, war or no war, they still are called Mikes, though they were renamed for the General shortly after Pearl Harbor. Army railroaders are conservative men, professionally. Renaming the Mikado the MacArthur, by the way, seems to be the nearest Americans have come in this war to those star-spangled variations of the last, during which we renamed sauerkraut Liberty cabbage, and German-fried potatoes Pershing-fried potatoes.

Of the crews that cowboyed the freight trains day and night from the ports up to Teheran and back, the conductors and engineers were sergeants, the firemen corporals, and the brakemen, if G.I., privates. Often a brakeman would be a native inherited from the Iranian State Railway. Whatever they were, they all worked sixteen or twenty hours at a belt in the early days. Just for laughs, one fireman corporal on the mountain run, on which the emergencies and wrecks were most frequent and the hours therefore the longest, kept a careful time book, as though he were still working at union scale back home, and soon he was earning more hypothetically than his colonel was actually. Once he made himself feel bad by figuring out how much income tax he would have had to pay on his imaginary earnings. In the Military Railway Service, the majority of the enlisted men were youngsters, but among the officers—former yard superintendents, trainmasters, maintenance-of-way men, and the like—there were lots of bald heads and upper plates and even a few snowy pates. Some of the officers must have been railroading when Pullman cars were still illuminated with gas lamps and the porters passed through at dusk lighting the lamps with long wax tapers. Standing behind a group of P.G.C. railroad officers bent over their wash troughs, you would notice chewing-tobacco sacks in quite a few hip pockets.

There was abundant bravery in the Persian Gulf Command when it was required, especially in the early days, before things were going smoothly. When disaster threatened, there was usually an officer or a man or a whole battalion to rush in and grab hold of it and never let go until it was conquered. Because this bravery was not the combat sort of bravery that gets written up in the papers, nobody thought of it as much more than part of the day's chores.

The construction of the Iranian State Railway, completed in 1938, after twelve years of labor, was, because of the mountainous terrain, one of the most spectacular engineering feats in history. The Iranian people are justly proud of it, and of the fact that it was built without the aid of foreign capital, its cost of $160,000,000 having been paid out of the proceeds of a government monopoly on sugar and tea. The road is single-tracked, which was ample for its peacetime traffic—a light passenger train every other day and a freight train of Middle East proportions once a week. Then our boys began to roll the Russian supplies over it around the clock. With long strings of loaded cars going north and long strings of empties coming south on the same single track, some very delicate dispatching had to be done. Everything would work out perfectly until a train ran away, which happened from time to time, and then a delightful afternoon or evening would be had by everyone on board and everyone all along the line.

Corporal Harry Slick was the fireman on a train that ran away. His Mike was pulling a train that had eight siding stops to make on its run through the Zagros Mountains. Slick was a quiet, well-spoken young soldier from Youngwood, Pennsylvania, whom everybody liked. Before joining up, he had worked on the Pittsburgh division of the Pennsy. One spring day in 1943, his train was made up of twenty-one cars, loaded with a thousand tons of supplies for the Russians. Ten of the cars were tankers filled with high-octane aviation gasoline; the eleven others were boxcars containing ammunition and explosives. There was no caboose, and the conductor, a soldier of Scandinavian descent, was riding in the cab with Slick and the engineer. Slick had just turned twenty-three; the two others were oldtimers and seasoned railroaders. The brakeman, who was as surefooted as anyone I've ever seen strolling up and down the tops of moving boxcars, was an Iranian. The engineer had brought along a can of those little G.I. alleged sausages, the kind nobody in the Army ever eats twice if he can help it, and shortly before the train started down its first long hill the conductor was kidding him about them. The mountains of the Zagros range are higher than our Rockies in a number of places, and in going through them the railroad ascends to more than seven thousand feet. Slick's train started to run away when it was going down a grade which dropped twenty-five hundred feet in forty-two miles, and the track down it was full of wicked curves. The engineer tried to shut off steam, but the throttle broke. It was as though, driving a car, your accelerator had stuck halfway to the floor and there was no way of turning your ignition off. As soon as the engineer realized that something was wrong, he applied his air brakes. Air brakes were scarce on the railroad in those days; only twenty per cent of the cars on this train were equipped with them. The engineer applied them, but it did no good. He whistled to the brakeman to start putting on all the hand brakes. On the next curve the three men in the cab leaned out and saw the wheels spitting great sparks under every car, but the train kept going faster. When Slick's Mike reached the bottom of the hill, it, with two and one-fifth million pounds of gas and ammunition and explosives behind it, was going ninety miles an hour.

The train slowed down to between sixty and seventy in the valley, but the engine was rocking so violently that the conductor lay on his belly on the engine deck and clung to the tender rail. The three men in the cab knew that there were southbound trains coming toward them over the single track. Twice the engineer tried to reverse the engine but couldn't. When the runaway tore past the first station it was supposed to wait at, a sergeant dispatcher named Seth Hood took one look at it and phoned down the line in time to get four trains cleared onto sidings and out of its way. As the runaway train roared through station after station, the three men were amazed that there was no collision; then it came to them that Hood had saved them, and when they were safely past the seventh station they bellowed at each other in delight. They knew that there were no trains beyond the eighth station at this time of day and they assumed that the one they were supposed to meet there would be on a siding. The Iranian brakeman waved from a boxcar at a gaping track gang. In literal-minded devotion to duty, he had faithfully sung out, from his car top, the name of each station the train had crashed through. Then the train rounded a blind curve and in the distance the three men saw the eighth station. Beside it they noticed three columns of smoke rising. To them this meant only one thing: there were three trains in the station—one on the main-line track and one on each of the station's two sidings. The engineer made one desperate last try at the reversing mechanism. Nothing happened. He jumped, and bounced ten feet into the air after he hit. The conductor waited until the train reached a fill and then jumped into the soft earth.

Slick stayed on the train. A few minutes later the train reached the station. To his amazement, it rushed through unharmed. Two of the three columns of smoke, it turned out, were from a double-header—two engines pulling one train—on one siding, and the third was from an engine on the other siding, so the main track was free. Slick hadn't known this, of course, when he took over. He just stuck there and kept on trying to reverse the engine. Thirty-five miles beyond the station, he finally stopped the train. He was always very modest afterward, insisting that the dispatcher deserved the real credit. When you tried to get him to explain why he hadn't jumped, the most he would say was "Well, you don't fool around with a railroad."

After the train stopped, Slick suddenly felt starved, and when an emergency squad arrived on the scene he was found dazedly hunting around the cab for the little sausages the engineer had brought. The engineer's skull and some of his ribs were broken, but he recovered after a year in a hospital. The conductor, who had missed a culvert by inches in his jump, was merely bruised. He had done some skiing and knew about falling. Slick received the Soldier's Medal, the award given by the Army for gallantry in non-combat areas, and the Russian Order of the Red Star, which entitles him to a monthly pension and free rides on all the common carriers in the Soviet Union, if he ever gets there. The last time I saw him, he was working on a pusher engine in the mountains and was still a corporal.

[March 17, 1945]

# D DAY, IWO JIMA

JOHN LARDNER

TWO divisions of Marines made the landing on Iwo Jima. These Marines were frankly apprehensive before the landing. I did not see a man, either in the staging areas before we boarded ship or on the journey north to Iwo Jima by transport, who expected anything but a bloody and disagreeable time of it. Iwo was far closer to the Japanese mainland than any enemy possession we had attempted to storm before, and our air observation showed that it was heavily fortified. Moreover, as officers kept pointing out to one another, Iwo was too small to provide room for maneuver, being only five miles long and, at the widest point, two and a half miles wide. Frontal attack was the only possible course, and the southeast beach, where we planned to land, was the only possible landing place. "You can't run the ends up there," one major said over and over again. "Every play is between the tackles." Another officer liked to say that we would have surprise on our side like a burglar with whooping cough. This, if it meant anything at all, may have been a reference to the sinking of some minesweepers and LCI gunboats of ours which had gone close to shore during the preliminary naval shelling of Iwo. Even a Japanese broadcaster had said that we would land on the southeast beach, but that, as I said, was the only possible landing place. Even so, the Jap announcer's remarks reinforced the cynical mood of the younger Marine officers.

The forebodings of these officers—all of which turned out to be perfectly justified except in one or two minor particulars—were uttered humorously, as a rule, but there were also cases of serious gloom among the officers and many gaudy premonitions among the enlisted men. These were examples of that detached professional pessimism which is ordinarily confined in war to intelligence officers, whose minds are top-heavy with knowledge of the enemy, his strength, his dispositions, and his potentialities. The Marines bound for Iwo spoke more flatly, and with less whimsical wood-rapping, of the expectation of death than any assault troops I had ever been with before. There were reasons for this apart from the special nature of the Iwo Jima operation. The number of Marine divisions is not large and nearly all of them have been badly mauled in the course of the past three years. Their work calls for it. All but two or three of the Pacific bastions attacked by Marine forces were

462

strongly held and bitterly defended, and even when this was not the case, the mere fundamentals of amphibious landings and assault caused them damage. In the Army, shock troops are a small minority supported by a vast group of artisans, laborers, clerks, and organizers. In the Marines there are practically nothing but shock troops. For such troops, in time, no matter how well trained and competent, a saturation point is bound to come. The Marines in the Pacific point all of this out themselves at the slightest provocation, and it's difficult, in the circumstances, to see what else they could do.

As it happened, the Marine division I went with to Iwo—the Fifth—was a new one, activated about a year ago and now engaged in its first combat mission. Most of its officers and many of its enlisted men, however, were veterans of earlier campaigns with other units. One of its enlisted men, Gunnery Sergeant John Basilone, had won the Congressional Medal of Honor at Guadalcanal. He was killed by mortar fire on Iwo Jima shortly after the division hit the beaches. Officers aboard our transport, especially those with large responsibilities, such as getting artillery ashore or conditioning amtracks and their crews for the first assault landing, stood on deck for two or three days before D Day, succumbing to bleak despair whenever the ocean swells ran high or the wind changed direction. "My God!" said Lieutenant Colonel Roose, a very young man from Toledo. "Imagine if that wind is blowing from the south when we hit!" "I'll tell you a couple of things that can happen to my artillery," said Lieutenant Colonel Duryea, not much older, "if it's rough like this at Iwo." And he did. It was gruesome.

Also unhappy for technical reasons was an officer known in his regiment—our passengers were mainly from the Twenty-seventh Regiment of the Fifth Division—as Purple Heart Louis, a high, broad, hulking man who presented an excellent target and invariably got hit in combat. He anticipated a great deal of bloodshed on Iwo Jima, but aboard the transport he was bothered chiefly by the fact that the cook for the commodore of our transport division fried everything he cooked, and Louis ate at the commodore's table. One of Louis's Purple Hearts had involved the loss of his gall bladder, and fried foods were poison to him. He relieved his misery by looting the junior officers in wardroom poker games at night. Ships in the Pacific are hot at night, with doors and blackened portholes closed and all air shut out, and Louis stripped to his gleaming torso when he played poker, revealing a cicatrix across his belly and abdomen which looked like the mother and father of all Caesarean scars. He was hit in the right arm about an hour and a half after landing on Iwo Jima.

D Day was Monday, February 19th, and H Hour was 0900. On D-minus-one, the regimental surgeon reported a hundred and twenty-five cases of diarrhea among the men and officers aboard. This had come from something they ate, but that evening the Navy cooks did better and served everyone a turkey dinner with ice cream. At the last meal, breakfast at 0500 the morning of the nineteenth, there were steak and eggs. Everyone had dressed in his green combat blouse and trousers and had strapped on his pistol belt, with a long knife, ammunition, a bandage roll, and one or two canteens attached, and had checked his carbine. After breakfast, everyone put on his helmet, which had a camouflage cover simulating sand, and went out on deck and over to the ladder nets. The sun was just coming up, so Iwo Jima was visible from our line of debarkation, which was several miles out at sea. There the larger transports halted, to keep beyond the range of shore batteries, and put off their cargoes of Marines into small boats. On Suribachi, the volcano at the south end of the island, we could see bursts of fire and smoke from our naval shelling, which continued till H Hour. Some of the men stared at the island. Others remarked that the wind was running in our favor, from the northwest, and that the sea was calmer than it had been, though still difficult. Many could think of nothing but the immediate necessity of climbing the slick, flaccid web of rope down the ship's side without looking silly or getting killed. Even young Marines have been killed on these descents when the sea has been rough, and for those over thirty-five the endless sequence of nets, Jacob's ladders, bouncing gangways, and lurching boats is a hazard and nightmare which can occupy their minds to the exclusion of all other dangers. Admirals and generals can look ridiculous in these circumstances. They are well aware of it, and their tempers during amphibious operations are correspondingly short.

I got into a small boat with Colonel Thomas Wornham, regimental commander, and some of his staff, his messengers, and his radio operators. We chopped and splashed through the ocean swells to Wornham's control ship, which was anchored nearer the shore, at the line at which the first assault troops formed up in their amtracks and began their long, slow, bobbing run for the beach. They went in in ragged waves, which left the departure line at intervals of a few minutes, coached hoarsely by a loudspeaker from the bridge of the control ship. The men in the amtracks were a fierce and stirring sight as they passed us to disappear in the valleys of water between us and the beach. I stood watching them as well as I could from the rail of the control ship beside a regimental messenger, a Navajo Indian named Galeagon, and we spoke of how most of the shock troops we could see, their hands and faces greased dead white for protection against possible flame barriers, sat up very straight and looked intently ahead. The first wave struck the beach approximately at the appointed hour of nine, and simultaneously the Navy shellfire, which had been raking the shoreline, jumped its range to the ridges and pillboxes farther inland. The central ridge was in our sector of the island. We could see the wreckage of Japanese planes piled at one edge of the plateau. We knew that an airfield lay just beyond this junk—one of the two airfields for which the Marines were beginning the dogged battle of Iwo Jima.

After a while, I walked to the cabin of the control ship where the radioman was receiving reports that were coming in to Wornham from the first radios set up on the beach. The first two hours' progress seemed to be good. The Japs had pulled back upland from the shore, leaving few dead behind them, and Wornham's regiment, which was second in the assault line striking north along the beach near Suribachi, had reached high ground, had crossed the southern end of the first airfield, and was beginning a descent to the western shore of the island, a half mile distant from the point where it had landed. I left the wireless room, where the radioman, earphones over his head, was now reading "The Case of the Caretaker's Cat."

Wornham's Higgins boat, a rectangular little launch with a hinged landing ramp in the bow, pulled up on the starboard quarter of our ship, and those of us who were going ashore with the Colonel climbed down a ladder and jumped in. It was exactly 1100, or two hours after the first landings, and this was the fourteenth wave. I should say that we were the fourteenth wave. As far as I could see, no other boat was moving shoreward at that moment. As we cast off, Galeagon came to the ship's rail and yelled something at us through a megaphone. Wornham, a short, stocky career Marine of about forty, smiling and convivial on our voyage north but now very taut and serious, leaned precariously over the stern of the boat, clutching at the rail, and cupped a hand to one ear. "Red One now under heavy mortar fire!" shouted the messenger. The Fifth Division's share of the beaches was Green Beach and Red Beaches One and Two. To the north, the Fourth Division had landed on Yellow One and Two and Blue One and Two. We were fifty feet from the control ship when Galeagon yelled another message. "Red Two under mortar fire," he said, the sound of his voice seeming to bounce across the waves. "Heavy mortar fire on both Red beaches." The others in the boat looked with expressionless faces at Wornham, who smiled wryly. "Head for a point about a hundred feet to the right of the line between Red One and Two," he told the coxswain. Then he turned to the rest of us and said, "All right, be ready to bail out of here goddam fast when we touch that beach."

We all crouched, whether sitting or standing, as the boat moved in. Now and then we wiped spray off our eyes and noses, and we paid no attention to a battleship and a cruiser through whose shadows we passed. I had some trouble crouching, because of my length and because the shelf on which I sat was only a foot or so beneath the stern rail. There was no special need, however, for crouching now, while we were still on water. It was the beaches the Japs were mortaring. We crouched in a sort of instinctive, shrinking alarm at what we were about to meet.

The Japs burst their mortar and artillery shells up and down the beaches for several days thereafter, but my own sharpest memories of this phase of the Iwo Jima battle are of D Day. That sort of shelling is a procedure someone can always use when he is defending a small area against an enemy who must get his supplies by water. At Iwo, as at Anzio, there quickly developed two fronts—the battle front forward and the shelling front on the beaches, where our supply and reinforcement lines were wholly dependent on boats and amphibious vehicles that were being stalled and pounded by surf and wind. And in the case of Iwo, the Marines depended also on motor or human convoys, which were slowed by drifting volcanic sand. The Japanese were limited only by their ammunition supply. As long as they could stay alive on Iwo Jima and keep their guns intact, they were all right, for they had observation over our supply beaches and we were within the range of their mortars. The mortar shell, a little bomb-shaped missile, travels in a high, lobbing trajectory and throws its fragments over a wide radius when it explodes. It makes for tearing, disfiguring wounds and for disfigured dead. Since the mortar fire continued steadily for nearly a week on the crowded shoreline, and hasn't stopped on the front lines yet, our casualties have not only been large but tend to be more slashed and mangled than usual.

We saw puffs of smoke—white, gray, and black—pluming from the beach as our boat came closer. Most of the men in the boat, whose first task was to set up a regimental command post somewhere between the beach and the front lines, were burdened with radio equipment. Alwyn Lee, an Australian war correspondent, and I were also fairly cumbrously loaded. A pack in three light pieces is more trouble than a single heavy pack, and I had, in addition to my Army musette bag, a typewriter and a blanket roll containing a poncho and a small spade, or entrenching tool. I also had a sash-type life belt buckled around my waist, in conformance a few hours earlier with a transport regulation. This belt dropped off and vanished that day on Iwo Jima, I don't know when or where.

The landing ramp slapped down on the beach and the passengers bustled out with their loads and disappeared behind the first low hummock in the sand. I was on the point of disembarking, second to last, just ahead of the Colonel, when I realized that I had forgotten my gear, and in the moment it took to turn and pick it up piecemeal, Wornham whizzed by me and was gone. I slogged up the beach across one wind-made ridge and trench and then another. Loose, dark sand came up to the tops of my high combat boots at each step, and my breathing was sharp and painful. I made it to the third and deepest trench, some thirty yards in from the shore, and fell to my face there alongside Lee and several men of the command-post detail. When you stopped running or slogging, you became conscious of the whine and bang of mortar shells dropping and bursting near you. All up and down Red Beaches One and Two, men were lying in trenches like ours, listening to shells and digging or pressing their bodies closer into the sand around them.

We were legitimately pinned down for about forty minutes. That is to say, the mortar fire was probably heavy enough and close enough during that time to make it impractical to go farther. However, there is such a thing as wishful pinned-down thinking, and it can become a more dangerous state of mind than any other in an area that is being shelled. A man tends to cling to his trench, even if it is in the center of a target, when the sensible thing is to proceed out of the target as quickly as possible, using his own best judgment about when it's prudent to dive for cover again. It seems to take about twenty minutes under shellfire to adjust your nerves and evolve a working formula by which you can make progress and gauge, very roughly, the nearness of hits and the pattern of fire.

Lee and I, by agreement, finally left our gear in a trench near the shore (we planned to salvage it later, if possible) and worked our way up the beach in the wake of Wornham and his men. There were Marines on all sides of us doing the same thing. Each man had a different method of progress. One, carbine in hand, walked along steadily, pausing and dropping to one knee only when something about the sound of the shells seemed to confuse him. Another made a high-hurdling jump into every trench or hole he used. At one point I listened to a frail Nisei interpreter arguing with an officer who wanted to help carry his pack. Again, at a moment when Lee and I were catching our breath, something stirred beside the dune just behind us. A wounded man, his face blackened by sand and powder, had roused himself from the lethargy in which he lay and noticed us. Shell fragments had hit him in one arm, one leg, the buttocks, and one eye. His eye, a red circle in his dark-stained face, worried him most. He wanted to know if there were any medical corpsmen with a litter nearby. He had been so deafened by the explosion of the shell that I had to go very close to make him hear me. There were no corpsmen or litters about. In fact, the enemy fire on the beach made it hard to get help to wounded men for the first two days, and then the process of evacuating them in boats, which had to bump their way through a high surf, was incredibly rough and painful. I promised this man to report him and get him help as soon as possible.

The next Marine we passed was dead, and so were a number of others on our diagonal course over the beach to the upland, but I didn't see a dead Japanese soldier until we got near the edge of the plateau. "That's the third one we've found on Red beaches today so far," said a soldier who sat near the mouth of a Jap concrete pillbox, which gave off a faint, foul smell. This pillbox, with walls three feet thick and built on a frame of metal tubing, was a good specimen of the Jap defenses on Iwo Jima, but in the days that followed I saw others even more substantial, with walls four to five feet thick, revolving gun turrets, and two or more approaches lined with neat stairs.

It seemed clear, by the time we reached Wornham's command post, now at least several minutes old, in a broad shellhole above the beach, that the Japs had quickly abandoned the beaches, after losing a few men, and had taken most of their dead with them. This worried Wornham, because he figured that it meant heavy counterattacks in the next night or two, and he was also worried, as regimental commanders are everywhere in battle, by the problem of keeping his combat battalions in communication with each other and with him. Sitting in his shellhole, along with a couple of dozen staff men, medical officers, messengers, radio operators, and stray visitors who just wanted to be in a hole with other people, we followed, by radio and courier, the adventures of three battalions a few hundred yards away. The battalions were known in Wornham's shellhole by their commanders' names—Robbie, Tony, and Butler. "Tony says he's ready to make his turn up the west beach," Wornham said fretfully, looking at a message in his hand. "I gotta get him." Now and then he looked around his hole and said plaintively, "Come on, let's break this up. Let's have some room here." At these words, a few of the strays would drift away in one direction or another, and a few minutes later others would take their places. The shells dropped more rarely in that neighborhood, but they were close enough. Tanks began to rumble up from the beach, at long intervals, and angle and stutter their way through a gap at the top of the ridge nearby. Purple Heart Louis came to the edge of the command post and had his right arm bandaged by a doctor to whom we had already reported the position of the wounded Marine on the beach. "I knew Louis would get it again," said a young captain. "Right where he deals the cards, too. I hope it will be a lesson to him."

We heard of death after death of men we had been with on the transport. One divisional surgeon had been killed and another had already had a breakdown from overwork. Visible Japanese dead were still scarce, even though one company had found a nest of Japs and killed a hundred. "Here's a report from F Company colonel, sir," said an aide. "He says the presence of a lot of flies in a trench suggests the Japs buried some dead there."

There were live Japs near enough, for whenever the Navy's Grumman fighter planes dived at a point just to our right, near the airfield, they drew machine-gun fire. Looking around, I had the leisure for the first time to think what a miserable piece of real estate Iwo Jima is. Later, when I had seen nearly all the island, I knew that there were no extenuating features. This place where thousands of men of two nations have been killed or wounded in less than three weeks' time has no water, few birds, no butterflies, no discernible animal life—nothing but sand and clay, humpbacked hills, stunted trees, knife-edged kuna grass in which mites who carry scrub typhus live, and a steady, dusty wind.

By midafternoon, Lee and I were ready to send our first dispatches. We decided that the only way to get them off quickly was to make for the flagship, several miles offshore. We did not feel very good about the prospect. The mortar fire on the beaches was as steady as ever and the surf was running higher than it had been in the morning. We reluctantly started down toward the shore, threading our way through a column of silent, apologetic-looking reinforcement troops, climbing uphill with boxes of ammunition from the beach. Occasionally a soldier stepped out of line and asked us if we knew where this column was bound. I don't know why the people going downhill inspired more confidence or looked better-informed than the leaders of the column moving uphill, unless it was that the very direction of our progress suggested that we were Iwo Jima tenants of long standing—five or six hours, perhaps—possessed of sweeping oracular powers and the ability to speak words that would restore confidence and banish fear and confusion. This was certainly untrue. Lee and I paused in a hole halfway down the beach to argue about where we had left our packs and typewriters. I thought it was somewhere to the left, but every time I pointed, a shell was dropped on the exact spot I had in mind. Shells were now also chasing amtracks, ducks, and other craft some little way out from the shore.

Lee said he thought we should head toward a place where we could see some boats bunching and where there might be a chance of our getting a ride. We started off, and a few minutes later we tumbled into a trench practically on top of our gear. There were a lot of men in this refuge now. Two Negro soldiers carrying supplies had stopped to give some water to a pair of Marines who were lying quietly at one end. The Marines had been hit by shrapnel and were waiting for litter bearers. After they drank the water, their only movement was a slight, mechanical stirring of their heads each time a shell burst close by. By now almost everyone on the beaches, even those not killed or wounded, had had some sort of direct contact with Japanese shells, if only to the extent of having tiny spent fragments, still burning hot, drop onto their clothing or into the sand right beside them.

By the time we reached a hole by the water's edge, near where we had landed, we had lost our sense of urgency and entered that stage, which comes after a certain amount of time in a shelled area, when you can no longer bring yourself to duck and run constantly, even when you are moving in the open. But the men in the boats along the shoreline immediately aroused us. Since they came into the fire zone only at intervals and remained as briefly as possible, they had no time to lose their awareness of danger. It suddenly seemed to us a matter of desperate importance to get out of there at once. An ammunition dump was beginning to grow up around us, and the shelling did not abate.

We went up to a boat whose ramp was slapping the waves a few feet out from the shoreline and whose coxswain was trying to hold her to shore by keeping her engine running. There we encountered a Marine named Connell, who for the next half hour gave the most spectacular demonstration of energy I have ever seen. Though he moved with great speed and fervor, there seemed to be no fear in him. He had been helping moor and unload supply boats all afternoon. He was stripped down to his green Marine shorts, and he spent as much time in the water as out of it, his lank, blond hair plastered to his skull. When he wanted to salvage a piece of equipment from the water, he made a long, flat power dive over the surf. His problem at the moment was to make this boat fast, so that the ammunition aboard her could be unloaded. With the coxswain's permission, we got into the boat and stowed our packs in the stern. It was quickly obvious that the crew of the boat, though they remained calm, were of no help to Connell whatever and considered the odds against unloading at this time overwhelming and the situation irremediable. Connell shouted orders or suggestions at them, but they simply stared at him and then stared up and down the beach at the shellbursts. Connell got hold of a rope, made it fast to the boat, then darted up the beach to tie the other end to a tractor, whose driver surveyed him curiously from the top of the vehicle. Connell persuaded the driver to start his engine and try to pull the boat in. The rope broke. Connell tied it again and it broke again. He swam out to get another rope, but by the time he returned to the beach the driver and tractor had disappeared. Swimming furiously, he then approached Lee and me, at the stern of the boat, and called out the courteous suggestion that we get ashore. "This is going to take a long time," he shouted over the sound of the surf, "and you fellows will do better somewhere else!" He never once showed the slightest sign of temper or desperation. He appeared to regard the wild scene and his own mighty efforts and constant frustrations as wholly rational and what was to be expected. He was wrong about the boat's being there a long time. A few minutes after Lee and I swam and struggled to shore—Connell made three personal amphibious trips to help us with our gear—the boat withdrew to sea, with its cargo still aboard, possibly to try a landing somewhere else. The last we saw of Connell, he was racing down the beach to grasp a mooring rope on another boat thirty yards away.

It was getting dark and our clothes and equipment were nearly dry again when we finally boarded an LCT bound for the general neighborhood of the flagship. Five sailors returning from a shore job were grouped in a corner of the hold aft, where the boat's sides rose above their heads. As the vessel pulled out, we saw that four of them were trying vaguely to soothe the fifth, who was in the throes of shock from a near miss by a shell. He was a small young man with an underslung lower jaw. His head lolled back against the bulwark and his eyes rolled violently. "They can't get you here," said one of his colleagues, pointing at the boat's high sides. "Look. They can't even see you." By the time we were a couple of miles out, the sailor had recovered to the point of asking questions about the battle, but these and the answers he himself supplied only had the effect of returning him to a state of shock. The four others stopped looking at him and talked listlessly among themselves.

We made the flagship that night, but my typewriter sank to the bottom of the sea during our transfer from the LCT to a smaller boat that could go alongside the gangplank of the flagship.

The nature of the Iwo Jima battle did not change much in the days that immediately followed. The Marines made slow and costly gains in ground as they fought northward—gains that struck me then, and still do, as very little short of miraculous. A week or so after D Day, in a little scrub grove halfway across the island, I recognized, behind his whiskers, a staff officer in our transport group who used to surprise me a little by the passion and complete engrossment with which he could discuss for two or three hours at a time such a question as whether or not certain items of battalion equipment should be distributed divisionally, or whether a brother officer of his named Logan, thirty-five hundred miles away, stood eighty-sixth or eighty-seventh on the promotion list. It now seemed to me that such preoccupations were useful indeed if they contributed to the professional doggedness with which this man and the troops of his unit moved forward against such overpowering intimations of mortality. "I hear that the mortar fire is easing up on the beaches," he said seriously. "That's good. There's no reason why everybody on the island should get killed."

# LETTER FROM LONDON

MOLLIE PANTER-DOWNES

*May 12, 1945*

THE big day started off here with a coincidence. In the last hours of peace, in September, 1939, a violent thunderstorm broke over the city, making a lot of people think for a moment that the first air raid had begun. Early Tuesday morning, V-E Day, nature tidily brought the war to an end with an imitation of a blitz so realistic that many Londoners started awake and reached blurrily for the bedside torch. Then they remembered, and, sighing with relief, fell asleep again as the thunder rolled over the capital, already waiting with its flags. The decorations had blossomed on the streets Monday afternoon. By six that night, Piccadilly Circus and all the city's other focal points were jammed with a cheerful, expectant crowd waiting for an official statement from Downing Street. Movie cameramen crouched patiently on the rooftops. When a brewer's van rattled by and the driver leaned out and yelled "It's all over," the crowd cheered, then went on waiting. Presently word spread that the announcement would be delayed, and the day, which had started off like a rocket, began to fizzle slowly and damply out. Later in the evening, however, thousands of Londoners suddenly decided that even if it was not yet V-E Day, it was victory, all right, and something to celebrate. Thousands of others just went home quietly to wait some more.

When the day finally came, it was like no other day that anyone can remember. It had a flavor of its own, an extemporaneousness which gave it something of the quality of a vast, happy village fête as people wandered about, sat, sang, and slept against a summer background of trees, grass, flowers, and water. It was not, people said, like the 1918 Armistice Day, for at no time was the reaction hysterical. It was not like the Coronation, for the crowds were larger and their gaiety, which held up all through the night, was obviously not picked up in a pub. The day also surprised the prophets who had said that only the young would be resilient enough to celebrate in a big way. Apparently the desire to assist in London's celebration combusted spontaneously in the bosom of every member of every family, from the smallest babies, with their hair done up in red-white-and-blue ribbons, to beaming elderly couples who, utterly without self-consciousness, strolled up and down the streets arm in arm

472

in red-white-and-blue paper hats. Even the dogs wore immense tricolored bows. Rosettes sprouted from the slabs of pork in the butcher shops, which, like other food stores, were open for a couple of hours in the morning. With their customary practicality, housewives put bread before circuses. They waited in the long bakery queues, the string bags of the common round in one hand and the Union Jack of the glad occasion in the other. Even queues seemed tolerable that morning. The bells had begun to peal and, after the night's storm, London was having that perfect, hot, English summer's day which, one sometimes feels, is to be found only in the imaginations of the lyric poets.

The girls in their thin, bright dresses heightened the impression that the city had been taken over by an enormous family picnic. The number of extraordinarily pretty young girls, who presumably are hidden on working days inside the factories and government offices, was astonishing. They streamed out into the parks and streets like flocks of twittering, gaily plumaged cockney birds. In their freshly curled hair were cornflowers and poppies, and they wore red-white-and-blue ribbons around their narrow waists. Some of them even tied ribbons around their bare ankles. Strolling with their uniformed boys, arms candidly about each other, they provided a constant, gay, simple marginal decoration to the big, solemn moments of the day. The crowds milled back and forth between the Palace, Westminster, Trafalgar Square, and Piccadilly Circus, and when they got tired they simply sat down wherever they happened to be—on the grass, on doorsteps, or on the curb—and watched the other people or spread handkerchiefs over their faces and took a nap. Everybody appeared determined to see the King and Queen and Mr. Churchill at least once, and few could have been disappointed. One small boy, holding onto his father's hand, wanted to see the trench shelters in Green Park too. "You don't want to see shelters today," his father said. "You'll never have to use them again, son." "Never?" the child asked doubtfully. "Never!" the man cried, almost angrily. *"Never!* Understand?" In the open space before the Palace, one of the places where the Prime Minister's speech was to be relayed by loudspeaker at three o'clock, the crowds seemed a little intimidated by the nearness of that symbolic block of gray stone. The people who chose to open their lunch baskets and munch sandwiches there among the flower beds of tulips were rather subdued. Piccadilly Circus attracted the more demonstrative spirits.

By lunchtime, in the Circus, the buses had to slow to a crawl in order to get through the tightly packed, laughing people. A lad in the black beret of the Tank Corps was the first to climb the little pyramidal Angkor Vat of scaffolding and sandbags which was erected early in the war to protect the pedestal of the Eros statue after the figure had been removed to safekeeping. The boy shinnied up to the top and took a tiptoe Eros pose, aiming an imaginary bow, while the crowd roared. He was followed by a paratrooper in a maroon beret, who, after getting up to the top, reached down and hauled up a blond young woman in a very tight pair of green slacks. When she got to the top, the Tank Corps soldier promptly grabbed her in his arms and, encouraged by ecstatic cheers from the whole Circus, seemed about to enact the classic role of Eros right on the top of the monument. Nothing came of it, because a moment later a couple of G.I.s joined them and before long the pyramid was covered with boys and girls. They sat jammed together in an affectionate mass, swinging their legs over the sides, wearing each other's uniform caps, and calling down wisecracks to the crowd. "My God," someone said, "think of a flying bomb coming down on this!" When a firecracker went off, a hawker with a tray of tin brooches of Monty's head happily yelled that comforting, sometimes fallacious phrase of the blitz nights, "All right, mates, it's one of ours!"

All day long, the deadly past was for most people only just under the surface of the beautiful, safe present, so much so that the Government decided against sounding the sirens in a triumphant "all clear" for fear that the noise would revive too many painful memories. For the same reason, there were no salutes of guns—only the pealing of the bells, and the whistles of tugs on the Thames sounding the doot, doot, doot, dooooot of the "V," and the roar of the planes, which swooped back and forth over the city, dropping red and green signals toward the blur of smiling, upturned faces.

It was without any doubt Churchill's day. Thousands of King George's subjects wedged themselves in front of the Palace throughout the day, chanting ceaselessly "We want the King" and cheering themselves hoarse when he and the Queen and their daughters appeared, but when the crowd saw Churchill there was a deep, full-throated, almost reverent roar. He was at the head of a procession of Members of Parliament, walking back to the House of Commons from the traditional St. Margaret's Thanksgiving Service. Instantly, he was surrounded by people—people running, standing on tiptoe, holding up babies so that they could be told later they had seen him, and shouting affectionately the absurd little nurserymaid name, "Winnie, Winnie!" One of two happily sozzled, very old, and incredibly dirty cockneys who had been engaged in a slow, shuffling dance, like a couple of Shakespearean clowns, bellowed, "That's 'im, that's 'is little old lovely bald 'ead!" The crowds saw Churchill again later, when he emerged from Commons and was driven off in the back of a small open car, rosy, smiling, and looking immensely happy. Ernest Bevin, following in another car, got a cheer too. One of the throng, an excited East Ender, in a dress with a bodice concocted of a Union Jack, shouted, "Gawd, fancy me cheering Bevin, the chap who makes us work!" Herbert Morrison, sitting unobtrusively in a corner of a third car, was hardly recognized, and the other Cabinet Ministers did no better. The crowd had ears, eyes, and throats for no one but Churchill, and for him everyone in it seemed to have the hearing, sight, and lungs of fifty men. His slightly formal official broadcast, which was followed by buglers sounding the "cease firing" call, did not strike the emotional note that had been expected, but he hit it perfectly in his subsequent informal speech ("My dear friends, this is your victory . . .") from a Whitehall balcony.

All day long, little extra celebrations started up. In the Mall, a model of a Gallic cock waltzed on a pole over the heads of the singing people. "It's the Free French," said someone. The Belgians in the crowd tagged along after a Belgian flag that marched by, its bearer invisible. A procession of students raced through Green Park, among exploding squibs, clashing dustbin lids like cymbals and waving an immense Jeyes Disinfectant poster as a banner. American sailors and laughing girls formed a conga line down the middle of Piccadilly and cockneys linked arms in the Lambeth Walk. It was a day and night of no fixed plan and no organized merriment. Each group danced its own dance, sang its own song, and went its own way as the spirit moved it. The most tolerant, self-effacing people in London on V-E Day were the police, who simply stood by, smiling benignly, while soldiers swung by one arm from lamp standards and laughing groups tore down hoardings to build the evening's bonfires. Actually, the police were not unduly strained. The extraordinary thing about the crowds was that they were almost all sober. The number of drunks one saw in that whole day and night could have been counted on two hands—possibly because the pubs were sold out so early. The young service men and women who swung arm in arm down the middle of every street, singing and swarming over the few cars rash enough to come out, were simply happy with an immense holiday happiness. They were the liberated people who, like their counterparts in every celebrating capital that night, were young enough to outlive the past and to look forward to an unspoilt future. Their gaiety was very moving.

Just before the King's speech, at nine Tuesday night, the big lamps outside the Palace came on and there were cheers and ohs from children who had never seen anything of that kind in their short, blacked-out lives. As the evening wore on, most of the public buildings were floodlighted. The night was as warm as midsummer, and London, its shabbiness now hidden and its domes and remaining Wren spires warmed by lights and bonfires, was suddenly magnificent. The handsomest building of all was the National Gallery, standing out honey-colored near a ghostly, blue-shadowed St. Martin's and the Charles I bit of Whitehall. The illuminated and floodlighted face of Big Ben loomed like a kind moon. Red and blue lights strung in the bushes around the lake in St. James's Park glimmered on the sleepy, bewildered pelicans that live there.

By midnight the crowds had thinned out some, but those who remained were as merry as ever. They went on calling for the King outside the Palace and watching the searchlights, which for once could be observed with pleasure and without apprehension. Tired couples sat down, holding hands, and watched livelier people dancing around the little bonfires that burned here and there in the parks. A Canadian boy said to his English girl, "I hope you never have to have another celebration like this in your lifetime, Pat, but if you do I'll be back to help out. You can depend on that."

At last, when the floodlights were turned off, people began to straggle home, some of them still singing. For thousands of them, home that night had to be a sheltered doorway or the grass under a tree in the park, because the tubes and buses had stopped running hours before and taxi-drivers, like everyone else, had taken the day off. The celebrating spirit continued through the next day, which was declared a holiday, and more crowds poured into the center of town to sing, cheer, wave their colors, and yell for Churchill. On V-E Day-plus-one, it seemed fitting that the first visit of the King and Queen should be to the East End, a section of town that had particularly good reason to celebrate. In Stepney, the visit was announced only at the last minute, by police who drove through the district in cars equipped with loudspeakers. Consequently, the narrow, dirty little streets were lined with hundreds of people instead of the thousands there would have been had there been more notice. In the crowd were three spectacled rabbis, some old ladies clutching shawls, lots of noisy, excited kids climbing up on walls, service men home on leave, and girls with frizzy, elaborate hair-dos. At one point along the route, there was a huge crater where the last V-2 to fall on London had crashed down one March morning among some large blocks of Council flats, destroying two of them and killing more than a hundred and thirty people, including the members of some family parties that had been celebrating the return of soldier sons. "As soon as ever I was told the King and Queen was coming, I knew they'd come to our incident," one of the shawled old ladies said proudly. Dozens of little flags made a good show among the ruined houses and the excitement of the people was, if anything, wilder than it had been in the West End the night before. When the royal car turned up, the people broke through the cordon of good-humored policemen and stormed toward the visitors. It was evident that everybody in the battered street interpreted the royal visit as a personal compliment. A young man with a pale, intelligent face said, "They're feeling fine round here. You should have seen the bonfires last night. Every little street had one. Burning the bunks out of the shelters, they were. Well, they've had a bad time and now it's over. They've got a right to feel fine if anybody has."

# LETTER FROM ROME

### PHILIP HAMBURGER

*May 8, 1945*

HAVING lived for a year in a troubled semblance of peace, Rome has accepted the news of peace itself with the helpless and tired shrug of the defeated. My guess is that few cities are sadder today. V-E Day has pointed up an unpleasant fact many people here had tried to forget: that Italy lost the war and can advance no claims for the rewards of peace. To the Italians I've talked with, peace in Europe means at the moment little more than a dreary continuation of their present misery—fantastic prices, black markets, unemployment, the struggle to regain national pride, and the even more difficult struggle to get people to think for themselves after two decades of stupefaction. The German surrender seems to have increased the Roman's capacity for introspection; his comprehension of the situation his country is in is almost morbid, and his personal problems have suddenly loomed larger and become more pressing: how can a young man get to Turin to discover whether his parents survived the German occupation; does the American know someone who will deliver a letter to a lady's husband, a partisan, in Milan; please, will the United States permit Italians to leave home and settle in America; at the far end of town a wealthy friend has food enough for his friends tonight, but can the American arrange to get them there and back by jeep?

Today, Tuesday, is V-E Day, but the bars and restaurants are deserted, the streets practically empty. No more bells than usual have been rung. To be sure, some flags are out and the sirens have sounded, but something is lacking. Occasional noisy groups of young Italians parade the streets, trying with almost pathetic desperation to crash the gate of victory, but the victory is not theirs and the enthusiasm is hollow. One such procession—fifteen to twenty poorly dressed young men, a boy beating a drum, and another boy carrying a large red flag—straggled down the Via Sistina this afternoon and stopped before a British mess. Through the door they could see men laughing and drinking. *"Finita, finita, la guerra è finita!"* cried the paraders, and a British sergeant, glass in hand, stepped outside, bowed gracefully, and thanked the parade for stopping by. "Good of you to come," he said, and went inside. The procession slowly moved down the street a few doors to a hotel where some

477

Americans live. *"Finita, finita, la guerra è finita!"* the Italians cried. Several Americans stuck their heads out of windows, and yelled "Hooray!," and one man with a camera leaned out and said, "Hold it till I get this!" Then everybody stuck his head back in again. The parade disappeared around a corner, the drummer halfheartedly sounding a roll. Of all the troops in town, only the British seem to be in a rejoicing mood. Arm in arm and six or eight abreast, groups of them have been marching through the city, singing. Victory in Europe appears to have accented only the homesickness of the American troops, and, knowing very well that for most of them the end of one war means simply the beginning of another, still farther from home, they have shown little enthusiasm. Tonight I saw hundreds of them sitting alone on curbstones staring into space or ambling along the streets, hands in pockets, looking into shop windows.

Italy last week was Milan, and, unlike Rome, Milan had its victory, a victory all the more pleasant, perhaps, because it came from within rather than from without. Our troops were greeted there almost with hysteria, but this exhilaration had already been touched off, first by the partisan uprising in the city and then by the execution of Mussolini and his most infamous henchmen. When the Germans in Italy finally surrendered, the news went almost unnoticed in Milan. The newspapers welcomed the capitulation in modest headlines but continued to devote their biggest ones to partisan activities. On the whole, the efficiency and triumph of the partisan tactics seemed to stun even the partisans, and for the first three or four days after the liberation large groups of them—almost all of whom were dashing around town in captured German cars, rounding up or finishing off lingering Fascists—could be seen embracing one another in the streets.

Because Milan is in the plains and would have been difficult to defend against any reinforcements the Germans might send in to aid the garrison troops, the Committee of National Liberation had to move slowly. Nevertheless, from the beginning of the German occupation, in September, 1943, at least fifteen thousand copies of clandestine newspapers were circulated every week. The newsprint for them was bought on the black market. In March, 1944, the Committee put on a successful eight-day general strike in Milan. In September of that year the partisans began to attack the Fascists and Germans in the mountains of northern Italy, but they knew that it would be futile to attempt a fight in Milan yet. "Justice and Liberty" squads—one squad to almost every block in the city—were formed and told to provide themselves with arms. The main source of weapons was the garrison of twenty thousand Fascist troops, many of whom were willing to sell their arms if paid high enough prices. Many others were killed at night and robbed of their arms. The acquiring of arms was accelerated last December, when the Allies gave the Committee of National Liberation the task of leading the resistance movement in northern Italy. The Allies not only began to supply arms but also gave a lot of money to a trusted partisan in Rome, a banker. By intricate financial maneuvering, he was able to transfer the money to the north.

Meanwhile, in Milan, the partisans shifted their headquarters about once a week, settling now in the office of an obscure razor-blade distributor, now across town in a dismal restaurant. Mussolini, who had a villa on Lake Garda, north of Verona, appeared less and less frequently in Milan. When he did appear, he and his heavily armed cavalcade usually raced through the city, bound for somewhere beyond. By last January, work in the factories making supplies for the Germans had almost entirely stopped because Allied bombing of the Brenner Pass had cut the railway over which coal was sent into the country. In April, the Committee of National Liberation ordered railroad and tramway workers in Milan to strike, snubbed the Fascists when they suggested that everybody let bygones be bygones and that one big brotherly "sacred union" of all Italians might be created, formed a Committee of Revolt, mobilized the Justice and Liberty squads, and finally, on the twenty-fifth, told its ten thousand armed and ten thousand unarmed partisans to start taking over the city. By noon the following day, a hundred Fascists had been killed and the Committee was in control of Milan. The Germans fought in the suburbs until the twenty-eighth, the day of Mussolini's execution, but those inside the town barricaded themselves in several hotels and refused to come out and fight, preferring to await the arrival of the Allies and to surrender to them.

Although many Romans—and quite a few American correspondents—deplore what went on in the Piazza Loreto on the morning of Sunday, the twenty-ninth, to the Milanese these events will probably always be symbols of the north's liberation. To an outsider like myself, who happened to be on hand to see Mussolini, Clara Petacci, Pavolini, Starace, and some of the other Fascists dangling by their heels from a rusty beam in front of a gas station, the breathless, bloody scene had an air of inevitability. You had the feeling, as you have at the final curtain of a good play, that events could not have been otherwise. In many people's minds, I think, the embellishments of this upheaval—thousands of partisans firing their machine guns into the air, Fascist bodies lying in a heap alongside the gas station, the enormous, pressing crowd—have been overemphasized and its essential dignity and purpose have been overlooked. This is best illustrated by the execution of Starace—the fanatical killer who was once secretary of the Fascist Party—who was brought into the square in an open truck at about ten-thirty in the morning. The bodies of Mussolini and the others had been hanging for several hours. I had reached the square just before the truck arrived. As it moved slowly ahead, the crowd fell back and became silent. Surrounded by armed guards, Starace stood in the middle of the truck, hands in the air, a lithe, square-jawed, surly figure in a black shirt. The truck stopped for an instant close to the grotesque corpse of his old boss. Starace took one look and started to fall forward, perhaps in a faint, but was pushed back to a standing position by his guards. The truck drove ahead a few feet and stopped. Starace was taken out and placed near a white wall at the rear of the gas station. Beside him were baskets of spring flowers—pink, yellow, purple, and blue—placed there in honor of fifteen anti-Fascists who had been murdered in the same square six months before. A firing squad of partisans shot Starace in the back, and another partisan, perched on a beam some twenty feet above the ground, turned toward the crowd in the square and made a broad gesture of finality, much like a highly dramatic umpire calling a man out at the home plate. There were no roars or bloodcurdling yells; there was only silence, and then, suddenly, a sigh— a deep, moaning sound, seemingly expressive of release from something dark and fetid. The people in the square seemed to understand that this was a moment of both ending and beginning. Two minutes later, Starace had been strung up alongside Mussolini and the others. "Look at them now," an old man beside me kept saying. "Just look at them now."

No city could long remain in the emotional fever of the first days of liberation in Milan, and by the middle of that week there were signs of weariness. Fewer partisans roamed the streets, and they were less rambunctious. Only isolated shootings took place, and these at night. The slow process of rounding up the twenty-four hundred Fascists in the city continued; they were placed in San Vittoria Jail, in cells recently occupied by their captors. A good many partisans dropped their clandestine names and resumed their own, which created some confusion among the partisans themselves, who had never known one another's real names. It suddenly became apparent that the days ahead, like any morning after, meant a slow and complicated readjustment.

As for the city itself, its population has, in a few years, jumped from a million to a million seven hundred thousand. A sixth of Milan's buildings were bombed, a considerable number of them in the center of town. The Duomo, however, has survived; only two of the hundreds of delicate statues along its sides were chipped by bomb fragments, although five of its seven organs were wrecked by the concussions of nearby explosions. On the first day of liberation, a crude sign over the door of La Scala (whose roof had been bombed out) said, "We Want Toscanini," but someone took it down after the entrance of the Allied troops and substituted the American, British, and Russian flags. Most of the church of Santa Maria delle Grazie and all of its cloisters are now rubble, but there are hopes that da Vinci's "Last Supper," in the refectory, is intact. Before the first bombings of the war, the fresco was lovingly buttressed with heavy wooden scaffolding and bags filled with stones. The framework withstood the bombings and looks sturdy enough from the outside, amid the wreckage, but so far, understandably, no one has had time to begin the painstaking work of removing the wood and the bags of stones to find out whether da Vinci's masterpiece has survived the second World War.

# OKINAWA

JOHN LARDNER

SOMETHING of the wide, vaudeville range of European warfare was seen in the Pacific Theatre for the first time when American Army and Marine troops, supported by hordes of ships, boats, planes, amphibious vehicles, land vehicles, and technicians and specialists of every description, invaded Okinawa on April 1st, Easter Sunday. Most of the items of this particular variety show had been seen singly on the Pacific stage before. The Philippines, for instance, offered the spectacle and problem of a large civilian population —something unknown till then in our series of Pacific landings. In the Marianas there were small-scale collaborations of the Army and the Marines, and it should be understood that in many points of training, equipment, and mental attitude the difference between the Army and the Marines is sharper than the difference between the American and the British armies in Europe. At Iwo Jima we employed our first full-dress armada of naval and air support, and in two or three other places there occurred that true rarity of the Pacific war, an artillery duel. But Okinawa had them all and in most respects had them bigger. On this island, filled to capacity by four hundred and fifty thousand somewhat bemused natives and seventy thousand desperate Japanese troops, as the Marines indulged in wild and hazardous bushwhacking, the Army simultaneously fought a great pitched battle of artillery, and ships and planes threw thousands of tons of shells in all directions, I felt for the first time that every piece in the complicated pattern of European war was present. There were also several weird and gaudy patches that were thoroughly and uniquely Pacific.

There was a great deal of Japanese suicide—a branch of hysteria the Japs have developed highly in this war—in many forms, all ingenious. It's true that our enemies on both fronts have turned to suicide, but the Germans saved it for what seems to the Western mind the logical time—the end—whereas there is no sure indication that the current Jap suicide trend means the finish of the Japanese war effort. The Japanese on Okinawa have used suicide as a battle tactic and an active defense measure. They had done so elsewhere, but never so extensively or earnestly. On land and sea, their arrangements for defense were both strong and emotional, and everywhere the emotional quality undermined and nullified the strength. A matter of two thousand Japanese planes, representing an enormous outlay of equipment and first-line pilot talent, were shot down in the Okinawa area in the period of slightly more than two weeks I watched the operation, and though they did some damage to our smaller craft, such as destroyers, minesweepers, and LCSs, and created tensions and minor wounds elsewhere in the huge regatta, the net effect of it all was disproportionately and pitifully weak. Similarly, ashore, the best defensive preparations, which included large ammunition supplies and very strong built-up positions, were not used against us until after we had a grip on the island fatal to its defense and had poured men and supplies in unmolested.

Of the planes shot down, the greater number were bent on suicide, under the terms of the Japanese Kamikaze, or special-attack-force, training, which calls for "death simultaneously with a mortal blow to the enemy." There are swimmers and small-boat crews, as well as airmen and other strange operatives still unmentionable, for security reasons, in this force whose members "are not expected to return." Okinawa was a headquarters for the training of suicide swimmers and suicide boatmen. One morning, I was in a ship off the west shore when daylight overtook fifteen suicide swimmers in a canoe and on a raft aboard which they were approaching a nearby destroyer, and to a man they killed themselves instantly with grenades. The suicide swimmers are so designated because they leave their small craft for the final, personal gesture of attack. Suicide boats are attack weapons in themselves, with explosives and rocket launchers, set to fire upon impact, in the bow.

Our ships were attacked at Okinawa by suicide swimmers, suicide boats, suicide planes, ordinary homespun bombing planes that "expected to return" (though they seldom did), shore batteries, mortars, torpedoes, and even a submarine or two, and on top of that they faced the passive threat of mines. On the day of the first suicide-plane raids, the Navy vessels and transports in the fleet just off our supply beaches shot down some hundred and twenty planes. In addition, a hundred and sixty Japanese aircraft were intercepted and shot down farther out at sea. There was no question that the planes were ticketed for suicide by the Kamikaze formula. Those fliers who managed to penetrate our awesome curtain of flak dived straight and with finality at the ships of their choice, apparently picked at random. None of them would ever have entered this abattoir at all if they had had any thought of escape. They all rammed, or tried to ram, and none got away from the area while I was watching, which I did from a bouncing seat that at times I would gladly have traded for any other, in spite of the grisly fascination of the scene. Planes were coming in at intervals, in small batches, as best they could, and there was no way of telling, when you stepped into a Higgins boat bound across the harbor, under a peaceful sky, what would happen before you got where you were going. I was in an Army messenger boat on its regular run between the flagship and the beach, with its usual cargo of a dozen couriers and passengers, and it was slapping blithely through the waves beneath a hot afternoon sun. The first warning of sudden visitors was an arm of anti-aircraft fire which shot up from a ship close by, to be joined immediately by other arms darting from every direction. Riding the apex of this cone of fire was a two-motored Japanese plane. Its purpose became obvious when the pilot went into a clean, deliberate dive instead of making for higher, freer spaces. Three ships loomed off our port bow—a white hospital ship, a gray transport, and an LST—and one of them was his target. They followed him, groping and clutching. I could see black slugs swarm around him, and red tracer bullets, and this made me realize how close he was—able to look down our personal throats in our personal small boat, if he cared to, and read the linings of our stomachs. I grabbed my helmet, put it on, and ducked behind the bulkhead. The others did the same. The coxswain had given up purposeful steering by now, having no idea which way to run, and we bounced around aimlessly and watched the wild race between a man intent on his destiny and guns that tried to forestall him. In spite of the plane's speed, it was an unequal race. Halfway down, a trimming of fire suddenly crept over the fuselage, and a moment later the plane twitched in its course just enough to make us doubtful about what its target was. Then the plane hit the water, skipped once, like a flat stone, and broke into pieces. We still couldn't tell which ship it was that the pilot had chosen for his altar of immolation. He crashed between the hospital ship and the transport, and a couple of hundred yards from us, but we did not note such points specifically until after we had picked ourselves off the bottom of the boat, to which we had dived to avoid the fragments of plane flying over our heads.

I was telling this story a few days later to a young soldier embroiled in the infantry and artillery business over on the far side of Okinawa, out of sight of the shipping, and he listened courteously. "Is that so?" he said, when I had ducked my final fragment of the suicide plane. "Listen, did you know I fell off a cliff once in Leyte? We were going along . . ."

The fact is that with three highly specialized operations in progress all at once in Okinawa and vicinity, the active, but submerged, combatants in each branch were apt to lose sight of those in the two others, and of the instruments of synchronization, which were applied at Okinawa on such a vast scale. The battle area was small enough so that wanderers from zone to zone, like myself and the other war correspondents, could watch all three, or parts of all three. But on another day, when a suicide-plane raid almost as big as the first one befell our shipping, I had little mind for anything but the shells from the Jap land guns that were dropping around an Army command post a dozen miles away from the anchorage. Down in Army territory, at the south end of the island, when they did speculate on life in other regions, they would ask, "What about those Marines? Are they making any headway?" Now, the Marines—Okinawa was invaded by one corps composed of two Marine divisions and one corps of four Army divisions—had turned north from the landing beaches into wild, thinly defended country, while the Army, turning south, had bumped square against prepared Japanese defenses and the main part of the Jap defense force. By the time I began to hear the Army's question about the Marines' whereabouts, the Marines had ranged northward, over hill and gully, for great distances—great island distances—and one light-footed battalion had reached the north tip of Okinawa, nearly fifty miles from the landing point. Reports of this sort of thing were mystifying to Army troops, considering their own circumstances, but they were hardly more mystified than the Marines themselves had been at the start of the jaunt north. So far as the Marines were concerned, the Okinawa invasion was like a fierce, bold rush by cops, hunting gunmen, into a house that suddenly turned out to be only haunted. Here and there, the Marines did get fleeting glimpses of an evil presence. One platoon was ambushed in a ravine by a small party of Jap soldiers. The first night ashore some infiltrating Japs slipped into a camp and bayoneted thirteen Marines in their foxholes. But mainly there was just open island, green, fresh, cool, scenic, and empty—empty except for thousands of civilians, whom the Marines firmly ignored and tried to avoid shooting. In their fury of frustration and puzzlement, however, they shot a little of everything else, including a horse that came down the road near an encampment one night sounding like fourteen Jap soldiers. It was mowed down by outposts of a company commanded by an adventurous young Marine from Atlantic City.

The sense of anticlimax was especially acute among the Marines to whom I was assigned during the landing operation. They belonged to the Fourth Marine Regiment, famous even among Marine regiments for its hardihood and fighting record. Its nucleus was a group of semi-Commandos known, at the time they began fighting on Guadalcanal, as the Marine Raiders, and it was commanded now by an old Raider leader, Colonel Alan Shapley, a big, golden-colored fellow with a golden past as the Naval Academy's greatest athletic hero of the twenties. On the way to Okinawa, Shapley had been depreciating to me the idea of supermen or supertroops—Raiders, Rangers, Commandos, and such. He said any regulation regiment of Army or Marines could do as well. But he added, "These boys of mine are very good, and they love to kill Japs. This will be a very tough show, but the boys are full of shooting." On D Day at Okinawa, these boys full of shooting rode in to the beaches in the amtracks, erect and fierce as always in their white war paint and steeled against the withering fire they had been promised for weeks. They rushed up the beaches and before they knew it—in two hours, to be accurate—had crossed their D-plus-three (or fourth-day) objective, the big Yontan airport. The thwarted Marines stared at the Okinawans and the otherwise empty landscape with twitching fingers. It was at this unfortunate juncture that a Japanese fighter-plane pilot elected to make a landing on Yontan Field. Plainly ignorant that Yontan was in our hands, he brought his neat little green fighter down gracefully and taxied to a stop near what had been the Japanese operations office. In five seconds his plane was full of holes of every calibre from every gun around the airstrip. Appreciating that the situation was unfavorable, the pilot got out of the plane with his revolver drawn and was immediately full of holes himself. "I'm sorry the boys were so damn impulsive," said Shapley later. "He would have been a good prisoner."

By dawn of the third day ashore, the Marines I was with were ready to jump off in the final move of forty-five hundred yards, which would bring them to the eastern shore of Ishikawa Isthmus, on the opposite side of the island from where they had landed. Three battalions were going to take part in the attack. The night had been an eerie one in our dew-drenched camp on a pine-covered ridge dividing two ravines. There had not been time to flush all the ravines and caves, and we had by now heard the story of the thirteen Marines who were bayoneted in their holes the night before. We watched the pink glow of a brush fire that exploding shells had started beyond the next hill. "By God, this is very mysterious. Know what I mean?" said Lieutenant Colonel Fred Beans, executive officer of the regiment, as the boys looked around desperately for something to shoot. In the matter of civilians, they showed commendable restraint, especially considering that every Marine regarded Okinawans as Japs and would split no Oriental hairs whatever except to concede that these "Japs" looked very harmless and beaten down. The Okinawans we saw at first, cowering in the thatched houses of the little village of China—an apt name, since Okinawans are more like Chinese peasants than anything else—or hiding in nearby caves, were all women, old men, and children, every male civilian between sixteen and forty having been herded south by the Jap Army for labor duty.

We learned with interest from a hand radio that an airborne invasion by Japs was expected that night. Those Marines who had gone to bed shivered under their blankets and ponchos; they were South Pacific fighters, unused to crisp, cool nights. Shapley became concerned about a faint wailing sound up ahead of us. Finally the regiment's operations officer, Major Orville Bergren, turned from our telephone with a message. "I got the word on that noise," he said. "The second battalion has a woman and a baby with them that are hurt and crying. They wish to hell we would do something about it, because it is driving them crazy. The man that was with them got killed in the Jap fire in that little counterattack they had this evening. You know how it is. These people are scared to move by day, so they move by night and get shot up. What about it?" "Tell them to take it easy and see that the civilians are doctored, and forget it," said Shapley. "They'll be jumping off soon."

All three battalions launched their final eastbound attack at 0830 and, except for one small-fire fight on the right flank, were delayed only by the roughness of the ground. By 1100, two battalions were on the eastern beaches, and by 1130 the third was in the little coast village of Ishikawa. "Being as how we are working with the Army on this invasion and have the loan of some of their vehicles, of which they got more than there are in the city of Detroit," said Beans, who, like other Marines, was never able to get over his astonishment at the Army's wealth of equipment on Okinawa, "we don't have to walk to catch up with those battalions." Then he turned to Shapley. "I'll go ahead, Colonel," he said, "and set up a new C.P. across the island, and you can follow with the other jeeps." So saying, Beans was off down the road. He returned five minutes later to recover his revolver, which he had left hanging from a branch of a pine tree. That was the kind of campaign it was.

I rode across the island in Shapley's jeep. The roads were narrow and dusty, the villages poor and dingy, but the green island around them was a fine thing to see. Some ridges were so thickly terraced for planting that it was hard to see how they remained standing. We passed across a coastal plain checkered with rice paddies and green squares of sugar cane. Potatoes, beans, garlic, onions, radishes grew everywhere. The civilians, who were now feeling easier, were walking along the roads and saluting us. Nobody returned these salutes until Shapley waved back at a jovial old gentleman with a dirty kimono and bare feet, and then conviviality was general, with some exceptions. A truck just ahead of us was carrying five young Marines and, in the uniform of the Jap labor troops, one young Okinawan who had been badly shot up that morning. Apparently his head wounds had brought on shock, headache, and nausea, for he huddled in a corner of the truck, refusing all attentions. When one of the Marines, during a stop in the journey, lighted a cigarette and put it between the Okinawan's lips, he shuddered violently and pulled back after one puff. The Marines watched intently.

"What do you want to treat a Jap so good for?" asked one of them, whose tow hair stuck out wildly in all directions.

"Why not?" said the man with the cigarette.

"Well, why don't they send some of them back to tell those other Japs how good we treat them?" the first man said. "Then maybe they would treat us good."

The man with the cigarette spat thoughtfully. "Why not?" he said.

"Why don't they send some of them back to tell those other Japs?" the tow-headed boy was yelling balefully as the truck moved on again.

We found Ishikawa to be a deserted village perched on a magnificent bathing beach. Colonel Beans, who had already set up a command post on a hill overlooking some rice and sugar fields, went swimming with the regimental surgeon. I wandered through the village, looking at the lights of a dozen barbecue fires that were beginning to flicker in the dusk. Pigs were roasting, and chickens. Assistant chefs were going up to the fires with handfuls of onions, garlic, and radishes. "They ought to be sticking to their rations, damn it, but I don't know what you can do about it," the doctor said to me as he came out of the sea and began to towel himself. "The main thing is if they just cook that stuff thoroughly enough. Otherwise there's going to be a lot of sick Marines." The doctor was in a disgruntled frame of mind because earlier in the day a man from the regiment's weapons company, following the combat troops into Ishikawa, had been shot through the abdomen while hunting souvenirs in an area not yet searched.

"How's he coming, Doc?" asked Beans sympathetically.

"Oh, he's got a fifty-fifty chance," the doctor said gruffly.

Back at the C.P., Shapley had put a sprig of blue flowers in the buttonhole of his shirt and was outlining the day's progress to the general commanding the division. A couple of mess sergeants were cooking soup in a bucket, against the chill of the coming evening; it got cold as soon as the sun went down. Other Marines were gathered around an old woman in an old black kimono, who was squatting in a corner of the camp and eating C rations with chopsticks. "I guess the Japs didn't cut her in on those new kimonos," one Marine said. A shipment of kimonos, just in from Japan, some lined with flaming red silk, had been found in the village. A Marine gave the woman a cigarette, which she began to smoke. Apparently all older Okinawan women smoke. She was an unusual case, however, for when she had only half smoked the cigarette, she threw it away and produced a long, slim opium pipe, with a tiny bowl, and got to work on that. "No kidding, this old dame startles me," said a Marine. Another Marine said, "I seen one of them with a pack this afternoon that I couldn't lift it myself and another guy helped me with it, and she put it on her head and she just walked away as easy as anything."

The good, rich smell of hot chicken broth filled the clean air, and the Marines went up to the bucket, dipped their canteen cups in, and stood around drinking. It looked a little like a picture of a Civil War camp, with troops lounging in their high-crowned, peaked utility caps and their green utility clothes, now gray with dust.

Over in a newly dug foxhole, two Navy photographers who had just caught up with the regiment began to swap dirty pictures for souvenirs. A great many photographers are traders, and they have evolved a smooth underground commercial arrangement whereby a set of pornographic negatives is kept in some such headquarters as Guam and made available to all photographers who wish to make their own prints for trading purposes. Bidding was brisk in our camp. One sailor gave a Marine twelve pictures for a little stained Japanese flag and an opium pipe. After a while everybody began to look around for a warm place to sleep.

Shapley's staff had lent me a cot and a blanket, and I spread the blanket and my poncho over me and lay thinking about infiltrators. The valleys and caves around the camp were mainly unflushed and unsearched. Pretty soon it was no longer necessary to imagine sounds or magnify little rustlings in the dark. I heard a good, substantial sound on my left, and it got closer and louder —it was something any lifetime subway passenger could immediately identify as a Jap soldier crawling on his hands and knees and making a slight added shuffling noise caused either by asthma or a knife held between his teeth. I glanced at Colonel Beans' cot and saw that he was healthily comatose. I reached under my bed for my canteen to use defensively, and felt my hand being nosed and then licked, in the slow, appreciative manner of a connoisseur, by something that gradually took shape in the darkness as a goat. I found in the morning that it was a white goat. It stayed with me all night, occasionally going under the cot and butting me morosely through the canvas. "It's not a matter of this goat liking you better than anybody else," said Beans when he woke up, apparently fearing that I might have derived some false vanity from the experience. "You're in a Marine camp, and goats are naturally attracted to Marines. We've been having this kind of infiltration all over the Pacific. It's a wonder more of them don't get shot."

Having crossed the island, the Marines now began a campaign of systematic bushwhacking through the wild and rugged northern two-thirds of Okinawa. The Fourth Regiment moved up the eastern coast in leapfrog style: the lead company of the lead battalion would turn left up the first road leading inland to search for Japs, while the next company went ahead to flush the next road, and so on till the first unit, its work done, moved up through the others to take the lead again. Warships cruised alongshore parallel to this advance, ready to lend support with their big guns in case of trouble. However, little game was found till the Marines began to scour the big Motobu Peninsula, on the west shore of the island. There—as on the tiny island of Ie, off Motobu, on which Ernie Pyle was killed, almost at the end of a quick and otherwise unnoteworthy little special campaign—Japs to the number of perhaps two regiments, scattered at the time of the landing, had reformed into tight defensive pockets, and it took some fighting to break these up. The Marines who had been baffled and gun-eager on landing day finally got their shooting on Motobu Peninsula. Some were killed and wounded, but not to the extent of really impressing their colleagues. One of my last memories of this phase of Okinawa is of a Marine six feet three in height running up to the field hospital carrying a dead snake, perhaps eighteen inches long, by the tail. "Look at this son of a bitch!" he yelled excitedly to the medical corpsmen who were tending the wounded on litters. "He almost got me! If I hadn't been expecting something like this ever since we landed, he would of got me!"

We had heard by now that the Army, at the other end of the island, had run into one of the greatest Jap defensive battles of the war, and since the story was now there and no longer among the Marines, I went south.

In the piebald campaign of Okinawa, the Japanese have reacted with two defenses, both suicidal in form: the violent, quick suicides of the Kamikaze forces, and the more orthodox but equally certain suicide of a strong, armed land force, dug into fine positions behind big guns, with no hope whatever of reinforcement or escape. Most of this force became pocketed voluntarily in the south end of the island, around the capital city of Naha, and fell to the lot of the Army branch of our landing team, four infantry divisions in strength. After completing their own job of bushwhacking and mopping up in the wilder northern part of Okinawa, the two Marine divisions that took part in the invasion stood by, along with strong naval sentinels out at sea, to watch the Army bending to its task. There was much opportunity in this situation for cynicism. Before Okinawa, little was known about Army troops in the Pacific outside the boundaries that formerly confined General MacArthur's zone of command, and in some quarters they were not too highly valued. Marines, carried and supported by Admiral Nimitz's ships, had done the bulk of the land fighting from Guadalcanal through Iwo Jima. On one or two occasions, especially in the Marianas, invasions had been joint Army-Marine operations, and these resulted in frictions that were fanned to the proportion of at least small grass fires by some participants and observers who took a unilateral, Marine view of the matter. The reputed Army inferiority was also talked up quite considerably in print. One deponent, a war correspondent, approached me in Joe Madden's restaurant, back in New York, on a summer evening in 1944 and said, "Tell me, is there such a thing anywhere as a good Army division?" The question startled and even shocked me somewhat, as it would anyone who had been watching Army divisions in action in the European Theatre. Three months before the Normandy landings, a number of Army divisions—the First, the Third, the Ninth, the Thirty-fourth, the Thirty-sixth, and the Forty-fifth—had already displayed great skill and bravery. I told him I didn't know exactly what he was talking about, and he said I would know when I got back to the Pacific (where I had been in the early days of the war).

It turns out, back in the Pacific, that many Marine leaders wave banners less violently in their own behalf than their unofficial spokesmen do. The episode of the Marianas, which involved basic differences in combat purpose, technique, and equipment between the Army and the Marine Corps, was certainly talked of, but I found that a great many Marine units had been frankly ignorant of the Army before Okinawa, and they were insatiably curious, when they saw the Army troops there, about how they looked and lived and performed. Some were astonished by the copious supply of Army vehicles. The Marine Corps is designed to move by foot on land, to take beachheads, to fight for quick decisions in small areas, and then to be shipped somewhere else. The Marines cannot, as a rule, proceed painstakingly against stubborn obstacles, because time is snapping at their heels and supply limitations are forcing them to hurry. The Army forces have the equipment to fight campaigns of attrition. Generally, as long as the enemy remains strong and organized, they do so. These, however, are textbook differences. Most Marine leaders admit that the man-for-man difference between Army and Marine troops in action is infinitesimal. I'm speaking, of course, of Army troops who belong to combat units and have had battle experience. These conditions are necessary to fair comparisons, since Marine units consist almost entirely of combat troops and have nearly all had long and bitter battle experience.

What the Marines saw to the south of them on Okinawa, after completing a good, characteristic job of rapid guerrilla work in the northern end of the island, was a line of Army divisions of various degrees of seasoning engaged in one of the most difficult pitched battles of the whole war. This fight is still in progress as I write. There are several ways of officially interpreting battle situations, and under some interpretations it would have been quite possible to put an official period to the Okinawa campaign some weeks ago. Strategic airfields had been won, our position was secure, and the enemy's was, broadly speaking, hopeless. Speaking more narrowly, he was still sixty thousand strong when I visited the Army line, was still throwing artillery shells as though he owned a mine of them, and was still, from richly prepared caves, hills, and bunkers, making our progress very slow and perilous indeed.

As you ride southward on the island of Okinawa, you find more and more tombs. These tombs are the hallmark of the war on Okinawa. They are not bunched and confined to cemeteries. They stud hillsides everywhere, terraced into the ground so that you see them only when you face the slope of a hill. In the most familiar type, there is a double circle of gray stone, in a sort of figure eight, laid on the slope of the land and with a square stone terrace at its foot. At the rear of the terrace, leading into the earth, is a low, oblong doorway, often barred, though not sealed, by a block of stone, and beyond the door, inside the crypt, are colonies of ancestors—from two to twenty in number—ranged in flimsy wooden coffins or in tall urns of rough glazed clay. We Americans were constantly sharing the privacy of these ancestors. In our Army's part of the island there was no better place to avoid the flying shrapnel from the heavy Jap barrages. We would sit and smoke quietly among the honored dead, keeping out of the line of the open door. There was no feeling among us that we were intruding; these tombs were often visited before we came. Okinawans live in close communion with their ancestors, and young girls who have earned the privilege are delegated from time to time to wash the bones of the forebears of their families with sweet-potato brandy, a product of the local distilleries.

On my way to the Army's front line, I hitched a ride on a big 6 x 6 quartermaster truck loaded with cases of rations. I sat on the summit of a plateau of food, along with several fellow-passengers—two Negro quartermaster men and two transient sailors—and I found it necessary to push one end of my canteen belt into a niche between two boxes to keep from sliding off as we rolled around curves or lurched down hills.

"What kind of rations are these?" asked one sailor.

"New-type C rations," said a quartermaster man.

"New-type C rations!" said the sailor, helping himself from a broken carton of chocolate bars. "What the hell can you do with C rations? You can't make them worse and you can't make them better."

The sailor had the loose, jerky movements and rolling, restless eyes you see in many thyroid cases. When traffic held us up briefly near a farm, he stood up on top of the cargo, with his cocked rifle in one hand, and looked from side to side. "I want to take a shot at one of them herons," he said. "I saw some herons a piece back on the road. I probably would miss it. Maybe I wouldn't miss it. I wonder if I could hit it. Where the hell is a big heron I could take a shot at?"

"There's a rat," said the other sailor suddenly, pointing at a ditch alongside the farmhouse.

"Where? Where? Where?" said the sailor with the gun, looking around in great excitement.

"It's over there, only it ain't a rat," the other sailor said. It looked to me like a mongoose or ferret.

"I see it! I see it!" shouted the sailor with the gun, and fired. The truck began to move again, and he hastily sat down. "I wonder if I hit it," he said. "I don't know if I hit it or not. Maybe I hit it." He continued to chatter as we moved along the rugged, beautiful east coast of Okinawa. The quartermaster man sitting next to me said in a low, grave voice, "That's foolish business, but those boys don't get off ship much—only when they got some errand down here." His finger swept two high-backed points of wooded land that jutted into the Pacific ahead of us to our left.

Two more hitched rides brought me to the neighborhood of the first of these points. I climbed a rocky path and found the command post of the Thirty-second Regiment of the Seventh Army Infantry Division, bivouacked among the tombs, either in tents or outdoors on cots and sleeping rolls and litters set up on the terraces of the tombs. The commander of the regiment, Colonel John M. Finn, commonly called Mickey, was undressing to take a sponge bath with water from a five-gallon fuel can. His orderly, Pfc. Peter Gomez, sat on another can close by, advising him.

"You certainly need this bath," said Gomez.

"I took one the day before yesterday," Finn said.

"You had to rush it too fast," said Gomez. "They certainly have been rushing us around here. I never saw so much Jap artillery."

A plane passed overhead and we all looked up.

"That's a Corsair—one of ours," Gomez said casually.

"My airplane spotter, orderly, valet, and strategist," said Finn, nodding at Gomez and washing himself. Gomez, a thin, brown young man with black sideburns and a hopeful wisp of a black goatee, looked down at his hands. There were four deep blisters on each of them. "Also your digger," he said. "I never dug so deep and so fast as yesterday."

The Finn-and-Gomez team, almost as old as the Seventh Division's combat record in this war, had been up to study the lines from an observation post just ahead of us the day before and had got caught in a Jap barrage. Shell fragments had wrecked the Colonel's telephone and his radio. Gomez dug a hole, between shellings, and his intensity, matching that of the Jap artillery fire, was such that the hole was four feet deep before he considered it adequate. He told me about it while Finn was putting on his clothes.

"You got your undershirt on backwards," the orderly interrupted himself to say.

"How in hell can you tell with these things?" said Finn cheerfully, pulling off the shirt and reversing it.

The Colonel is as thin and dark as Gomez, but his button-nosed face, with its tilted chin, is strictly Hibernian. He is an easygoing commander, known for his great bravery. Gomez shares this reputation, but he has added certain private aspects to his share of it. He has also won himself a place in the regiment as a sort of combined buffoon and historian. He used to be a bartender in Chicago—at the Club Alabam, the 885 Club, Michael Todd's Theatre Café, and other night spots, or, as he calls them, "buckets of plasma." He gets hurt quite often but never in a run-of-the-mill fashion. In addition to suffering from foxhole hands, an occupational disease of diggers, Gomez has fallen off a horse, fallen off a cliff, and been bitten by a snake. The snake was in the Philippines and the bite made Gomez mildly ill. The horse that threw him was an Okinawan horse he was trying to ride with a lasso bridle. The cliff he fell off was in Leyte, and this experience, which Colonel Finn and twenty-three other members of the regiment all had together, was one of the Thirty-second's most noteworthy and cherished adventures before Okinawa. It followed the familiar theme of the Pearl White movie serials of long ago, except that the camera, after backing the heroine up to the edge of the cliff, where she had been cornered by the villains on horseback, would suspend the action till next week, frequently leaving Miss White in mid-air, whereas the action in the case of Finn and Gomez and their companions was continuous and sustained. The Japs had cornered them and they had no choice but to go over the cliff, slowing their descent from time to time by clutching rocks or bushes. After hitting the bottom with considerable violence, they spent six and a half hours eluding Jap patrols on the way back to their own lines. It took another four days for the men to get back into combat trim.

The Seventh reminds me of the more seasoned Army divisions of the European war. Okinawa is its fourth campaign, following Attu, Kwajalein, and Leyte, and it has acquired the easy, informal, facetious attitude of a veteran combat outfit, which is deceptive because it conceals a skill and efficiency the greener divisions do not have. In some non-combat details, this efficiency may be, and often is, relaxed. The men of the command post, when I visited there, were deriving considerable relish from a blotch on the record of ingenuity built up with great care by Gomez and three of his close associates—Jones, Parks, and Gavan. On a recent evening, these four had been assigned to guard an Okinawa civilian, picked up near camp, pending his examination and classification by the Military Government the next day. They put him into a pup tent and elected to stand guard in shifts, one man watching for an hour and a quarter while the three others slept. It was not till near the end of the fourth shift, some five hours later, that they discovered that the Okinawan had taken leave of them at some unidentified point in the procedure, leaving his hat placed strategically at one end of the tent, just in view of the watchman. Parks, in answer to critics, insisted that they would get him when he returned for his hat, but the Okinawan had not done this by the time I left camp.

I had supper with Finn the evening I arrived at his command post. He and his staff were in the midst of a discussion of the astonishing quantities of Japanese artillery here and of the excellence of Jap observation and concealment when the enemy suddenly began to illustrate these remarks with 150-millimetre shells, interspersed with large mortar shells. They hit very close to the command post. "Holy smoke!" said Finn, reaching for his helmet. "It looks like we don't sleep again tonight. I'd rather have them hitting here, though, than on top of the battalions."

We went behind a tent and squatted against a stone wall that formed one wing of a large tomb to our left. Finn counted the shellbursts under his breath, trying to get a record of the rate and extent of the barrage. "Thirty-seven, thirty-eight," he was murmuring when a clerk came along with pencil and tablet to pick up the count. The clerk followed the familiar scoring system of groups of five—four vertical marks crossed diagonally by a fifth. Sometimes the shells came so fast that he had to race his pencil over the paper to keep up. After a few minutes, I was jarred by a sort of clout, as if a hand had been dropped heavily on my shoulder. The thud was loud enough to make everybody look at me, and I in turn looked guiltily at my left shoulder, which was where I had felt the clout. A fragment of shell about the size of a spool of thread had ripped the sleeve of my field jacket, but it had not penetrated my heavy shirt. It left a small burn and a bruise. I picked up the fragment, found it too hot to hold, and quickly threw it down. Finn's tiny dog, a native of Okinawa called Okie, leaped for it, burned her nose, and leaped back. "Well," Finn said after a slight pause, "there's the old Thirty-second hospitality for you. Visitors come and get their clothes torn off. Did it hurt you?"

"No," I said, somewhat embarrassed.

"Well, anyway," said Finn, "we better go join somebody's ancestors. It's too public out here."

We went into a tomb, crawling through a low, narrow door, and then settled down along one wall in darkness. Since the door had been open for several days, the atmosphere was not especially close. Four tall urns stood just behind me. Back in the darkness of the recess, I could detect the outlines of two rows of coffins. There was a great sense of security in these crypts during a shelling. They would not withstand a direct hit, but direct hits are few and far between and flying shrapnel, always the chief hazard of a barrage, would need a high degree of cunning indeed to find its way through a tomb's low door. Outside, a shell banged very near and we all winced instinctively. Jones, the luckless guardian of civilians but a good mess sergeant, popped into the tomb and groped his way to a seat among us. He threw something down on the floor. "Somehow, I can't get interested in that book," he said.

"What are you talking about?" said Finn.

"'Arrowsmith,' by Sinclair Lewis," said Jones. "I been trying to read out there, sir. Somehow, it don't seem to grip my imagination."

Tomb life becomes as conventional as any other after a while. Now and then, from the night outside, someone would call, "Is Mr. Drake in there?" or "Is Mr. Stainback in that tomb?," and someone within would reply, "No, he's in the next tomb" or "The radio is in the third tomb to your right."

As we sat in our tomb that night, Finn remarked that the intervals between attacks, when "you just sit and take the Jap stuff instead of fighting," are harder on men than the attack phase itself. It's true that in the long, formless gamut of "non-wound" casualties—shock cases, concussion cases, combat-fatigue cases, "psycho" cases—a good many can be traced to the effects of continuous bombardment during lulls in infantry action. It's also true that many shock and concussion casualties suffer physically. A company commander, credited with killing more Japs than any other man in the Thirty-second Regiment, suffered concussion, from a near miss by a shell, which affected his kidneys to such an extent that he needed the most delicate hospital treatment to survive. The difficulty is that the borderline between such a case and the purely mental, or "psycho," cases is dim. And "psycho" cases may turn out to be just as hard to treat. Standing on the terrace of a tomb in the Thirty-second Regiment camp one night, I heard the sound of uncertain footsteps on the hill just behind me and turned to see two medical corpsmen helping a third man down a path. The feet of the third man were dragging, and he was saying over and over, in a high, hysterical voice that had a queer, inhuman sound among the shellbursts in the dark night, "They'll get every one of you! They'll get every one of you!"

"Casualty?" asked a soldier standing beside me.

"Yeah, mental," answered one of the medical corpsmen over his shoulder, and the three men disappeared in the darkness.

I was with the Thirty-second Regiment on the morning of April 13th, Okinawa time, when Colonel Finn got the news over the telephone, at our early breakfast, of the death of President Roosevelt. There were men near our table and more men out in front of the tent, so within twenty minutes the news was all over the command post. But it spread quietly and the reaction was quiet. Some men were nonplussed and unable to put their thoughts into words; others were shocked into stillness and went about their work in a sort of walking reverie. Now and then, when two men met, they would stop to speak of what had happened, but they spoke slowly, with long pauses between their sentences, and when at last a pause grew into a silence, they would part and move on, as though it were impossible to understand the event and therefore to discuss it. I had never seen any news have an effect quite like this one. Finn, after exchanging fragments of low-voiced, half-unbelieving conversation with his staff, lapsed into a sort of brown daydream. Along about the middle of the morning, he suddenly said, "Well, damn it, the sooner we attack again the better it will be for everybody."

The Army line, of which the Thirty-second was on the extreme left flank, attacked again a few days later, and against the best-prepared line the Japanese had yet established in the Pacific, except possibly on Iwo Jima. It may be, as some say, that an infusion of Marines in the line would speed things up, but this is always true of fresh troops when fresh troops are available for replacement. The issue between the Marines and the Army is hard to determine. The Japanese are the only ones on Okinawa in a position to settle concrete points, and what they have proved is that their orthodox land defense against our troops is more effective in inflicting damage, if not in changing the course of the war, than the wild novelties of their land and water defense against our ships. Ashore, they have worked along the classic lines of war in both theatres, with counterattacks supported by massed artillery, machine-gun fire, and grenades, with minefields and tank traps, and, above all, with prepared gun positions in bunkers and caves. These cave positions surpass those of Iwo Jima in ingenuity and complexity. They are of great depth, set in a succession of communicating tiers like the setbacks on an apartment house, and equipped with food, water, ammunition, and mobile gun bases, some of which are surprisingly hard for our counter-battery fire to spot. In solving this problem, of course, our troops have had the amphibious advantage of side and rear views as well as front and bird's-eye. A battleship lying close offshore put four-

teen direct hits on five caves in one morning, probably destroying three ammunition dumps. Five caves is not many on Okinawa—an Army leader
questioned on this point before we landed said, "I don't wish to seem morbid,
but we believe there are more caves on Okinawa than in the rest of the world
put together"—but ammunition dumps and the Japs in their neighborhood,
when they blow up, are not replaceable in this campaign.

At sea, meanwhile, the inflexible students of Kamikaze have continued to
operate in the manner of a brigade of stylized moths storming the Wrigley
sign on Broadway. Because these Japs never attempt to dogfight or defend
themselves, our interceptor planes shoot down the suicide craft in droves. And
because they dive straight into anti-aircraft fire, in attempting to ram ships,
they are fat targets for flak gunners. They try again and again, and occasionally one of them does manage to make up for the failure of another. On
April 6th, the suicide plane I saw shot down and break up in the water seemed
to be aiming at a white hospital ship. Three weeks later another Kamikaze
pilot got home to this same hospital ship, whose nature it was impossible to
mistake in the midst of a fleet of ships otherwise solidly gray in color. This
ramming caused death and injuries aboard the hospital vessel, but I was impressed by the waste and inefficiency of the Japanese form of cripple-kicking
when I remembered a field hospital in Italy where I once saw a single German
dive-bomber pilot late one afternoon kill just as many people. The German
flier was not a Kamikaze. He went home to supper.

Furthermore, the Germans, being cool, practical men, never inserted
workingmen—not even Poles, Czechs, or Russians—into their flying bombs.
They used radio control at the Anzio beachhead and made the bombs do their
own work when sinking ships robot style. The Japanese produced a flying
bomb for the first time at Okinawa. If the Germans had not been otherwise
occupied, they might have gone into fits of scientific mirth over the Jap improvement on their own device, an improvement which consisted simply of
adding a cockpit and a not too large young man to a flying bomb and in-
structing him to join his ancestors in as many pieces as possible. The suicide
bomb has been used sparingly till now, but it will probably be used more lib-
erally as time goes on. By Kamikaze standards, it is an extremely reasonable
little gadget.

# LETTER FROM BERCHTESGADEN

## PHILIP HAMBURGER

*June 1, 1945*

LIKE the Reich that Hitler built to last a thousand years, his Berchtesgaden is now a grotesque and instructive heap of rubbish. A visit here can be rewarding, especially to archeologists, anthropologists, isolationists, and anyone who has ideas of sometime becoming a Führer. Better still, it makes nice sightseeing for American troops, hundreds of whom swarm over the charred grounds every day and poke through the dismal relics of the man who brought them to Europe in the first place. I have been doing a little poking myself.

To begin at the beginning, or at the foot of the Obersalzberg, you drive through the village of Berchtesgaden, pass American Army signs reading "To Hitler's Home," cross a simple, rustic bridge at the edge of town, and shift into low gear for the steep climb up the mountain. The glistening concrete highway is intact and very smooth. The vistas are breath-taking—now acres of pine forest, now snow-capped Alps, now green valleys below—and all along the roadside you see neat fences and dainty flowers. The first gatehouse is disarming, a naïve wooden chaletlike structure with an archway across the road. Except for two M.P.s standing guard, this could be the entrance to the estate of a gentleman, a gentleman with an appreciation of the countryside. The second gatehouse is more ominous. It is of wood and stone, standing forbiddingly on the hillside, and it is the first break with the setting, the first hint that perhaps the master of the estate was afraid of someone. Turn sharp right, inch up a steeper grade, and the road becomes broad and level as it runs along a shelf of the mountain lined on both sides, as far as you can see, with a vast tangle of camouflaged, bombed-out buildings, all green. Instantly you realize that, even when these buildings were intact, they were a desecration of the surroundings, utterly without beauty—a bulky, brutal set of structures thrown together in haphazard fashion, spreading every which way, as though to satisfy a boundless and ugly dream. "In the name of God," said the corporal who drove me up, "who ever called this place a retreat?"

There are few signs that Hitler had, or wanted, solitude. On the contrary, he seems to have had a passion for providing accommodations for hundreds of his cohorts. Above and behind his house, the Berghof, he constructed a massive,

*497*

rectangular barracks to house eight hundred S.S. men. The barracks is badly in need of repair; there are gaping holes in the roof and piles of debris in the courtyard. Large sheets of ragged green metal, once used for camouflage, have been blasted from the roof and lie scattered over the ground. In the basement are garages, with their gasoline pumps and No Smoking signs. Except for one Mercedes-Benz, telescoped and fallen into a bomb crater, the cars are gone. The S.S. men are gone, too. According to German workmen around the place, they were the last to leave, after the heavy bombardment of April 25th. Adjoining the barracks are the remains of a long, low administrative building, and across the road is a hothouse, which catered to Hitler's love for flowers. Also on the estate were another building for S.S. men, close to the master's house; a guest house; a home for Göring, which is now crushed and silly-looking, as though stagehands at the Metropolitan had taken hatchets and ripped apart a setting for "Hänsel and Gretel"; a home for Bormann, successor to Hess, and reputedly commanding officer of the estate in Hitler's absence; a nursery for the sturdy *Kinder* of the élite (the little Führers of the future); tunnels connecting all these buildings with one another and with Hitler's house, and leading up the hill to the final proof that privacy was certainly not wanted—a three-story hotel known as the Platterhof, with three hundred and fifty rooms and hot and cold running water.

Important visitors—field marshals, satellite premiers, high Party officials, and so on—were put in the guest house, but lesser Nazis always stopped at the Platterhof. The Führer's hospitality didn't include free room and board for the guests at the Platterhof; they paid their way. Now the 101st Airborne Division, Army of the United States, occupies its low-ceilinged, cell-like rooms, each with two pine beds and a desk lamp. Most of the furnishings were destroyed by the French troops who were the first to break into the place and who, apparently under the impression that it was Hitler's house, smashed most of the windows and made off with china, glassware, wall decorations, and the hotel's plentiful stocks of fine wines. (Senator Wheeler, who came along several weeks later to view the wreckage of an establishment where he might easily have been made to feel right at home in the old days, was seen by someone tearing a telephone from a wall as a souvenir.) Behind the desk in the bare, uninviting lobby, a sergeant divides his time between acting as room clerk and passing out, to visiting troops, maps of the estate politely labelled "Obersalzberg, Hitler's Mountain Retreat." A model of the unsuccessful camouflage plan for Berchtesgaden, designed by a Munich architect, stands in the lobby; it is dotted with tiny buildings, trees, green nets, and so on.

Guests at the Platterhof ate their meals under gold-and-white wooden chandeliers in a vaulted pavilion adjoining the hotel. It sits on a bluff overlooking Hitler's house and has a large hat-check room, a kitchen with a *caffè espresso* machine, some deep-freeze tubs for ice cream, and a beer tap. A German electrician detailed by our Army to clean up some debris told me that

Hitler's final military conference at Berchtesgaden took place in the pavilion last June, after our invasion. Two hundred generals, including Keitel and Guderian, attended. The meeting went on for more than two days, almost without pause. Hitler shouted so loudly that workmen in remote parts of the estate could hear his rasping voice as it pierced the clear mountain air. "He kept banging so *verdammt* hard on the table," the electrician said, "that on the second afternoon he knocked a heavy lamp onto the floor and I had to rush in with a new bulb." While the bulb was being put in, the Führer stopped his harangue and the generals watched the electrician in silence. The moment the electrician stepped outside, the Führer resumed.

The right wing of Hitler's house received a direct hit in the great raid. The resulting fire spread to the rest of the building, destroying all the fittings in the main entrance hall except some squat red marble pillars. The big front room, with its famous large window, is charred and empty. There is only the frame of the window and, at the opposite side, a large wrought-iron fireplace decorated with the figures of three German soldiers. The main staircase is in fairly good condition. Where its marble balustrade is chipped, you can see that the marble is no more than an inch-thick veneer on concrete. Hitler's workroom, upstairs, runs the width of the house; its walls have been thoroughly scorched and only the sockets of three windows and a hideous brown *Kachelofen* remain. His bedroom, which adjoins the workroom, has also been burned. The Führer's bathroom is in better shape. It has green tiled walls, in the best *Good Housekeeping* tradition.

In the basement, I came upon a narrow, gray-walled shooting gallery, the sort of thing you'd expect to find in an F.B.I. school. There are also numerous pantries and kitchens; the entrances to many tunnels, mostly blocked, into which vast quantities of food were put in the last months before Germany's defeat; a room cluttered with overturned chairs and tables, phonograph records, birth certificates, X-ray plates, and piles of old magazines, including a November 15, 1930, issue of the *Kölnische Illustrierte Zeitung* containing an article violently demanding that outworn treaties be discarded.

The German workmen I have talked with here agree that Hitler left the Berghof last June, after his meeting with the generals, and never returned. "Eva Braun drove off in June, too, with a captain and lots of luggage," one of the men said. Göring hung around the place long after Hitler had gone, prowling through the hills in Alpine shorts and with a hunting gun. During the bombardment of April 25th, he took to his bomb shelter. "He trembled tremendously," this man said. The last gay times at Berchtesgaden came shortly after the conference, when Eva Braun's sister married a colonel general and then five hundred guests went to Hitler's Adlerhorst, or Eagle's Nest, on the Kehlstein and got plastered. In March of this year, after Hitler consulted a stomach specialist in the nearby town of Bischofswiesen, orders were given to install a diet kitchen in the Berghof; this started the rumor that he would soon return. Some people thought they saw his car in Berchtesgaden shortly afterward, but nobody saw the Führer.

During his last weeks at the Berghof, Hitler walked with a slight limp and carried a cane. He occasionally visited some Gestapo cronies at the nearby Schloss Klesheim, once the castle of one of Franz Josef's brothers. When he did, all roads in the neighborhood were closed off. He also enjoyed short walks down the mountainside to a summer house known as Mooslahner Kopf, adjoining some farm lands he owned. He was invariably preceded and trailed by three or four hundred Gestapo men. Inside the Berghof, Heil Hitlers were forbidden. His housekeeper, a Frau Middelstrasse, was instructed to say *"Grüss Gott"* whenever she encountered him. *"Führt euch Gott,"* he would reply, sweeping past. Just before his final departure, he told her, "Now that I am going away, you will no longer have to bother with my needs and you can busy yourself with many things about the house."

Four o'clock on Sunday afternoon was the Führer's brooding hour. He was driven rapidly up the Kehlstein, past long lines of Gestapo guards, and then took the elevator to the building on its summit, the Adlerhorst, known to everybody on the estate as the Tearoom. While he brooded, as many as a thousand S.S. and Gestapo men surrounded the place.

I went up to the Adlerhorst. I drove along the twisting mountain road (hundreds of Yugoslavs are said to have died building it) until I reached the end, a thousand feet below the summit. At this point, in a broad pocket cut out of the mountain, I faced two bronze doors leading to the elevator that reaches the building itself. An inscription over the doors says *"Erbaut* 1938." The day I was there, the elevator wasn't running and Army engineers were in the shaft removing mines, so I took a footpath to the peak. It was a brisk fifteen-minute walk, past ice fields and small, snow-covered shrubs. Perched on the top of the mountain and surrounded on all sides by the jagged peaks of other mountains is the Adlerhorst, a hexagonal granite structure from which an L-shaped rear juts out. Both inside and out it reveals Hitler's madness and his exquisite bad taste. Taking Nietzsche's words literally—Superman lives on the mountaintop —the master of Europe went into the clouds. And what did he build? From the outside, the place could be the guardhouse of a state penitentiary. Inside, everything is out of proportion or off key—ceilings too low, windows too small, bronze doors here, wooden doors there, some rooms right out of an ad for Men of Distinction, others designed like a cheap bar-and-grill. Clouds sweep in through the doorways and windows. The master went so high that for only a few hours a day, and then only when the weather was very good, is there any view at all. The elevator opens on the entrance hall, and beside it is a metal panel with thirteen lights to show the position of the car. On it, too, are the words *"Vorsicht! Aufzug!"* and the information that the capacity of the elevator is 1125 kilograms, or fifteen persons. Twenty-four bronze hat-and-coat hooks hang in the hallway, and opposite them are lavatories large enough to handle a Music Hall crowd. At one end of the hallway is a taproom with a bright-blue table and seats with bright-red leather cushions. In the kitchen are shiny pots and pans, stoves, and a meat block that has never been touched; there isn't a cleaver mark on it.

Off the main hall is a long conference room with an oak table, twenty-six chairs, and blackout curtains, and off that is a huge hexagonal room—the brooding room, the room where Hitler could think his long, lonely, megalo-maniac, bloody thoughts. And into this room he crowded forty-six chairs, one more ugly than the next—low-slung chairs covered with sickly blue imitation needle point. On the floor is a machine-made imitation Chinese rug. Before a massive red marble fireplace stands an overstuffed rust-colored sofa that no Kansas farmer would allow in his house. A huge white circular table is in the center of the room. The wall lights are garish gold strips arranged fanwise to simulate tongues of flame.

Furthermore, the Adlerhorst had mice. In a closet, I found a half-empty cardboard box of powder. An absolute guarantee against *Feldmäuse,* the label said.

[July 28, 1945]

# LETTER FROM BERLIN

JOEL SAYRE

*July 14, 1945*

SOME days ago, on Unter den Linden, I was staring through an iron gate barring the approach to what is left of the Ehrenmal, the Prussian equivalent of our Tomb of the Unknown Soldier, when two girls stopped beside me, also to stare. Each had a rucksack filled with wood on her back. There is no cooking gas in Berlin, no coal, no oil; householders burn wood from ruined buildings and dwellings, and they have no trouble finding plenty. The Ehrenmal, dedicated in 1931, is in the Alte Wache, or Old Guardhouse, a small, once handsome structure with walls of chaste limestone, built about a century and a quarter ago. For generations, at twelve-thirty in the afternoon every Sunday, Wednesday, and Friday, the guard outside the Alte Wache was changed while Berliners looked on with the same delight with which Londoners used to watch the changing of the guard at Buckingham Palace. The Ehrenmal, a slab of black granite bearing a wreath of silver and gold oak leaves and an inscription honoring the Prussians who died in the last war, was placed so that the illumination from a round skylight in the dome of the guardhouse shone on it. There is no guard outside the Alte Wache now. Its limestone walls are no longer chaste and the illumination from the shattered skylight is augmented by the light that comes through the jagged holes in the dome. The slab and the wreath of the Ehrenmal are still there, visible through the entrance, but the wreath has been jarred off the slab and both are littered with rubble, muck, and charred lumps of wood. "*Ach, ja,* poor Berlin," one of the girls said as they turned away. "How they beat us to pieces!"

The R.A.F. and our Eighth Air Force together dropped more than a hundred and fifty-six million pounds of bombs on Berlin. No one knows which section got it worst, for the complete figures on the damage won't be in for several months. Perhaps they will show that the parts worst hit were the workers' districts like Wedding and Köpenick. Nevertheless, Unter den Linden, the center of a target known to the Eighth Air Force as "Big B," or downtown Berlin, certainly got its share. The street, which, as everyone must remember, got its name from the rows of linden trees down its middle, is a hundred and ninety-eight feet wide and nearly a mile long, and it is the hub of

Berlin's east-west axis. In prewar days, with its jewelry shops, bureaus for luxury travel, salesrooms for custom-made automobiles, hotels such as the Adlon and the Bristol, and restaurants whose food, drink, and service made you think of Ernst Lubitsch pictures, it was one of the world's great avenues. On it, too, were the University, the State Library, Frederick the Great's State Opera, the Ministries of Interior and Finance, and the American, French, and Soviet Embassies. Not much is left of these buildings; most of them are shells, at best.

Take the Adlon, down at the street's western end, close to the Brandenburg Gate. If you ignore the fact that its doors and windows are bricked up as a precaution against bomb blast, it looks from the outside as you might expect a first-rate metropolitan hotel to look. Inside, it is a fire-gutted shambles, a circumstance for which, it appears, the cupidity of the proprietor, Herr Adlon, is responsible. Before Berlin fell, on May 2nd, the Adlon had nearly four hundred thousand bottles of vintage wine in its cellar. As the Russian Army closed in on the city, somebody on the hotel's staff began worrying about these treasures and went to the boss. *"Um Gottes willen,* Herr Adlon," he is supposed to have said, "what are you going to do about all that wine? The Russians are coming and you don't want them to get it, do you? Give it to the people in the streets. Pour it down the sewers. *Um Christi willen,* Herr Adlon!" Herr Adlon replied that he would think it over. He thought it over so carefully, weighing and counterweighing every possibility with such thoroughness, that he had disposed of only a few gross of bottles, to his employees, at nine marks apiece, before the Red Army arrived in Berlin. Its enlisted men, as the enlisted men of any army in the world would have done, got into the wine cellar of the Adlon. They had succeeded in drinking only a few hundred bottles, however, when the hotel caught fire from, it is said, a lighted cigar dropped on a carpet by an exhilarated staff sergeant. Four hundred and ten of the Adlon's four hundred and fifty bedrooms and all of its two hundred and fifty-five baths were burned out, and the remainder of Herr Adlon's stock of bottled goods was turned into a pool of molten glass.

Or take the State Opera House, grandfather to the Scala in Milan and great-great-grandfather to the Metropolitan in New York. Its façade, including the Latin inscription on the lintel above its columns, announcing that Fredericus Rex gave the building to Apollo and the Muses, is intact. When you go inside, you realize that even a massed choir of Carusos and Chaliapins couldn't fill it with sound, for there is practically nothing left to fill. This is not the building's first bit of bad luck. It was opened in 1743, and its interior was burned out a century later; then it was restored, and in 1928 completely modernized. It was burned out again, by the R.A.F.'s incendiaries, two centuries after its erection, but was quickly restored by the Nazis and reopened. I suspect that Fredericus Rex would have had some rather strong reactions had he been present on that reopening night. "Lohengrin," sung by the Reich's foremost artists, nourished the Führer's passion for Wagner and was at least a nod in Apollo's direction, but for those of the Party's leaders whose favorite muse was Terpsichore, there was a *Nackt-ballet,* or a posse of *Tanzgirls* with no clothes on, which performed fulsomely in each of the opera's intermissions. Later, the Eighth got the building again, for the third time, on one of its Big B operations.

With some friends, I walked one day down the short, narrow Oberwall-strasse, which runs off Unter den Linden. What we saw there can, with a few variations, be seen today in hundreds of Berlin side streets. There had been fighting in the Oberwallstrasse; a wrecked American half-track with S.S. license plates lay keeled over to starboard, and other military vehicles were strewn along behind it. A howitzer from the last war, which residents of the district told us had been taken from the Zeughaus, Berlin's military museum, and pressed into service, lay on its side. Clearly, the Russian heavy artillery had found the range. The Oberwallstrasse had also been bombed. Half of one large dwelling house had been sheared off, leaving four stories of rooms exposed to view. In one ground-floor room stood a small lathe which had doubtless been used to make parts of military instruments; during the war there was a great deal of *Heimarbeit,* or parlor manufacture, in Berlin.

Halfway up the street, an elderly woman and a little girl were foraging for fuel in another wrecked house. A sign on one wall of it said, in German, "Warning! As per order of the Herr Police President of Berlin, this property has been strewn with a highly poisonous rat exterminator. Children and domestic animals are to be kept at a distance." The old woman and the little girl hadn't read the sign or, more likely, didn't care. Under a fallen joist the child found a man's left shoe, in fairly good condition, and this she put into her rucksack. Single shoes are a commodity on Germany's black market.

In the gutter in front of another house we came across a soggy, coverless book that turned out to be Longfellow. "Life is real! Life is earnest!" and "Under a spreading chestnut tree" look funny in German; so does *"Auf den Ufern Gitschigummi sass der kleine Hiawatha."* Two youths who had been watching us came over. One said that in better days he had enjoyed Long-fellow; the other had been fascinated by Edgar Allan Poe. They were medical students waiting for the University to reopen and give them a chance to go on with their studies. That would not be for some time, I told them rather magisterially, as though I were a member of the Allied Control Commission. I pointed out that although we took Aachen last October, only the first four grades of its grammar schools had been opened so far and that nobody expected the university in Heidelberg to resume operation for at least another year. The two young men were surprised to learn that so little educational progress had been made elsewhere in Germany. Shortly after the capture of Berlin, they said, the Russians had reopened all the pre-University schools that were still standing. The only reason the University hadn't reopened, they said, was that it had been *ausgebombt*.

My friends and I walked back to Unter den Linden. A pale, bald man with protruding black eyes pedalled slowly by on a bicycle with no tires on its wheels. A hunchback, whose legs accounted for three-quarters of his height, trudged past in a blue windbreaker and checked trousers, pushing a handcart loaded with three empty barrels. Two trucks came along. One was a Studebaker 4 x 6, driven by a Russian soldier and carrying three Holstein cows, who looked poorly. The other was a German vehicle, painted black and powered by a wood-burning gas generator. Unter den Linden used to swarm with pedestrians and traffic, but now there was little of either. In front of the Brandenburg Gate a pretty Russian Wac, with the help of two flags, was directing what traffic there was. Above the gate's arches hung a Russian banner inscribed "Long live the Soviet Armies that planted their victory standards in Berlin!" On top of the gate, the outside right horse in the famous sculptured team of four steeds pulling Victory's chariot badly needed a veterinary.

A thin old man, who must have taken us for Russians, approached and said in a whining voice, "*Guten Tag,* comrades. Can you spare me a little tobacco?" He wore a black homburg that almost covered his ears, a wing collar and a string tie, a dark suit and overcoat that were very neatly brushed and pressed, and beautifully shined black shoes. We turned him down, and he sorrowfully walked on with his hands clasped behind him. A curly-haired, actorish-looking fellow in his thirties, wearing plus-fours and a canary pullover, came up to us and offered to pay cash for cigarettes. We said that we had all the cash we wanted, and he too went away. Next we got talking with a pale youth who was carrying a portfolio. He told us that he was a Jew and showed us his card to prove it. Jews and half-Jews in Berlin have identification cards issued by the Russians. Each card has the bearer's photograph, declares that he is a victim of National Socialism, and asks that he be given special consideration. This youth didn't mention tobacco. When one of us handed him a cigarette, he was overwhelmed.

No tobacco has been sold legally in Berlin since May 2nd. On the black market a single cigarette costs from fifteen to twenty marks (a dollar and a half to two dollars, at the official rate of exchange), depending on its quality. American cigarettes are considered the best, and the standard black-market price for a pack of twenty is three hundred marks, or thirty dollars. This ten-cent valuation of the mark is the arbitrary one set by our Army Finance Department, and the mark's actual purchasing power, even in the open market, is often two and a half to three times greater. The value of a pack of Chesterfields can thus run as high as seventy-five to ninety dollars.

The German word for the butt of a cigarette or cigar is *Kippe*. I'd conservatively estimate that at least two million of the three million Berliners left in the city that was once home for nearly four and a half million are now engaged in *Kippensammlung,* or butt collecting. The butt collecting in Berlin, I do not hesitate to say, is the most intensive on earth, and I am not forgetting the *Kippensammlung* on the Bowery and in the Middle East. Remain stationary on a Berlin street while you smoke a cigarette, and likely as not you will soon have around you a circle of children, able-bodied men, and whiskered old men, all waiting to dive for the butt when you throw it away. A riddle that has achieved wide circulation in the city runs as follows: If you can make one whole cigarette out of three butts, how many can you make out of ten butts? The answer is five. The explanation is that from nine of the ten butts you make three cigarettes, and from the butts of those three you make your fourth cigarette. You make the fifth cigarette from the butt of your fourth, plus the tenth original butt, *plus* a butt you borrow from a friend whom you pay back with the butt of the fifth cigarette after you've smoked it.

Butts are legal tender in the economic system that prevails in Berlin. The other afternoon, I was at the home of a woman who was having some glass put in the blown-out windows of her apartment. The glazier had been on the job all day, using old bent nails instead of putty. The woman's fifteen-year-old daughter came into the living room to say that the glazier had finished and was waiting to be paid. *"Na, wo hast du die Kippen gesteckt?* [Come now, where have you put the butts?]" the mother asked the child, who went out and shortly returned with a silver bowl containing about twenty butts. Her mother took the bowl into the next room, where the glazier had been working, and through the open door I could hear him expressing his ecstatic thanks. "They taste so *wunderschön* in my pipe!" he said. Plainly he was more than satisfied with his day's pay.

# HIROSHIMA

JOHN HERSEY

## I—A NOISELESS FLASH

AT EXACTLY fifteen minutes past eight in the morning, on August 6, 1945, Japanese time, at the moment when the atomic bomb flashed above Hiroshima, Miss Toshiko Sasaki, a clerk in the personnel department of the East Asia Tin Works, had just sat down at her place in the plant office and was turning her head to speak to the girl at the next desk. At that same moment, Dr. Masakazu Fujii was settling down cross-legged to read the Osaka *Asahi* on the porch of his private hospital, overhanging one of the seven deltaic rivers which divide Hiroshima; Mrs. Hatsuyo Nakamura, a tailor's widow, stood by the window of her kitchen, watching a neighbor tearing down his house because it lay in the path of an air-raid-defense fire lane; Father Wilhelm Kleinsorge, a German priest of the Society of Jesus, reclined in his underwear on a cot on the top floor of his order's three-story mission house, reading a Jesuit magazine, *Stimmen der Zeit;* Dr. Terufumi Sasaki, a young member of the surgical staff of the city's large, modern Red Cross Hospital, walked along one of the hospital corridors with a blood specimen for a Wassermann test in his hand; and the Reverend Mr. Kiyoshi Tanimoto, pastor of the Hiroshima Methodist Church, paused at the door of a rich man's house in Koi, the city's western suburb, and prepared to unload a handcart full of things he had evacuated from town in fear of the masive B-29 raid which everyone expected Hiroshima to suffer. A hundred thousand people were killed by the atomic bomb, and these six were among the survivors. They still wonder why they lived when so many others died. Each of them counts many small items of chance or volition—a step taken in time, a decision to go indoors, catching one streetcar instead of the next—that spared him. And now each knows that in the act of survival he lived a dozen lives and saw more death than he ever thought he would see. At the time, none of them knew anything.

The Reverend Mr. Tanimoto got up at five o'clock that morning. He was alone in the parsonage, because for some time his wife had been commuting with their year-old baby to spend nights with a friend in Ushida, a suburb to the north. Of all the important cities of Japan, only two, Kyoto and Hiroshima, had not been visited in strength by *B-san,* or Mr. B, as the Japanese, with a mixture of respect and unhappy familiarity, called the B-29; and Mr. Tanimoto, like all his neighbors and friends, was almost sick with anxiety. He had heard uncomfortably detailed accounts of mass raids on Kure, Iwakuni, Tokuyama, and other nearby towns; he was sure Hiroshima's turn would come soon. He had slept badly the night before, because there had been several airraid warnings. Hiroshima had been getting such warnings almost every night for weeks, for at that time the B-29s were using Lake Biwa, northeast of Hiroshima, as a rendezvous point, and no matter what city the Americans planned to hit, the Superfortresses streamed in over the coast near Hiroshima. The frequency of the warnings and the continued abstinence of Mr. B with respect to Hiroshima had made its citizens jittery; a rumor was going around that the Americans were saving something special for the city.

Mr. Tanimoto is a small man, quick to talk, laugh, and cry. He wears his black hair parted in the middle and rather long; the prominence of the frontal bones just above his eyebrows and the smallness of his mustache, mouth, and chin give him a strange, old-young look, boyish and yet wise, weak and yet fiery. He moves nervously and fast, but with a restraint which suggests that he is a cautious, thoughtful man. He showed, indeed, just those qualities in the uneasy days before the bomb fell. Besides having his wife spend the nights in Ushida, Mr. Tanimoto had been carrying all the portable things from his church, in the close-packed residential district called Nagaragawa, to a house that belonged to a rayon manufacturer in Koi, two miles from the center of town. The rayon man, a Mr. Matsui, had opened his then unoccupied estate to a large number of his friends and acquaintances, so that they might evacuate whatever they wished to a safe distance from the probable target area. Mr. Tanimoto had had no difficulty in moving chairs, hymnals, Bibles, altar gear, and church records by pushcart himself, but the organ console and an upright piano required some aid. A friend of his named Matsuo had, the day before, helped him get the piano out to Koi; in return, he had promised this day to assist Mr. Matsuo in hauling out a daughter's belongings. That is why he had risen so early.

Mr. Tanimoto cooked his own breakfast. He felt awfully tired. The effort of moving the piano the day before, a sleepless night, weeks of worry and unbalanced diet, the cares of his parish—all combined to make him feel hardly adequate to the new day's work. There was another thing, too: Mr. Tanimoto had studied theology at Emory University, in Atlanta, Georgia; he had graduated in 1940; he spoke excellent English; he dressed in American clothes; he had corresponded with many American friends right up to the time the war began; and among a people obsessed with a fear of being spied upon— perhaps almost obsessed himself—he found himself growing increasingly uneasy. The police had questioned him several times, and just a few days before he had heard that an influential acquaintance, a Mr. Tanaka, a retired officer of the Toyo Kisen Kaisha steamship line, an anti-Christian, a man famous in Hiroshima for his showy philanthropies and notorious for his personal tyrannies, had been telling people that Tanimoto should not be trusted. In compensation, to show himself publicly a good Japanese, Mr. Tanimoto had taken on the chairmanship of his local *tonarigumi,* or Neighborhood Association, and to his other duties and concerns this position had added the business of organizing air-raid defense for about twenty families.

Before six o'clock that morning, Mr. Tanimoto started for Mr. Matsuo's house. There he found that their burden was to be a *tansu,* a large Japanese cabinet, full of clothing and household goods. The two men set out. The morning was perfectly clear and so warm that the day promised to be uncomfortable. A few minutes after they started, the air-raid siren went off—a minutelong blast that warned of approaching planes but indicated to the people of Hiroshima only a slight degree of danger, since it sounded every morning at this time, when an American weather plane came over. The two men pulled and pushed the handcart through the city streets. Hiroshima was a fan-shaped city, lying mostly on the six islands formed by the seven estuarial rivers that branch out from the Ota River; its main commercial and residential districts, covering about four square miles in the center of the city, contained three-quarters of its population, which had been reduced by several evacuation programs from a wartime peak of 380,000 to about 245,000. Factories and other residential districts, or suburbs, lay compactly around the edges of the city. To the south were the docks, an airport, and the island-studded Inland Sea. A rim of mountains runs around the other three sides of the delta. Mr. Tanimoto and Mr. Matsuo took their way through the shopping center, already full of people, and across two of the rivers to the sloping streets of Koi, and up them to the outskirts and foothills. As they started up a valley away from the tight-ranked houses, the all-clear sounded. (The Japanese radar operators, detecting only three planes, supposed that they comprised a reconnaissance.) Pushing the handcart up to the rayon man's house was tiring, and the men, after they had maneuvered their load into the driveway and to the front steps, paused to rest awhile. They stood with a wing of the house between them and the city. Like most homes in this part of Japan, the house consisted of a wooden frame and wooden walls supporting a heavy tile roof. Its front hall, packed with rolls of bedding and clothing, looked like a cool cave full of fat cushions. Opposite the house, to the right of the front door, there was a large, finicky rock garden. There was no sound of planes. The morning was still; the place was cool and pleasant.

Then a tremendous flash of light cut across the sky. Mr. Tanimoto had a distinct recollection that it travelled from east to west, from the city toward the hills. It seemed a sheet of sun. Both he and Mr. Matsuo reacted in terror— and both had time to react (for they were 3,500 yards, or two miles, from the center of the explosion). Mr. Matsuo dashed up the front steps into the house and dived among the bedrolls and buried himself there. Mr. Tanimoto took four or five steps and threw himself between two big rocks in the garden. He bellied up very hard against one of them. As his face was against the stone, he did not see what happened. He felt a sudden pressure, and then splinters and pieces of board and fragments of tile fell on him. He heard no roar. (Almost no one in Hiroshima recalls hearing any noise of the bomb. But a fisherman in his sampan on the Inland Sea near Tsuzu, the man with whom Mr. Tanimoto's mother-in-law and sister-in-law were living, saw the flash and heard a tremendous explosion; he was nearly twenty miles from Hiroshima, but the thunder was greater than when the B-29s hit Iwakuni, only five miles away.)

When he dared, Mr. Tanimoto raised his head and saw that the rayon man's house had collapsed. He thought a bomb had fallen directly on it. Such clouds of dust had risen that there was a sort of twilight around. In panic, not thinking for the moment of Mr. Matsuo under the ruins, he dashed out into the street. He noticed as he ran that the concrete wall of the estate had fallen over—toward the house rather than away from it. In the street, the first thing he saw was a squad of soldiers who had been burrowing into the hillside opposite, making one of the thousands of dugouts in which the Japanese apparently intended to resist invasion, hill by hill, life for life; the soldiers were coming out of the hole, where they should have been safe, and blood was running from their heads, chests, and backs. They were silent and dazed.

Under what seemed to be a local dust cloud, the day grew darker and darker.

At nearly midnight, the night before the bomb was dropped, an announcer on the city's radio station said that about two hundred B-29s were approaching southern Honshu and advised the population of Hiroshima to evacuate to their designated "safe areas." Mrs. Hatsuyo Nakamura, the tailor's widow, who lived in the section called Nobori-cho and who had long had a habit of doing as she was told, got her three children—a ten-year-old boy, Toshio, an eight-year-old girl, Yaeko, and a five-year-old girl, Myeko—out of bed and dressed them and walked with them to the military area known as the East Parade Ground, on the northeast edge of the city. There she unrolled some mats and the children lay down on them. They slept until about two, when they were awakened by the roar of the planes going over Hiroshima.

As soon as the planes had passed, Mrs. Nakamura started back with her children. They reached home a little after two-thirty and she immediately turned on the radio, which, to her distress, was just then broadcasting a fresh warning. When she looked at the children and saw how tired they were, and when she thought of the number of trips they had made in past weeks, all to no purpose, to the East Parade Ground, she decided that in spite of the instructions on the radio, she simply could not face starting out all over again. She put the children in their bedrolls on the floor, lay down herself at three o'clock, and fell asleep at once, so soundly that when planes passed over later, she did not waken to their sound.

The siren jarred her awake at about seven. She arose, dressed quickly, and hurried to the house of Mr. Nakamoto, the head of her Neighborhood Association, and asked him what she should do. He said that she should remain at home unless an urgent warning—a series of intermittent blasts of the siren— was sounded. She returned home, lit the stove in the kitchen, set some rice to cook, and sat down to read that morning's Hiroshima *Chugoku*. To her relief, the all-clear sounded at eight o'clock. She heard the children stirring, so she went and gave each of them a handful of peanuts and told them to stay on their bedrolls, because they were tired from the night's walk. She had hoped that they would go back to sleep, but the man in the house directly to the south began to make a terrible hullabaloo of hammering, wedging, ripping, and splitting. The prefectural government, convinced, as everyone in Hiroshima was, that the city would be attacked soon, had begun to press with threats and warnings for the completion of wide fire lanes, which, it was hoped, might act in conjunction with the rivers to localize any fires started by an incendiary raid; and the neighbor was reluctantly sacrificing his home to the city's safety. Just the day before, the prefecture had ordered all able-bodied girls from the secondary schools to spend a few days helping to clear these lanes, and they started work soon after the all-clear sounded.

Mrs. Nakamura went back to the kitchen, looked at the rice, and began watching the man next door. At first, she was annoyed with him for making so much noise, but then she was moved almost to tears by pity. Her emotion was specifically directed toward her neighbor, tearing down his home, board by board, at a time when there was so much unavoidable destruction, but undoubtedly she also felt a generalized, community pity, to say nothing of self-pity. She had not had an easy time. Her husband, Isawa, had gone into the Army just after Myeko was born, and she had heard nothing from or of him for a long time, until, on March 5, 1942, she received a seven-word telegram: "Isawa died an honorable death at Singapore." She learned later that he had died on February 15th, the day Singapore fell, and that he had been a corporal. Isawa had been a not particularly prosperous tailor, and his only capital was a Sankoku sewing machine. After his death, when his allotments stopped coming, Mrs. Nakamura got out the machine and began to take in piecework herself, and since then had supported the children, but poorly, by sewing.

As Mrs. Nakamura stood watching her neighbor, everything flashed whiter than any white she had ever seen. She did not notice what happened to the man next door; the reflex of a mother set her in motion toward her children. She had taken a single step (the house was 1,350 yards, or three-quarters of a mile, from the center of the explosion) when something picked her up and she seemed to fly into the next room over the raised sleeping platform, pursued by parts of her house.

Timbers fell around her as she landed, and a shower of tiles pommelled her; everything became dark, for she was buried. The debris did not cover her deeply. She rose up and freed herself. She heard a child cry, "Mother, help me!," and saw her youngest—Myeko, the five-year-old—buried up to her breast and unable to move. As Mrs. Nakamura started frantically to claw her way toward the baby, she could see or hear nothing of her other children.

In the days right before the bombing, Dr. Masakazu Fujii, being prosperous, hedonistic, and, at the time, not too busy, had been allowing himself the luxury of sleeping until nine or nine-thirty, but fortunately he had to get up early the morning the bomb was dropped to see a house guest off on a train. He rose at six, and half an hour later walked with his friend to the station, not far away, across two of the rivers. He was back home by seven, just as the siren sounded its sustained warning. He ate breakfast and then, because the morning was already hot, undressed down to his underwear and went out on the porch to read the paper. This porch—in fact, the whole building—was curiously constructed. Dr. Fujii was the proprietor of a peculiarly Japanese institution, a private, single-doctor hospital. This building, perched beside and over the water of the Kyo River, and next to the bridge of the same name, contained thirty rooms for thirty patients and their kinfolk—for, according to Japanese custom, when a person falls sick and goes to a hospital, one or more members of his family go and live there with him, to cook for him, bathe, massage, and read to him, and to offer incessant familial sympathy, without which a Japanese patient would be miserable indeed. Dr. Fujii had no beds—only straw mats—for his patients. He did, however, have all sorts of modern equipment: an X-ray machine, diathermy apparatus, and a fine tiled laboratory. The structure rested two-thirds on the land, one-third on piles over the tidal waters of the Kyo. This overhang, the part of the building where Dr. Fujii lived, was queer-looking, but it was cool in summer and from the porch, which faced away from the center of the city, the prospect of the river, with pleasure boats drifting up and down it, was always refreshing. Dr. Fujii had occasionally had anxious moments when the Ota and its mouth branches rose to flood, but the piling was apparently firm enough and the house had always held.

Dr. Fujii had been relatively idle for about a month because in July, as the number of untouched cities in Japan dwindled and as Hiroshima seemed more and more inevitably a target, he began turning patients away, on the ground that in case of a fire raid he would not be able to evacuate them. Now he had only two patients left—a woman from Yano, injured in the shoulder, and a young man of twenty-five recovering from burns he had suffered when the steel factory near Hiroshima in which he worked had been hit. Dr. Fujii had six nurses to tend his patients. His wife and children were safe; his wife and one son were living outside Osaka, and another son and two daughters were in the country on Kyushu. A niece was living with him, and a maid and a manservant. He had little to do and did not mind, for he had saved some money. At fifty, he was healthy, convivial, and calm, and he was pleased to pass the evenings drinking whiskey with friends, always sensibly and for the sake of conversation. Before the war, he had affected brands imported from Scotland and America; now he was perfectly satisfied with the best Japanese brand, Suntory.

Dr. Fujii sat down cross-legged in his underwear on the spotless matting of the porch, put on his glasses, and started reading the Osaka *Asahi*. He liked to read the Osaka news because his wife was there. He saw the flash. To him —faced away from the center and looking at his paper—it seemed a brilliant yellow. Startled, he began to rise to his feet. In that moment (he was 1,550 yards from the center), the hospital leaned behind his rising and, with a terrible ripping noise, toppled into the river. The Doctor, still in the act of getting to his feet, was thrown forward and around and over; he was buffeted and gripped; he lost track of everything, because things were so speeded up; he felt the water.

Dr. Fujii hardly had time to think that he was dying before he realized that he was alive, squeezed tightly by two long timbers in a V across his chest, like a morsel suspended between two huge chopsticks—held upright, so that he could not move, with his head miraculously above water and his torso and legs in it. The remains of his hospital were all around him in a mad assortment of splintered lumber and materials for the relief of pain. His left shoulder hurt terribly. His glasses were gone.

Father Wilhelm Kleinsorge, of the Society of Jesus, was, on the morning of the explosion, in rather frail condition. The Japanese wartime diet had not sustained him, and he felt the strain of being a foreigner in an increasingly xenophobic Japan; even a German, since the defeat of the Fatherland, was unpopular. Father Kleinsorge had, at thirty-eight, the look of a boy growing too fast—thin in the face, with a prominent Adam's apple, a hollow chest, dangling hands, big feet. He walked clumsily, leaning forward a little. He was tired all the time. To make matters worse, he had suffered for two days, along with Father Cieslik, a fellow-priest, from a rather painful and urgent diarrhea, which they blamed on the beans and black ration bread they were obliged to eat. Two other priests then living in the mission compound, which was in the Nobori-cho section—Father Superior LaSalle and Father Schiffer—had happily escaped this affliction.

Father Kleinsorge woke up about six the morning the bomb was dropped, and half an hour later—he was a bit tardy because of his sickness—he began to read Mass in the mission chapel, a small, Japanese-style wooden building which was without pews, since its worshippers knelt on the usual Japanese matted floor, facing an altar graced with splendid silks, brass, silver, and heavy embroideries. This morning, a Monday, the only worshippers were Mr. Take-moto, a theological student living in the mission house; Mr. Fukai, the secretary of the diocese; Mrs. Murata, the mission's devoutly Christian housekeeper; and his fellow-priests. After Mass, while Father Kleinsorge was reading the Prayers of Thanksgiving, the siren sounded. He stopped the service and the mission-aries retired across the compound to the bigger building. There, in his room on the ground floor, to the right of the front door, Father Kleinsorge changed into a military uniform which he had acquired when he was teaching at the Rokko Middle School in Kobe and which he wore during air-raid alerts.

After an alarm, Father Kleinsorge always went out and scanned the sky, and in this instance, when he stepped outside, he was glad to see only the single weather plane that flew over Hiroshima each day about this time. Satisfied that nothing would happen, he went in and breakfasted with the other Fathers on substitute coffee and ration bread, which, under the circum-stances, was especially repugnant to him. The Fathers sat and talked awhile, until, at eight, they heard the all-clear. They went then to various parts of the building. Father Schiffer retired to his room to do some writing. Father Cieslik sat in his room in a straight chair with a pillow over his stomach to ease his pain, and read. Father Superior LaSalle stood at the window of his room, thinking. Father Kleinsorge went up to a room on the third floor, took off all his clothes except his underwear, and stretched out on his right side on a cot and began reading his *Stimmen der Zeit*.

After the terrible flash—which, Father Kleinsorge later realized, reminded him of something he had read as a boy about a large meteor colliding with the earth—he had time (since he was 1,400 yards from the center) for one thought: A bomb has fallen directly on us. Then, for a few seconds or minutes, he went out of his mind.

Father Kleinsorge never knew how he got out of the house. The next things he was conscious of were that he was wandering around in the mis-sion's vegetable garden in his underwear, bleeding slightly from small cuts along his left flank; that all the buildings round about had fallen down ex-cept the Jesuits' mission house, which had long before been braced and double-braced by a priest named Gropper, who was terrified of earthquakes; that the day had turned dark; and that Murata-*san,* the housekeeper, was nearby, cry-ing over and over, "*Shu Jesusu, awaremi tamai!* Our Lord Jesus, have pity on us!"

On the train on the way into Hiroshima from the country, where he lived with his mother, Dr. Terufumi Sasaki, the Red Cross Hospital surgeon, thought over an unpleasant nightmare he had had the night before. His mother's home was in Mukaihara, thirty miles from the city, and it took him two hours by train and tram to reach the hospital. He had slept uneasily all night and had wakened an hour earlier than usual, and, feeling sluggish and slightly feverish, had debated whether to go to the hospital at all; his sense of duty finally forced him to go, and he had started out on an earlier train than he took most mornings. The dream had particularly frightened him because it was so closely associated, on the surface at least, with a disturbing actuality. He was only twenty-five years old and had just completed his training at the Eastern Medical University, in Tsingtao, China. He was something of an idealist and was much distressed by the inadequacy of medical facilities in the country town where his mother lived. Quite on his own, and without a permit, he had begun visiting a few sick people out there in the evenings, after his eight hours at the hospital and four hours' commuting. He had recently learned that the penalty for practicing without a permit was severe; a fellow-doctor whom he had asked about it had given him a serious scolding. Nevertheless, he had continued to practice. In his dream, he had been at the bedside of a country patient when the police and the doctor he had consulted burst into the room, seized him, dragged him outside, and beat him up cruelly. On the train, he just about decided to give up the work in Mukaihara, since he felt it would be impossible to get a permit, because the authorities would hold that it would conflict with his duties at the Red Cross Hospital.

At the terminus, he caught a streetcar at once. (He later calculated that if he had taken his customary train that morning, and if he had had to wait a few minutes for the streetcar, as often happened, he would have been close to the center at the time of the explosion and would surely have perished.) He arrived at the hospital at seven-forty and reported to the chief surgeon. A few minutes later, he went to a room on the first floor and drew blood from the arm of a man in order to perform a Wassermann test. The laboratory containing the incubators for the test was on the third floor. With the blood specimen in his left hand, walking in a kind of distraction he had felt all morning, probably because of the dream and his restless night, he started along the main corridor on his way toward the stairs. He was one step beyond an open window when the light of the bomb was reflected, like a gigantic photographic flash, in the corridor. He ducked down on one knee and said to himself, as only a Japanese would, "Sasaki, *gambare!* Be brave!" Just then (the building was 1,650 yards from the center), the blast ripped through the hospital. The glasses he was wearing flew off his face; the bottle of blood crashed against one wall; his Japanese slippers zipped out from under his feet—but otherwise, thanks to where he stood, he was untouched.

Dr. Sasaki shouted the name of the chief surgeon and rushed around to the man's office and found him terribly cut by glass. The hospital was in horrible confusion: heavy partitions and ceilings had fallen on patients, beds had overturned, windows had blown in and cut people, blood was spattered on the walls and floors, instruments were everywhere, many of the patients were running about screaming, many more lay dead. (A colleague working in the laboratory to which Dr. Sasaki had been walking was dead; Dr. Sasaki's patient, whom he had just left and who a few moments before had been dreadfully afraid of syphilis, was also dead.) Dr. Sasaki found himself the only doctor in the hospital who was unhurt.

Dr. Sasaki, who believed that the enemy had hit only the building he was in, got bandages and began to bind the wounds of those inside the hospital; while outside, all over Hiroshima, maimed and dying citizens turned their unsteady steps toward the Red Cross Hospital to begin an invasion that was to make Dr. Sasaki forget his private nightmare for a long, long time.

Miss Toshiko Sasaki, the East Asia Tin Works clerk, who is not related to Dr. Sasaki, got up at three o'clock in the morning on the day the bomb fell. There was extra housework to do. Her eleven-month-old brother, Akio, had come down the day before with a serious stomach upset; her mother had taken him to the Tamura Pediatric Hospital and was staying there with him. Miss Sasaki, who was about twenty, had to cook breakfast for her father, a brother, a sister, and herself, and—since the hospital, because of the war, was unable to provide food—to prepare a whole day's meals for her mother and the baby, in time for her father, who worked in a factory making rubber earplugs for artillery crews, to take the food by on his way to the plant. When she had finished and had cleaned and put away the cooking things, it was nearly seven. The family lived in Koi, and she had a forty-five-minute trip to the tin works, in the section of town called Kannon-machi. She was in charge of the personnel records in the factory. She left Koi at seven, and as soon as she reached the plant, she went with some of the other girls from the personnel department to the factory auditorium. A prominent local Navy man, a former employee, had committed suicide the day before by throwing himself under a train—a death considered honorable enough to warrant a memorial service, which was to be held at the tin works at ten o'clock that morning. In the large hall, Miss Sasaki and the others made suitable preparations for the meeting. This work took about twenty minutes.

Miss Sasaki went back to her office and sat down at her desk. She was quite far from the windows, which were off to her left, and behind her were a couple of tall bookcases containing all the books of the factory library, which the personnel department had organized. She settled herself at her desk, put some things in a drawer, and shifted papers. She thought that before she began to make entries in her lists of new employees, discharges, and departures for the Army, she would chat for a moment with the girl at her right. Just as she turned her head away from the windows, the room was filled with a blinding light. She was paralyzed by fear, fixed still in her chair for a long moment (the plant was 1,600 yards from the center).

Everything fell, and Miss Sasaki lost consciousness. The ceiling dropped suddenly and the wooden floor above collapsed in splinters and the people up there came down and the roof above them gave way; but principally and first of all, the bookcases right behind her swooped forward and the contents threw her down, with her left leg horribly twisted and breaking underneath her. There, in the tin factory, in the first moment of the atomic age, a human being was crushed by books.

## II — THE FIRE

IMMEDIATELY after the explosion, the Reverend Mr. Kiyoshi Tanimoto, having run wildly out of the Matsui estate and having looked in wonderment at the bloody soldiers at the mouth of the dugout they had been digging, attached himself sympathetically to an old lady who was walking along in a daze, holding her head with her left hand, supporting a small boy of three or four on her back with her right, and crying, "I'm hurt! I'm hurt! I'm hurt!" Mr. Tanimoto transferred the child to his own back and led the woman by the hand down the street, which was darkened by what seemed to be a local column of dust. He took the woman to a grammar school not far away that had previously been designated for use as a temporary hospital in case of emergency. By this solicitous behavior, Mr. Tanimoto at once got rid of his terror. At the school, he was much surprised to see glass all over the floor and fifty or sixty injured people already waiting to be treated. He reflected that, although the all-clear had sounded and he had heard no planes, several bombs must have been dropped. He thought of a hillock in the rayon man's garden from which he could get a view of the whole of Koi—of the whole of Hiroshima, for that matter—and he ran back up to the estate.

From the mound, Mr. Tanimoto saw an astonishing panorama. Not just a patch of Koi, as he had expected, but as much of Hiroshima as he could see through the clouded air was giving off a thick, dreadful miasma. Clumps of smoke, near and far, had begun to push up through the general dust. He wondered how such extensive damage could have been dealt out of a silent sky; even a few planes, far up, would have been audible. Houses nearby were burning, and when huge drops of water the size of marbles began to fall, he half thought that they must be coming from the hoses of firemen fighting the blazes. (They were actually drops of condensed moisture falling from the turbulent tower of dust, heat, and fission fragments that had already risen miles into the sky above Hiroshima.)

Mr. Tanimoto turned away from the sight when he heard Mr. Matsuo call out to ask whether he was all right. Mr. Matsuo had been safely cushioned within the falling house by the bedding stored in the front hall and had worked his way out. Mr. Tanimoto scarcely answered. He had thought of his wife and baby, his church, his home, his parishioners, all of them down in that awful murk. Once more he began to run in fear—toward the city.

Mrs. Hatsuyo Nakamura, the tailor's widow, having struggled up from under the ruins of her house after the explosion, and seeing Myeko, the youngest of her three children, buried breast-deep and unable to move, crawled across the debris, hauled at timbers, and flung tiles aside, in a hurried effort to free the child. Then, from what seemed to be caverns far below, she heard two small voices crying, *"Tasukete! Tasukete!* Help! Help!"

She called the names of her ten-year-old son and eight-year-old daughter: "Toshio! Yaeko!"

The voices from below answered.

Mrs. Nakamura abandoned Myeko, who at least could breathe, and in a frenzy made the wreckage fly above the crying voices. The children had been sleeping nearly ten feet apart, but now their voices seemed to come from the same place. Toshio, the boy, apparently had some freedom to move, because she could feel him undermining the pile of wood and tiles as she worked from above. At last, she saw his head, and she hastily pulled him out by it. A mosquito net was wound intricately, as if it had been carefully wrapped, around his feet. He said he had been blown right across the room and had been on top of his sister Yaeko under the wreckage. She now said, from underneath, that she could not move, because there was something on her legs. With a bit more digging, Mrs. Nakamura cleared a hole above the child and began to pull her arm. *"Itai!* It hurts!" Yaeko cried. Mrs. Nakamura shouted, "There's no time now to say whether it hurts or not," and yanked her whimpering daughter up. Then she freed Myeko. The children were filthy and bruised, but none of them had a single cut or scratch.

Mrs. Nakamura took the children out into the street. They had nothing on but underpants, and although the day was very hot, she worried rather confusedly about their being cold, so she went back into the wreckage and burrowed underneath and found a bundle of clothes she had packed for an emergency, and she dressed them in pants, blouses, shoes, padded-cotton air-raid helmets called *bokuzuki,* and even, irrationally, overcoats. The children were silent, except for the five-year-old, Myeko, who kept asking questions: "Why is it night already? Why did our house fall down? What happened?" Mrs. Nakamura, who did not know what had happened (had not the all-clear sounded?), looked around and saw through the darkness that all the houses in her neighborhood had collapsed. The house next door, which its owner had been tearing down to make way for a fire lane, was now very thoroughly, if crudely, torn down; its owner, who had been sacrificing his home for the community's safety, lay dead. Mrs. Nakamoto, wife of the head of the local air-raid-defense Neighborhood Association, came across the street with her head all bloody, and said that her baby was badly cut; did Mrs. Nakamura have any bandage? Mrs. Nakamura did not, but she crawled into the remains of her house again and pulled out some white cloth that she had been using in her work as a seamstress, ripped it into strips, and gave it to Mrs.

Nakamoto. While fetching the cloth, she noticed her sewing machine; she went back in for it and dragged it out. Obviously, she could not carry it with her, so she unthinkingly plunged her symbol of livelihood into the receptacle which for weeks had been her symbol of safety—the cement tank of water in front of her house, of the type every household had been ordered to construct against a possible fire raid.

A nervous neighbor, Mrs. Hataya, called to Mrs. Nakamura to run away with her to the woods in Asano Park—an estate, by the Kyo River not far off, belonging to the wealthy Asano family, who once owned the Toyo Kisen Kaisha steamship line. The park had been designated as an evacuation area for their neighborhood. Seeing fire breaking out in a nearby ruin (except at the very center, where the bomb itself ignited some fires, most of Hiroshima's city-wide conflagration was caused by inflammable wreckage falling on cookstoves and live wires), Mrs. Nakamura suggested going over to fight it. Mrs. Hataya said, "Don't be foolish. What if planes come and drop more bombs?" So Mrs. Nakamura started out for Asano Park with her children and Mrs. Hataya, and she carried her rucksack of emergency clothing, a blanket, an umbrella, and a suitcase of things she had cached in her air-raid shelter. Under many ruins, as they hurried along, they heard muffled screams for help. The only building they saw standing on their way to Asano Park was the Jesuit mission house, alongside the Catholic kindergarten to which Mrs. Nakamura had sent Myeko for a time. As they passed it, she saw Father Kleinsorge, in bloody underwear, running out of the house with a small suitcase in his hand.

Right after the explosion, while Father Wilhelm Kleinsorge, S. J., was wandering around in his underwear in the vegetable garden, Father Superior LaSalle came around the corner of the building in the darkness. His body, especially his back, was bloody; the flash had made him twist away from his window, and tiny pieces of glass had flown at him. Father Kleinsorge, still bewildered, managed to ask, "Where are the rest?" Just then, the two other priests living in the mission house appeared—Father Cieslik, unhurt, supporting Father Schiffer, who was covered with blood that spurted from a cut above his left ear and who was very pale. Father Cieslik was rather pleased with himself, for after the flash he had dived into a doorway, which he had previously reckoned to be the safest place inside the building, and when the blast came, he was not injured. Father LaSalle told Father Cieslik to take Father Schiffer to a doctor before he bled to death, and suggested either Dr. Kanda, who lived on the next corner, or Dr. Fujii, about six blocks away. The two men went out of the compound and up the street.

The daughter of Mr. Hoshijima, the mission catechist, ran up to Father Kleinsorge and said that her mother and sister were buried under the ruins of their house, which was at the back of the Jesuit compound, and at the same time the priests noticed that the house of the Catholic-kindergarten teacher at the front of the compound had collapsed on her. While Father LaSalle and Mrs. Murata, the mission housekeeper, dug the teacher out, Father Kleinsorge went to the catechist's fallen house and began lifting things off the top of the pile. There was not a sound underneath; he was sure the Hoshijima women had been killed. At last, under what had been a corner of the kitchen, he saw Mrs. Hoshijima's head. Believing her dead, he began to haul her out by the hair, but suddenly she screamed, "*Itai! Itai!* It hurts! It hurts!" He dug some more and lifted her out. He managed, too, to find her daughter in the rubble and free her. Neither was badly hurt.

A public bath next door to the mission house had caught fire, but since there the wind was southerly, the priests thought their house would be spared. Nevertheless, as a precaution, Father Kleinsorge went inside to fetch some things he wanted to save. He found his room in a state of weird and illogical confusion. A first-aid kit was hanging undisturbed on a hook on the wall, but his clothes, which had been on other hooks nearby, were nowhere to be seen. His desk was in splinters all over the room, but a mere papier-mâché suitcase, which he had hidden under the desk, stood handle-side up, without a scratch on it, in the doorway of the room, where he could not miss it. Father Kleinsorge later came to regard this as a bit of Providential interference, inasmuch as the suitcase contained his breviary, the account books for the whole diocese, and a considerable amount of paper money belonging to the mission, for which he was responsible. He ran out of the house and deposited the suitcase in the mission air-raid shelter.

At about this time, Father Cieslik and Father Schiffer, who was still spurting blood, came back and said that Dr. Kanda's house was ruined and that fire blocked them from getting out of what they supposed to be the local circle of destruction to Dr. Fujii's private hospital, on the bank of the Kyo River.

Dr. Masakazu Fujii's hospital was no longer on the bank of the Kyo River; it was in the river. After the overturn, Dr. Fujii was so stupefied and so tightly squeezed by the beams gripping his chest that he was unable to move at first, and he hung there about twenty minutes in the darkened morning. Then a thought which came to him—that soon the tide would be running in through the estuaries and his head would be submerged—inspired him to fearful activity; he wriggled and turned and exerted what strength he could (though his left arm, because of the pain in his shoulder, was useless), and before long he had freed himself from the vise. After a few moments' rest, he climbed onto the pile of timbers and, finding a long one that slanted up to the riverbank, he painfully shinnied up it.

Dr. Fujii, who was in his underwear, was now soaking and dirty. His undershirt was torn, and blood ran down it from bad cuts on his chin and back. In this disarray, he walked out onto Kyo Bridge, beside which his hospital had stood. The bridge had not collapsed. He could see only fuzzily without his glasses, but he could see enough to be amazed at the number of houses that were down all around. On the bridge, he encountered a friend, a doctor named Machii, and asked in bewilderment, "What do you think it was?"

Dr. Machii said, "It must have been a *Molotoffano hanakago*"—a Molotov flower basket, the delicate Japanese name for the "bread basket," or self-scattering cluster of bombs.

At first, Dr. Fujii could see only two fires, one across the river from his hospital site and one quite far to the south. But at the same time, he and his friend observed something that puzzled them, and which, as doctors, they discussed: although there were as yet very few fires, wounded people were hurrying across the bridge in an endless parade of misery, and many of them exhibited terrible burns on their faces and arms. "Why do you suppose it is?" Dr. Fujii asked. Even a theory was comforting that day, and Dr. Machii stuck to his. "Perhaps because it was a Molotov flower basket," he said.

There had been no breeze earlier in the morning when Dr. Fujii had walked to the railway station to see his friend off, but now brisk winds were blowing every which way; here on the bridge the wind was easterly. New fires were leaping up, and they spread quickly, and in a very short time terrible blasts of hot air and showers of cinders made it impossible to stand on the bridge any more. Dr. Machii ran to the far side of the river and along a still unkindled street. Dr. Fujii went down into the water under the bridge, where a score of people had already taken refuge, among them his servants, who had extricated themselves from the wreckage. From there, Dr. Fujii saw a nurse hanging in the timbers of his hospital by her legs, and then another painfully pinned across the breast. He enlisted the help of some of the others under the bridge and freed both of them. He thought he heard the voice of his niece for a moment, but he could not find her; he never saw her again. Four of his nurses and the two patients in the hospital died, too. Dr. Fujii went back into the water of the river and waited for the fire to subside.

The lot of Drs. Fujii, Kanda, and Machii right after the explosion—and, as these three were typical, that of the majority of the physicians and surgeons of Hiroshima—with their offices and hospitals destroyed, their equipment scattered, their own bodies incapacitated in varying degrees, explained why so many citizens who were hurt went untended and why so many who might have lived died. Of a hundred and fifty doctors in the city, sixty-five were already dead and most of the rest were wounded. Of 1,780 nurses, 1,654 were dead or too badly hurt to work. In the biggest hospital, that of the Red Cross, only six doctors out of thirty were able to function, and only ten nurses out of more than two hundred. The sole uninjured doctor on the Red Cross Hospital staff was Dr. Sasaki. After the explosion, he hurried to a storeroom to fetch bandages. This room, like everything he had seen as he ran through the hospital, was chaotic—bottles of medicines thrown off shelves and broken, salves spattered on the walls, instruments strewn everywhere. He grabbed up some bandages and an unbroken bottle of mercurochrome, hurried back to the chief surgeon, and bandaged his cuts. Then he went out into the corridor and began patching up the wounded patients and the doctors and nurses there. He blundered so without his glasses that he took a pair off the face of a wounded nurse, and although they only approximately compensated for the errors of his vision, they were better than nothing. (He was to depend on them for more than a month.)

Dr. Sasaki worked without method, taking those who were nearest him first, and he noticed soon that the corridor seemed to be getting more and more crowded. Mixed in with the abrasions and lacerations which most people in the hospital had suffered, he began to find dreadful burns. He realized then that casualties were pouring in from outdoors. There were so many that he began to pass up the lightly wounded; he decided that all he could hope to do was to stop people from bleeding to death. Before long, patients lay and crouched on the floors of the wards and the laboratories and all the other rooms, and in the corridors, and on the stairs, and in the front hall, and under the porte-cochère, and on the stone front steps, and in the driveway and court-yard, and for blocks each way in the streets outside. Wounded people supported maimed people; disfigured families leaned together. Many people were vomiting. A tremendous number of schoolgirls—some of those who had been taken from their classrooms to work outdoors, clearing fire lanes—crept into the hospital. In a city of two hundred and forty-five thousand, nearly a hundred thousand people had been killed or doomed at one blow; a hundred thousand more were hurt. At least ten thousand of the wounded made their way to the best hospital in town, which was altogether unequal to such a trampling, since it had only six hundred beds, and they had all been occupied. The people in the suffocating crowd inside the hospital wept and cried, for Dr. Sasaki to hear, "*Sensei! Doctor!*," and the less seriously wounded came and pulled at his sleeve and begged him to come to the aid of the worse wounded. Tugged here and there in his stockinged feet, bewildered by the numbers, staggered by so much raw flesh, Dr. Sasaki lost all sense of profession and stopped working as a skillful surgeon and a sympathetic man; he became an automaton, mechanically wiping, daubing, winding, wiping, daubing, winding.

Some of the wounded in Hiroshima were unable to enjoy the questionable luxury of hospitalization. In what had been the personnel office of the East Asia Tin Works, Miss Sasaki lay doubled over, unconscious, under the tremendous pile of books and plaster and wood and corrugated iron. She was wholly unconscious (she later estimated) for about three hours. Her first sensation was of dreadful pain in her left leg. It was so black under the books and debris that the borderline between awareness and unconsciousness was fine; she apparently crossed it several times, for the pain seemed to come and go.

At the moments when it was sharpest, she felt that her leg had been cut off somewhere below the knee. Later, she heard someone walking on top of the wreckage above her, and anguished voices spoke up, evidently from within the mess around her: "Please help! Get us out!"

Father Kleinsorge stemmed Father Schiffer's spurting cut as well as he could with some bandage that Dr. Fujii had given the priests a few days before. When he finished, he ran into the mission house again and found the jacket of his military uniform and an old pair of gray trousers. He put them on and went outside. A woman from next door ran up to him and shouted that her husband was buried under her house and the house was on fire; Father Kleinsorge must come and save him.

Father Kleinsorge, already growing apathetic and dazed in the presence of the cumulative distress, said, "We haven't much time." Houses all around were burning, and the wind was now blowing hard. "Do you know exactly which part of the house he is under?" he asked.

"Yes, yes," she said. "Come quickly."

They went around to the house, the remains of which blazed violently, but when they got there, it turned out that the woman had no idea where her husband was. Father Kleinsorge shouted several times, "Is anyone there?" There was no answer. Father Kleinsorge said to the woman, "We must get away or we will all die." He went back to the Catholic compound and told the Father Superior that the fire was coming closer on the wind, which had swung around and was now from the north; it was time for everybody to go.

Just then, the kindergarten teacher pointed out to the priests Mr. Fukai, the secretary of the diocese, who was standing in his window on the second floor of the mission house, facing in the direction of the explosion, weeping. Father Cieslik, because he thought the stairs unusable, ran around to the back of the mission house to look for a ladder. There he heard people crying for help under a nearby fallen roof. He called to passersby running away in the street to help him lift it, but nobody paid any attention, and he had to leave the buried ones to die. Father Kleinsorge ran inside the mission house and scrambled up the stairs, which were awry and piled with plaster and lathing, and called to Mr. Fukai from the doorway of his room.

Mr. Fukai, a very short man of about fifty, turned around slowly, with a queer look, and said, "Leave me here."

Father Kleinsorge went into the room and took Mr. Fukai by the collar of his coat and said, "Come with me or you'll die."

Mr. Fukai said, "Leave me here to die."

Father Kleinsorge began to shove and haul Mr. Fukai out of the room. Then the theological student came up and grabbed Mr. Fukai's feet, and Father Kleinsorge took his shoulders, and together they carried him downstairs and outdoors. "I can't walk!" Mr. Fukai cried. "Leave me here!" Father

Kleinsorge got his paper suitcase with the money in it and took Mr. Fukai up pickaback, and the party started for the East Parade Ground, their district's "safe area." As they went out of the gate, Mr. Fukai, quite childlike now, beat on Father Kleinsorge's shoulders and said, "I won't leave. I won't leave." Irrelevantly, Father Kleinsorge turned to Father LaSalle and said, "We have lost all our possessions but not our sense of humor."

The street was cluttered with parts of houses that had slid into it, and with fallen telephone poles and wires. From every second or third house came the voices of people buried and abandoned, who invariably screamed, with formal politeness, *"Tasukete kure!* Help, if you please!" The priests recognized several ruins from which these cries came as the homes of friends, but because of the fire it was too late to help. All the way, Mr. Fukai whimpered, "Let me stay." The party turned right when they came to a block of fallen houses that was one flame. At Sakai Bridge, which would take them across to the East Parade Ground, they saw that the whole community on the opposite side of the river was a sheet of fire; they dared not cross and decided to take refuge in Asano Park, off to their left. Father Kleinsorge, who had been weakened for a couple of days by his bad case of diarrhea, began to stagger under his protesting burden, and as he tried to climb up over the wreckage of several houses that blocked their way to the park, he stumbled, dropped Mr. Fukai, and plunged down, head over heels, to the edge of the river. When he picked himself up, he saw Mr. Fukai running away. Father Kleinsorge shouted to a dozen soldiers, who were standing by the bridge, to stop him. As Father Kleinsorge started back to get Mr. Fukai, Father LaSalle called out, "Hurry! Don't waste time!" So Father Kleinsorge just requested the soldiers to take care of Mr. Fukai. They said they would, but the little, broken man got away from them, and the last the priests could see of him, he was running back toward the fire.

Mr. Tanimoto, fearful for his family and church, at first ran toward them by the shortest route, along Koi Highway. He was the only person making his way into the city; he met hundreds and hundreds who were fleeing, and every one of them seemed to be hurt in some way. The eyebrows of some were burned off and skin hung from their faces and hands. Others, because of pain, held their arms up as if carrying something in both hands. Some were vomiting as they walked. Many were naked or in shreds of clothing. On some undressed bodies, the burns had made patterns—of undershirt straps and suspenders and, on the skin of some women (since white repelled the heat from the bomb and dark clothes absorbed it and conducted it to the skin), the shapes of flowers they had had on their kimonos. Many, although injured themselves, supported relatives who were worse off. Almost all had their heads bowed, looked straight ahead, were silent, and showed no expression whatever.

After crossing Koi Bridge and Kannon Bridge, having run the whole way,

Mr. Tanimoto saw, as he approached the center, that all the houses had been crushed and many were afire. Here the trees were bare and their trunks were charred. He tried at several points to penetrate the ruins, but the flames always stopped him. Under many houses, people screamed for help, but no one helped; in general, survivors that day assisted only their relatives or immediate neighbors, for they could not comprehend or tolerate a wider circle of misery. The wounded limped past the screams, and Mr. Tanimoto ran past them. As a Christian he was filled with compassion for those who were trapped, and as a Japanese he was overwhelmed by the shame of being unhurt, and he prayed as he ran, "God help them and take them out of the fire."

He thought he would skirt the fire, to the left. He ran back to Kannon Bridge and followed for a distance one of the rivers. He tried several cross streets, but all were blocked, so he turned far left and ran out to Yokogawa, a station on a railroad line that detoured the city in a wide semicircle, and he followed the rails until he came to a burning train. So impressed was he by this time by the extent of the damage that he ran north two miles to Gion, a suburb in the foothills. All the way, he overtook dreadfully burned and lacer- ated people, and in his guilt he turned to right and left as he hurried and said to some of them, "Excuse me for having no burden like yours." Near Gion, he began to meet country people going toward the city to help, and when they saw him, several exclaimed, "Look! There is one who is not wounded." At Gion, he bore toward the right bank of the main river, the Ota, and ran down it until he reached fire again. There was no fire on the other side of the river, so he threw off his shirt and shoes and plunged into it. In midstream, where the current was fairly strong, exhaustion and fear finally caught up with him —he had run nearly seven miles—and he became limp and drifted in the water. He prayed, "Please, God, help me to cross. It would be nonsense for me to be drowned when I am the only uninjured one." He managed a few more strokes and fetched up on a spit downstream.

Mr. Tanimoto climbed up the bank and ran along it until, near a large Shinto shrine, he came to more fire, and as he turned left to get around it, he met, by incredible luck, his wife. She was carrying their infant son. Mr. Tani- moto was now so emotionally worn out that nothing could surprise him. He did not embrace his wife; he simply said, "Oh, you are safe." She told him that she had got home from her night in Ushida just in time for the explo- sion; she had been buried under the parsonage with the baby in her arms. She told how the wreckage had pressed down on her, how the baby had cried. She saw a chink of light, and by reaching up with a hand, she worked the hole bigger, bit by bit. After about half an hour, she heard the crackling noise of wood burning. At last the opening was big enough for her to push the baby out, and afterward she crawled out herself. She said she was now going out to Ushida again. Mr. Tanimoto said he wanted to see his church and take care of the people of his Neighborhood Association. They parted as casually—as bewildered—as they had met.

Mr. Tanimoto's way around the fire took him across the East Parade Ground, which, being an evacuation area, was now the scene of a gruesome review: rank on rank of the burned and bleeding. Those who were burned moaned, *"Mizu, mizu!* Water, water!" Mr. Tanimoto found a basin in a nearby street and located a water tap that still worked in the crushed shell of a house, and he began carrying water to the suffering strangers. When he had given drink to about thirty of them, he realized he was taking too much time. "Excuse me," he said loudly to those nearby who were reaching out their hands to him and crying their thirst. "I have many people to take care of." Then he ran away. He went to the river again, the basin in his hand, and jumped down onto a sandspit. There he saw hundreds of people so badly wounded that they could not get up to go farther from the burning city. When they saw a man erect and unhurt, the chant began again: *"Mizu, mizu, mizu."* Mr. Tanimoto could not resist them; he carried them water from the river—a mistake, since it was tidal and brackish. Two or three small boats were ferrying hurt people across the river from Asano Park, and when one touched the spit, Mr. Tanimoto again made his loud, apologetic speech and jumped into the boat. It took him across to the park. There, in the underbrush, he found some of his charges of the Neighborhood Association, who had come there by his previous instructions, and saw many acquaintances, among them Father Kleinsorge and the other Catholics. But he missed Fukai, who had been a close friend. "Where is Fukai-*san?*" he asked.

"He didn't want to come with us," Father Kleinsorge said. "He ran back."

When Miss Sasaki heard the voices of the people caught along with her in the dilapidation at the tin factory, she began speaking to them. Her nearest neighbor, she discovered, was a high-school girl who had been drafted for factory work, and who said her back was broken. Miss Sasaki replied, "I am lying here and I can't move. My left leg is cut off."

Some time later, she again heard somebody walk overhead and then move off to one side, and whoever it was began burrowing. The digger released several people, and when he had uncovered the high-school girl, she found that her back was not broken, after all, and she crawled out. Miss Sasaki spoke to the rescuer, and he worked toward her. He pulled away a great number of books, until he had made a tunnel to her. She could see his perspiring face as he said, "Come out, Miss." She tried. "I can't move," she said. The man excavated some more and told her to try with all her strength to get out. But books were heavy on her hips, and the man finally saw that a bookcase was leaning on the books and that a heavy beam pressed down on the bookcase. "Wait," he said. "I'll get a crowbar."

The man was gone a long time, and when he came back, he was ill-tempered, as if her plight were all her fault. "We have no men to help you!" he shouted in through the tunnel. "You'll have to get out by yourself."

"That's impossible," she said. "My left leg . . ." The man went away.

Much later, several men came and dragged Miss Sasaki out. Her left leg was not severed, but it was badly broken and cut and it hung askew below the knee. They took her out into a courtyard. It was raining. She sat on the ground in the rain. When the downpour increased, someone directed all the wounded people to take cover in the factory's air-raid shelters. "Come along," a torn-up woman said to her. "You can hop." But Miss Sasaki could not move, and she just waited in the rain. Then a man propped up a large sheet of corrugated iron as a kind of lean-to, and took her in his arms and carried her to it. She was grateful until he brought two horribly wounded people—a woman with a whole breast sheared off and a man whose face was all raw from a burn— to share the simple shed with her. No one came back. The rain cleared and the cloudy afternoon was hot; before nightfall the three grotesques under the slanting piece of twisted iron began to smell quite bad.

The former head of the Nobori-cho Neighborhood Association to which the Catholic priests belonged was an energetic man named Yoshida. He had boasted, when he was in charge of the district air-raid defenses, that fire might eat away all of Hiroshima but it would never come to Nobori-cho. The bomb blew down his house, and a joist pinned him by the legs, in full view of the Jesuit mission house across the way and of the people hurrying along the street. In their confusion as they hurried past, Mrs. Nakamura, with her children, and Father Kleinsorge, with Mr. Fukai on his back, hardly saw him; he was just part of the general blur of misery through which they moved. His cries for help brought no response from them; there were so many people shouting for help that they could not hear him separately. They and all the others went along. Nobori-cho became absolutely deserted, and the fire swept through it. Mr. Yoshida saw the wooden mission house—the only erect building in the area—go up in a lick of flame, and the heat was terrific on his face. Then flames came along his side of the street and entered his house. In a paroxysm of terrified strength, he freed himself and ran down the alleys of Nobori-cho, hemmed in by the fire he had said would never come. He began at once to behave like an old man; two months later his hair was white.

As Dr. Fujii stood in the river up to his neck to avoid the heat of the fire, the wind blew stronger and stronger, and soon, even though the expanse of water was small, the waves grew so high that the people under the bridge could no longer keep their footing. Dr. Fujii went close to the shore, crouched down, and embraced a large stone with his usable arm. Later it became possible to wade along the very edge of the river, and Dr. Fujii and his two surviving nurses moved about two hundred yards upstream, to a sandspit near

Asano Park. Many wounded were lying on the sand. Dr. Machii was there with his family; his daughter, who had been outdoors when the bomb burst, was badly burned on her hands and legs but fortunately not on her face. Although Dr. Fujii's shoulder was by now terribly painful, he examined the girl's burns curiously. Then he lay down. In spite of the misery all around, he was ashamed of his appearance, and he remarked to Dr. Machii that he looked like a beggar, dressed as he was in nothing but torn and bloody underwear. Late in the afternoon, when the fire began to subside, he decided to go to his parental house, in the suburb of Nagatsuka. He asked Dr. Machii to join him, but the Doctor answered that he and his family were going to spend the night on the spit, because of his daughter's injuries. Dr. Fujii, together with his nurses, walked first to Ushida, where, in the partially damaged house of some relatives, he found first-aid materials he had stored there. The two nurses bandaged him and he them. They went on. Now not many people walked in the streets, but a great number sat and lay on the pavement, vomited, waited for death, and died. The number of corpses on the way to Nagatsuka was more and more puzzling. The Doctor wondered: Could a Molotov flower basket have done all this?

Dr. Fujii reached his family's house in the evening. It was five miles from the center of town, but its roof had fallen in and the windows were all broken.

All day, people poured into Asano Park. This private estate was far enough away from the explosion so that its bamboos, pines, laurel, and maples were still alive, and the green place invited refugees—partly because they believed that if the Americans came back, they would bomb only buildings; partly because the foliage seemed a center of coolness and life, and the estate's exquisitely precise rock gardens, with their quiet pools and arching bridges, were very Japanese, normal, secure; and also partly (according to some who were there) because of an irresistible, atavistic urge to hide under leaves. Mrs. Nakamura and her children were among the first to arrive, and they settled in the bamboo grove near the river. They all felt terribly thirsty, and they drank from the river. At once they were nauseated and began vomiting, and they retched the whole day. Others were also nauseated; they all thought (probably because of the strong odor of ionization, an "electric smell" given off by the bomb's fission) that they were sick from a gas the Americans had dropped. When Father Kleinsorge and the other priests came into the park, nodding to their friends as they passed, the Nakamuras were all sick and prostrate. A woman named Iwasaki, who lived in the neighborhood of the mission and who was sitting near the Nakamuras, got up and asked the priests if she should stay where she was or go with them. Father Kleinsorge said, "I hardly know where the safest place is." She stayed there, and later in the day, though she had no visible wounds or burns, she died. The priests went farther along the river and settled down in some underbrush. Father LaSalle lay down and went right to sleep. The theological student, who was wearing slippers, had carried with him a bundle of clothes, in which he had packed two pairs of leather shoes. When he sat down with the others, he found that the bundle had broken open and a couple of shoes had fallen out and now he had only two lefts. He retraced his steps and found one right. When he rejoined the priests, he said, "It's funny, but things don't matter any more. Yesterday, my shoes were my most important possessions. Today, I don't care. One pair is enough."

Father Cieslik said, "I know. I started to bring my books along, and then I thought, 'This is no time for books.'"

When Mr. Tanimoto, with his basin still in his hand, reached the park, it was very crowded, and to distinguish the living from the dead was not easy, for most of the people lay still, with their eyes open. To Father Kleinsorge, an Occidental, the silence in the grove by the river, where hundreds of gruesomely wounded suffered together, was one of the most dreadful and awesome phenomena of his whole experience. The hurt ones were quiet; no one wept, much less screamed in pain; no one complained; none of the many who died did so noisily; not even the children cried; very few people even spoke. And when Father Kleinsorge gave water to some whose faces had been almost blotted out by flash burns, they took their share and then raised themselves a little and bowed to him, in thanks.

Mr. Tanimoto greeted the priests and then looked around for other friends. He saw Mrs. Matsumoto, wife of the director of the Methodist School, and asked her if she was thirsty. She was, so he went to one of the pools in the Asanos' rock gardens and got water for her in his basin. Then he decided to try to get back to his church. He went into Nobori-cho by the way the priests had taken as they escaped, but he did not get far; the fire along the streets was so fierce that he had to turn back. He walked to the riverbank and began to look for a boat in which he might carry some of the most severely injured across the river from Asano Park and away from the spreading fire. Soon he found a good-sized pleasure punt drawn up on the bank, but in and around it was an awful tableau—five dead men, nearly naked, badly burned, who must have expired more or less all at once, for they were in attitudes which suggested that they had been working together to push the boat down into the river. Mr. Tanimoto lifted them away from the boat, and as he did so, he experienced such horror at disturbing the dead—preventing them, he momentarily felt, from launching their craft and going on their ghostly way—that he said out loud, "Please forgive me for taking this boat. I must use it for others, who are alive." The punt was heavy, but he managed to slide it into the water. There were no oars, and all he could find for propulsion was a thick bamboo pole. He worked the boat upstream to the most crowded part of the park and began to ferry the wounded. He could pack ten or twelve into the boat for each crossing, but as the river was too deep in the center to pole his way across, he had to paddle with the bamboo, and consequently each trip took a very long time. He worked several hours that way.

Early in the afternoon, the fire swept into the woods of Asano Park. The first Mr. Tanimoto knew of it was when, returning in his boat, he saw that a great number of people had moved toward the riverside. On touching the bank, he went up to investigate, and when he saw the fire, he shouted, "All the young men who are not badly hurt come with me!" Father Kleinsorge moved Father Schiffer and Father LaSalle close to the edge of the river and asked people there to get them across if the fire came too near, and then joined Tanimoto's volunteers. Mr. Tanimoto sent some to look for buckets and basins and told others to beat the burning underbrush with their clothes; when utensils were at hand, he formed a bucket chain from one of the pools in the rock gardens. The team fought the fire for more than two hours, and gradually defeated the flames. As Mr. Tanimoto's men worked, the frightened people in the park pressed closer and closer to the river, and finally the mob began to force some of the unfortunates who were on the very bank into the water. Among those driven into the river and drowned were Mrs. Matsumoto, of the Methodist School, and her daughter.

When Father Kleinsorge got back after fighting the fire, he found Father Schiffer still bleeding and terribly pale. Some Japanese stood around and stared at him, and Father Schiffer whispered, with a weak smile, "It is as if I were already dead." "Not yet," Father Kleinsorge said. He had brought Dr. Fujii's first-aid kit with him, and he had noticed Dr. Kanda in the crowd, so he sought him out and asked him if he would dress Father Schiffer's bad cuts. Dr. Kanda had seen his wife and daughter dead in the ruins of his hospital; he sat now with his head in his hands. "I can't do anything," he said. Father Kleinsorge bound more bandage around Father Schiffer's head, moved him to a steep place, and settled him so that his head was high, and soon the bleeding diminished.

The roar of approaching planes was heard about this time. Someone in the crowd near the Nakamura family shouted, "It's some Grummans coming to strafe us!" A baker named Nakashima stood up and commanded, "Everyone who is wearing anything white, take it off." Mrs. Nakamura took the blouses off her children, and opened her umbrella and made them get under it. A great number of people, even badly burned ones, crawled into bushes and stayed there until the hum, evidently of a reconnaissance or weather run, died away.

It began to rain. Mrs. Nakamura kept her children under the umbrella. The drops grew abnormally large, and someone shouted, "The Americans are dropping gasoline. They're going to set fire to us!" (This alarm stemmed from one of the theories being passed through the park as to why so much of Hiroshima had burned: it was that a single plane had sprayed gasoline on the city and then somehow set fire to it in one flashing moment.) But the drops were palpably water, and as they fell, the wind grew stronger and stronger, and suddenly—probably because of the tremendous convection set up by the blazing city—a whirlwind ripped through the park. Huge trees crashed down; small ones were uprooted and flew into the air. Higher, a wild array of flat things revolved in the twisting funnel—pieces of iron roofing, papers, doors, strips of matting. Father Kleinsorge put a piece of cloth over Father Schiffer's eyes, so that the feeble man would not think he was going crazy. The gale blew Mrs. Murata, the mission housekeeper, who was sitting close by the river, down the embankment at a shallow, rocky place, and she came out with her bare feet bloody. The vortex moved out onto the river, where it sucked up a waterspout and eventually spent itself.

After the storm, Mr. Tanimoto began ferrying people again, and Father Kleinsorge asked the theological student to go across and make his way out to the Jesuit Novitiate at Nagatsuka, about three miles from the center of town, and to request the priests there to come with help for Fathers Schiffer and LaSalle. The student got into Mr. Tanimoto's boat and went off with him. Father Kleinsorge asked Mrs. Nakamura if she would like to go out to Nagatsuka with the priests when they came. She said she had some luggage and her children were sick—they were still vomiting from time to time, and so, for that matter, was she—and therefore she feared she could not. He said he thought the fathers from the Novitiate could come back the next day with a pushcart to get her.

Late in the afternoon, when he went ashore for a while, Mr. Tanimoto, upon whose energy and initiative many had come to depend, heard people begging for food. He consulted Father Kleinsorge, and they decided to go back into town to get some rice from Mr. Tanimoto's Neighborhood Association shelter and from the mission shelter. Father Cieslik and two or three others went with them. At first, when they got among the rows of prostrate houses, they did not know where they were; the change was too sudden, from a busy city of two hundred and forty-five thousand that morning to a mere pattern of residue in the afternoon. The asphalt of the streets was still so soft and hot from the fires that walking was uncomfortable. They encountered only one person, a woman, who said to them as they passed, "My husband is in those ashes." At the mission, where Mr. Tanimoto left the party, Father Kleinsorge was dismayed to see the building razed. In the garden, on the way to the shelter, he noticed a pumpkin roasted on the vine. He and Father Cieslik tasted it and it was good. They were surprised at their hunger, and they ate quite a bit. They got out several bags of rice and gathered up several other cooked pumpkins and dug up some potatoes that were nicely baked under the ground, and started back. Mr. Tanimoto rejoined them on the way. One of the people with him had some cooking utensils. In the park, Mr. Tanimoto organized the lightly wounded women of his neighborhood to cook. Father Kleinsorge offered the Nakamura family some pumpkin, and they tried it, but they could not keep it on their stomachs. Altogether, the rice was enough to feed nearly a hundred people.

Just before dark, Mr. Tanimoto came across a twenty-year-old girl, Mrs. Kamai, the Tanimotos' next-door neighbor. She was crouching on the ground with the body of her infant daughter in her arms. The baby had evidently been dead all day. Mrs. Kamai jumped up when she saw Mr. Tanimoto and said, "Would you please try to locate my husband?"

Mr. Tanimoto knew that her husband had been inducted into the Army just the day before; he and Mrs. Tanimoto had entertained Mrs. Kamai in the afternoon, to make her forget. Kamai had reported to the Chugoku Regional Army Headquarters—near the ancient castle in the middle of town— where some four thousand troops were stationed. Judging by the many maimed soldiers Mr. Tanimoto had seen during the day, he surmised that the barracks had been badly damaged by whatever it was that had hit Hiroshima. He knew he hadn't a chance of finding Mrs. Kamai's husband, even if he searched, but he wanted to humor her. "I'll try," he said.

"You've got to find him," she said. "He loved our baby so much. I want him to see her once more."

## III—DETAILS ARE BEING INVESTIGATED

EARLY in the evening of the day the bomb exploded, a Japanese naval launch moved slowly up and down the seven rivers of Hiroshima. It stopped here and there to make an announcement—alongside the crowded sandspits, on which hundreds of wounded lay; at the bridges, on which others were crowded; and eventually, as twilight fell, opposite Asano Park. A young officer stood up in the launch and shouted through a megaphone, "Be patient! A naval hospital ship is coming to take care of you!" The sight of the ship-shape launch against the background of the havoc across the river; the un-ruffled young man in his neat uniform; above all, the promise of medical help —the first word of possible succor anyone had heard in nearly twelve awful hours—cheered the people in the park tremendously. Mrs. Nakamura settled her family for the night with the assurance that a doctor would come and stop their retching. Mr. Tanimoto resumed ferrying the wounded across the river. Father Kleinsorge lay down and said the Lord's Prayer and a Hail Mary to himself, and fell right asleep; but no sooner had he dropped off than Mrs. Murata, the conscientious mission housekeeper, shook him and said, "Father Kleinsorge! Did you remember to repeat your evening prayers?" He answered rather grumpily, "Of course," and he tried to go back to sleep but could not. This, apparently, was just what Mrs. Murata wanted. She began to chat with the exhausted priest. One of the questions she raised was when he thought the priests from the Novitiate, for whom he had sent a messenger in midafternoon, would arrive to evacuate Father Superior LaSalle and Father Schiffer.

The messenger Father Kleinsorge had sent—the theological student who had been living at the mission house—had arrived at the Novitiate, in the hills about three miles out, at half past four. The sixteen priests there had been doing rescue work in the outskirts; they had worried about their colleagues in the city but had not known how or where to look for them. Now they hastily made two litters out of poles and boards, and the student led half a dozen of them back into the devastated area. They worked their way along the Ota above the city; twice the heat of the fire forced them into the river. At Misasa Bridge, they encountered a long line of soldiers making a bizarre forced march away from the Chugoku Regional Army Headquarters in the center of the town. All were grotesquely burned, and they supported themselves with staves or leaned on one another. Sick, burned horses, hanging their heads, stood on the bridge. When the rescue party reached the park, it was after dark, and progress was made extremely difficult by the tangle of fallen trees of all sizes that had been knocked down by the whirlwind that afternoon. At last—not long after Mrs. Murata asked her question—they reached their friends, and gave them wine and strong tea.

The priests discussed how to get Father Schiffer and Father LaSalle out to the Novitiate. They were afraid that blundering through the park with them would jar them too much on the wooden litters, and that the wounded men would lose too much blood. Father Kleinsorge thought of Mr. Tanimoto and his boat, and called out to him on the river. When Mr. Tanimoto reached the bank, he said he would be glad to take the injured priests and their bearers upstream to where they could find a clear roadway. The rescuers put Father Schiffer onto one of the stretchers and lowered it into the boat, and two of them went aboard with it. Mr. Tanimoto, who still had no oars, poled the punt upstream.

About half an hour later, Mr. Tanimoto came back and excitedly asked the remaining priests to help him rescue two children he had seen standing up to their shoulders in the river. A group went out and picked them up—two young girls who had lost their family and were both badly burned. The priests stretched them on the ground next to Father Kleinsorge and then embarked Father LaSalle. Father Cieslik thought he could make it out to the Novitiate on foot, so he went aboard with the others. Father Kleinsorge was too feeble; he decided to wait in the park until the next day. He asked the men to come back with a handcart, so that they could take Mrs. Nakamura and her sick children to the Novitiate.

Mr. Tanimoto shoved off again. As the boatload of priests moved slowly upstream, they heard weak cries for help. A woman's voice stood out especially:

"There are people here about to be drowned! Help us! The water is rising!" The sounds came from one of the sandspits, and those in the punt could see, in the reflected light of the still-burning fires, a number of wounded people lying at the edge of the river, already partly covered by the flooding tide. Mr. Tanimoto wanted to help them, but the priests were afraid that Father Schiffer would die if they didn't hurry, and they urged their ferryman along. He dropped them where he had put Father Schiffer down and then started back alone toward the sandspit.

The night was hot, and it seemed even hotter because of the fires against the sky, but the younger of the two girls Mr. Tanimoto and the priests had rescued complained to Father Kleinsorge that she was cold. He covered her with his jacket. She and her older sister had been in the salt water of the river for a couple of hours before being rescued. The younger one had huge, raw flash burns on her body; the salt water must have been excruciatingly painful to her. She began to shiver heavily, and again said it was cold. Father Kleinsorge borrowed a blanket from someone nearby and wrapped her up, but she shook more and more, and said again, "I am so cold," and then she suddenly stopped shivering and was dead.

Mr. Tanimoto found about twenty men and women on the sandspit. He drove the boat onto the bank and urged them to get aboard. They did not move and he realized that they were too weak to lift themselves. He reached down and took a woman by the hands, but her skin slipped off in huge, glove-like pieces. He was so sickened by this that he had to sit down for a moment. Then he got out into the water and, though a small man, lifted several of the men and women, who were naked, into his boat. Their backs and breasts were clammy, and he remembered uneasily what the great burns he had seen during the day had been like: yellow at first, then red and swollen, with the skin sloughed off, and finally, in the evening, suppurated and smelly. With the tide risen, his bamboo pole was now too short and he had to paddle most of the way across with it. On the other side, at a higher spit, he lifted the slimy living bodies out and carried them up the slope away from the tide. He had to keep consciously repeating to himself, "These are human beings." It took him three trips to get them all across the river. When he had finished, he decided he had to have a rest, and he went back to the park.

As Mr. Tanimoto stepped up the dark bank, he tripped over someone, and someone else said angrily, "Look out! That's my hand." Mr. Tanimoto, ashamed of hurting wounded people, embarrassed at being able to walk upright, suddenly thought of the naval hospital ship, which had not come (it never did), and he had for a moment a feeling of blind, murderous rage at the crew of the ship, and then at all doctors. Why didn't they come to help these people?

Dr. Fujii lay in dreadful pain throughout the night on the floor of his family's roofless house on the edge of the city. By the light of a lantern, he had examined himself and found: left clavicle fractured; multiple abrasions and lacerations of face and body, including deep cuts on the chin, back, and legs; extensive contusions on chest and trunk; a couple of ribs possibly fractured. Had he not been so badly hurt, he might have been at Asano Park, assisting the wounded.

By nightfall, ten thousand victims of the explosion had invaded the Red Cross Hospital, and Dr. Sasaki, worn out, was moving aimlessly and dully up and down the stinking corridors with wads of bandage and bottles of mercurochrome, still wearing the glasses he had taken from the wounded nurse, binding up the worst cuts as he came to them. Other doctors were putting compresses of saline solution on the worst burns. That was all they could do. After dark, they worked by the light of the city's fires and by candles the ten remaining nurses held for them. Dr. Sasaki had not looked outside the hospital all day; the scene inside was so terrible and so compelling that it had not occurred to him to ask any questions about what had happened beyond the windows and doors. Ceilings and partitions had fallen; plaster, dust, blood, and vomit were everywhere. Patients were dying by the hundreds, but there was nobody to carry away the corpses. Some of the hospital staff distributed biscuits and rice balls, but the charnel-house smell was so strong that few were hungry. By three o'clock the next morning, after nineteen straight hours of his gruesome work, Dr. Sasaki was incapable of dressing another wound. He and some other survivors of the hospital staff got straw mats and went outdoors —thousands of patients and hundreds of dead were in the yard and on the driveway—and hurried around behind the hospital and lay down in hiding to snatch some sleep. But within an hour wounded people had found them; a complaining circle formed around them: "Doctors! Help us! How can you sleep?" Dr. Sasaki got up again and went back to work. Early in the day, he thought for the first time of his mother, at their country home in Mukaihara, thirty miles from town. He usually went home every night. He was afraid she would think he was dead.

Near the spot upriver to which Mr. Tanimoto had transported the priests, there sat a large case of rice cakes which a rescue party had evidently brought for the wounded lying thereabouts but hadn't distributed. Before evacuating the wounded priests, the others passed the cakes around and helped themselves. A few minutes later, a band of soldiers came up, and an officer, hearing the priests speaking a foreign language, drew his sword and hysterically asked who they were. One of the priests calmed him down and explained that they were Germans—allies. The officer apologized and said that there were reports going around that American parachutists had landed.

The priests decided that they should take Father Schiffer first. As they prepared to leave, Father Superior LaSalle said he felt awfully cold. One of the Jesuits gave up his coat, another his shirt; they were glad to wear less in the muggy night. The stretcher bearers started out. The theological student led the way and tried to warn the others of obstacles, but one of the priests got a foot tangled in some telephone wire and tripped and dropped his corner of the litter. Father Schiffer rolled off, lost consciousness, came to, and then vomited. The bearers picked him up and went on with him to the edge of the city, where they had arranged to meet a relay of other priests, left him with them, and turned back and got the Father Superior.

The wooden litter must have been terribly painful for Father LaSalle, in whose back scores of tiny particles of window glass were embedded. Near the edge of town, the group had to walk around an automobile burned and squatting on the narrow road, and the bearers on one side, unable to see their way in the darkness, fell into a deep ditch. Father LaSalle was thrown onto the ground and the litter broke in two. One priest went ahead to get a handcart from the Novitiate, but he soon found one beside an empty house and wheeled it back. The priests lifted Father LaSalle into the cart and pushed him over the bumpy road the rest of the way. The rector of the Novitiate, who had been a doctor before he entered the religious order, cleaned the wounds of the two priests and put them to bed between clean sheets, and they thanked God for the care they had received.

Thousands of people had nobody to help them. Miss Sasaki was one of them. Abandoned and helpless, under the crude lean-to in the courtyard of the tin factory, beside the woman who had lost a breast and the man whose burned face was scarcely a face any more, she suffered awfully that night from the pain in her broken leg. She did not sleep at all; neither did she converse with her sleepless companions.

In the park, Mrs. Murata kept Father Kleinsorge awake all night by talking to him. None of the Nakamura family were able to sleep, either; the children, in spite of being very sick, were interested in everything that happened. They were delighted when one of the city's gas-storage tanks went up in a tremendous burst of flame. Toshio, the boy, shouted to the others to look at the reflection in the river. Mr. Tanimoto, after his long run and his many hours of rescue work, dozed uneasily. When he awoke, in the first light of dawn, he looked across the river and saw that he had not carried the festered, limp bodies high enough on the sandspit the night before. The tide had risen above where he had put them; they had not had the strength to move; they must have drowned. He saw a number of bodies floating in the river.

Early that day, August 7th, the Japanese radio broadcast for the first time a succinct announcement that very few, if any, of the people most concerned with its content, the survivors in Hiroshima, happened to hear: "Hiroshima suffered considerable damage as the result of an attack by a few B-29s. It is believed that a new type of bomb was used. The details are being investigated." Nor is it probable that any of the survivors happened to be tuned in on a short-wave rebroadcast of an extraordinary announcement by the President of the United States, which identified the new bomb as atomic: "That bomb had more power than twenty thousand tons of TNT. It had more than two thousand times the blast power of the British Grand Slam, which is the largest bomb ever yet used in the history of warfare." Those victims who were able to worry at all about what had happened thought of it and discussed it in more primitive, childish terms—gasoline sprinkled from an airplane, maybe, or some combustible gas, or a big cluster of incendiaries, or the work of parachutists; but, even if they had known the truth, most of them were too busy or too weary or too badly hurt to care that they were the objects of the first great experiment in the use of atomic power, which (as the voices on the short wave shouted) no country except the United States, with its industrial know-how, its willingness to throw two billion gold dollars into an important wartime gamble, could possibly have developed.

Mr. Tanimoto was still angry at doctors. He decided that he would personally bring one to Asano Park—by the scruff of the neck, if necessary. He crossed the river, went past the Shinto shrine where he had met his wife for a brief moment the day before, and walked to the East Parade Ground. Since this had long before been designated as an evacuation area, he thought he would find an aid station there. He did find one, operated by an Army medical unit, but he also saw that its doctors were hopelessly overburdened, with thousands of patients sprawled among corpses across the field in front of it. Nevertheless, he went up to one of the Army doctors and said, as reproachfully as he could, "Why have you not come to Asano Park? You are badly needed there."

Without even looking up from his work, the doctor said in a tired voice, "This is my station."

"But there are many dying on the riverbank over there."

"The first duty," the doctor said, "is to take care of the slightly wounded."

"Why—when there are many who are heavily wounded on the riverbank?"

The doctor moved to another patient. "In an emergency like this," he said, as if he were reciting from a manual, "the first task is to help as many as possible—to save as many lives as possible. There is no hope for the heavily wounded. They will die. We can't bother with them."

"That may be right from a medical standpoint—" Mr. Tanimoto began, but then he looked out across the field, where the many dead lay close and intimate with those who were still living, and he turned away without finishing his sentence, angry now with himself. He didn't know what to do; he had promised some of the dying people in the park that he would bring them medical aid. They might die feeling cheated. He saw a ration stand at one side of the field, and he went to it and begged some rice cakes and biscuits, and he took them back, in lieu of doctors, to the people in the park.

The morning, again, was hot. Father Kleinsorge went to fetch water for the wounded in a bottle and a teapot he had borrowed. He had heard that it was possible to get fresh tap water outside Asano Park. Going through the rock gardens, he had to climb over and crawl under the trunks of fallen pine trees; he found he was weak. There were many dead in the gardens. At a beautiful moon bridge, he passed a naked, living woman who seemed to have been burned from head to toe and was red all over. Near the entrance to the park, an Army doctor was working, but the only medicine he had was iodine, which he painted over cuts, bruises, slimy burns, everything—and by now everything that he had painted had pus on it. Outside the gate of the park, Father Kleinsorge found a faucet that still worked—part of the plumbing of a vanished house—and he filled his vessels and returned. When he had given the wounded the water, he made a second trip. This time, the woman by the bridge was dead. On his way back with the water, he got lost on a detour around a fallen tree, and as he looked for his way through the woods, he heard a voice ask from the underbrush, "Have you anything to drink?" He saw a uniform. Thinking there was just one soldier, he approached with the water. When he had penetrated the bushes, he saw there were about twenty men, and they were all in exactly the same nightmarish state: their faces were wholly burned, their eye sockets were hollow, the fluid from their melted eyes had run down their cheeks. (They must have had their faces upturned when the bomb went off; perhaps they were anti-aircraft personnel.) Their mouths were mere swollen, pus-covered wounds, which they could not bear to stretch enough to admit the spout of the teapot. So Father Kleinsorge got a large piece of grass and drew out the stem so as to make a straw, and gave them all water to drink that way. One of them said, "I can't see anything." Father Kleinsorge answered, as cheerfully as he could, "There's a doctor at the entrance to the park. He's busy now, but he'll come soon and fix your eyes, I hope."

Since that day, Father Kleinsorge has thought back to how queasy he had once been at the sight of pain, how someone else's cut finger used to make him turn faint. Yet there in the park he was so benumbed that immediately after leaving this horrible sight he stopped on a path by one of the pools and discussed with a lightly wounded man whether it would be safe to eat the fat, two-foot carp that floated dead on the surface of the water. They decided, after some consideration, that it would be unwise.

Father Kleinsorge filled the containers a third time and went back to the riverbank. There, amid the dead and dying, he saw a young woman with a needle and thread mending her kimono, which had been slightly torn. Father Kleinsorge joshed her. "My, but you're a dandy!" he said. She laughed.

He felt tired and lay down. He began to talk with two engaging children whose acquaintance he had made the afternoon before. He learned that their name was Kataoka; the girl was thirteen, the boy five. The girl had been just about to set out for a barbershop when the bomb fell. As the family started for Asano Park, their mother decided to turn back for some food and extra clothing; they became separated from her in the crowd of fleeing people, and they had not seen her since. Occasionally they stopped suddenly in their perfectly cheerful playing and began to cry for their mother.

It was difficult for all the children in the park to sustain the sense of tragedy. Toshio Nakamura got quite excited when he saw his friend Seichi Sato riding up the river in a boat with his family, and he ran to the bank and waved and shouted, "Sato! Sato!"

The boy turned his head and shouted, "Who's that?"

"Nakamura."

"Hello, Toshio!"

"Are you all safe?"

"Yes. What about you?"

"Yes, we're all right. My sisters are vomiting, but I'm fine."

Father Kleinsorge began to be thirsty in the dreadful heat, and he did not feel strong enough to go for water again. A little before noon, he saw a Japanese woman handing something out. Soon she came to him and said in a kindly voice, "These are tea leaves. Chew them, young man, and you won't feel thirsty." The woman's gentleness made Father Kleinsorge suddenly want to cry. For weeks he had been feeling oppressed by the hatred of foreigners that the Japanese seemed increasingly to show, and he had been uneasy even with his Japanese friends. This stranger's gesture made him a little hysterical.

Around noon, the priests arrived from the Novitiate with the handcart. They had been to the site of the mission house in the city and had retrieved some suitcases that had been stored in the air-raid shelter and had also picked up the remains of melted holy vessels in the ashes of the chapel. They now packed Father Kleinsorge's papier-mâché suitcase and the things belonging to Mrs. Murata and the Nakamuras into the cart, put the two Nakamura girls aboard, and prepared to start out. Then one of the Jesuits who had a practical turn of mind remembered that they had been notified some time before that if they suffered property damage at the hands of the enemy, they could enter a claim for compensation with the prefectural police. The holy men discussed this matter there in the park, with the wounded as silent as the dead around them, and decided that Father Kleinsorge, as a former resident of the destroyed mission, was the one to enter the claim. So, as the others went off with the handcart, Father Kleinsorge said goodbye to the Kataoka children and trudged to a police station. Fresh, clean-uniformed policemen from another town were in charge, and a crowd of dirty and disarrayed citizens crowded around them, mostly asking after lost relatives. Father Kleinsorge filled out a claim form and started walking through the center of town on his way to Nagatsuka. It was then that he first realized the extent of the damage; he passed block after block of ruins, and even after all he had seen in the park, his breath was taken away. By the time he reached the Novitiate, he was sick with exhaustion. The last thing he did as he fell into bed was request that someone go back for the motherless Kataoka children.

Altogether, Miss Sasaki was left two days and two nights under the piece of propped-up roofing with her crushed leg and her two unpleasant comrades. Her only diversion was when men came to the factory air-raid shelters, which she could see from under one corner of her shelter, and hauled corpses up out of them with ropes. Her leg became discolored, swollen, and putrid. All that time, she went without food and water. On the third day, August 8th, some friends who supposed she was dead came to look for her body and found her. They told her that her mother, father, and baby brother, who at the time of the explosion were in the Tamura Pediatric Hospital, where the baby was a patient, had all been given up as certainly dead, since the hospital was totally destroyed. Her friends then left her to think that piece of news over. Later, some men picked her up by the arms and legs and carried her quite a distance to a truck. For about an hour, the truck moved over a bumpy road, and Miss Sasaki, who had become convinced that she was dulled to pain, discovered that she was not. The men lifted her out at a relief station in the section of Inokuchi, where two Army doctors looked at her. The moment one of them touched her wound, she fainted. She came to in time to hear them discuss whether or not to cut off her leg; one said there was gas gangrene in the lips of the wound and predicted she would die unless they amputated, and the other said that was too bad, because they had no equipment with which to do the job. She fainted again. When she recovered consciousness, she was being carried somewhere on a stretcher. She was put aboard a launch, which went to the nearby island of Ninoshima, and she was taken to a military hospital there. Another doctor examined her and said that she did not have gas gangrene, though she did have a fairly ugly compound fracture. He said quite coldly that he was sorry, but this was a hospital for operative surgical cases only, and because she had no gangrene, she would have to return to Hiroshima that night. But then the doctor took her temperature, and what he saw on the thermometer made him decide to let her stay.

That day, August 8th, Father Cieslik went into the city to look for Mr. Fukai, the Japanese secretary of the diocese, who had ridden unwillingly out of the flaming city on Father Kleinsorge's back and then had run back crazily into it. Father Cieslik started hunting in the neighborhood of Sakai Bridge, where the Jesuits had last seen Mr. Fukai; he went to the East Parade Ground, the evacuation area to which the secretary might have gone, and looked for him among the wounded and dead there; he went to the prefectural police and made inquiries. He could not find any trace of the man. Back at the Novitiate that evening, the theological student, who had been rooming with Mr. Fukai at the mission house, told the priests that the secretary had remarked to him, during an air-raid alarm one day not long before the bombing, "Japan is dying. If there is a real air raid here in Hiroshima, I want to die with our country." The priests concluded that Mr. Fukai had run back to immolate himself in the flames. They never saw him again.

At the Red Cross Hospital, Dr. Sasaki worked for three straight days with only one hour's sleep. On the second day, he began to sew up the worst cuts, and right through the following night and all the next day he stitched. Many of the wounds were festered. Fortunately, someone had found intact a supply of *narucopon,* a Japanese sedative, and he gave it to many who were in pain. Word went around among the staff that there must have been something peculiar about the great bomb, because on the second day the vice-chief of the hospital went down in the basement to the vault where the X-ray plates were stored and found the whole stock exposed as they lay. That day, a fresh doctor and ten nurses came in from the city of Yamaguchi with extra bandages and antiseptics, and the third day another physician and a dozen more nurses arrived from Matsue—yet there were still only eight doctors for ten thousand patients. In the afternoon of the third day, exhausted from his foul tailoring, Dr. Sasaki became obsessed with the idea that his mother thought he was dead. He got permission to go to Mukaihara. He walked out to the first suburbs, beyond which the electric-train service was still functioning, and reached home late in the evening. His mother said she had known he was all right all along; a wounded nurse had stopped by to tell her. He went to bed and slept for seventeen hours.

Before dawn on August 8th, someone entered the room at the Novitiate where Father Kleinsorge was in bed, reached up to the hanging light bulb, and switched it on. The sudden flood of light, pouring in on Father Kleinsorge's half sleep, brought him leaping out of bed, braced for a new concussion. When he realized what had happened, he laughed confusedly and went back to bed. He stayed there all day.

On August 9th, Father Kleinsorge was still tired. The rector looked at his cuts and said they were not even worth dressing, and if Father Kleinsorge kept them clean, they would heal in three or four days. Father Kleinsorge felt uneasy; he could not yet comprehend what he had been through; as if he were guilty of something awful, he felt he had to go back to the scene of the violence he had experienced. He got up out of bed and walked into the city.

He scratched for a while in the ruins of the mission house, but he found nothing. He went to the sites of a couple of schools and asked after people he knew. He looked for some of the city's Japanese Catholics, but he found only fallen houses. He walked back to the Novitiate, stupefied and without any new understanding.

At two minutes after eleven o'clock on the morning of August 9th, the second atomic bomb was dropped, on Nagasaki. It was several days before the survivors of Hiroshima knew they had company, because the Japanese radio and newspapers were being extremely cautious on the subject of the strange weapon.

On August 9th, Mr. Tanimoto was still working in the park. He went to the suburb of Ushida, where his wife was staying with friends, and got a tent which he had stored there before the bombing. He now took it to the park and set it up as a shelter for some of the wounded who could not move or be moved. Whatever he did in the park, he felt he was being watched by the twenty-year-old girl, Mrs. Kamai, his former neighbor, whom he had seen on the day the bomb exploded, with her dead baby daughter in her arms. She kept the small corpse in her arms for four days, even though it began smelling bad on the second day. Once, Mr. Tanimoto sat with her for a while, and she told him that the bomb had buried her under their house with the baby strapped to her back, and that when she had dug herself free, she had discovered that the baby was choking, its mouth full of dirt. With her little finger, she had carefully cleaned out the infant's mouth, and for a time the child had breathed normally and seemed all right; then suddenly it had died. Mrs. Kamai also talked about what a fine man her husband was, and again urged Mr. Tanimoto to search for him. Since Mr. Tanimoto had been all through the city the first day and had seen terribly burned soldiers from Kamai's post, the Chugoku Regional Army Headquarters, everywhere, he knew it would be impossible to find Kamai, even if he were living, but of course he didn't tell her that. Every time she saw Mr. Tanimoto, she asked whether he had found her husband. Once, he tried to suggest that perhaps it was time to cremate the baby, but Mrs. Kamai only held it tighter. He began to keep away from her, but whenever he looked at her, she was staring at him and her eyes asked the same question. He tried to escape her glance by keeping his back turned to her as much as possible.

The Jesuits took about fifty refugees into the exquisite chapel of the Novitiate. The rector gave them what medical care he could—mostly just the cleaning away of pus. Each of the Nakamuras was provided with a blanket and a mosquito net. Mrs. Nakamura and her younger daughter had no appetite and ate nothing; her son and other daughter ate, and lost, each meal they were offered. On August 10th, a friend, Mrs. Osaki, came to see them and told them that her son Hideo had been burned alive in the factory where he worked. This Hideo had been a kind of hero to Toshio, who had often gone to the plant to watch him run his machine. That night, Toshio woke up screaming. He had dreamed that he had seen Mrs. Osaki coming out of an opening in the ground with her family, and then he saw Hideo at his machine, a big one with a revolving belt, and he himself was standing beside Hideo, and for some reason this was terrifying.

On August 10th, Father Kleinsorge, having heard from someone that Dr. Fujii had been injured and that he had eventually gone to the summer house of a friend of his named Okuma, in the village of Fukawa, asked Father Cieslik if he would go and see how Dr. Fujii was. Father Cieslik went to Misasa station, outside Hiroshima, rode for twenty minutes on an electric train, and then walked for an hour and a half in a terribly hot sun to Mr. Okuma's house, which was beside the Ota River at the foot of a mountain. He found Dr. Fujii sitting in a chair in a kimono, applying compresses to his broken collarbone. The Doctor told Father Cieslik about having lost his glasses and said that his eyes bothered him. He showed the priest huge blue and green stripes where beams had bruised him. He offered the Jesuit first a cigarette and then whiskey, though it was only eleven in the morning. Father Cieslik thought it would please Dr. Fujii if he took a little, so he said yes. A servant brought some Suntory whiskey, and the Jesuit, the Doctor, and the host had a very pleasant chat. Mr. Okuma had lived in Hawaii, and he told some things about Americans. Dr. Fujii talked a bit about the disaster. He said that Mr. Okuma and a nurse had gone into the ruins of his hospital and brought back a small safe, which he had moved into his air-raid shelter. This contained some surgical instruments, and Dr. Fujii gave Father Cieslik a few pairs of scissors and tweezers for the rector at the Novitiate. Father Cieslik was bursting with some inside dope he had, but he waited until the conversation turned naturally to the mystery of the bomb. Then he said he knew what kind of bomb it was; he had the secret on the best authority—that of a Japanese newspaperman who had dropped in at the Novitiate. The bomb was not a bomb at all; it was a kind of fine magnesium powder sprayed over the whole city by a single plane, and it exploded when it came into contact with the live wires of the city power system. "That means," said Dr. Fujii, perfectly satisfied, since after all the information came from a newspaperman, "that it can only be dropped on big cities and only in the daytime, when the tram lines and so forth are in operation."

After five days of ministering to the wounded in the park, Mr. Tanimoto returned, on August 11th, to his parsonage and dug around in the ruins. He retrieved some diaries and church records that had been kept in books and were only charred around the edges, as well as some cooking utensils and pottery. While he was at work, a Miss Tanaka came and said that her father had been asking for him. Mr. Tanimoto had reason to hate her father, the retired shipping-company official who, though he made a great show of his charity, was notoriously selfish and cruel, and who, just a few days before the bombing, had said openly to several people that Mr. Tanimoto was a spy for the Americans. Several times he had derided Christianity and called it unJapanese. At the moment of the bombing, Mr. Tanaka had been walking in the street in front of the city's radio station. He received serious flash burns, but he was able to walk home. He took refuge in his Neighborhood Association shelter and from there tried hard to get medical aid. He expected all the doctors of Hiroshima to come to him, because he was so rich and so famous for giving his money away. When none of them came, he angrily set out to look for them; leaning on his daughter's arm, he walked from private hospital to private hospital, but all were in ruins, and he went back and lay down in the shelter again. Now he was very weak and knew he was going to die. He was willing to be comforted by any religion.

Mr. Tanimoto went to help him. He descended into the tomblike shelter and, when his eyes were adjusted to the darkness, saw Mr. Tanaka, his face and arms puffed up and covered with pus and blood, and his eyes swollen shut. The old man smelled very bad, and he moaned constantly. He seemed to recognize Mr. Tanimoto's voice. Standing at the shelter stairway to get light, Mr. Tanimoto read loudly from a Japanese-language pocket Bible: "For a thousand years in Thy sight are but as yesterday when it is past, and as a watch in the night. Thou carriest the children of men away as with a flood; they are as a sleep; in the morning they are like grass which groweth up. In the morning it flourisheth and groweth up; in the evening it is cut down, and withereth. For we are consumed by Thine anger and by Thy wrath are we troubled. Thou hast set our iniquities before Thee, our secret sins in the light of Thy countenance. For all our days are passed away in Thy wrath: we spend our years as a tale that is told. . . ."

Mr. Tanaka died as Mr. Tanimoto read the psalm.

On August 11th, word came to the Ninoshima Military Hospital that a large number of military casualties from the Chugoku Regional Army Headquarters were to arrive on the island that day, and it was deemed necessary to evacuate all civilian patients. Miss Sasaki, still running an alarmingly high fever, was put on a large ship. She lay out on deck, with a pillow under her leg. There were awnings over the deck, but the vessel's course put her in the sunlight. She felt as if she were under a magnifying glass in the sun. Pus oozed out of her wound, and soon the whole pillow was covered with it. She was taken ashore at Hatsukaichi, a town several miles to the southwest of Hiroshima, and put in the Goddess of Mercy Primary School, which had been turned into a hospital. She lay there for several days before a specialist on fractures came from Kobe. By then her leg was red and swollen up to her hip. The doctor decided he could not set the breaks. He made an incision and· put in a rubber pipe to drain off the putrescence.

At the Novitiate, the motherless Kataoka children were inconsolable. Father Cieslik worked hard to keep them distracted. He put riddles to them. He asked, "What is the cleverest animal in the world?," and after the thirteen-year-old girl had guessed the ape, the elephant, the horse, he said, "No, it must be the hippopotamus," because in Japanese that animal is *kaba*, the reverse of *baka*, stupid. He told Bible stories, beginning, in the order of things, with the Creation. He showed them a scrapbook of snapshots taken in Europe. Nevertheless, they cried most of the time for their mother.

Several days later, Father Cieslik started hunting for the children's family. First, he learned through the police that an uncle had been to the authorities in Kure, a city not far away, to inquire for the children. After that, he heard that an older brother had been trying to trace them through the post office in Ujina, a suburb of Hiroshima. Still later, he heard that the mother was alive and was on Goto Island, off Nagasaki. And at last, by keeping a check on the Ujina post office, he got in touch with the brother and returned the children to their mother.

About a week after the bomb dropped, a vague, incomprehensible rumor reached Hiroshima—that the city had been destroyed by the energy released when atoms were somehow split in two. The weapon was referred to in this word-of-mouth report as *genshi bakudan*—the root characters of which. can be translated as "original child bomb." No one understood the idea or put any more credence in it than in the powdered magnesium and such things. Newspapers were being brought in from other cities, but they were still confining themselves to extremely general statements, such as Domei's assertion on August 12th: "There is nothing to do but admit the tremendous power of this inhuman bomb." Already, Japanese physicists had entered the city with Lauritsen electroscopes and Neher electrometers; they understood the idea all too well.

On August 12th, the Nakamuras, all of them still rather sick, went to the nearby town of Kabe and moved in with Mrs. Nakamura's sister-in-law. The next day, Mrs. Nakamura, although she was too ill to walk much, returned to Hiroshima alone, by electric car to the outskirts, by foot from there. All week, at the Novitiate, she had worried about her mother, brother, and older sister, who had lived in the part of town called Fukuro, and besides, she felt drawn by some fascination, just as Father Kleinsorge had been. She discovered that her family were all dead. She went back to Kabe so amazed and depressed by what she had seen and learned in the city that she could not speak that evening.

A comparative orderliness, at least, began to be established at the Red Cross Hospital. Dr. Sasaki, back from his rest, undertook to classify his patients (who were still scattered everywhere, even on the stairways). The staff gradually swept up the debris. Best of all, the nurses and attendants started to remove the corpses. Disposal of the dead, by decent cremation and enshrinement, is a greater moral responsibility to the Japanese than adequate care of the living. Relatives identified most of the first day's dead in and around the hospital. Beginning on the second day, whenever a patient appeared to be moribund, a piece of paper with his name on it was fastened to his clothing. The corpse detail carried the bodies to a clearing outside, placed them on pyres of wood from ruined houses, burned them, put some of the ashes in envelopes intended for exposed X-ray plates, marked the envelopes with the names of the deceased, and piled them, neatly and respectfully, in stacks in the main office. In a few days, the envelopes filled one whole side of the impromptu shrine.

In Kabe, on the morning of August 15th, ten-year-old Toshio Nakamura heard an airplane overhead. He ran outdoors and identified it with a professional eye as a B-29. "There goes Mr. B!" he shouted.

One of his relatives called out to him, "Haven't you had enough of Mr. B?"

The question had a kind of symbolism. At almost that very moment, the dull, dispirited voice of Hirohito, the Emperor Tenno, was speaking for the first time in history over the radio: "After pondering deeply the general trends of the world and the actual conditions obtaining in Our Empire today, We have decided to effect a settlement of the present situation by resorting to an extraordinary measure. . . ."

Mrs. Nakamura had gone to the city again, to dig up some rice she had buried in her Neighborhood Association air-raid shelter. She got it and started back for Kabe. On the electric car, quite by chance, she ran into her younger sister, who had not been in Hiroshima the day of the bombing. "Have you heard the news?" her sister asked.

"What news?"

"The war is over."

"Don't say such a foolish thing, sister."

"But I heard it over the radio myself." And then, in a whisper, "It was the Emperor's voice."

"Oh," Mrs. Nakamura said (she needed nothing more to make her give up thinking, in spite of the atomic bomb, that Japan still had a chance to win the war), "in that case . . ."

Some time later, in a letter to an American, Mr. Tanimoto described the events of that morning. "At the time of the Post-War, the marvelous thing in our history happened. Our Emperor broadcasted his own voice through radio directly to us, common people of Japan. Aug. 15th we were told that some news of great importance could be heard & all of us should hear it. So I went to Hiroshima railway station. There set a loudspeaker in the ruins of the station. Many civilians, all of them were in boundage, some being helped by shoulder of their daughters, some sustaining their injured feet by sticks, they listened to the broadcast and when they came to realize the fact that it was the Emperor, they cried with full tears in their eyes, 'What a wonderful blessing it is that Tenno himself call on us and we can hear his own voice in person. We are thoroughly satisfied in such a great sacrifice.' When they came to know the war was ended—that is, Japan was defeated, they, of course, were deeply disappointed, but followed after their Emperor's commandment in calm spirit, making whole-hearted sacrifice for the everlasting peace of the world—and Japan started her new way."

## IV — PANIC GRASS AND FEVERFEW

ON AUGUST 18th, twelve days after the bomb burst, Father Kleinsorge set out on foot for Hiroshima from the Novitiate with his papier-mâché suitcase in his hand. He had begun to think that this bag, in which he kept his valuables, had a talismanic quality, because of the way he had found it after the explosion, standing handle-side up in the doorway of his room, while the desk under which he had previously hidden it was in splinters all over the floor. Now he was using it to carry the yen belonging to the Society of Jesus to the Hiroshima branch of the Yokohama Specie Bank, already reopened in its half-ruined building. On the whole, he felt quite well that morning. It is true that the minor cuts he had received had not healed in three or four days, as the rector of the Novitiate, who had examined them, had positively promised they would, but Father Kleinsorge had rested well for a week and considered that he was again ready for hard work. By now he was accustomed to the terrible scene through which he walked on his way to the city: the large rice field near the Novitiate, streaked with brown; the houses on the outskirts of the city, standing but decrepit, with broken windows and dishevelled tiles; and then, quite suddenly, the beginning of the four square miles of reddish-brown scar, where nearly everything had been buffeted down and burned; range on range of collapsed city blocks, with here and there a crude sign erected on a pile of ashes and tiles ("Sister, where are you?" or "All safe and we live at Toyosaka"); naked trees and canted telephone poles; the few standing, gutted buildings only accentuating the horizontality of everything else (the Museum of Science and Industry, with its dome stripped to its steel frame, as if for an autopsy; the modern Chamber of Commerce Building, its tower as cold, rigid, and unassailable after the blow as before; the huge, low-lying, camouflaged city hall; the row of dowdy banks, caricaturing a shaken economic system); and in the streets a macabre traffic—hundreds of crumpled bicycles, shells of streetcars and automobiles, all halted in mid-motion. The whole way, Father Kleinsorge was oppressed by the thought that all the damage he saw had been done in one instant by one bomb. By the time he reached the center of town, the day had become very hot. He walked to the Yokohama Bank, which was doing business in a temporary wooden stall on the ground floor of its building, deposited the money, went by the mission compound just to have another look at the wreckage, and then started back to the Novitiate. About halfway there, he began to have peculiar sensations. The more or less magical suitcase, now empty, suddenly seemed terribly heavy. His knees grew weak. He felt excruciatingly tired. With a considerable expenditure of spirit, he managed to reach the Novitiate. He did not think his weakness was worth mentioning to the other Jesuits. But a couple of days later, while attempting to say Mass, he had an onset of faintness and even after three attempts was unable to go through with the service, and the next morning the rector, who had examined Father Kleinsorge's apparently negligible but unhealed cuts daily, asked in surprise, "What have you done to your wounds?" They had suddenly opened wider and were swollen and inflamed.

As she dressed on the morning of August 20th, in the home of her sister-in-law in Kabe, not far from Nagatsuka, Mrs. Nakamura, who had suffered no cuts or burns at all, though she had been rather nauseated all through the week she and her children had spent as guests of Father Kleinsorge and the other Catholics at the Novitiate, began fixing her hair and noticed, after one stroke, that her comb carried with it a whole handful of hair; the second time, the same thing happened, so she stopped combing at once. But in the next three or four days, her hair kept falling out of its own accord, until she was quite bald. She began living indoors, practically in hiding. On August 26th, both she and her younger daughter, Myeko, woke up feeling extremely weak and tired, and they stayed on their bedrolls. Her son and other daughter, who had shared every experience with her during and after the bombing, felt fine.

At about the same time—he lost track of the days, so hard was he working to set up a temporary place of worship in a private house he had rented in the outskirts—Mr. Tanimoto fell suddenly ill with a general malaise, weariness, and feverishness, and he, too, took to his bedroll on the floor of the half-wrecked house of a friend in the suburb of Ushida.

These four did not realize it, but they were coming down with the strange, capricious disease which came later to be known as radiation sickness.

Miss Sasaki lay in steady pain in the Goddess of Mercy Primary School, at Hatsukaichi, the fourth station to the southwest of Hiroshima on the electric train. An internal infection still prevented the proper setting of the compound fracture of her lower left leg. A young man who was in the same hospital and who seemed to have grown fond of her in spite of her unremitting preoccupation with her suffering, or else just pitied her because of it, lent her a Japanese translation of de Maupassant, and she tried to read the stories, but she could concentrate for only four or five minutes at a time.

The hospitals and aid stations around Hiroshima were so crowded in the first weeks after the bombing, and their staffs were so variable, depending on their health and on the unpredictable arrival of outside help, that patients had to be constantly shifted from place to place. Miss Sasaki, who had already been moved three times, twice by ship, was taken at the end of August to an engineering school, also at Hatsukaichi. Because her leg did not improve but swelled more and more, the doctors at the school bound it with crude splints and took her by car, on September 9th, to the Red Cross Hospital in Hiroshima. This was the first chance she had had to look at the ruins of Hiroshima; the last time she had been carried through the city's streets, she had been hovering on the edge of unconsciousness. Even though the wreckage had been described to her, and though she was still in pain, the sight horrified and amazed her, and there was something she noticed about it that particularly gave her the creeps. Over everything—up through the wreckage of the city, in gutters, along the riverbanks, tangled among tiles and tin roofing, climbing on charred tree trunks—was a blanket of fresh, vivid, lush, optimistic green; the verdancy rose even from the foundations of ruined houses. Weeds already hid the ashes, and wild flowers were in bloom among the city's bones. The bomb had not only left the underground organs of plants intact; it had stimulated them. Everywhere were bluets and Spanish bayonets, goosefoot, morning glories and day lilies, the hairy-fruited bean, purslane and clotbur and sesame and panic grass and feverfew. Especially in a circle at the center, sickle senna grew in extraordinary regeneration, not only standing among the charred remnants of the same plant but pushing up in new places, among bricks and through cracks in the asphalt. It actually seemed as if a load of sickle-senna seed had been dropped along with the bomb.

At the Red Cross Hospital, Miss Sasaki was put under the care of Dr. Sasaki. Now, a month after the explosion, something like order had been reestablished in the hospital; which is to say that the patients who still lay in the corridors at least had mats to sleep on and that the supply of medicines, which had given out in the first few days, had been replaced, though inadequately, by contributions from other cities. Dr. Sasaki, who had had one seventeen-hour sleep at his home on the third night, had ever since then rested only about six hours a night, on a mat at the hospital; he had lost twenty pounds from his very small body; he still wore the ill-fitting glasses he had borrowed from an injured nurse.

Since Miss Sasaki was a woman and was so sick (and perhaps, he afterward admitted, just a little bit because she was named Sasaki), Dr. Sasaki put her on a mat in a semi-private room, which at that time had only eight people in it. He questioned her and put down on her record card, in the correct, scrunched-up German in which he wrote all his records: *"Mittelgrosse Patien-*

*tin in gutem Ernährungszustand. Fraktur am linken Unterschenkelknochen mit Wunde; Anschwellung in der linken Unterschenkelgegend. Haut und sichtbare Schleimhäute mässig durchblutet und kein Oedema,"* noting that she was a medium-sized female patient in good general health; that she had a compound fracture of the left tibia, with swelling of the left lower leg; that her skin and visible mucous membranes were heavily spotted with *petechiae,* which are hemorrhages about the size of grains of rice, or even as big as soybeans; and, in addition, that her head, eyes, throat, lungs, and heart were apparently normal; and that she had a fever. He wanted to set her fracture and put her leg in a cast, but he had run out of plaster of Paris long since, so he just stretched her out on a mat and prescribed aspirin for her fever, and glucose intravenously and diastase orally for her undernourishment (which he had not entered on her record because everyone suffered from it). She exhibited only one of the queer symptoms so many of his patients were just then beginning to show—the spot hemorrhages.

Dr. Fujii was still pursued by bad luck, which still was connected with rivers. Now he was living in the summer house of Mr. Okuma, in Fukawa. This house clung to the steep banks of the Ota River. Here his injuries seemed to make good progress, and he even began to treat refugees who came to him from the neighborhood, using medical supplies he had retrieved from a cache in the suburbs. He noticed in some of his patients a curious syndrome of symptoms that cropped out in the third and fourth weeks, but he was not able to do much more than swathe cuts and burns. Early in September, it began to rain, steadily and heavily. The river rose. On September 17th, there came a cloudburst and then a typhoon, and the water crept higher and higher up the bank. Mr. Okuma and Dr. Fujii became alarmed and scrambled up the mountain to a peasant's house. (Down in Hiroshima, the flood took up where the bomb had left off—swept away bridges that had survived the blast, washed out streets, undermined foundations of buildings that still stood—and ten miles to the west, the Ono Army Hospital, where a team of experts from Kyoto Imperial University was studying the delayed affliction of the patients, suddenly slid down a beautiful, pine-dark mountainside into the Inland Sea and drowned most of the investigators and their mysteriously diseased patients alike.) After the storm, Dr. Fujii and Mr. Okuma went down to the river and found that the Okuma house had been washed altogether away.

Because so many people were suddenly feeling sick nearly a month after the atomic bomb was dropped, an unpleasant rumor began to move around, and eventually it made its way to the house in Kabe where Mrs. Nakamura lay bald and ill. It was that the atomic bomb had deposited some sort of poison on Hiroshima which would give off deadly emanations for seven years; nobody could go there all that time. This especially upset Mrs. Nakamura, who remembered that in a moment of confusion on the morning of the explosion she had literally sunk her entire means of livelihood, her Sankoku sewing machine, in the small cement water tank in front of what was left of her house; now no one would be able to go and fish it out. Up to this time, Mrs. Nakamura and her relatives had been quite resigned and passive about the moral issue of the atomic bomb, but this rumor suddenly aroused them to more hatred and resentment of America than they had felt all through the war.

Japanese physicists, who knew a great deal about atomic fission (one of them owned a cyclotron), worried about lingering radiation at Hiroshima, and in mid-August, not many days after President Truman's disclosure of the type of bomb that had been dropped, they entered the city to make investigations. The first thing they did was roughly to determine a center by observing the side on which telephone poles all around the heart of the town were scorched; they settled on the torii gateway of the Gokoku Shrine, right next to the parade ground of the Chugoku Regional Army Headquarters. From there, they worked north and south with Lauritsen electroscopes, which are sensitive to both beta particles and gamma rays. These indicated that the highest intensity of radioactivity, near the torii, was 4.2 times the average natural "leak" of ultra-short waves for the earth of that area. The scientists noticed that the flash of the bomb had discolored concrete to a light reddish tint, had scaled off the surface of granite, and had scorched certain other types of building material, and that consequently the bomb had, in some places, left prints of the shadows that had been cast by its light. The experts found, for instance, a permanent shadow thrown on the roof of the Chamber of Commerce Building (220 yards from the rough center) by the structure's rectangular tower; several others in the lookout post on top of the Hypothec Bank (2,050 yards); another in the tower of the Chugoku Electric Supply Building (800 yards); another projected by the handle of a gas pump (2,630 yards); and several on granite tombstones in the Gokoku Shrine (385 yards). By triangulating these and other such shadows with the objects that formed them, the scientists determined that the exact center was a spot a hundred and fifty yards south of the torii and a few yards southeast of the pile of ruins that had once been the Shima Hospital. (A few vague human silhouettes were found, and these gave rise to stories that eventually included fancy and precise details. One story told how a painter on a ladder was monumentalized in a kind of bas-relief on the stone façade of a bank building on which he was at work, in the act of dipping his brush into his paint can; another, how a man and his cart on the bridge near the Museum of Science and Industry, almost under the center of the explosion, were cast down in an embossed shadow which made it clear that the man was about to whip his horse.) Starting east and west from the actual center, the scientists, in early September, made new measurements, and the highest radioactivity they found this time was 3.9 times the natural "leak." Since radioactivity of at least a thousand times the natural "leak" would be required to cause serious effects on the human body, the scientists announced that people could enter Hiroshima without any peril at all.

As soon as this reassurance reached the household in which Mrs. Nakamura was concealing herself—or, at any rate, within a short time after her hair had started growing back again—her whole family relaxed their extreme hatred of America, and Mrs. Nakamura sent her brother-in-law to look for the sewing machine. It was still submerged in the water tank, and when he brought it home, she saw, to her dismay, that it was all rusted and useless.

By the end of the first week in September, Father Kleinsorge was in bed at the Novitiate with a fever of 102.2, and since he seemed to be getting worse, his colleagues decided to send him to the Catholic International Hospital in Tokyo. Father Cieslik and the rector took him as far as Kobe and a Jesuit from that city took him the rest of the way, with a message from a Kobe doctor to the Mother Superior of the International Hospital: "Think twice before you give this man blood transfusions, because with atomic-bomb patients we aren't at all sure that if you stick needles in them, they'll stop bleeding."

When Father Kleinsorge arrived at the hospital, he was terribly pale and very shaky. He complained that the bomb had upset his digestion and given him abdominal pains. His white blood count was three thousand (five to seven thousand is normal), he was seriously anemic, and his temperature was 104. A doctor who did not know much about these strange manifestations—Father Kleinsorge was one of a handful of atomic patients who had reached Tokyo—came to see him, and to the patient's face he was most encouraging. "You'll be out of here in two weeks," he said. But when the doctor got out in the corridor, he said to the Mother Superior, "He'll die. All these bomb people die—you'll see. They go along for a couple of weeks and then they die."

The doctor prescribed suralimentation for Father Kleinsorge. Every three hours, they forced some eggs or beef juice into him, and they fed him all the sugar he could stand. They gave him vitamins, and iron pills and arsenic (in Fowler's solution) for his anemia. He confounded both the doctor's predictions; he neither died nor got up in a fortnight. Despite the fact that the message from the Kobe doctor deprived him of transfusions, which would have been the most useful therapy of all, his fever and his digestive troubles cleared up fairly quickly. His white count went up for a while, but early in October it dropped again, to 3,600; then, in ten days, it suddenly climbed above normal, to 8,800; and it finally settled at 5,800. His ridiculous scratches puzzled everyone. For a few days, they would mend, and then, when he moved around, they would open up again. As soon as he began to feel well, he enjoyed himself tremendously. In Hiroshima he had been one of thousands of sufferers; in Tokyo he was a curiosity. American Army doctors came by the dozen to observe him. Japanese experts questioned him. A newspaper interviewed him.

And once, the confused doctor came and shook his head and said, "Baffling cases, these atomic-bomb people."

Mrs. Nakamura lay indoors with Myeko. They both continued sick, and though Mrs. Nakamura vaguely sensed that their trouble was caused by the bomb, she was too poor to see a doctor and so never knew exactly what the matter was. Without any treatment at all, but merely resting, they began gradually to feel better. Some of Myeko's hair fell out, and she had a tiny burn on her arm which took months to heal. The boy, Toshio, and the older girl, Yaeko, seemed well enough, though they, too, lost some hair and occasionally had bad headaches. Toshio was still having nightmares, always about the nineteen-year-old mechanic, Hideo Osaki, his hero, who had been killed by the bomb.

On his back with a fever of 104, Mr. Tanimoto worried about all the funerals he ought to be conducting for the deceased of his church. He thought he was just overtired from the hard work he had done since the bombing, but after the fever had persisted for a few days, he sent for a doctor. The doctor was too busy to visit him in Ushida, but he dispatched a nurse, who recognized his symptoms as those of mild radiation disease and came back from time to time to give him injections of Vitamin $B_1$. A Buddhist priest with whom Mr. Tanimoto was acquainted called on him and suggested that moxibustion might give him relief; the priest showed the pastor how to give himself the ancient Japanese treatment, by setting fire to a twist of the stimulant herb moxa placed on the wrist pulse. Mr. Tanimoto found that each moxa treatment temporarily reduced his fever one degree. The nurse had told him to eat as much as possible, and every few days his mother-in-law brought him vegetables and fish from Tsuzu, twenty miles away, where she lived. He spent a month in bed, and then went ten hours by train to his father's home in Shikoku. There he rested another month.

Dr. Sasaki and his colleagues at the Red Cross Hospital watched the unprecedented disease unfold and at last evolved a theory about its nature. It had, they decided, three stages. The first stage had been all over before the doctors even knew they were dealing with a new sickness; it was the direct reaction to the bombardment of the body, at the moment when the bomb went off, by neutrons, beta particles, and gamma rays. The apparently uninjured people who had died so mysteriously in the first few hours or days had succumbed in this first stage. It killed ninety-five per cent of the people within a half mile of the center, and many thousands who were farther away. The doctors realized in retrospect that even though most of these dead had also suffered from burns and blast effects, they had absorbed enough radiation to kill them. The rays simply destroyed body cells—caused their nuclei to degenerate and broke their walls. Many people who did not die right away came down with nausea, headache, diarrhea, malaise, and fever, which lasted several days. Doctors could not be certain whether some of these symptoms were the result of radiation or nervous shock. The second stage set in ten or fifteen days after the bombing. The main symptom was falling hair. Diarrhea and fever, which in some cases went as high as 106, came next. Twenty-five to thirty days after the explosion, blood disorders appeared: gums bled, the white-blood-cell count dropped sharply, and *petechiae* appeared on the skin and mucous membranes. The drop in the number of white blood corpuscles reduced the patient's capacity to resist infection, so open wounds were unusually slow in healing and many of the sick developed sore throats and mouths. The two key symptoms, on which the doctors came to base their prognosis, were fever and the lowered white-corpuscle count. If fever remained steady and high, the patient's chances for survival were poor. The white count almost always dropped below four thousand; a patient whose count fell below one thousand had little hope of living. Toward the end of the second stage, if the patient survived, anemia, or a drop in the red blood count, also set in. The third stage was the reaction that came when the body struggled to compensate for its ills—when, for instance, the white count not only returned to normal but increased to much higher than normal levels. In this stage, many patients died of complications, such as infections in the chest cavity. Most burns healed with deep layers of pink, rubbery scar tissue, known as keloid tumors. The duration of the disease varied, depending on the patient's constitution and the amount of radiation he had received. Some victims recovered in a week; with others the disease dragged on for months.

As the symptoms revealed themselves, it became clear that many of them resembled the effects of overdoses of X-ray, and the doctors based their therapy on that likeness. They gave victims liver extract, blood transfusions, and vitamins, especially $B_1$. The shortage of supplies and instruments hampered them. Allied doctors who came in after the surrender found plasma and penicillin very effective. Since the blood disorders were, in the long run, the predominant factor in the disease, some of the Japanese doctors evolved a theory as to the seat of the delayed sickness. They thought that perhaps gamma rays, entering the body at the time of the explosion, made the phosphorus in the victims' bones radioactive, and that they in turn emitted beta particles, which, though they could not penetrate far through flesh, could enter the bone marrow, where blood is manufactured, and gradually tear it down. Whatever its source, the disease had some baffling quirks. Not all the patients exhibited all the main symptoms. People who suffered flash burns were protected, to a considerable extent, from radiation sickness. Those who had lain quietly for days or even hours after the bombing were much less liable to get sick than those who had been active. Gray hair seldom fell out. And, as if nature were protecting man against his own ingenuity, the reproductive processes were affected for a time; men became sterile, women had miscarriages, menstruation stopped.

For ten days after the flood, Dr. Fujii lived in the peasant's house on the mountain above the Ota. Then he heard about a vacant private clinic in Kaitaichi, a suburb to the east of Hiroshima. He bought it at once, moved there, and hung out a sign inscribed in English, in honor of the conquerors:

M. FUJII, M.D.

MEDICAL & VENEREAL

Quite recovered from his wounds, he soon built up a strong practice, and he was delighted, in the evening, to receive members of the occupying forces, on whom he lavished whiskey and practiced English.

Giving Miss Sasaki a local anesthetic of procaine, Dr. Sasaki made an incision in her leg on October 23rd, to drain the infection, which still lingered on eleven weeks after the injury. In the following days, so much pus formed that he had to dress the opening each morning and evening. A week later, she complained of great pain, so he made another incision; he cut still a third, on November 9th, and enlarged it on the twenty-sixth. All this time, Miss Sasaki grew weaker and weaker, and her spirits fell low. One day, the young man who had lent her his translation of de Maupassant at Hatsukaichi came to visit her; he told her that he was going to Kyushu but that when he came back, he would like to see her again. She didn't care. Her leg had been so swollen and painful all along that the doctor had not even tried to set the fractures, and though an X-ray taken in November showed that the bones were mending, she could see under the sheet that her left leg was nearly three inches shorter than her right and that her left foot was turning inward. She thought often of the man to whom she had been engaged. Someone told her that he was back from overseas. She wondered what he had heard about her injuries that made him stay away.

Father Kleinsorge was discharged from the hospital in Tokyo on December 19th and took a train home. On the way, two days later, at Yokogawa, a stop just before Hiroshima, Dr. Fujii boarded the train. It was the first time the two men had met since before the bombing. They sat together. Dr. Fujii said he was going to the annual gathering of his family, on the anniversary of his father's death. When they started talking about their experiences, the Doctor was quite entertaining as he told how his places of residence kept falling into rivers. Then he asked Father Kleinsorge how he was, and the Jesuit talked about his stay in the hospital. "The doctors told me to be cautious," he said. "They ordered me to have a two-hour nap every afternoon."

Dr. Fujii said, "It's hard to be cautious in Hiroshima these days. Everyone seems to be so busy."

A new municipal government, set up under Allied Military Government direction, had gone to work at last in the city hall. Citizens who had recovered from various degrees of radiation sickness were coming back by the thousand —by November 1st, the population, mostly crowded into the outskirts, was already 137,000, more than a third of the wartime peak—and the government set in motion all kinds of projects to put them to work rebuilding the city. It hired men to clear the streets, and others to gather scrap iron, which they sorted and piled in mountains opposite the city hall. Some returning residents were putting up their own shanties and huts, and planting small squares of winter wheat beside them, but the city also authorized and built four hundred one-family "barracks." Utilities were repaired—electric lights shone again, trams started running, and employees of the waterworks fixed seventy thousand leaks in mains and plumbing. A Planning Conference, with an enthusiastic young Military Government officer, Lieutenant John D. Montgomery, of Kalamazoo, as its adviser, began to consider what sort of city the new Hiroshima should be. The ruined city had flourished—and had been an inviting target—mainly because it had been one of the most important military-command and communications centers in Japan, and would have become the Imperial headquarters had the islands been invaded and Tokyo been captured. Now there would be no huge military establishments to help revive the city. The Planning Conference, at a loss as to just what importance Hiroshima could have, fell back on rather vague cultural and paving projects. It drew maps with avenues a hundred yards wide and thought seriously of preserving the half-ruined Museum of Science and Industry more or less as it was, as a monument to the disaster, and naming it the Institute of International Amity. Statistical workers gathered what figures they could on the effects of the bomb. They reported that 78,150 people had been killed, 13,983 were missing, and 37,425 had been injured. No one in the city government pretended that these figures were accurate—though the Americans accepted them as official—and as the months went by and more and more hundreds of corpses were dug up from the ruins, and as the number of unclaimed urns of ashes at the Zempoji Temple in Koi rose into the thousands, the statisticians began to say that at least a hundred thousand people had lost their lives in the bombing. Since many people died of a combination of causes, it was impossible to figure exactly how many were killed by each cause, but the statisticians calculated that about twenty-five per cent had died of direct burns from the bomb, about fifty per cent from other injuries, and about twenty per cent as a result of radiation effects. The statisticians' figures on property damage were more reliable: sixty-two thousand out of ninety thousand buildings destroyed, and six thousand more damaged beyond repair. In the heart of the city, they found only five modern buildings that could be used again without major repairs. This small number was by no means the fault of flimsy Japanese construction. In fact, since the 1923 earthquake, Japanese building regulations had required that the roof of each large building be able to bear a minimum load of seventy pounds per square foot, whereas American regulations do not normally specify more than forty pounds per square foot.

Scientists swarmed into the city. Some of them measured the force that had been necessary to shift marble gravestones in the cemeteries, to knock over twenty-two of the forty-seven railroad cars in the yards at Hiroshima station, to lift and move the concrete roadway on one of the bridges, and to perform other noteworthy acts of strength, and concluded that the pressure exerted by the explosion varied from 5.3 to 8.0 tons per square yard. Others found that mica, of which the melting point is 900°C., had fused on granite gravestones three hundred and eighty yards from the center; that telephone poles of *Cryptomeria japonica,* whose carbonization temperature is 240°C., had been charred at forty-four hundred yards from the center; and that the surface of gray clay tiles of the type used in Hiroshima, whose melting point is 1,300°C., had dissolved at six hundred yards; and, after examining other significant ashes and melted bits, they concluded that the bomb's heat on the ground at the center must have been 6,000°C. And from further measurements of radiation, which involved, among other things, the scraping up of fission fragments from roof troughs and drainpipes as far away as the suburb of Takasu, thirty-three hundred yards from the center, they learned some far more important facts about the nature of the bomb. General MacArthur's headquarters systematically censored all mention of the bomb in Japanese scientific publications, but soon the fruit of the scientists' calculations became common knowledge among Japanese physicists, doctors, chemists, journalists, professors, and, no doubt, those statesmen and military men who were still in circulation. Long before the American public had been told, most of the scientists and lots of nonscientists in Japan knew—from the calculations of Japanese nuclear physicists —that a uranium bomb had exploded at Hiroshima and a more powerful one, of plutonium, at Nagasaki. They also knew that theoretically one ten times as powerful—or twenty—could be developed. The Japanese scientists thought they knew the exact height at which the bomb at Hiroshima was exploded and the approximate weight of the uranium used. They estimated that, even with the primitive bomb used at Hiroshima, it would require a shelter of concrete fifty inches thick to protect a human being entirely from radiation sickness. The scientists had these and other details which remained subject to security in the United States printed and mimeographed and bound into little books. The Americans knew of the existence of these, but tracing them and seeing that they did not fall into the wrong hands would have obliged the occupying authorities to set up, for this one purpose alone, an enormous police system in Japan. Altogether, the Japanese scientists were somewhat amused at the efforts of their conquerors to keep security on atomic fission.

Late in February, 1946, a friend of Miss Sasaki's called on Father Kleinsorge and asked him to visit her in the hospital. She had been growing more and more depressed and morbid; she seemed little interested in living. Father Kleinsorge went to see her several times. On his first visit, he kept the conversation general, formal, and yet vaguely sympathetic, and did not mention religion. Miss Sasaki herself brought it up the second time he dropped in on her. Evidently she had had some talks with a Catholic. She asked bluntly, "If your God is so good and kind, how can he let people suffer like this?" She made a gesture which took in her shrunken leg, the other patients in her room, and Hiroshima as a whole.

"My child," Father Kleinsorge said, "man is not now in the condition God intended. He has fallen from grace through sin." And he went on to explain all the reasons for everything.

It came to Mrs. Nakamura's attention that a carpenter from Kabe was building a number of wooden shanties in Hiroshima which he rented for fifty yen a month—$3.33, at the fixed rate of exchange. Mrs. Nakamura had lost the certificates for her bonds and other wartime savings, but fortunately she had copied off all the numbers just a few days before the bombing and had taken the list to Kabe, and so, when her hair had grown in enough for her to be presentable, she went to her bank in Hiroshima, and a clerk there told her that after checking her numbers against the records the bank would give her her money. As soon as she got it, she rented one of the carpenter's shacks. It was in Nobori-cho, near the site of her former house, and though its floor was dirt and it was dark inside, it was at least a home in Hiroshima, and she was no longer dependent on the charity of her in-laws. During the spring, she cleared away some nearby wreckage and planted a vegetable garden. She cooked with utensils and ate off plates she scavenged from the debris. She sent Myeko to the kindergarten, which the Jesuits reopened, and the two older children attended Nobori-cho Primary School, which, for want of buildings, held classes out of doors. Toshio wanted to study to be a mechanic, like his hero, Hideo Osaki. Prices were high; by midsummer Mrs. Nakamura's savings were gone. She sold some of her clothes to get food. She had once had several expensive kimonos, but during the war one had been stolen, she had given one to a sister who had been bombed out in Tokuyama, she had lost a couple in the Hiroshima bombing, and now she sold her last one. It brought only a hundred yen, which did not last long. In June, she went to Father Kleinsorge for advice about how to get along, and in early August, she was still considering the two alternatives he suggested—taking work as a domestic for some of the Allied occupation forces, or borrowing from her relatives enough money, about five hundred yen, or a bit more than thirty dollars, to repair her rusty sewing machine and resume the work of a seamstress.

When Mr. Tanimoto returned from Shikoku, he draped a tent he owned over the roof of the badly damaged house he had rented in Ushida. The roof still leaked, but he conducted services in the damp living room. He began thinking about raising money to restore his church in the city. He became quite friendly with Father Kleinsorge and saw the Jesuits often. He envied them their Church's wealth; they seemed to be able to do anything they wanted. He had nothing to work with except his own energy, and that was not what it had been.

The Society of Jesus had been the first institution to build a relatively permanent shanty in the ruins of Hiroshima. That had been while Father Kleinsorge was in the hospital. As soon as he got back, he began living in the shack, and he and another priest, Father Laderman, who had joined him in the mission, arranged for the purchase of three of the standardized "barracks" which the city was selling at seven thousand yen apiece. They put two together, end to end, and made a pretty chapel of them; they ate in the third. When materials were available, they commissioned a contractor to build a three-story mission house exactly like the one that had been destroyed in the fire. In the compound, carpenters cut timbers, gouged mortises, shaped tenons, whittled scores of wooden pegs and bored holes for them, until all the parts for the house were in a neat pile; then, in three days, they put the whole thing together, like an Oriental puzzle, without any nails at all. Father Kleinsorge was finding it hard, as Dr. Fujii had suggested he would, to be cautious and to take his naps. He went out every day on foot to call on Japanese Catholics and prospective converts. As the months went by, he grew more and more tired. In June, he read an article in the Hiroshima *Chugoku* warning survivors against working too hard —but what could he do? By July, he was worn out, and early in August, almost exactly on the anniversary of the bombing, he went back to the Catholic International Hospital, in Tokyo, for a month's rest.

Whether or not Father Kleinsorge's answers to Miss Sasaki's questions about life were final and absolute truths, she seemed quickly to draw physical strength from them. Dr. Sasaki noticed it and congratulated Father Kleinsorge. By April 15th, her temperature and white count were normal and the infection in the wound was beginning to clear up. On the twentieth, there was almost no pus, and for the first time she jerked along a corridor on crutches. Five days later, the wound had begun to heal, and on the last day of the month she was discharged.

During the early summer, she prepared herself for conversion to Catholicism. In that period she had ups and downs. Her depressions were deep. She knew she would always be a cripple. Her fiancé never came to see her. There was nothing for her to do except read and look out, from her house on a hillside in Koi, across the ruins of the city where her parents and brother died. She was nervous, and any sudden noise made her put her hands quickly to her throat. Her leg still hurt; she rubbed it often and patted it, as if to console it.

It took six months for the Red Cross Hospital, and even longer for Dr. Sasaki, to get back to normal. Until the city restored electric power, the hospital had to limp along with the aid of a Japanese Army generator in its back yard. Operating tables, X-ray machines, dentist chairs, everything complicated and essential came in a trickle of charity from other cities. In Japan, face is important even to institutions, and long before the Red Cross Hospital was back to par on basic medical equipment, its directors put up a new yellow brick veneer façade, so the hospital became the handsomest building in Hiroshima—from the street. For the first four months, Dr. Sasaki was the only surgeon on the staff and he almost never left the building; then, gradually, he began to take an interest in his own life again. He got married in March. He gained back some of the weight he lost, but his appetite remained only fair; before the bombing, he used to eat four rice balls at every meal, but a year after it he could manage only two. He felt tired all the time. "But I have to realize," he said, "that the whole community is tired."

A year after the bomb was dropped, Miss Sasaki was a cripple; Mrs. Nakamura was destitute; Father Kleinsorge was back in the hospital; Dr. Sasaki was not capable of the work he once could do; Dr. Fujii had lost the thirty-room hospital it took him many years to acquire, and had no prospects of rebuilding it; Mr. Tanimoto's church had been ruined and he no longer had his exceptional vitality. The lives of these six people, who were among the luckiest in Hiroshima, would never be the same. What they thought of their experiences and of the use of the atomic bomb was, of course, not unanimous. One feeling they did seem to share, however, was a curious kind of elated community spirit, something like that of the Londoners after their blitz—a pride in the way they and their fellow-survivors had stood up to a dreadful ordeal. Just before the anniversary, Mr. Tanimoto wrote in a letter to an American some words which expressed this feeling: "What a heartbreaking scene this was the first night! About midnight I landed on the riverbank. So many injured people lied on the ground that I made my way by striding over them. Repeating 'Excuse me,' I forwarded and carried a tub of water with me and gave a cup of water to each one of them. They raised their upper bodies slowly and accepted a cup of water with a bow and drunk quietly and, spilling any remnant, gave back a cup with hearty expression of their thankfulness, and said, 'I couldn't help my sister, who was buried under the house, because

I had to take care of my mother who got a deep wound on her eye and our house soon set fire and we hardly escaped. Look, I lost my home, my family, and at last my-self bitterly injured. But now I have gotted my mind to dedicate what I have and to complete the war for our country's sake.' Thus they pledged to me, even women and children did the same. Being entirely tired I lied down on the ground among them, but couldn't sleep at all. Next morning I found many men and women dead, whom I gave water last night. But, to my great surprise, I never heard any one cried in disorder, even though they suffered in great agony. They died in silence, with no grudge, setting their teeth to bear it. All for the country!

"Dr. Y. Hiraiwa, professor of Hiroshima University of Literature and Science, and one of my church members, was buried by the bomb under the two storied house with his son, a student of Tokyo University. Both of them could not move an inch under tremendously heavy pressure. And the house already caught fire. His son said, 'Father, we can do nothing except make our mind up to consecrate our lives for the country. Let us give *Banzai* to our Emperor.' Then the father followed after his son, '*Tenno-heika, Banzai, Banzai, Banzai!*' In the result, Dr. Hiraiwa said, 'Strange to say, I felt calm and bright and peaceful spirit in my heart, when I chanted *Banzai* to Tenno.' Afterward his son got out and digged down and pulled out his father and thus they were saved. In thinking of their experience of that time Dr. Hiraiwa repeated, 'What a fortunate that we are Japanese! It was my first time I ever tasted such a beautiful spirit when I decided to die for our Emperor.'

"Miss Kayoko Nobutoki, a student of girl's high school, Hiroshima Jazabuin, and a daughter of my church member, was taking rest with her friends beside the heavy fence of the Buddhist Temple. At the moment the atomic bomb was dropped, the fence fell upon them. They could not move a bit under such a heavy fence and then smoke entered into even a crack and choked their breath. One of the girls begun to sing *Kimi ga yo,* national anthem, and others followed in chorus and died. Meanwhile one of them found a crack and struggled hard to get out. When she was taken in the Red Cross Hospital she told how her friends died, tracing back in her memory to singing in chorus our national anthem. They were just 13 years old.

"Yes, people of Hiroshima died manly in the atomic bombing, believing that it was for Emperor's sake."

A surprising number of the people of Hiroshima remained more or less indifferent about the ethics of using the bomb. Possibly they were too terrified by it to want to think about it at all. Not many of them even bothered to find out much about what it was like. Mrs. Nakamura's conception of it—and awe of it—was typical. "The atom bomb," she would say when asked about it, "is the size of a matchbox. The heat of it is six thousand times that of the sun. It exploded in the air. There is some radium in it. I don't know just how it works, but when the radium is put together, it explodes." As for the use of the bomb, she would say, "It was war and we had to expect it." And then she would add, *"Shikata ga nai,"* a Japanese expression as common as, and corresponding to, the Russian word *"nichevo"*: "It can't be helped. Oh, well. Too bad." Dr. Fujii said approximately the same thing about the use of the bomb to Father Kleinsorge one evening, in German: *"Da ist nichts zu machen.* There's nothing to be done about it."

Many citizens of Hiroshima, however, continued to feel a hatred for Americans which nothing could possibly erase. "I see," Dr. Sasaki once said, "that they are holding a trial for war criminals in Tokyo just now. I think they ought to try the men who decided to use the bomb and they should hang them all."

Father Kleinsorge and the other German Jesuit priests, who, as foreigners, could be expected to take a relatively detached view, often discussed the ethics of using the bomb. One of them, Father Siemes, who was out at Nagatsuka at the time of the attack, wrote in a report to the Holy See in Rome: "Some of us consider the bomb in the same category as poison gas and were against its use on a civilian population. Others were of the opinion that in total war, as carried on in Japan, there was no difference between civilians and soldiers, and that the bomb itself was an effective force tending to end the bloodshed, warning Japan to surrender and thus to avoid total destruction. It seems logical that he who supports total war in principle cannot complain of a war against civilians. The crux of the matter is whether total war in its present form is justifiable, even when it serves a just purpose. Does it not have material and spiritual evil as its consequences which far exceed whatever good might result? When will our moralists give us a clear answer to this question?"

It would be impossible to say what horrors were embedded in the minds of the children who lived through the day of the bombing in Hiroshima. On the surface, their recollections, months after the disaster, were of an exhilarating adventure. Toshio Nakamura, who was ten at the time of the bombing, was soon able to talk freely, even gaily, about the experience, and a few weeks before the anniversary he wrote the following matter-of-fact essay for his teacher at Nobori-cho Primary School: "The day before the bomb, I went for a swim. In the morning, I was eating peanuts. I saw a light. I was knocked to little sister's sleeping place. When we were saved, I could only see as far as the tram. My mother and I started to pack our things. The neighbors were walking around burned and bleeding. Hataya-*san* told me to run away with her. I said I wanted to wait for my mother. We went to the park. A whirlwind came. At night a gas tank burned and I saw the reflection in the river. We stayed in the park one night. Next day I went to Taiko Bridge and met my girl friends Kikuki and Murakami. They were looking for their mothers. But Kikuki's mother was wounded and Murakami's mother, alas, was dead."